Characteristics of Emotional and Behavioral Disorders of Children and Youth

Sixth Edition

JAMES M. KAUFFMAN
University of Virginia

Merrill
an imprint of Prentice Hall

Upper Saddle River, New Jersey
Columbus, Ohio

Library of Congress Cataloging-in-Publication Data
Kauffman, James M.
    Characteristics of emotional and behavioral disorders of children and youth / James M. Kauffman.—6th ed.
      p.   cm.
    Includes bibliographical references and index.
    ISBN 0-13-515974-1 (case)
    1. Behavior disorders in children. 2. Emotional problems of children.   I. Title.
    RJ506.B44K38   1997
    618.92′89′002437—dc20

                                               96-17542
                                                  CIP

Cover art: © Mark Ari/Superstock
Editor: Ann Castel Davis
Production Editor: Louise N. Sette
Photo Researcher: Angela Jenkins
Design Coordinator: Julia Zonneveld Van Hook
Text Designer: Kip Shaw/Pageworks
Cover Designer: Scott Rattray
Production Manager: Pamela D. Bennett
Director of Marketing: Kevin Flanagan
Advertising/Marketing Coordinator: Julie Shough
Electronic Text Management: Marilyn Wilson Phelps, Matthew Williams, Karen L. Bretz, Tracey Ward

This book was set in Galliard by Prentice Hall and was printed and bound by Quebecor Printing/Book Press.
The cover was printed by Phoenix Color Corp.

© 1997 by Prentice-Hall, Inc.
Simon & Schuster/A Viacom Company
Upper Saddle River, New Jersey 07458

Earlier edition © 1993 by Macmillan Publishing Company. Earlier editions, entitled *Characteristics of Behavior
Disorders of Children and Youth*, © 1989, 1985, 1981, 1977 by Merrill Publishing Company.

Photo credits: Scott Cunningham/Merrill, pp. 136, 164, 216, 276, 394, 430, 510; Corbis-Bettmann, p. 64;
KS Studios/Merrill, p. 108; Gail Meese/Merrill, p. 330; Skjold Photographs, pp. 192, 458; David Strickler/Strix Pix,
p. 306; Todd Yarrington/Merrill, pp. 4, 482; Anne Vega/Merrill, pp. 38, 240; Tom Watson/Merrill, p. 374.

Printed in the United States of America

10 9 8 7 6 5 4 3 2

ISBN: 0-13-515974-1

Prentice-Hall International (UK) Limited, *London*
Prentice-Hall of Australia Pty. Limited, *Sydney*
Prentice-Hall of Canada, Inc., *Toronto*
Prentice-Hall Hispanoamericana, S. A., *Mexico*
Prentice-Hall of India Private Limited, *New Delhi*
Prentice-Hall of Japan, Inc., *Tokyo*
Simon & Schuster Asia Pte. Ltd., *Singapore*
Editora Prentice-Hall do Brasil, Ltda., *Rio de Janeiro*

For my children, Tim and Missy

Preface

This book, like its earlier editions, serves primarily as an introductory text in special education for children and youths with emotional and behavioral disorders (those called "seriously emotionally disturbed" in federal regulations). Because emotional and behavioral disorders are commonly observed in children and youths in all special education categories, the book will also be of value in courses dealing with the characteristics of mental retardation, learning disabilities, or students in cross-categorical special education. Students in school psychology, educational psychology, or abnormal child psychology may also find the book useful.

Several comments are necessary to clarify my intent in writing this book. First, developmental processes have been an important concern of mine in trying to understand the problem of emotional and behavioral disorders. I have tried to integrate the most relevant parts of the vast and scattered literature on child development and show their relevance to understanding the children and youths who have these disorders. In struggling with this task, I have attempted not only to summarize what is known about why disorders occur but also to suggest how emotional and behavioral development can be influenced for the better, particularly by educators. Second, in concentrating primarily on research and theory grounded in reliable empirical data, I have revealed my bias toward social learning principles. I believe that when we examine the literature with a willingness to be swayed by empirical evidence rather than by devotion to humanistic ideology alone, then a social learning bias is understandable. Third, this book is not, by any stretch of the imagination, a comprehensive treatment of the subject. An introductory book must leave much unsaid and many loose ends that need tying up. Unquestionably, the easiest thing about writing this book was to let it fall short of saying it all and hope that readers will pursue the information in the works cited in the references.

I have tried to address the interests and concerns of teachers and of students preparing to become teachers. Consequently, I have described many interventions, particularly in the chapters in Part Four. However, I emphasize that the descriptions are cursory; this text does not provide the details of educational methods and behavioral interventions that are necessary for competent implementation by teachers. This is not a methods or how-to-do-it book.

New to This Edition

Users of previous editions will notice several new features of the sixth edition.

- I have added a brief case description at the end of each chapter, accompanied by several study questions, to help readers apply the chapter content to real-life problems. The cases are drawn from real life; they are not hypothetical.

- In each of the seven chapters in Part Four—Facets of Disordered Behavior—the case is followed by an excerpt from the individualized education program (IEP) for the child or youth just described. I added this feature to help readers consider how they might implement the central feature of special education under the Individuals with Disabilities Education Act (IDEA)—the IEP, which requires assessing individual needs and planning teaching strategies to address them.

- Chapter 3, on the history of the field, now includes a discussion of current issues in the field, linking historical developments to contemporary trends and problems.

- In chapter 4 I have added case illustrations for each of the conceptual models I discuss to help readers better understand how theories are translated to practice.

- Chapter 17 has a new title—Schizophrenia and Pervasive Developmental Disorders—and has been completely rewritten to focus on current issues in childhood schizophrenia, autism, and related disorders.

Besides these new features, I have rewritten much of the material to reflect recent research.

Organization of the Text

The organization of this book differs noticeably from that of most alternative texts. The emphasis is on clear description of emotional and behavioral disorders and interpretation of research on the factors implicated in their development. Unlike other texts in this discipline, this book is not organized around theoretical models or psychiatric classifications but around basic concepts: the nature, extent, and history of the problem and conceptual approaches to it; assessment of the problem; major causal factors; the many facets of disordered emotions and behavior; and a personal statement about teaching pupils with these disorders. This organization, I hope, encourages students to become critical thinkers and problem solvers.

Part One introduces major concepts and historical antecedents of contemporary special education for children and youths with emotional and behavioral disorders. Chapter 1 begins with a series of vignettes to orient the reader to disorders and the ways they disturb others. The vignettes are followed by discussion of the problems in defining these disorders, especially for educational purposes. In chapter 2, prevalence is discussed from a conceptual, problem-solving perspective rather than as an exercise in memory of facts and figures. Chapter 3 traces the growth of the field—how it grew out of the disciplines of psychology, psychiatry, and public education—and summarizes major current trends. Chapter 4 abstracts the major conceptual models that guide thinking about educating students with emotional and behavioral disorders and provides a sketch of the conceptual model underlying the orientation of the book.

Part Two deals with procedures and problems in assessing emotional and behavioral disorders. Chapter 5 reviews not only the problems in screening student populations but also the difficulties encountered in classifying disorders. Chapter 6 takes up the topics of evaluation for eligibility and intervention, with attention to social validation and the IEP.

Part Three examines the origins of disordered behavior, with attention to the implications of causal factors for special educators. Chapter 7 discusses biological factors; chapter 8, the role of the family; chapter 9, the influence of the school; and chapter 10, cultural factors. Each chapter integrates current research findings that may help us understand why children and youths acquire emotional or behavioral disorders and what preventive actions might be taken.

Types of disorders are discussed in Part Four. The chapters are organized around major behavioral dimensions derived from factor analyses of behavioral ratings by teachers and parents. Although no categorical scheme produces unambiguous groupings of all disorders, the chapters are devoted to the behavioral dimensions emerging most consistently from empirical research. Each chapter emphasizes issues germane to special education, including definition, assessment, and intervention.

Part Five contains only one chapter, my interpretation and application of all of the preceding material to teaching practices. This is a personal statement intended only to suggest some basic assumptions about teaching pupils who exhibit seriously troublesome behavior.

Acknowledgments

Any shortcomings of this book are my responsibility alone, but its worth has been enhanced very substantially by others who have assisted me in a variety of ways. I acknowledge with thanks the reviewers of the fifth edition, who offered advance suggestions for this, the sixth edition. The perceptive suggestions of Anne M. Bauer, University of Cincinnati; Lisa Bloom, Western Carolina University; Marion Boss, University of Toledo; E. Paula Crowley, Illinois State University; Beth Fouse, University of Texas at Tyler; and Pamela H. Wheeler, Lewis University, resulted in substantial improvements in my work. Many other users of the book, both students and instructors, have given me helpful feedback over the years, and I encourage those who are willing to share their comments on the book to write or call me with their suggestions. I am also grateful to the contributors of the "Personal Reflections" features for their willingness to share their knowledge and views on important questions and to Jeanne Bauwens for contributing cooperative learning activities to the instructor's manual. Finally, I offer special thanks to Teresa Zutter for supplying many of the case studies and the IEP excerpts in the chapters in Part Four and for preparing the instructor's manual.

J.M.K.
Charlottesville, VA

Contents

PART ONE
The Problem and Its History

Introduction to Part One

In one of his best known short stories, humorist James Thurber describes the private fantasies of Walter Mitty. While Walter Mitty's wife was getting her hair done and he ran errands, and while he drove and she prattled about things to which he paid no attention, he fantasized that he was a daring naval pilot, an eminent surgeon, a debonair marksman on the witness stand in a sensational murder trial, and a captured soldier facing execution with nonchalance. Walter Mitty's imaginings are seen as both humorous and adaptive. His internal dialogue is seen as a way of coping with his life circumstances and enhancing his self-image. An actual person who thinks and behaves like Walter Mitty is not likely to be described as having serious emotional or behavioral problems.

Fantasy and internal dialogue are parts of everyone's experience, but they are not always adaptive or self-enhancing. Consider Calvin, the little boy who, with his stuffed animal companion, has a rich fantasy life in the cartoon feature, "Calvin and Hobbes." Much of the time, Calvin's behavior and internal dialogue are what most of us would consider "cute" or "normal" for a little boy, but at times they cross the border into what many would describe as "demented," "sick," or "disturbed" if they characterized an actual child. Think of the television cartoon characters Beavis and Butthead. How would you judge their behavior if exhibited by actual boys their age? Reflect on the famous Bart Simpson statement, "An underachiever, and proud of it." If

an actual student in your classroom said this to you, apparently repeated it to himself, and behaved accordingly, would you find it amusing? Troubling? An indication of an emotional or behavioral disorder?

Thinking about emotional or behavioral disorders requires asking a lot of questions about the way people think and behave. Once you begin asking questions, you are likely to find that the answers aren't as simple as they seemed at first—at least, not if you're the one trying to answer. One of the most effective strategies for learning about any topic is making yourself try to answer the questions you ask—to ask the questions of yourself. Much of my thinking about my professional work is an internal dialogue in which I imagine myself being asked questions about things I am presumed to know or expected to learn about. Sometimes I envision the questions coming from friends in easy conversation or from students eager to know what I think and why. At other times I see myself being grilled mercilessly by an adversarial audience. In my worst moments, I am being cross-examined by a hostile attorney in court or in a Congressional hearing, or by a panel of arrogant experts who *really do* know the answers.

Many of the questions I fantasize myself being asked are unanswerable, but my imagined questioners are relentless in putting me on the spot. I struggle to refine my answers, never feeling entirely satisfied with my responses. In some cases I can think of no better statement than, simply, "I don't know." Frequently, the only thing that keeps my internal dialogue from becoming a nightmare is that I realize I am in control of what I ask myself as well as how I answer. I breathe a sigh of relief, knowing that my questioners are, at least for the moment, purely imaginary. Then, as is the prerogative of self-questioners, I take the offensive. I become the questioner and imagine someone else sweating out their answers to the questions I ask. After all, if I can put myself on an imaginary griddle, I can fry my imaginary interrogators in return! I become an academic Walter Mitty, pinning my opponents down in withering cross-examination.

And so it goes inside my head. I hope that reading this book will launch you on a similar adventure of self-questioning. If reading my text helps you formulate answers to questions, it should also help you raise more questions, some that neither you nor anyone else is likely to answer in a lifetime of study. In the introductions to the five parts of this book, I present for you some of the questions I've asked myself—and tried to answer, always with only partial success—in the chapters that follow. This book is about difficult questions regarding people's emotions and behavior. There are no simple, easy answers to these questions, and few of the answers are unequivocal. That is the nature of the topic of emotional or behavioral disorders. It is not an appealing area of study for students who feel a need for more answers than questions or who want straightforward answers to complex problems. We don't know much compared to what we need to know, partly because the field of study is relatively young and the necessary research hasn't been done. In addition, some of the important questions we might ask call for value judgments and can't be answered directly by research. For answers to many questions, we have to be satisfied with educated guesses or personal opinions.

As you begin your study of emotional or behavioral disorders, you should be asking yourself some of the most obvious yet profound questions about this field of inquiry. For example, "What is an emotional or behavioral disorder?" As you will see in chapter 1, we have a very difficult problem right off the bat. As simple as this first question might seem, we're immediately faced with an ambiguous answer and continuing controversy.

In chapter 2, we turn to such questions as "What is the scope of the problem?" "What is the percentage of students with emotional or behavioral disorders in most schools?" "How do we estimate the number of such students in a district, a state, or the country?" "Why should we?" As you may already have asked yourself, "How can we measure accurately the extent of a problem we can't define precisely?" Reading chapter 2 should help you formulate questions about what might be required to meet the needs of students with emotional or behavioral disorders if there are as many such students as we estimate there are.

"How and where did special education for children and youths with emotional or behavioral disorders begin?" "What influences shaped the field into what it is today?" "What are the implications of current trends in the field?" Historical analysis should enable us to answer the first of these rather precisely, it would seem. As I indicate in chapter 3, however, the beginning of the field is difficult to describe precisely, partly because it is submerged in the beginnings of related professions. If finding the roots of the field is difficult, predicting where it is going is more so. Some of the questions I hope reading chapter 3 will prompt you to ask when you read about "new" developments are: "Have we heard this before?" "Who had this idea, and how did it work out?" "If this is a 'recycled' idea, what is different about it as it is being presented today?"

Before you finish reading chapter 3—probably before you finish reading chapter 1—you will be asking yourself questions about a framework for thinking about emotional or behavioral disorders. It is frustrating to try to discuss something with someone who is on a different wavelength. The experience is much like listening to a badly tuned radio that picks up two stations at once. So you might be asking, "What are the major frequency bands that I can tune in?" Other ways of asking this are, "What foundation concepts and principles guide people's thinking about emotional or behavioral disorders?" "How do we make sense of behavior that people call 'crazy,' 'sick,' or 'deviant'?" In chapter 4, I summarize some of the major theories (conceptual models) that scholars have used to explain both strange and commonplace behavior. These theories are of value for our purposes primarily because they help us when we ask, "How do we conceptualize efforts to help students who exhibit unacceptable behavior?" The way we think about things—the way we go about analyzing problems and testing solutions—will have a profound effect on what we do with students.

Perhaps the questions I've posed for Part One seem very basic. They are. But basic questions are often among the most difficult to answer. Their seeming simplicity is deceptive; complete and satisfactory answers to them have eluded the best minds for generations. As you begin reading this book, I hope it will be with a mixture of curiosity about how researchers and teachers have tried to address these questions and excitement about the questions you might ask yourself or others.

1

Definition: The Nature of the Problem

As you read this chapter, keep these guiding questions in mind:

- Why should an emotional or behavioral disorder (EBD) be considered a disability?
- What is the difference between emotional or behavioral disorder and serious emotional disturbance?
- What criteria should one use in deciding that behavior is disordered or abnormal?
- Why is defining emotional or behavioral disorders so difficult?
- How is the current federal definition inconsistent with Bower's research and his intention in writing a definition?
- Why is the judgment of teachers or a multidisciplinary team a necessary part of any school-based definition of emotional or behavioral disorder?

This book is about children and youths who arouse negative feelings and induce negative behavior in others. They are not often popular or leaders among their peers. Typically, they experience academic failure in addition to social rejection or alienation. Most adults choose to avoid them as much as possible. Their behavior is so persistently irritating to authority figures that they seem to be asking for punishment or rebuke. Even in their own eyes, these children and youths are usually failures; they obtain little gratification from life and repeatedly fall short of their aspirations. They have disabilities; compared to nondisabled individuals, their options in important aspects of daily living are highly restricted. Their disabilities are the result of their behavior, which is discordant with their social-interpersonal environments; their behavior costs them many opportunities for gratifying social interaction and self-fulfillment.

EMERGING TERMINOLOGY

This book is about children and youths who have been called **emotionally disturbed** or **behaviorally disordered**. *Seriously emotionally disturbed* is the label currently used in federal legislation and regulations regarding special education. *Behaviorally disordered* is preferred by some professionals in the field of special education, however, because it is a more accurate descriptor of the socialization difficulties of children and youths. *Behaviorally disordered* also seems to be a less stigmatizing label than *emotionally disturbed* (Feldman, Kinnison, Jay, & Harth, 1983; Smith, Wood, & Grimes, 1988). Yet in the professional literature and in the laws and regulations of various states, many additional terms refer to the same population. For the most part, these terms are combinations of one of the terms from column A and another from column B in Table 1.1. Thus, in a given state, the label may be **emotionally handicapped** or **emotionally impaired**, while in another it may be **behaviorally impaired**. Occasionally, combinations of two words from column A appear with one from column B—*socially and emotionally maladjusted, socially and emotionally disturbed, personally and socially maladjusted*, and so on. The point is that the terminology of the

Table 1.1
Combinations of Terms

Column A	Column B
Emotionally	Disturbed
Behaviorally	Disordered
Socially	Maladjusted
Personally	Handicapped
	Conflicted
	Impaired

field is confused—sometimes as confused as the children and youth to whom we apply the labels.

Confusing combinations of terms are beginning to give way to a commonly accepted label for this category. The term **emotional or behavioral disorders** was adopted in the late 1980s by the National Mental Health and Special Education Coalition, a group formed in 1987 to foster collaboration among various professional and advocacy organizations (Forness, 1988b; Forness & Knitzer, 1992). By 1991, more than 30 professional and advocacy organizations were members of the Coalition, and it now appears that after decades of disagreement the terminology **children and youths with emotional or behavioral disorders** will be widely accepted. Although this terminology may not be adopted in state and federal laws and regulations, we use it in this book with the understanding that it is the language now preferred by many parent and professional organizations. The Coalition chose **emotional or behavioral disorders** over other possible labels simply to indicate that the children and youths to whom it refers may exhibit disorders of emotions or behavior or both. It is a more clearly inclusive term than many others.

DEVELOPMENTAL NORMS VERSUS SOCIOCULTURAL EXPECTATIONS

Some of the behaviors that disabled children and youths exhibit are recognized as abnormal in nearly every cultural group and all social strata. Muteness, serious self-injury, eating feces, and murder are examples of disorders that are seldom or never considered culture-specific. These disordered behaviors represent discrepancies from universally accepted developmental norms. On the other hand, children and youths are often handicapped simply because their behavior violates standards peculiar to their culture or the social institutions in their environment, such as their school. Academic achievement, various types of aggression, sexual behavior, language patterns, and so on will be judged deviant or normal depending on the prevailing attitudes in the individual's ethnic and religious group, family, and school. Failing to read, hitting others, taking others' belongings, and swearing, for example, are evaluated according to the standards of the child's community. A given act or pattern of behavior may be considered disordered or deviant in one situation or context, but not in another—simply because of differences in the expectations of the people with whom the child or youth lives (cf. Peterson & Ishii-Jordan, 1994). The majority of emotional or behavioral disorders are defined by such sociocultural expectations, not by universal developmental norms. Research now indicates, however, that behaviors violating some sociocultural expectations may also be developmental disorders. Hyperaggression and covert antisocial behavior, for example, are disorders of conduct that not only violate social expectations but also create developmental risk (Kazdin, 1995; Walker, Colvin, & Ramsey, 1995).

BEHAVIOR SHAPED BY ITS SOCIAL CONTEXT (ECOLOGY)

Many emotional or behavioral disorders, though not all, originate or are made worse by the child's or youth's social interactions. The disorders are learned through modeling, reinforcement, extinction, and punishment—learning processes that shape and maintain much of everyone's behavior, both normal and deviant (Bandura, 1986). Adults and youngsters in the child's or youth's environment may accidentally arrange conditions that cause and support undesirable, inappropriate behavior. Ironically, the same adults who unwittingly shape inappropriate behavior may then initiate action to have the child or youth labeled "disturbed," "disordered," or "maladjusted." The child or youth might behave quite differently if these adults changed their own behavior in relation to the youngster's, or if he or she were placed in a different social environment. The problem in these cases is partly, and sometimes mostly, in the caretakers' or peers' behavior.

One might be tempted to conclude that the child or youth with an emotional or behavioral disorder is not "to blame" for the way others react. But youngsters' behavior influences the actions of their parents, their teachers, their peers, and others who interact with them. Children "teach" their parents, teachers, and peers how to behave toward them as surely as they are taught by these others (Bell & Harper, 1977; Emery, Binkoff, Houts, & Carr, 1983). It is not appropriate to ascribe "fault" exclusively to either the youngster with an emotional or behavioral disorder or to others in the environment. Teaching and learning are interactive processes in which teacher and learner frequently, and often subtly, exchange roles. When a youngster has difficulty with teachers, peers, or parents, it is as important to consider their responses to the behavior as it is to evaluate the youngster's reactions to others. It is not surprising, therefore, that an ecological perspective has become popular.

An ecological perspective takes into account the interrelationships between the child or youth and various aspects of the environment. The problem of emotional or behavioral disorders is not viewed simply as a youngster's inappropriate actions but, rather, as undesirable **interactions** and **transactions** between the youngster and other people. For example, a child's temper tantrums in school could indeed be a problem. An ecological perspective demands that the behavior of the child's teachers, peers, and parents—their expectations, demands, and reactions to the child's tantrums and other behavior—be taken into consideration to explain and deal with the problem (Walker, 1995).

TYPES OF DISORDERS AND CAUSES

The environmental conditions under which children and youths display disordered emotions and behavior vary widely. Some youngsters endure extremely adverse circumstances, including abuse, neglect, and pervasive disadvantage, without developing emotional or behavioral disorders; others succumb to adverse circumstances; and some develop disorders in environments that are clearly conducive to normal development.

Although environmental conditions affect how children and youths behave, biological factors also exert a strong influence. We do not know precisely why some children are relatively vulnerable and others invulnerable to environmental conditions. A wide variety of causal factors may give rise to a wide variety of emotional or behavioral disorders, and the relationships among causes and disorders is exceedingly complex, as will become apparent in subsequent chapters. We can seldom determine the cause of the disorder in individual cases.

EXAMPLES OF DISORDERED EMOTIONS AND BEHAVIOR

Children and youths can cause negative feelings and reactions in others in many different ways. As we will see in following chapters, disordered emotions or behavior may be described according to two primary dimensions: **externalizing** (aggressive, acting-out behavior) and **internalizing** (social withdrawal). The following cases illustrate the range in types of emotional or behavioral disorders and the variety of factors that can cause children and youths to become disabled. We have chosen these examples to show that disordered emotions and behavior have been reported in the literature of earlier centuries as well as in current writings; they appear in young children as well as adolescents; they are exhibited by individuals who have grown up in privileged homes of caring parents as well as by those who have been reared in poverty or under abusive conditions; they are often accompanied by lower than average intelligence but sometimes by intellectual brilliance; they may be characterized by externalizing (acting out) or internalizing (withdrawn) behavior or alternation between the two; and they may be described from the perspective of an observer or of the self.

In the case of Tony quoted below, notice that the youth's disordered emotions and behavior obviously are disturbing to the community, are of long standing, have been resistant to intervention by a variety of individuals (including teachers), and seem related to adverse environmental conditions.

Tony

When he was 8, Tony Singleton [not his real name] was getting high on dope and booze he says he stole from his mother.

At 14, he was incarcerated after being convicted of breaking and entering, and petit larceny.

When, as a 17-year-old, he attacked two women near the University of Virginia, authorities decided juvenile court was no longer appropriate. And, in February, a Charlottesville Circuit judge sentenced 18-year-old Singleton to 11 years behind bars.

Court documents based on statements by Singleton and interviews with people who have tried to help him produce a picture of a troubled youth who throughout his short life has received services from an assortment of psychologists, social workers, probation officers, and teachers. . . .

A psychiatric evaluation of Singleton prepared this year [1987] by Park E. Dietz of the Forensic Psychiatry Clinic at the University of Virginia paints a portrait of a confused and desperate young man. Singleton told Dietz he was neglected by his mother, a local plant worker who was often away from home. She never married Singleton's father but lived with a succession of boyfriends, one of whom would regularly beat Singleton.

Singleton said his mother had . . . marijuana, and at a very young age he began to steal both [drugs] and money from her.

He said he sometimes smoked the dope. Other times he sold it to kids on the streets of Charlottesville.

Between 1974 and 1976, the . . . Social Services Department, which investigates complaints of abused and neglected children, received reports that Singleton, between 5 and 7 years old at the time, was not properly cared for.

A worker from the department observed that Singleton's mother left him free to roam. While unsupervised, he would break into cars and houses. Singleton was not properly dressed and occasionally slept outdoors.

Social workers arranged to have Singleton taken from his mother and placed with his paternal grandmother.

The grandmother lived in a three-bedroom house with 11 other people, including a mentally retarded daughter.

A probation officer who visited the home in 1983 described it:

> There was no front doorknob on the inside of the front door. She (the grandmother) has a rug pushed up against the door to prevent cold air from coming inside as the door does not meet the base of the frame tightly.
>   The blue walls have a few holes in them and the drapes are falling down. (Her) clothes hang on a clothesline which extends along the wall of her living room. . . . A foul odor permeates the air. . . . She sleeps in the den on a sofa.

When Singleton entered school, a psychologist found the youngster was functioning below average. Almost a decade later, Singleton, 15 at the time, was reading and doing arithmetic at the fifth grade level.

Singleton was placed in special education classes at . . . elementary and . . . middle schools.

A [middle school] teacher described him as "desperate for friends but . . . has difficulty establishing relationships."

Schoolmates teased him about his unpleasant odor, caused by bedwetting.

To avoid the taunts, Singleton built a partition around his desk.

Early in 1983, Singleton was convicted of burglary and theft and placed on probation.

While on probation, he violated curfew and exhibited behavior problems, and was placed in the Boys Attention Home, a house in Charlottesville for juveniles whose next step into the juvenile justice system would place them in a more restrictive state learning center.

His probation officer said that while Singleton was there he "refused to follow rules or complete chores and on several occasions left the program without permission."

He was transferred that summer to the Barrett Learning Center, a state juvenile detention facility in Hanover.

Authorities there initially noticed gradual improvement in Singleton's behavior. But eventually, he started cursing the staff and breaking the rules daily. (McHugh, 1987, pp. A1, A6)

In Tony's case we see obvious environmental factors contributing to his troublesome behavior. At first glance, at least, his behavior seems less puzzling than Mark's (whose story follows) because we understand how unfavorable home and school environments can make a child want to strike out at others. It is harder to understand the hostility or nastiness of a youth who has been reared in an economically privileged environment. We find fewer ready explanations for a "chip on the shoulder" attitude, particularly when the youth is blessed with intellectual superiority in addition to economic advantage.

Mark

The nervous, anxious, and seemingly hostile adolescent sat on the far side of the 6-foot classroom table. He fingered a pack of Marlboros, turning them over and over. His concentration was intense, unrelenting, compulsive, almost as if he hoped, by concentrating on the cigarettes, to direct the thoughts of the alternative school's staff away from him.

At first glance, he looked more like a candidate for admission to one of the better prep schools than for a slot in an alternative program. He was wearing a blue, oxford-cloth shirt, cream-colored cords, and docksiders. He hadn't bothered to tuck the shirt in and one button too many had been left open. . . .

He arrived at school early enough on the first day to claim the coveted last desk in the last row. He systematically walled in his space. The back of his chair was always against the classroom wall. Books, papers, pencils, pens; anything he owned was strewn, like a fortress, on the floor around his desk. . . .

Mark was maniacal about keeping his space for himself. He wanted no one near him and would become verbally abusive if anyone touched him. He was struggling for attention, and at the same time refusing to accept it.

Mark's verbal contortions ranged from sophisticated wit to murderous descriptions of the ways he would eliminate his prime adversary in the classroom (me) to new and unheard of vulgarities.

When a very slow student in the class was awed on learning that Mark lived in the best section of town, he explained that the only difference was that Perrier® came out of the Matthews' faucets.

At least once a day he would consider himself victimized, and me the victimizer. Requests for classwork were considered irrational. Requests for a halt to a variety of obscenities were considered unfounded. Any request that required some form of cooperation was considered untimely. After refusing to participate, Mark would offer vivid details on his latest plan for my elimination. These would often come after I would reach out to him and especially after I would try to touch him.

Mark created many new vulgarities and embellished old ones with disarmingly picturesque terms. The adults associated with the program were well over 30 and none of us had heard many of Mark's vulgarities. One staff member began compiling a working dictionary of Mark's barbarisms. . . .

He was often sent to the solitary confinement of "the cubicle" to stop his disruption of the class and permit other students to work. I spent hours there with him looking at and talking to the hurt, intelligent eyes of a superior being. Repeatedly, he rejected verbal or physical contact.

As the school year drew to a close, his nervous, compulsive, repetitive behavior intensified. Even while sitting still, he seemed to be pacing the walls in the parameters of his being. His concentrated mental isometrics were increasingly painful, trying, and irrational. . . . (Maruskin-Mott, 1986, p. 53)

We are tempted to see students like Mark as products of our time. We may conclude that they are "spoiled" beyond belief or victims of the hidden stresses of modern life, the products of economically privileged but emotionally destructive families (which confuse the child with conflicting and inconsistent messages). But similar cases and similar explanations (e.g., the heightened levels of stress in contemporary life or inconsistent discipline) have been presented in the literature for many decades. Consider the case of N. B., presented more than a century and a half ago.

N. B.

N. B., aged 16, was described to me by his father, who came to consult me, in regard to his management, as a boy of singularly unruly and intractable character; selfish, wayward, violent without ground or motive, and liable under the paroxysm of his moodiness to do personal mischief to others; not, however, of a physically bold character. He is of a fair understanding, and exhibits considerable acuteness in sophisticated apologies for his wayward conduct. He has made little progress in any kind of study. His fancy is vivid, supplying him profusely with sarcastic imagery. He has been subjected at different times, and equally without effect, to a firmly mild and to a rigid discipline. In the course of these measures, solitary confinement has been tried; but to this he was impassive. It produced no effect.

He was last in a very good [school] in a town in —, where he drew a knife upon one of the officers of the establishment, while admonishing him; and produced a deep feeling of aversion in the minds of his companions, by the undisguised pleasure which he showed at some bloodshed which took place in this town during the disturbance of 18—.

He has not appeared to be sensually disposed, and he is careful of property. His bodily health is good, and he has never had any cerebral affection. This boy was further described to me as progressively becoming worse in his conduct, and more savagely violent to his relatives. Still I easily discovered that he was unfavourably situated; for his relations appeared to be at once irritable and affectionate; and the total failure of various plans of education was throwing him entirely upon their hands.

As an instance of the miserable pleasure which he took in exciting disgust and pain, I was told, that when 13 years old, he stripped himself naked and exposed himself to his sisters. (Mayo, 1839, pp. 68–69)

The behavior of Tony, Mark, and N. B. illustrate externalizing behavior of boys, and indeed the most typical child or youth with an emotional or behavioral disorder is an acting-out male. Moreover, we tend to focus our concern on externalizing or acting-out behavior; it is difficult, and sometimes dangerous, to ignore it. However, professionals and the public are becoming increasingly aware of two facts: first, both boys and girls have externalizing and internalizing disorders; second, internalizing behavior can be extremely serious. Eating disorders (particularly **anorexia** and **bulimia**), which are most common among adolescent girls, have received much attention in the professional literature and the popular press for several decades. The case of Char illustrates anorexia in early adolescence.

Char

Char is a 12-year-old . . . only child and lives with her parents in a middle-class urban area. She was referred by her family physician for an assessment following weight loss during the preceding 6 months from 100 pounds to 75 pounds. She had lost approximately 5 pounds in the 10 days prior to the assessment interview. Char complained that she had felt depressed over the past year and indicated that she did not understand why everyone was so concerned about her weight. Her parents were distressed because Char had become increasingly withdrawn and would not eat with the family. Their attempts to prod her into eating had been met with increasing resistance, with fights around mealtime becoming the norm. (Garner & Parker, 1993)

The case goes on to explain that Char had been of average weight in elementary school but had, beginning about six months before her referral, become increasingly self-conscious and begun complaining that she was too fat. At first, her parents, who themselves were health-conscious, supported and praised her dieting. But after several months they became terrified that Char would waste away. Char felt depressed but did not want to gain weight, as her weight loss was the only accomplishment that had given her positive feelings about herself in many months. Eating disorders like Char's, which are related to anxiety and depression, may or may not directly involve a student's schooling. However, depression and anxiety disorders can severely impede a child's psychological development and academic progress, as illustrated by the following case.

Kenny

Kenny is a 10-year-old boy who . . . is extremely fearful of going to school and has refused to go for the past several months. In addition to school refusal, Kenny is unable to enter all other situations that involve his being separated from his parents (e.g., playing in the backyard or at other children's homes, going to Little League practice, staying home with the babysitter). When "pushed" to go to school, or to be separated from his parents when at home, Kenny responds with crying and tantrums. He also has threatened to hurt himself (e.g., jump out of the classroom window) if forced to go to school.

Kenny's separation problems began about 1 year prior to his evaluation at the clinic. At that time, Kenny's father was having problems with alcohol abuse and was frequently absent from the home for prolonged periods of time. Kenny's separation anxiety worsened gradually over the course of the year, resulting in complete school refusal. Help had been sought at a local mental health clinic where psychotherapy was provided, but Kenny continued to deteriorate. He developed significant depressive symptomatology, including dysphoric mood, guilty feelings about his problems, occasional wishes to be dead, and periodic early morning awakening. (Last, 1992, p. 89)

Some children and youths acquire severe disorders in late childhood or adolescence after years of normal development. However, children may begin exhibiting disorders at a very early age. When the onset is very early, children are often diagnosed as having some form of **pervasive developmental disorder**, such as autism or Asperger's disorder. Some young children exhibit behavior that appears to be the early onset of conduct disorder (cf. Loeber, Green, Lahey, Christ, & Frick, 1992) or that appears to have some unspecified neurological cause and carries no specific diagnostic label. In some cases, it is difficult or impossible to distinguish one severe disorder from another. Regardless of the eventual diagnosis, if these very serious problems are not addressed early and effectively, the consequences for the child and family can be tragic. The early onset of severe disorders of unspecified type are illustrated by the cases of Frankie and Albert.

Frankie

At age four, Frankie was referred to a therapeutic preschool program by his day care center. He had been expelled from the center for severe behavior problems, disobedience, tantrums, hurting other children, and disrupting the program. At the home he shared with his 18-year-old mother and alcoholic grandmother, Frankie deliberately drank charcoal starter fluid. At first his mother denied that Frankie had problems. Gradually, she responded to the staff and parents at the therapeutic preschool, and Frankie began to change his behavior. (Knitzer, 1982, pp. 3–4)

Albert

When I observed Albert just before Christmas in the resource room where he was taught one-on-one, he was noncompliant with reasonable requests (e.g., "Sit in your chair"), and verbally and physically aggressive toward his full-time aid, his teacher, and his classmates on the playground. He had frequent tantrums, vomited and ate his vomitus, blew his nose and wiped the mucous on others.

Albert had not started his academic life isolated in the resource room. When his parents registered him at school, they requested that Albert be fully included in the general education classroom. And even though the psychological folder from a school in another state delineated Albert's difficult behaviors, the strong medications he took every day, and his institutionalization for three months the previous year, the school agreed to the parents' request. They placed him in a second grade class. Albert was a rising third grader, but was so small that parents and school administrators decided that he would do better in the second grade.

I was consulting in this school, and as part of this process I interviewed the teachers who were responsible for Albert's education. Mrs. Tinsley, the regular second grade teacher, had volunteered to have Albert as part of her class. She had special education training, had fully included other children with disabilities successfully in her class, and was looking forward to Albert's coming. Her second grade class consisted of "mostly well-behaved achieving students." Albert was coming to the Dream Team—to experienced teachers who wanted him and to classmates who would be good role models for him.

But Albert had not read the textbooks. He continued the unpleasant behaviors mentioned in the psychological folder; wiping mucous on others when his will was thwarted, screaming constantly, vomiting (once into the printer because he didn't wish to stop using the computer), pulling and grabbing the other children's clothes, biting adults for no apparent reason other than that they were there. At first, according to Mrs. Tinsley, the other students wanted to help him. They became "big brother" or "big sister" to him. Most of the interactions his classmates initiated with him consisted of trying to cue him to comply with teacher requests, and praising him on the rare occasions when he did—just what we would have taught them to do as peer confederates. Although a few students encouraged him to misbehave, most wanted to help him. After a while, according to Mrs. Tinsley, the students were afraid and confused by Albert's behavior. School personnel could not find strong enough rewards (or effective response cost procedures) to moderate Albert's behavior. He continued to vomit and eat it, to yell and scream. Even though all the teachers involved with Albert tried to cue him about appropriate and inappropriate comments, he still initiated conversations with classmates by asking them if they loved him or if they would marry him. He continued to pull and to grab the other children's clothing and tried to urinate on the boys when he went to the bathroom. (Kauffman & Pullen, 1996, p. 10)

Children and youths with emotional or behavioral disorders usually present problems to many of the people with whom they have contact. Most relevant to the focus of this book are the difficulties they cause teachers and peers at school. All veteran teachers of students with emotional or behavioral disorders recall incidents in which the pupils defeated their best efforts to instruct or maintain order. In many cases, teachers marvel at the wild antics of their students or the seemingly unsolvable puzzle their behavior presents. And, in retrospect, many leading experts are amused by their naiveté—which sometimes served them well and sometimes was disastrous—in dealing with students who are difficult to manage and teach (see Foster, 1986; Kauffman & Lewis, 1974; Patton, Kauffman, Blackbourn, & Brown, 1991). Pearl Berkowitz, an important figure in the development of special education for students with emotional and behavioral disorders, relates some of her early experiences as follows.

Pearl Berkowitz

If you could look back and focus on my most vivid memory, you might see me, now the teacher in Mrs. Wright's former classroom, futilely hovering over two hyperactive twelve-year-old girls who are fighting about which one should use the free half of an easel, while on the other side of this easel, a big, burly, belligerent boy is calmly painting, secure in the knowledge that no one would dare question his right to do so. Standing near the window is a small, thin-faced, pale, remote-looking boy who is staring at the fish tank, apparently just watching the fish swim around. Next to him, another boy is sitting on the rocker tickling himself under the chin with the mink tails he has just cut off the collar of the school secretary's new spring coat. Two children, a boy and a girl, perched on the old dining table, are playing a loud game of checkers, while another boy is silently resting, stretched out atop an old upright piano which I had inveigled into my room. Sporadically, in the midst of this magnificent atmosphere for learning, some child says to another, "Your mother," and the entire class seems to leap together and land in a football pile-up on the floor, while I stand helplessly by.

Of course I made many mistakes, but I hope I also learned something from each. Let me share just one of these early mistakes with you. I was doing my weekly planning when a brilliant idea occurred to me. I decided that the greatest contribution I could make that week would be to bring some culture into the lives of those poor, deprived, disturbed children at Bellevue. To start on this enriching experience, I elected to read to them a favorite poem from my own elementary school days, "The Owl and the Pussycat." Imagine my consternation at the chaos I caused when I reached the lines, "What a beautiful pussy you are, you are. What a beautiful pussy you are." The children actually tumbled out of my room with noisy screaming and guffawing. Within minutes, I was left alone in the classroom, bewildered and unaware of what had caused the difficulty. I had a lot to learn. (Berkowitz, 1974, pp. 30–31)

Surprises are part of teaching children with emotional or behavioral disorders, even after one has been at it many years and become highly skilled; mistakes and disappointments, as well as successes and gratification, are part of the territory. Patricia L. Pullen describes an unexpected response to a good teaching procedure with Barry, a 9-year-old youngster who exhibited a variety of problem behaviors.

Patricia L. Pullen

Perhaps my most frustrating and surprising experience with Barry involved an attempt to reinforce him with praise for appropriate behavior. One day as I was working with another group of children across the room I observed him playing quietly and appropriately with a classmate. Because this was something he seldom did that I wanted to encourage, I decided to do what I'd been taught will "reinforce" good behavior. I walked over to Barry, knelt beside him, gave him a hug, and commented, "Barry, I really like the way you're playing quietly with the blocks and having fun with Susie." He looked at me strangely, jumped to his feet, and screamed at me, "Well, fuck you, shitload!" (Patton et al., 1991, p. 31)

When a teacher has success with a student whose disordered emotions and behavior have presented major problems, the gratification is enormous. Consider the sense of accomplishment the teacher must have felt in the following case.

Andy

Andy started in my class on Valentine's day. He was no Valentine. He didn't think teacher directions (e.g., "It's time to line up for lunch") were very important. When Andy wanted to play in the free-time area, he expected to be allowed to do so, and he protested loudly when he wasn't. In short, Andy wanted to do what he wanted to do when he wanted to do it without any interference from anyone, including teachers. He reminded me of a line from a Bogart movie: "I want what I want when I want it." Andy soon found out that I was not Lauren Bacall.

His teacher from the previous school in another system called me after he had been at school for two days. She was loaded with information about his family and academic information not included in the psychological folder, such as cues to give him to stop some of his undesirable behavior.

I also made a home visit. Andy's mother, Mrs. Johnson, received me in her immaculately clean dining area. She never looked at the IEP changes I wished to make in Andy's educational plan. She never looked at me. She looked at the razor strap on the table. This strap had been cut in two, had a leather thong in the top which she pulled onto her wrist. Twice, while I was there, she banged the strap on the table when one of the children was too loud or too close for her comfort. Mrs. Johnson signed the addendum to the IEP, and I left. I also vowed that Andy would get *lots* more attention from me, my aid, the principal, the speech pathologist, and anybody else I could strong-arm into doing a favor for me.

It was imperative that we get Andy in his seat, get him to stay in his seat, and to complete work that his previous teacher assured me he could do. He was fascinated with the box of shells I had collected at the beach the previous summer. I sorted them into sizes and promised him one of the tiny shells for every problem he worked correctly. I had bags and bags of shells at home that had cost me nothing, and he loved them. Soon he asked, "Instead of all those little shells, how about if I get a bigger one for a whole sheet?" We discussed that the papers had to be neat, mostly correct, as well as completed. He thought that was fair. My aid found an old pencil box, covered it, and helped him glue his shells onto the box—a treasure chest. In the meantime, I sent him with good notes all over the school; to the principal, the guidance counselor, the secretary, and anybody else who expressed an interest in Andy.

Andy's work habits improved. His behavior improved. And, after a while, he began to give his shells to the younger children in the class, or back to me at the end of the day. It wasn't long before a sticker on his paper displayed on the bulletin board was enough for him.

Instead of going to the guidance counselor, principal, or secretary for stickers for his papers, he began to give his good papers to them, happy for their praise and their thanks.

The following year, he needed much less reinforcement. It seemed he was proud just to finish a paper. "I do good work, don't I?" (Kauffman & Pullen, 1996, p. 6)

Finally, it is important to consider how disordered emotions and behavior look and feel from the perspective of the child or youth. As Bower (1980) notes, "Of all the afflictions to which human beings are heir, none is more difficult to understand, conceptualize, or assess than that called 'emotional'" (p. 201). Our conceptualizations cannot be complete until we have been able to set aside the analysis of "problem" or "disorder" from the adult's perspective and see it through the child's eyes. We can find many examples of the child's perspective in contemporary literature. Let us first consider two examples of the youngster's view of school-related problems taken from the personal retrospectives of two noted special educators, Esther P. Rothman and Sheldon R. Rappaport.

Esther P. Rothman

From the start, I hated school, deeply, irrevocably, and silently. Kindergarten was anathema. Rather than take me to the doctor every other day with sore throats and stomachaches that were strictly school-induced, my mother finally capitulated and let me stay at home. First grade was no better, however, and as my sore "threats" would no longer work, and as the compulsory school laws prevented my mother from withdrawing me, I had no alternative but to start off for school daily and then divert myself to the rocks and crevices that then underlay the Hellsgate Bridge in the new and growing suburb of Queens, twenty minutes away by subway from the lower East Side where I was born.

I wonder if teachers really appreciate how overwhelmingly frightening it is to be a truant. Fear possessed me completely—fear of ridicule by school-loving seat-mates, each of whom was smarter than ten of me put together; fear of God, who was certainly going to punish me by striking my parents dead; but, most of all, fear of tongue-lashings by arm-twisting teachers, who were going to debase me by "leaving me back." Which indeed they did. I was a "holdover." My teacher didn't bother to explain to my mother why I was left back, but she clearly told everyone else. I couldn't read. And I couldn't read because I played hooky—or so she said. The fact that I was already reading Hebrew and the exotic adventures of Dickie Dare in my friend Lilly's third-grade reader was totally unknown to my teacher, yet I am certain, even now, that if she had known it, she would not have altered her decision.

My teacher was what I knew she was—anti-Semitic—because my mother told me so. This was a word I learned very early in life, and I accepted it casually as I accepted being an alien, one of only four Jewish children in the entire school. I felt special—not a bad feeling, but not completely good either.

I was never permitted to hold the American flag in front of the class for our morning class salute—a sacrosanct ceremony in every classroom in the entire school. My shoes were never clean enough. Once I was told I had lice. Or sometimes I did not have a handkerchief safety-pinned to the lower shoulder of my dress; this handkerchief always had to be in that exact same spot—never elsewhere. I never figured out how it was that we were supposed to blow our noses, and I never asked. I settled it myself. I had a handkerchief for showing and a handkerchief for blowing. And usually I forgot one or the other or both deliberately because I firmly believed that good little girls should never need to blow their noses at all. It was too crass. Instead, I stuffed pencil tip erasers up my nostrils. As for boys, I never even wondered what they did. Handkerchiefs were not within their generic classification.

These memories come flooding over me as I write—the hurt of being labeled a liar by a seventh-grade teacher who did not believe I had written a composition using the word *chaos* because I could not give him a definition of it. Did he never understand that I knew the word *chaos* down to my very toes because I felt it deeply every day of my life in school? Then there was the day my fifth-grade teacher threw into the garbage can the chocolate cake my mother had baked for a class party and which the children had voted to give to the teacher because it was the prettiest cake of all. And going farther back, I remember staring at the school map that hung—large, frightening, and overwhelming—from the border of the chalkboard and trying desperately to find New York State while not another child spoke—every eye, especially the teacher's, was glued to me. But worst of all was the indignity, fear, and humiliation of having to cheat on a test because I could not remember whether four-fifths equalled 80 percent. (Rothman, 1974, pp. 221–222)

Sheldon R. Rappaport

That school day had been like all others—bright with the joy of being with children and blurred in a kaleidoscope of activity. But in late afternoon, there was something different in the way Miss Joseph asked us to take our seats. Her customary calm and warmth were missing. On top of that, she announced that the principal had come to talk to us. My stomach squinched "danger."

The principal, small, grayed, and austere, spoke in her usually clipped fashion about the importance of working hard in school. As her train of thought thundered by, I was aware only of its ominous roar. The meaning of her words did not come into focus until she made the pronouncement: "Those boys and girls who have frittered away their time, and as a consequence will not be promoted to second grade, will stand when I call their names." Then she called my name.

The shock and mortification staggered me, making it difficult to struggle out of my seat and stand beside my desk. Who stood when she called the other names, the faces of those who remained seated, and what further remarks she intoned all blurred into a macabre dance that encircled my shame. Breathing was painful and had, I was sure, a ridiculously loud rasp which was heard by everyone. My legs rebelled at supporting my weight, so my fingers, aching tripods of ice, shared the burden. In contrast to the cold of my numbed face were the hot tears that welled in my eyes and threatened to spill down my cheeks to complete my degradation.

The principal left. Class was over. Amid joyous shouts, children milled through the door that for them was the entrance to summer fun and freedom. Some may have spoken to me, to tease or to console, but I could not hear them. The warm and pretty Miss Joseph was there, speaking to me, but I could neither hear nor respond. The borders of my mind had constricted like a hand clutching my pain.

Daily I sat staring at a book that would not surrender to me its meaning. In my war with the book, now and again I was victorious over an isolated word, but the endless legion of pages ultimately defeated me. Repeatedly, I looked back over the unfriendly, unyielding rows of print to find a word that I could recognize. In doing so, my failures amassed by the minute, like a swelling mob jeering at me. Finally, the fury rising within me burst from my fists, while from between clenched teeth I silently cursed the head I was pounding. To me, the immutable reality was that my head was bad. It caused my frustration. It sponsored my shame. I knew no alternative but to beat it into becoming a smarter head. That failed, too, adding daily to my feelings of frustration and worthlessness.

Daily terrors were walking the eight blocks to and from school and going into the school yard for recess. Being all flab and clumsiness and wearing thick glasses made me a ready target for any kid who needed to prove his prowess by beating me up. And the number who needed that were legion. Consequently, a rainy day became a reprieve. To awaken to a rainy morning was like an eleventh-hour stay of execution. It meant no recess outdoors. And nobody who wanted to fight. But even better than a rainy morning was being ill. Only then, in my bed, in my room, did I feel really secure. In the fall of third grade I missed twenty-two days of school. I was confined to bed with rheumatic fever, as I learned from the family doctor when I didn't have the desired wind for distance running while in college. Despite pains which I can still vividly recall, that confinement is the most peaceful of all my childhood memories.

The only outdoor activities I enjoyed were pretend ones. (The woman who lived in the next row house must have been sainted.) To get me out of the house, my mother put on the open porch the piano stool I played with. It became the steering wheel of a huge, powerful truck (you know how loud they are), which I guided flawlessly along endless highways, gaining the admiration of all whom I passed. At other times, I ventured across the street where the vacant lot became a battlefield on which I, clothed in my father's army tunic and overseas cap, performed feats of heroism and distinction for which I received countless medals and accolades. Those fantasized moments of glory apparently nourished my thin strand of self-respect enough to enable it to withstand the daily siege on my pride.

At night, when the cannonade of derision was still and my imperiled pride temporarily safe, I implored God and the Christ, Jesus, to see to it that tomorrow would not hold for me the tortures of today. I offered all possible concessions and deals, but relentlessly the tomorrows of Monday to Friday were no better. (Rappaport, 1976, pp. 347–350)

Although Rothman and Rappaport clearly experienced serious and painful problems of adjustment in childhood, neither was identified as mentally ill. However, children sometimes do experience major mental illnesses. Very occasionally, a young child may have **schizophrenia**, a disorder that is usually diagnosed in young adulthood and affects about 1 in 100 adults. Schizophrenia is a mental illness with physiological causes that are poorly understood (Leutwyler, 1996). It involves major disorders of thought processes and perceptions, such as delusions or hallucinations, and it is often episodic—people with it may go through alternating periods of acute illness and remission. Treatment with psychotropic drugs is the primary form of intervention in schizophrenia, although certain forms of psychotherapy can be helpful in some cases, and support from the child's family is critical. For children and youths, appropriate education is also an extremely important part of treatment. In the following case, an anonymous youth provides a first-person account of what it is like to experience schizophrenia as a child. (We shall return to Elizabeth's experience in later chapters.)

Elizabeth

I have schizophrenia. Actually I have childhood-onset schizophrenia. This is a very rare form of schizophrenia, especially in girls.

I have had problems ever since I started school. I remember trying to hide under the tables in kindergarten so I wouldn't have to do any work. In first grade I was in the top reading group, even though my mom and grandma had to come to school every day to make sure I got my work done. By the third grade I was in the bottom reading group. I started the fourth grade, and I was doing better because I was taking Ritalin. But something happened in October. All of a sudden I couldn't read or write or do math anymore. Everything was so confusing because I couldn't understand anything that was going on around me. By November I was so sick I couldn't go to school anymore. On November 13 I went to the hospital and I stayed there for 2 months.

I got on a medicine called Mellaril and that helped me on my way to recovery. A doctor told my family that one-third of schizophrenia patients get well all by themselves, one-third can be helped with medicine, and one-third cannot be helped by medicine. But getting better took me a long, long time. In the middle of the seventh grade, I was proclaimed to be in remission. . . .

I have been in remission for over 2 years. Whenever we ask either my psychiatrist or my psychologist what my future will be, they say they just don't know. Childhood schizophrenia is just too rare (especially in girls), and my recovery and improvement have been like miracles. My psychologist says I am high functioning. I don't know exactly what he means. But every night I pray that I will stay in remission. So far that has worked along with my therapy, my medicine, and all the help I get from my family and some of my teachers. (Anonymous, 1994, pp. 587, 589-590)

A severe mental illness such as schizophrenia does not necessarily exclude a child or youth from participation in typical activities and preclude a successful career, given that the illness can be treated successfully and necessary family and school supports are provided. The following information about Elizabeth puts her account into perspective and strikes a very hopeful note.

Elizabeth (continued)

Elizabeth was in 10th grade when this was written [with the help of her mother]. She is now a senior in high school and has been able to mainstream all academic classes while maintaining a B average. Every weekday afternoon she tutors two fourth-grade students who are having difficulty with reading at her former elementary school. She is looking forward to attending a junior college next year. It is her dream to be an elementary school teacher. (Anonymous, 1994, p. 590)

Other descriptions of disordered emotions and behavior and their treatment are scattered throughout this book. In each case it is important to consider not only the unpleasant or disturbing features of the youngster's behavior, but also the circumstances that may have contributed to the problem and the reactions of others (both peers and adults). Children and youths with emotional or behavioral disorders should not be viewed merely as youngsters who cause others to experience anger, grief, anxiety, or other unpleasantness. They are troubled as well as troubling, and they often must live in situations that are not conducive to satisfactory interpersonal relations. Teachers must be sensitive to the students' pain, even while they themselves are being pained by the youngsters' misbehavior, puzzling responses, or academic failures in their classrooms.

PROBLEMS OF DEFINITION

The cases you have read about so far may clearly illustrate what children and youths with emotional or behavioral disorders can be like; nevertheless, descriptions are not a definition. These youngsters' problems may seem obvious, but the way they should be defined as a category is not obvious.

The children and youths who are the topic of this book etch pictures in one's memory that are not easy to erase. The foregoing discussion and descriptions provide the basis for an intuitive grasp of what an emotional or behavioral disorder is, but the definition of such a disorder—the construction of guidelines that will foster valid and reliable judgments about who does and who does not have it—is anything but simple. One reason it is so difficult to arrive at a reliable definition is that an emotional or behavioral disorder is not a thing that exists outside a social context, but a label assigned according to cultural rules (Burbach, 1981; Peterson & Ishii-Jordan, 1994). Perhaps a science of behavior exists, but the objective methods of natural science play a relatively minor role in designating someone as deviant. An emotional or behavioral disorder is whatever behavior a culture's chosen authority figures designate as intolerable. Typically, it is behavior that is perceived to threaten the stability, security, or values of that society (Moynihan, 1993; Rhodes & Paul, 1978).

Defining an emotional or behavioral disorder is unavoidably subjective, at least in part. We can be objective and precise in measuring specific responses of individuals, and we can be painstakingly explicit in stating social norms, cultural rules, or community expectations for behavior. But we must ultimately realize that norms, rules, and expectations, and the appraisal of the extent to which particular individuals deviate from them, require subjective judgment. The problem of definition is made all the more difficult by differences in conceptual models, differing purposes of definition, the complexities of measuring emotions and behavior, the range and variability of normal and deviant behavior, the relationships among emotional or behavioral disorders and other exceptionalities, the transience of many problems during human development, and the disadvantages inherent in labeling deviance.

Differences in Conceptual Models

Distinctly different conceptual models have been developed to guide intervention. Psychodynamic, biological, sociological, behavioral, ecological, psychoeducational, educational, and phenomenological models have been described (see McDowell,

Adamson, & Wood, 1982; Smith et al., 1988; Van Hasselt & Hersen, 1991a, 1991b). Each conceptual model includes a set of assumptions about why children behave as they do and what must be done to correct disorders. Unsurprisingly, a definition derived from the tenets of one conceptual model does little but baffle or disappoint those who hold the assumptions of a different model. Writing a definition to which all can subscribe, regardless of conceptual persuasion, may be impossible. An additional problem is that many concepts about the emotional or behavioral disorders of children and youths are merely adaptations of conceptual models of adult psychopathology and do not consider the developmental differences of youngsters at various ages. We discuss conceptual models more fully in chapter 4; suffice to say here that people who disagree about what emotional or behavioral disorders are at a theoretical or philosophical level are unlikely to agree on a practical definition.

Differing Purposes of Definitions

Definitions serve the purposes of the social agents who use them. Courts, schools, clinics, and families rely on different criteria for definition. Courts give greatest attention to law-violating behavior, schools primarily to academic failure, clinics to reasons for referral, and families to behavior that violates their rules or strains their tolerance. Perhaps formulating a single definition that is useful to all the various social agents who are responsible for youngsters' conduct is impossible. In this book we are primarily concerned with definitions that serve the purposes of public education. Consequently, our focus is on school-related issues, and we often refer to the children and youths in question as "students."

Surveys reveal that the definitions of state education agencies often include statements regarding the supposed causes (often citing biological or family factors), requirements for certification of the youngster (often specifying who may legitimately classify the child or youth), and exclusions (for example, a statement that the disorders cannot be caused by mental retardation or serious health impairments) (Cullinan & Epstein, 1979). School administrative definitions vary so much that a student might be classified in one state but not in another. Clearly, definitions are seriously problematic if a student can change from "normal" to "disturbed" merely by moving across a state line. States may be moving slowly toward aligning their definitions with the definition used in federal regulations; nevertheless, great variability remains in terminology and definition from state to state. Moreover, the current federal definition itself presents serious problems, as we will see.

Difficulties in Measuring Emotions and Behavior

No tests measure personality, adjustment, anxiety, or other relevant psychological constructs precisely enough to provide a sound basis for defining emotional or behavioral disorders. Psychometric tests may contribute to understanding a youngster's behavior, but the tests' reliability and validity are inadequate for purposes of identification. Although the problems of reliability and validity are especially great for projective tests, which purportedly measure unconscious mental processes, these problems also occur in personality inventories, behavior rating scales, and screening tests designed to sift out students who may have a disorder (Piacentini, 1993; Merrell, 1994).

Some of the difficulty in measurement is a result of attempts to assess supposed internal states or personality constructs that cannot be observed directly. Direct observation and measurement of behavior have begun to reduce reliance on indirect measurement, but these newer assessment techniques have not resolved the problem of definition. Although it may be more useful to a teacher to know how frequently a student hits classmates or sasses an adult than to know the student's responses to psychometric tests, there is no consensus among teachers or psychologists as to what frequency of a given behavior indicates a disorder. Local norms for given behavior problems may be useful in screening, but they do not provide a general definition.

To compare students for purposes of classification, behavior must be measured under specified environmental conditions. This standard is required because behavior is typically quite sensitive to social context: students behave differently under different circumstances. Even if environmental conditions are specified and students' behaviors are measured directly and reliably under those conditions, however, we are still not likely to derive a satisfactory definition. The reason is that, given a single set of environmental circumstances, disordered and adaptive behavior are defined by more than behavioral frequencies. Adaptive and disordered behavior are defined by the student's ability or inability to modulate his or her behavior in everyday environments to avoid the censure of others and obtain their approval. The problem of measurement here is analogous to that in the fields of vision and hearing. Central visual acuity and pure tone auditory thresholds can be measured rather precisely under carefully controlled conditions, but these measures do not indicate how efficiently one will see or hear in one's everyday environment (except within very broad limits). Two people with the same auditory acuity, for example, may function quite differently, one as hearing (using oral language almost exclusively) and the other as deaf (relying mostly on manual communication). Visual and auditory efficiency must be assessed by observing how the individual adapts to the changing demands of the environment for seeing and hearing. Behavioral adaptation must also be judged by observation and according to how well one meets environmental demands that often change subtly. This judgment calls for experienced "clinical" appraisal, which includes precise measurement of behavior but goes beyond quantitative assessment. It also demands knowledge of cultural influences on behavior.

Range and Variability of Normal and Deviant Behavior

A wide range of behavior may be considered normal; the difference between normal and disordered behavior is usually one of degree rather than kind, and there is no sharp line between the two. Most children and youths do nearly everything done by those who have emotional or behavioral disorders, but they perform these acts under different conditions, at a different age, or at a different rate. Crying, throwing temper tantrums, fighting, whining, spitting, urinating, screaming, and so on are all behaviors that can be expected of all youngsters. Only the situations in which children and youths with emotional or behavioral disorders perform these acts, or the intensity and rate at which they do them, sets them apart. Longitudinal studies and surveys of youngsters' and parents' perceptions of problem behavior show clearly that a large number of children and youths who are considered "normal" show disturbing behaviors, such as tantrums, destructiveness, fearfulness, and hyperactivity to some degree and at some time during their development (see, for example, Achenbach & Edelbrock, 1981). Most students are considered to be a behavior problem at some time in school by one of their teachers (Campbell, 1983; Rubin & Balow, 1978). The problem of definition involves comparison against a nebulous and constantly changing standard. For most behaviors, there are inadequate quantitative norms to which we can compare a student's behavior.

There is also great variability in deviant behavior. Deviant acts can range from physical assault on others to extreme withdrawal. An individual may exhibit behavior that alternates between these extremes, and the degree of deviance may change markedly over time or with changes in the environment. It is thus inappropriate to consider most classifications of human behavior as mutually exclusive, such that one must be considered either aggressive or nonaggressive, withdrawn or gregarious, and so on. Writing a definition that deals adequately with the many types and degrees of disorder is extremely difficult.

Relationships Among Emotional or Behavioral Disorders and Other Exceptionalities

As Hallahan and Kauffman (1977) pointed out decades ago, there are many similarities among students with mild mental retardation, learning disabilities, and emotional or behavioral disorders. Students with severe disabilities in these three categories have many common characteristics. There is considerable literature regarding emotional or behavioral disorders in individuals with mental retardation (Barrett, 1986; Epstein, Cullinan, & Polloway, 1986; Menolascino, 1990). Not only is it often difficult to distinguish among students with such pervasive developmental disorders as autism or mental retardation, but in some cases it may also be difficult to distinguish very young children with severe emotional or behavioral disorders from those who are deaf, blind, or have suffered brain injury.

A student may have more than one type of disability. Disordered behavior may occur in combination with any other type of exceptionality; indeed, emotional or behavioral disorders probably occur more frequently in combination with other disabilities than alone. Defining emotional or behavioral disorders in a way that excludes other handicapping conditions, therefore, is unrealistic. A disorder should be defined specifically enough for its definition to be of value in working with children and youths whose single or primary disability is maladaptive emotions or behavior, but broadly enough to admit its coexistence with other disabilities. This is no easy matter.

Transience of Many Emotional and Behavioral Problems

Emotional and behavioral problems are often transitory. Behavior problems exhibited by young children seem likely to disappear within a few years unless the problems are severe or include high levels of hostile aggression and destructiveness. Definitions must take into account age-specific and developmentally normal problems that do not persist over a long period of time.

Disadvantages in Labeling Deviance

A problem associated with the issue of definition is the unavoidable practice of labeling—attaching a diagnostic or classifying label to the student or behavior (Burbach, 1981; Hallahan & Kauffman, 1994, 1997; Kauffman & Pullen, 1996). Assigning any label is dangerous because the label is likely to stigmatize and can significantly alter the youngster's opportunities for education, employment, and socialization. This seems to be true regardless of the conceptual foundation of the definition with which the label is associated or the semantics of the label. Furthermore, once a student has been labeled, changing the label may be difficult or impossible. However, we cannot talk about things, including disabilities, without using labels (language) to describe them. Our definitions should be couched in language that will minimize damage to students when they are identified as members of a particular deviant group.

IMPORTANCE OF DEFINITION

The issue of definitions may not appear serious at first. If a student has an emotional or behavioral disorder when adult authorities say so, then why not concern ourselves with the more important issue of effective intervention and leave the question of definition to those who enjoy arguing about words? Serious reflection leads us ultimately to conclude that definition is too important to leave to chance or whim.

The definition we accept reflects how we conceptualize the problem and, therefore, what intervention strategies we consider appropriate. A definition communicates succinctly a conceptual framework that has direct implications for practitioners. Medical definitions imply the need for medical interventions, educational definitions imply the need for educational solutions, and so on. Furthermore, a definition specifies the population to be served and thereby has a profound effect on who receives intervention as well as how they will be served. It follows that if a definition specifies a population, then it will provide the basis for estimates of prevalence. Finally, decisions of legislative bodies, government executives, and school administrators concerning allocation of funds and training and employment of personnel are guided by the implications of working definitions. Vague and inappropriate definitions contribute to confused and inadequate legislation, foggy administrative policies, nonfunctional teacher training, and ineffective intervention. Definition is a crucial as well as a difficult problem, and it behooves special educators to construct the soundest possible definition.

A case in point—definitional problems affecting services to students—is the current federal definition, which has been widely criticized as inadequate or inappropriate for a variety of reasons. The federal definition seems to indicate that a student must be failing academically to be classified as "seriously emotionally disturbed" for special education purposes. This feature of the definition may result in denial of services to a large number of students with serious disorders but academic skills judged adequate for their grade placement (Kauffman, 1986a; Morse, 1985; Smith et al., 1988).

THE CURRENT FEDERAL DEFINITION: ITS DERIVATION AND STATUS

During the past 30 years, numerous definitions of emotional or behavioral disorders have been constructed. Each has served the particular purposes of the writer, but none has resolved the problems of terminology, specificity, clarity, and usefulness that we have discussed. Only one has had a significant influence on public policy at the national level—that of Bower (1981). The current federal definition derives from Bower's research involving thousands of students in California in the 1950s. Although Bower's definition is a logical interpretation of his findings, the version that was adopted by the U.S. Department of Education has been widely criticized as illogical (see Bower, 1982; Council for Children with Behavioral Disorders Executive Committee, 1987; Forness & Knitzer, 1992; Kauffman, 1986a). To understand the issues, one must first understand Bower's definition and then compare it to the federal version, point by point.

In a classic treatise on definition and identification, Bower defined "emotionally handicapped" students as those exhibiting one or more of five characteristics to a marked extent and over a period of time:

1. An inability to learn which cannot be explained by intellectual, sensory, or health factors . . .

2. An inability to build or maintain satisfactory interpersonal relationships with peers and teachers . . .

3. Inappropriate types of behavior or feelings under normal conditions . . .

4. A general, pervasive mood of unhappiness or depression . . .

5. A tendency to develop physical symptoms, pains, or fears associated with personal or school problems (Bower, 1981, pp. 115–116)

According to Bower, the first of these characteristics, problems in learning, is possibly the most significant school-related aspect of emotionally handicapped youngsters' behavior. Another important feature of his definition is the inclusion of degrees or levels of severity.

Emotional handicaps may be displayed in transient, temporary, pervasive, or intensive types of behavior. To complete the definition, it would be necessary to establish a continuum in which the degree of handicap can be perceived and perhaps estimated, especially as it relates to possible action by the school. One could begin such a continuum with (1) children who experience and demonstrate the normal problems of everyday living, growing, exploration, and reality testing. There are some, however, who can be observed as (2) children who develop a greater number and degree of symptoms of emotional problems as a result of normal crises or stressful experiences, such as death of father, birth of sibling, divorce of parents, brain or body injury, school entrance, junior high school entrance, or puberty. Some children move beyond this level of adjustment and may be described as (3) children in whom moderate symptoms of emotional maladjustment persist to some extent beyond normal expectations but who are able to manage an adequate school adjustment. The next group would include (4) children with fixed and recurring symptoms of emotional maladjustment who can with help profit by school attendance and maintain some positive relationships in the school setting. Beyond this are (5) children with fixed and recurring symptoms of emotional difficulties who are perhaps best educated in a residential school setting or temporarily in a home setting. (Bower, 1981, p. 119)

Bower's definition has many good points, particularly its specification of five characteristic types of behavior. Still, it does not easily enable one to determine that a particular child or youth is or is not emotionally handicapped. There is much latitude in terms like *to a marked extent* and *over a period of time*. There is also a need for subjective judgment about each of the five characteristics. Consider the problems in answering these questions:

Just what is an inability to learn? Is it evidenced by a 1-year lag in achievement, or 6 months, or 2 years? Does it include inability to learn appropriate social behavior, or only academic skills?

How do you establish that an apparent inability to learn is not explainable by intellectual factors or health factors? Do health factors include mental health factors?

Exactly what are satisfactory interpersonal relationships with peers?

What behavior is inappropriate, and what are normal conditions?

When is unhappiness pervasive?

Bower's definition is widely criticized because it obviously lacks the precision necessary to take much of the subjectivity out of decision making. This may not be a fault of his definition. It may be the nature of the problem of definition. Bower's definition has had a tremendous impact on public policy not because of its accuracy, but primarily because it is included, with a few changes, in the rules and regulations governing implementation of Public Law 94–142 (now the Individuals with Disabilities Education Act, IDEA). Section 121a.5 of the rules and regulations, with the most significant differences between it and Bower's definition indicated by italics, reads as follows:

"*Seriously* emotionally *disturbed*" is defined as follows:
(i) The term means a condition exhibiting one or more of the following characteristics over a long period of time and to a marked degree, *which adversely affects educational performance*:
(A) An inability to learn which cannot be explained by intellectual, sensory, or health factors;

(B) An inability to build or maintain satisfactory interpersonal relationships with peers and teachers;

(C) Inappropriate types of behavior or feelings under normal circumstances;

(D) A general, pervasive mood of unhappiness or depression; or

(E) A tendency to develop physical symptoms or fears associated with personal or school problems.

(ii) The term includes children who are schizophrenic [or autistic].[1] *The term does not include children who are socially maladjusted, unless it is determined that they are seriously emotionally disturbed.* (45 C.F.R. 121a.5[b][8][1978])

Bower's terminology "emotionally handicapped" was changed to "seriously emotionally disturbed." As noted by our use of italics, the federal rules and regulations contain three statements not found in Bower's original definition. These added statements do not make the definition clearer; in fact, they come close to making nonsense of it. The additional clause "which adversely affects educational performance" is particularly puzzling. One might speculate that it is a pro forma statement (that is, set up in advance) that the regulation is concerned only with educational matters. The clause is redundant, however, with characteristic A, "An inability to learn," if educational performance is considered to mean academic achievement. Moreover, a student is extremely unlikely to exhibit one or more of the characteristics listed to a marked degree and for a long time without adverse effects on academic progress. But what should one conclude about a student who exhibits, for example, characteristic D, "A general, pervasive mood of unhappiness or depression," and is academically advanced for his or her age and grade? If educational performance is interpreted to mean academic achievement, then the student would seem to be excluded from the category of seriously emotionally disturbed; however, if educational performance is interpreted to include personal and social satisfaction in the school setting, then the clause is superfluous.

Even greater confusion is created by part ii regarding schizophrenia and autism and social maladjustment. Any youngster with schizophrenia would clearly be included under the original definition; that is, any such child or youth will exhibit one or more of the five characteristics listed (especially B and/or C) to a marked degree and over a long period of time. Therefore, the addendum is unnecessary. The final addendum regarding social maladjustment is incomprehensible. A youngster cannot be socially maladjusted by any credible interpretation of the term without exhibiting one or more of the five characteristics (especially B and/or C) to a marked degree and over a long period of time (Bower, 1982; Cline, 1990).

Many professionals are very unhappy with the current definition because of the limitations we have discussed, and hope that it will soon be replaced. In "So, Who's Crazy?" a distinguished leader in special education muses about how our assumptions regarding problem "ownership" influence our definitions. Before considering an alternative definition, however, we should consider additional perspectives on the problem.

---

[1]The federal definition was revised in the 1980s to exclude autistic students. Autism was made a subcategory under "Other Health Impaired" because of the belief that it is a condition having biological causes. Bower (1982) notes the logical problems inherent in excluding autistic and socially maladjusted students from his definition and from the federal version. In 1990, autism was made a separate category.

So, Who's Crazy?

As a past president of the Council for Children with Behavioral Disorders, C. Michael Nelson wrote the following thought-provoking comments about who "owns" the problems of troubled and troubling children and youths.

"I intentionally chose [the term *crazy*] over the jargon preferred in our profession, such as psychotic, emotionally disturbed, or behaviorally disordered, because it more accurately conveys my impression that such labels are readily applied to anything or anybody we don't understand or with whom we disagree. The judgment that someone or something is crazy is relative and situational. It depends upon who is doing the judging, the standards against which they are judging, and the limits of the context in which the judgment is applied. . . .

"So, who's crazy? The way I see it, there are several candidates for the title. You might think of this as a multiple choice test. Is it (a) children and youth—our traditional choice; (b) ourselves—by which I mean teachers, teacher trainers, and other professional caretakers; (c) the 'system'—which includes schools, agencies of state and federal government, as well as professional organizations; (d) society itself; or (e) all of the above?" (Nelson, 1985, p. 9)

PERSPECTIVES ON DEFINITION

In the early part of the twentieth century, psychiatric perspectives on definition tended to be accepted with little question by school personnel. Bower's work in California public schools in the 1950s and 1960s and the growth of special education programs for students with emotional or behavioral disorders led to definitions becoming more closely related to students' behavior in the classroom. Most professionals recognize that a given definition is never adequate for all purposes. As Knitzer (1982) commented, "It is hard to talk about children and adolescents who need mental health services. Terms like 'mentally ill,' 'behaviorally disordered,' or 'psychotic' take away their uniqueness and pain" (p. 3). The most useful definition for educators is one that clearly focuses on the behavior problems of students in schools.

Ironically, the current federal definition may be contributing to underservice of students with emotional or behavioral disorders. The addenda to Bower's definition allow so many interpretations that students who need services can be excluded relatively easily. Some can be excluded because they are not academically retarded; others because they are judged to be socially maladjusted but not emotionally disturbed (see Center & Obringer, 1987; Cline, 1990; Forness & Knitzer, 1992). Legal arguments continue over such issues as whether a student must be academically retarded under the definition and whether adjudication as delinquent qualifies a juvenile as "seriously emotionally disturbed."

The definition of emotional or behavioral disorders remains partly subjective, even though several relevant characteristics of a student's behavior can be described clearly. The definition of disturbance or disorder eludes complete objectivity for the same reasons that happiness and depression defy completely objective definition. This does not mean that the effort to devise more objective means of identifying students must be abandoned (as we discuss further in Part Two). Nor does it mean that it is impossible to improve the definition. For the definition to be most useful to educators, however, the subjective judgments that go into identifying students must include those of the teachers who work with them. In decisions made by groups of professionals, the *teacher*, not the psychologist, social worker, or psychiatrist, should be viewed as the most important "imperfect test" in determining that a student needs help in school (Gerber & Semmel, 1984). Reliance on teachers' judgments puts great responsibility on teachers for moral and ethical conduct in decision making, but it is a responsibility they cannot avoid (cf. Howe & Miramontes, 1992; Kauffman, 1992).

AN EMERGING DEFINITION

Although the problems presented by the current federal definition have been recognized for many years, professionals have not until recently been able to reach agreement on a substitute definition, much less to persuade the U.S. Congress to adopt a new one. When the National Mental Health and Special Education Coalition was formed in the late 1980s, it created a working group assigned to propose a new definition. The working group represented more than a dozen different professional associations and advocacy groups, assuring that the proposed definition would initially have a strong base of support. The proposed new definition reads as follows:

I. The term emotional or behavioral disorder means a disability characterized by behavioral or emotional responses in school programs so different from appropriate age, cultural, or ethnic norms that they adversely affect educational performance, including academic, social, vocational or personal skills, and which:
    (a) is more than a temporary, expected response to stressful events in the environment;
    (b) is consistently exhibited in two different settings, at least one of which is school-related; and
    (c) persists despite individualized interventions within the education program, unless, in the judgment of the team, the child's or youth's history indicates that such interventions would not be effective.
    Emotional or behavioral disorders can co-exist with other disabilities.
II. This category may include children or youth with schizophrenic disorders, affective disorders, anxiety disorders, or other sustained disturbances of conduct or adjustment when they adversely affect educational performance in accordance with section I. (Forness & Knitzer, 1992, p. 13)

This definition obviously does not solve all the problems in identifying and serving children and youths with emotional or behavioral disorders. Nevertheless, the Coalition and many of its member organizations believe it is a significant improvement over the current federal definition. Forness and Knitzer (1992) note the following: (1) it uses terminology that reflects current professional preferences and concern for minimizing stigma, (2) it includes both disorders of emotions and disorders of behavior, (3) it is school centered but acknowledges that disorders exhibited outside the school setting are also important, (4) it is sensitive to ethnic and cultural differences, (5) it does not include minor or transient problems or ordinary responses to stress, (6) it acknowledges the importance of pre-referral interventions but does not require slavish implementation of them in extreme cases, (7) it acknowledges that children and youth can have multiple disabilities, and (8) includes the full range of emotional or behavioral disorders of concern to mental health and special education professionals without arbitrary exclusions. Nelson, Rutherford, Center, and Walker (1991) point out that a major problem of the current federal definition is its exclusion of many antisocial children and youth who need special education and related mental health services.

The Coalition and many of the more than 30 professional and advocacy groups have formally endorsed the proposed definition and are working toward its incorporation into federal laws and regulations. Those who support the definition hope that it will eventually become the standard adopted by the states as well.

SUMMARY

Children and youths with emotional or behavioral disorders are disabled by behaviors that are discordant with their social-interpersonal environments. The definition of these disorders is a difficult matter complicated by differences in conceptual models, differences in the purposes of various social agencies, problems in measuring social-interpersonal behavior, variability in normal behavior, confusing relationships among emotional or behavioral disorders and other exceptionalities, the transience of many childhood disorders, and the effects of pejorative labels. No definition can be made completely objective. No definition has been universally accepted. The most common definition used in educational contexts is that proposed originally by Bower and incorporated in the federal rules and regulations for IDEA. This definition specifies marked and persistent characteristics having to do with the following:

1. School learning problems
2. Unsatisfactory interpersonal relationships
3. Inappropriate behavior and feelings
4. Pervasive unhappiness or depression
5. Physical symptoms or fears associated with school or personal problems

Inclusion and exclusion clauses of questionable meaning have been appended to these characteristics in the federal definition. Although improvements in definition are possible, and more objective criteria for identification are being developed, teachers' responsibility for judging students' behavior cannot be avoided.

A new definition has been proposed by the National Mental Health and Special Education Coalition using the terminology **emotional or behavioral disorder**. The proposed definition has been endorsed by many organizational members of the

Coalition, which hopes to achieve incorporation of the new definition in federal laws and regulations. Major points of the proposed definition are these:

1. Emotional or behavioral responses in school
2. Difference from age, cultural, or ethnic norms
3. Adverse effect on educational performance (academic, social, vocational, or personal)
4. More than temporary or expected responses to stress
5. Consistent problem in two different settings, including school
6. Persistent disorder despite individualized interventions
7. Possibility of coexistence with other disabilities
8. Includes full range of disorders of emotions or behavior

Case for Discussion

"Where Does He Fit?"

Allan Zook

I did not realize they were "shopping" for the ideal class for their son when Allan's parents came to observe my classroom. Just prior to their observing, Allan had qualified for special education services as a student with multiple disabilities. But neither the school system nor the parents could decide where he could best be served. A week after their visit, my supervisor brought me Allan's folder and directed me to meet with the parents that week and develop an IEP for him. "You win!" she said as she patted my shoulder. My question was, "Why?"

My "prize" was 7 years old. He had received speech and language services since he was 2, took massive doses of anticonvulsant medication, and thought compliance with adults' requests or commands was disabling. He also had a repertoire of behaviors guaranteed to distress his teachers and peers. For example, he liked to pick his nose and wipe the results on teachers or students. He routinely exposed himself during the time he spent in mainstream classes. He was big for his age, aggressive, and had justifiably earned the description "bully." I was not surprised to observe that he played by himself and did not approach other students. They did not approach him, either.

Testing Allan was, according to the school psychologists who had tried, an extraordinary challenge. The full-scale IQ of 73 was to be taken with a grain of salt, as his responses were "unusual." Allan's academic skills were as delayed as his social skills. Most of the normative and curriculum-based measurement data placed him 2 to 3 years behind his age mates in reading and math. His fine motor skills were almost nonexistent, and requiring him to do any handwriting, cutting, or painting was for him a fate worse than death. "It's too hard," he always whined before he threw a tantrum.

Individual and small group instruction was almost impossible for Allan. Even when he tried to pay attention (which wasn't very often), he was distracted by anything and everything—people walking by the room, other students shifting in their seats, a newly decorated bulletin board, someone's clothing, a strange noise.

Some days he came to school late because he had experienced a seizure earlier in the day. On those days, he was subdued and not so eager to misbehave, but neither did he remember many of the skills he had mastered prior to the seizure. If he had a seizure in school, which happened occasionally, the rest of the day was a waste as far as academic work was concerned.

"So, why me, Lord?" I asked myself repeatedly. Allan's parents and the special education administrators considered classes designed for kids with learning disabilities, physical disabilities, and emotional disturbance, but they decided my class of kids with mild mental retardation was the best place for him. They liked my highly structured, directive program. They liked the fact that my kids were happy and learning lots of social and academic skills. They believed he'd fit in better in my class than in any of the others. Besides, I had room to take another student in my class without asking for a state waiver. So, I won the lottery.

Questions About the Case

1. Does Allan fit the definition of "serious emotional disturbance" in IDEA? Does he fit the definition of "emotional or behavioral disorder" of the National Mental Health and Special Education Coalition?

2. How would you determine which of Allan's disabilities was foremost for purposes of education?

3. Was Allan's placement in this class appropriate? Was it legal under IDEA? (You may want to revisit this question after you have read chapter 6.)

PERSONAL REFLECTIONS

Definition

Steven R. Forness, Ed.D., is Principal, Inpatient School, and an educational psychologist in the Outpatient Clinic at the UCLA Neuropsychiatric Hospital. He is also a Professor in the Department of Psychiatry and Biobehavioral Sciences at UCLA.

Why should an emotional or behavioral disorder be considered a disability?

Children who have emotional or behavioral disorders are disabled in an especially critical way. They are cut off in one way or another from the fullness of life itself. A boy with schizophrenia may at times be so bombarded by "voices in his head" that he can pay only intermittent attention to what the real people around him are saying. A girl with clinical depression may feel so withdrawn or sad that she can scarcely get out of bed in the morning, let alone enjoy the company of others. An adolescent with an anxiety disorder may be so fearful or preoccupied with what others may think that he or she avoids a whole variety of wonderful situations that are part of growing up. A young boy with an attention deficit may be so hyperactive or impulsive that the simplest of school tasks becomes arduous and cannot be finished without tremendous and exhaustive effort at concentration. Even a youngster with a conduct disorder may be so impelled to follow his or her own instincts as to be constantly drawn into conflicts, arguments, or physical aggression, even with close family members. Children like these have real and tragic disabilities.

These children may also have associated problems that add to their disability, especially in school. As many as half of them have serious academic problems. I have almost daily contact with youngsters whose schooling has been interrupted by their emotional or behavioral disorders for a wide variety of reasons. Some are so depressed or anxious that they never even make it to school for days or weeks at a time. Others are so prone to verbal conflict or physical aggression with classmates or teachers that they are frequently truant or suspended from school. Still others show behavioral or emotional responses to typical situations that are so unusual or bizarre that their schoolmates either begin to shun their company or, worse yet, tease them unmercifully. School becomes a particularly unhappy place for them. When someone asks the degree to which these youngsters are disabled, I answer as a special educator that a great many are perhaps even *more* disabled than children or adolescents with learning disabilities or mental retardation. As a matter of fact, recent annual reports by the U.S. Department of Education have shown that the long-term outcomes for youngsters with emotional or behavior disorders are among the worst in special education and that we are serving only the most seriously impaired in this category.

Why and how are these children disabled?

To answer that question, one has only to ask their parents, their teachers, and even the youngsters themselves. They will tell you not only of the devastating personal distress and stigma that go with having these disorders but also of the abysmal failure of education, mental health, child welfare, juvenile justice, and health insurance agencies to ease their plight. It is indeed this current combination of personal anguish and public neglect that leads me to see emotional or behavioral disorders as one of the most disabling conditions of the children with whom I work.

Why do professionals find it so difficult to agree on a definition?

I have observed the process of definition and diagnosis of emotional or behavioral disorders from several vantage points. I have worked as a special educator in a psychiatric setting for nearly 30 years. For several years, I have also been a member of the National Mental Health and Special Education Coalition, a group of about 30 professional associations representing school and mental health professionals as well as families of youngsters with emotional or behavioral disorders. I have also worked with others on the revision of the American Psychiatric Association's diagnostic manual. All these experiences lead me to wonder how we ever arrive at *any* definition of emotional or behavioral disorders!

Part of the problem stems from the limited perspective of each professional discipline. Parents tend to focus on the problems of living with their children, teachers often see only classroom management or academic issues, social workers tend to view family interactions as a primary focus, psychologists sometimes are preoccupied with the child's inner world or behavioral interactions that can be shaped and modified, and psychiatrists may concentrate on a search for effective medication. Seldom, if ever, does everyone sit in the same room and "pool" these fragments of knowledge. It is also exceedingly rare that professionals are trained in a truly *inter*disciplinary fashion. More often than not, they are taught in a *multi*disciplinary fashion where they work side-by-side, yet seldom interact with each other in any significant way.

Part of the problem also involves how we determine when an emotional or behavioral response actually crosses the line and becomes "deviant." Psychiatric diagnoses are not very reliable and often consist of selecting a critical but limited number of symptoms from a larger list of common characteristics of a particular disorder. Emotional or behavioral rating scales often depend on a rather arbitrary clinical cutoff point determined from a limited sample of patients. Projective tests depend greatly on the skill of individual clinicians who determine whether responses are outside normal limits. Case histories of a child with a potential emotional or behavioral disorder are frequently filtered through both the selective memories of parents or guardians and the biases of the interviewing clinician.

Finally, society itself shifts its tolerance for deviant behavior from generation to generation (witness the difference between the button-down era of the 1950s and the wild rebelliousness of the 1960s), from community to community (behavior that seems quite common to residents in an inner-city neighborhood may seem intolerable to those living in a wealthy suburb), and from age to age (behavior tolerated from a preschooler becomes unacceptable just a few years later). Given all of these barriers to consensus, the definition of emotional or behavioral disorders will continue to be the most elusive category in special education.

Is it useful to draw distinctions between emotional disorders and behavioral disorders?

In actual fact, it is sometimes difficult if not impossible to separate emotional from behavioral disorders. When I read case histories of children admitted to our psychiatric hospital for so-called "emotional" disorders, such as depression, the first thing that parents or teachers noticed in many cases was not necessarily the emotion of sadness but a behavior such as the child's acting agitated or aggressive or withdrawing from social situations. We often have to infer emotional states from a child's overt behaviors. I have also studied a rather large group of children with depression in our outpatient clinic and found that more than half of them had a separate diagnosis of conduct or attention deficit disorder *in addition* to their underlying depression. This comorbidity or co-occurrence of two disorders in the same child may be much more common in children referred for services, i.e., the ones referred for special education or mental health services. Dick Mattison, a psychiatrist whom I helped to train at UCLA, has done extensive research on children referred to special education for emotional or behavioral disorders. He found that nearly half of these students had two different diagnoses, usually an emotional *and* a behavioral disorder. Having one disorder does not confer any "immunity" from developing a second disorder; it may in fact even *predispose* a child to having another disorder. Seldom do disorders come in nice tidy packages.

Differentiating between these two types of disorders may be useful or even possible only at the extremes. Historically, the primary public school term for these disorders in federal special education law was "serious emotional disturbance." Most mental health clinicians and special educators nonetheless realize that it is not useful, and most of the time not even possible, to make these distinctions.

Are there other points you would like to make about this topic?

Three things about these children continue to amaze me. One is the incredible diversity of this population. We have from 20 to 40 children in our psychiatric hospital at any given time, ranging in age from 2 to early 20s. Most present challenging problems, even for an experienced special education teacher. Our inpatient school, therefore, has a variety of small preschool, elementary, and secondary classrooms to address the functional levels of these youngsters' learning and behavioral problems, with a variety of special or remedial curriculum materials and individualized token economy systems. But we also have an elementary classroom and a secondary classroom in which we have regular textbooks, put relatively little or no emphasis on token or checkmark systems, and focus more on academic progress than on classroom behavior or social skills. Kids who attend these latter two classrooms do so because they have been admitted to a psychiatric hospital for a range of *serious* psychiatric disorders. The expression of their particular emotional or behavioral disorders just doesn't seem to affect their ability to comply with most school expectations or do academic work. The educators in their community schools were completely (and probably appropriately) unaware that these children had serious psychiatric disorders such as schizophrenia, anxiety disorder, or depression.

Second, the children we serve often need many different types of services. I spoke earlier of comorbidity, i.e., two or more psychiatric disorders occurring in the same child. It turns out, however, that many of the children I work with have what I call "*tri*morbidity," i.e., two or more psychiatric disorders along with a learning disability or even mental retardation. Several also come with histories of child abuse and even chronic medical disorders, in addition to their emotional or behavioral disorders. Almost daily I come across kids who will need the services of at least four or five professionals when they leave the hospital—e.g., a psychiatrist to regulate their medication, a psychologist to assist their parents in developing and monitoring a home behavioral management system, a social worker for family therapy sessions, perhaps one of these three or even a fourth person to also be the child's therapist, a consulting special education teacher for learning disability materials in school, and even a pediatrician for medical problems that may be related to physical or sexual abuse or for a chronic medical problem that may be unrelated. It is not all that unusual that a single case may require the coordination of agencies for mental health, special education, child welfare, health services, and juvenile justice.

Third, time and time again, even after reading what looks like a catastrophic case history and steeling myself for the worst, the kid I meet is essentially just a kid. Relatively seldom is his or her behavior especially bizarre. More often than not the behavioral or emotional responses we see are crying, tantrums, mouthing off, fighting, and other things that most kids occasionally do in the course of growing up. Kids with emotional or behavioral disorders do these things but do them much more frequently and with less provocation. Emotional or behavioral disorders are, in all but a few cases, mostly a matter of degree. What separates them is the frequency (not the kind) of emotional or behavioral response. In most cases, there is just a kid underneath all that behavioral or emotional excess, a kid who is hurt or scared or misunderstood, either because of what has happened in the past or because of the insidiousness of the disorder itself. Some few disorders are, of course, extreme and require very specific treatments. In every case, however, we do well to remember that we treat a child, not a disorder.

2

Prevalence: The Extent of the Problem

As you read this chapter, keep these guiding questions in mind:

- In what sense does identification of students with emotional or behavioral disorders require arbitrary decisions?

- What is the difference between prevalence and incidence?

- Why have special educators been more concerned with prevalence than with incidence?

- Why is it difficult to arrive at precise prevalence figures?

- How can we use false positive and false negative scores on a behavior rating scale to estimate prevalence?

- What arguments can one use to defend the position that 2 percent of the student population is a conservative estimate of prevalence?

- Approximately what percentage of the public school population is now served by special education under the *seriously emotionally disturbed* category?

- Why does it seem unlikely that 2 percent of the school-age population will be served by special education (under the category of *seriously emotionally disturbed*) in the foreseeable future?

Nearly all children and youths at some time, in some social context, could be said to exhibit an emotional or behavioral disorder. But classifying nearly all children and youths as disabled by these isolated, transitory, or minor problems would be silly. Indeed, suggestions that 20 percent or more of children and youths have serious psychological problems create public disbelief and professional skepticism (cf. Smith et al., 1988). A typical reaction is that "bleeding hearts" are making much ado about the normal pains of growing up, bemoaning the usual slings and arrows that people must suffer as part of their daily lives. The general public and administrators also tend to dismiss teachers' reports of problems as unreliable. Teachers do sometimes mistake their own ineptitude in teaching and managing behavior for the emotional or behavioral disorders of students, and skeptics use this fact to discount all teachers' opinions. If we want to argue convincingly for special services, we must present the strongest possible case that the emotional and behavioral problems we are concerned about are unusual, debilitating, and not the result of teachers' inadequacies.

How frequently do students' emotional or behavioral problems clearly stand out from the usual difficulties of childhood and youth and seriously limit their options for social and personal development in spite of adequate teachers? The answer to this question cannot be entirely objective. Addressing the question requires that we establish arbitrary criteria. These criteria may be quite objective, but choosing the criteria requires subjective judgment. Consider similar questions: "How heavy (or thin or tall or short) must a person of given age be to qualify as exceptional for medical purposes?" "How little income must a person have to be considered poor for purposes of public assistance?" "How different from the average in intelligence and social adaptation must a student be to qualify as having mental retardation (or giftedness) for special education purposes?" In each case, we can "make" more people deviant—obese, poor, retarded, or disturbed, for example—simply by changing an arbitrary definition. Physicians, economists, social workers, psychologists, or educators may make their case for a given criterion, and their arguments may be convincing to legislators or others who make public policy or establish standards for judgment. The standards and policy are merely a matter of consensus, and they can be changed at will (cf. Moynihan, 1993).

The number or percentage of children and youths who are judged to have emotional or behavioral disorders, then, is a matter of choice. Disordered emotion or behavior is not a "thing," an objective entity that can be detached from the observer. Emotional or behavioral disorder, like poverty, is a social reality that we construct on the basis of our judgment as to what is tolerable and what is desirable (Kauffman, Gerber, & Semmel, 1988). Our task as professionals is to struggle with issues of prevalence, to make the most intelligent and caring choices we can about the lives of children and youths. We must seek to identify those students—and only those—for whom the risks associated with identification (such as social stigma) are outweighed by the advantages (effective intervention). This is no easy task. While we can and must make difficult judgments about the risks and advantages entailed in identification, we can seldom be absolutely certain that our judgment of the individual case is correct (Kauffman, 1984).

Try to decide which of the students in the following descriptions has an emotional or behavioral disorder. The descriptions are very brief, and you probably believe you should have more information before making judgments. You should, in fact, have more information; *anyone* should, and anyone would probably be unprofessional in making a judgment based solely on this information.

WHO HAS A DISORDER?

These descriptions are based on actual case histories. Some of the children and youths were labeled as having an emotional or behavioral disorder; others were not. Some were placed in regular classrooms; others in special classes or institutions. These brief case descriptions illustrate the difficulties even experts face in deciding who does and who does not have an emotional or behavioral disorder.

Barry

Barry has five older siblings, the youngest of whom is 10 years older than he. He has always been the "baby of the family" in everyone's eyes, especially his mother's. He is now a rotund third-grader whose torpor is remarkable. His obesity, sluggishness, and infantile behavior (e.g., he prefers to play with small stuffed animals) make him a constant and easy target for teasing by his classmates. Since he entered kindergarten, Barry's mother has brought him to school daily, sat in her car in the parking lot during the entire school day in case he should "need" her at any time, brought his lunch to him and fed him in the hall or in her car, and whisked him home after school. Her life seems absurdly devoted to his safety and comfort, yet ironically calculated to impair his psychological and physical growth and development. School officials suspect that Barry was bottle-fed until he was in the second grade, and they know that his diet now consists primarily of junk foods. He has no friends his age, and he will not participate in age-appropriate play in the classroom or on the playground. He is constantly teased by other children because of his weight and infantile behavior.

Darlene

Darlene's mother was a 12-year-old sixth-grader when Darlene was conceived. Recently graduated from high school, the mother is now pregnant with her third child. Darlene is a first-grader who frequently gets into trouble because she hits or pokes other children, fails to do her work, and disobeys the teacher. Other children are beginning to shy away from her in fear. She is bright-eyed and gregarious with adults, and the casual observer may not suspect that the teacher sees her as a significant problem.

Nathan

Nathan is an eighth-grader with an IQ in the gifted range. Although he is highly intelligent and creative and scores high on standardized achievement tests, his report cards contain only Ds and Fs. All his teachers and the school principal are exasperated with his constant clowning in class, his refusal to complete assignments (and his insistence that sloppy, incomplete work is sufficient), and his frequent "macho" behavior that gets him into fights with other students. His mother, a divorced former teacher, is at her wit's end with him at home; he is slovenly, refuses to do chores, threatens her and his older sister with physical violence, and was recently caught shoplifting.

Claudia

Claudia is the wispy 16-year-old daughter of a wealthy attorney. Her favorite book is the Bible; she is preoccupied with remaining slender in this life and earning the right to ecstatic happiness forever in the next. Her schoolwork is always perfect, or nearly so. She has only one close friend, a woman in her early 20s who has a history of suicide attempts. Claudia complains constantly of being tired, of being unable to sleep, and of being too fat. She is forever dieting and exercising, and she frequently vomits immediately after she eats a normal meal. She offers profuse apologies for any imperfection anyone points out in her behavior or academic performance.

Now let us look at a somewhat more detailed description. Does T. J. has an emotional or behavioral disorder?

T. J.

T. J. is an 11-year-old fifth-grader. His IQ is 115. He has no significant physical anomalies and no history of developmental delay in motor development or language. He had no particular difficulties academically until fourth grade. His academic performance was about average until last year, when his grades suddenly began to deteriorate. This year he is earning mostly Ds and Fs.

T. J. was not known as a problem child in school until last year. But every teacher who has dealt with him in the past 18 months has commented on his frequent misbehavior. He is difficult to manage because of his high rates of out-of-seat behavior, talking out, teasing, and temper outbursts. He is usually defiant of teachers and argumentative with his peers. These problems are, in the opinion of his current teachers, increasing. His belligerence recently resulted in several fights in and around school, including one in which another child was injured and required medical attention. Two weeks ago he was caught shoplifting a bag of candy from the local drugstore. Ratings by his teachers on a problem checklist indicate that his behavior is a problem more often than that of 90 percent of his schoolmates.

T. J. has no close friends, although he is sometimes tolerated briefly in school situations by other boys who exhibit similar behavior patterns. He and his two older brothers live with his mother and stepfather, who provide little supervision or control. His parents have never shown any interest in his school progress or lack of it, and they have refused to recognize that any of his behavior, including the fights and shoplifting, is a problem.

T. J.'s current teachers are quite concerned about him for several reasons. He does not complete most of his academic work and is failing in most subjects. He disrupts the class frequently by hitting or taunting other students or mumbling complaints about the teacher and assignments. He spends a lot of his time in class drawing "tattoos" on his arms with felt-tip pens. None of his three experienced teachers, who manage 63 fifth-graders as a team, has been able to establish a close relationship with T. J. or produce significant improvement in his behavior. (Kauffman, 1984, p. 62)

For special education purposes, should one consider T. J. to have a disorder? On the basis of the information presented, experts may disagree. Of course, one may argue that additional information is necessary to justify a decision. But regardless of how much additional information one might amass, the decision would probably remain questionable. Some would argue that T. J. presents a problem but does not have an emotional or behavioral disorder. Perhaps he needs help but not in the form of special education. Some might suggest that his home life and his teachers' lack of expertise are responsible for his behavior. T. J. and everyone else involved would have more to lose than to gain by his being identified as a student with an emotional or behavioral disorder. His problems can best be addressed through consultation with his regular class teachers on how to manage his behavior in the classroom and by providing social workers to help his parents do a better job at home.

Others would argue that T. J. shows all the classic signs of a student in trouble, one who is unlikely to improve without direct intervention. He is certainly headed for more social and academic trouble unless something is done, probably through provision of special education and related services. Special educators are the most appropriate professionals to deal with the situation, and the benefits of identifying him for special education would clearly outweigh the risks. He can be taught academic and social skills most effectively through placement in a special program for part of the school day with a smaller group of students and a teacher specially trained to manage such problems. After weighing all the outcomes—for T. J., his classmates, his teachers, and his parents—the greatest benefits and least damage will be done by providing special education.

Understandably, heated arguments about prevalence will continue into the foreseeable future. After all, the issues are both complex and emotional; they include economics, statistics, law, public policy, and concern for the welfare of children.

MEANING OF PREVALENCE AND INCIDENCE

Prevalence refers to the total number of individuals with X disorder in a given population. The prevalence of a disorder is calculated for a given period or for a point in time. Federal reports typically include the number of students with emotional or behavioral disorders counted at a particular time during the school year. Prevalence is often expressed as a percentage of the population; the total number of cases is divided by the total number of individuals in the population. Thus, if 40 students out of a total student population of 2,000 in a school or school district are identified as having emotional or behavioral disorders, then the prevalence rate is 2 percent.

Incidence refers to the rate of *inception*—the number of *new* cases of X disorder in a given population. **Cases** can refer to *individuals* or to *episodes* of the disorder (which means that an individual might be counted more than once during the incidence period if he or she exhibits the disorder, subsequently does not exhibit the disorder or goes into remission, and then again exhibits the disorder). Incidence, like prevalence, may be expressed as a percentage of the population, but this can be misleading when episodes rather than individuals are counted. Incidence addresses the question "How often does this disorder occur?" whereas prevalence addresses the question "How many individuals are affected?"

For special education purposes, prevalence has usually had more meaning than incidence. Prevalence has been the statistic of interest because most exceptionalities with which special educators deal have been assumed to be developmental, life-long characteristics. Consequently, teachers and school administrators have most often been concerned about knowing or estimating the number of students who have emotional or behavioral disorders or mental retardation or some other disability in any given school year.

Incidence of certain disorders or problems is often also important, however, particularly when making judgments regarding trends in the school population. The incidence of pregnancy, suicidal behavior, or drug and alcohol use among public school students, for example, may be critical for planning and evaluating intervention programs. Moreover, special educators are becoming increasingly aware that exceptionalities can be episodic. A student may function quite differently in one grade than in another, or even change rather drastically over a period of weeks or months. Emotional or behavioral disorders, as well as giftedness, mental retardation, and learning disabilities, are not necessarily immutable characteristics. To the extent that disorders are transient or episodic, incidence becomes equally as important as prevalence.

PREVALENCE AND INCIDENCE ESTIMATES: WHY SHOULD WE CARE?

Prevalence and incidence estimates have little meaning for the classroom teacher. When your responsibility is to teach a class of difficult children and you know that many teachers or parents are anxiously awaiting the day when their child can enter your class, what difference does it make whether 2 percent or 5 percent or 10 percent of the school's students have emotional or behavioral disorders?

For those who plan and administer special education programs at a districtwide or statewide or nationwide level, however, prevalence and incidence are extremely important. Prevalence estimates and incidence rates are the basis for requesting budgets, hiring staff, planning inservice programs, and so on. Frequently, school boards or school administrators decide to cut budgets or allocate additional funds because the percentage of children served by a program is more than or less than that of neighboring school districts or state or national averages. Thus, although prevalence issues may seem irrelevant or purely academic to classroom teachers, these issues can ultimately affect their working conditions.

PROBLEMS OF ESTIMATION

Estimates of the prevalence of emotional or behavioral disorders vary from about 0.5 percent of the school population to 20 percent or more. It is easy to see why estimates are varied and confused. First, because the definition is unsettled, the number of students cannot be determined accurately or reliably. It is difficult, if not impossible, to count the instances of a phenomenon that has no precise definition. Second, there are numerous ways to estimate the number of students with emotional or behavioral disorders, and differences in methodology can produce drastically different results. Third, the number of students counted by any definition and methodology can be influenced more by powerful social policy and economic factors than by professional training or clinical judgment. Judgments about who is and who is not disabled for special education purposes are surely influenced by social consequences and their economic implications (Kauffman et al., 1988; Moynihan, 1993). We will discuss each of these problems—definition, methodology, and policy and economic factors.

Lack of Standard Definition

The effect of differences in definitions on estimates of prevalence needs no more elaboration here (see Anderson & Werry, 1994 for discussion). But even when the same definition is used, estimates of prevalence differ. Consider that a survey long ago of state directors of special education (Schultz, Hirshoren, Manton, & Henderson, 1971) found prevalence estimates ranging from 0.5 percent to 15 percent in various states. A quarter century later, extreme variation—0.05 percent to 2.08 percent—was reported among the states in the percentage of pupils identified as having emotional or behavioral disorders and receiving special education under the federal category "serious emotional disturbance" (U.S. Department of Education, 1995). Even using a standard written definition, people seem to carry their own private definitions in their heads; they differ greatly in how they match the written definition to students' behavior.

The Methodology of Estimation

Prevalence and incidence are usually estimated from a sample of the population in question. It is not feasible to count every case in an entire state or nation, or even in an extremely large school district. The estimate must be generated from standard screening procedures applied to a carefully selected sample. The methodological problems are similar to those of conducting a poll or making a projection during an election. Different numbers will tend to be obtained, depending on how the sample is selected and what questions are asked.

The methodology of estimating emotional or behavioral disorders has not been well developed (see Anderson & Werry, 1994). How data are gathered and from whom they are taken make a difference in the number of cases or episodes counted. Should teachers, parents, psychologists, students, or some combination of these be consulted? What should be the criteria, and who should serve as judges? Should one rely on mailed questionnaires, personal interviews, referrals to social agencies, behavior ratings, or direct observation of behavior? And how should the survey sample be selected? For reasons of economy, most prevalence surveys have relied on questionnaires or behavior ratings. For purposes of identifying disorders in the schools, teacher judgment is obviously relevant and has been shown to be effective and reliable as well.

Because no standard methodology has been developed, and perhaps for other reasons as well, estimates of prevalence and incidence of emotional or behavioral disorders among child populations have varied wildly. Moreover, most studies of prevalence and incidence are open to criticism on methodological grounds. Methodological problems notwithstanding, we can make reasonable estimates of prevalence. One way to make a rough estimate is to compare behavior ratings of students who are already identified and receiving services to the ratings of nonidentified students. False negatives (students who should be but have not been identified) and false positives (students who have been identified but should not have been) can be estimated by establishing cutoff scores for behavior ratings, noting the extent to which distributions of scores for referred and nonreferred (or identified and nonidentified) individuals are overlapping. Achenbach and Edelbrock (1981) provide a rationale for this approach using parents' ratings of children who were referred and of children who were not referred for mental health services:

> In the absence of any litmus test for either mental health or disorder in children, it appears that actual referral for mental health services is an appropriate morbidity criterion against which to validate discrimination procedures, at least where mental health services are available regardless of family income. The value of actual referral is that it typically reflects persisting problems on the part of the child in one or more important life areas. Thus, even when parents do not perceive problems, pressure from school personnel and others seeing the child's behavior in natural settings often compels parents to seek help. Although false positives can certainly result from parental intolerance of normal child behavior or from parents' seeking help for themselves, and false negatives can result from parents' intransigence despite pressure to seek help, actual referral is probably as good a criterion as any other currently available. It may often be better than direct psychiatric assessments and mental health workers' ratings of parents' reports. (pp. 56–57)

Into Achenbach and Edelbrock's paragraph, we could substitute school-related phrases (for example, "actual identification of students for special education") for those related to mental health (for example, "actual referral for mental health services"). That is, one could argue that actual identification of students for special education is an appropriate criterion against which to judge the definition of emotional or behavioral disorder and procedures intended to discriminate between students who have a disorder and those who do not. A score on a behavior rating scale can be taken as an indication, but only one indication, that the student may need special education or mental health services. Given these assumptions, the question then becomes, "What percentage of the nonidentified group is similar enough to students in the already identified sample that they could reasonably be considered candidates for the same treatment?" This methodology is a comparison of two frequency distributions, such that areas of overlap in the distributions are of concern, as illustrated in Figure 2.1.

As shown by the hypothetical distributions in Figure 2.1, some nonidentified students will score as high as or higher than some identified students; conversely, some identified students will score lower than some who have not been identified. If an arbitrary cutoff score is chosen as the criterion, then false negatives and false positives can be identified. False negatives can be considered candidates for identification or as potentially in need of services; false positives can be considered candidates for reclassification as "nonhandicapped" (perhaps as a result of misclassification, perhaps as a result of therapeutic intervention). Table 2.1 shows the results of one study

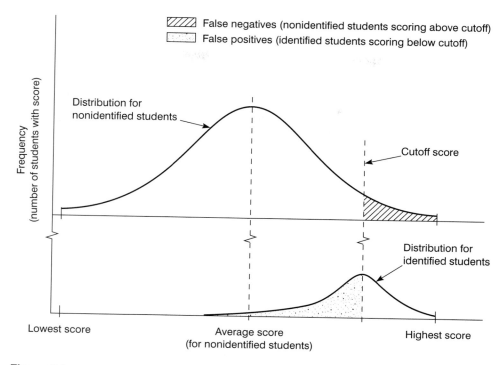

Figure 2.1

Hypothetical Frequency Distribution of Behavior Rating Scores for Nonidentified and Identified Students Showing Cutoff Score as Criterion for False Negatives and False Positives

involving teachers' behavior ratings on the *Behavior Problem Checklist* (Quay & Peterson, 1975) for 727 identified and 1,116 nonidentified students (Cullinan, Epstein, & Kauffman, 1984). Note that the percentage of false positives increased and the percentage of false negatives decreased with a higher cutoff score.

Using a similar methodology with parents' ratings, Achenbach and Edelbrock (1981) found that about 9 percent of a group of nonreferred children scored outside the normal range (that is, were false negatives) and about 26 percent of referred children scored within the normal range (that is, were false positives) when the cutoff score was the ninetieth percentile for the nonreferred group. These results are strikingly similar to those of Cullinan et al. (1984), except for senior high school students in the Cullinan et al. sample (see also Achenbach, Howell, Quay, & Conners, 1991).

Could one reasonably conclude on the basis of the Achenbach and Edelbrock (1981) and Cullinan et al. (1984) studies that about 9 percent of the nonidentified population has an emotional or behavioral disorder? Probably not. The behavior rating scores alone are not convincing, and a substantial percentage of the identified students were false positives. Allowing for a considerable margin of error in the classifications that would result from the behavior ratings, is it a reasonable guess that 3

Table 2.1
False Negatives and False Positives for 90 and 95 Percentile Cutoff Scores Based on Nonhandicapped Students on Total-Problems BPC Score, By Age-by-Sex Subgroups

Subgroups	90 Percentile Criterion			95 Percentile Criterion		
	Cutoff Score	% False Negative[a]	% False Positive[b]	Cutoff Score	% False Negative[b]	% False Positive[b]
Male						
elementary	21	10.6	22.4	28	5.5	57.8
middle	26	9.0	45.2	34	4.9	73.5
senior high	28	9.9	59.9	32	4.5	73.8
Female						
elementary	16	9.5	25.0	21	5.1	41.7
middle	20	8.8	27.3	25	5.3	34.1
senior high	25	10.1	66.2	37	4.0	90.9

Source: From "Teachers' Ratings of Students' Behaviors: What Constitutes Behavior Disorder in Schools?" by D.Cullinan, M.H. Epstein, and J.M. Kauffman, 1984, *Behavioral Disorders, 10*, p. 17. Copyright 1984 by The Council for Exceptional Children. Reprinted with permission.

percent to 6 percent of the population has an emotional or behavioral disorder? Probably so. To illustrate, let us assume that 2 percent of the school population is now classified as having an emotional or behavioral disorder (a high estimate). Let us also assume that half of these students are misclassified, such that only 1 percent "truly" have a disorder or "actually" belong in special education. Let us also assume that only one fourth of the false negatives (or one fourth of 9 percent) in the Achenbach and Edelbrock and Cullinan et al. studies "actually" have disorders (a conservative estimate). The percentage of the population "actually" having emotional or behavioral disorders would thus be estimated at 3.25 percent.

Social Policy and Economic Factors

At any given time, 2 percent is a very modest estimate of the school population whose emotional or behavioral disorders are deserving of special education. Because IDEA requires that *all* children with disabilities be identified and provided special education appropriate for their individual needs, it could be expected that at least 2 percent of the school population has been identified and is being served. Recent reports from the U.S. Department of Education, however, indicate that less than half that prevalence estimate (about 0.7 percent) is receiving services (U.S. Department of Education, 1995). It seems unlikely that services will be expanded to approximate reasonable prevalence estimates.

The definition is sufficiently vague and subjective that just about any student can be included or excluded, so long as inclusion or exclusion can be said to serve a useful purpose. School systems and states find it useful to stay within their budgets. Official nonrecognition of the needs of students whose problems can be ignored is a convenient way for many school officials to avoid the hassles, risks, and costs of expanded services. In addition, many professionals find it easy to rationalize non-identification of students whose behavior is not disordered in the extreme (Kauffman, 1984, 1988).

REASONABLE ESTIMATES OF PREVALENCE

The question most relevant to discussion here is, "What is a reasonable estimate of the percentage of students whose behavior is so persistently troublesome that special education is desirable?" The best available evidence indicates that the estimate of 2 percent is too conservative, although it was used for more than two decades (approximately 1955–1980) by the U.S. Department of Education. The Department of Education revised its prevalence estimate downward to a range of 1.2 percent to 2.0 percent for several years during the mid-1980s, but since then has not published an estimate.

More reasonable estimates based on population surveys appear to be in the range of 3 to 6 percent of the student population (see Achenbach & Edelbrock, 1981; Anderson & Werry, 1994; Brandenburg, Friedman, & Silver, 1990; Cullinan et al., 1984; Graham, 1979; Juul, 1986). Longitudinal studies play a critical role in establishing reasonable estimates (Power, 1994). An early, important estimate of prevalence for educators is a longitudinal study by Rubin and Balow (1978). Each year they asked teachers to report via questionnaire whether the children in their study sample had shown behavior problems. The decision as to what constituted a problem was left to the individual teacher. Over half of the 1,586 children Rubin and Balow studied were at *some* time during their school years considered by at least *one* of their teachers to show a behavior problem. In any given year, about 20 to 30 percent of the children were considered by at least one teacher to show a problem. Most importantly, 7.4 percent of the children (11.3 percent of the boys and 3.5 percent of the girls) were considered to show a problem by *every* teacher who rated them over a period of 3 years. An estimate derived from the Achenbach and Edelbrock study (1981) indicated the prevalence of behavioral disorder as judged by parents to be well above 2 percent; and teachers' ratings of students identified as "disturbed" and those not identified also suggested that considerably more than 2 percent of the school population could reasonably be considered to have emotional or behavioral disorders (Cullinan et al., 1984).

Several findings are consistent across a variety of studies that span nearly four decades (Achenbach & Edelbrock, 1984; Bower, 1981; Bradenburg et al., 1990; Cullinan et al., 1984; Glidewell & Swallow, 1968; Griffiths, 1952; Institute of Medicine, 1989; Rubin & Balow, 1978; Rutter, Tizard, Yule, Graham, & Whitmore, 1976; see also Graham, 1979; Juul, 1986). First, *most* children and youths exhibit seriously troublesome behavior at some time during their development. Second, more than 2 percent of school-age youngsters are considered by teachers and other adults—consistently and over a period of years—to exhibit disordered behavior and to fit the federal definition of "seriously emotionally disturbed." For example, the 7.4

percent of the child population that Rubin and Balow (1978) found to be consistently identified as having behavior problems over a period of 3 years appears to fit a reasonable definition: when compared to other children, they scored significantly lower on achievement tests in language, reading, spelling, and arithmetic in addition to their persistently and pervasively troublesome behavior in school. These children also scored significantly lower on tests of intelligence, were classified by significantly lower socioeconomic levels, totalled significantly higher numbers of grade retentions, and required more special services (remedial reading, speech therapy, psychological evaluation, and so on), all of which are characteristics associated with emotional or behavioral disorders. The picture emerging from studies of the characteristics of students now in programs for students with emotional or behavioral disorders, and of those not identified but who show similar characteristics, is one of serious academic and social difficulties that are not likely to be overcome without intervention (Colvin, Greenberg, & Sherman, 1993; Cullinan et al., 1984; Kauffman et al., 1987; Sabornie, Cullinan, & Epstein, 1993).

TRENDS IN PREVALENCE ESTIMATES AND PERCENTAGE OF STUDENTS SERVED BY SPECIAL EDUCATION

During the decade of the mid-1970s to the mid-1980s, the percentage of the public school population receiving special education services under the "seriously emotionally disturbed" category grew from about 0.5 percent to about 1.0 percent; however, since 1986, growth in services has been negligible or even declined, according to federal reports. The percentage of students served varies drastically from state to state and among school districts. Hallahan, Keller, and Ball (1986) have shown that *seriously emotionally disturbed* is one of the most variable categories of special education in terms of differences among states. This variability is probably attributable, at least partly, to confusion regarding the definition.

As noted, the federal government used a prevalence estimate of 2.0 percent for about 25 years before suggesting a range of 1.2 to 2.0 percent in the mid-1980s and then dropping the estimate entirely. The government obviously prefers not to allow wide discrepancies between prevalence estimates and the actual number of students served. It is easier to cut prevalence estimates than to serve more students. Moreover, if an appearance of compliance is to be maintained, it is best to work from the assumption that the number of students served is the number who need service.

Social policy and economic realities have effectively precluded the public schools' identification of 2 percent or more of the school age population as having emotional or behavioral disorders. Consideration of the economic realities alone illustrates the difficulty in increasing services to match a 2-percent prevalence estimate. A quarter century ago, calculations indicated that nearly one billion dollars more per year would be needed from the federal government, plus nearly 1.4 billion dollars from state and local sources, to serve 2 percent of the students in public schools (Grosenick & Huntze, 1979). These figures did not include funds for training personnel or allowances for inflation. Today, services for 2 percent of the public school population would require several billion dollars more from federal sources alone than is currently budgeted. It is highly unlikely that federal or state legislatures or local schools will make the required amounts of money available for training personnel and operating programs for 2 percent of the public school population.

Faced with a shortage of adequately trained personnel and insurmountable budget problems, what can we expect of school officials? They cannot risk litigation and loss of federal funds by identifying students they cannot serve. It is reasonable to expect that they will identify as many students as they can find resources to serve. The tragedy is that social policy (IDEA) mandates the impossible and that the public—and a growing number of professionals—are likely to change their perceptions to match economic realities. The social policy mandate changes the question, at least for those who manage budgets, from "How many students with emotional or behavioral disorders are there in our schools?" to "How many can we afford to serve?" And to save face and try to abide by the law, it is tempting to conclude that there are, indeed, precisely as many students with emotional or behavioral disorders as one is able to serve.

Pressures *not* to identify students as having emotional or behavioral disorders are powerful (Kauffman, 1986b, 1988; Peacock Hill Working Group, 1991). Distaste for identifying students as exceptional and for providing special programs outside the regular class, even on a part-time basis, has led to efforts to merge or restructure special and general education, known in the 1980s as the *regular education initiative* (REI) (see Hallahan, Kauffman, Lloyd, & McKinney, 1988; Lloyd, Singh, & Repp, 1991) and in the 1990s as the *full inclusion movement* (Fuchs & Fuchs, 1994, 1995; Kauffman & Hallahan, 1995). Proponents of full inclusion argue that most students now considered disabled are either not disabled at all or have such mild disabilities that we can expect regular classroom teachers, with little additional training or assistance, to deal with them effectively. This viewpoint, however well intentioned, has a strong negative effect on the recognition of emotional or behavioral disorders as disabilities for which special education and related services are appropriate (Braaten, Kauffman, Braaten, Polsgrove, & Nelson, 1988; Kauffman, 1988). The trend appears to be toward identification of only those students whose behavior offends or disturbs others most egregiously—those with the most severe disorders (Peacock Hill Working Group, 1991). We do not seem to be nearing the day when special education and related services will be provided even for most of the 3 percent of the child population that Morse (1985) considers "very seriously impaired" (p. ix).

In 1986, a meeting of education and mental health experts resulted in the following conclusions regarding underservice of students with emotional or behavioral disorders by special education (National Mental Health Association, 1986).

> A majority of SED [seriously emotionally disturbed] children are never identified as such and consequently do not receive the services they need. The reasons for this underidentification are many:
>
> There is concern about the stigma of labeling a child as "severely emotionally disturbed."
>
> No clear definition of SED eligibility exists in the law; therefore, states have had to operationalize a definition, resulting in a tremendous disparity among states.

A lack of uniformity in identification procedures exists in states and localities.

Because of funding constraints, states may set limits on the number of SED children they will identify.

Children may not be identified, not only because of limited funding, but also because few or no appropriate services may be available in their community or because communities lack confidence in their ability to develop appropriate services due to lack of funding or because this is a difficult population to serve.

A lack of clarity among clinicians in the mental health field on definitions and diagnoses compounds the difficulty educators have in making an assessment that a child is severely emotionally disturbed.

The law explicitly excludes children who are "socially maladjusted," yet the distinctions between socially maladjusted and severely emotionally disturbed are confusing and meaningless. This confusion in labeling can result in some children not being identified or served.

There is a tendency to identify children who present significant behavioral problems, and to overlook those who do not act out. In some communities, this, in part, results in an over-representation of black males identified as SED and an under-identification of females of all races, who may not be labeled as troublesome.

There are limited outreach efforts by schools and education systems to parents and professionals in the community to identify SED youths.

There are also differences for SED children, compared to other populations with handicaps, in the degree of their handicap. SED children tend to be more disturbed before they are identified; those with mild or moderate disturbances may never be identified. (p. 5)

Nothing has changed during the past decade that would make this statement inaccurate. In fact, as the need for services for more children and youths with emotional or behavioral disorders has grown, American society's response has been to trim funding for social programs, including special education, that provide services to those in need.

FACTORS AFFECTING PREVALENCE AND PLACEMENT FOR SERVICES

Assuming that we can agree about the definition of children and youths who should be identified as having emotional or behavioral disorders, what are the factors that might increase or decrease the prevalence of these disorders? This is the primary question we address in the four chapters in Part Three.

At this point it is sufficient to note that a variety of biological, family, school, and cultural conditions might make emotional or behavioral disorders occur more frequently. Thus we might expect that these disorders will be somewhat more prevalent in some communities and schools than in others. Nevertheless, these factors that might be expected to affect prevalence do not explain the extreme range of rates of service (from 0.05 percent of the school population in one state to 2.08 percent in another; see U. S. Department of Education, 1995).

Emotional or behavioral disorders are not identified at the same rate across age groups, partly because of the nature of these disorders and the way our society responds to them. As shown in Figure 2.2, the distribution of students identified as having emotional or behavioral disorders at different ages is almost an exact mirror image of the distribution for students with learning disabilities, and it is quite unlike the relatively flat distribution for those with mental retardation. We might speculate that the age trends for students with emotional or behavioral disorders are related to the increasing social difficulties they face as they enter adolescence, which is a stressful period for all youngsters. Students with learning disabilities and mental retardation may tend to have more obvious academic difficulties early in their school careers. Those with mental retardation show steady and persistent school difficulties through adolescence, and some of those with learning disabilities begin to find a resolution of their difficulties by early adolescence.

The patterns shown in Figure 2.2 are consistent with other indications that the problems of children with emotional or behavioral disorders tend to be overlooked or neglected for as long as possible—until they become painfully obvious and intolerable to adults. By the time these children obtain services, they are older and their problems are more severe than those identified in other categories. Adults tend to respond to them by being more demanding and punitive. This may account, in part, for the fact that students with emotional or behavioral disorders leave school at higher rates and are placed more frequently in more restrictive settings than are students in other categories (see Kauffman, Lloyd, Hallahan, & Astuto, 1995a; National Mental Health Association, 1986, 1989; Peacock Hill Working Group, 1991).

Students identified as having emotional or behavioral disorders and requiring special education are placed frequently in settings seen as more restrictive than their home schools and regular classes (Stephens & Lakin, 1995). The federal data for the 1993–94 school year showed that about 20 percent of children with emotional or behavioral disorders (compared to 35 percent of those with learning disabilities) were placed primarily in regular classrooms; 27 percent in resource rooms (compared to 44 percent of those with learning disabilities); 35 percent in separate classes (compared to 20 percent of those with learning disabilities); and nearly 19 percent in separate schools, residential facilities, or homebound or hospital environments (compared to about 1 percent of those with learning disabilities) (U.S. Department of Education, 1995). The reasons that parents, educators, and other professionals select particular placements are poorly understood. Smith et al. (1988) concluded, "Unfortunately, there is relatively little research available on decision making regarding behavioral disorders labeling and placement decisions" (p. 108). Their conclusion is supported by other researchers and more recent reviews (e.g., Denny, Gunter, Shores, & Campbell, 1995; Grosenick, George, & George, 1987; Grosenick, George, George, & Lewis, 1991; Jennings, Mendelsohn, May, & Brown, 1988; Knitzer, Steinberg, & Fleisch, 1990; Martin, Hallenbeck, Kauffman, & Lloyd, 1995; Mattison, Morales, & Bauer, 1992; Stephens & Lakin, 1995).

Research has shown that the reintegration of many students with emotional or behavioral disorders into less restrictive placements is possible but that it requires considerable effort and a high level of attention to individual needs on a case-by-case

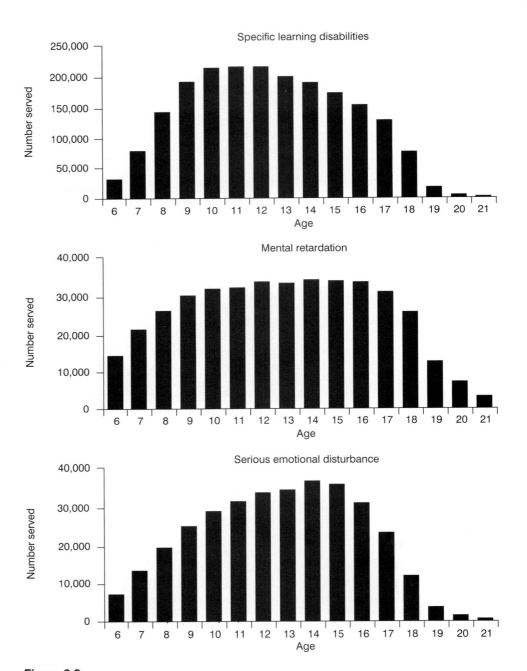

Figure 2.2
Number of Students in Three Special Education Categories Receiving Special Education
Services in 1989–90
Source: From U.S. Department of Education (1991), *Thirteenth annual report to Congress on the implementation of the Individuals with Disabilities Education Act*. Washington, DC: Author, p. 11.

basis if it is to be successful (Fuchs, Fuchs, Fernstrom, & Hohn, 1991; Sack, Mason, & Collins, 1987). The great variability across states and communities in prevalence and placement suggests, however, that many students with emotional or behavioral disorders are poorly or inappropriately served. As noted by the National Mental Health Association:

> Clinically, the most appropriate mode of treatment for children with mental and emotional problems is often a community-based service that is centered on the needs of the child and focused on the family unit. However, policymakers and third party payers have supported the development of few of these kinds of services. Often no professional help is available in the child's immediate community so that the family cannot be as actively involved as they should be. . . . Thus, children with emotional problems tend to be placed in more restrictive settings than they need (1989, pp. 1–2).

Other literature indicates that the outcomes of placement for special education and treatment may depend in part on the types of disorders children exhibit (i.e., their diagnoses). For example, in a long-term follow-up of children from a psychiatric day treatment center, Sack et al. (1987) found much better outcomes for children with emotional disorders (e.g., anxiety, depression) than for those with behavioral disorders (e.g., conduct disorder, attention deficit disorder). Moreover, Sack et al. and others (e.g., Mattison & Forness, 1995; Mattison et al., 1992; Kazdin, 1991) note that aggressive behavior and the presence of variables related to placement decisions—other than the child's or youth's psychiatric diagnosis—are associated with poor prognosis, even with the best available treatment. These factors include physical or sexual abuse, parental neglect or nonsupervision, parental criminality or psychiatric disturbance, low parental socioeconomic and education level, and broken (single parent) family.

Only very recently has substantial information become available regarding important features of separate day and residential schools serving students with emotional or behavioral disorders and other handicapping conditions. Data from the work of Stephens, Lakin, Brauen, and O'Reilly (1990) "provide the first national picture of the current status of separate facilities serving children with disabilities" (U.S. Department of Education, 1991, p. ii; see also Stephens & Lakin, 1995). Highlights of the findings specific to students with emotional or behavioral disorders revealed the following, based on a large sample of students placed in separate day or residential facilities:

- There have been an increasing percentage of students served in separate facilities of all types.

- They were both placed in and discharged from both day and residential facilities at higher rates than students with other handicapping conditions; admission and discharge rates were higher in residential than in day facilities; discharge rates paralleled admission rates.

- They comprised by far the largest segment (slightly over half) of the total population of students with disabilities placed in separate residential schools; those with a primary diagnosis of serious conduct/behavior disorder (22.6 percent) or attention deficit disorder (9.9 percent) comprised one third of all disabled students placed in separate residential facilities.

■ Slightly more than half of those placed in separate day schools were in public facilities; more than two thirds of those placed in residential schools were in private facilities.

■ Most were between the ages of 12 and 17 when first admitted to day or residential facilities. Private residential programs reported increased referrals of youngsters in middle to late adolescence.

■ Approximately 48 percent of those in day schools and 44 percent of those in residential schools carried a primary diagnosis of serious conduct/behavior disorder.

■ The second most common primary diagnosis was attention deficit disorder, accounting for approximately 17 percent of day students and 19 percent of residential students.

■ The proportion of students placed in certain settings was skewed for some ethnic groups. For example, the proportion of African-American students tended to be higher than average among students placed in public day schools; Hispanic and Asian students tended to be placed less frequently than average in residential schools.

■ Most of the new admissions to separate day schools were previously placed in special classes in regular schools (about 38 percent) or regular classes with or without resource services (about 23 percent); about 11 percent came from other special day schools, and about 6 percent from residential schools.

■ Most of the new admissions of day students in separate residential schools were previously placed in special classes in regular schools (about 43 percent) or regular classes with or without resource services (about 23 percent); about 13 percent came from other residential schools and about 7 percent from day schools.

■ Most of the new admissions of residential students in separate residential schools were previously placed in regular classes with or without resource services (about 28 percent) or special classes in regular schools (about 27 percent); about 16 percent came from other residential schools and about 9 percent from day schools.

■ A substantial percentage of new admissions to separate day and residential facilities had received no prior instruction—approximately 5 percent of new admissions to day schools, 9 percent of new day students in residential schools, and 9 percent of new residential students in residential schools.

■ Approximately 3 percent of new admissions to day and residential facilities had previously been placed in home-based instruction.

■ Providing opportunities to interact with nondisabled peers is difficult.

■ Most students below age 17 exited separate day or residential schools to regular schools, often to special classes. Finding appropriate educational or vocational placements for students who reached maximum age for the facility was a serious problem.

■ A higher percentage of those exiting residential schools entered a college or university degree program (13 percent) than of those exiting day schools (5 percent).

PREVALENCE AND INCIDENCE OF SPECIFIC DISORDERS

So far we have considered emotional or behavioral disorders in the general case. But because there are many types of disorders, it is possible to estimate the prevalence of some specific problems. Unfortunately, many of the same difficulties of estimation we have discussed for the general case also arise when considering more specific disorders (Anderson & Werry, 1994). The classification of emotional or behavioral disorders is almost as problematic as the general definition. In addition, the methodology of estimation is at least as varied for many specific disorders as for the general case. Consequently, estimates of prevalence and incidence of specific disorders vary and are confusing. Whenever possible, we will provide prevalence estimates in chapters dealing with specific disorders.

SUMMARY

Nearly all children and youths sometimes exhibit behavior that is problematic. Emotional and behavioral problems are a part of normal development. Labeling 20 percent or more of the child population as having an emotional or behavioral disorder, however, results in disbelief by the general public and alternative explanations by educators. Prevalence figures must be accompanied by convincing arguments that the identified population is in need of special services because their problems are highly unusual, debilitating, and not the result of teacher inadequacy. Establishing criteria for identification, however, requires arbitrary judgment regarding what degree of difference is tolerable as well as a judgment as to the relative risks of identification and nonidentification.

Prevalence refers to the number or percentage of individuals exhibiting a disorder at or during a given time. **Incidence** refers to the number of new cases of a disorder occurring during a given internal. Prevalence has been of greatest interest to special educators because most disabilities have been assumed to be developmental and to entail life-long characteristics. However, special educators are increasingly aware that types of disability, particularly some disorders of learning and behavior, are episodic. Consequently, incidence is becoming of greater interest. Prevalence and incidence may seem irrelevant to the everyday work of the teacher, but they are important issues for those who plan and administer programs, with consequent implications for the teacher's working conditions.

Estimates of prevalence and incidence are made difficult by the lack of a standard definition, by methodological problems, and by social policy and economic factors. If no standard definition is accepted, then it is difficult to count cases. Because the methodology of estimation is not well developed, we can expect arguments about the meaning of existing studies and difficulties in designing adequate studies. One way to estimate prevalence is to compare behavior ratings of identified populations to the ratings of students who have not been identified. Nonidentified students whose scores are above a cutoff score (for example, the ninetieth percentile) may be false negatives or candidates for services (that is, *possibly* in need of services). Identified students whose scores fall below the same cutoff may be false positives (perhaps not in need of services).

The U.S. Department of Education for many years used a prevalence estimate of 2 percent, although the federal government now publishes no estimate. Reasonable estimates based on the best available research are that 3 to 6 percent of the school-age population are in need of special education and related services because of their emotional or behavioral disorders. Although the percentage of students served increased from about 0.5 percent to about 1.0 percent from the mid-1970s to the mid-1980s, it does not seem likely that dramatic increases in the percentage will occur in the foreseeable future. Economic factors and other constraints, such as the full inclusion movement and other pressures toward nonidentification, appear likely to limit future estimates of prevalence.

The prevalence of emotional or behavioral disorders is affected by causal factors, the nature of the disorders themselves, and society's response to them. Compared to students with learning disabilities, those with emotional or behavioral disorders tend to be identified at later ages and to be placed for education in more restrictive settings. Most students with emotional or behavioral disorders who are receiving special education are in the 12 to 17 year age range. A disproportionate number, compared to children and youths in other categories, are placed in highly restrictive settings, such as separate day schools and residential schools.

Case for Discussion

"Is This a Sick County?"

Carrie Dobbs

Marion County school board member Frank Lott scowled at the county special education director, Carrie Dobbs. "Ms. Dobbs, I simply don't understand. Here we are in Marion County with 2 percent of our kids identified as seriously emotionally disturbed, and right next to us in the Circle City Schools only 1 percent of the kids are identified. And, if I'm to believe the consultants you brought in, only about 1 percent of the public school population nationwide is identified. Now, why should we have *double* the rate of identification of other places, including the school system next to us? Are you telling me that something about this county makes kids emotionally disturbed?"

"No, Mr. Lott, I think we use better identification procedures than Circle City and most other school systems in the country, and we're doing our best to serve all of our students who need special education because of their emotional or behavioral problems."

School board member Sandi Mosher leaned back in her chair, staring intently at Carrie Dobbs. "Like Mr. Lott, I don't understand what's happening. But I know we're spending a lot more money on these kids than Circle City. I wonder if that isn't because you use the term 'behavior improvement' instead of 'seriously emotionally disturbed.'"

"That might be part of the reason, I admit," Carrie said cautiously. "But we think BI is a better choice than SED. It carries less stigma, and we'd rather label a program than kids."

"But that's just the point, isn't it?" asked Mr. Lott. "You make it easier to identify students, so parents are more likely to go along with it—until they find out that the kids are actually labelled "emotionally disturbed" in our reports to state and federal authorities, and then they're really upset."

"Besides," Ms. Mosher joined in, "it seems to me you're including a lot of kids who are just behavior problems, but they're not really seriously emotionally disturbed. I don't like this BI label, and I don't think it's reasonable for us to be identifying kids in this county who wouldn't be identified in most other systems and using labels in this county that aren't consistent with state and federal language."

"I respectfully disagree, Ms. Mosher. The students we've identified have serious and persistent behavior problems that put them at a severe disadvantage in school. They're very likely to fail or drop out of school without a special program. We feel the BI program is the most effective and least stigmatizing way of providing the needed services. Our identification procedures and our prevalence are consistent with the best available research."

Questions About the Case

1. If you were a school board member, what line of questioning would you pursue in challenging Ms. Dobbs?

2. If you were Ms. Dobbs, how would you defend serving 2 percent of the school population in a "Behavior Improvement" program?

3. If you were asked to investigate the BI program in the Marion County Schools, what would you want to know to help you understand whether serving 2 percent of the students is justified?

PERSONAL REFLECTIONS

Prevalence

Teresa Zutter, M.Ed., is principal of the Herndon Center, a special program for students with emotional or behavioral disorders. The Herndon Center is located in a special wing of Herndon Middle School in Herndon, Virginia.

Why is it important for you as an administrator to be able to estimate the number of students who will be identified as having emotional or behavioral disorders?

Obviously, school administrators need to plan many months in advance of the beginning of a new school year. An accurate estimate of how many students will need services at various grade levels and the degree of support each will need is invaluable in deciding how many teachers to hire. We have to budget for textbooks, materials, supplies, and equipment for each student. We have to provide physical accommodations in compliance with federal and state requirements as well. And at cofacilities like ours, use of communal areas such as the lunchroom, the gymnasium, the playing fields, the auditorium, etc., must be discussed with the general education administrators for smooth coexistence and integration of our programs and students. Transportation must be budgeted as well, and this is especially complex when one facility is serving a wide area in a particular district.

Teaching every student is our most important task, but the preliminary steps of initial referral, screening, evaluation, eligibility, placement, and follow-up triennial reviews are also crucial. Furthermore, inservice training for both special educators and general education teachers is required for comprehensive educational services. We can manage our time efficiently only if all involved personnel know in advance approximately how many students must be accommodated in planning these other crucial components of special education. Finally, prevalence figures can be enormously helpful when planning for community-based programming. Negative community attitudes about a program, especially if they are based on exaggeration or rumor, can intensify the fears and uncertainties of students and parents. We administrators are responsible for communicating to the public how many students will be served at a particular site in the course of explaining the educational program.

Why is a higher percentage of students identified in some school districts and states than others?

Some states and localities still see public education as a critical element of a strong community. The local high school football games are still attended every fall Friday by families, friends, and neighbors. There is community spirit and concern for the young. These people still feel free to care for and watch over each other's children. These communities may be urban or rural, and the citizens of them may be highly educated or relatively uneducated. But one characteristic differentiating these communities from others is their willingness to provide for the well-being of others. This public attitude affects the establishment and support of community- and school-based services, the quality of public employees, and the degree to which educators are professionally and financially rewarded for their work. Prevalence may be higher in these caring communities because the process of identification is sound.

In the best of circumstances, a school district has the financial and political backing of its citizens to honestly and objectively assess the needs of its young people. Although the risk of false positives may be greater in these communities, the risk of false negatives is lower, as eligibility criteria may be less stringent. When a public service is well established and well run, it stands a higher chance of being used regularly and more comfortably. High-quality services promote accuracy in assessing needs. Citizens with disabled children often choose to move into a particular district or state because of its fine reputation for readily accessible and high quality public school special education services.

High prevalence may also be due to the difficulty of school personnel in discriminating true emotional or behavioral disorders from serious general student difficulties. Many general education teachers have never taken even an introductory special education course. Most general education teacher training does not include a course in behavior management. In school districts where teachers are poorly trained and unsupported, "problem children" are at higher risk for being incorrectly labeled as disabled. Lack of professional training and competence in basic classroom behavior management skills can contribute directly to high prevalence rates.

Many teachers report seeing disturbing behaviors in more of their students today than they saw in the past. Many highly competent teachers worry that more of today's children are exhibiting behaviors that warrant identification as a disorder or disability. Some suggest that this is due to the overall dysfunction, chaos, and moral decay in contemporary American society. And it is important to recognize that some states and localities have higher rates of poverty and other environmental conditions that we know contribute to emotional and behavioral disorders.

What factors do you think account for the increasing prevalence of emotional and behavioral disorders?

There appear to be a multitude of reasons that might explain it. Unfortunately, the explosion of student referrals is due to many factors that fall beyond the control of the public schools. There appears to have been a fundamental change in children's basic sense of security. Many children are afraid of the future. They worry that they will not live out a natural life span, and they express pessimism regarding the future of Earth itself. Many have adopted the attitude "What's the use? We're all going to die anyway!"

Learned helplessness seems to be sweeping the nation, as children recognize at younger and younger ages that the chances of a successful life-long marriage and prosperous life may be extremely difficult or impossible to attain and sustain. The fairy tale endings of previous generations have evaporated in the light of harsh realities being portrayed through the music, media, and daily exposure to role models who lead increasingly frenetic lives. Even in the midst of increasingly crowded areas, children experience loneliness, isolation, and depression. Large numbers of children seem to be mourning the loss of certain fundamental human social elements without being able to express exactly what is missing. Technological developments and family priorities and structure rob many children of opportunities to learn about interpersonal intimacy, acquire social skills, and achieve psychological and physiological well-being. Many developmentally significant social traditions are being diminished in frequency and importance. It appears that the lack of stability, permanence, and unwavering commitment in so many areas of young people's lives has contributed to mistrust on their part that anyone is really in control.

Children affected by their mothers' use of drugs during pregnancy and by drug use in their homes are reaching school age in significant numbers. Drug abuse in the home or neighborhood is often accompanied by child neglect, violence, poverty, and the inevitable deterioration of the fabric of family and community. Ineffective teaching methods and rising teacher burnout exacerbate the situation. Most teachers have neither the training nor the desire to be surrogate parent, psychologist, and social worker in addition to teacher. One response is to place students in special education where, theoretically, there is more time to pay attention to the serious symptoms of a societal problem that is larger than any school system can successfully overcome.

On a more positive note, reports of higher prevalence of emotional and behavioral problems also may be due to a more open attitude nationwide that no longer allows children's problems to be swept under society's rug. Instead of being hidden away, these children are being acknowledged and assisted by effective school programs. These children have always been a part of the public school scene, but there may be more public support to help troubled children before their destructive behaviors become a way of life. In part, this may be due to adult citizens feeling the same unease or even outright fear commonly expressed by youths that our society is raging out of control. While it may be a sobering experience for a nation to contend openly with its suffering children, the rational and reasonable approach of attacking today's concerns head-on is to be applauded.

What are the major reasons that fewer students have been identified than we would expect based on prevalence studies?

Demographic fluctuations may be a contributing factor. Budgets for education initiatives may shrink as the population of taxpayers changes. For instance, if households with no school-age children outnumber those with children, then a school bond vote might be defeated in favor of other public spending, such as new roads. A school system faced with a budget crisis, inadequately trained personnel, poorly defined procedures, rigid criteria for eligibility, or a weakness in available programs may underidentify students. Limited services may be provided to only the most obviously in need.

Second, when money is tight special education may have to compete with other worthy education programs for limited resources. For example, a region may become popular for immigrants from a war-torn country. Costly programs for incorporating these new students may force another look at current funding. With no hard-and-fast rules for eligibility for many programs, including special education and English as a Second Language, school districts may manipulate identification procedures to raise or lower prevalence to more closely fit the available local funding.

A lower identification rate does not necessarily stem from such negative situations. Another notable possibility includes implementation of extremely effective inservice training of general education teachers. Teachers who are supported and rewarded for success with children who might otherwise be referred for special education may lower the prevalence of disabilities. The actual number of at-risk children in a particular area may remain the same, but more children escape the disability label due to efficient pre-referral assistance in the regular classroom setting. Likewise, identified children who are properly educated by special educators and then mainstreamed back into general education may be found ineligible for services at the next triennial review. In these circumstances, the school system may have chosen to invest in proactive educational strategies, with less emphasis on sustaining large numbers of children in long-term separate programs.

Finally, the phenomenon of "resilient children" has only recently been examined closely on a national level. Researchers have always wondered why some children successfully overcome extremely distressful and traumatic circumstances, while others succumb to emotional despair and ineffective coping mechanisms. However, more attention is now being given to learning how we can help more children achieve personal success despite incredible adversity. States or districts that promote innovative research and program development to foster resiliency in children may exhibit lower prevalence due to a true decrease in the number of students who, without this assistance, might otherwise be identified.

3

The History of the Problem: Development of the Field

As you read this chapter, keep these guiding questions in mind:

- What factors make it difficult to trace the history of special education for students with emotional or behavioral disorders?

- What events in the late 1700s set the stage for more humane and effective treatment of children and youth with emotional or behavioral disorders?

- What was moral therapy, and why was it abandoned in the nineteenth century?

- What events and trends in the late 1800s led to a decline in effective treatment for youngsters with emotional or behavioral disorders and mental retardation?

- In the first half of the 1900s, what were the predominant emphases in programs for children and youth with emotional or behavioral disorders?

- What were the theoretical roots and social forces behind the conceptual models that emerged after 1960?

- What are recent trends in the field, and what new problems are emerging?

We have seen that the issues of definition and prevalence are difficult matters to resolve. Has this always been the case, or is the difficulty peculiar to the present era of rapid technological development, social change, and the tendency to take conflicts to court? We are tempted to believe that in an earlier era, when life was simpler, the issues were less difficult. Perhaps life was simpler long ago, but much of the historical literature suggests that questions of how to identify social deviance and what to do about it once it is recognized have always been perplexing.

The connectedness of current issues to past problems is an important concept. We cannot understand today's difficulties very well if we assume they emerge from present circumstances alone. Although knowledge of history is no guarantee that we will not repeat our mistakes, ignorance of history virtually ensures that we will make no real progress (Kauffman, 1981, 1993; Kauffman & Smucker, 1995). Consideration of the historical background of current issues and contemporary practices will serve us well.

Teachers in every era have faced the problem of disorderly and disturbing student behavior (Braaten, 1985; Winzer, 1993). Throughout history one can find examples of youngsters' behavior that angered and disappointed their parents or other adults and violated established codes of conduct. The historical roots of special education for students with emotional or behavioral disorders are not easy to identify, however. Although these disorders of children and youth have long been recognized, it is only relatively recently that systematic special educational provisions for these students have been devised.

To the extent possible, this chapter focuses on the history of the *education* of students with emotional or behavioral disorders and other interventions directly relevant to educational concerns. A purely educational emphasis is not possible, however, because the conceptual foundations of special education lie for the most part in the disciplines of psychology and psychiatry. Its historical origins are intertwined inseparably with the histories of other fields of study and practice (Lewis, 1974).

Over the years education has come to play a prominent role in the treatment of youngsters' emotional or behavioral disorders. As this historical sketch unfolds, therefore, it will become increasingly educational in focus.

LATE 1700s: DISPELLING IGNORANCE, NEGLECT, AND ABUSE

Before 1800, children and youths with nearly any significant disability were at best protected from abuse, and we know of few systematic attempts to teach them. Emotional or behavioral disorders were believed to be evidence of Satan's power, and children and adolescents were often punished under the law as adults (Bremner, 1970; Despert, 1965). Abuse, neglect, cruel medical treatment (e.g., bleeding and purging), and harsh punishment were common and often accepted matter-of-factly. Not until the period following the American and French Revolutions in the closing years of the eighteenth century did kind and effective treatment of the "insane" and "idiots" (terms then used to designate people with mental illness and mental retardation) begin to appear. In that era of political and social revolution, emphasis on individual freedom, human dignity, philanthropy, and public education set the stage for humane treatment and education of people with disabilities.

Immediately after the French Revolution, Phillipe Pinel, a distinguished French physician and one of the earliest psychiatrists, unchained several people who were chronically mentally ill and had been brutally confined for years in the Bicêtre Hospital in Paris. When treated with kindness, respect, and the expectation that they would behave appropriately, these formerly deranged, regressed patients showed dramatic improvement. Pinel's revolutionary and humane methods were widely known and used in Europe and the United States during the first half of the nineteenth century. His approach, later elaborated by his students and admirers, became known as **moral treatment**.

One of Pinel's students was Jean Marc Gaspard Itard, another French physician. In the late 1700s and early 1800s, Itard attempted to teach the "wild boy of Aveyron" (Itard, republished in English translation, 1962). This boy, Victor, was found in the forest where he had apparently been abandoned at an early age. Pinel believed him to have profound mental retardation ("idiocy," in the language of the day), but it is clear from Itard's description that Victor exhibited many of the behaviors characteristic of severe mental illness. Itard was convinced that Victor could be taught practical skills, including speech. Although Victor never uttered more than a few words, Itard was remarkably successful in teaching him many skills. Itard's work with Victor provided the basis for the teaching methods of Edward Seguin and other late-nineteenth-century educators of "idiots." Itard's book remains a fascinating and moving classic in the education of students with disabilities. Contemporary educational methods for students with mental retardation and emotional or behavioral disorders are grounded in many of the principles expounded by Itard almost two centuries ago (Lane, 1976). Moreover, Itard's work remains a reference point for intervention today with children who are found to have been closeted away and abused by their parents (cf. Raymer, 1992).

Besides the work of Pinel and Itard in Europe, developments in America in the late 1700s were also a prelude to education for children and youth with emotional or behavioral disorders. Most important was the influential writing of Dr. Benjamin Rush of Philadelphia, often considered the father of American psychiatry. Following the American Revolution, Dr. Rush became a strong proponent of public education and public support for schools for poor children.[1] His writings argue vehemently and eloquently against corporal punishment and cruel discipline and for kind and prudent methods of behavior control. His words, first published in 1790 in *The Universal Asylum and Columbian Magazine*, have the ring of present-day child advocacy and appeal for more caring relationships with children:

> I conceive corporal punishments, inflicted in an arbitrary manner, to be contrary to the spirit of liberty, and that they should not be tolerated in a free government. Why should not children be protected from violence and injuries, as well as white and black servants? Had I influence enough in our legislature to obtain only a single law, it should be to make the punishment for striking a schoolboy, the same as for assaulting and beating an adult member of society.
>
> The world was created in love. It is sustained by love. Nations and families that are happy, are made so only by love. Let us extend this divine principle, to those little communities which we call schools. Children are capable of loving in a high degree. They may therefore be governed by love. (Bremner, 1970, pp. 222–223)

Rush does not advocate the abandonment of discipline. He suggests mild forms of punishment in school: admonishing the child privately, confining the child after school hours, and requiring the child to hold a small sign of disgrace in the presence of the other children. If the child does not respond to these methods, Rush recommends dismissing the child from school and turning the business of discipline over to the parents. His emphasis on education and love-oriented methods of control had a profound influence on the early years of American psychiatry and the moral therapy employed in many American "lunatic asylums" during the first half of the nineteenth century.

THE 1800s: THE RISE AND FALL OF MORAL THERAPY[2]

Most twentieth-century descriptions of nineteenth-century treatment of youngsters with emotional or behavioral disorders have been brief and negative (Despert, 1965; Kanner, 1957, 1962; Lewis, 1974; Rubenstein, 1948). Only relatively recently has the history of public education for such children and youth been traced (Berkowitz

---

[1]For excerpts from the writings of Benjamin Rush, see Bremner (1970), pp. 218–223, 249–251.

[2]Section adapted from J.M. Kauffman, "Nineteenth-Century Views of Children's Behavior Disorders: Historical Contributions and Continuing Issues," *Journal of Special Education* (1976) 10, 335–349. Used with permission.

& Rothman, 1967a; Hoffman, 1974, 1975). The literature of the nineteenth century is meager by current standards; children in this literature are often looked upon and treated psychologically as miniature adults; and bizarre ideas (such as the notions that insanity could be caused by masturbating, by studying too hard, or by watching someone have an epileptic seizure) are persistent. However, most histories of childhood emotional or behavioral disorders consistently contain certain inaccuracies and distortions that lead to underestimating the value of the nineteenth-century literature in approaching present-day problems (Kauffman, 1976).

Mental Retardation and Emotional or Behavioral Disorders

One reason the nineteenth century is often dismissed as an unimportant era in the field of emotional or behavioral disorders is that the relationship between them and mental retardation is overlooked. Nineteenth-century writers recognized the great similarity between mental retardation (then called "idiocy" or "imbecility") and mental illness (then called "insanity" or "madness"). Not until 1886 was there a legal separation between "insanity" and "feeblemindedness" in England (Hayman, 1939).

Some nineteenth-century descriptions of "idiocy" and its varieties present a picture of youngsters who today might well be said to have **schizophrenia** or **autism**. Itard's (1962) description of Victor, written at the end of the eighteenth century, is important as a study of emotional or behavioral disorder as well as a treatise on mental retardation. Esquirol (1845), a French physician, describes in considerable detail the physical and behavioral features of an 11-year-old "imbecile" admitted to the Salpetriere hospital. The description of Charles Emile, a 15-year-old "idiot" at the Bicêtre, also contains reference to severely disordered behavior. Brigham (1845) summarized the observations of Voisin, a physician at the Bicêtre, who said of Charles:

> He was wholly an animal. He was without attachment; overturned everything in his way, but without courage or intent; possessed no tact, intelligence, power of dissimulation, or sense of propriety; and was awkward to excess. His *moral sentiments* are described as *null*, except the love of approbation, and a noisy instinctive gaiety, independent of the external world. . . . Devouring everything, however disgusting, brutally sensual, passionate—breaking, tearing, and burning whatever he could lay his hand upon; and if prevented from doing so, pinching, biting, scratching, and tearing himself, until he was covered with blood. He had the particularity of being so attracted by the eyes of his brothers, sisters, and playfellows, as to make the most persevering efforts to push them out with his fingers. . . . When any attempt was made to associate him with the other patients, he would start away with a sharp cry, and then come back to them hastily. (p. 336)

Some of the children and youths served in institutions for the deaf and the blind, as well as institutions for those with mental retardation, served children and youth who today would likely be said to have autism or other severe developmental disorders. The eminent American educator of students with disabilities, Samuel Gridley Howe, understood the difficulty in distinguishing students with mental retardation from those with emotional or behavioral disorders. He used the term *simulative idiocy* (Howe, 1852) to describe the problem that today would be termed **pseudoretardation**—the *appearance* of mental retardation presented by a nonretarded person. In short, the close relationship between mental retardation and emotional or behavioral disorders was known in the nineteenth century, and the observations of many nineteenth-century writers are surprisingly consonant with today's emphasis on the similarities and overlapping characteristics, etiologies, and interventions for these two groups.

Theories of Etiology

By the end of the eighteenth century, the belief that emotional or behavioral disorders were caused by demon possession was no longer in vogue among the experts. Nineteenth-century writers were, however, undeniably preoccupied with the relationship between masturbation and insanity, particularly insanity in children and youths. The prevailing belief was that masturbation caused (or at least aggravated) insanity (Hare, 1962; Rie, 1971).[3] Nevertheless, some writers questioned the causal relationship between masturbation and insanity long before the beginning of the twentieth century. Although Stribling (1842) referred to masturbation as a "detestable vice" and a "degrading habit," he clearly understood that it was often mistaken as a cause of insanity.

Many of the "causes" of mental illness listed by nineteenth-century writers are laughable indeed: "idleness and ennui," "pecuniary embarrassment," "sedentary and studious habits," "inhaling tobacco fumes," "gold fever," "indulgence of temper" (Stribling, 1842); "suppression of hemorrhoids," "kick on the stomach," "bathing in cold water," "sleeping in a barn filled with new hay," "study of metaphysics," "reading vile books," "license question," "preaching sixteen days and nights," "celibacy," "sudden joy," "ecstatic admiration of works of art," "mortified pride," "Mormonism," "duel," "struggle between the religious principle and power of passion" (Jarvis, 1852). Nevertheless, writers of the day did question supposed cause-effect relationships, as we see in Jarvis's comment that masturbation could not be evaluated as a factor in any increase of insanity because "we have no means of knowing whether masturbation increases or diminishes" (Jarvis, 1852, p. 354).

However, some psychiatrists of the early nineteenth century identified etiological factors in youngsters' emotional or behavioral disorders that are today given serious consideration. For example, Parkinson in 1807 and West in 1848 (in Hunter & Macalpine, 1963) pointed to the interaction of temperament and child rearing, overprotection, overindulgence, and inconsistency of discipline as factors in the development of troublesome behavior. Parkinson's perspectives are consistent with the twentieth century findings of Thomas, Chess, and Birch (1968), and his comments on inconsistency in child rearing and discipline are compatible with those of Haring and Phillips (1962) and Patterson (1982).

---

[3]The idea that masturbation was an intolerably horrible and debasing practice had not been laid to rest by the end of the nineteenth century. Castration and ovariotomy were still used in the 1890s and early 1900s in attempts to stop masturbation and sexual interests of "idiotic," "imbecile," "feebleminded," and "epileptic" children and youth, many of whom exhibited other disturbing behaviors (Bremner, 1971, pp. 855–857).

Summary of Theories   Although biological causes of mental retardation and emotional or behavioral disorders were recognized during the first half of the nineteenth century, the emphasis was on environmental factors, especially early discipline and training. It is not surprising that interventions in that period center on environmental control—providing the proper sensory stimulation, discipline, and instruction.

As Hoffman (1974, 1975) notes, the impact of Darwinist thought in the late nineteenth century was profound. British philosopher Herbert Spencer and spokesman for social Darwinism in the United States William Graham Sumner saw the seeds of social decay and destruction in the unchecked propagation of the lower classes and defective individuals, as did Dr. Walter E. Fernald (1893), distinguished medical superintendent of the Massachusetts School for the Feebleminded. The ideas of social evolution, survival of the fittest, and eugenics were to lead inevitably to the writing and influence of Henry H. Goddard, an early twentieth-century progenitor of special education (Balthazar & Stevens, 1975; Smith, 1962). The favored position in the late nineteenth and early twentieth centuries was that undesirable behavioral traits represented inherited flaws and that intervention should be limited to selective breeding.

Intervention

One cannot deny that many children and youth, including those with emotional or behavioral disorders and limited intellect, were neglected and abused in the nineteenth century. Bremner (1970, 1971), Hoffman (1974, 1975), and Rothman (1971) amply document the cruel discipline, forced labor, and other inhumanities suffered by children and youth in the 1800s (see also Forehand & McKinney, 1993). Although many nineteenth-century attempts at education and treatment were primitive compared to the best that can now be offered, some youngsters with emotional or behavioral disorders in the nineteenth century received considerably better care than many such children receive today. If one were to concentrate on the neglect and abuse in institutions, schools, detention centers, and homes in the late twentieth century, one might justifiably conclude that the plight of children and youth has not improved much in the past hundred years. Contrasting the best contemporary thinking and treatment to the worst of the nineteenth century creates a dark and distorted vision of the last century, with its references to imprisonment, cruelty, punishment, neglect, ignorance, bizarre ideas (masturbatory insanity), and absence of effective education and treatment for youngsters with emotional or behavioral disorders (Despert, 1965; Kanner, 1962; Rie, 1971; Rubenstein, 1948). As it happens, many nineteenth-century leaders in the treatment of children with emotional or behavioral disorders were more enlightened than their critics have assumed. Unfortunately, some of their brightest successes, such as moral treatment, have usually been ignored.

Seldom has moral treatment been mentioned in connection with children and youths. "Moral treatment, in modern technical jargon, is what we mean by resocialization by means of a growing list of therapies with prefaces such as recreational, occupational, industrial, music—with physical education thrown in for good measure" (Bockoven, 1956, p. 303). Bockoven points out that these therapies do not add up to moral treatment, which implies an integrated total treatment program (see

Brigham, 1847, for a succinct description of moral treatment).[4] Rie (1971) discusses moral treatment of the 1800s but largely discounts its relevance for child psychopathology because youngsters were not admitted to institutions in great numbers. Yet children and youth did find their way into institutions and were treated by moral therapists during the first half of the nineteenth century (Esquirol, 1845; Hunter & Macalpine, 1974; Mayo, 1839). For example, Francis Stribling, a prominent moral therapist of the early 1800s, reports that of 122 patients in Western Lunatic Asylum in Staunton, Virginia during 1841, 9 were under the age of 20 and 2 under the age of 15 (Stribling, 1842). Thus, we need to include moral treatment in the types of care offered to children and youths in that era.

Moral therapists emphasized constructive activity, kindness, minimum restraint, structure, routine, and consistency in treatment. Furthermore, obedience to authority and conformity to rules were primary features of child-care institutions and child-rearing dogma in mid-nineteenth century America (Rothman, 1971). Rothman indicates that the emphasis on obedience and conformity was sometimes carried to a ridiculous or even harmful extreme, that some youngsters languished in jails or poorhouses, and that the concepts of structure, consistency, and reeducation were sometimes distorted to include cruel and excessive punishment. Still, it is evident from the writing of moral therapists that humane, nonpunitive care was the goal.

By the middle of the nineteenth century, educators were providing programs for students with limited intelligence and emotional or behavioral disorders. Schools in asylums for "insane" and "idiotic" students flourished for a time under the leadership of humanistic teachers who developed explicit teaching methods (Brigham, 1845, 1847, 1848; Howe, 1851, 1852; Ray, 1846). As Bockoven (1956) notes, education was a prominent part of moral treatment. Teaching and learning were considered conducive to mental health—a concept that can hardly be considered bizarre or antiquated.

Most of the education for students with severe emotional or behavioral disorders, aside from the academic instruction offered in asylums for "the insane," was provided under the rubric of education for "idiots." The teaching techniques employed by leading educators of students with mental retardation were amazingly modern in many respects—based on individual assessment, highly structured, systematic, directive, and multisensory, with emphasis on training in self-help and daily living skills for those with severe disabilities, frequent use of games and songs, and suffusion with positive reinforcement (Brigham, 1848; Itard, 1962; Ray, 1846; Seguin, 1866). Despite the overenthusiasm and excessive claims of success by moral therapists and early educators of students with mental retardation (Howe, Itard, and Seguin), the basic soundness of their work and the changes they were able to produce remain impressive (Balthazar & Stevens, 1975). At midcentury the prevailing attitude was one of hope and belief that every student with disabilities could be helped.

---

[4]The term *moral treatment* did not, as some have surmised, connote religious training. Originally, as translated from Pinel's work, moral treatment meant *psychological* as opposed to *medical* treatment of insanity and included every therapeutic endeavor other than medication or surgery. For further discussion of moral treatment, see Bockoven (1972), Caplan (1969), Carlson and Dain (1960), Dain and Carlson (1960), Grob (1973), Menninger (1963), Rees (1957), and Ullmann and Krasner (1969).

In the nineteenth century, considerable concern was shown for children and youths who were delinquent, vagrant, aggressive, disobedient, or disadvantaged (poor or orphaned), but not considered "insane" or "idiotic" (Bremner, 1970, 1971; Eggleston, 1987; Rothman, 1971). Many of these youngsters, who today might be said to have mild or moderate disabilities, found their way into jails and almshouses. There was, however, a strong movement to establish child care institutions (orphan asylums, reformatories, houses of refuge, and so on) for the purpose of reforming and rehabilitating children and youths. The intent was to protect wayward, disabled, and poor youngsters and to provide for their education and training in a humane, familiar atmosphere. Concern for the futures of those exhibiting acting-out behavior was not entirely misguided. Contemporary longitudinal studies tend to confirm what nineteenth-century writers suspected: aggressive, acting-out, delinquent behavior in youngsters predicts misfortune for their later adjustment (Robins, 1966, 1979; Walker, Colvin, & Ramsey, 1995).

Intervention in the public schools became a reality only after the enactment of compulsory attendance laws in the closing decades of the nineteenth century. One reason for enacting compulsory attendance laws was the large number of non-English-speaking, immigrant youngsters who poured into the United States during this period. Immigrant children and youths, authorities felt, should be compelled to be socialized and Americanized by the schools. Once the attendance laws were enacted and enforced, many students obviously interfered with the education of the majority and benefitted little from the regular classes themselves. Before these youngsters had been compelled to go to school, they had merely dropped out, causing no problems except by roaming the streets and committing delinquent acts. Partly out of concern for such problems, the public schools established ungraded classes. In 1871, authorities in New Haven, Connecticut, opened an ungraded class for truant, disobedient, and insubordinate children. Soon afterward, other cities followed suit, and classes for the socially maladjusted and "backward" students (those with mental retardation) grew rapidly (Berkowitz & Rothman, 1967a; Hoffman, 1974). These special classes, as well as corporate schools and similar institutions, became little more than dumping grounds for all manner of misfits. Whether the students or the public school administrators were the misfits was as pertinent a question for that era as it is for the present (Cruickshank, Paul, & Junkala, 1969).

Changes within the 1800s

The nineteenth century cannot be viewed as a unitary or homogeneous historical period. In the years between 1850 and 1900, important changes took place in attitudes toward severe and profound emotional or behavioral disorders and mental retardation, and rather dramatic differences appeared in the type of care afforded in institutions. Optimism, pragmatism, inventiveness, and humane care, associated with moral treatment and model social programs in the first half of the century, gave way to pessimism, theorizing, rigidity, and dehumanizing institutionalization after the Civil War. The failure of private philanthropy and public programs to solve the problems of "idiocy," "insanity," and delinquency and to rectify the situations of the poor led to cynicism and disillusionment. More and larger asylums and houses of refuge were not the answers. The many complex reasons for the retrogression after 1850 include economic, political, social, and professional factors analyzed by Bockoven (1956, 1972), Caplan (1969), Deutsch (1948), Grob (1973), Kanner (1964), Menninger (1963), Rothman (1971), and Ullmann and Krasner (1969).

Ironically, most historical comment on children's emotional or behavioral disorders seems to favor the last decades of the nineteenth century as more auspicious in the development of child psychiatry (Alexander & Selsnick, 1966; Harms, 1967; Kanner, 1973c; Rie, 1971; Walk, 1964). MacMillan's (1960) review of the literature suggests that the earlier decades provided a richer body of information. His observations seem to be borne out by examination of some of the literature published during the last decades of the century. Certainly, there is little or nothing to be found in the writings of Hammond (1891), Maudsley (1880), or Savage (1891) that improves on earlier works insofar as treatment is concerned. The valuable and insightful work of the late-nineteenth century psychiatrists (such as Griesinger) reviewed by Harms (1967) is concerned with the theory and diagnosis of psychological disturbances in children and youth.

After the demise of moral treatment about midcentury, psychiatry became increasingly engrossed in varieties of psychodynamic theory, and therapeutic action on behalf of patients often gave way to interest in diagnosis and classification. Educational and reform efforts with problem children and delinquents increased in number and size, but not in quality or effectiveness. Hoffman (1974) notes that "in each case, what began as sincere, humanistic efforts toward change were turned into near caricatures of their original purposes" (p. 71). Before 1900 it was clear that institutionalization did not mean treatment and that special class placement could mar a child's identity.

By the end of the nineteenth century, several textbooks had been published about the psychiatric disorders of children and youths. These books deal primarily with etiology and classification and, as Kanner (1960) notes, tend toward fatalism. Psychiatric disorders were assumed to be the irreversible results of such widely varied causes as masturbation, overwork, hard study, religious preoccupation, heredity, degeneracy, or disease. The problems of obstreperous children and juvenile delinquents had not been solved, but new efforts were being made: Lightner Witmer established a psychoeducational clinic at the University of Pennsylvania in 1896; Chicago and Denver established the country's first juvenile courts in 1899. Events and trends during the first decades of the twentieth century represented a gradual increase in concern for children and youths with emotional or behavioral disorders.

1900 TO 1960: ESTABLISHMENT OF INTERVENTION PROGRAMS

1900 to 1910

Several important events in the first years of the twentieth century gave direction and impetus to concern for children and youths for many years to come. Ellen Key, the Swedish sociologist, awakened great interest with her prophecy that the twentieth century would be "the century of the child" (Key, 1909). Clifford W. Beers, a bright young man who experienced a nervous breakdown in 1900 and later recovered, wrote of his experiences in a mental hospital. His autobiography, *A Mind that Found Itself* (Beers, 1908), had a profound influence on public opinion. Along with the psychiatrist Adolph Meyer and the philosopher and psychologist William James, Beers founded the National Committee for Mental Hygiene in 1909. The mental hygiene movement resulted in efforts at early detection and prevention, including the establishment of mental hygiene programs in schools and the opening of child guidance clinics.[5] Dr. William Healy founded the Juvenile Psychopathic Institute for the psychological and sociological study of juvenile delinquents in 1909. Healy and his wife, Augusta Bronner, along with Grace M. Fernald, Julia Lathrop, and others in Chicago, began their systematic study of repeated juvenile offenders that influenced research and theory for many years.[6] Also during these years, Alfred Binet introduced an intelligence scale to measure children's performance and to predict their success at school. Sigmund Freud and his contemporaries began writing widely on the topics of infant sexuality and human mental development. The work of Freud and other psychoanalysts was to have a profound effect on the way children's behavior was viewed and, eventually, on attempts to educate children and youths with emotional or behavioral disorders (Fine, 1991). Finally, during these years Drs. Henry Goddard and Walter Fernald forwarded the notion that mental retardation is inseparably linked to criminality and degeneracy (Doll, 1967; Hoffman, 1974; Smith, 1962).

1911 to 1930

Concern for the mental and physical health of children expanded greatly after 1910 (Ollendick & Hersen, 1983). In 1911, Dr. Arnold Gesell founded the Clinic for Child Development at Yale, and in 1912, Congress created the U.S. Children's Bureau "to investigate and report upon all matters pertaining to the welfare of children and child life among all classes of our people." The first teacher training program in special education began in Michigan in 1914. By 1918, all states had compulsory education laws, and in 1919, Ohio passed a law for statewide care of handicapped children. By 1930, sixteen states had enacted laws allowing local school districts to recover the excess costs of educating exceptional children and youths (Henry, 1950). Educational and psychological testing were becoming widely used and school psychology, guidance, and counseling were emerging. Mental hygiene and child guidance clinics became relatively common by 1930; by that time child psychiatry was a new discipline (Kanner, 1973c). According to Kanner, child guidance clinics of this era made three major innovations: (1) interdisciplinary collaboration, (2) treatment of any child whose behavior was annoying to parents and teach-

---

[5]For descriptions of mental hygiene programs and special school provisions for maladjusted children during this era, see the historical account of Berkowitz & Rothman (1967a).

[6]See Healy (1915a, b; 1931) and Healy and Bronner (1969 [original work published in 1926]); also Eggleston, 1987.

ers, not just the severe cases, and (3) attention to the effects of interpersonal relation-ships and adult attitudes on child behavior (Kanner, 1973c, pp. 194–195).

In the 1920s, demand arose for mental hygiene programs in the schools, and some school systems established such programs. Thomas Haines, director of the Division of Mental Deficiency of the National Committee for Mental Hygiene, called for statutes governing the study and training of *all* exceptional children in the public schools, including the "psychopathic, the psychoneurotic, and those who exhibit behavior problems" (Haines, 1925). In an article in *New Republic*, Dr. Smiley Blanton (1925), director of the Minneapolis Child Guidance Clinic and a practicing child psychiatrist, describes the operation of mental hygiene clinics in the public schools of Minneapolis.[7] The staff consisted of 1 psychologist, 3 psychiatric social workers (who had been teachers before they became social workers), 20 visiting teachers, and 10 corrective speech teachers. One of the functions of the clinic was to organize a course in mental hygiene for high school juniors and seniors. Another objective was to establish behavior clinics in kindergartens. The clinic took referrals from teachers and parents and also served preschool and juvenile court cases. After referral to the clinic, a child was studied carefully and a staff meeting was held to determine a course of action. Typically, the staff talked things over with the parents and teacher and tried to change their attitudes toward the child. Specific instructions were given on behavior management, and a social worker would then go to the home or classroom to help carry out the program.

Two professional organizations that are particularly important to the education of children with emotional or behavioral disorders were founded in the 1920s. The Council of Exceptional Children, organized in 1922, was then made up primarily of educators but included other professionals and parents. The group became a power-ful force for the appropriation of monies and enactment of legislation concerning the education of all handicapped children. The American Orthopsychiatric Association (AOA), dominated by the professions of child psychiatry, clinical psychology, and social work but including education and other disciplines as well, was founded in 1924. The AOA did much to encourage research and dissemination of information regarding therapy and education for children and youths with emotional or behav-ioral disorders.

1931 to 1945

The Depression and World War II necessarily diverted attention and funds from education of students with disabilities. There were, however, more students with disabilities in special education in 1940 than in 1930, and by 1948, 41 of the 48 states had enacted laws authorizing or requiring local school districts to make special educational provisions for at least one category of exceptional children (Henry, 1950). The vast majority of special classes were for children with mild mental retar-dation. Programs for students with emotional or behavioral disorders were relatively

---

[7]See Bremner (1971), pp. 947–957, 1040–1057.

few and were designed primarily for acting-out and delinquent children and youths in large cities.

Hitler's rise to power in Europe provided several unanticipated benefits for the education of disabled children in the United States. Several people who were later to influence special education fled to America, including Bruno Bettelheim, Marianne Frostig, Alfred Strauss, and Heinz Werner.[8] (We will touch on some of their contributions later; see also Hallahan, Kauffman, & Lloyd, 1996.)

Several significant developments in child psychiatry occurred during this period. The first psychiatric hospital for children in the United States, the Bradley Home, was established in Rhode Island in 1931 (Davids, 1975). Leo Kanner of Johns Hopkins University contributed immeasurably to the field with the first edition of his textbook *Child Psychiatry* in 1935 and with his initial descriptions of early infantile autism (Kanner, 1943, 1973a, b, c). Here is his description of his first experience with children who would later be said to have "Kanner's syndrome."

> In October 1938, a 5-year-old boy was brought to my clinic from Forest, Mississippi. I was struck by the uniqueness of the peculiarities which Donald exhibited. He could, since the age of 2½ years, tell the names of all the presidents and vice-presidents, recite the letters of the alphabet forwards and backwards, and flawlessly, with good enunciation, rattle off the Twenty-Third Psalm. Yet he was unable to carry on an ordinary conversation. He was out of contact with people, while he could handle objects skillfully. His memory was phenomenal. The few times when he addressed someone—largely to satisfy his wants—he referred to himself as "You" and to the person addressed as "I." He did not respond to any intelligence tests but manipulated intricate formboards adroitly. (Kanner, 1973a, p. 93)

During the 1930s, Despert (a 1968 collection of her papers) and Potter (1933), with Kanner and others, tried to clarify the characteristics of various categories of youngsters with severe emotional and behavioral disorders. Dr. Lauretta Bender pioneered the education of children with schizophrenia. Having organized the children's ward at Bellevue Psychiatric Hospital in New York City in 1934, she appealed in 1935 to the New York City Board of Education for teachers to staff special classrooms at Bellevue for children with severe emotional or behavioral disorders. The Board responded by assigning two substitute teachers to teach ungraded classes (the category used for children with mental retardation) at Bellevue under the administration of the school for students with physical disabilities. Despite inadequate facilities and a complete lack of instructional materials in the beginning, the program succeeded (Wright, 1967). The Bellevue school was to become a fertile training ground for future leaders, most notably Pearl Berkowitz and Esther Rothman (Berkowitz, 1974; Rothman, 1974).

By the end of the 1930s, the literature on children's emotional or behavioral disorders had grown to sizable proportions (Baker & Stullken, 1938). Attempts had been made to define emotional disturbance and to delineate several subclassifications. Surveys of children's behavior problems and teachers' attitudes toward misbe-

---

[8]See Frostig (1976), Hallahan and Cruickshank (1973), and Hallahan and Kauffman (1976, 1977).

havior (Wickman, 1929) had been completed, and there had been efforts to estimate the prevalence of emotional or behavioral disorders. Various plans of special education such as special rooms, schools, classes, and consultative help, had been tried.

The Post-War Years and the 1950s

Following World War II, additional varieties of emotional or behavioral disorders were described by the psychiatric profession.[9] Mahler (1952) delineated a form she called *symbiotic infantile psychosis* (overattachment to the mother); Rank (1949) introduced the term *atypical child* (any severe disturbance of early development resulting from problems of relationship between mother and child); Bergman and Escalona (1949) described children with unusual sensitivity to sensory stimulation; and Robinson and Vitale (1954) wrote about children with circumscribed interest patterns. All of these children with severe disorders fit under the general category of childhood psychosis.

The 1940s and 1950s saw a rising wave of interest in the education of children with emotional or behavioral disorders. In 1944, Bruno Bettelheim began his work at the Sonja Shankman Orthogenic School at the University of Chicago. His concept of a "therapeutic milieu" (Bettelheim, 1950; Bettelheim & Sylvester, 1948) continues to be used in educational methods based on psychoanalytic thought (Bettelheim, 1961, 1970; Redl, 1959a, 1966; Trieschman, Whittaker, & Brendtro, 1969). During the 1940s, Fritz Redl and David Wineman began their work with hyperaggressive youngsters in Detroit. Basing their strategies on the ideas of Bettelheim and others who were psychoanalytic in their thinking regarding delinquency (Aichorn, 1935; Eissler, 1949; Freud, 1946), Redl and Wineman described their use of a therapeutic milieu and a technique called the *life space interview* at Pioneer House, a residential setting for young aggressive and delinquent boys (Redl & Wineman, 1951, 1952). The efforts and thoughts of Redl and Wineman influenced an entire generation of educators (Long, 1974; Morse, 1974).

The New York City Board of Education organized its "600" schools in 1946.[10] These schools, arbitrarily numbered from 600 to 699, were established specifically for the purpose of educating "disturbed" and "maladjusted" youngsters. Some were day schools located in regular school buildings; others were located in residential diagnostic and treatment settings (Berkowitz & Rothman, 1967a).

One of the most important publications of the 1940s was a book by Alfred A. Strauss and Laura E. Lehtinen, *Psychopathology and Education of the Brain-Injured Child* (1947). This book summarizes the work of Strauss and his colleagues (especially Heinz Werner) and students at the Wayne County Training School in

---

[9]For succinct summaries of the contributions of numerous individuals working in this era, see Haring and Phillips (1962).

[10]The designation "600" has now been dropped in favor of a random numbering system. This decision was made in 1965, after it became apparent that 600 was stigmatizing. For additional description of education in schools of this type, see Tobin (1971).

Northville, Michigan, and the Cove Schools in Racine, Wisconsin. Although much of the work of Werner and Strauss was with children whose mental retardation was assumed to be exogenous (resulting from postnatal brain damage), Strauss and Lehtinen recognized that learning problems exist in some children of normal intelligence. They attributed these learning difficulties to brain injury; however, they recognized that emotional maladjustment is characteristic of such children:

> The response of the brain-injured child to the school situation is frequently inadequate, conspicuously disturbing, and persistently troublesome. The following excerpts from a teacher's reports are illustrative.
>
> J.M., 7 years old: " . . . doesn't pay attention to any directions. He is unaware of anything said, yet at times he surprises me by noticing things that others don't."
>
> D.J., 7 years old: " . . . attention hard to hold. Asks constantly: "When can I go? Can I go now?" etc. No initiative. Little self-control. Seems high strung and nervous. . . . "
>
> D.H., 8 years old: " . . . has proven quite a serious problem in behavior. Has acquired the habit of throwing himself into tantrums at the slightest provocation. . . . "
>
> J.K., 8 years old: " . . . has made scarcely any social adjustments in relationships with other children, he loses all self-control, becoming wild and uncontrollable; he is extremely nervous and excitable; his attention span is very short and he is unable to concentrate for more than a few minutes. During work periods he jumps from one activity to another. . . . " (Strauss & Lehtinen, 1947, p. 127)[11]

For such children, Strauss and Lehtinen recommended a highly structured educational approach and a highly consistent, distraction-free environment. Besides general educational principles, they described special methods for teaching arithmetic, reading, and writing. Their work is particularly important because it provided the foundation for the later efforts of Cruickshank (Cruickshank, Bentzen, Ratzeburg, & Tannhauser, 1961) and Haring and Phillips (1962).

By the early 1950s, interest in special education for students with emotional or behavioral disorders gained considerable momentum. In fact, one could say that this area of special education came of age by the end of the 1950s, for one no longer had to be content with examining developments in psychiatry or with citing references in mental retardation. Education of students with emotional or behavioral disorders had become a field of specialization in its own right. One early indication of mental health professionals' recognition of the importance of education was publication of a symposium on the education of emotionally disturbed children (Krugman, 1953). This issue was one of the first attempts by the *American Journal of Orthopsychiatry* to devote an appreciable number of pages specifically to a collection of papers on the importance of schools and education. Among the papers of the symposium are those of Louis Hay (1953), detailing the Junior Guidance Class Program in New York City, and Dr. J. Cotter Hirschberg (1953), explaining the important roles of educa-

---

[11]From *Psychopathology and Education of the Brain-Injured Child* by A.A. Strauss and L.L. Lehtinen, 1947, pp. 127, 129–130. Copyright 1947 by Grune & Stratton. Reprinted by permission.

tion in residential treatment. It is noteworthy that the second part of the *Forty-ninth Yearbook of the National Society for the Study of Education* on the education of exceptional children (the first in its history, published in 1950) includes a chapter on the education of socially maladjusted children and youths (Stullken, 1950).

Another landmark event of the early 1950s was the founding of the League School by Carl Fenichel in 1953 (Fenichel, 1974; Fenichel, Freedman, & Klapper, 1960). The League School was the first private day school for seriously emotionally disturbed children in the United States. Fenichel, who had training in psychoanalysis, began the school using a permissive, psychoanalytic orientation, but soon gave this up in favor of a more directive, psychoeducational approach (Fenichel, 1966, 1974).

In 1955, the first book describing classroom teaching of children with emotional or behavioral disorders appeared.[12] Leonard Kornberg (1955) recounted his experiences in teaching 15 boys at Hawthorn-Cedar Knolls, a residential school near New York City. His teaching approach was based primarily on psychoanalytic thought and drew heavily on the interpersonal therapeutic process—"dialogue" and responding to "I" and "otherness." As he put it, "The essential classroom event is the transaction of meaning among more than two persons, as contrasted with the two-person contact of a therapy situation" (Kornberg, 1955, p. 132). This emphasis on interpersonal relationship and psychiatric-dynamic ideas is predominant in the literature of the 1950s.

By the mid-1950s, researchers recognized that systematic procedures were needed to identify students with emotional or behavioral disorders in the public schools. Eli Bower and others began research in California that culminated in publication of the screening instrument devised by Bower and Lambert (1962) and other writings of Bower (1981). Concern for teaching children and youths with emotional or behavioral disorders had grown by the late 1950s to the extent that an initial study of teacher preparation was reported by Mackie, Kvaraceus, and Williams (1957). The last years of the decade were auspicious for the field because numerous individuals were attaining new vantage points on education: Pearl H. Berkowitz and Esther P. Rothman were collaborating in New York City; William C. Morse and Nicholas J. Long were working at the University of Michigan's Fresh Air Camp; Frank M. Hewett was beginning his studies at the University of California at Los Angeles; Nicholas Hobbs and William C. Rhodes began conceptualizing new strategies at George Peabody College in Nashville, Tennessee; William M. Cruickshank and Norris G. Haring were conducting research projects in the public schools of Maryland and Virginia; and Richard J. Whelan was developing a directive, structured behavioral approach at the Menninger Clinic in Topeka, Kansas. These activities resulted in a wave of publications and research that burst upon the field in the 1960s and 1970s.

---

[12]The books that appeared before 1955 are not primarily descriptions of classroom teaching, although Redl and Wattenberg (1951) discuss mental health in teaching and others (e.g., Bettelheim, 1950; Hymes, 1949; Pearson, 1954; Prescott, 1954; Redl & Wineman, 1951, 1952; Slavson, 1954) examine the relationship between psychoanalysis, psychotherapy, other forms of treatment, and mental health efforts and education. Also Axline (1947) and Moustakas (1953) describe play therapy with children. Until the early 1960s, the most explicit teaching methods for children with emotional or behavioral disorders were probably found in the classic books by Strauss and Lehtinen (1947) and Strauss and Kephart (1955).

THE 1960s AND 1970s: THE EMERGENCE OF CONCEPTUAL MODELS

A steady stream of events after 1960 led to the current diversity of theory and practice in the education of students with emotional or behavioral disorders. While much of the groundwork was laid prior to 1960, only after that point were specific classroom practices articulated. Then, special classes in the public schools proliferated to such a degree that planning guidelines were published (Hollister & Goldston, 1962) and a nationwide survey of special classes was conducted (Morse, Cutler, & Fink, 1964). Professionals banded together in 1964 to form a new division of the Council for Exceptional Children, the Council for Children with Behavioral Disorders. Various curriculum designs were outlined (Kauffman, 1974a; Rhodes, 1963), and curricula to teach specific social-interpersonal skills were developed (Fagen, Long, & Stevens, 1975; Walker, Hops, & Greenwood, 1981). A series of three annual conferences on the education of emotionally disturbed children was held at Syracuse University, bringing together educators and psychologists of divergent viewpoints (Knoblock, 1965, 1966; Knoblock & Johnson, 1967). Preparation of personnel to work with children with emotional or behavioral disorders received federal support in 1963 with the enactment of Public Law 88–164 (amending PL 85–926 of 1958). The Autism Society of America (initially called the National Society for Autistic Children) was founded in 1965.

Reviewing all the important events and trends of the years between 1960 and 1985 is impossible, so what follows are brief summaries of some of the more critical developments. I have organized the summaries around conceptual models, because distinctly different and competing concepts of emotional or behavioral disorders and intervention emerged during this era. (I discuss the implications of various conceptual models more thoroughly in chapter 4.)

Psychoanalytic View

In 1960, Berkowitz and Rothman published their now-classic book, *The Disturbed Child: Recognition and Psychoeducational Therapy in the Classroom*. After describing various classifications of children, they devote four chapters to the teacher's role and classroom procedures. The underlying theory is psychoanalytic, and their suggested approach is quite permissive. In a later book, Berkowitz and Rothman (1967b) pulled together descriptions by several individuals of a variety of programs in New York City. Together they further delineated their concept of clinical teaching (Rothman & Berkowitz, 1967b), proposed a paradigm for a clinical school (Rothman & Berkowitz, 1967a), and described methods of teaching reading to students with emotional or behavioral disorders (Rothman & Berkowitz, 1967c). In other works Berkowitz (1974) reported the status of public schools in treatment centers and described her continued work in institutional schools in New York City; Rothman (1970, 1974) wrote more about her involvement with the Livingston School.

Psychoeducational Approach

Just as Berkowitz and Rothman's later publications reflected movement from a strictly psychoanalytic perspective toward a more pragmatic stance, the work of Morse and others at the University of Michigan in the 1960s showed a tendency to emphasize practical considerations and ego development. Morse and Long, in collaboration with Ruth G. Newman, published the first edition of a landmark volume, *Conflict in the Classroom* (Long, Morse, & Newman, 1965). This book brought together the ideas of Redl and Morse regarding the life space interview (LSI) but included several disparate viewpoints, ranging from the psychoanalytic (Freud, 1965) to the behavioral (Haring & Whelan, 1965). The LSI grew out of Redl's work at Pioneer House in Detroit in the 1940s and 1950s (see Heuchert & Long, 1980). At or shortly after a behavioral crisis, the teacher (or other child worker) conducts an LSI to strengthen the youngster's ego and help the youngster understand and interpret correctly the problems he or she has just encountered (Long & Newman, 1965; Morse, 1953, 1965b; Morse & Wineman, 1965; Redl, 1959b). Also in the 1960s, Morse explained his idea of the crisis teacher—a teacher skilled in LSI techniques and remedial teaching who would be prepared to take over the management and teaching of a difficult student for a short period of time (during a behavioral crisis), and to obviate the need for full-time special class placement (Morse, 1965a, 1971a, b). More recently, Fagen et al. (1975) presented a psychoeducational self-control curriculum, and Fagen (1979) described psychoeducational methods for adolescents (see also Dembinski, Schultz, & Walton, 1982; Rezmierski, Knoblock, & Bloom, 1982; Rich, Beck, & Coleman, 1982; Wood & Long, 1991).

Humanistic Education

As Martin (1972) noted, individualism and humanism were the forces shaping special education in the 1960s and 1970s. There was concern for the particular educational needs of African American and other minority group youngsters, especially those from inner-city areas and poverty backgrounds (Dennison, 1969; Dokecki, Strain, Bernal, Brown, & Robinson, 1975; Johnson, 1969, 1971; Rothman, 1970, 1974). For students with emotional or behavioral disorders it was suggested that radical departures from past educational practices were needed. **Countertheorists**, who depart markedly from tradition and are not accepted as fellow professionals by established authorities in their fields, became a strong force in the mid-1960s. Many who were part of this countertheory group considered themselves humanists and subscribers to the freedom and openness called for by Carl Rogers (1983) and others (Kohl, 1970; Kozol, 1972; Leonard, 1968; Neill, 1960).

Pleas for freedom, openness, and humanism were made by Dennison (1969), Grossman (1972), Knoblock (1970, 1973, 1979), Knoblock and Goldstein (1971), and Trippe (1970). Humanistic education tends to emphasize the affective side of learning and teaching (see Morse, Ardizzone, MacDonald, & Pasick, 1980; Schultz, Heuchert, & Stampf, 1973).

Ecological Approach

The 1960s also saw the rise of the ecological approach. Based primarily on the writing of Hobbs (1965, 1966, 1974) and Rhodes (1965, 1967, 1970), this approach calls for intervention not only with the child or youth, but also with the child's home, school, and community.[13] The most important project associated with the ecological approach was Project Re-ED. After having worked extensively in the mental health field in this country and having observed the European educateur programs,[14] Hobbs, along with Rhodes, Matthew J. Trippe, Wilbert W. Lewis, Lloyd M. Dunn, and others, began Re-ED programs in Tennessee and North Carolina in the early 1960s. Re-ED schools focused on health rather than illness, teaching rather than treatment, learning rather than fundamental personality change, the present and future rather than the past, and on the child's total social system rather than his or her intrapsychic processes exclusively (Hobbs, 1965). In the initial Re-ED schools, youngsters were served in a residential setting during the week but returned home on weekends. A central aspect of Project Re-ED was the selection and training of the teacher-counselors, who carried out the moment-to-moment and day-to-day work with youngsters, and the liaison teachers, who maintained communication and coordination with the home and regular school class (Hobbs, 1966, 1974). Work with the Re-ED and educateur models continues, and most evaluations appear to support the efficacy of an ecological approach (Daly, 1985; Lee, 1971; Lewis, 1982; Votel, 1985; Weinstein, 1969). Furthermore, the initial work of Hobbs and Rhodes apparently gave impetus to the research and writing of others who emphasize ecological concepts (Apter & Conoley, 1984; Graubard, 1976; Graubard, Rosenburg, & Miller, 1971; Rosenburg & Graubard, 1974; Swap, 1974, 1978; Swap, Prieto, & Harth, 1982).

Behavioral Approach

In the late 1950s and early 1960s, some special educators began to make explicit use of basic behavior principles and behavior modification techniques (cf. Forness & MacMillan, 1970; Kazdin, 1978; Cullinan, Epstein, & Kauffman, 1982). The behavior modification frame of reference was derived primarily from B.F. Skinner's (1953) basic research and writing; however, its initial application to the education of students with emotional or behavioral disorders was the work of many individuals, a number of whom were influenced by the work of Heinz Werner, Alfred Strauss, Laura Lehtinen, Newell Kephart, and others who devised methods of teaching brain-injured children at the Wayne County Training School in the 1940s.

William M. Cruickshank and his colleagues conducted an experimental public school program for brain-injured and hyperactive children (many of whom had emo-

---

[13]Hobbs, Rhodes, and others draw upon the theoretical formulations and field work of ecological psychologists such as Roger C. Barker and Herbert F. Wright (Barker & Wright, 1949, 1954; Barker, 1968; see also Gump, 1975).

[14]See Linton (1969, 1970) as well as Hobbs (1974) for descriptions of the educateur programs.

tional difficulties) in Montgomery County, Maryland, in the late 1950s. The report of this project (Cruickshank et al., 1961) described a highly structured program similar in many ways to that outlined earlier by Strauss and Lehtinen (1947). The report emphasized control of extraneous stimuli and use of a consistent routine and consistent consequences for behavior. Shortly after the Montgomery County Project, Norris G. Haring and E. Lakin Phillips extended the concept of structure to work with students with emotional or behavioral disorders in the public schools of Arlington, Virginia (Haring & Phillips, 1962; Phillips, 1967; Phillips & Haring, 1959). Their major hypothesis is that these youngsters lack order, predictability, and consistency in their environment and need the stability and consistent demands of Cruickshank's program. They particularly emphasize the use of consistent consequences for behavior (a basic behavior modification principle). A structured approach as defined by Haring and Phillips consists of three primary elements: clear directions; firm expectations that the child will perform as directed; and consistent follow-through in applying consequences for behavior.

Later in the 1960s, Haring collaborated with Richard J. Whelan at the University of Kansas Medical Center to refine and extend the concept of structure (Haring & Whelan, 1965; Whelan & Haring, 1966), which was extended even further in the late 1960s and into the 1970s by Haring and Phillips to include the behavior modification technology of direct daily measurement of behavioral rates (Haring, 1968, 1974b; Haring & Phillips, 1972). Whelan, Haring's collaborator at Kansas University, had previously developed a structured approach to teaching at the Southard School of the Menninger Clinic in Topeka, Kansas (Whelan, 1963, 1966). Whelan has expanded and refined the concept of structure and the use of behavior principles (Whelan, 1974; Whelan & Gallagher, 1972).

Others were also pioneering the behavioral approach. The report of Zimmerman and Zimmerman (1962) was a prelude to an outpouring of behavior modification research in the late 1960s and 1970s. Their simple anecdotal reports of how they resolved two behavior problems—temper tantrums and refusal to write spelling words—by systematic use of consequences was followed by a spate of technically sophisticated reports in the behavior modification literature. Many behavioral psychologists, including those interested in special education, made tremendous strides in therapeutic endeavors in this era (Goodall, 1972). For example, Herbert C. Quay and his associates contributed immeasurably to the classification of disordered behavior (Quay, 1975). Gerald R. Patterson and his colleagues studied the families of aggressive children and contributed many insights into the coercive processes that operate in such families, as well as effective techniques for managing aggression (Patterson, 1982; Patterson, Reid, Jones, & Conger, 1975). Hill Walker and colleagues, working often with Patterson's research group, applied behavior principles to managing acting out behavior in the classroom and teaching social skills (e.g., Walker & Buckley, 1973; Walker, Hops, & Fiegenbaum, 1976; Walker, McConnell, Holmes, Todis, Walker, & Golden, 1983).

One behavioral psychologist interested in special education was Frank Hewett. Two of his areas of activity are particularly noteworthy. First, in the middle 1960s, he designed an *engineered classroom* that employed a token (point) system as well as special curricula and centers of activity. The Santa Monica Project, an early trial of his program, has become a frequently cited and widely emulated behavioral approach (Hewett, 1967, 1968). As part of his research and training activities, Hewett also proposed a hierarchy of educational tasks (Hewett, 1964a) and a hierarchy of competencies for teachers (Hewett, 1966). He continued to write of his research and training using behavioral methods (Hewett, 1970, 1971, 1974). His second area of interest was teaching children with severe disorders. Through systematic use of operant conditioning (reinforcement) techniques, he was able to teach speech and reading skills to a boy with autism (Hewett, 1964b, 1965).

Finally, during the 1960s and 1970s, there was a dramatic increase in interest and effort to educate children and youths with severe disabilities, including those with severe emotional or behavioral disorders.[15] The intervention techniques that gained widest acceptance in this era and proved to be most effective with students having severe disabilities were behavior modification methods. Although the professionals who made contributions in this area are too numerous to name, the work of O. Ivar Lovaas is particularly notable. First at the University of Washington and later at the University of California at Los Angeles, Lovaas and his colleagues researched the teaching of language and daily living skills to autistic and schizophrenic children (Lovaas, 1966, 1967, 1982; Lovaas & Koegel, 1973; Lovaas, Koegel, Simmons, & Long, 1973; Lovaas, Young, & Newsom, 1978; Devany, Rincover, & Lovaas, 1981). His work, along with that of others who employed operant conditioning techniques, demonstrates that students with severe disabilities can learn when appropriate conditions are arranged and that one need not wait for this learning to occur spontaneously.

PROJECTS AND ISSUES OF THE 1970s AND 1980s

Many special projects with long-range implications for children and youths with emotional or behavioral disorders were conducted in the 1970s, most under the sponsorship of federal agencies. I briefly describe three projects that illustrate the scope and diversity of efforts to improve the education of these youngsters: a project on conceptual models, one involving labeling, and another focused on analysis of needs.

To delineate clearly and to synthesize the diverse ideologies and practices in the field, William C. Rhodes and others at the University of Michigan began the Conceptual Project in Emotional Disturbance in the early 1970s. Recognizing the fragmentation and conflict in the field, but also the commonalities and the mood of ecumenicalism among various factions, Rhodes set about to clarify the conceptual models and their associated methods of intervention (Rhodes & Head, 1974;

---

[15]Part of the reason for this growing interest and effort was the litigation in which the parents of exceptional children were plaintiffs. Court decisions that all children, including those with the most severe disabilities, have a right to public education gave impetus to local schools to make provisions for such children and to the Office of Special Education Programs (U.S. Department of Education) to support training programs for teachers of such students.

Rhodes & Tracy, 1972a, 1972b), and his work has become a classic reference in the field. The Project on Classification of Exceptional Children was directed by Nicholas Hobbs in the early 1970s. This project was conducted (at the request of the U.S. Secretary of Health, Education and Welfare) to examine the consequences of labeling exceptional children of all categories, including those with emotional or behavioral disorders. The results (Hobbs, 1975a, 1975b) reflect the stigmatizing and damaging effects of an inadequate classification and labeling process, an issue of intense concern in the first half of the 1970s.

Beginning in the late 1970s, a federally funded project on national needs analysis and leadership training was launched at the University of Missouri. The work of Judith Grosenick and Sharon Huntze documented the unmet needs of children with emotional or behavioral disorders in the nation's schools and outlined many unanswered questions regarding educational programs (Grosenick & Huntze, 1979, 1983).

An issue of the 1980s—and one continuing to the present day—is whether most children and youths with emotional or behavioral disorders are receiving an appropriate education as required under IDEA, which went into effect in 1978. IDEA, originally known as Public Law 94–142, is a complex and prescriptive law (see Bateman & Chard, 1995; Bateman & Herr, 1981; Hallahan & Kauffman, 1997). Its central feature is the requirement that every child with a disability, including those considered to have serious emotional disturbance, receive a free, appropriate education. The intention of the law certainly cannot be faulted, and some of its effects have undoubtedly been salutary. Because they are defined under the law as disabled, troubled students who are identified as having serious emotional disturbance cannot now legally be excluded from school or denied an appropriate education. The promise of the law to ensure appropriate education for every child and youth with a disability, however, remains unfulfilled.

The prospect that all students with emotional or behavioral disorders will be served by special education and mental health remains dim, as we saw in chapter 2. However, two important organizations formed in the late 1980s brought new hope of progress. In 1987, the National Mental Health Association and the Council for Exceptional Children joined efforts to form the National Mental Health and Special Education Coalition (Forness, 1988b). The Coalition brings together the leadership of diverse groups, including parents, special educators, school psychologists, clinical psychologists, psychiatrists, social workers, and others involved in serving children and youths with emotional or behavioral disorders. It provides a forum for communication among various groups and encourages joint efforts to improve services. It has proposed a new definition and terminology (Forness & Knitzer, 1992), and its continuing efforts are geared toward improving mental health and special education legislation and increasing collaboration among disciplines. Another important milestone in the field was the organization in 1989 of the Federation of Families for Children's Mental Health. The Federation now offers support and advocacy for parents and families of children and youths with emotional or behavioral disorders.

Because the federal definition of "seriously emotionally disturbed" excludes those who are "only" socially maladjusted, providing services to incarcerated youths has been particularly problematic (Murphy, 1986a, 1986b; Nelson, Rutherford, &

Wolford, 1987). Incarcerated youths obviously exhibit disordered behavior, but controversy regarding their inclusion in the special education category "seriously emotionally disturbed" continues. Studies of the needs of incarcerated youths for special education and efforts to define appropriate education for youths in prisons and detention centers were funded by the federal government in the 1980s (Rutherford, Nelson, & Wolford, 1985, 1986). The first book devoted to special education in the criminal justice system was published in 1987 (Nelson et al., 1987). In 1989, the National Juvenile Justice Coalition was formed to address problems of education and treatment of youths involved with the juvenile justice system. It brings together a variety of organizations concerned with these youths for the purpose of obtaining a strong national voice for juvenile justice issues.

During the late 1980s, calls were made for greater integration of special and regular education for *all* students with disabilities. In fact, some proposed a merger of regular and special education or called for abandonment of "pull-out" programs in which students are taught in any setting other than the regular class. These calls for radically integrating or merging were known in the 1980s as the *regular education initiative* (REI) (see Braaten, Kauffman, Braaten, Polsgrove, & Nelson, 1988; Hallahan & Kauffman, 1991; Hallahan et al., 1988; Lloyd, Singh, & Repp, 1991). In the 1990s, similar calls for radical reform have been called the *full inclusion movement* (Fuchs & Fuchs, 1994, 1995). The probable effects of full inclusion on teachers, students with emotional or behavioral disorders, and students without disabilities are matters of considerable controversy, and many special educators appear to be skeptical of the outcome (Braaten et al., 1988; Hallahan et al., 1988; Kauffman, 1989, 1993, 1994, 1995; Kauffman & Hallahan, 1993; Kauffman, Lloyd, Baker, & Riedel, 1995; Walker & Bullis, 1991). Although mainstreaming, or at least increased integration, may indeed be desirable and feasible for many or most students, there are questions about the limits to which the concept of integration can be pushed without becoming counterproductive (Kauffman et al., 1995). The problems of students with disabilities in secondary schools present particularly difficult questions.

By the late 1980s, programs at the secondary level, particularly the transition from school to work, had become a national priority in special education (Rusch & Phelps, 1987). Many students whose disabilities are serious but not typically considered severe, particularly those with emotional or behavioral disorders and learning disabilities, were known to drop out or be "elbowed out" of high schools (Edgar, 1987; Edgar & Siegel, 1995; Wagner, 1991). Most of these youths, in addition to being disabled, are poor, minority, male students. Should we make greater efforts to integrate them into high school academic programs that do not meet their needs and in which their continued presence or success are highly improbable? Or should they be offered a special curriculum, a separate educational track? Edgar (1987) states the difficult choices succinctly: "What a dilemma—two *equally* appalling alternatives, integrated mainstreaming in a nonfunctional curriculum which results in horrendous outcomes (few jobs, high dropout rate) or separate, segregated programs for an already devalued group, a repugnant thought in our democratic society" (p. 560). The complex issues persist, and, as Edgar points out, the answer to the issue of integration may differ somewhat for many disabled students at the secondary level (see also Schumaker & Deshler, 1988).

The issue of special education's service to very young children with emotional or behavioral disorders emerged in the 1980s. In 1986 Congress passed PL 99–457, which extended (beginning with the 1990–91 school year) the requirements of PL 94–142 (now IDEA) to all children with disabilities 3 to 5 years of age. PL 99–457 applies even in states that do not provide free public education to nondisabled children 3 to 5 years of age. The law also includes incentives for states to develop early intervention programs for disabled infants and infants at risk, from birth to age 36 months.

Finally, the conceptual models that emerged during the 1960s and 1970s evolved into more sophisticated, integrative approaches during the 1980s (Van Hasselt & Hersen, 1991a, 1991b). Based on a melding of behavioral and cognitive research, many leaders in the field are embracing intervention strategies variously called *cognitive-behavior modification* (see Bandura, 1986; Mahoney, 1974; Meichenbaum, 1977, 1979, 1980) and *individual psychology* (see Morse, 1985). These strategies take into consideration how individuals think and feel about their behavior as well as how people's social environments influence the way they behave. In short, many of the simplistic notions of the past—that behavior can always be modified effectively merely by manipulating its consequences, or that behavior cannot be changed until the student gets insight into the nature of the problem—have been put to rest. Today's best practices ignore neither the realities of human affective and cognitive experiences nor the reality that people's behavior is powerfully influenced by its consequences.

CURRENT ISSUES AND TRENDS

Current issues and trends in the field seem to suggest a heightened level of attention to the empirical and conceptual foundations of special education. Given this circumstance, it is tempting to believe that we are finally emerging into an era of enlightenment in which progress will be coherent, dramatic, and sustained. Perhaps we are entering such an era, but careful analyses of current trends and issues in the light of history will remind us that today's issues are not new, nor are current suggestions for addressing them likely to be completely successful.

Special education has perpetual issues, including who should be served and how and where they should be served (Bateman, 1994). Many or most of the issues of today have been issues for well over half a century, as reflected in the following: early identification (e.g., Brown, 1943), placement options (e.g., Berry, 1936; Postel, 1937), similarities between general and special education (e.g., Baker, 1934), and training in social skills (e.g., Farson, 1940). Our approaches to these issues may be somewhat more sophisticated today, but we clearly do not have the wisdom or the technical knowledge to put these problems behind us. Although the issues and trends we review here may be prominent in the final years of the twentieth century, they all have historical roots many decades deep and will likely remain vexing problems for many decades to come. These issues and trends are not entirely separate and distinct; inevitably, we find that addressing one demands that we consider others simultaneously.

Early Identification and Prevention

A persistent and self-defeating response of educators and parents is to let emotional or behavioral problems fester until they become disorders of serious if not dangerous proportions. The problems inherent in early identification and prevention have been well understood for more than 30 years (Bower, 1960), yet few measures to address the problems have been taken. We know that the early signs of emotional and behavioral disorders can be detected through careful observation or use of reliable screening instruments (Loeber, Green, Lahey, Christ, & Frick, 1992; Walker & Severson, 1990; Walker, Severson, & Feil, 1994). There is now, as there has been for decades, recognition that we need intervention that is early in two ways: We need to catch problems when the child is young, and we need to catch the early stages of misbehavior regardless of the person's age (Kauffman, 1994b; Walker et al., 1995). Early intervention—both types—is the essence of prevention, yet early identification, intervention, and prevention remain unresolved problems.

Will schools use the knowledge and tools we have to identify students early, before problems become very serious? Having identified the students, will schools take preventative action? These are the same questions raised by Bower in 1960 and by many others in the intervening years. The answers are in doubt for reasons that are both readily apparent and exasperating.

■ Many people are tempted to maintain a "developmental optimism" in the face of signs that a young child is at high risk. "He'll grow out of it," "Don't worry, it's just a passing phase she's going through," and similar explanations provide a convenient excuse not to intervene.

■ Others worry about the stigma associated with any identification of deviance or risk status. Their concern to avoid the stigma of identification prevents intervention, not the development of the disorder. Identification requires labeling—words used to describe the particular group of children under consideration. People who oppose all labeling also oppose all identification and, therefore, all procedures not used with all children. Universal interventions play an important role in primary prevention, but they are insufficient to address the problems of students for whom secondary prevention is necessary (Walker et al., 1995).

■ Still others point to the less-than-perfect prediction that any early identification procedure or preventative effort entails. Early screening and prevention inevitably mean that some children are misidentified, because no such system is perfect, and the chance of making an error can be used as an excuse not to identify a child and intervene.

■ Another complicating factor is concern for bias. If a disproportionate number of children belonging to any particular group of concern is identified—those who are poor, male, or belong to an ethnic, religious, or color group, for example—then early identification and prevention may be undermined by charges of discrimination.

■ Finally, early screening, identification, and intervention are interrelated and costly. Screening makes no sense if children are not identified; identification makes no sense in the absence of intervention; intervention, other than the procedures used indiscriminately with all children, cannot be provided without identification. All cost money. There is always competition for public funds, and many taxpayers and their governmental representatives seem to prefer paying the costs of problems that cannot be skirted to paying the costs of preventing problems that are still avoidable. Many agree to pay for prisons but not for early intervention.

Early identification and prevention are compelling ideas embraced by many special educators in the 1990s. Turning the ideas into coherent, consistent, sustained action will require scientific and political finesse that previous generations could not muster. In the mid-1990s, it was still the case that children were unlikely to be identified for special services until their problems had grown severe and existed for a period of years (see Duncan, Forness, & Hartsough, 1995; Forness, Kavale, MacMillan, Asarnow, & Duncan, in press).

Education of Antisocial and Violent Students

Antisocial, delinquent, and violent behavior in schools and communities has been a perplexing issue for a very long time. In contemporary American culture, youth violence has become a major problem demanding intervention on multiple fronts (American Psychological Association, 1993; Kauffman, 1994b; Kauffman & Burbach, in press; Walker et al., 1995). In fact, the education of antisocial and violent students has become a central issue in both general and special education in the 1990s. The problem is complex and demands that we struggle with difficult questions, including the following:

■ When is antisocial and violent behavior legitimately declared a disability, and when should it be considered criminal or delinquent behavior for which special education is inappropriate? There is great controversy about the kind of behavior that demonstrates a disability and that which merely demonstrates delinquency, criminality, or moral failure.

■ What level of antisocial and violent behavior can be tolerated in a general education classroom? No doubt, behavior that is tolerated in many classrooms today would not have been in decades past. Moreover, conduct varies widely from school to school and class to class. There is much disagreement about the kind of behavior that should be tolerated or accommodated in general education classrooms. And, because behavior cannot be separated from the student who exhibits it, there is much controversy about which students, if any, should be removed from general education classrooms.

- If students "cross the line" of what is tolerable in a classroom or school, then where and how should their education be continued? Alternative schools, special classes, homebound instruction—these placement options and the kinds of instruction offered in them are matters of much conflict.

- What are legitimate means of controlling antisocial and violent behavior? Punishment of various types and the legitimate uses of it provide the basis of heated arguments about the treatment of children and youths.

- How can schools best function as a part of a larger community effort to lessen antisocial and violent behavior? Most people today seem to recognize that the problem of antisocial and violent behavior is not one the schools can handle alone. However, there is much disagreement about just what schools can and should do and how they can best work with other social agencies to address the problem.

Decades of research suggest how some of these issues might be addressed (American Psychological Association, 1993; Walker et al., 1995). However, the educational treatment of students who bring weapons to school, threaten and intimidate their peers or teachers, disrupt the education of their classmates, or are incarcerated will likely be controversial for decades to come.

Comprehensive, Collaborative, Community-based Services

A strong trend in the 1990s is the integration of a variety of services for children and families, "wrapping services around" children in their homes and communities rather than sending them to a succession of intervention programs in other environments (Clark & Clarke, 1996). These attempts to coordinate and improve the effectiveness of multiple social service programs such as special education, child protective services, child welfare, foster care, and so on are built on the observation that individual programs are seldom sufficient to meet children's needs and that a closer working relationship of all service providers is required (e.g., Armstrong & Evans, 1992; Clarke, Schaefer, Burchard, & Welkowitz, 1992; Nelson & Pearson, 1991; Rosenblatt & Attkisson, 1992; Quinn, Epstein, & Cumblad, 1995). Making the school a center for social welfare programs of all kinds, an idea now at least three decades old (cf. Rothman & Berkowitz, 1967a), is part of the current trend.

The idea of comprehensive, coordinated social services, including general and special education, delivered through the neighborhood school is compelling. It is particularly appealing in the case of children whose lives are in great disarray, as are the lives of many children who have emotional or behavioral disorders and are also in foster care (Smucker, Kauffman, & Ball, 1996). However, implementing the ideas and demonstrating that the service delivery system is effective are far from simple. At this point we understand relatively little about how to design and evaluate research on such complex service delivery systems (Knapp, 1995). The issue is likely to be kept alive for decades to come for several reasons.

- Simply combining inadequate services will solve few problems, and in many communities the services to be integrated are insufficient in quantity and quality. If individual agencies have too few resources to be "wrapped around" children, then the combined or integrated service delivery system, too, will leave many children ill-served.

■ Creating the needed expertise and availability of services, integrated and collaborative or not, is an expensive proposition that voters in many states and communities appear unwilling to fund. If wrap-around services are going to be found adequate in the long run—after the initial hyperbole about reform, restructuring, and "systems change" have given way to reality—then they must have highly trained personnel who can coordinate a sufficient number of adequately trained direct service personnel. Serving the needs of difficult children and youths is a highly personnel-intensive proposition, and there is no real short-cut or cheap path to addressing these needs.

■ The proposition to provide varied services through local schools inevitably becomes enmeshed in controversies about what schools are for—the scope of their mission in their communities. In many communities, schools are poorly funded even to accomplish their academic goals for students, and those who control the schools seem reluctant to expand their mission to include collaborative work with other social agencies.

The ideal of comprehensive, collaborative, community-based services is highly appealing, but not new. Whether such services become a reality in many American communities will depend on how Americans come to view their schools and value their children. Barring a dramatic change in the political will of the nation, the promise of the ideal will remain unfulfilled for decades to come (cf. Knitzer & Aber, 1995).

Focus on Academic and Social Skills

Since the report of Knitzer, Steinberg, and Fleisch (1990), there has been increased concern about the quality of instruction in special education programs for students with emotional or behavioral disorders. Knitzer and her colleagues suggested that in far too many classrooms serving these students the emphasis is almost exclusively on controlling acting-out behavior, meaning that students are being given neither the academic proficiency nor the social skills they will need to be reintegrated into general education or become employable adolescents and adults.

It is widely recognized that effective instruction is at the heart of both effective special education (e.g., Kauffman, 1994a) and behavior management (e.g., Kauffman et al., 1993; Walker et al., 1995). In fact, researchers have devised procedures in which teachers approach predictable misbehavior as an instructional problem and devise teaching procedures for desirable behavior similar to those used for academic instruction (Colvin, Sugai, & Patching, 1993). Emphasis on teaching will likely continue as a trend in special education programs for at least two reasons.

■ Good instruction is now known by researchers to be the first line of defense in behavior management. That is, a good instructional program prevents many behavior problems from arising, and an emphasis on instruction is compatible with the clearest mission of public schools. For several decades, beginning in the early 1960s, special educators working from a behavioral model emphasized the use of consequences to alter problem behavior (e.g., Haring & Phillips, 1962). More recently, it has become apparent that the antecedents of behavior—the events preceding an act and the context or setting in which it occurs—are powerful teaching tools that have been neglected in working with students with problem behavior (Alberto & Troutman, 1995; Mayer, 1995). Researchers are helping teachers understand how the classroom conditions they create and the instructional procedures they use may contribute to behavior problems and their resolution (e.g., Colvin et al., 1993; Gunter, Denny, Jack, Shores, & Nelson, 1993; Walker et al., 1995).

■   Empirical evidence to support an instructional approach to behavioral problems is accumulating, and a clear consensus may be reached that teaching appropriate behavior explicitly is a central mission of special education programs. Given that teaching both academics and appropriate social behavior are seen as the central role of schools, there may be less tolerance for programs in which the objectives are merely behavioral containment.

This trend in special education may be one of the most promising, but it is not without controversy and danger. If students who are antisocial, disruptive, and violent are disqualified for special education and seen as simply "bad," then they may be expelled or placed in alternative programs designed to be more punitive than instructive. The controversy is whether such students should be considered to need special education; the danger is that they will be found to deserve only exclusion from general education and that their school experience, if they continue to have one, will not emphasize instruction in academic and social skills.

Functional Analysis of Behavior

In a *functional analysis*, the teacher or researcher determines what specific purposes or goals the student's behavior may have. The objective then becomes teaching the student to achieve essentially the same goal but with different and more acceptable behavior (Alberto & Troutman, 1995; Dunlap et al., 1993; O'Neill, Horner, Albin, Storey, & Sprague, 1990). Although functional analysis is, in concept, at least as old as behavioral psychology, the current trend in research and practice is primarily a phenomenon of the 1990s.

The emphasis on functional analysis is a result of considering the communicative intent of behavior—the function the behavior has in telling others what one likes, dislikes, wants, cannot tolerate, and so on. It grows out of work with individuals who have severe mental retardation or other disorders that prevent them from using oral language, but it applies also to verbal individuals who are inept at communicating their goals appropriately through language. It is also a way of responding nonpunitively to behavior. Whereas a less thorough behavioral analysis may suggest using punishing consequences for misbehavior, functional analysis is an attempt to respond with support for appropriate alternatives to misbehavior.

An emphasis on functional analysis is completely consistent with increased attention to the academic and social skills curricula. It is also a more explicit and narrow focus on the environmental events that trigger undesirable social behavior and what the student obtains as a consequence of behaving in a given way. Functional analysis may reveal, for example, that a student misbehaves out of frustration, boredom, or overstimulation. It may uncover the fact that misbehavior is maintained because of the attention it garners or because it allows the student to avoid difficult tasks or unpleasant demands. Although it is a highly useful tool in teaching, conducting a functional analysis and basing teaching procedure on it requires careful training, especially in the case of students whose behavioral problems are severe or of long standing (see Dunlap et al., 1993; Walker et al., 1995). Consider these potential limitations:

- Functional analysis of behavior is not necessarily simple. Identifying the function of the behavior—what it "says" or the role it plays in the student's life—may require extensive assessment by trained observers. Without support staff trained in functional analysis, teachers may be unable to carry out the required observations and other evaluation procedures.

- Intervention procedures suggested by a functional analysis are sometimes difficult for classroom teachers to carry out without extra help.

Nevertheless, research on functional analysis will likely provide increasingly effective teaching procedures and become an increasingly important part of special education teachers' repertoire.

Continuum of Alternative Placements

The inclusion of students with disabilities in general education classrooms is perhaps one of the most controversial and divisive issues in education in the 1990s (Kauffman & Hallahan, 1995, 1997). Inclusion of students with emotional or behavioral disorders is particularly controversial (Kauffman & Lloyd, 1995; Kauffman, Lloyd, Baker, & Riedel, 1995; Kauffman, Lloyd, Hallahan, & Astuto, 1995b). The controversy is not generated by suggestions that *some* students with emotional or behavioral disorders should be included in regular classes but by the suggestion that *all* students should be accommodated in general education (e.g., Lipsky & Gartner, 1991; Van Dyke, Stallings, & Colley, 1995; Stainback & Stainback, 1991).

Many different definitions of *inclusion* have been offered, and much confusion about the term and its meaning persists. Virtually no one opposes the partial or total inclusion of most students with disabilities in as normal an educational experience as possible. In fact, placement in the least restrictive environment (LRE) has been a basic concept in special education for at least several decades. What has become a central issue in the 1990s is whether, as some reformers propose, the regular classroom should be considered the LRE for literally all students (cf. Kauffman, 1995; Kauffman & Hallahan, 1995). Proponents of "full" inclusion often discuss special education with little or no reference to the different types and levels of disabilities represented and assume that no students will fail to benefit from placement in a regular classroom (e.g., comments by Sapon-Shevin in O'Neil, 1995).

Federal law (IDEA) and regulations mandate a continuum of alternative placements, which has included the following options since the early 1960s:

- Regular classroom with supports, including aides, counselling, or mental health services
- Crisis or resource teachers in regular schools, including consultation with regular classroom teachers and students spending minimum time in the resource room
- Self-contained special classes in regular schools, including mainstreaming for part of the school day
- Special day schools, including those organized on a cooperative or regional basis
- Day treatment or partial hospitalization programs attached to hospitals or residential centers, including those placing some students in regular classrooms in the community
- Residential treatment centers and inpatient hospitals, including those sending some students home on weekends and to regular classrooms in the community
- Homebound instruction, in which teachers visit students' homes to provide instruction
- Schools in juvenile detention centers and prisons. (Kauffman & Smucker, 1995, pp. 36-37)

Reformers' suggestion that this continuum be abandoned in favor of one (i.e., regular classroom in the neighborhood school) or very few placement options is seen by many special educators as ill-advised, unworkable, and detrimental to many children and youths with disabilities, especially to many with emotional or behavioral disorders (e.g., Diamond, 1993; Idstein, 1993; Kauffman, Lloyd, Baker, & Riedel, 1995; Morse, 1994). In addition, under IDEA it is illegal not to maintain the continuum of alternative placements and to make placement decisions on the basis of each individual student's needs (Bateman & Chard, 1995; Huefner, 1994). Nevertheless, as ideological and political pressures for full inclusion build, maintenance of placement options becomes a serious concern (Hallenbeck, Kauffman, & Lloyd, 1993).

Throughout history, the purposes of placement have been to create and control social ecologies that are conducive to appropriate behavior and mental health, both of the children and their families. Kauffman and Smucker (1995) listed the following purposes:

- Protecting others (family, community, schoolmates) from children's uncontrolled or intolerable behavior
- Protecting children from themselves or others
- Educating or training children in academics and other life skills and appropriate emotional responses, attitudes, and conduct
- Educating or training children's families or teachers and peers in order to provide a more supportive environment
- Keeping children available and amenable to therapies—psychotherapy, pharmacotherapy, or behavior therapy

■ Providing opportunity for observation and assessment of children's behavior and its contexts. (p. 37)

It is extremely unlikely that these purposes can be achieved without a continuum of alternative placements (cf. Kauffman, 1995). However, advocates for students with emotional or behavioral disorders will undoubtedly fight a continuing battle to maintain placement options in the face of reform proposals that would eliminate or severely limit them.

Transition to Work or Further Education

Since 1990, IDEA has required that individual plans be written for the transition of older students with disabilities from high school to higher education or work (Halla-han & Kauffman, 1997). IDEA, in combination with societal concern for education of the work force and efforts to reform public schooling, has thus made transition an issue sure to continue.

The primary controversial issues in transition have to do with the curricular and placement options that should be available to students with disabilities at the secondary level (Edgar & Siegel, 1995). Plans for the transition of students with emotional or behavioral disorders, as well as other disabilities, may founder on the following points, as Edgar (1987) noted:

■ The college-bound secondary curriculum may be inappropriate for the interests, life goals, and abilities of some students with disabilities, even with special supports in regular classes. Forcing students into these classes not only fails to prepare them for technical education or work but creates an environment in which students are likely to misbehave, fail, and drop out.

■ Any alternative curriculum or placement option makes the student vulnerable to stigma, neglect, and second-class status. Any alternative to inclusion in the regular, college-bound curriculum is open to charges of discrimination, tracking, and abuse.

The early 1990s saw reports of the National Longitudinal Transition Study (NLTS), a major effort to assess the outcomes of secondary education for students with disabilities. As noted by the U.S. Department of Education (1995),

> The NLTS shows that secondary school programs can produce post-school benefits for students with disabilities—but only for students who can succeed in them. Perhaps the greatest positive contribution schools can make to the post-school success of students with disabilities is to contribute to the in-school success of those students, regardless of their placement. As the inclusion movement gains momentum, great care must be paid to issues of quality and support. (p. 88)

Differentiated education is always controversial. If all students are not treated equally, we assume that some are treated unfairly. We have great difficulty reconciling difference and equality in spite of our commitment to individualization. The dilemmas inherent in helping secondary students plan for life after school are not easily resolved; perhaps they are unresolvable. They are likely to be issues with which every generation will continue to struggle throughout their professional lives.

Multicultural Special Education

The rapidly changing age, social class, and ethnic demographics of the United States have brought multicultural concerns to the forefront of educators' thinking in the 1990s. Teaching students with any type of exceptionality demands understanding of multicultural issues (Hallahan & Kauffman, 1997). Teaching students with emotional or behavioral disorders requires particularly keen attention to the cultural aspects of behavior and behavioral change (Anderson & Webb-Johnson, 1995; Council for Children with Behavioral Disorders, 1989; Peterson & Ishii-Jordan, 1994; Trent & Artiles, 1995).

It is difficult to know exactly how to define culture for purposes of multicultural education. Banks (1994) suggested the concepts of microculture and macroculture. The *macroculture* is a national or shared culture to which smaller microcultures belong. For example, American culture is made up of many *microcultures* based on gender, social class, race, ethnicity, disability, religion, region, and so on. Gay and lesbian youths may be considered to have their own microculture (McIntyre, 1992). Microcultures may differ in a variety of ways relevant to special education, including the discipline procedures they recommend, condone, or reject (McIntyre & Silva, 1992). Moreover, a basic concept of multiculturalism is that there is enormous individual variation among the members of any microculture. Although a culture, however defined, may have identifiable group characteristics, any individual member may or may not share those characteristics.

Regardless of the microculture under consideration, the multicultural aspects of special education for students with emotional or behavioral disorders raise difficult questions that point to continuing controversies.

- How can behavior be assessed without cultural bias? Behavior cannot be assessed without a cultural perspective, so it is critically important to understand one's own cultural frame of reference and how it might affect perceptions and judgments.

- What behavior is normative and what behavior is deviant in the student's culture? Clearly, cultures differ in their standards and expectations for the behavior of children and youths, what they consider acceptable and what they consider inappropriate or intolerable. It is essential to understand the cultural demands of the child's family and community.

- What interventions are acceptable in the culture of the student? Cultures vary considerably in what is considered appropriate behavior of adults toward children. Educators must understand how proposed interventions will be viewed by students' parents and communities.

- How might racism, sexism, and other forms of discrimination have contributed to and how might they still contribute to the creation, labelling, and inappropriate treatment of "deviance"?

- Whose culture should be the standard for making judgments about behavior and interventions?

The challenge of multicultural education is not new. Americans have always faced the daunting task of dealing with cultural diversity (Banks, 1993, 1994). Historically, we Americans have failed, as have most if not all other nations of the world, to provide a macroculture that is inviting and supportive of all of our desirable microcultures. The next few decades may determine whether a humane, democratic American macroculture exists and can be sustained.

A National Agenda for Improving Outcomes for Students

Partly in response to the issues and trends we have discussed so far and partly in response to recognition that the outcomes for students with emotional or behavioral disorders have been unsatisfactory, the federal government launched an effort in the early 1990s to establish a national agenda for education. Students with emotional or behavioral disorders typically have low grades and other indications of unsatisfactory academic outcomes, have higher dropout and lower graduation rates than other student groups, are often placed in highly restrictive settings, are disproportionately from poor and minority families, and frequently encounter the juvenile justice system (Chesapeake Institute, 1994; U.S. Department of Education, 1994). By 1992, the national agenda consisted of seven interdependent, strategic targets (notice that the terminology used is that of federal legislation—serious emotional disturbance):

Target 1   *Expand Positive Learning Opportunities and Results*: To foster the provision of engaging, useful, and positive learning opportunities. These opportunities should be result-driven and should acknowledge as well as respond to the experiences and needs of children and youths with a serious emotional disturbance.

Target 2   *Strengthen School and Community Capacity*: To foster initiatives that strengthen the capacity of schools and communities to serve students with serious emotional disturbance in the least restrictive environments appropriate.

Target 3   *Value and Address Diversity*: To encourage culturally competent and linguistically appropriate exchanges and collaborations among families, professionals, students, and communities. These collaborations should foster equitable *outcomes* for all students and result in the identification and provision of services that are responsive to issues of race, culture, gender, and social and economic status.

Target 4   *Collaborate with Families*: To foster collaborations that fully include family members on the team of service providers that implements family-focused services to improve educational *outcomes*. Services should be open, helpful, culturally competent, accessible to families, and school-based as well as community-based.

Target 5   *Promote Appropriate Assessment*: To promote practices ensuring that assessment is integral to identification, design, and delivery of services for children and youths with SED. These practices should be culturally appropriate, ethical, and functional.

Target 6   *Provide Ongoing Skill Development and Support*: To foster the enhancement of knowledge, understanding, and sensitivity among all who work with children and youths who have or who are at risk of developing SED. Support and development should be ongoing and should aim at strengthening the capacity of families, teachers, service providers, and other stakeholders to collaborate, persevere, and improve outcomes for children and youths with SED.

Target 7 *Create Comprehensive and Collaborative Systems*: To promote systems change resulting in the development of coherent services built around the individual needs of children and youths who have or who are at risk of developing SED. These services should be family-centered, community-based, and appropriately funded. (U.S. Department of Education, 1994, pp. 119-120)

The national agenda is ambitious, and it remains to be seen whether sufficient resources will be allocated to make achievement of these targets possible (cf. Smith & Couthino, in press).

PAST AND FUTURE

At the close of the twentieth century, it is easy to be discouraged by the history of the treatment of children and youths with emotional or behavioral disorders. Not a single critical issue seems to have been truly resolved; current issues and trends seem only to be a recycling of those that have been with us for well over a century (cf. Kauffman, 1976, 1981; Kauffman & Smucker, 1995). In spite of the best intentions of those who have struggled with the problems of educating students with emotional or behavioral disorders, the most promising innovations nearly always seem to have gone awry, to have produced results that are disappointing in the eyes of some, or to have been abandoned at least temporarily. Our disappointment may be partly a result of unrealistic expectations and partly a result of our failure to see that good intentions are not enough to ensure success.

It is difficult to define success in special education, especially in the education of students with emotional or behavioral disorders. If special education really "works," then what would we expect the outcomes to be? For many or most students who have severe disorders of conduct, it is unrealistic to expect a "cure" if intervention is not begun early (Walker et al., 1995). How much improvement under what conditions would we define as "success"? These are important questions that are seldom directly, explicitly addressed among special educators. Too often, perhaps, our expectations are simply not reasonable, and we define ourselves or our programs as failures by criteria that are quixotic—extravagantly, unreasonably idealistic.

Many of the efforts special educators have made have been at least moderately successful by a reasonable standard, but few have been spectacularly successful and none has been totally successful. Charges of failure and calls for radical reform have been based in some cases on distorted perceptions of the effects special education might be expected to produce, given the resources allocated to the effort (Kauffman, 1994a; Kauffman, Lloyd, Hallahan, & Astuto, 1995b; Peacock Hill Working Group, 1991). We must constantly strive to balance the recognition that special education needs improvement and should produce better outcomes than it does for children with the acknowledgement that special education has a history of improving the lives of many students. In a sense, our situation is like that of the students with whom we work: we need to recognize our failures, limitations, and need for improvement without becoming unrealistic in our expectations for change, success, or approximations of perfection.

The road special education has traveled from eugenics to euphemisms in the past century has been paved with good intentions. The people who, in retrospect, we may see as "monsters" who seemingly set out to stigmatize, dehumanize, and disenfranchise children and youths with disabilities are bogeymen, not the real people who chose labels, built institutions, established special classes, emptied institutions, tinkered with new labels, mainstreamed students and called for full inclusion, or wrote the laws and regulations we see as cumbersome, inadequate, or counterproductive. Their intentions were good, but good intentions are not and never have been enough to make hope a reality.

If it had succeeded as planned, special education's history would be a tale of success—of cures and caring, fully realized potential, freedom from stigma and discrimination, efficient management, and social harmony. Well-laid, best-intentioned plans can miss their mark for many reasons, including the failure of planners to see their designs in socio-historical context and to adhere strictly to what is actually known at the time about intervention in human behavior (Moynihan, 1993). Our failure to see how our own designs are enmeshed in the context of current sociopolitical trends and our false claims of knowledge about our interventions could make us the bugbears of future generations. If we are going to avoid many mistakes of the past, then we need to proceed with greater awareness of our history, more caution in assuming that any change will bring real progress, and heightened attention to staying within the scientific foundations of our work (Kauffman, 1993).

SUMMARY

Children and youths with emotional or behavioral disorders have been recognized throughout history. Before 1800, most of them were thought to be possessed, wicked, or idiotic. Efforts to educate these students began in the nineteenth century, first in "lunatic" asylums and institutions for "idiots" and later in houses of refuge, detention centers, and public school classes for truants, troublemakers, and "backward" pupils. The mental hygiene and child study movements of the early twentieth century highlighted the emotional or behavioral disorders of children and youths and led to efforts to deal more effectively with such youngsters in homes and schools. In the 1940s, several syndromes were clearly described. Several psychoanalytically oriented educational programs began in the late 1940s and the 1950s. The 1960s and early 1970s were periods of rapid growth in educational interventions. Diverse theories ranging from psychoanalytic to behavioral led to divergent educational practices. Besides the forces of psychoanalysis and behaviorism, the field was influenced by the growth of ecological and humanistic psychology. New issues emerged in the 1970s and 1980s as federal legislation and initiatives took effect. However, many current issues are a recycling of concerns that have never been and may never be completely resolved.

The history of the field cannot be captured merely by reviewing a chronology of events, but a chronology can help one grasp the development of ideas and trends. Some of the important events in the history of the field are listed in Table 3.1.

Table 3.1

Chronology of Important Events Relating to Children with Emotional or Behavioral Disorders. 1799–1992.

Year	Event
1799	Itard publishes his report of the wild boy of Aveyron
1825	House of Refuge, first institution for juvenile delinquents in the U.S., founded in New York; similar institutions founded in Boston (1826) and Philadelphia (1828)
1841	Dorothea Dix begins crusade for better care of the insane
1847	State Reform School for Boys, the first state institution for juvenile delinquents, established in Westborough, Massachusetts
1850	Massachusetts incorporates school for idiotic and feebleminded youths at urging of Samuel Gridley Howe; Edward Seguin moves to the United States
1866	Edward Seguin publishes *Idiocy and Its Treatment by the Physiological Method*
1871	Ungraded class for truant, disobedient, and insubordinate children opens in New Haven, Connecticut
1898	New York City Board of Education assumes responsibility for two schools for truant children
1899	First U.S. juvenile court established in Chicago
1908	Clifford Beers publishes *A Mind That Found Itself*
1909	National Committee for Mental Hygiene founded; Ellen Key publishes *The Century of the Child;* William Healy founds the Juvenile Psychopathic Institute in Chicago
1911	Arnold Gesell founds the Clinic for Child Development at Yale University
1912	Congress creates the U.S. Children's Bureau
1919	Ohio passes law for statewide education of the handicapped
1922	Council for Exceptional Children founded
1924	American Orthopsychiatric Association founded
1931	First psychiatric hospital for children in the U.S. founded in Rhode Island
1935	Leo Kanner publishes *Child Psychiatry;* Loretta Bender and others begin school for psychotic children at Bellevue Psychiatric Hospital in New York City
1943	Leo Kanner describes early infantile autism
1944	Bruno Bettelheim opens the Orthogenic School at the University of Chicago
1946	New York City Board of Education designates "600" schools for disturbed and maladjusted pupils; Fritz Redl and David Wineman open Pioneer House in Detroit
1947	Alfred Strauss and Laura Lehtinen publish *Psychopathology and Education of the Brain-Injured Child* based on work at Wayne County Training School in Northville, Michigan
1950	Bruno Bettelheim publishes *Love is Not Enough*
1953	Carl Fenichel founds the League School, first private day school for severely emotionally disturbed children, in Brooklyn
1955	Leonard Kornberg publishes *A Class for Disturbed Children,* first book describing classroom teaching of disturbed children
1960	Pearl Berkowitz and Esther Rothman publish *The Disturbed Child,* describing permissive, psychoanalytic educational approach

Year	Event
1961	William Cruickshank et al. publish *A Teaching Method for Brain-Injured and Hyperactive Children,* reporting results of a structured educational program in Montgomery County, Maryland; Nicholas Hobbs and associates begin Project Re-ED in Tennessee and North Carolina
1962	Norris Haring and Lakin Phillips publish *Educating Emotionally Disturbed Children,* reporting results of a structured program in Arlington, Virginia; Eli Bower and Nadine Lambert publish *An In-School Process for Screening Emotionally Handicapped Children* based on research in California
1963	PL 88–164 provides federal money for support of personnel preparation in the area of emotionally disturbed
1964	William Morse, Richard Cutler, and Albert Fink publish *Public School Classes for the Emotionally Handicapped: A Research Analysis;* Council for Children with Behavioral Disorders established as a division of Council for Exceptional Children
1965	Nicholas Long, William Morse, and Ruth Newman publish *Conflict in the Classroom;* Autism Society of America founded; First Annual Conference on the Education of Emotionally Disturbed Children held at Syracuse University
1968	Frank Hewett publishes *The Emotionally Disturbed Child in the Classroom,* reporting use of an engineered classroom in Santa Monica, California
1970	William Rhodes begins Conceptual Project in Emotional Disturbance, summarizing theory, research, and intervention
1974	Association for Persons with Severe Handicaps founded
1975	Nicholas Hobbs publishes *Issues in the Classification of Children and The Futures of Children,* reporting the work of the Project on the Classification of Exceptional Children
1978	PL 94–142 (enacted in 1975) requires free, appropriate education for all handicapped children, including the seriously emotionally disturbed; federal funding for National Needs Analysis studies at University of Missouri
1986	PL 99–457 enacted, extending provisions of PL 94–142 to all handicapped children three to five years of age by school year 1990–91; statistics show that about one percent of students enrolled in public schools are receiving special education services as seriously emotionally disturbed, only about one-half a conservative estimate of prevalence
1987	National Mental Health and Special Education Coalition formed; C. Michael Nelson, Robert B. Rutherford, and Bruce I. Wolford publish *Special Education in the Criminal Justice System*
1989	Federation of Families for Children's Mental Health founded; National Juvenile Justice Coalition formed
1990	Individuals with Disabilities Education Act (IDEA) amends PL 94–142; National Mental Health and Special Education Coalition proposes new definition and terminology
1992	National Agenda for Students with Serious Emotional Disturbance proposed

Definition, prevalence, and terminology remain current issues of great importance to special educators. Issues of increasing importance revolve around the settings in which students with emotional or behavioral disorders should be taught. Proposals to merge or radically integrate regular and special education have, however, met with considerable skepticism, particularly as such integration might be applied at the secondary level. Extension of special education to incarcerated youths and provision of special services to very young children with emotional or behavioral disorders are emerging trends. Conceptual models are evolving into more sophisticated and integrated approaches that address students' behavior and cognitions in social systems. New coalitions of parents, professionals, and advocates and a new organization for parents and families have brought renewed hope to the field.

In the 1990s, issues and trends include early identification and prevention; education of antisocial and violent students; comprehensive, collaborative, community-based services; a focus on instruction in academic and social skills; functional analysis of behavior; maintaining a continuum of alternative placements; transition of students to work or further education; and multicultural education. In 1992, a national agenda was proposed, launching efforts to achieve seven strategic targets that should improve outcomes for students with emotional or behavioral disorders.

Case for Discussion

"She's All Yours"

Cindy Lou

I began my teaching career in a special self-contained class In a small town in the South. I was not certified to teach, but the school district was desperate for someone to take positions in special education. Two days before my first students arrived, the principal handed me a cum folder and said, "Mrs. Jones and I have decided that this young man would do better in your room." He offered no verbal or written explanation about *why* the young man in question would do better in a class for students with mild mental retardation. As the year progressed, I began to understand how students qualified for my class. If the principal and the regular classroom teacher agreed, they pulled that child's folder from behind the regular classroom teacher's name in the file drawer and placed the folder behind my name. He or she was then "retarded." It was that simple—a process uncluttered by procedures the teacher and principal deemed unnecessary.

The most interesting student in my class that year was Cindy Lou, one of the few who had actually had a score on an IQ test. Her full-scale score, obtained 4 years before she came to my class, was 92.

Cindy Lou always sat in the back of the room, in spite of my best efforts to place her anywhere else. I soon learned to appreciate her self-imposed exile. Whenever she completed seat work, she talked and muttered to herself constantly. Sometimes she supplemented this soliloquy with yells and threats directed at anyone unfortunate enough to catch her eye. Early on, some of my other students laughed at her or teased her about talking and muttering to herself. But they soon learned to keep a healthy distance from Cindy Lou. She was a big girl and not above punching someone who offended her. And it soon became apparent that she didn't require an excuse to knock someone into the middle of next week. Any insult, real or imagined, would suffice.

In spite of Cindy Lou's angry outbursts, she was the best student in my room—when she was there. She was always first to grasp a concept, completed her work first, and answered oral and written questions correctly. But even with my efforts combined with those of her mother, the principal, the school social worker, Cindy Lou was absent at least one day each week.

Cindy Lou was a seventh grader who had been retained twice. She was large, full-bosomed, and sexually active. It wasn't long before the town madame called me to say, "Listen here, you restrain that Cindy Lou!" According to her, Cindy Lou waited outside her establishment, offering herself for less money than the whores inside. "She's undercutting my girls. And furthermore, I'll have you know I run a clean establishment. None of my girls is underage!" she bellowed.

Just before Christmas, Cindy Lou brought me a pretty glass candle holder shaped like a star. Since we spent part of every day in angry confrontation with each other, I was touched that she would give me a present. An hour later, the principal asked me to come to his office. The manager of a store was there. He had seen Cindy Lou take the candle holder. When he confronted her, she had become violent and he had retreated. There were other witnesses, and he intended to press charges unless someone paid for the candle holder. I was new, unskilled, and a bit stupid. I paid for the candle holder.

Questions About the Case

1. In what historical period do you think this case *could have* taken place? Why?

2. In what historical period do you think this case *did* take place? What developments in the field lead you to this conclusion?

3. Historically, what attempts have been made to guard against misidentification and misplacement of students with special needs? Can you propose better safeguards than have been devised so far?

PERSONAL REFLECTIONS

History

Richard J. Whelan, Ed.D., is the Ralph L. Smith Distinguished Professor of Child Development and Professor of Special Education and Pediatrics at the University of Kansas Medical Center, where he is also the Director of Education.

What do you think are the most important current forces influencing the direction of the field of special education for children with emotional and behavioral disorders?

I see four overlapping, yet integrated, current forces that are major influences in the field today. The first is the long overdue coalition among mental health service providers and special education professionals. I also include in this group parent organizations that are now making every effort to have their needs identified and responded to at the federal and state levels.

The second force is legislation that is largely the product of lobbying efforts by the coalition and parent groups. Legislation (and changes in regulations supporting federal initiatives) will continue to provide money for preparing professional personnel in education and for supporting research and demonstration projects that show how an integrated approach to mental health services and education can be developed at the local level. This effort will take the form of transdisciplinary or interdisciplinary efforts between community level mental health personnel and special educators in local school systems. If such interdisciplinary, integrated service functions successfully at the local level, it should be implemented at the state and national levels. Local initiatives that are successful and efficient have a higher probability of growth and spread to state and national levels. If we have learned anything about the integration of educational and mental health services over the past 40 years, it is that top-down laws without local accep-

tance are rarely successful in bringing about deep change as contrasted to surface compliance.

A third force is an initiative to decertify certain students as eligible for special education. This initiative has its foundations in efforts among administrators—of general and special education programs, plus some professionals in the field—to separate students with conduct problems from students who are identified as seriously emotionally disturbed. The rationale behind this movement is that youngsters with conduct problems are capable of deciding or differentiating among behavior patterns that are acceptable to society and those that are not: if students with conduct problems do not make the right behavioral choices, they should be held accountable to the rules and regulations of the school system and society at large with the same consequences for them as are imposed on other students. Although on the surface this approach seems to make sense, the question is whether the so-called general education personnel are capable of serving the very complex needs of youngsters who act out their affectively based problems. In all likelihood, the general education organization is not capable at this time of offering these students what they need in the way of counseling or specialized instruction. Unfortunately, one of the propelling forces that is driving this decertification movement is economic. Perhaps both general education and special education administrators believe that by limiting the number of children served under the category of seriously emotionally disturbed they can reduce the special education budget. This force is also paradoxical because the numbers of seriously emotionally disturbed children currently being served in special education programs are far fewer than the federal government's estimated 2 percent. However, if this decertification movement is successful, the young people who are denied services at a time when special education might make a difference will surely be frequent and comprehensive users of the mental health system as adults.

Finally, the fourth current force is one of educational restructuring to produce "payoffs" of large achievement gains for the majority of students. On the surface, who wants to challenge reforms that may increase learning? But beware, special educators, because reformers are looking at disability-targeted dollars to reduce teacher–pupil ratios in general education classrooms (see Odden, Monk, Nakib, & Picus, 1995). After all, if 12 percent of the students are using 25 percent of the education dollars, some may say, "Let's just redistribute the funds to reduce teacher-pupil ratios from 1:25 to 1:13." And who will provide instruction to students with disabilities in these smaller classrooms? General education teachers, of course! This is "back to the past" thinking, yet it is one more way to support an agenda called "reform" on the backs of students who are few in number and have little political clout to protect their interests. It is a reversal of the hard-won rights embodied in IDEA.

Furthermore, research findings on smaller class size do not support the assumption of benefits to be gained by the dollar redistribution, nor does research support the assumption that general educators are competent in teaching extremely diverse student groups. Instead, the *Kappan* article lists a reference on service coordination to support a statement that there is conclusive research that special education dollars produce few achievement effects. The source listed doesn't address program efficacy, but it does argue for coordinated services, a worthwhile goal. The implication for special educators is that we must look behind the assertions of reformers for a foundation of evidence. If the evidence to support an assertion is not there, or is distorted, then we must be prepared to respond strongly and quickly. Students with special needs deserve no less than our strongest possible response to protect their rights to an appropriate education that is equitable, but not necessarily identical, to the education general education students receive.

How do you think the field will be different in the first decade of the twenty-first century?

This question reminds me of a statement that Albert Einstein made: "I never think of the future. It comes soon enough." Nevertheless, if our society wants to reduce the number of children with serious emotional and behavioral disorders, it will have to function differently than it does today. I believe the trends in the 1990s are moving in the right direction. For example, if the federal government and states will carry through current initiatives to expand Head Start services, perhaps we can finally move into prevention rather than wait to initiate treatment at the point of crisis or after several crises have occurred in a child's life. Prevention must include a strategy of care that begins during pregnancy and follows throughout the child's educational experience. This means that our local, state, and national governmental agencies must provide instruction for parents and potential parents in healthy living, child development, and other topics that will ensure that their children have the capacity and skills to respond to the vagaries of everyday living.

When children come to school unprepared to deal with teaching and learning environments, the cost of that neglect is an increased frequency of serious affective problems that forever influence children's ability to respond appropriately in situations that require cognitive, social, and related competence. Neither the children nor we as a society in general are served well by such neglect, and as citizens of a demographically diverse nation that requires capable citizens for its very existence, we must insist that this neglect stop now. The first decade of the twenty-first century should see not only responsive intervention programs in the public schools and at the preschool level but also a necessary emphasis on the prevention of childhood emotional problems. This prevention must take a proactive approach in terms of children acquiring knowledge and skills to allow them to be resilient and adaptive to the problems they confront in everyday life.

In your professional lifetime, what do you think have been the most important developments affecting the education of children with emotional or behavioral disorders?

In addition to my responses to your earlier questions, I think one of the most important changes in the field since I began, well over 40 years ago, is the willingness of professionals to look at various ways of understanding children's behavior and the interventions designed to deal with them. When I started there were two, perhaps three, very divergent approaches to understanding and treating the problems children presented to mental health personnel and to professionals in the schools. Unfortunately, there was very little understanding of positions or the language used by the major supporters of each philosophy or theory. Over the past 40 years, there has been a steady progression toward integration of theories—understanding of causes and methods of intervention—to the point at which professionals who adhere to different theoretical approaches can now converse with a more common language and compare research findings associated with their particular positions. The common language that I have seen adopted across theoretical models is that of measurement, particularly that brought to the profession by the strategies and tactics of applied behavior analysis (ABA). It is now relatively common, for example, to use ABA measurement procedures to test the efficacy of a life-space-interview approach with students. I view this as a "healthy" change because an increased understanding of other views often leads to effective communication, which in turn results in useful approaches to prevention and intervention. Also, children in pain could not care less about the theory espoused by their teacher or counselor—they want relief and help toward a better life.

Another development of critical importance is the role of the federal government in providing programs to serve children with emotional and behavioral disorders. Without the federal catalytic initiatives to provide dollars to serve children and support teacher education, I believe that our field would not have progressed very much since the late 1950s. In the late 1950s, there were fewer than 15 programs in the United States preparing teachers to serve this group of children. The federal initiative to prepare large numbers of professional personnel has increased service options manyfold. No longer are children and their advocates faced with the choices of no intervention or total hospitalization—there is a continuum of choices between the two extremes. And the federal government has backed up access to these increased services by a strong system of due-process protections and guarantees for a free, appropriate public education. But our field must be forever vigilant, because during economic hard times the hard-won rights of children with special needs can be lost easily. Children can't vote, and professional voices are rarely loud enough or numerically sufficient to counter voices that call for the dismantling of effective programs upon the altars of "wasteful spending" and "bootstrap" slogans.

Perhaps the most important development is the recognition that special education has something to offer in the way of therapeutic experiences for children with emotional and behavioral disorders. No longer do we hear statements like this from our colleagues in mental health: "We will fix the youngsters and send them back to you teachers, and you need not worry about the therapy process." Now we teachers are viewed as important, essential people on the transdisciplinary or interdisciplinary team and function as co-equals with mental health personnel. After all, the business of children is school; next to home, they spend more hours per day in the school environment than anyplace else. Even if a home situation is dysfunctional, there is still hope that the hours in school can be used to instill within a child the skills, strength, and resilience to cope successfully with life outside of school.

What are the most important lessons to be learned from the history of our field?

Clarence Darrow once remarked, "History repeats itself, and that is one of the things that is wrong with history." I hope that Mr. Darrow was wrong in his analysis of history. Certainly there are important lessons to be learned from our past, and we should avoid the obvious errors we've made. At the same time, we must be selective in pulling from our history those achievements that are still functional today and will be long into the future. In using the past to learn lessons, we must avoid the pitfall of wanting to predict the future so precisely that we alter the past to make our prediction true. After all, we don't know whether our present projections of the future are correct until they become the present. If we are going to learn from our past, then let's be sure that we don't change it to fit our present needs and plans for the future. There must be a careful balance between the positions of "seeing is believing" and "believing is seeing"; either position alone may produce policy errors of considerable magnitude. For example, must the best of 24-hour intervention models be closed because a current paradigm declares that community-based services are best for all children with disabilities? Of course not, but if conventional wisdom based on one-sided policy visions prevails, intensive intervention programming could be unavailable for children with 24-hour needs. Add to this the reality that community service models—no matter how functional the grand plan—have rarely had access to the human and dollar resources required to deliver the services they were designed to provide. Commitment to provide services for children with special needs is the essential vision. Now let's bring historical fact plus balancing of policies to the process of realizing this vision.

Perhaps the most important lesson that we can learn from our history relates back to the concept of preventing the high prevalence of children with emotional and behavioral disorders. We somehow have not arrived at the position of knowing that early commitment of resources functions to preclude even larger commitments of them in the future. The citizens and leaders of our country seem not to be able to operate over the long term; instead, they are making crisis decisions that at best serve as Band-Aids™ for very fundamental problems in our society. Clearly, the goals of the President and the Governors' America 2000 Initiatives are important. Very few people can argue with the position that every child should come to school ready to learn. But unless our society is willing to back up that goal with funding for validated programs, we will not have learned critical lessons from our history.

Another lesson is that we must prepare all educators to be mental health providers in the sense that we offer children nurturing environments with opportunities to learn and time in which to do it. We must abandon our lockstep notion that the curriculum and the time available to teach it must be the same for all children. Having a set curriculum and a set time to complete it is simply not responsive to the needs of all children. Just as children's needs vary, so must curriculum and teaching time vary to get that all-important "fit" between them. If this can be accomplished, many of the affective and cognitive problems children present today can be prevented from becoming realities tomorrow.

4
Conceptual Models: Approaches to the Problem

As you read this chapter, keep these guiding questions in mind:

- How are beliefs about human nature linked to one's choice of intervention strategies?

- Under what circumstances might someone use nonbiological interventions even though a behavior problem is known to be caused by a physiological disorder?

- What assumptions might prevent someone who accepts a psychodynamic model from trying to change disordered behavior immediately?

- What are the major goals of the life space interview, an intervention strategy associated with the psychoeducational approach?

- What role does the teacher play in a humanistic approach? In what ways is an ecological approach compatible with behavioral and social-cognitive theory?

- From the perspective of a behavioral model, what is the most important strategy in changing maladaptive behavior?

- What is the most important concept underlying social-cognitive theory, and what implication does it have for understanding the disordered emotions and behavior of children and youth?

People in every culture have sought to conceptualize unusual or disturbing human behavior in terms of causal factors and to trace back to those same factors ways to eliminate, control, and prevent deviant acts. From the innumerable causes and remedies that have been suggested over the centuries, we can identify several conceptual themes. These themes have remained remarkably consistent for thousands of years, and contemporary versions are merely elaborations and extensions of their ancient counterparts (Kauffman, 1974b). For purposes of explanation and control of behavior, humans have been variously conceptualized, for example, as spiritual beings, biological organisms, rational and feeling persons, and products of their environments.

Educators have always struggled with how human behavior—both troublesome and desirable—should be conceptualized. What we believe people *are* determines what explanations of behavior we seek and accept. If people are thought to be spiritual beings, then mystical or religious approaches to changing their behavior will be adopted. If people are conceptualized as biological organisms, then medical, surgical, or dietary treatments will be prescribed. If people are said to be rational and feeling persons, then cognitive and affective interventions will be attempted. And if people are analyzed as products of environmental events, then antecedent and consequent events will be controlled in efforts to modify behavior. How we respond to disordered behavior is linked to what we believe about the nature and causes of human conduct.

Today we recognize so many possible causes of troublesome behavior that sorting through them has become a troubling task. It does not take professional training to see how nearly all aspects of young people's lives are fraught with potential for psychological problems. Adults now recognize that children and youths feel stress in everyday life and that school experiences can be particularly stressful. For example, a front-page story in *The Washington Post* noted that "For many Washington area teenagers, stress is a ubiquitous and inescapable fact of life" (Boodman, 1995, A1).

Recognizing that children and youths face stress, however, does not bring understanding of the causes of disordered emotions or behavior or a remedy. It is one thing to recognize stress; it is quite another to articulate a coherent view of how stress affects human development and to determine what kinds are most significant. It is one thing to note that self-concept is an important aspect of emotional and behavioral development; it is quite another to understand how self-esteem fits into the web of other influences on behavior. The accompanying feature discusses popular oversimplifications about the origins and effective treatment of emotional and behavioral disorders. To have more than a superficial understanding of emotional and behavioral disorders, we need a complex set of organizing principles, a conceptual model or framework for organizing and making sense of the vast array of ideas and information about causes and cures. Any simple explanation of human behavior will have its day in the popular imagination, but all such oversimplifications have a common fate—becoming today's cliche and tomorrow's jest.

Popular Views of Emotional or Behavioral Disorders of Children and Youths

Browse through the current titles in a bookstore, sample the magazines at a newsstand, or scan nearly any newspaper and you will probably find more than one statement about why so many children and youths have emotional or behavioral problems. The popular press provides a steady stream of commentary from presumed experts and laypeople on the reasons for youngsters' emotional pain and misconduct. Sometimes a conceptual model is carefully articulated in these commentaries, but more often the underlying model is implicit in the discussion. Sometimes an integrated, sophisticated view is articulated, but too often an overly simplified explanation is offered. Simplistic views often have great popular appeal. For example, the simplistic idea that emotions are more important than IQ in determining personal adjustment and occupational success, popularized in Goleman's (1995) book *Emotional Intelligence,* led *Time* to comment, "if it were that simple, the book would not be quite so interesting or its implications so controversial" (Epperson, Mondi, Graff, & Towle, 1995, p. 62).

One popular notion of the 1980s and 1990s is that emotional and behavioral disorders are caused by stress. For example, in *Childstress! Understanding and Answering Stress Signals of Infants, Children, and Teenagers,* Miller (1982) attempted to explain youngsters' troubling behavior as a reaction to the stressful circumstances of contemporary life—competition, overindulgence by parents, parental divorce, lack of support from extended family or community, and so on. Certainly, Miller describes real and significant sources of stress. Furthermore, nearly every teacher can attest to the pernicious effects of stress on students' learning and behavior. Miller's view of contemporary infants, children, and youths suggests, however, that the causes of emotional or behavior disorders are everywhere, lurking amid all youngsters' experiences. Few children, it seems, will escape the curse of our stress-ridden society. The only apparent solution is a radical change in societal values to relieve the stress our children and youths are experiencing. Too often, such observations are turned into a popular, simplistic formula: stress causes emotional or behavioral problems; if we want to reduce these problems, we must alleviate stress. We must go beyond a simple formula to learn how youngsters cope with stress—why some succumb to a given stressor but others don't—and to discover why some sources of stress are particularly debilitating but others are not.

Another popular idea is that emotional and behavioral problems are a reflection of low self-esteem. The suggested cure, as you might expect, is lifting self-esteem. Among the most popular views of the 1990s is the assumption that low self-esteem is the origin of every human foible and that raising self-esteem will solve every problem from the poor academic performance of school children to the mismanagement of corporations. The fixation on self-esteem as cause and cure for every manner of behavior problem of people of every age was featured in *Newsweek* (Adler et al., 1992). Low self-esteem, some suggest, is behind delinquents' behavior (which is interpreted as an attempt to enhance their self-esteem by showing off), the motivation for "sin" (and also the basis for self-righteousness), the basis for underachievement (and overachievement) and aggression (and passivity)—any behavior that is seen as undesirable. In the 1990s, psychologists, ministers, business executives, educators—even legislators, who have made the enhancement of self-esteem a matter for government action—are embracing what Adler et al. describe as naive optimism about the curative effect of higher self-esteem. The simplistic view of self-esteem as a universal cause and cure, Adler et al. suggest, is giving feeling good about oneself a bad name.

Among the "hottest" issues of the 1990s is youth violence, especially its causes and cures. From *Parade Magazine* (Moyers, 1995) to *Education Week* (Kauffman, 1974b) to *School Psychology Review* (Morrison, Furlong, & Morrison, 1994) and many other popular and professional journals, we read the suggestion that violence has no single cause and no single cure, that we must integrate what we know about biological, psychological, sociological, and all other verifiable influences on behavior if we are to understand the causes of violence and address the problem effectively. This is not a simplistic view. However, some articles in the popular press focus on particular explanations of violent behavior that many are tempted to oversimplify. For example, *The New Yorker* featured a thoughtful discussion of certain biological aspects of violence and the controversy surrounding evolutionary psychology (Wright, 1995a). Evolutionary psychologists study the interplay of behavior, neurochemicals, and the individual's environment—how each affects the other and how behavior has been shaped through genetic processes during human evolution. However, glib statements about evolutionary psychology can be seriously misleading and be broadened to explain nearly all human emotional or behavioral problems.

Evolutionary psychology deals not only with the problem of violence but with other social behavior as well. In fact, the notions of evolutionary psychologists have been so popularized that *Time* carried a cover story on how the mismatch between genetic inheritance and the contemporary social environment may account for high rates of not only violence but also depression and feelings of isolation, disconnectedness, and mistrust (Wright, 1995b). In short, the genetics of human evolution is another in a long series of important ideas that can be turned into facile explanations of behavior. We must guard against both the oversimplified view that behavior is simply genetic and controllable by biochemicals and the opposite oversimplification—that the biological aspects of behavior are trivial or irrelevant.

Nearly every reader of this book will know that there are alternative theories of behavior (or schools of psychology). Each conceptual model offers an explanation of human behavior and suggests how to change it. The challenge we face is choosing or constructing a defensible theory and using it consistently to evaluate alternative conceptual models. More simply, the challenge is to decide what is believable and what is not believable about the causes of human behavior.

Besides believability, there is also the matter of deciding how to group and analyze ideas. We offer three different levels of analysis or grouping. First, we provide a traditional exposition of models. Since the early 1970s, when Rhodes and his colleagues published summaries of the Conceptual Models Project, teacher educators and researchers have provided this now traditional grouping of concepts: biogenic, psychodynamic, psychoeducational, humanistic, ecological, and behavioral (see Van Hasselt & Hersen, 1991a, 1991b). Second, we discuss a conceptual model derived primarily from social learning principles. Third, we describe an integrated model applied to the classification of disordered emotions and behavior, analysis of causal factors, methodology of assessment, and intervention.

TRADITIONAL EXPOSITION OF CONCEPTUAL MODELS

This exposition provides a very brief description of the basic assumptions and an application of several conceptual models. Each description of assumptions is followed by a brief case report illustrating how the theory might be applied. Keep two cautions in mind as you read these expositions and the accompanying cases:

- The descriptions of these models are cursory, and much additional reading is required to obtain a full understanding of each model.

- The descriptions and cases are purposely unidimensional and do not reflect the multiple perspectives that competent practitioners typically bring to bear.

The descriptions and cases presented here are purposeful oversimplifications intended to highlight particular conceptual models. Very seldom would a competent teacher, psychologist, or psychiatrist view a child or youth through only one of these "lenses." Finally, we should note that each of these models has gone through periods of popularity and disrepute. Some are being gradually abandoned as evidence to support them fails to materialize; others are being gradually strengthened through the accumulation of scientific evidence. Some are more readily applicable to certain disorders than to others (e.g., a biogenic approach may be more relevant to schizophrenia and autism than to conduct disorder).

Biogenic Approach

Human behavior involves neurophysiological mechanisms; that is, a person cannot perceive, think, or act without the involvement of his or her anatomy and physiology. One set of conceptual models begins with one or both of two hypotheses:

1. Emotional or behavioral disorders represent a physiological flaw.
2. These disorders can be brought under control through physiological processes.

Some writers suggest that disorders such as autism, hyperactivity, depression, or hyperaggression are manifestations of genetic factors, brain dysfunction, food additives, biochemical imbalance, or are simply disorders most responsive to or most easily ameliorated by chemicals or, in rare cases, neurosurgery. According to these models, recognition of the underlying biological problem is critical; however, successful treatment may or may not be aimed at resolving the physiological flaw. In many cases, we know of no way to repair or ameliorate the brain damage, genetic process, or metabolic disorder. Consequently, we must be satisfied with understanding the physiological cause of the disorder and making appropriate adaptations to it. Some management strategies are based on hypotheses about physiological processes but do not address known physiological disorders. For example, students may be given stimulant drugs to help control hyperactivity or schizophrenia, or they may be taught biofeedback techniques to help them gain self-control, even though the physiological cause(s) have not been isolated. Interventions associated with a biogenic approach include drug therapy, dietary control, exercise, surgery, biofeedback, and alteration of environmental factors that exacerbate the physiological problem. (See Brown & Pollitt, 1996; Cossairt, Marlowe, Stellern, & Jacobs, 1985; deCatanzaro, 1978; DesLauriers & Carlson, 1969; Feingold, 1975, 1976; Leibowitz, 1991; Rimland, 1964; and Werry, 1986a; Wolraich, Wilson, & White, 1995, for examples and discussion.)

Elizabeth (continued)

We first met Elizabeth in chapter 1. She was diagnosed with schizophrenia as a young child. She is now a tenth grader, and her illness has been in remission for 2 years. However, she has gone through years of struggle with a variety of emotional and behavioral disorders for which medications were prescribed. In elementary school, her academic performance deteriorated markedly between first and third grade, and she had trouble getting along with other children. She also had difficulty paying attention and completing her school work.

The first psychiatrist who treated Elizabeth thought she had attention deficit disorder because of her difficulty in paying attention, completing tasks, and getting along with other children. Consequently, the psychiatrist prescribed Ritalin for Elizabeth. Her performance improved considerably early in the fourth grade when she was taking Ritalin. However, within a few months it became apparent that Elizabeth was suffering from another disorder.

When psychiatrists discovered that Elizabeth was having auditory hallucinations and sometimes visual hallucinations accompanying the voices she heard, she was hospitalized. Because she had terrible headaches along with the hallucinations, imaging techniques were used to check her brain for tumors or other neurological problems that could cause her symptoms. Nothing was found wrong with her brain. Consequently, the psychiatrist's decision was to place Elizabeth on a **neuroleptic** (antipsychotic) drug, a major tranquilizer called Mellaril. This drug kept the effects of her illness under enough control that Elizabeth could go home and return to school. Although Mellaril has been very helpful, her support from her family and teachers has also been very important in allowing her to function well in school and at home. [Note: This case is based on the first-person account described by Anonymous (1994).]

Psychodynamic Approach

Dynamic psychiatry is concerned with hypothetical mental mechanisms and their interplay in the developmental process. **Psychodynamic models**, sometimes called **psychoanalytic** models because psychoanalytic theory provides so many of their tenets, rest on the assumption that the essence of emotional and behavioral disorders is *not* the behavior itself but a "pathological" imbalance among the dynamic parts of one's personality (the id, ego, and superego). Disturbed behavior is merely symptomatic of an underlying "mental illness"; the cause of mental illness is usually attributed to excessive restriction or excessive gratification of the individual's instincts at a critical stage of development or to early traumatic experiences. Interventions based on a psychodynamic model stress the importance of individual psychotherapy for the child (and often for the parents as well) and the necessity of a permissive, accepting classroom teacher. Problems in relating to youngsters, whether as teacher or therapist, are often interpreted in terms of the adult's own unconscious conflicts. Extreme importance is placed on understanding the unconscious motivation for behavior, on the assumption that once it is understood (and not until), the problem will be resolved. Another assumption is that if the underlying, unconscious conflict is not understood and resolved, then any improvement in the "symptomatic" behavior is trivial or even harmful, and the symptom will be replaced by another. (See Axline, 1947; Berkowitz & Rothman, 1960; Bettelheim, 1970; Fine, 1991; Freud, 1965; Gartner, 1985; Kornberg, 1955; Scharfman, 1978; Tuma & Sobotka, 1983; and Watkins & Schatman, 1986, for examples and discussion.)

Bertha

Bertha, a 4-year-old diagnosed as "psychotic" and unmanageable, was in residential treatment. She exhibited many symptoms of severe mental illness, one of which was that she frequently attempted to smash people's eyeglasses. If she was prevented from doing this, her behavior became extremely wild. The assumption of those designing a therapeutic program for Bertha was that if she were ever to be helped, they would have to understand why she engaged in this behavior; and she would have to be helped to understand her own behavior as well. To achieve this understanding, it would be necessary to simply accept her breaking glasses, not to try to suppress this symptom of her underlying mental illness. Consequently, breaking glasses was accepted for 3 years, until Bertha was able to reveal the hidden, unconscious meaning of her behavior.

Through listening to Bertha talk about her past and observing her behavior, those responsible for her treatment arrived at the following interpretation: Bertha's mother had had chronic schizophrenia and was a person extremely difficult to understand. Bertha decided that because her mother wore glasses, which helped her see better and therefore understand things, she would try to understand her mother by putting on her mother's glasses. But when she put on the glasses, she saw worse instead of better. This infuriated Bertha—the injustice that her mother could see better but she saw worse with the glasses and still could not understand her mother's behavior. She was so infuriated that she felt compelled to break all reminders or symbols of this injustice. The intervention consisted of unraveling an interpretation of the unconscious motivation of Bertha's misbehavior, not on any procedures designed to control it directly. [Note: This case is based on one described by Bettelheim (1970).]

Psychoeducational Approach

The **psychoeducational model** shows concern for unconscious motivations and underlying conflicts (hallmarks of psychodynamic models) yet also stresses the realistic demands of everyday functioning in school, home, and community. A basic assumption of the psychoeducational model is that teachers must understand unconscious motivations if they are to deal most effectively with academic failure and misbehavior. This does not mean that they must focus on resolving unconscious conflicts as a psychotherapist might. It means focusing on how to help the student acquire self-control through reflection and planning. Intervention based on a psychoeducational model may include therapeutic discussions or **life space interviews** (LSI) to help youngsters understand that what they are doing is a problem, recognize their motivations, observe the consequences of their actions, and plan alternative responses to use in similar future circumstances. Emphasis is on the youngster's gaining insight that will result in behavioral change, not on changing behavior directly. (See Dembinski et al., 1982; Fagen, 1979; Fenichel, 1974; Heuchert & Long, 1980; Long, 1974; Long & Newman, 1965; Morse, 1974; Redl, 1966; Rezmierski et al., 1982; Rich et al., 1982; Wood, 1990; and Wood & Long, 1991, for examples and discussion.)

Aaron

Fourteen-year-old Aaron was referred for special education because of his oppositional and sometimes verbally threatening behavior. In addition to being noncompliant with adults' instructions, he frequently leaves the classroom without permission and roams the hallways. He appears to enjoy confrontations with teachers and taunts his peers, especially a deaf student in the class, Drew, who also has minimal social skills. The type of intervention his teacher used is illustrated by the way she handled a particular incident.

One morning, Drew came to school very agitated, requiring the teacher to spend most of her time before lunch calming him down. At lunch, Aaron persistently aggravated Drew. When the teacher told Aaron to stop and return to his desk, Aaron began yelling that Drew had called him a "fag" and that he, Drew, was the one who should return to his desk. When the teacher repeated her instruction, Aaron shoved a desk across the room and left the classroom without permission. Pacing the hall, he began disturbing other students. The teacher and another staff member then escorted Aaron to a quiet room, to which he went without resistance. In the quiet room, the teacher used LSI techniques to help Aaron think through the reasons for his behavior and how he might behave in more adaptive ways.

Through skillful interviewing about the incident with Drew, the teacher was able to help Aaron see that he is jealous and resentful of the time she spends with Drew. Aaron lives with his mother and an older sister who has multiple disabilities, is very low functioning, and demands a lot of his mother's attention. His father left home when Aaron was 8 years old, and his mother is not in good health. This means that Aaron has had to take on some adult responsibilities at an early age. The goals of the teacher's LSI about this particular incident were to get Aaron to understand that she cares about him, that she wants to prevent him from disrupting the group, and, most importantly, that there are similarities in his situation at home and at school that give rise to similar feelings and behavior.

Aaron's teacher used what James and Long (1992) have called a "Red Flag Interview," a discussion that addresses the problem of transferring problems from home to school. A Red Flag Interview follows a predictable sequence in which a student like Aaron is helped to understand that: (1) he experiences a stressful situation at home (e.g., a beating, overstimulation, etc.), (2) his experience triggers intense feelings of anger, helplessness, etc., (3) these feelings are not expressed to the abusive person at home because he is fearful of retaliation, (4) he contains his feelings until he is getting on the bus, entering the school, or responding to a demand, and (5) he acts out his feelings in an environment that is safer and directs his behavior toward someone else.

Although the LSI may be based on psychoanalytic notions of defense mechanisms, it also must end with a return to the reality of the situation. In Aaron's situation, this meant his return to the class and anticipation of future problems. His teacher ended the LSI as follows:

Interviewer: "What do you think Drew might do when we walk into the room?"
Aaron: "He will probably point at me and laugh."
Interviewer: "That might happen. How can you deal with that?"
Aaron: "I can ignore him."
Interviewer: "That will not be easy for you. It will take a lot of emotional strength to control your urge to tease him back. And if you do that and Drew teases you, who is going to get into trouble?"
Aaron: "Drew."
Interviewer: "That's right. You are now beginning to think more clearly about your actions. Also, I will set up a behavior contract for you. If you are able to ignore Drew's teasing, you will earn positive one-on-one time with me."
Aaron: "Agreed." (James & Long, 1992, p. 37)

Source: This case is based on one described by James and Long (1992).

Humanistic Approach

Humanistic education draws heavily from humanistic psychology, the sociopolitical movement of the late 1960s and early 1970s known as the counterculture or countertheory movement, and the free school, open education, alternative school, and deschooling ideas of the same era. A humanistic approach emphasizes self-direction, self-fulfillment, self-evaluation, and free choice of educational activities and goals, but the theoretical underpinnings of humanistic models are hard to identify. A teacher who devises education based on a humanistic model will be more a resource and catalyst for learning than a director of activities. The teacher is unauthoritarian and promotes a classroom atmosphere best described as open, free, nontraditional, affectively charged, and personal. An assumption underlying most humanistic approaches is that youngsters will find their own solutions to their problems if they are merely freed to do so in a loving and supportive environment. (See Burke, 1972; Dennison, 1969; Knoblock, 1970, 1973, 1979, 1983; Neill, 1960; and Rogers, 1983, for examples and discussion.)

Some of the elements of affective education (Morse et al., 1980) and some characteristics of alternative schools, sometimes called "schools of choice" fit the model of humanistic education (see Fizzell, 1987; Knoblock, 1983). The **holistic education** of the 1990s, which rejects the traditional "mechanistic" view of the natural sciences and emphasizes one's personal construction of reality, appears in many ways to be an extension of the humanistic approach of the 1960s and 1970s or a blending of psychoeducational and humanistic elements (see Blair, 1992; Rhodes, 1992; Rhodes & Doone, 1992). The **life-impact curriculum** described by Rhodes and Doone (1992) and Blair (1992) has as its objectives changing students' higher order thinking abilities by:

a. awakening children to the pattern of meaningful experiences that they project and build into an object, space, time, and causal reality.

b. teaching mental patterning and projection skills that give children a greater sense of control over the development of themselves.

c. extending the range of variability and flexibility in the acceptance and projection of reality in their actual world, both in and out of school. (Rhodes & Doone, 1992, p. 13)

Denny

Denny was one of 15 boys attending a regional alternative school for troubled youths. He was streetwise, functioning academically at an elementary-school level, and apparently headed for a life of work at menial jobs or criminal behavior. He had been seen as a troublemaker by all of his teachers during his 10-year school career because he showed no interest in the curriculum and was frequently disruptive and aggressive toward adults and his peers. His teacher in the alternative school began with the premise that Denny must first learn something about himself, then about the world closest to him before he could choose what he needed to do to prepare for the future. Rather than starting with something like a discussion of job prospects or abstract vocational goals, his teacher began by asking Denny to keep track of how he spent his time—to record his hourly and daily experiences in a simple log. Then Denny and his teacher discussed—and Denny wrote sentences and brief paragraphs about—the major themes of this life, the consistent threads of his daily experience. This led to Denny's formulating questions about his existence, feelings, desires, and goals. Then the stage was set for him to begin using reference and resource materials to learn about his career prospects.

With these experiences as background, Denny was in a position to begin a new phase in his personal, self-selected curriculum; he found out first what he was, and then he was ready to explore what he might become. With his teacher's assistance, he constructed an interview protocol and practiced interviewing techniques. Then he went into the community to interview adults, who had been previously contacted by his teacher, about their lives and careers. It was at this point, several months into the school year, that Denny began to take an interest in basic academics, selecting for himself the curriculum that would help him acquire the skills he would need to pursue his career. At the alternative school, he received minimal demands and guidance from his teacher and maximum freedom to explore his world on his own terms and plot his own course for learning.

Note: This case was constructed from program descriptions by Knoblock (1979, 1983).

Ecological Approach

An **ecological model** is based on concepts in ecological psychology and community psychology. In its early years, the approach drew also on the model of European **educateurs**, who work with youngsters in their homes and communities as well as their schools. The student is considered an individual enmeshed in a complex social system, both a giver and a receiver (excitor and responder) in social transactions with other students and adults in a variety of roles and settings. Emphasis is on study of the child's entire social system, and intervention is directed, ideally, toward all facets of the student's milieu. Interventions used in ecological programs have tended to emphasize behavioral and social learning concepts and the ways they can be used to alter an entire social system. (See Daly, 1985; Hobbs, 1966, 1974; Lewis, 1982; Muskal, 1991; Rhodes, 1965, 1967, 1970; Schroeder, 1990; Swap, 1974, 1978; Swap et al., 1982; and Votel, 1985, for examples and discussion.)

In the 1980s and 1990s, the melding of ecological concepts and social learning or behavioral theory has been described as **ecobehavioral analysis** (see Kamps, Leonard, Dugan, Boland, & Greenwood, 1991; Schroeder, 1990; Teare et al., 1995). An ecobehavioral analysis is an attempt to identify and use naturally occurring, functional events more skillfully and consistently to improve instruction and behavior management. If naturally occurring strategies, such as peer tutoring, can be validated as effective and applied consistently, then supportive, habilitative social systems might be built or strengthened with less reliance on artificial interventions that tend to be more costly, intrusive, temporary, and unreliable.

Emelda

Emelda, a 10-year-old with autism, attended a special self-contained class in a public school. She spoke in complete sentences but exhibited echolalia, parroting words, phrases, or sentences she heard. Academically, she was performing at about second grade level. The primary objective of intervention was to increase her rate of correct academic responding. The first step was to observe the naturally occurring ecological, teacher, and student variables in the class. Ecological variables included such things as the particular activity (e.g., language), tasks being presented (e.g., discussion, use of media), physical arrangement (e.g., class divided into groups), and instructional grouping (e.g., one-to-one or small group). Teacher variables included who (teacher or aide) was giving instruction, whether the teacher was at the desk or among the students, and various categories of the teacher's behavior (e.g., whether demanding an academic response, focusing on one student, giving approval or disapproval). Student variables were such things as whether Emelda was participating in the task, moving about the classroom, paying attention, or engaging in off-task behavior such as self-stimulation.

Through correlation of ecological, teacher, and student variables with Emelda's correct responding to academic tasks, teachers and researchers found the naturally occurring procedures that were most effective in helping her learn. The conditions under which Emelda and other students learned most effectively included the following:

- 3 to 5 students per group
- combinations of verbal interaction (discussion formats) with media (e.g., pictures or drawings of what is being discussed)
- individualized sets of media materials for each student
- 5-minute rotations of media/concept presentations
- a minimum of 3 sets of materials to teach each concept
- frequent group (choral) responding
- fast-paced *random* responding (i.e., not calling on students in a predictable order)
- serial responding—3 to 5 quick responses per student
- frequent student-to-student interactions (Kamps et al., 1991, p. 377)

Emelda's case demonstrated how the study of multiple, naturally-occurring variables in a classroom environment can reveal which ones are most effective in controlling a student's progress. An ecological approach may encompass multiple variables in a classroom, but it could also involve multiple variables in the school, community, family, or a combination of these environments.

Note: This case is based on research described by Kamps et al. (1991).

Behavioral Approach

Two major assumptions underlie a **behavioral model**:

1. The essence of the problem is the behavior itself.
2. Behavior is a function of environmental events.

Maladaptive behavior is viewed as inappropriate learned responses; therefore, intervention should consist of rearranging antecedent events and consequences to teach more adaptive behavior. A behavioral model derives from the work of behavioral psychologists. With its emphasis on precise definition and reliable measurement, careful control of the variables thought to maintain or change behavior, and establishment of replicable cause-effect relationships, it represents a natural science approach. Interventions based on a behavioral model consist of choosing target responses, measuring their current level, analyzing probable controlling environmental events, and changing antecedent or consequent events until reliable changes are produced in the target behaviors. (See Alberto & Troutman, 1995; Cipani, 1991; Cooper, Heron, & Heward, 1987; Cullinan et al., 1982; Kerr & Nelson, 1989; Kerr, Nelson, & Lambert, 1987; Morris, 1985; Walker, 1995; Walker, Colvin, & Ramsey, 1995; Walker, Reavis, Rhode, & Jenson, 1985, for examples and discussion.)

Sven

Sven was an 11-year-old attending a special, self-contained class for students with emotional or behavioral disorders. His teacher described him as showing inadequate attention to tasks, inappropriate and aggressive talk, and physically aggressive behavior. An observer recorded Sven's behavior during brief (15-second) intervals for 15-30 minutes of his English lesson each day. These observations showed that he was engaged in academic tasks less than 60 percent of the time on average and that his behavior was disruptive about 40 percent of the time.

Those working with Sven assumed that students who exhibit maladaptive behavior may do so for a variety of reasons, including not only the consequences of behavior but the setting in which it occurs and the demands for performance—the antecedents. In this case, antecedents related to Sven's maladaptive behavior were changed. The antecedents of his off-task, disruptive behavior—what he was assigned to do, especially if it was an assignment he did not like—seemed to be at least as much a problem as the consequences of his behavior. Therefore, the primary strategy used to modify Sven's behavior was to give him his choice of six to eight task options in his English class. The task options were constructed as variations on the work he normally would do, any one of which was acceptable and would lead to the same instructional objective. Under these conditions, Sven engaged in academic tasks about 95 percent of the time, and his disruptive behavior dropped to an average of about 10 percent.

Clearly, giving Sven choices about his assignments—all of the choices being acceptable variations—improved his attention to his tasks and decreased his disruptive behavior very markedly. Although rewarding consequences for appropriate behavior and academic performance are critically important, teachers may also use knowledge of behavior principles to alter the conditions of instruction in ways that defuse task resistance and encourage task attention. [Note: This case is based on one described by Dunlap et al. (1994).]

Cullinan, Epstein, and Lloyd (1991) have compared important features of three of these conceptual models: psychoeducational, behavioral, and ecological. Figure 4.1 shows their evaluation of the three models on causation (the extent to which each relies on formal principles, past events, internal determinants, and a holistic view to explain behavior), intervention (the extent to which each suggests methods that are replicable, efficient, and have broad applicability), and scientific rigor (the extent to which each relies on empirical data, shows evidence of behavior change restricted to the treatment setting, and shows evidence that treatment effects extend to other environments than the treatment setting). This kind of comparison among conceptual models helps us see the particular strengths and weaknesses of various frameworks for special educators.

Figure 4.1
Comparisons of Models of
Behavior Disorder

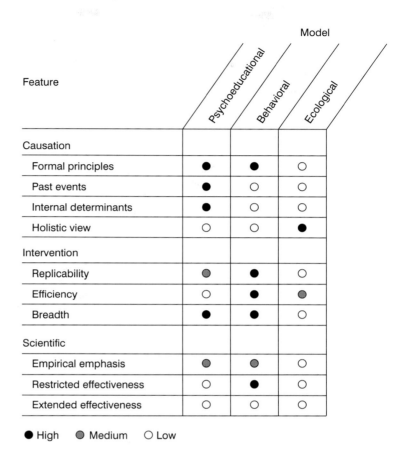

Feature	Psychoeducational	Behavioral	Ecological
Causation			
Formal principles	●	●	○
Past events	●	○	○
Internal determinants	●	○	○
Holistic view	○	○	●
Intervention			
Replicability	◓	●	○
Efficiency	○	●	◓
Breadth	●	●	○
Scientific			
Empirical emphasis	◓	◓	○
Restricted effectiveness	○	●	○
Extended effectiveness	○	○	○

● High   ◓ Medium   ○ Low

Source: Cullinan, D., Epstein, M. H., & Lloyd, J. W. (1991). Evaluation of conceptual models of
behavior disorders. *Behavioral Disorders, 16,* 150.

DEVELOPING AN INTEGRATED MODEL

The education of children and youth with emotional or behavioral disorders is not now governed by a consistent philosophy or conceptual model that is linked to instructional methodology. Only about half of the local school district programs surveyed by Grosenick, George, and George (1988) had a written program philosophy regarding the education of students with emotional or behavioral disorders. One might expect such a written document to serve as a guide for establishing goals and designing interventions; its absence suggests lack of a coherent conceptual basis for teaching practices. A random sample of more than 200 teachers of students with emotional or behavioral disorders revealed little consistency among teachers' training, theoretical orientations, and use of intervention strategies (Beare, 1991). Beare concluded that "this lack of common goal and philosophy delays the development of our field and leads to programs that may not reflect the best current appropriate educational practices" (1991, p. 216). Although slavish devotion to a single conceptual model is not desirable and diverse theories can be the basis for productive debate, our field would be advanced by a more integrated, less haphazard conceptual approach.

In practice, few professionals adhere rigidly to a single conceptual model. Most realize that multiple perspectives are needed for competent practice. Yet there is a limit to the degree to which one can be eclectic, picking and choosing concepts and strategies from various models, without being simple-minded and self-contradictory. Some conceptual models are not complementary; they suggest radically different and incompatible approaches to a problem. Acceptance of one set of assumptions about human behavior sometimes implies rejection of another. We must therefore consider the possible bases for choosing and using conceptual models.

Selection and Use of Conceptual Models

We have several distinct options in treating the issue of conceptual models. First, we can adopt a single model as an unvarying theme, a template by which to judge all hypotheses and research findings. Although this option has the advantages of consistency and clarity, it is disconcerting to many careful thinkers because it rests on the questionable assumption that reality is sufficiently encompassed by one set of hypotheses about human behavior.

Second, we can take a nonevaluative stance, a posture that treats all concepts equally, as deserving the same attention and respect. This option has immediate appeal in its acknowledgment that every model has limitations, and it allows the reader to choose from an unbiased treatment of all contestants. There are, however, many drawbacks; under the guise of eclecticism, this option rests on the implicit assumption that we have no sound reasons for discriminating among ideas. It fosters the attitude that behavior management and education, like religion and political ideology, are better left to personal belief than to scientific scrutiny, and it leads inevitably to witless self-contradiction. Finally, it supports fads based on little more than a bold assertion that something is true or "works," and such fads are a serious impediment to progress in education (Carnine, 1993).

A third option, and the one I chose for this book, is to focus on hypotheses that can be supported or refuted by replicable and public empirical data—ideas that lend themselves to investigation by the methods of natural science. The result of this choice is that most of the discussion is consistent with a social-cognitive model and useful concepts from other models are discussed as they are related to social learning. The psychodynamic approach is ignored, for the most part, and psychoeducational and humanistic approaches are given limited coverage because relatively little reliable evidence (from a natural science point of view) is available to support them. Biogenic models are discussed because they are open to empirical investigation, but these models are not treated extensively because of their limited implications for the work of educators.

My choice for this book does not mean I believe there is only one "way of knowing"; I do believe, however, that some ways of knowing are better than others for certain purposes. For educators who work with troubled children and youths, I believe the natural science tradition provides the firmest foundation for competent professional practice. The most useful knowledge is derived from experiments that can be repeated and that consistently produce similar results—in short, information obtained from investigations conducted according to well-established rules of scientific inquiry. Not every problem can be approached through scientific experiment, and in such cases one must rely on other sources of wisdom—clinical experience, intuition, expert opinion, logical analysis, and so forth. But to the extent that reliable, quantitative, experimental evidence is available or can be obtained, I believe educators should make it the basis for their practice (see Kauffman, 1987, 1993, 1994a for further discussion). Furthermore, the most useful scientific information for teachers is that which is derived from controlled experiments that reveal how the social environment can be arranged to modify behavior and how individuals can be taught self-control.

Biological experiments have relatively few implications for the work of teachers. Teachers do not choose students' genes, perform surgery, prescribe drugs, control diet, or do physical therapy. Teachers do, however, have enormous power over the social environment of the classroom, as well as a significant measure of control over how they think about behavioral and emotional problems and how they act. Therefore, our emphasis is on social learning.

A Social-Cognitive Approach

Social-cognitive theory is an attempt to explain human behavior from a natural science perspective by integrating what is known about the effects of the environment (the behaviorist position) and what is known about the role of cognition (cognitive psychology). Scientific research indicates indisputably that the consequences of our behavior—environmental responses created by our actions—affect the way we are likely to behave in the future. But behavioral research alone cannot explain the subtleties and complexities of human conduct. Social-cognitive theory emphasizes **personal agency**: the ability of humans to use symbols for communication, to anticipate future events, to learn from observation or vicarious experience, to evaluate and regulate themselves, and to be reflectively self-conscious. Personal agency adds a needed dimension to a behavioral analysis and provides a more complete explanation of human behavior (see Bandura, 1995; Mahoney, 1995; Meyers & Cohen, 1990).

Social-cognitive theory is *not*, however, merely a combination of behavioral and cognitive psychology. It is also a reconceptualization of the direction, interaction, and reciprocality of effects. It suggests that people are not merely products of their environments, as described by radical behaviorists; nor are they simply driven to behave as they do by internal forces, the view of radical psychodynamic theorists. It suggests, in addition, that behavior results from reciprocal influences among the environment (both social and physical), personal factors (thoughts, feelings, perceptions), and the individual's behavior itself. This "triadic reciprocality," described by Bandura (1977, 1978, 1986), is depicted in the center of Figure 4.2, showing that behavior (B), person variables (P), and environment (E) constantly influence one another.

Figure 4.2
Triadic Reciprocality in Social-Cognitive Theory. Environment (*E*), behavior (*B*), and person variables (*P*) influence each other reciprocally. Solid lines connecting *B, P,* and *E* represent strong reciprocal effects; dashed lines represent weaker influence. Circles represent environment, behavior, and person variables and their shared (intersecting) reciprocal effects.

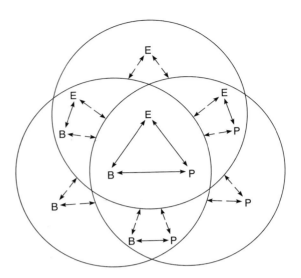

Under some conditions, one of the three factors shown in Figure 4.2 may play a more influential role than another, but usually all three elements are involved. As Bandura (1986) notes,

> Reciprocality does not mean symmetry in the strength of bidirectional influences. Nor is the patterning and strength of mutual influences fixed in reciprocal causation. The relative influence exerted by the three sets of interacting factors will vary for different activities, different individuals, and different circumstances. (p. 24)

Thus, the three sets of interacting factors might be depicted as in the outer portions of Figure 4.2. Under many circumstances, all three factors exert reciprocal influence, as shown by the central part of the figure in which the three circles (representing sets of factors) intersect. Under other circumstances, the intersections of and interactions between two of the sets of factors, or the effects of only one set, are of primary concern.

An example of strong reciprocal causal connections between two factors, with only weak connection to the third, is the extremely fearful child who will not make any approach to dogs. In this case, environment and person variables intersect and are closely tied, as shown in the upper right section of Figure 4.2. Environment, *E*, and person variables, *P*, interact reciprocally, as shown by the solid line connecting them; but the connection to behavior is weaker, as indicated by the broken lines connecting them to behavior, *B*. Dogs may arouse great fear in the child, and the fear may lead the child to avoid environments that include dogs and seek dog-free environments, which effectively reduce anxiety. But the child's behavior involving dogs may be extremely limited, consisting almost entirely of stereotyped avoidance rather than varied and adaptive responses (see Kauffman, 1979; Kauffman & Kneedler, 1981).

An example of person variables affecting each other reciprocally but having only weak connections to behavior and environment is an individual who becomes more and more anxious on the basis of thoughts and affective states. "In the personal realm of affect and thought, there exist reciprocal escalating processes, as when frightening thoughts arouse internal turmoil that, in turn, breeds even more frightening thoughts" (Bandura, 1986, p. 25). Such processes are represented in the lower right section of Figure 4.2, in which an isolated subset of person variables, P, is connected to behavior and environment by dashed lines, indicating weaker causal connections.

As I use the term in this book, **social-cognitive theory** also takes into consideration the developmental features of behavior. That is, we recognize that behavior must be evaluated in the context of normal development. There is continuity across developmental stages in the type of behavior that is adaptive or maladaptive, yet the same behavior may have different meanings at different ages. For example, a pronounced lack of social skills may be maladaptive at all developmental stages, but the particular behaviors that indicate social retardation may differ considerably, depending on the child's age and social circumstances (see Ross & Jennings, 1995).

A detailed exposition of social-cognitive theory is far beyond the scope of this book. Full understanding of the theory demands study of the work of its foremost proponent, Albert Bandura (see, for example, Bandura, 1977, 1978, 1986, 1995). We have sketched the theory here merely to provide a framework for later discussion. The primary concept to keep in mind is Bandura's notion of **triadic reciprocality**. An important implication of this concept is that emotional or behavioral disorders are comprehensible only in the contexts, both personal and social, in which they occur. For example, studies of how teachers control their students' behavior must be extended to include students' effects on teachers; that is, **transactions**, or mutual influences. The emphasis of social-cognitive theory on reciprocality of effects in human transactions is entirely consistent with an ecological approach.

A STRUCTURE FOR DISCUSSION

Given a social-cognitive model for conceptualizing human behavior, what is the best way to structure a coherent discussion of the characteristics of the emotional or behavioral disorders of children and youths? As Bandura (1986) notes, it is impossible to study all possible reciprocal actions at once; trying to examine all causal factors simultaneously paralyzes scientific study because the task is overwhelmingly complex. We must study behavior, its assessment, its causes, and its effects in simpler, more manageable segments. This is true whether one is conducting research or summarizing and interpreting it.

Figure 4.3 indicates that assessment and intervention are overlapping activities. It also indicates that types of disorders and causal factors are interconnected. We might choose to analyze a particular "slice" of the model, such as the assessment of genetic factors in depression, but we can never completely separate the particular problem we are analyzing from all other problems. If we are studying the assessment of genetic factors in depression, then we cannot totally ignore the assessment of temperament as a causal factor and the design of interventions involving peers and par-

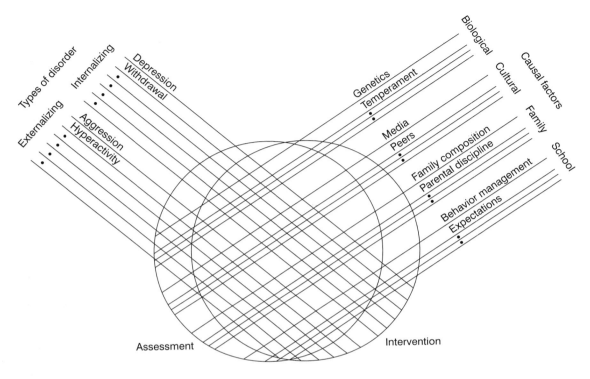

Figure 4.3
Structure for Analysis of Emotional or Behavioral Disorders

ents. While we focus on one particular topic, we must be aware of its connectedness to others. Our focus in the following chapters will first be on assessment (part 2), then on causal factors (part 3), then on types of disorders (part 4), and finally on a personal statement about teaching (part 5).

SUMMARY

Beliefs about the nature of human beings determine what explanations one seeks for behavior and the strategies one uses in approaching emotional or behavioral disorders. Throughout history, people have been conceptualized as spiritual beings, as biological organisms, as rational and feeling individuals, and as products of their environments. Each conceptualization has led to intervention approaches. Conceptual models, which help organize and interpret information, are necessary for making sense of the vast array of ideas and information about the causes and cures of disordered emotions or behavior. Traditional expositions of conceptual models include descriptions of biogenic, psychodynamic, psychoeducational, humanistic, ecological, and behavioral models. Although practitioners and scholars seldom employ one model exclusively, they must have a rational basis for choosing among models; some are logically incompatible and suggest opposite courses of action. A model derived from scientific experiments in social learning and self-control provides the most defensible basis for professional practice. A social-cognitive approach, which emphasizes triadic reciprocity among behavior, person variables, and environment provides a consistent theme for this book.

Case for Discussion

"Where Do You Start with One Like This?"

Derrick Yates

Derrick is a 12-year-old placed in a class of high average and gifted fifth graders, although his academic skills are at about third-grade level. He has been known as a terror, as unmanageable, by every teacher he has had in his school career. He is large for his age and is described as being a "scary kid" with crooked, bucked teeth, a chilling laugh, and an odd look in his eyes. Because of his disruptive behavior, he has been allowed to attend school for only half days for protracted periods. The school's teacher assistance team has recommended that he be evaluated for possible special education services.

At home, Derrick's behavior is also highly problematic, threatening, and intimidating. His mother and father are divorced, and Derrick lives with his mother and younger sister and brother. He is enraged about the divorce and blames his mother for the family's breakup. The school social worker reports that Derrick killed the family dog with a butcher knife—beheaded and dismembered the dog and scattered the parts in the yard. His mother has had locks installed on the kitchen drawers for fear that Derrick would use knives and other kitchen utensils to harm her or his siblings. She has also had double locks installed on her bedroom door and lets the two younger children sleep with her for fear of Derrick. She reports that in a fit of rage stemming from her not asking him to talk with his father (who had called regarding child support) on the phone, Derrick one night assaulted her bedroom door with a butcher knife. Derrick's mother is at her wit's end, terrified of him and not able to get help from social services or mental health services.

Derrick's teacher this year is an experienced special educator who asked for reassignment to a general education classroom. Although she is well aware of Derrick's history, she has agreed to take Derrick in her class until the evaluation for special education is completed. Derrick knows that teachers and other students are afraid of him. He says that he likes to do mean things and glories in his bad reputation. However, for the first few days of this school year his teacher has kept her cool, seemed unafraid of him, and observed no serious misbehavior. One day he approaches her with this question: "You don't know about me, do you?" [Note: This case was adapted from Kauffman, Mostert, Nuttycombe, Trent, and Hallahan (1993).]

Questions About the Case

1. What conceptual model offers the best understanding of the cause(s) of Derrick's behavior?

2. How would you describe the most important behavior, environment, and person variables (using a social-cognitive model) in the case of Derrick, and how are these variables interrelated?

3. Were you to design an intervention strategy for working with Derrick, where would you begin, and why?

4. What concepts would you draw upon in deciding how best to respond to Derrick's question to his teacher?

PERSONAL REFLECTIONS

Conceptual Models

Frank H. Wood, Ph.D., is Professor of Educational Psychology and Special Education at the University of Minnesota.

How would you describe the importance of theoretical concepts for teachers' everyday work?

Theories are interrelationships among complex ideas expressed in a condensed form. Being so condensed, with complex ideas often signified by single key words, theories often seem "unfriendly" at first meeting. Getting to know them takes work, requires learning a new vocabulary, or more often, learning a new meaning for old vocabulary. For example, in behavioral psychology **reinforcement** means reward, and thus **negative reinforcement** must have something to do with reward rather than punishment.

Our impatience with the time it takes to learn how to read a theoretical statement is frequently compounded by the perception that, once learned, the statement does not tell us anything we didn't already know. It's not surprising that many educators feel that theories are hard-to-understand descriptions of the obvious. But the value of theories should not be so quickly dismissed. Theories help us recognize common patterns in differing situations. They help us pull out and remember the most significant details in situations. They help us predict what will happen if key factors in a situation are manipulated. When theories help us to do these things, they're useful to us.

No theory that has been seriously put forward by people who have carefully studied human behavior is entirely lacking in value. But some theories are certainly more useful than others to teachers. "Usefulness" is an appropriate criterion against which an educational theory can be measured. The usefulness of a theory depends on *who* wants to use it and for *what*. Given those constraints, "by whom" and "for what," any theory can be evaluated

for its usefulness to us as educators. The theory we are studying at the moment may appear to have no application in our particular classroom, but to dismiss all theories as irrelevant and impractical would deprive us of very useful tools. As a matter of fact, there is almost no teacher—certainly no good teacher—who does not use theories or some of their component parts, principles, or models, in generating ideas useful for instruction. Often, we may simply be unaware that we are doing so.

For you personally, what are the most important guiding concepts for teachers of children with emotional or behavioral disorders?

Consider a well-known principle of human learning, sometimes called the law of effect: A response that is followed (timing factor) by a reward (reward factor) will increase in strength and frequency of occurrence. Many of the behavior management procedures good teachers use in the their classrooms are well-timed applications of an effective reward. Teachers praise students who are working on assigned tasks, predicting that this verbal reward will strengthen their application to their work. Teachers give higher grades to students whose work is of higher quality, predicting that all students will be motivated to produce higher quality work. In each case, teachers are demonstrating a belief in the relevance and usefulness of the law of effect.

Most of the time teachers can apply the law of effect and other important theoretical principles of learning without knowing they are doing so. However, for especially challenging situations—such as when we plan an intervention program for a student who is *not* responding well to praise or grades—it is often helpful to bring to mind this theoretical principle of the effect of reward. Considering alternative applications of the principle may help us develop a strategy for solving the problem. Perhaps the reward is not being applied at the right time or in the right manner. The student may be embarrassed by praise given in front of others but respond to praise given quietly or privately at a later time. More fundamentally, perhaps praise and grades are not effective rewards for this student. Opportunities to earn free time or time at the computer may stimulate greater efforts to achieve. The law of effect tells us that the nature of the reward and its timing are important. Exploring alternative patterns of timing and reward can help us come up with a combination that will make the principle work for this student.

Often the interrelationship of several different concepts or principles can be illustrated in a diagram that is easier to remember than the ideas in their written form. An example shown elsewhere in this book (see Figure 4.2) is the diagram illustrating the concept of "triadic reciprocality." Such a diagram is a graphic representation of the principle that persons and environments affect and are reciprocally affected by each other. Try writing out in words what this diagram illustrates and you will see how usefully the diagram summarizes several complex ideas.

I ask teachers to learn the diagram of triadic reciprocality before using it to understand, in a systems context, the behavior of individual students. I think several other diagrams efficiently capture theoretical concepts that are useful to teachers. One is the familiar *Antecedents → Behavior ← Consequences* diagram summarizing the theoretical concept that behavior (B) is influenced by events that precede (A for antecedents) and follow it (C for consequences). The A and C of this diagram are both aspects of the E (for environmental factors) of the triadic reciprocality diagram. We can add a personal dimension (P from the triadic reciprocality diagram) to our diagram by differentiating between (1) As and Cs that are characteristic of the setting in which the behavior occurs and the behavior of the people in that setting and (2) As and Cs that are characteristic of the individual whose behavior is the focus of attention. In the second sense, As may include what the individual brings to the setting, such as physical characteristics and previously learned behavior, whereas Cs are the meaning the individual gives to his or her behavior in the context of the responses (consequences) for that behavior. Again, most of us will find it easier to understand and remember these ideas by studying the figure than by reading the words. Translating pieces of theories into figures makes them easier to remember and apply—it makes them more useful to us.

There are many other theoretical models with which teachers should be familiar because they are useful in the same sense as those I've already discussed: in a school setting, they help teachers understand present student behavior more adequately and suggest ways they may promote student growth. Theoretical models provide mental frameworks on which teachers can organize the enormously complex information they acquire about an individual student or group in ways that help it "makes sense." Used this way, theories are useful and relevant to the work of the teacher—well worth knowing about.

What basic values do you think should guide teachers of children with emotional or behavioral disorders?

Ethical principles incorporating values provide another example of the application of theoretical ideas to real-world situations. I'll mention just two such principles. First, there is *the professional's commitment to serve*. The basic ethical commitment made by all people who take on the special role of providing professional service to others is to give a higher priority to the needs of those they serve than is expected in human relationships in general. Thus, parents are expected to give a higher priority to the general care of their children than are other members of the lay public. Medical professionals give a higher priority to healing sick persons than is expected by others in the society. Teachers are expected to give a higher priority than others to helping their students develop and use their abilities to acquire useful knowledge and skills.

I carefully say "a higher priority than is expected in human relationships in general" because this ethical commitment is sometimes misunderstood as meaning that teachers should give to the growth of their students a priority that is absolute. Such an idealized commitment has been described in fiction, but in practice it cannot be maintained for long. Teachers who neglect too seriously the meeting of their own needs often become exhausted and disillusioned. They may eventually find it difficult to meet their minimal professional obligations to their students. This is particularly the case when the students behave in ways that cause discomfort or injury to others and arouse a strong sense of disapproval or anger in the teacher. Teachers must learn to balance their high professional commitment with their care for their own physical and mental well-being.

Professional teachers must ask themselves two important questions. The first is what may be called the "professional question": Am I doing more to help my students develop and use their abilities to acquire useful knowledge and skills than those in their lives who make no claim to be professional teachers? The professional answer must be "yes." The second question is the "personal question": Am I successfully balancing the effort required to teach with my own mental, emotional, and physical resources so that I can continue to be an effective teacher for as long as I wish? The answer to this question should also be "yes," but it makes no sense to ask it if we have not already answered the professional ethics question affirmatively.

Second, there are *the limits of the service provided*. Educating means arranging experiences for students that encourage them to learn. Among the most difficult of the decisions educators must make are those about the limits to be placed on the experiences provided. Some experiences from which students might learn cannot be ethically used because they are too stimulating, too frightening, or too physically dangerous to students. The use of punishment to discourage the expression of problem behavior provides a good test case. How much discomfort or stress can teachers ethically apply in managing problem behavior? This decision is especially difficult for educators who teach students with emotional and behavioral disorders because these students are characteristically vulnerable to fear- or anger-producing situations.

Is there an ethical principle that can help us make wise decisions when punishing procedures may be necessary to control the behavior of a student? Can the same principle help us decide whether or not to continue remaining immediately available to a student who refuses to respond positively to any request or task unless our constant attention is given (knowing that withdrawing our attention will lead to severe and prolonged tantrums)?

Ann and Rud Turnbull provide a thoughtful discussion of this important issue in their book, *Families, Professionals, and Exceptionality* (1990). Although they discuss several alternatives, the decision rule they recommend as helpful in the widest variety of situations is the principle of "empathetic reciprocity," a secular version of the principle of the "Golden Rule," common to all the great religious traditions. Paraphrased, this rule asks that we take the perspective of the student and then respond to the question, "In this setting, given the alternatives available and the probable outcomes of each, what experience would be the best one for me?" The ultimate responsibility for the effects of the action we take always rests with us, but the process of thinking through the principle of empathetic reciprocity helps us make decisions consistent with the high priority we professional educators must give to meeting the needs of our students.

PART TWO
Assessment

Introduction to Part Two

As you read the next two chapters, I hope your self-questioning will turn to important practical matters having to do with intervention. If we are going to do something about emotional or behavioral disorders, we have to have some means of determining who has a disorder. We must also decide what kind of information we are going to rely on in screening, classifying, and teaching the students we believe have a disorder. The major problems we address in Part Two might be expressed as two questions:

- How do we turn a definition into practical procedures for identifying students who have disorders and classifying their disorders in a useful way?

- How do we get and use information about students that will help us teach them most effectively?

In chapter 5, we discuss issues in screening and classification. At first blush, screening seems an easy problem to tackle. After all, children and youths with severe emotional or behavioral disorders are usually easy for anyone to identify. They typically stand out immediately and clearly as different—obviously peculiar or deeply troubled in most people's perceptions. Rational people do not typically have much difficulty reaching a consensus that certain ways of behaving are deviant, and most people will admit that clearly deviant behavior requires some sort of intervention. If we were interested only in children and youths with severe disorders, screening would be a snap. But the majority of emotional or behavioral disorders are not so severe, nor are youngsters with them so readily identified.

Most emotional or behavioral disorders of children and youths are not so severe that they are immediately obvious to the casual observer. They are serious enough that at least one adult is upset or concerned; they are mild enough that someone might argue that most of the youngster's behavior is within the normal range and that the problem will work itself out with little or no help. Indeed, mild disorders fade into normal behavior in a haze of conjecture about where to "draw the line" or what to "make" of particular behavior. Differences of opinion about whether an individual should be identified as having an emotional or behavioral disorder are common, even among experts. Consequently, it is often helpful to use screening procedures to help focus attention on the marginal cases. Screening procedures are designed to answer questions like these:

- Which students should we be most concerned about?

- How should we select those we are going to study more carefully?

- How do we decide that one student has problems but doesn't need special education, but that another student with problems does need special education?

The variety of youngsters' perplexing behavior is dazzling, even to people who have had many years of experience working with those who have emotional or behavioral disorders. Saying that a student has an emotional or behavioral disorder and needs special education is thus not very informative. "What kind of disorder does this student have?" is a reasonable question to ask, and the answer must be a category or classification. The classifications we use should tell us more about what kind of behavior the student exhibits— the problems we might expect. We cannot treat every individual in *every* respect as a unique case; we must identify the similar or critical features of cases so that we have some basis for communicating about types of problems and deciding what interventions to try. Classification is not just basic to all science: it is essential for effective communication and intervention. The issue, then, is this: What is the most helpful way to categorize or classify the types of problems we encounter?

In chapter 6, we get to important questions about how assessment is related to what we do in the classroom:

■ What kinds of information are most helpful in planning an educational program?

■ How should I use the information I have about a student in writing an educational plan, choosing a curriculum, and evaluating progress?

Significant changes in the assessment of exceptional children and youths have occurred in recent years. One change is a shift in terminology. Psychologists and educators still occasionally use the term *diagnosis*, and psychiatrists typically use that term with reference to emotional or behavioral disorders. However, *diagnosis* has largely been replaced in the language of educators by *evaluation* or *assessment*, because *diagnosis* connotes the classification of disease. In the vast majority of cases, there is no evidence that disordered emotions or behavior is a disease in any physiological sense of the term. *Evaluation* and *assessment* are more appropriate for educational purposes because they connote measurement of nonphysiological and nonmedical factors related to social learning and adaptation.

During the past several years, there has been a large increase in the availability of assessment devices and technical information about the assessment process. If you are preparing to teach students with emotional or behavioral disorders, you will need to study assessment procedures in greater detail than this book provides.

Besides the increase in available instruments and technical information, legal issues have recently taken a prominent place in assessment. A student who is referred for special education must be evaluated to determine whether he or she is eligible for services under IDEA and related state legislation. Federal regulations require that this assessment be completed by an interdisciplinary team of qualified specialists, because the results will be useful not only for determining eligibility for special education but also for planning instruction regardless of the student's placement in special or general education classes. If the student receives special education, then the evaluation data must be used in writing an individualized education program (IEP). The law requires a new IEP for each year the student receives special education; it demands a reevaluation of eligibility for special education at least every 3 years.

The assessment of a student's abilities and problems is no easy task. It can easily be botched in either of two ways. On the one hand, it is easy to be too imprecise—so subjective and so reliant on general impressions that we miss important details or end up with a decision that simply does not fit the objective facts of the case. On the other hand, it is easy to get so absorbed in precise measurement and quantitative details that we miss the big picture or ignore the affective, human aspects of the case. Perhaps assessment is the task that presents the greatest challenge to maintaining balance between objective data and subjective interpretation. I think the challenge of becoming skilled at assessment is much like the challenge of becoming a sensitive scientist, and I hope you will complete your reading of the next two chapters with an appreciation of the difficulty of giving balanced attention to what can be recorded objectively and what can only be sensed.

5

Screening and Classification

As you read this chapter, keep these guiding questions in mind:

- What is the primary purpose of any screening procedure?
- Why do few school systems use systematic screening procedures for emotional or behavioral disorders?
- Why does early detection usually involve secondary rather than primary prevention?
- What factors make screening for infants' and preschoolers' emotional or behavioral disorders particularly difficult?
- What criteria should we use in devising and selecting screening procedures?
- In what ways should screening represent convergence and confirmation of concerns?
- Why and how should pre-referral strategies precede a teacher's referral of a student for evaluation for special education?
- Why is classification of disorders important?
- What are the greatest drawbacks of using psychiatric classifications in special education?
- How do dimensional systems of classification come closer to the ideal than do psychiatric systems?
- What assumption prevents *individuals* from being classified using a dimensional approach?
- In what ways can we differentiate autism and childhood schizophrenia?

SCREENING

Effective screening means becoming a good "suspectition" (Bower, 1981). It means being able to pick out cases that are not immediately obvious and identify incipient problems (those that are just beginning) with a high degree of accuracy. The reason for screening youngsters with emotional or behavioral disorders (or any other disability, for that matter) is based on the assumption that early identification and treatment are more effective, efficient, and humane than letting problems fester until they arouse the concern of even hardened observers. Furthermore, IDEA requires efforts to identify *all* children and youths with disabilities. Still, few school systems carry out systematic and effective screening for students with emotional or behavioral disorders. One reason for failure to screen systematically is that many more students than could be served by special education would likely be referred. Students who are referred must be carefully evaluated, and evaluation is a costly and potentially stigmatizing, anxiety-provoking process for both student and parents. Students who are identified must, by law, be provided with appropriate special education and related services, which is even more costly and stigmatizing. So it is not really surprising that many school systems rely primarily on teacher-initiated referral; typically, only those students who trouble their teachers to the breaking point become targets for evaluation (see National Mental Health Association, 1986; Peacock Hill Working Group, 1991; Walker, Colvin, & Ramsey, 1995).

Early Identification and Prevention

Screening is often justified by the argument that early identification will lead to prevention. Although this argument is both rational and supported by various research findings, translating concern for prevention into effective screening procedures is difficult. Chief among the difficulties are defining the disorders to be prevented and separating serious from trivial problems. Effective screening must eliminate concern for common problems that do not carry serious consequences or that are virtually certain to resolve themselves without intervention (Achenbach & Edelbrock, 1981). Efforts to prevent problems demand a developmental perspective that takes into account developmental milestones associated with chronological age, life events, different environments, and intervention strategies (Gelfand et al., 1986; Ross & Jennings, 1995).

The purpose of screening for emotional or behavioral disorders is usually **secondary prevention**, as opposed to **primary prevention**. "Primary prevention is the prevention of the occurrence, or at least the expression, of the disability; secondary prevention is something less ambitious" (Ornitz, 1986, p. 75). Secondary prevention is the prevention of side effects or exacerbation of an existing disorder; thus secondary prevention is intended to minimize the stress experienced by the family, teachers, and peers of a youngster who exhibits disordered emotions or behavior and to minimize the complications or worsening of the disorder itself.

Screening for emotional or behavioral disorders among infants and preschool children is particularly problematic. Children with pervasive developmental disorders such as autism have often been perceived by their parents as "different" from birth or from a very early age. Pediatricians often identify these and other cases in which extremely troublesome behavior is part of a pervasive developmental disorder. But trying to select infants and preschoolers who need special education and related services because of relatively *mild* disorders is quite another matter. Several factors make selection difficult. First, large and rapid changes occur during development from infancy to middle childhood. Infants and preschoolers have not yet acquired the language skills that are the basis for much of the older child's social interaction. Second, a child's behavioral style or temperament in infancy interacts with parenting behavior to determine later behavior patterns. For example, "difficult" behavior x at the age of 10 months is not predictive of inappropriate behavior y at 6 years. Behavior management techniques that parents and teachers use from 10 months to 6 years need to be taken into account (Thomas & Chess, 1984; Thomas et al., 1968). Third, parents vary markedly in their tolerance of emotional and behavioral differences in children. Because a problem *is* a problem primarily by parental definition in the preschool years, it is difficult to decide on a standard set of behaviors that are deviant (Achenbach & Edelbrock, 1981; Campbell, 1983, 1995). (Exceptions, as we have said, are obvious developmental lags.) Finally, the school itself is a potential source of problems—its structure, demands for performance of new skills, and emphasis on uniformity may set the stage for disorders that simply do not appear until the child enters school. Nevertheless, it is now possible to identify preschoolers who are at high risk for developing antisocial behavior and other serious behavioral problems (Loeber et al., 1992; Walker et al., 1995).

Criteria for Selecting and Devising Screening Procedures

Some screening procedures are more effective and efficient than others. Care is required to select procedures that meet reasonable psychometric and practical criteria for use in schools. Walker et al. (1995) suggested four criteria for screening and identifying antisocial behavior, and the same criteria could be applied to all types of emotional or behavioral disorders:

1. The procedure should be proactive rather than reactive. The school should take the initiative in seeking out students who are at high risk for exhibiting disorders, not simply wait for these students to demonstrate serious maladaptive behavior and then respond.

2. Whenever possible, a variety of people (e.g., teacher, parent, trained observer) should be employed, and students' behavior should be evaluated in a variety of settings (e.g., classroom, playground, lunch room, home). The objective should be to obtain as broad as possible a perspective on the nature and extent of any problems that are detected (see also Orvaschel, Ambrosini, & Rabinovich, 1993).

3. Screening should take place as early as possible in students' school careers, ideally at preschool and kindergarten levels. If screening is to serve its intended function well, then target students need to be identified and intervention programs begun before the child develops a history of maladaptive behavior and school failure.

4. Teacher nominations and rankings or ratings are appropriate in the beginning of the screening process but should be supplemented, if possible, by direct observation, examination of school records, peer or parent ratings, and other sources of information that might be available. The process should be increasingly broad and thorough at successive stages to minimize the chances of misidentification.

ALTERNATIVE SCREENING INSTRUMENTS

Hundreds of behavioral rating scales are available, nearly all of which are potentially useful as screening instruments. Many other procedures, including self-reports, sociometrics, direct observation, and interviewing are used in assessing children's social-emotional behavior (Hersen & Ammerman, 1995; Merrell, 1994; Ollendick & Hersen, 1993). We cannot discuss the whole range of instruments that might be used for screening emotional or behavioral disorders but will concentrate on several representative instruments. Use and interpretation of these instruments require careful study of the test materials and manuals.

Behavior Rating Profile (Brown & Hammill, 1990)[1]

The *Behavior Rating Profile*, second edition (BRP-2), is a battery of six subtests or components: Teacher Rating Scale, Parent Rating Scale, three Student Rating Scales (Home, School, and Peer), and Sociogram. Because separate norms are available for each part, each component can be used independently or in combination with any of the other parts. The entire instrument can be used to derive an "ecological profile." The ecological profile indicates how different respondents (self, teachers, parents, and peers) perceive the student in different settings (home, school, and social life). Norms for ages 6 through 18 allow classification of the student's behavior as within the "normal" range or within a "deviant" range.

Students complete three *Student Rating Scales* (self-rating scales) with "true" or "false" responses to a variety of statements. The three scales consist of 20 items each, intermingled into one 60-item list.

These are representative items for the Student Rating Scale: Home:

    1. My parents "bug" me a lot.
  33. I have lots of nightmares and bad dreams.
  47. I often break rules set by my parents.

These are items for the Student Rating Scale: School:

  14. I sometimes stammer or stutter when the teacher calls on me.
  29. My teachers give me work that I cannot do.
  59. The things I learn in school are not as important or helpful as the things I learn outside of school.

These are items for the Student Rating Scale: Peer:

    6. Some of my friends think it is fun to cheat, skip school, etc.
  10. Other kids don't seem to like me very much.
  31. I seem to get into a lot of fights.

The *Teacher Rating Scale* requires teachers to rate each of 30 items as "Very Much Like the Student," "Like the Student," "Not Much Like the Student," or "Not At All Like the Student." These are representative items:

    4. Tattles on classmates
  17. Is an academic underachiever
  30. Doesn't follow class rules

The *Parent Rating Scale* requires parents to rate each of 30 items as "Very Much Like My Child," "Like My Child," "Not Much Like My Child," or "Not At All Like My Child," using items like these:

    1. Is verbally aggressive to parents
  10. Is shy; clings to parents
  27. Won't share belongings willingly

---

[1]From L. L. Brown & D. D. Hammill, *Behavior Rating Profile: An Ecological Approach to Behavioral Assessment* (2nd ed.). Austin, Texas: Pro-Ed. 1990. Used with permission.

The *Sociogram* is a peer-nominating technique in which teachers ask students questions such as "Which of the girls and boys in your class would you most like to work with (or least like to work with) on a school project?" Each student in the class is asked to name three of his or her classmates for each question.

Child Behavior Checklist (Achenbach & Edelbrock, 1991)[2]

The *Child Behavior Checklist* (CBCL) is available in parent's report, teacher's report, and self-report forms. It is one of the most thoroughly researched rating scales available (McMahon, 1984). The CBCL, unique among rating instruments, reflects behavioral competencies (e.g., forming peer relationships, doing household chores) as well as maladaptive behavior (Beck, 1995). The teacher's report, adapted from the parent version, includes items for rating problem behavior as well as school performance and adaptive behavior. The teacher rates each of the 112 behavior problems on the checklist on a three-point scale, "Not True (as far as you know)," "Somewhat or Sometimes True," or "Very True or Often True." Representative items are as follows:

2. Hums or makes other odd noises in class
9. Can't get his/her mind off certain thoughts; obsessions (describe)
10. Can't sit still, restless, or hyperactive
11. Clings to adults or too dependent
12. Complains of loneliness
13. Confused or seems to be in a fog
14. Cries a lot
15. Fidgets
16. Cruelty, bullying, or meanness to others
47. Overconforms to rules
48. Not liked by other pupils
57. Physically attacks people
58. Picks nose, skin, or other parts of body (describe)
74. Showing off or clowning
82. Steals
84. Strange behavior (describe)
86. Stubborn, sullen, or irritable
96. Seems preoccupied with sex
101. Truancy or unexplained absence
105. Uses alcohol or drugs (describe)
107. Dislikes school

The teacher's report form of the CBCL can be used with students ages 5 through 18. Scores can be plotted on a Child Behavior Profile form that relates specific items to problem factors such as these (specific factors depend on the age and sex group): social withdrawal, anxious, unpopular, obsessive-compulsive, immature, self-

---

[2]From T. M. Achenbach, *Manual for the Child Behavior Checklist/4-18 and 1991 Profile*. Burlington, Vermont: University of Vermont, Department of Psychiatry, 1991. Copyright by T. M. Achenbach. Reproduced by permission.

destructive, hyperactive, and aggressive. Items describing adaptive functioning are related to factors such as working hard, behaving appropriately, learning, and being happy. Depending on the concerns about a particular child, teachers might administer only items related to a specific subscale, such as aggression (Walker et al., 1995).

Systematic Screening for Behavior Disorders (Walker & Severson, 1990)

Walker and Severson (1990) have devised *Systematic Screening for Behavior Disorders* (SSBD) for use in elementary schools based on the assumption that teacher judgment is a valid and cost-effective (though greatly underused) method of identifying students with emotional or behavioral disorders (Walker, Severson, Nicholson, Kehle, Jenson, & Clark, 1994). Teachers tend to over-refer students who exhibit **externalizing behavior problems**—those who act out or exhibit conduct disorder. Teachers tend to under-refer students with **internalizing problems**—those who are characterized by anxiety and social withdrawal. To make certain that students are not overlooked in screening, and to minimize time and effort, a three-step or "multiple gating" process is used (Walker et al., 1988).

In the first step, or "gate," the teacher lists and rank-orders students with externalizing and internalizing problems, listing those who best fit descriptions of externalized problems and internalized problems and ranking them from most like to least like the descriptions. The second step requires that the teacher complete two checklists for the three highest-ranked students on each list—those who have passed through the first "gate." One checklist asks the teacher to indicate whether the pupil exhibited specific behaviors during the past month ("steals," "has tantrums," "uses obscene language or swears"); the other requires that the teacher judge how often ("never," "sometimes," "frequently") each student shows certain characteristics ("follows established classroom rules," "cooperates with peers in group activities or situations"). The third step requires observation of students whose scores on the checklists exceed established norms—those who have passed through the second "gate." Students are observed in the classroom and on the playground by a school professional other than the usual classroom teacher (a school psychologist, counselor, or resource teacher). Classroom observations indicate the extent to which the student meets academic expectations; playground observations assess the quality and nature of social behavior. These direct observations, in addition to teacher ratings, are then used to decide whether the student has problems that warrant full evaluation for special education. The procedures that Walker and his colleagues devised are the most fully developed screening system currently available for use in school settings.

The Early Screening Project: A Proven Child-Find Process (Walker, Severson, & Feil, 1994)

The Early Screening Project (ESP) is a downward extension of the SSBD of Walker and Severson (1990). It is designed and normed specifically for children ages 3 to 5.

School Archival Records Search (Walker, Block-Pedego, Todis, & Severson, 1991)

The *School Archival Records Search* (SARS) is designed to code and quantify existing school records of elementary students. It involves collecting and systematically coding certain information from a student's school records. Eleven variables are examined: demographics, attendance, achievement test information, school failure (i.e., retentions in grade), disciplinary contacts, within-school referrals, certification for special education, placement out of the regular classroom, receiving Chapter I services, out-of-school referrals, and negative narrative comments. The SARS was originally intended as a fourth level of screening in the SSBD, but it can be used for a variety of other purposes. Because it is a systematic way of searching out important data about a student's school career, however, the SARS can be used to assist in three other decision-making tasks: identifying students who are at risk for dropping out of school, validating school assessments, and determining eligibility for special programs.

SCREENING AS CONVERGENCE AND CONFIRMATION OF CONCERNS

One person's opinion or a single score on a rating scale or other instrument should never be considered adequate for screening. A student should be selected for evaluation only when several observers share the suspicion that he or she may have a disorder and their shared suspicion is confirmed by data obtained from structured observations or ratings. Otherwise, the risk is too high that the student will be unnecessarily labeled and stigmatized, that his or her privacy rights will be violated, and that resources will be wasted on fruitless evaluations.

The goal of screening should be to obtain information from a variety of sources and to use instruments that facilitate hypotheses regarding the reciprocal influence of the behavior, the environments in which it occurs, and the student's personal perspectives. This goal is consistent with an ecological approach and with a social-cognitive conceptual model.

A special concern in screening and identification is the accommodation of cultural diversity and individual differences. Students who are members of some ethnic or cultural minorities are at particularly high risk for identification as having disabilities requiring special education or other special services, while other ethnic groups are at risk of under-identification (see Artiles & Trent, 1994; Hallahan & Kauffman, 1997; Peterson & Ishii-Jordan, 1994). On the one hand, behavioral differences that are not truly disorders may be misinterpreted if the person doing the assessment is not sensitive to cultural or ethnic patterns of behavior. On the other hand, misperception or misunderstanding of cultural or ethnic patterns of behavior could lead to serious behavioral problems being overlooked or dismissed as of little consequence. Bias about the characteristics of various cultural groups could thus result in over-identification or under-identification of students with these characteristics (cf.

Anderson & Webb-Johnson, 1995; Peterson & Ishii-Jordan, 1994). Teachers often need guidance in how to evaluate the influence of cultures on students' behavior (McIntyre, 1994). The available data suggest that African American students, especially those in urban middle schools, are at risk of over-identification and that children from Hispanic or Asian-American families are at risk of under-identification (Peterson & Ishii-Jordan, 1994).

The Council for Children with Behavioral Disorders (1989) issued a white paper calling for particular care in assessment to guard against unfair discrimination on the basis of cultural or individual differences. Among the recommendations of the white paper were the following:

- Focus attention on assessment of classroom and school learning environments that may foster behavioral problems.
- Attend to predisposing factors (e.g., cultural expectations, prior learning, family conditions) that may play a role in students' behavior.
- Focus on observable student and teacher behavior in the classroom and the conditions under which these occur.
- Establish specific, measurable, and instructionally relevant standards for acceptable academic performance and social behavior.
- Develop and implement careful pre-referral interventions.
- Implement effective and efficient instructional approaches.

These recommendations deserve especially careful attention because we live in a particularly pluralistic society with many problems in accommodating diverse cultures. Consequently, in chapters 9 and 10, we discuss in much more detail the possible roles of school and cultural factors in causing emotional and behavioral disorders.

PRE-REFERRAL STRATEGIES

Before students are evaluated for special education services, teachers must try to accommodate their needs in regular classes. These efforts must be documented and must show that the student is not responding well to reasonable adaptations of the curriculum and behavior management techniques used in the regular classroom (see Noll, Kamps, & Seaborn, 1993; Wood, Smith, & Grimes, 1985). Pre-referral strategies aim to reduce the number of "false positives," (that is, to prevent misidentification) and to avoid wasting effort on unnecessary formal evaluations. The following feature summarizes what a teacher must do before referring a student for a full evaluation.

What Do I Do Before Making a Referral?

Before making a referral, you will be expected to document the strategies you have used in your class to meet the student's educational needs. Regardless of whether the student is later found to have a disability, your documentation will be useful in the following ways:

(1) you will have evidence that will be helpful to or required by the committee of professionals who will evaluate the student, (2) you will be better able to help the student's parents understand that methods used for other students in the class are not adequate for their child, and (3) you will have records of successful and/or unsuccessful methods of working with the student that will be useful to you and any other teacher who works with the student in the future.

Your documentation of what you have done may appear to require a lot of paperwork, but careful record keeping will pay off. If a student is causing you serious concern, then you will be wise to demonstrate your concern by keeping written records. Your notes should include items such as the following:

- Exactly what you are concerned about

- Why you are concerned about it

- Dates, places, and times you have observed the problem

- Precisely what you have done to try to resolve the problem

- Who, if anyone, helped you devise the plans or strategies you have used

- Evidence that the strategies have been successful or unsuccessful

---

Pre-referral strategies sometimes result in successful management of the student in a general education classroom without the need for special education (see Noll et al., 1993, and the accompanying feature, "Amy"). Early detection of problems increases the likelihood of finding effective solutions without removing the student from the problem situation. Even with the best available pre-referral strategies and flawless teamwork of general and special educators, however, some students' needs will not be met in regular classes (see Bateman & Chard, 1995; Braaten et al., 1988; Lloyd, Crowley, Kohler, & Strain, 1988).

Amy

Characteristics: Amy was a fifth-grade student more than 2 years behind academically, with Chapter I remedial assistance in reading and math. Family stressors included a blended family (stepfather, stepsisters), alcoholic grandmother, and a disorganized home life, but family members were loving toward the child. Two instances of sexual molestation by an acquaintance had been reported.

Behaviors: Student self-reported feelings of unworthiness; explosive behaviors occurred when corrected. She also exhibited unpredictable mood swings, made loud and irrelevant comments, and stole from and displayed aggression toward peers. The student reported people were following her and that she could hear negative thoughts of others.

Monitoring system: Amy requested earning points; thus, a point sheet was designed for academics (i.e., begin work, ask for help when needed, work without disturbing others) and behaviors (i.e., follow directions, accept correction, keep hands to self). The student self-recorded warnings or reminders, with a review every hour by the teacher and a tally at the end of each day with the school nurse. Points earned activities with selected persons.

Follow-up/maintenance: Eventually, the student was able to control her behaviors, with less-frequent reporting to the teacher. In additions, a social skills and problem-solving group including other fifth-grade girls was conducted twice per week to assist in maintaining positive peer interactions. (Noll et al., 1993, p. 209)

Screening should result in prompt attempts to find solutions to the problems of selected students in general education without evaluating them for special education. Failure to find solutions within a reasonable time should result in prompt referral for evaluation; eternal hope should not spring from failure. Furthermore, specialized pre-referral procedures should not be conducted without parental consent, and keeping students in general education classrooms when pre-referral procedures have not been successful could be a violation of IDEA (see Katsiyannis, 1994). When has a teacher done enough to circumvent referral? The answer requires careful consideration of the individual, as the cases of Don and Bill illustrate.

When Has a Referral Been Justified?

Nearly all professionals agree that a referral is not justified just because a teacher observes that a student misbehaves or has an academic problem in the classroom. Nevertheless, professionals often disagree about how much effort to expend on accommodating the student's needs before the teacher requests an evaluation for special education.

School systems are increasingly likely to require teachers to complete referral forms on which they describe behavioral characteristics and pre-referral strategies. Consider Don and Bill, and imagine that you had to make decisions based solely on the information provided here. Are the referrals justifiable? If so, why? If not, what additional information or level of detail or specificity would make them justifiable?

Don

Don is a second grader whose teacher provides the following reasons for referral. "His behavior is continually disruptive. He is verbally abusive and physically aggressive. He will not follow instructions (such as to get proper book out, put candy away, ask for permission to leave the room, etc.). He uses vulgar, offensive words. He is untruthful." The teacher judges his academic performance to be average in spelling, handwriting, social studies, and physical education; below average (but not failing) in reading, language, arithmetic, science, and music. No recent test scores are reported.

Don's mother was contacted about a month ago—when she was asked to come to school following Don's suspension. She is aware of Don's behavior problems and is cooperative with school personnel. She is aware of Don's referral and is in agreement with it.

Don was retained in first grade. He has so far attended three different schools. His current teacher reports that she contacted Don's previous teachers, who reported similar problems but had no suggestions for his management. The resource teacher has suggested and tried several different behavior management strategies, none of which has been successful. Don's current teacher has tried behavioral contracting, preferential seating, and peer tutoring, as well as reasoning with him, trying to help him see the consequences of unacceptable behavior, isolating him from peers, withholding all or part of his recess, sending him to the principal, and changing his placement to a classroom with fewer troublesome students. These strategies have been tried for a period of about two months; none has been successful.[3]

Bill

Bill is a 14-year-old eighth grader with a history of fighting, defiance, disruption, and lewd conduct. His present placement is in a special education resource room, with participation in as many regular classes as possible. School staff, including a behavioral consultant, have been devising special behavior management plans for him during the past year. He is now being referred for possible placement in a more restrictive residential setting.

At the beginning of the school year, Bill was harassing certain female staff members. This was dealt with by teaching Bill alternatives to staring (such as glancing) and by informing him of the severe consequences that would result from his staring, making slurping noises, and vocalizing or mouthing lewd remarks. He has responded well to this program and has been penalized only once for lewd behavior.

The program in effect at the beginning of the school year included a general behavior checklist on which Bill's behavior was rated each period on each of five behaviors: followed directions, participated, paid attention, completed classwork, and turned in homework. Teachers rated each behavior on the following scale: 3 = Great!, 2 = OK, 1 = Not Acceptable, ? = Not Applicable. Points could be earned for scoring threes and lost for scoring ones. Earned points could be exchanged in homeroom and during seventh period for activities and free time. Instruction in desirable classroom behavior was provided in homeroom. This plan was in effect from the beginning of school to mid-October. Bill could exhibit the desired behaviors, but he performed them sporadically.

In mid-October a set of consequences for resource and regular class settings was added for Bill's disruptive behavior. Regular classroom teachers were given the option of a quick ejection from their class (ignore, warn, eject); resource teachers were given the option of keeping him after school and having him walk home.

Because Bill was ending up in the office too much to suit the principal, even with the added consequences, additional interventions were tried. Direct observations were made to determine the extent to which Bill was following directions, including obeying classroom rules. He was found to be compliant with directions and rules about 60 to 75 percent of the time on the average; he was engaging in a high level of disruptive and defiant behavior, and his compliance tended to fluctuate wildly (for example, from zero to 86-percent compliance on one day). More explicit systems of penalties and rewards were devised; a "levels" plan was implemented, in which Bill could earn greater freedom and independence in school, plus food rewards, for improved behavior. Bill earned edible rewards on two occasions, and then stated that he was no longer interested in "behaving for burgers."

In addition to the contingencies devised for Bill, the behavioral consultant has been providing instruction in social skills. These skills include asking for help from staff and responding appropriately to confusing and/or contradictory instructions or queries from staff.

---

[3]I am grateful to Betty Hallenbeck for providing the information about Don.

Bill's behavior has been extremely variable from day to day since the beginning of school. Although he has reached several specific goals (e.g., not being ejected from more than four classes in 10 days), there has been no general trend toward improvement. In fact, Bill was recently suspended from school for 1 day.[4]

CLASSIFICATION

Classification should be based on reliably observed phenomena, and the classification of a given disorder should have a clear relationship to its nature, origin, course, and treatment. Ideally, a classification system should include *operationally-defined categories*—categories defined in such a way that the behaviors comprising them can be measured. The system should also be *reliable*: an individual should be classified consistently by different observers, and the assignment of someone to a category should be consistent over a reasonable period of time. The categories should be *valid*: assignment to a category should be determinable in a variety of ways (by a variety of observational systems or rating scales), and it should be highly predictive of particular behaviors (Waldman & Lillenfeld, 1995).

We shall briefly discuss two major types of classification: psychiatric and dimensional. Of the alternative systems available, psychiatric classification typically carries the greatest legal authority, but dimensional classification has greatest relevance for educators and most closely approximates the ideal system.

Psychiatric Classification

Psychiatry, mimicking the empirical classification of diseases in physical medicine, has devised systems of classification based on demonstrated or presumed *mental diseases*. Historically, many psychiatric classifications have been unreliable and have had few or no implications for treatment, particularly educational interventions (Achenbach, 1985; Merrell, 1994; Sinclair, Forness, & Alexson, 1985). However, psychiatric classifications are widely used, and educators will encounter psychiatric labels in working with students with emotional or behavioral disorders. Much progress has been made in psychiatric classification during the past 2 decades in making categories more objective and reliable. Nevertheless, psychiatric categories are not aligned with eligibility criteria for special education; students are not identified for special education through psychiatric diagnosis (Duncan, Forness, & Hartsough, 1995).

The most widely accepted psychiatric system of classification is the one devised by the American Psychiatric Association. The standard psychiatric diagnoses are those included in the most recent edition of the American Psychiatric Association's *Diagnostic and Statistical Manual of Mental Disorders*, or *DSM*. The fourth edition of the manual is known as *DSM-IV* (American Psychiatric Association, 1994). Besides the classifications it lists, the *DSM-IV* system includes multiaxial assessment that is

---

[4]I am grateful to Lee Jones for the information about Bill.

designed to help in planning treatment and predicting outcomes. **Multiaxial assessment** is a way of organizing information on five axes or strands of information. The five axes are an attempt to include all relevant information and to see the problem in the context of its biological and social ecologies.

Axis I   *Clinical Disorders* are listed, including not only the primary presenting complaint but all *Other Conditions That May Be a Focus of Clinical Attention*. On this axis, the clinician lists the diagnostic category or categories of the individual's psychopathology (e.g., Conduct Disorder; Attention Deficit/Hyperactivity Disorder, Hyperactive-Impulsive Type).

Axis II   *Personality Disorders* and *Mental Retardation* are listed on a separate axis to make sure that these are not overlooked when the primary complaint is a more florid disorder listed on Axis I.

Axis III   *General Medical Conditions* includes the current medical conditions that might be relevant to understanding or managing the disorder(s) listed on Axes I and II (e.g., physical illnesses that might be related to anxiety or depression).

Axis IV   *Psychosocial and Environmental Problems* is meant to indicate factors that might affect the diagnosis, treatment, or prognosis of disorders listed on Axes I and II. These would include such categories as problems with a primary support group or educational, occupational, or economic problems. The purpose is to take into account the life circumstances of the individual that may be relevant to the diagnosed disorder.

Axis V   *Global Assessment of Functioning* is the clinician's estimate of the client's overall functioning in everyday life.

The actual diagnostic categories are listed under 18 broad headings, the first of which is "Disorders Usually First Diagnosed in Infancy, Childhood, or Adolescence." Although children and youths may receive diagnoses from other categories, they are most likely to be categorized under this general heading. The first four categories under this heading are Mental Retardation, Learning Disorders, Motor Skills Disorder, and Communication Disorders. These disorders may, indeed, accompany emotional or behavioral disorders of other types, but they are typically considered in detail in books or chapters devoted exclusively to them (e.g., Hallahan, Kauffman, & Lloyd, 1996; Shames, Wiig, & Secord, 1994).

For purposes of this book, we will examine the *DSM-IV* listing of diagnostic categories and subcategories beginning with the fifth major category, Pervasive Developmental Disorders (see Table 5.1). We shall not attempt to define all of these categories here, but definitions of all are found in the glossary and most are discussed in later chapters. In *DSM-IV*, each category and subcategory is associated with a number (e.g., Autistic Disorder is 299.00), which we have not included. Many categories in *DSM-IV* include a subcategory NOS for "not otherwise specified," a catch-all that, as we discuss later, is necessary in any comprehensive diagnostic system.

All of the categories and subcategories listed in *DSM-IV* are accompanied in the manual by extensive diagnostic guidelines that include explicit criteria for inclusion and exclusion. These guidelines and criteria have done much to improve the reliabil-

Table 5.1

Selected *DSM-IV* Categories of Disorders Usually First Diagnosed in Infancy, Childhood, or Adolescence

---

Pervasive Developmental Disorders

Autistic disorder

Rett's disorder

Childhood disintegrative disorder

Asperger's disorder

Pervasive developmental disorder NOS

Attention-Deficit and Disruptive Behavior Disorders

Attention-deficit/Hyperactivity disorder

Combined type

Predominantly inattentive type

Predominantly hyperactive-impulsive type

Attention-deficit/hyperactivity disorder NOS

Conduct disorder (*Specify type:* Childhood-onset type/Adolescent-onset type)

Oppositional defiant disorder

Disruptive behavior disorder NOS

Feeding and Eating Disorders of Infancy or Early Childhood

Pica

Rumination disorder

Feeding disorder of infancy or early childhood

TIC Disorder

Tourette's disorder

Chronic motor or vocal tic disorder

Transient tic disorder (*Specify if:* Single episode/Recurrent)

Tic disorder NOS

Elimination Disorders

Encopresis

With constipation and overflow incontinence

Without constipation and overflow incontinence

Enuresis (Not due to a general medical condition) (*Specify type:* Nocturnal only/ Diurnal only/Nocturnal and Diurnal)

Other Disorders of Infancy, Childhood, or Adolescence

Separation anxiety disorder (*Specify if:* Early onset)

Selective mutism

Reactive attachment disorder of infancy or early childhood (*Specify type:* Inhibited type/Disinhibited type)

Stereotyped movement disorder (*Specify if:* With self-injurious behavior)

Disorder of infancy, childhood, or adolescence NOS

---

ity of psychiatric diagnosis (cf. Waldman & Lillenfeld, 1995) Just because a child or youth carries a *DSM-IV* diagnosis does not mean that he or she is eligible for special education services. Although many of those who carry psychiatric labels are eligible for special education, it is important to remember that identification for special education is independent of and uses criteria different from those in any DSM classification system (Duncan et al., 1995; Sinclair, Forness, & Alexson, 1985).

Behavioral Dimensions

Psychiatric classification is focused primarily on differentiating among *kinds* of disorders. Dimensional classification indicates how much individuals differ in the *degree* to which they exhibit a type of behavior (Waldman & Lilienfeld, 1995). Behavioral dimensions are descriptions of behavioral clusters (highly intercorrelated behaviors). Statistical procedures, such as factor analysis, are used to find behavioral dimensions based on behavior ratings. The statistical analyses reveal which behavior problems tend to occur together to form a dimension. In early studies (e.g., Ackerson, 1942; Hewitt & Jenkins, 1946), behavior traits were obtained from reports in children's case histories. The behaviors were listed and then clustered by visual inspection of the data. Current statistical analyses are much more precise.

Two behavior rating scales from which dimensional classifications are commonly extracted are the *Revised Behavior Problem Checklist* (RBPC) (Quay & Peterson, 1987) and the *Child Behavior Checklist* (CBCL) (Achenbach & Edelbrock, 1991). (The teacher report form of the CBCL was briefly described earlier in this chapter.) We describe each rating scale briefly and summarize the nature of the dimensions that have been found using them.

Revised Behavior Problem Checklist (RBPC)   During many years of research with a previous version of the Behavior Problem Checklist (BPC), Quay and others identified four pervasive patterns in youngsters' problem behavior (Quay, 1975, 1977; Von Isser, Quay, & Love, 1980). These are generally described as follows:

Conduct disorder—characterized by verbal and overt physical aggression, disruptiveness, negativism, irresponsibility, and defiance of authority

Anxiety-withdrawal (also called Personality problem)—characterized by overanxiety, social withdrawal, seclusiveness, shyness, sensitivity, and other indications of retreat from the environment

Immaturity (also sometimes referred to as Inadequacy-immaturity)—characterized by preoccupation, short attention span, passivity, daydreaming, sluggishness, and other failures to meet developmental expectations

Socialized aggression—typically involving gang activities, group stealing, truancy, and identification with a delinquent subculture

Research over many years has consistently found several or all of these dimensions of disordered behavior among samples of disabled and nondisabled youngsters (Cullinan et al., 1984; McCarthy & Paraskevopoulos, 1969; Quay, Morse, & Cutler,

1966). Those with emotional or behavioral disorders are nearly always rated higher than any other identified group on all dimensions of problem behavior, and the differences tend to be greatest on the conduct disorder dimension. Boys usually have higher problem scores than girls. The results of a large-scale study (Cullinan & Epstein, 1985) are displayed in Figure 5.1. In this study, the behavior problem scores of the behaviorally disordered (BD) group were significantly higher than those of the other groups, compared across all behavioral dimensions, age levels, and both sexes. Boys' problem scores were significantly higher than girls' scores on the conduct disorder dimension, but not on the others.

Factor analyses of the RBPC indicate six dimensions or scales, some of which are essentially the same as the four usually found in studies with the earlier version of the rating scale (Quay & Peterson, 1987). Table 5.2 shows the six scales and representative items from them.

Child Behavior Checklist   Achenbach and his colleagues have researched the behavior ratings of identified (for treatment) and nonidentified youngsters using both par-

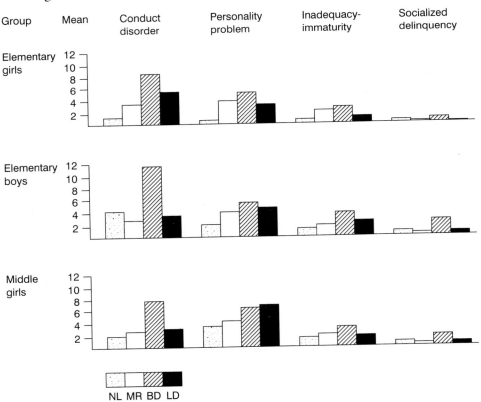

Figure 5.1
Means of Four Behavior Problem Checklist Factor Scores (for nonhandicapped [NL], educable mentally retarded [MR], behaviorally disordered [BD], and learning disabled [LD] groups of boys and girls at each of three age levels [elementary = 8–10, middle = 11–13, senior = 14–16]).

ent and teacher forms of the CBCL (Achenbach, 1985, 1991; Achenbach & Edelbrock, 1981, 1984, 1989). They have identified several *broad-band* factors or syndromes, the most common being *overcontrolled* and *undercontrolled*. Similar broadband or general factors have also been called *internalizing* and *externalizing*. More specific or *narrow-band* syndromes identified through statistical analyses or behavioral ratings include those labeled *aggressive, hyperactive, delinquent, schizoid, depressed,* and *social withdrawal.*

Using different labels for similar dimensions is somewhat confusing. Achenbach and Edelbrock's undercontrolled (or externalizing) is a rough approximation of Quay and Peterson's conduct disorder and socialized aggression dimensions; their overcontrolled (or internalizing) syndrome approximates Quay and Peterson's anxiety-withdrawal and immaturity dimensions.

An important concept underlying the classification of behavioral dimensions is that all individuals exhibit the characteristics of all the dimensions, but to varying degrees (Quay, 1986a; Waldman & Lilienfeld, 1995). It is erroneous to assume that an individual may be rated high on only one dimension. Many students with emo-

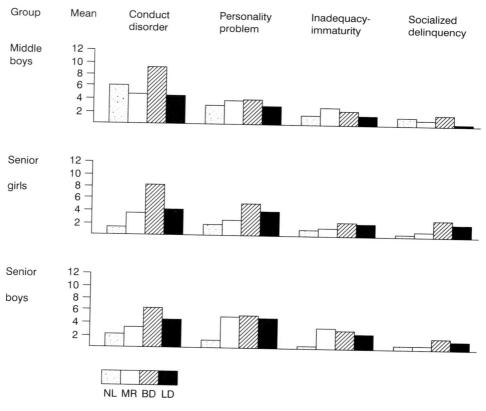

Figure 5.1 (*continued*)
Data from "Adjustment Problems of Mildly Handicapped and Nonhandicapped Students" by D. Cullinan and M. H. Epstein, 1985, *Remedial and Special Education,* 6(2), pp. 5–11.

Table 5.2
Representative Items from the Six Scales of the RBPC

Scale	Item No.	Item
I. Conduct Disorder (CD) (22 items)	2	Seeks attention; "shows-off"
	5	Disruptive; annoys and bothers others
	17	Fights
	19	Has temper tantrums
II. Socialized Aggression (SA) (17 items)	7	Steals in company with others
	18	Loyal to delinquent friends
	20	Truant from school, usually in company with others
	24	Has "bad" companions, ones who are always in some kind of trouble
	54	Freely admits disrespect for moral values and laws
III. Attention Problems— Immaturity (AP) (16 Items)	13	Short attention span; poor concentration
	31	Distractible; easily diverted from the task at hand
	35	Sluggish, slow moving, lethargic
	44	Answers without stopping to think
IV. Anxiety-Withdrawal (AW) (11 items)	4	Self-conscious; easily embarrassed
	21	Hypersensitive; feelings are easily hurt
	22	Generally fearful; anxious
	27	Depressed; always sad
V. Psychotic Behavior (PB) (6 items)	12	Repetitive speech; says same thing over and over
	39	Expresses strange, far-fetched ideas
VI. Motor Excess (ME) (5 items)	1	Restless; unable to sit still
	25	Tense; unable to relax

Source: From *Manual for the Revised Behavior Problem Checklist* (pp. 20–22) by H. C. Quay and D. R. Peterson, 1987, Coral Gables, FL: Author.

tional or behavioral disorders have multiple problems, and they may receive high ratings on several dimensions. Students' behavior is classified according to certain statistical clusters of items on the rating scale; individuals are not classified. Although the same perspective is taken in some psychiatric classifications (that is, disorders are classified, not people), dimensional classification has the advantage of being based on more reliable, empirically-derived categories.

These observations bring us back to a foundational concept related to the definition of disorder: emotional or behavioral disorder is not an all-or-nothing phenomenon. How different an individual's behavior must be from that of others before we invoke the label *disordered* is a matter of judgment, an arbitrary decision based on an explicit or implicit value system. The same concept applies to the subclassification of disorders within the general category. How high an individual's rating must be on a particular factor or dimension before his or her behavior is said to be problematic is a matter of judgment. That judgment may be guided by statistical analyses, but the statistics themselves are not sufficient. Classification using a dimensional system, like psychiatric classification, is not by itself sufficient to make a child or youth eligible for special education services.

Multiple Classifications and the Issue of Comorbidity

Regardless of whether psychiatric or dimensional classification systems are used, researchers and clinicians frequently find that children and youths exhibit more than one type of problem or disorder (see Forness, Kavale, & Lopez, 1993; Richardson, McGauhey, & Day, 1995). Multiple classifications may be more common than single classifications. For example, a youngster who exhibits conduct disorder may also be depressed, one with schizophrenia may exhibit conduct disorder as well, a pervasive developmental disorder may be accompanied by an elimination disorder, or a child may be rated high on both externalizing and internalizing items because his or her behavior vacillates quickly from one extreme to the other.

A word commonly used to describe the co-occurrence of disorders is **comorbidity**. Waldman and Lilienfeld (1995) caution that comorbidity is a medical term referring to the co-occurrence of well-understood physical diseases and may be misleading when applied to emotional or behavioral disorders. Nevertheless, the term is used frequently, and children and youths who are referred for special education or other clinical services often carry multiple diagnostic labels.

Classification of Severe Disorders

Behavior along the different dimensions can vary from minor, even trivial, to extremely serious problems; however, some youngsters' behavior is characterized by differences that appear to be qualitatively as well as quantitatively different (Wenar, Ruttenberg, Kalish-Weiss, & Wolf, 1986). These children are frequently described as inaccessible to others, as unreachable or out of touch with reality, or as having mental retardation. They are often unresponsive to other people, have bizarre language and speech patterns or no functional language at all, exhibit grossly inappropriate behavior, lack everyday living skills, or perform stereotypical, ritualistic behavior. There is not much debate about whether children can exhibit the severe disorders that are often referred to in the general case as **psychosis** (cf. American Psychiatric Association, 1994). Prior and Werry (1986) provide a nontechnical definition of psychotic behavior: "The interpretation of oneself, of the world, and of one's place in it, is so seriously at variance with the actual facts of the matter as to interfere with everyday adaptation and to strike the impartial observer as incomprehensible" (p. 156). Many of the children classified as having a pervasive developmental disorder (PDD) fit such a description.

There is considerable debate about how to subdivide severe disorders in a reliable and helpful way (Gottesman, 1991). The most common distinction between two major groups is made on the basis of age of onset. If the onset of the disorder occurs before the child is about 3 years old, the label **autistic disorder** is typically applied; if after the age of 3 years, the youngster is usually said to have **schizophrenia**, a psychosis usually seen in adults and very rare in young children. Although we can see much overlap in the behavioral characteristics of children with autism and those with schizophrenia, the reason for the distinction by age of onset is easy to understand. One need only examine the age distribution of first-observed symptoms. Figure 5.2 shows that onset is more frequent before the age of about 3 years and after the age of 12 years than between those ages. Parents describe many children with autism as seeming odd or obviously different from birth—aloof, cold, and unresponsive. According to the data in Figure 5.2, the onset of psychotic behavior during

Figure 5.2
Approximate Distribution of Cases of Childhood Psychotic Behavior by Age of Onset

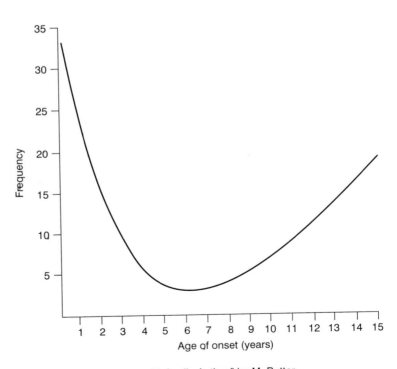

Source: Curve sketched from data presented in "The Development of Infantile Autism" by M. Rutter, 1974, *Psychological Medicine, 4*, p. 148.

middle childhood is quite unusual. Thus autism (onset before the age of 3 years) and schizophrenia (onset in later childhood or adolescence) are typically differentiated primarily on the basis of first appearance of symptoms. However, Rutter and Schopler (1987) note several other important distinctions between autism and schizophrenia: schizophrenia tends to run in families, autism rarely does; delusions and hallucinations are characteristic of schizophrenia but rare in autism; schizophrenia is often episodic—periods of normal or near normal functioning interspersed with psychotic behavior—but autism is characterized by persistent symptoms; and epileptic seizures are seen in about 25 percent of children with autism, whereas youngsters with schizophrenia rarely have seizures.

Confusion and disagreement regarding diagnostic classification persist. Debate about just what is necessary and sufficient to distinguish psychotic behavior from mental retardation goes back more than a century and continues today. Autism is considered a pervasive developmental disorder because the characteristics are present from birth or from a very early age and affect all or nearly all areas of functioning. But uncertainty about exactly what characteristics distinguish autism from other pervasive developmental disorders and early childhood-onset schizophrenia is common (Gottesman, 1991; Prior & Werry, 1986; see also Schopler & Mesibov, 1994, 1995). Aside from an apparent consensus that someone can have both mental retardation and autism or schizophrenia and that autism is distinguished from schizophrenia primarily by age of onset, there is little agreement. However, when the onset of symptoms of schizophrenia is during childhood or adolescence, the child's condition may be indistinguishable from schizophrenia as it occurs in adults (Gottesman, 1991; Asarnow, Tompson, & Goldstein, 1994). Moreover, children with autism are sometimes diagnosed with schizophrenia as adolescents or adults.

The three major diagnostic criteria for autistic disorder given by *DSM-IV* include, in addition to onset prior to 3 years:

1. qualitative impairment in social interaction
2. qualitative impairments in communication
3. restricted repetitive and stereotyped patterns of behavior, interests, and activities (American Psychiatric Association, 1994)

We discuss the characteristics of autism and other pervasive developmental disorders in more detail in other chapters, especially chapters 7 and 17 (see Kanner, 1973a; Kanner, Rodriguez, & Ashenden, 1972; Sacks, 1995; and Kanner's original 1943 articles [reprinted in Howells, 1971] for further descriptions of children and adults with autism.)

Schizophrenia is most fundamentally a disorder of thinking and perception. Children or youths with schizophrenia may exhibit bizarre behavior, delusions, and distorted perceptions, sometimes including hallucinations, and their affect is typically inappropriate in many social circumstances. They may believe they are being controlled by alien forces. Delusions and hallucinations are rare in preadolescents, but they are sometimes a part of severe disorders such as schizophrenia. The case of Elizabeth, whose case we first introduced in chapter 1, illustrates the experience of hallucinations by a preadolescent with childhood onset schizophrenia.

Elizabeth (continued)

I certainly heard voices. They started in the fourth grade when I was really sick. At first the voices were friendly; then they got mean and scared me to pieces. I got so I couldn't even go into my bedroom because I was so scared that a voice who lived there might get me. Then for a while some other voices came, and they were good voices who protected me from the bad voices. The good voices were the first to disappear when I started taking medicine, and then I just had to be frightened of the bad voices again.

It was 6 years ago that this happened, so I really don't remember what the voices said to me. But I do remember that it was a very bad experience. I always had a terrible headache when the voices came, so the doctors x-rayed my head to see if they could find anything wrong with my brain, but there was nothing wrong.

When I was sickest, I could even see the voices. They were very weird. They were like ghosts (one of them had three heads). When I was in the hospital, I drew pictures of them and some even had names like "Greenie." I have wallpaper in my bedroom of old-fashioned girls with bonnets, and it used to seem to me that they would come alive and come off the walls to attack me, which was pretty scary.

My psychiatrist said I shouldn't spend any time thinking about the voices. Whenever I felt a voice attack coming on, I would go to my mother. She could always tell I was in trouble because I would get big, dark circles under my eyes. She would say "Distract," and she would make me lie down and relax. It worked.

Now the voices seem like a bad dream. I don't ever, ever want them to come back. Schizophrenia is a very painful disease.

Once while I was in the hospital, the voices told me to jump out of the window. But I didn't want to because I was afraid of heights (I was on the sixth floor). I told my nurse about this and I was put within constant sight. I had to sleep in two chairs pushed together next to the nurse's station. (Anonymous, 1994, p. 589)

The Necessity of Classification

The search continues for reliable, valid classifications with relevance for intervention. Although classification of disordered behavior carries the risk that individuals will be needlessly stigmatized by labels for their differences, it would be foolish to abandon the task of classifying people's problems. Giving up all uses of classification is tantamount to abandoning the scientific study of social and behavioral difficulties. Indeed, we need labels for problems to communicate about them (Waldman & Lilienfeld, 1995). Nevertheless, we must try to reduce the social stigma of the words that describe behavioral differences.

The Complexity and Ambiguity of Classification

Classification is a complex undertaking, and scholars frequently disagree about how particular behavioral characteristics should be categorized. Furthermore, any set of categories yet devised leaves the categorical "home" of some behaviors in doubt. All comprehensive systems of classification produce a residual or miscellaneous category for behavioral odds and ends, or they result in arbitrary assignment of certain behaviors to a category of questionable homogeneity. As we shall see in parts three and four, both the disorders of behavior and their causes are usually multidimensional; life seldom refines disorders or their causes into pure, unambiguous forms. Youngsters seldom show teachers or researchers a single disorder uncontaminated by elements of other problems, and the cause of a disorder is virtually never found to be a single factor. As a case in point, consider the interrelationships among hyperactivity, conduct disorder, and delinquency. Hyperactivity is a prominent feature of the behavior of many children who have a conduct disorder. Conduct disorder and delinquency are overlapping categories because **conduct disorder** is characterized by overt aggression or covert antisocial behavior, such as stealing, lying, and fire setting; **delinquency** is also often characterized by such behavior but involves breaking the law. The same factors that cause conduct disorder and delinquency may also contribute to hyperactivity. Thus, grouping specific types of disorders is necessarily somewhat subjective, and classifications always contain a certain amount of ambiguity.

SUMMARY

Screening means narrowing the field to those students most likely to have emotional or behavioral disorders. It involves becoming a good "suspectition," so that incipient cases and those that are not immediately obvious are reliably identified. Although IDEA requires identification of all children with disabilities, few school systems use systematic screening procedures to identify students with emotional or behavioral disorders. If schools were to use such screening procedures, they would be likely to identify more students than could be served by special education.

One rationale for screening is that early identification will result in effective early intervention. Although this rationale is supportable, translating concern into screening procedures is difficult. Screening for emotional or behavioral disorders involves, for the most part, secondary prevention—preventing complications and exacerbation of existing problems. Effective screening of infants and young children with mild disorders is particularly difficult for educators because young children's behavior is sensitive to parental management, and parents, not teachers, define preschoolers' problem behavior. Criteria for selecting screening instruments include proactive (rather than reactive) procedures, information obtained from a variety of sources, implementation in the early grades, and use of teacher identification followed by additional procedures such as direct observation and ratings by parents and peers.

Many rating scales and other instruments can be used for screening. Screening should never consist of a single individual's judgment or be based on data from a single instrument. Convergence of judgments based on confirmation from a variety of sources should be the basis for screening decisions. Accommodation of cultural diversity and individual differences is necessary to avoid bias in screening children and youths who are members of ethnic or cultural minorities.

Pre-referral strategies are a necessary intermediate step between screening and referral for evaluation. Before formal evaluation for special education, school personnel must make documented efforts to resolve the student's problems and provide appropriate education in the regular classroom. When pre-referral strategies fail, the teacher should not delay in referring the student for evaluation.

Classification is basic to any science, including the science of human behavior. Classifications should help us understand the nature, origin, and course of whatever is being classified. Psychiatric classification systems have not been especially useful to educators because they are not highly reliable or valid for teaching purposes. Teachers will probably encounter the most widely accepted psychiatric classification system, that of the American Psychiatric Association (various editions and revisions of *DSM*, the official diagnostic and statistical manual).

Dimensional classifications more closely approximate the ideal system in terms of reliability, validity, and utility in education. An assumption underlying the dimensional approach is that all individuals exhibit behavior that is classifiable but to varying degrees; thus we classify *behavior*, not individuals. The broadest categories in a quantitative, dimensional approach to disordered behavior are internalizing (withdrawal) and externalizing (acting out). Within these broad dimensions, more specific categories have been described. Some of these are called *conduct disorder, socialized aggression, attention problem, immaturity, anxiety-withdrawal,* and *psychotic behavior*. Students with emotional or behavioral disorders typically obtain higher ratings on all or most problem dimensions than do students in other special education categories. Boys usually obtain higher problem scores than girls. Differences between categories of students tend to be greatest for the conduct disorder dimension.

The most severe disabilities present particular difficulties for classification. Two common categories are autism and schizophrenia. Autism is distinguished from schizophrenia primarily by age of onset, although other differences may be noted as well. Children whose characteristics are first noticed before the age of about 3 years are usually considered to have autism; if the onset is later, then the child or youth is usually said to have schizophrenia. Children with autism often lack functional language and do not usually show the disordered thought patterns of those with schizophrenia, which may include hallucinations or delusions.

Classification cannot be avoided because categories and labels are essential for human communication about disorders. All systems of classification include some miscellaneous categories and ambiguities. Many children and youths with emotional or behavioral disorders exhibit more than one type or dimension of disorder. The co-occurrence of disorders is often referred to as comorbidity.

Case for Discussion

"A Problem or a Disorder?"

Laura Brown

Laura Brown enjoys her 20 second graders, an interesting mix of general and special education students. Her class has equal numbers of males and females, with both genders including students of Caucasian, African-American, Hispanic, and Chinese descent. But she is concerned about Song, an 8-year-old girl who is an only child and the daughter of Chinese immigrants who arrived in the United States about 2 years before she was

born. Song is bilingual and seems to be just another of the American children in this culturally diverse class. However, she exhibits a variety of problem behaviors, both academic
and social, that are not typical of her classroom peers.

Much of the time, Song appears to be off in her own little world, oblivious to everything going on around her. She usually does not respond to Laura's instructions. Even
more troubling to Laura, Song seldom initiates interactions with her peers during free time
or recess and is frequently left out of her peers' games and activities. On numerous occasions, Laura has found Song in the classroom after all of the other children have left, simply because Song has not paid attention to directions to prepare for recess, lunch, music,
or some other activity and to line up with the other children. Song seldom begins work on
assignments until she has been given numerous prompts and reminders, and she typically fails to complete assignments once she has begun working on them. She spends
most of her time reading at her desk or on the floor. Laura sees Song as a bright child,
and her scores on IQ and achievement tests suggest that she may be gifted. Nevertheless, Song's academic performance is lagging due to her deficits in following directions
and completing assignments.

Song is not well liked by her peers, in part because she pretends to be a chicken
(squawking and making chicken-like movements) or impersonates the voices and actions
of video game characters with such frequency that her peers find her irritating. At first,
these behaviors elicited laughter from her peers, but now the other children are expressing exasperation with her.

Laura has sent notes home to Song's parents expressing her concern about Song's
failure to pay attention, follow instructions, and complete assignments, but she has
received no replies. She has made one home visit, during which Song's parents were
polite, concerned, and had no suggestions for helping Song be more compliant or complete her work. At this point, Laura attributes much of Song's behavior to what she calls
"The Little Princess" syndrome. Song is not only the only child of her parents but is surrounded by a large extended family of grandparents, aunts, and uncles who dote on her
and allow her so much freedom to do as she pleases that she is not accustomed to meeting specific expectations. Perhaps, Laura thinks, Song's behavior is merely a reflection of
her home life and cultural background. Still, she worries that unless Song learns to pay
attention to the teacher, comply with requests, complete assignments, and interact positively with her peers she is at very high risk of academic and social failure.[5]

Questions About the Case

1. How might Laura proceed to determine whether Song should be referred for evaluation for special services?
2. How would you describe Song's behavior within the framework of a dimensional
   classification system?
3. What are the possible multicultural aspects of this case, and what steps could Laura
   take to make sure she neither mistakes cultural variation for problem behavior nor
   mistakes a serious problem for cultural variation?
4. Given that Laura and other school personnel are committed to early identification
   and prevention, what steps might they take at this point?

---

[5]Information for this case was contributed by Laura Brown.

PERSONAL REFLECTIONS

Screening and Classification

Hill M. Walker, Ph.D., is Professor and Associate Dean for Research and Outreach and Director of the Center on Human Development at the University of Oregon.

How would you describe the signs that a child is likely to develop antisocial behaviors?

Antisocial behavior refers to the persistent violation of social norms relating to appropriate or expected behavior in a range of settings (home, school, or community, for example). This behavior pattern is usually expressed as antisocial behavior directed either toward persons (that is, coercion, victimization, aggression, and so on) and/or property (such as stealing, property destruction, fire-setting). The frequency of antisocial behavior has escalated dramatically in our society over the last decade, and it is *the* best predictor of future delinquent behavior that we have. Delinquency, in turn, is highly predictive of adult criminality.

The behavioral indications of antisocial behavior can be either overt and/or covert in nature. Overt indicators include adult defiance, problems with rule-governed behavior, aggression that often results in assault, humiliation of peers, and extreme negativism. Covert indicators include lying, cheating and stealing, drug and alcohol abuse at very early ages, and very serious offenses such as burglary, shoplifting, and fire-setting. Children who are likely to adopt one or both of these patterns typically come from home environs that are characterized by (a) harsh and inconsistent discipline; (b) ineffective and infrequent monitoring of children's activities, whereabouts, and peer affiliations; (c) low levels of parent involvement in the child's life; (d) infrequent use of positive family management techniques; and (e) poor conflict-resolution and crisis-management skills. Families displaying this profile are often under intense stress from such factors

as unemployment; physical, sexual, and/or psychological abuse; and drug and alcohol abuse.

These conditions provide a fertile setting for the development of an antisocial behavior pattern. If this behavior pattern persists into the school setting and is maintained there, it is very likely that the child will affiliate with deviant peers by about the fourth or fifth grade. Once a member of such a peer group, a child's first felony arrest occurs within 2 years in about 60 percent to 70 percent of cases. So, it is *extremely* important to identify this problem early and to intervene in both home and school settings in order to try preventing its full-scale development. Once established, antisocial behavior is extremely difficult to change.

Why did you devise a screening procedure for students' emotional and behavioral disorders?

Actually, part of the reason has to do with my answer to your first question. Our best intervention is the early identification and prevention of these disorders. We have the means and resources to screen for antisocial behavior patterns and other disorders that disrupt the development of academic and social-behavioral competence. However, we rarely do so in a systematic or standardized manner.

School provides an ideal setting for the regular screening of children who may be at risk for developing behavior problems and disorders that can have a dramatically negative impact on their lives and those around them, yet schools do not usually assume responsibility for early and systematic screening in this domain. They prefer, instead, to rely upon the idiosyncratic referrals of regular teachers to identify children in need of assessment, diagnosis, and intervention. Studies show that teachers typically under-refer students with acting-out behavior problems (disruption, aggression) and rarely refer students with personality problems (depression, social isolation).

My colleagues and I developed a systematic screening procedure for behavioral disorders to facilitate the earliest possible identification of students at risk for development of social-behavioral adjustment problems. We think teachers can play a very important role in this screening process—and we have incorporated them, along with other information sources, into our screening procedure.

Why do so few schools use systematic screening procedures?

The answer to this question remains partially a mystery to me. My best guesses are as follows: (1) if you don't screen for and identify problems, then you avoid having to address them; (2) social-behavioral problems are often viewed by school authorities as child- and parent-owned problems rather than as school-owned problems; and (3) schools are so overwhelmed with the current demands on their skills, capacity, and resources, that the prospect of adding any number of additional demands through the vehicle of systematic and regular screening for behavioral disorders is viewed as simply not feasible or realistic. Unfortunately, both children and teachers suffer as a result of these policies and views.

What do you see as the most useful subcategory or classification in emotional and behavioral disorders?

There are many exotic and esoteric classification systems for describing disorders of children's and adults' emotions and behavior. In my view, many of these systems are only tangentially related to school-based behavioral disorders. I think the bipolar *externalizing-internalizing* classification scheme developed by Alan Ross and Tom Achenbach is the best system for use in accounting for school-related disorders. *Externalizing* refers to acting-out problems that involve excess behavior that is problematic. Disorders such as aggression, disruption, oppositional behavior, noncompliance, and negativism are illustrative of "externalizing" disorders. In contrast, *internalizing* refers to insufficient amounts of behavior that often involve skill deficits. Examples of internalizing disorders are depression, social isolation and neglect, phobias, anxiety, and immaturity.

Once classification schemes become more fine-grained than bipolar systems of this type, their usefulness is limited by an inability of professionals to agree on which categories best represent an individual child's problems. Externalizing problems suggest a behavioral reduction and replacement-intervention strategy, while internalizing problems suggest a skill-building, acceleration strategy. Thus, I believe educators would be well served in adopting this type of bipolar classification scheme in dealing with school-related emotional or behavioral disorders.

6

Evaluation for Instruction

As you read this chapter, keep these guiding questions in mind:

- How has evaluation of exceptional children changed?

- How is evaluation for eligibility different from and similar to evaluation for intervention?

- What are the implications of the fact that youngsters seldom refer themselves for evaluation?

- How can professionals work to overcome unpredictability, unreliability, and bias in evaluation for eligibility?

- What types of procedures should be used to evaluate a student referred because of disordered behavior?

- How does curriculum-based evaluation differ from the more traditional approach?

- What is a functional analysis, and why is it an important aspect of evaluation for instruction?

- What are the advantages of an instructional approach to assessment?

- What is involved in social validation, and why is it important?

- How do direct observation, curriculum-based evaluation, and social validation relate to writing individualized education programs (IEPs)?

- What is the proper relationship between educational placement and the IEP?

When a youngster exhibits behavior troublesome enough to result in referral and evaluation, it is important to assess his or her behavior and its context so as to plan an appropriate intervention. Determining precisely the nature and extent of the problem, finding its possible causes and exacerbating factors, designing methods for changing it, and monitoring the outcome are necessary components of evaluation for educational purposes. This type of evaluation is an ongoing process that is an integral part of teaching and intervention.

Evaluation thus serves two major purposes: first, determining whether the student should be identified or classified for special education or other purposes; second, providing information relevant to intervention. These purposes are not mutually exclusive; information gained during initial evaluation for purposes of classification should obviously be helpful in designing initial teaching and management strategies. The same evaluation procedures are, in large measure, appropriate for both eligibility and intervention. Nevertheless, the focus of initial evaluation is clearly a yes/no decision for special education and related services, whereas the primary concerns of ongoing evaluation are designing the intervention and measuring progress. Furthermore, evaluation for eligibility must be multidisciplinary, with emphasis on ruling out as many causes of the problem as possible. Evaluation for intervention, on the other hand, focuses more on classroom performance and what can be done to improve the student's behavior. The general rules for evaluation for special education are explained in the accompanying feature.

What General Rules Apply to Evaluation for Special Education?

The general rules governing evaluation for special education are laid down by federal law in the Individuals with Disabilities Education Act (IDEA) and its accompanying code of regulations. State rules may be no less strict than the federal rules.

An evaluation entails individualized assessment of the student's educational needs. It typically includes four components: medical, psychological, social, and educational. All evaluation procedures must be completed before the student's eligibility for special education can be determined. The assessment must be completed by a group of professionals qualified to evaluate the student's problems, at least one of whom must be a teacher or specialist qualified to teach students with disabilities like the one the child is suspected of having.

The student must be assessed in each area of known or suspected disability. Evaluation must be done using methods or tests that are not racially or culturally discriminatory, and it must be done in the student's native language or usual mode of communication. The tests must be reliable and valid for the purposes for which they are used. Furthermore, no single test or method of evaluation can be used as the sole criterion for determining the student's eligibility for special education. After parental permission for evaluation is obtained, the school must complete all components within 65 days. (Note: 65 days is a federal requirement; some state laws set a limit of less than 65 days.)

The test results and other records about the student must be kept confidential. No one but teachers and other professionals who work with the student is allowed to review the records without parental permission. It is unprofessional and illegal to share information from the evaluation with professionals who are not directly involved with the student's education. However, parents must, by law, be informed of the results of the evaluation in language they can understand, and the school must allow parents to see their child's records if they so request.

If parents disagree with the school's evaluation data, they have a right to have their child evaluated somewhere else and present the results to the school. Then, if parents and the school cannot reach an agreement about an accurate evaluation, by law either party may request a hearing.

After a student is placed in special education, his or her progress is assessed each year by the teacher. However, a full reevaluation involving an interdisciplinary team must be completed at least every 3 years. This is called a *triennial* evaluation and is done to decide whether the student's placement is still appropriate.

Whether evaluation is for eligibility or intervention, two considerations are important: the source of referral and the initial appearance of a problem. Young children almost never refer themselves for evaluation; even youths seldom do. Children and youths are usually brought to the attention of mental health workers or special educators by their parents, teachers, or other adults. The evaluation is thus almost always prompted by adults' judgments of youngsters' behavior rather than by the children's opinions about themselves. Adult referral of children and youths has two immediate implications:

- The evaluation must involve appraisal of at least one referring adult as well as the youngster. Appraisal of the adult who refers the child or youth is necessary to validate the concern about the disturbing behavior and to discover how the adult's responses to the student might be contributing to the problem.

■ Attempts must be made to determine the youngster's own view of the situation.

No humane and ethical approach to the disorder can disregard or trivialize the child's opinions of his or her problems and treatment. Some youngsters' opinions are not accessible because of their lack of communication skills, and some young people's opinions must be overruled because they are clearly not in their own best interests. Nevertheless, the rights of children and youths must be protected, and their opinions, when they can be determined, should be weighed seriously in decisions about identification and treatment.

Emotional or behavioral problems are not always what they seem at first. Sometimes an explanation is difficult to find, not because the disorder is buried deep in the individual's psyche, but simply because some of the most relevant facts are hard to extract from the situation. Consider the case of Ray.

Ray

Throughout elementary school, Ray's teachers described him as a bright, cooperative, and sociable student. His work habits and general attitude toward school were very good. He achieved at or above grade level in all subjects and was popular among his peers. During the first few months of junior high school, all of Ray's teachers gave a similar general description. By the middle of seventh grade, however, Ray's behavior had changed dramatically.

Ray was absent from school with increasing frequency. He dropped out of all the extracurricular activities in which he had formerly participated. His teachers reported that he did not often complete assignments, frequently daydreamed in class, and was generally uninvolved in class activities. His grades dropped below passing.

Ray's teachers attempted to alter his behavior by a variety of means. They gave verbal praise, additional privileges, and points exchangeable for tangible rewards contingent upon appropriate behavior, but these techniques did not produce the desired behavior changes. Curricular modifications were made repeatedly, but Ray remained uninvolved in classroom activities. In fact, he was absent from school more and more frequently as time went on. He was unwilling to discuss the problem with his teachers or the guidance counselor. Phone calls and letters to his parents went unanswered. Only after being warned of a potential fine for truancy did Ray's parents agree to discuss the situation with school personnel. A conference was arranged with Ray, his parents, teachers, and the guidance counselor.

During the conference, Ray's parents stated that he remained at home during his absences from school. The relationship between Ray and his mother appeared to be overly solicitous (they greeted each other with a kiss and held hands during most of the discussion). Ray's father was attentive but generally silent throughout the conference. Both parents agreed to make certain that Ray would attend school regularly.

Over the next few weeks, Ray's attendance improved only slightly. The case was then referred to the school mental health team, which was comprised of the teachers, guidance counselor, social worker, school psychologist, and a psychiatrist. Reviewing the case, the psychiatrist emphasized that Ray had unmet dependency needs and was experiencing separation anxiety. The teachers initiated activities the psychiatrist recommended to enhance Ray's self-concept, increase his independence, and develop his sense of autonomy and control. Demonstrable results, in terms of improved attendance rates, were not evident after a month of such efforts.

As the final effort before taking legal action against Ray's parents, the social worker made a home visit one day when Ray was absent. Upon her arrival, the social worker found Ray comforting his obviously battered mother. His mother then revealed that her husband, an alcoholic, had been fired from his job a few months earlier. During this period of unemployment, he frequently drank excessively and became physically abusive toward her. When Ray was home, however, his father was usually not abusive or beat Ray's mother less severely.

Note: This case was contributed by James Krouse.

Ray's case illustrates the point that evaluation may need to involve assessment of more than just the student's problem behavior. The reasonable explanation for Ray's behavior was not immediately obvious, and it is often the case that family factors in apparent emotional or behavioral problems are difficult to ferret out (cf. Reitman & Gross, 1995). Appropriate intervention in this case would have focused on resolving the abuse of Ray's mother as well as increasing his school attendance.

Sometimes evaluation focuses too much on the student's behavior and does not tap some critical item of information, which is often difficult to obtain. If the student's behavior is understood in the context of the circumstances of his or her life, then decisions regarding eligibility and intervention can be made with greater confidence.

EVALUATION FOR ELIGIBILITY

Federal regulations require that evaluation for eligibility involve multiple sources of data and assessment by a multidisciplinary team (MDT). Evaluation of academic performance is critical because most students suspected of or identified as having emotional or behavioral disorders have serious academic problems as well as problems of social adjustment (Kauffman et al., 1987; Lloyd, Kauffman, Landrum, & Roe, 1991). Evaluations of physical status, cognitive development, and language skills are also important because problems in any one of these areas can contribute to disorders. Evaluations of the social environment of the home and the student's emotional responses to parents, teachers, and peers are essential for understanding the social influences that may be contributing to the problem. Ideally, the MDT carefully weighs information obtained from evaluations in all these areas before deciding the student's eligibility for special education.

Unfortunately, the MDT seldom functions with ideal care and reliability. In practice, decisions are often made with information from limited sources, and the decision-making process tends to be unreliable—not predictable on the basis of objective data from tests and observations alone (Smith et al., 1988). One reason for the lack of predictability is the absence of guidelines specifying exactly how the MDT must function. Another reason is the lack of clear criteria for defining disorders. Still another reason is the tendency of some evaluation procedures to turn up irrelevant or unhelpful information; for example, physiological or psychological tests may have little value for educational decisions. Decision making might become more objective along some dimensions by tightening the criteria for definition and by using expert systems, in which computer programs use multiple sources of data to establish complex and entirely objective criteria. Such efforts to objectify the decision-making process do not, unfortunately, take into consideration the fact that the definition of disordered behavior is necessarily subjective, as we discussed in chapter 1. More objective and reliable instruments and computer programs may *help* people make better decisions, but they cannot become the sole bases for decision making.

A major problem in evaluation is that the decisions of those who declare a student eligible for special education tend to be unreliable (unpredictable or inconsistent) when judged against criteria such as standardized test scores and objective behavioral observations. Different groups and different individuals may evaluate according to different criteria; they may use different criteria for students who differ in sex, race, socioeconomic status, and so forth. Inconsistency is a serious concern because it can indicate bias or inappropriate discrimination in evaluation. However, the solution is not to make the judgments conform to objective psychometric criteria alone (such as test scores or quantitative values in computer programs), nor is it to abandon the goal of more reliable, predictable, or consistent decisions. The most desirable response is to stress professional responsibility in decision making (see Bateman, 1992; Merrell, 1994; Smith et al., 1988). These are key actions in discharging that responsibility:

- Obtaining in-service training in appropriate evaluation procedures

- Refusing to use evaluation procedures that you are not qualified to use and refusing to accept evaluation data from unqualified personnel

- Functioning as a member of an MDT to ensure that a single individual does not make the eligibility decision

- Insisting that multiple sources of data be made available to the MDT and that the eligibility decision be made on the basis of all relevant data

- Requiring implementation of documented pre-referral strategies prior to evaluation for eligibility

- Involving the parents and, if appropriate, the student in the eligibility decision, to be sure they are informed of the nature of the problem and the implications of identification

- Documenting disordered behavior, its adverse effects on the student's education, and the need for special education and related services

- Considering the interests of all parties affected by the eligibility decision—student, peers, parents, and teachers

■ Estimating the probable risks and benefits of identifying and not identifying the student for special education

■ Remaining sensitive to the possibility of bias in the use of procedures and interpretation of data

EVALUATION FOR INTERVENTION

Adequate evaluation for the purpose of intervention requires careful attention to a wide range of factors that may be important in the origin and modification of problem behavior. Thus, whenever possible, information must be obtained from parents, teachers, peers, the student, and impartial observers.

Evaluation for special education interventions also requires focusing on the student's problems as they are manifested in school. The data obtained during screening may be helpful in further evaluating the student for intervention. Procedures for evaluating referred students should include at least standardized tests of intelligence and achievement, behavior ratings, assessment of peer relations, interviews, self-reports, and direct observations. An important approach to evaluation, particularly of academic achievement, is curriculum-based assessment (CBA). CBA may also be applied to social skills.

An important question to answer in evaluation is "What purpose or function does the behavior serve in the student's life?" **Functional analysis** is an approach to assessment designed to answer this question. The function of behavior is a critical issue to be addressed in an evaluation, and a competent functional analysis may draw on all of the types of assessment information we discuss in this section.

Finally, we might approach the assessment of behavior much the same as we do the assessment of academic skills. Social-emotional behavior can be analyzed as an instructional problem: How can we teach the student a better way of behaving? A clear focus on teaching helps educators tie assessment directly to instruction and prevent misbehavior from occurring. Ultimately, the goal of assessment should be **precorrection**—guiding the student away from misbehavior and toward the desired response through skillful, carefully planned instruction linked directly to assessment (Colvin, Sugai, & Patching, 1993).

Standardized Tests of Intelligence and Achievement

Standardized tests can be used to estimate what a student has learned and to compare his or her performance to the norms of age mates. They can provide a description of current abilities and point to areas in need of instruction. A test of intelligence provides evidence of a student's learning in general skill areas; a test of academic achievement taps more specific skills. Neither type of test, however, provides much information about just what a student should be taught.

There are good reasons for using standardized intelligence and achievement tests; it is helpful, for example, to know how a student's progress in learning skills compares to other students' progress in a national sample. One must, however, avoid serious pitfalls, which include possible bias in favor of certain cultural, ethnic, or socioeconomic groups (bias in terms of a disproportionate number of students from one of these groups who score within a certain range on a given test). Other pitfalls are a margin of error in the scores students achieve at a given testing, changes in scores over time or after instruction, and failure of the scores to predict important outcomes. An IQ derived from a standardized test is not a measure of intellectual potential, nor is it static or immutable; it is merely a measure of general learning in certain areas compared to the learning of other students of the same age who comprised the normative sample. An IQ is only a *moderately* accurate predictor of what a student is likely to learn in the future *if no special intervention is provided*. Remember that a student's performance on a given test on a given day can be influenced by many factors, and even under the best conditions, the score is an *estimate* of a range in which the student's true score is likely to fall.

Considering the pitfalls in standardized testing is particularly important in evaluating students with emotional or behavioral disorders. These disorders tend to interfere with learning and academic performance during both instruction and testing. Consequently, students with such disorders are likely to perform below their true abilities on standardized tests. As a group, they tend to score lower than average on intelligence and achievement tests. Careful evaluation of their abilities is warranted, therefore, to avoid mistakes in setting expectations for their performance.

Many standardized tests are **normative**: a student's score is compared to the scores of a large, presumably similar, sample of individuals on which the test was normed. Some standardized tests are **criterion-referenced**; that is, they do not explicitly compare a student's performance to that of a normative group but, rather, indicate whether the student has or has not achieved a specific skill (criterion). Ultimately, a criterion-referenced test is a standardized test with a single yes/no score or criterion rather than an aggregate score. The criterion was probably chosen because most students of the same age in a comparison group have reached it. Thus, a criterion-referenced test presents many of the same problems as norm-referenced tests: possible bias because of the criteria chosen, invalidity of the criteria as measures of true ability to perform, variability of the student's performance, and so on.

Objections to well-known intelligence and achievement tests, as well as to other standardized measures, are often based on criticism of the inappropriate use and interpretation of test scores—unintelligent or unprofessional psychometric procedures that can ruin the value of any evaluation procedure. The value and limitations of standardized and normative testing have been discussed in detail (Salvia & Ysseldyke, 1991; Wallace, Larsen, & Elksnin, 1992). Despite their limitations, standardized tests of intelligence and achievement, used with appropriate caution, can be helpful in assessing important areas of strength, weakness, and progress in students with emotional or behavioral disorders (Kaufman & Ishikuma, 1993; Lincoln, Kaufman, & Kaufman, 1995).

Behavior Ratings

The behavior rating scales described in chapter 5 are commonly used in evaluation of emotional or behavioral disorders. Sometimes several individuals (parents and teachers, for instance) complete rating scales, and then the ranges are compared to assess the level of agreement about the student's behavior. In fact, one should be very wary of making judgments based on the ratings of a single observer, be it parent or teacher (McConaughy, 1993). Ratings by several individuals should be aggregated to reduce the possibility of bias (Merrell, 1994). The scores obtained on rating scales can be compared to norms that are helpful in judging whether behavior demands intervention and in describing or classifying the types of problems a child or youth exhibits.

In addition to their usefulness for description and classification, rating scales can be administered repeatedly and the scores used to evaluate progress in reaching intervention goals. However, behavior ratings are not adequate for pinpointing specific behaviors as targets for change, something for which direct observation is required (Merrell, 1994).

Rating scales are subject to the same dangers of misuse and misinterpretation as any other standardized assessment instrument regarding reliability, validity, inappropriate application, and bias (cf. Piacentini, 1993). Another possible misuse is to ask teachers who are not sufficiently acquainted with a student to complete a behavior rating scale.

Direct Observation and Measurement

A large body of behavioral research supports the commonsense practice of observing students in the environments in which problems are reported (Alberto & Troutman, 1995; Barrios, 1993; Beck, 1995). Direct observation means that an observer (e.g., teacher, psychologist, parent) sees the behavior as it occurs; direct measurement means that the occurrence of the behavior is recorded immediately. Thus, direct observation and measurement yields information on the frequency, rate, percent of opportunities, and so on with which a behavior occurs rather than a rating. A rating represents cumulative subjective judgment reduced to a number; direct observation and measurement represents objective reporting of the occurrence of behavior.

Direct observation and measurement involves not only recording the behavior of the student in question but also selecting the setting(s) or context(s) in which behavior will be measured, a systematic method of observing and recording, procedures designed to ensure reliability of observation, and means of accumulating, displaying, and interpreting the data. In addition to observation of the behavior itself, the immediate antecedents (what happens just before) and consequences (what happens just after) are typically observed and recorded in an initial assessment. The reason for recording antecedents and consequences is that these are often conditions or events that help to explain why the behavior occurs and that, if altered, may change the behavior.

An extensive technology of direct observation and measurement has been developed, much of which is directly applicable to teaching. As Barrios (1993) notes, however, observation and measurement systems can become very complex and costly, resulting in their being used only by specialists. Keeping observation and recording systems simple and inexpensive enough to be used in everyday teaching practice is a major goal in assessment strategies. Such teacher-friendly systems are readily available for use in classroom intervention (see Alberto & Troutman, 1995; Kerr & Nelson, 1989; Kerr et al., 1987; Morgan & Jenson, 1988; Morris, 1985).

Direct observation is a particularly important approach to evaluating disorders that involve externalized problems, those in which the student strikes out at and disturbs others. Regardless of the type of behavior involved, direct observation can address questions like these:

- In what settings (home, school, math class, or playground) is the problem behavior or behavioral deficit exhibited?

- With what frequency, duration, or force does the behavior occur in various settings?

- What happens immediately before the behavior occurs—what seems to set the occasion for it?

- What happens immediately after the behavior occurs that may serve to strengthen or weaken it?

- What other inappropriate responses are observed?

- What appropriate behavior could be taught or strengthened to lessen the problem?

- What does the student's behavior communicate to others?

Direct observation requires careful definition of observable target behaviors and frequent—usually daily—recording of occurrence. Some interventions and evaluation procedures depend on this methodology. A behavioral approach to teaching makes direct observation a central feature of intervention. Curriculum-based assessment depends on direct observation and recording of academic and social behavior, and direct observation is a required part of functional analysis. Direct observation is also an important aspect of many interventions derived from a social-cognitive model. Thus, of all the alternative means of evaluation for intervention, direct observation and measurement of behavior is perhaps the most central in importance.

Interviews

Interviews vary widely in structure and purpose. They can be freewheeling conversations or can follow a prescribed line of questioning for obtaining information about specific behaviors or developmental milestones. They can be conducted with verbal children as well as with adults. They may be designed to assess a wide range of problems or to assess particular types of disorders such as depression or anxiety (Hodges & Zeman, 1993; Merrell, 1994).

Skillful interviewing is no simple matter. When troublesome behavior is in question, it is not easy to keep the interviewee(s) from becoming defensive. Differences in cultural backgrounds of the interviewer and interviewee may foster miscommunication. And an interview in which answers represent half-truths, misleading information, avoidance, or misunderstandings will not be much help in evaluation. (Consider the difficulty in obtaining helpful information from Ray and his parents in the case discussed earlier.) Furthermore, one must maintain a healthy skepticism about the accuracy of interview responses that require memory of long-past events. It is also important to weigh carefully the interviewees' subjective opinions, especially when their responses are emotionally charged or seriously discrepant from other subjective reports or objective evidence. Finally, extracting and accurately recording the most relevant information from an interview requires keen judgment and excellent communication skills (Merrell, 1994).

Interviews should help the evaluator get an impression of how the student and significant others interact and feel about each other. They should also help members of the evaluation team decide what additional types of information they need. But interviews can accomplish these ends only to the extent that the interviewer has great interpersonal skills, the experience and sensitivity to make sound clinical judgments, and the ability to focus on information about the relevant behavior and its social contexts.

Descriptions of behavior, competencies, environmental conditions, and consequences obtained from interviews may be helpful but are often inaccurate and cannot be relied on without verification from other sources. It is important to note discrepancies between reports given to interviewers and information obtained from direct observation, as those discrepancies can sometimes be crucial in designing interventions. If, for example, teachers or parents report that they frequently praise appropriate behavior and ignore misconduct but direct observation shows the opposite, then the adults' misperceptions must be taken into account in designing an intervention plan.

Assessment of Peer Relations

Interaction with and acceptance by the peer group are necessary for normal social development. Students with emotional or behavioral disorders often do not develop normal peer relations (Rhode, Jenson, & Reavis, 1992; Sabornie, 1985; Sabornie & Kauffman, 1985; Walker, Colvin, & Ramsey, 1995). Some are socially withdrawn and maintain a low profile with their classmates by avoiding peer interaction. Others are aggressive toward peers; a disruptive influence in any group activity, they maintain a high profile with their classmates, although their peers actively reject them. In either case, the student ends up alone because he or she does not have the necessary social skills for the positive reciprocal exchanges that characterize friendships.

Research increasingly indicates that problems in social interaction with peers are a prominent feature of a variety of emotional or behavioral disorders, a highly significant problem of exceptional children and youths that demands evaluation and intervention in its own right (Coie, 1990; Shores, 1987; Simpson, 1987; Walker et al., 1995). Assessment of peer relations is a critical aspect of research and practice, including the identification of subtypes of disorders, determining social status, selecting students for social skills training, judging the outcomes of intervention, and predicting long-term outcomes (Gresham & Little, 1993).

Peer relations may be evaluated by a variety of methods. Some screening instruments include rating scales that are completed by peers; some include sociometric questions for assessing acceptance or rejection among peers or interviews regarding social relationships. Sociometric techniques are not necessarily part of a screening procedure but are often used in research and evaluation in which peer relations are a central concern. Direct observation is sometimes used to measure how often the student makes social initiations or responds appropriately to peers' initiations.

Self-Reports

Self-reports typically require students to respond to checklists, rating scales, or interviews in which they describe their behavior or feelings. How students perceive themselves and how they respond emotionally to various circumstances is an important part of the assessment of **person variables,** the cognitive processes and affective states that are part of Bandura's (1986) social-cognitive model (see chapter 4). Self-reports are particularly important when evaluating disorders such as substance abuse, anxiety, fears, and depression—disorders that involve high levels of affect and often are not open to direct observation (Merrell, 1994; Reynolds, 1993). Useful in identifying the points of stress a student feels most acutely, self-reports are also critical in evaluating covert self-verbalizations that are part of cognitive-behavioral interventions such as self-monitoring (see Harris, Wong, & Keogh, 1985; Shapiro & Cole, 1993). Self-reports are of limited value, however, for youngsters who are nonverbal or unable to organize their responses coherently.

Some behavior rating scales include self-reports, along with ratings by teachers and parents, and may yield scores on multiple dimensions of behavior. Other self-report scales are designed to tap particular self-perception, affective, or behavioral domains such as self-concept, loneliness, alcohol use, depression, and so on. Like all other assessment strategies, self-reports must be interpreted with caution regarding their reliability and validity and in the context of other sources of information.

Curriculum-Based Evaluation

An evaluation methodology involving frequent, direct measurement of students' performance using their typical curriculum materials began to emerge in the mid-1980s (Deno, 1985; Shinn & Marston, 1985). In the literature, it has been called curriculum-based measurement (Deno, 1985), curriculum-based assessment (Germann & Tindal, 1985), and curriculum-based evaluation (Howell, Fox, & Morehead, 1993). This methodology is a sharp contrast to more traditional approaches to evaluation in which students are given tests that include many items they have never seen before. The assumption underlying the traditional approach is that the test items are representative of a pool of similar items on which the student has been or should have been instructed. The assumption of curriculum-based methodology is that it is more accurate and useful to measure student performance with the curriculum materials used in the students' daily instruction.

Proponents of curriculum-based evaluation stress that the most important information for planning intervention and evaluating instruction is obtained from students' responses to daily instruction, not from standardized normative tests on which items may be only obliquely related to what the students actually have been taught. Students are therefore tested frequently—often daily—by being asked to complete brief tasks taken from their current instructional materials. Individual students' performances are compared to those of others in the same school using the same curriculum. For example, students might be asked to read aloud for 1 minute from a passage in their usual reader, perhaps three times per week. Their reading rates (words read correctly per minute and/or errors per minute) are then recorded. To evaluate written language, students might be asked to provide a 3-minute sample of their writing in response to a topic sentence. Math performance might be evaluated by asking students to complete as many computation problems as they can in 2 minutes, with the problems taken from their basal text. Students who are having difficulty, and who might be considered exceptional for special education purposes, are thus identified on the basis of their usual educational performance compared to that of their classroom peers.

Curriculum-based evaluation is important because most students who receive special education because of emotional or behavioral disorders have academic deficits (cf. Rhode et al., 1992; Walker et al., 1995). Furthermore, proponents of curriculum-based methods include social skills among measurable performances (Germann & Tindal, 1985; Howell, 1985; Howell et al., 1993). A student's and his or her classmates' specific behavioral problems or social skills (such as hitting classmates, making derogatory comments about self, making positive social initiations, and taking turns) can be recorded systematically for comparison. If the student's behavior is significantly different from that of other students, then he or she may be identified as needing a special teaching procedure to change the targeted behavior, and the results can be evaluated by noting changes in the student's behavior compared to the peer group. The significant difference between this kind of curriculum-based evaluation and direct observation is this: a curriculum-based approach assumes that the school is using a coherent social skills curriculum, that is, that social skills are being taught systematically. Unfortunately, social skills curricula are not yet well developed, and many schools have not implemented existing curricula (Hollinger, 1987; Walker et al., 1995).

Functional Analysis

Since the early 1990s, increasing emphasis has been placed on analyzing the function of students' behavior (O'Neill, Horner, Albin, Storey, & Sprague, 1990). A **functional analysis** is a process of obtaining and analyzing assessment data to better understand the nature and causes of problem behavior and develop more effective and positive interventions. As noted by Walker (1995),

> Functional analysis has three main goals: (1) to describe the undesirable or problem behavior in operational terms, (2) to predict the occasions and situations in which the behavior of interest is and is not likely to occur, and (3) to identify and define the purpose(s) the problem behavior serves. (p. 77)

The way a functional analysis is conducted is not mysterious, but it is time-consuming and requires knowledge of a variety of assessment strategies. It usually begins with a structured teacher interview (or self-interview) in which the objective is to clarify the nature of the problem behavior, including its form, frequency, duration, and intensity, and the contexts (e.g., time, situations) in which it tends to occur. The responses of others to the student's behavior are assessed, including the responses of peers, teachers, and parents. The student's behavior is tracked throughout the day to see how and when and where it occurs and what consequences it produces—what it gets for the student and what it allows the student to avoid. Then, in the light of all the assessment data, the teacher forms a hypothesis about *why* the behavior is occurring and what might be altered to resolve the problem.

For example, Umbreit (1995) found through functional analysis that the disruptive behavior of a student with attention deficit hyperactivity disorder (ADHD) appeared to be maintained by the attention he received when he behaved badly and by the fact that he was able to get out of his work by misbehaving. A simple, four-part intervention quickly reduced the student's disruptive behavior to near zero:

1. Giving him independent assignments in a location away from other students
2. Assigning him to cooperative learning activities with students who were not his friends and who would ignore his inappropriate behavior
3. Allowing him to request a small break (a minute or two) from his work whenever he asked
4. Training his teachers to ignore disruptive behavior

Functional analyses like those described by Umbreit (1995) provide the basis for arranging classroom conditions and instructional procedures that give students maximum freedom and self-control while resolving their behavior problems.

Assessment as an Instructional Problem: Pre-Correction

Teachers often forget that the most effective strategies for teaching academic skills can be applied to teaching appropriate social-emotional behavior. Whether the instructional problem is academic or social-emotional, taking careful note of the situations or contexts in which a particular mistake is most likely to occur is the first step in resolving the problem. Having noted the likely context of a typical error, the teacher may then modify the context to make the error less likely. Other techniques for decreasing the chances that the student will make an error include helping the student rehearse (practice) the correct response, reinforcing (rewarding) correct responses, prompting (reminding or assisting) the student to give the correct response when necessary, and monitoring the student's progress. This approach—combining assessment with proactive teaching strategies—may be used to prevent much misbehavior. Therefore, Colvin, Sugai, and Patching (1993) use the term *pre-correction* to describe strategies for avoiding the need to correct behavior (see also Walker, Colvin, & Ramsey, 1995).

An example provided by Gina Stetter, a teacher of at-risk second graders, helps clarify the concept and procedures of pre-correction (Stetter, 1995). Ms. Stetter observed that her students frequently forgot necessary items (e.g., eating utensils, napkins) when going through the cafeteria serving line. Consequently, they often left the lunch table, returning to the serving line to retrieve these items. This may seem an insignificant matter to those uninitiated into teaching students who are at high risk of school failure—students Rhode, Jenson, and Reavis (1992) refer to as "tough kids." However, the experienced teacher knows that more serious problems often grow around such mundane, seemingly trivial behavior. Leaving one's place and food at the lunch table, returning to (and, likely, butting into) the serving line, and coming back to the table are events rife with possibilities for conflict (e.g., pushing, accusations, verbal confrontations, tussles that may escalate to more serious antisocial conduct). Ms. Stetter's approach to assessment focused on the question "How can I teach the desired behavior?" rather than "How can I put a stop to the problem behavior?" Her observations indicated that students tended to forget items in the context of preparing to leave the classroom for lunch and entering the cafeteria line; therefore, she decided to work on teaching students to remember all necessary items while going through the line so that they would not need to return. Her teaching procedures were straightforward:

- *Emphasize the expected behavior*: Remember all needed items while in the serving line.

- *Modify the context*: In the classroom before leaving for lunch, list all items needed (milk, fork, napkin, straw, etc.).

- *Conduct behavioral rehearsal*: Ask students to repeat the list of needed items.

- *Provide strong reinforcement*: Give students rewards such as small candies, points, or extra recess time for remembering everything.

- *Prompt desired behavior just prior to performance*: Just before entering the cafeteria, provide the reminder, "Now, be sure to remember everything you need."

- *Monitor performance*: Keep count of the number of times students return to the serving line.

Ms. Stetter's assessment of the problem and her teaching procedures related to the assessment—her pre-correction plan—resulted in an immediate and dramatic drop in the number of students returning to the serving line. During the 10 school days before she implemented her pre-correction plan, she observed 6 or 7 returns daily; during the 10 days following her implementation of the plan, she observed 2 returns on the first day and 1 or 0 returns thereafter. Furthermore, after she implemented her pre-correction plan she observed her students engaging in **prosocial behavior** such as sharing items appropriately or reminding each other not to forget items. She described the advantages as follows:

> I spent time setting up the expectations, prompting, and following through on the reward. I did not, however, spend time "fussing" or correcting children. If they chose to go back, so be it; they would just not get a treat. I did not cajole or discourage their behavior. They made their own choices and very often made the "right" choice. It was a positive experience for both me and the children.

We discuss pre-correction further in chapter 12 because it is a particularly useful strategy for managing antisocial behavior.

EVALUATION AND SOCIAL VALIDATION

Those who are responsible for assessing students must be concerned with the scientific or technical quality of their work as well as the social validity of the outcomes. **Social validity** means that the clients (parents, teachers, and students) who are ostensibly being helped, as well as those who intervene, are convinced that (1) a significant problem is being addressed, (2) the intervention procedures are acceptable, and (3) the outcome of intervention is satisfactory (cf. Schwartz & Baer, 1991; Wolf, 1978). Social validation is the process of evaluating the clinical importance and personal/social meaningfulness of intervention. As Kazdin (1977) pointed out, social validation involves social comparison and subjective evaluation (that is, comparison to peers who do not exhibit the disorder). It requires subjective judgments of specially trained and/or nonprofessional persons about the client's behavior.

To the extent that a student's behavior is markedly different from that of a valid comparison group before intervention but indistinguishable from the comparison group's behavior after intervention, social validity is established by social comparison. (This is consistent with curriculum-based methodology.) And, to the extent that clients and trained observers perceive that the quality of the student's behavior is unacceptable before intervention but markedly improved or desirable after intervention, social validity is indicated by subjective evaluation. Social validation is a particularly important issue for special educators when radical reform or merging of general and special education is proposed (see Kauffman, Lloyd, Baker, & Riedel, 1995; Kauffman & Hallahan, 1995; Landrum & Kauffman, 1992; Walker & Bullis, 1991).

USE OF EVALUATION DATA IN WRITING INDIVIDUALIZED EDUCATION PROGRAMS

Evaluation for special education carries legal as well as professional implications. Ultimately, evaluation data must be used to arrive at legitimate decisions about the student's identification, instruction, and placement. At the center of the federal law known as IDEA is the requirement that every student who has a disability and needs special education because of the disability will have a written, individualized education program (IEP) describing the appropriate education the student will receive (Bateman, 1996).

There has been much misunderstanding of the process of writing and using IEPs, and we cannot provide all of the relevant information here.[1] Writing IEPs demands not only knowledge of what an IEP is but of the requirements regarding who writes the IEP and how the IEP team functions. Some of the basic questions about IEPs are answered in the following feature.

---

[1]See Bateman, 1996, for detailed description and guidelines for writing IEPs that are both legally defensible and educationally useful.

Notes on the IEP

What Is an IEP?

An IEP is a written agreement between the parents and the school about what the student needs and what will be done to address those needs. It is, in effect, a contract about services to be provided for the student. By law, an IEP must include the following:

- the student's present levels of academic performance
- annual goals for the student, including short-term instructional objectives
- the special education and related services that will be provided and the extent to which the student will participate in regular education programs
- for older students, specific plans for transition to work or further education
- plans for starting the services and the anticipated duration of the services
- appropriate plans for evaluating, at least annually, whether the objectives are being achieved

Who Writes the IEP?

For the student's first IEP, the following must be involved

- the student's teacher
- one or both of the student's parents or someone acting legally as the parent
- a representative of the public agency or school other than the student's teacher who is qualified to provide or supervise special education
- the student, if appropriate
- other individuals at the discretion of the student's parent or the school
- at least one person who was a member of the team that evaluated the student or someone who is knowledgeable about the evaluation procedures used with the student
- a representative of each agency involved, if transition services are being considered

Are Teachers Legally Liable for Reaching IEP Goals?

Teachers are not legally liable for reaching IEP goals. Federal law does not require that the stated goals be met. However, teachers and other school personnel are responsible for seeing that the IEP is written to include the required components, that the parents have an opportunity to review and participate in developing the IEP, that it is approved by the parents before placement, and that the services called for in it are actually provided. Teachers and other school personnel are responsible for making a good-faith effort to achieve the goals and objectives of the IEP.

All types of evaluation procedures may yield relevant information about a student's education. Several procedures are particularly important, however, for the IEPs of students with emotional or behavioral disorders. Although not every acceptable IEP includes them, direct observation, curriculum-based evaluation, and social validation procedures offer rich sources of information that should be the basis for instructional planning. Direct observational data allows the teacher to choose specific behavioral targets for intervention and to set quantitative goals and objectives for behavioral change. Curriculum-based procedures allow the teacher to be precise about academic goals and objectives in the student's everyday curriculum. A curriculum-based approach also encourages the teacher to select or devise a social skills curriculum, an essential area of learning for students with emotional or behavioral disorders. Both direct behavioral observation and curriculum-based evaluation encourage appropriate social comparisons and provide the basis for social validation. The legal mandates for involving a multidisciplinary team in the eligibility decision and encouraging parents to participate in development of the IEP require at least a minimal level of social validation.

IEPs differ greatly in format, level of detail, and conceptual orientation. This may be understandable, given the freedom of schools to choose their formats, the range of conceptual models in the field of emotional or behavioral disorders, and the differences in individual students' needs as well as their parents' wishes and demands. However, a legally correct and useful IEP must contain certain types of information:

- the student's unique characteristics or needs

- the special education, related services, or modifications that must be made to accommodate these characteristics or needs

- the beginning date and duration of the special education and related services that are to be provided

- the present levels, short-term objectives, and annual goals related to the special education and related services

Figure 6.1 is a segment from an actual IEP for Curt, a low-achieving ninth-grader who was considered poorly motivated and a disciplinary problem with a "bad attitude." Figure 6.2 is a segment from an IEP for Aaron, a third-grader who exhibited troubling behavior. The same categories of information are included in figures 6.1 and 6.2, although the formats differ.

The full IEPs for Curt and Aaron are considerably longer than the segments shown in figures 6.1 and 6.2, because the full IEPs include characteristics and instructional strategies for academic as well as behavioral problems. In chapters 11 through 17, an IEP segment addressing behavioral problems is included along with the case for discussion. Figures 6.1 and 6.2 and the segments in chapters 11 through 17 are not presented as excerpts from perfect IEPs but as illustrations of how behavioral problems and intervention plans can be presented in legally defensible and educationally useful ways.

Figure 6.1
IEP Segment for Curt

Unique characteristics or needs	Special education, related services, modifications	Time	Present Levels, Objectives, Annual goals (objectives to include procedure, criteria, schedule)
Social needs: to learn anger management skills, especially regarding swearing to learn to comply with requests	1. Teacher and/or counselor consult with behavior specialist regarding techniques and programs for teaching social skills, especially anger management.		*Goal:* During the last quarter of the academic year, Curt will have 2 or fewer detentions for any reason.

Objective #1: At the end of the 1st quarter, Curt will have had 10 or fewer detentions.

Objective #2: At the end of 2nd quarter, Curt will have had 7 or fewer detentions.

Objective #3: At the end of 3rd quarter, Curt will have had 4 or fewer detentions. |
| | 2. Provide anger management training for Curt. | 30 min., 3 × week | |
| | 3. Establish a peer group which involves role playing, etc. so Curt can see positive role models and practice newly learned anger management skills. | 30 min., 2 × week | |
| Present level: Lashes out violently when not able to complete work, uses profanity, and refuses to follow further directions from adults | 4. Develop a behavior plan for Curt that gives him responsibility for charting his own behavior. | | *Goal:* Curt will manage his behavior and language in a reasonably acceptable manner as reported by faculty and peers.

Objective #1: At 2 weeks, asked at end of class if Curt's behavior/language was acceptable or not, 3 out of 6 teachers will say "acceptable."

Objective #2: At 6 weeks, asked same question, 4 out of 6 teachers will say "acceptable."

Objective #3: At 12 weeks, 6 out of 6 will say "acceptable." |
| | 5. Provide a teacher or some other adult mentor to spend time with Curt (could be talking, game play, physical activity). | 30 min., 2 × week | |
| | 6. Provide training for the mentor regarding Curt's needs/goals. | | |

Note: Adapted from Bateman, 1996, p. 89.

Figure 6.2
IEP Segment for Aaron

Unique characteristics/ needs	Special education, related services, and modifications	Objectives (including procedures, criteria, and schedule)	Annual Goal
Social behavior: talks and draws inappropriately about monsters, torture, blood, etc. Present level of performance: Inappropriate talk and/or drawing 10–20 times daily	1. Behavior contract 2. Social skills program 3. In-room display of appropriate work	1. No more than twice daily by 10/1/95 2. No more than once weekly by 10/15/95	Appropriate talking and drawing

Note: Adapted from Bateman, 1996, p. 92.

THE IEP AND PLACEMENT

The educational placement of students with disabilities, especially those with emotional or behavioral disorders, has been one of the most controversial issues in special education in the 1990s. We know that students with emotional or behavioral disorders:

■ are frequently placed in restrictive environments (Stephens & Lakin, 1995; U.S. Department of Education, 1995)

■ are frequently moved from one placement to another (Denny, Gunter, Shores, & Campbell, 1995)

■ are often placed with little or no involvement of teachers (Lloyd, Martin, & Kauffman, 1995)

■ are often placed without adequate parent involvement, such that parents feel blamed, confused, patronized, or ignored (Duchnowski, Berg, & Kutash, 1995)

■ are often placed without adequate involvement of mental health professionals (Mattison & Forness, 1995)

Research about how placement decisions are made and about the effects of various types of placements is inadequate (Martin, Hallenbeck, Kauffman, & Lloyd, 1995). Predictably, therefore, policies regarding placement are matters of great debate among administrators and teachers (Leone & McLaughlin, 1995; Kauffman, Lloyd, Baker, & Riedel, 1995). The issues regarding placement are complex, and we cannot explore all of them here. However, it is critically important that administrators and teachers understand the following requirements of federal law (IDEA) and regulations (see Bateman, 1996; Bateman & Chard, 1995; Huefner, 1994):

1. Schools must provide a full continuum of alternative placements, ranging from placement in general education with needed supports to placement in residential treatment centers and hospitals. It is illegal to place all students in a single type of setting regardless of their disabilities or to refuse to provide a particular alternative (e.g., special self-contained class) that will meet the student's needs.

2. Students must be placed in the least restrictive environment in which their appropriate education can be offered. Potential negative effects of a placement on the student and on regular classroom peers must be considered in making placement decisions.

3. Placement decisions must be individualized, be based on the student's IEP, and be made *after* appropriate education is described in the IEP. Placements must be chosen on the basis of the student's individual educational needs, not on the basis of a label or category.

SUMMARY

Significant changes have occurred in evaluation of exceptional students: terminology has shifted from diagnosis to assessment and evaluation; available information has increased dramatically, and legal mandates have influenced the evaluation process. Evaluation should produce helpful information for deciding eligibility for special education and planning for intervention. Youngsters seldom refer themselves for evaluation, and problems are often not what they first appear. Thus evaluation must include the adult(s) who referred the student, as well as the student's own perceptions of the problem, and the evaluator must seek all relevant information.

Evaluation for eligibility must be handled by a multidisciplinary team (MDT). Ideally, the MDT considers all relevant information and makes unbiased, reliable decisions. In practice, MDTs do not always make predictable, unbiased decisions. Although better evaluation instruments and expert systems may help to improve the reliability of eligibility decisions, improving reliability and reducing bias will also depend on individuals' commitment to higher professional standards of conduct.

Evaluation for intervention should typically include standardized tests of intelligence and achievement, behavior ratings, assessment of peer relations, interviews, self-reports, and direct behavioral observations. An emerging approach is **curriculum-based evaluation**, in which students' performance is measured frequently (often daily) using the curriculum materials in which they are working. Curriculum-based methods can be applied to social skills as well as to the traditional academic curriculum. **Functional analysis** may indicate how classroom conditions and instructional procedures may be arranged to give students maximum freedom and self-control while resolving their behavior problems. An instructional approach to assessment, known as *pre-correction*, helps integrate assessment and teaching procedures and allows teachers to prevent many behavior problems.

Social validation is an evaluation strategy involving comparisons between behavior disordered students and their peers, as well as comparisons between the target student's behavior before and after intervention. It emphasizes obtaining objective evidence and consensus among the principal parties that (1) the problem is important, (2) the intervention is appropriate, and (3) the outcome is satisfactory.

Evaluation data should be useful in writing the IEP for a student who is placed in special education. Direct observation, curriculum-based evaluation, and social validation are procedures with special relevance for the IEPs of students with emotional or behavioral disorders. IEPs vary greatly in format and content, but all must contain certain elements: unique characteristics or needs; special education, related services, or modifications; beginning date and duration of services; and present levels, short-term objectives, and annual goals. Schools must offer a full continuum of placement options. Students must be placed in the least restrictive environment in which an appropriate education can be provided. Placement decisions must be individualized and must be made after, not before, appropriate education is described.

Case for Discussion

"Challenging Behavior, Indeed!"

Sal

Sal is brooding again. Brooding followed by agitation and a blow-up seem to be his typical pattern. Today, as usual, all of us—teachers and support personnel in this special unit in a middle school—are wondering and worrying aloud whether he and we would be able to make it through the day. Everyone is cringing at the prospect of the next struggle, realizing that today will likely be another "one of those days" when we end up in a physical struggle. Physical struggles with seventh-graders like Sal do not make you feel good, competent, or wise. They make you feel defeated and stupid. I think Sal knows that.

The rage Sal carries around seems to have no end. We are struggling to try to find its beginning. Venting his rage on his hapless victims appears to be highly reinforcing to Sal. Our first goal is to keep him from hurting someone. I often think we must seem like a commando team, positioned along the hallway ready for the inevitable punch, push, or flying chair that will mark the beginning of Sal's seething, full-blown tantrum. "Fuck you! Fuck everybody! Nobody better try to stop me! That's not a threat, that's a PROMISE!" Screaming, ripping books, overturning desks . . . we all hope that in the process of restraining Sal nobody, including Sal, gets hurt; that we'll be able to contain him more quickly than last time; and that we'll soon find some way to reduce the frequency and severity of his tantrums.

I've heard people refer euphemistically to behaviors like Sal's as "challenging." Challenging, indeed! We are challenged to find out how to change it. Whatever academic task we give Sal, whatever academic expectation we set, he seems to follow the same pattern: brooding, becoming more and more agitated, eventually engaging the teacher or other staff in a full-tilt struggle. We've tried modifying his assignments, lowering our expectations, requiring only a minimum amount of work. So far, Sal's been "winning," in that he doesn't conform to any expectations we set for doing actual school work. Maybe if we just left him alone, let him sit there in the classroom without being asked to do anything. . . . But he'd be winning then, too, wouldn't he?

Questions About the Case

1. If you were to work with Sal, what assessment strategies would you emphasize?

2. Write an IEP segment based on the information given in this case.

3. Imagine that you are interviewing Sal's parents and teachers. What questions would you ask of them that, if answered, might help you find a way of teaching him more successfully?

PERSONAL REFLECTIONS

Evaluation for Instruction

Angela Gaviria, Ed.S., has taught students with a variety of disabilities, including emotional and behavioral disorders.

How is the information you take to an eligibility meeting different from the information needed to design an intervention?

Actually, I think that all of the information discussed in an eligibility meeting is important to consider when designing an intervention. However, when you're designing an intervention, you need to focus more on what is actually going on in the classroom, rather than on the history of the problem. For example, to develop an intervention, you may consider the teacher's procedures and the different strategies that the teacher has implemented with the child. You also may consider how the child interacts with other students, the classroom rules, and the rewards and consequences incorporated in the classroom. Information such as this has direct implications for the intervention.

What kinds of information do you find most helpful in planning educational programs and writing IEPs?

I have found that classroom observations are very pertinent to consider when writing an IEP. Observations are, to a certain extent, free from a referring teacher's subjective point of view and provide a picture of what actually is going on in the classroom. This is not to downplay the value of teachers' impressions and accounts. In fact, I think that it is useful to obtain descriptions of students' behavioral and academic strengths and weaknesses from several teachers, because children may interact differently in different classroom settings. Along these lines, I think it is important to see how a child may act during less structured times, such as in the hallway or cafeteria. It's important to address in the IEP the behavior of a child in these settings as well

as in the classroom. Also, some of the information obtained through the eligibility meeting may be important to consider when writing the IEP. For example, standardized academic scores are often reported in eligibility meetings and could be useful when planning for instruction.

You entered school speaking only Spanish. As someone who has experienced the process of adapting to a different culture, what do you think are the most important things teachers should be aware of in evaluating students from cultural backgrounds different from their own?

I feel it's very important for teachers to see kids as individuals, not simply to deal with what they can or cannot do in a particular language. Many teachers seem to believe that children who cannot speak English are not intelligent and do not have the capacity to succeed, or that their cultural differences may impede them from functioning adequately in the regular classroom setting. I think it's important for teachers to be flexible enough to look at a child's strengths and what motivates that child. From that perspective, teachers can build on the things the child needs to learn and be successful in school. I think that teachers have to look at the demands of school and the demands of interacting with other children, and realize that a child who speaks a language other than English is living in a different world. Teachers must be sensitive to how difficult it has to be for that child and provide an opportunity for that child to succeed.

187

I was lucky. My first-grade teacher was always willing to give me a chance. She was flexible. She saw that I had a strength in math and she built on that, giving me the opportunity to start succeeding. Instead of placing me in a lower-ability-level group and forgetting me, she gave me the opportunity to learn what other children were doing. If she had not given me the chance, I could have been stuck in that low group for years.

To what extent do you evaluate the student's classroom environment as well as the student's behavior?

I make a considerable effort to evaluate children's classroom environments because I think that it is difficult to evaluate behavior in isolation. Different children need different classroom guidelines. Many children need clear, consistent boundaries in order to maintain control of their behavior. A teacher may be too flexible, allowing boundary limits to be changed and extended. This mismatch may contribute to a child's behavior problems.

I think that it is important to assess the classroom environment often, because small changes in the classroom can make a difference to some children. Recently, I noticed that some students who were previously successful in mainstream classes began failing. To investigate the possible reasons for this failure, my first step was to observe in the mainstream class to see if there had been a change in the way in which the classroom operated. Changes in the classroom environment, such as different consequences and reinforcement or even a different seating arrangement, can influence the behavior of some students. Also, by looking at the classroom environment, I can offer suggestions for behavior management to the mainstream teacher and to the student.

What do you think is the most challenging aspect of evaluating students with emotional or behavioral disorders?

I believe that one of the most difficult aspects of evaluating children with emotional or behavioral disorders is teachers—or, rather, teachers' criteria for determining that a child does or does not have an emotional or behavioral disorder. Often, teachers do not look at the specific characteristics of children in relation to the definition of emotional or behavioral disorders. Instead, they decide because of a particular behavior that the child has an emotional or behavioral disorder. These decisions seem to have less to do with what may constitute a disorder than with a teacher's frustration in dealing with an individual child.

More often than not, when asked about a child's behavior, teachers will make broad, general statements, such as, "This student is awful all day long, and he doesn't do anything!" When evaluating a child for an emotional or behavioral disorder, statements of this kind are not helpful. It is important for teachers to be specific and objective about the behavior of the children they refer for evaluation, to determine exactly *what* it is that the child is doing, *when* it occurs, and *how frequently* it is occurring. Without such information, it is difficult to provide guidelines for behavior management or to make decisions about eligibility for special education services.

Do you have other reflections on planning for these students?

Many regular and special educators are not prepared to manage children with emotional and behavioral problems. I don't think the emphasis in teacher preparation is on what to do and how to decide what techniques or behavior management approaches to use when working with a child with emotional or behavioral problems. It seems to me that the students who are receiving special educational services today—especially students who are identified as emotionally and behaviorally disordered—have a host of problems.

It's hard to evaluate children for special education services and not take the family situation or home and community environment into account. As a result, I think teachers are not as willing to try to address problems in their classrooms. Instead, they refer these children and simply wait for the child to be assessed and identified. I believe that there are a lot of things teachers can do in their classrooms that go undone because they are waiting for formal assessment. Teachers need to assess what is going on within their classrooms and see what they can do to mediate some of the problems their difficult students have.

PART THREE
Causal Factors

Introduction to Part Three

When we are confronted by someone's disturbing behavior, we often wonder "Why?" We search for a conceptual model that will help us understand what has gone wrong and what to do about it. We want to know what causes the person to behave this way. In part, perhaps, we want to know what or whom to blame. If we know what or whom to blame, we believe, we will know how to correct the problem and, perhaps, prevent future occurrences. In the chapters in this section, we discuss the four most frequent answers to the "Why?" question about emotional or behavioral disorders: biology, family, school, culture. As you read these chapters, keep the following questions in mind:

- How are causal factors interrelated?

- How is knowledge of cause related to intervention?

- What are the implications of the way we assess blame?

The fact that we discuss biological, family, school, and cultural causal factors in separate chapters does not mean that they are entirely separate issues. In fact, biological, family, school, and cultural factors are all interrelated; seldom, if ever, does one factor alone cause an emotional or behavioral disorder. Seldom can we answer the "Why?" question about emotional or behavioral disorders with much confidence, and rarely can we pinpoint a single cause. In most cases, we should think about how causal factors work together—what each factor contributes to the individual's risk or vulnerability. As we consider the factors that heighten an individual's risk for emotional or behavioral disorders, we should also be thinking about those factors that offset risk—the conditions that build a person's resilience and help to prevent disorders. We need to ask not only "What supporting role do these factors play in creating conditions under which emotional or behavioral disorders are likely to develop?" but also "What events and conditions help to counteract risk factors?"

Often, we assume that knowing the cause of troublesome behavior will help us find a better way of dealing with it. If we believe an individual's behavior is a sign of "illness" or "disorder," we may hope that finding the cause will lead to a cure. But finding a contributing cause does not always lead us directly to an intervention because we may have no feasible way of changing the causal condition. We may know that watching lots of television programs is associated with increases in the aggressive behavior of already hyperaggressive children, but we may not have effective means of controlling these children's television watching. Furthermore, finding an effective cure or intervention does not necessarily imply that we know the cause.

We might find that medication reduces a child's hyperactivity, but we cannot necessarily conclude from that finding that this child's hyperactivity has a biochemical cause. Some medications work even though physicians do not understand how they are related to the cause of the illness. Reasoning backward from effective treatment to a cause is a common error of logic: *post hoc, ergo propter hoc* (after the fact, therefore because of it). To take an example from medicine, the observation that penicillin cures strep throat does not lead logically to the conclusion that a lack of penicillin causes strep throat. Similarly, in classroom practice, the observation that praise for a student's on-task behavior increases attention to task does not necessarily support the conclusion that lack of reinforcement for on-task behavior caused this student's inattention.

In considering what we know about causal factors, you might ask yourself these questions:

■ What does knowing or suspecting this cause suggest that I should do?

■ Are there effective ways of dealing with this problem even if we don't know the cause?

These are important questions for teachers, and at the end of each chapter in this section, I summarize the implications for educators of what we know about causal factors. How we think about blame or responsibility for behavior is crucial in determining the interventions we choose for children and youths who are troubling to us.

The relationship between presumed cause and blame has important implications not only for our choice of intervention but for the survival of a humane society. An enduring moral precept of our society is that we do not hold people responsible for misfortunes that are beyond their control. Sick people are not usually blamed for their illness. To the extent that we assume children or youths are suffering from mental illness or social circumstances beyond their control, we do not blame them for their misconduct. In modern America, and in most Western cultures, we seldom blame

children or youths for serious misconduct. In most cases, we shift blame to something other than the individual—to a biological disorder, parental mismanagement or abuse, dissolution of the family, peer pressure, teachers' incompetence, bad school organization, or social decadence. The extent to which we are prone to look for ways to absolve ourselves of blame for our own behavior and give others an excuse for inappropriate behavior is illustrated by the insistence of a character in a popular television situation comedy of the 1990s, *Designing Women*, that she is a helpless victim of "obnoxious personality disorder."

To what extent should we depersonalize blame and attribute misbehavior to external factors? Under what conditions should we view young people who exhibit unacceptable behavior as victims of their environments or biology rather than as responsible persons who should be held accountable for their choices? The depersonalization of blame may carry substantially different implications, depending on the nature, seriousness, and severity of social deviance and the age of the person who exhibits it. Blaming children and youths with autism or schizophrenia—assuming that they choose to behave the way they do and holding them morally responsible for their deviant behavior—hardly seems justifiable on any grounds, partly because evidence so clearly connects these disorders with biological processes. Nevertheless, children and youths who exhibit disorders in which biological factors are less obvious and personal volition is more clearly involved—conduct disorders and juvenile delinquency, for example—might be expected to share some measure of moral responsibility for their behavior.

Questions about the attribution of cause and personal responsibility are pervasive and critical issues in the field of emotional or behavioral disorders. They are at the heart of the controversy regarding whether students with conduct disorders or "social maladjustment" should be considered to have a handicapping condition or to behave in ways that merit prosecution and punishment. The personalization of blame almost certainly accounts for the punitive approaches to dealing with most students who misbehave in school and the underidentification of students who have emotional or behavioral disorders. Yet, the depersonalization of blame may also have undesirable outcomes, including disproportionate increases in social attention and benefits to youngsters who misbehave and a depreciation of individual integrity. In an era of concern for individual responsibility and self-actualization, special educators must weigh carefully the evidence that individual students are able to exercise self-control, as well as the evidence that they are victims of circumstances and have little or no personal, moral responsibility for their behavior.

7

Biological Factors

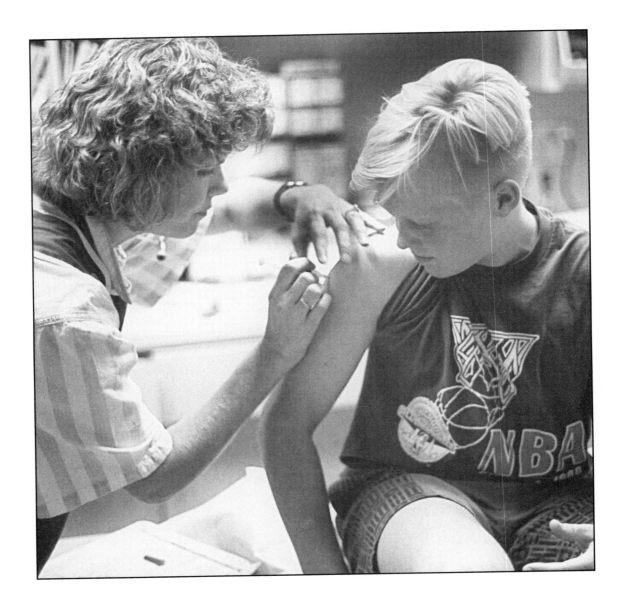

As you read this chapter, keep these guiding questions in mind:

- What is the relationship between the cause of an emotional or behavioral disorder and its cure?

- To what extent should youngsters with emotional or behavioral disorders be held accountable for their conduct?

- Why do biological factors have such great appeal as explanations of deviant behavior?

- Under what conditions is it most likely that a person will develop schizophrenia?

- What can one conclude about the relationship between brain damage or dysfunction and emotional or behavioral disorders?

- In what way might nutritional factors and youngsters' deviant behavior be interactional or exert reciprocal influence?

- What is temperament, and how might it affect pupil-teacher interactions?

- What is the relationship between physical illness and emotional or behavioral disorders?

- What are the primary implications of biological causes of emotional or behavioral disorders for educators?

THE APPEAL OF BIOLOGICAL FACTORS AS CAUSAL EXPLANATIONS

A biological view of emotional or behavioral disorders has particular appeal. On the one hand, psychological models of behavior cannot account for all behavioral variations in children. On the other hand, advances in genetics, physiology, and medical technologies such as imaging and medications make the suggestion of a biological basis for all emotional or behavioral disorders seem plausible. The central nervous system is undeniably involved in all behavior, and all behavior involves neurochemical activity. Furthermore, scientists long ago established that genetic factors alone are *potentially* sufficient to explain all variation in human behavior (Eiduson, Eiduson, & Geller, 1962). It may seem reasonable to believe, therefore, that disordered emotion or behavior always implies a genetic accident, bacterial or viral disease, brain injury, brain dysfunction, allergy, or some other biochemical imbalance.

Attractive as biological explanations may appear on the surface, however, the assumption that disorders are simply a result of biological misfortune is misleading. Although biological processes have a pervasive influence on behavior, they affect behavior only in interaction with environmental factors (see Plomin, 1995; Rutter, 1995). In the case of genetics, Plomin (1995) noted, "Twenty years ago, the message from behavioural genetics research was that genetic factors play a major role in behavioural/dimensions and disorders. The message today is that these same data provide strong evidence for the importance of environmental factors as well as genetic factors" (p. 34).

Knowing that a disorder has a biological cause does not always lead to a prescription for treatment. This does not mean that biologically-based disorders are untreatable; it means that scientists may not be able to devise a biological treatment designed to reverse the cause but may only be able to treat its effects, the symptoms of the biological process. Furthermore, because biological and environmental processes are interactive, sometimes the best treatment for a biological disorder is an alteration of the environment—arrangement of the social environment to ameliorate the effects of the biologically-based disorder. For example, **Tourette's disorder**, a neurological disorder with symptoms including **tics** and often accompanied by obsessions, compulsions, hyperactivity, distractibility, and impulsivity, may be treated with a combination of medication and cognitive-behavioral approaches involving changes in the social environment (March, 1995; Silva, Munoz, Barickman, & Friedhoff, 1995). The social environment may have significant effects on the symptoms of Tourette's disorder, although the basic cause of the disorder is neurological.

The biological processes involved in behavioral deviance are extremely complex, and new discoveries are being made rapidly. Moreover, nearly every type of biological factor has been suggested as a possible cause of nearly every type of psychopathology (see Klorman, 1995; Werry, 1986a). We may conclude that the effects of biological factors on behavioral development are considerable, but frequently neither demonstrable nor simple. And, although biological factors influence behavior, environmental conditions modify biological processes. Knowledge of biological causes may carry significant implications for prevention or medical treatment, but such knowledge usually has few direct implications for the work of educators. Educators work almost exclusively with environmental influences, relying on biological scientists and medical personnel to diagnose and treat the physiological aspects of emotional or behavioral disorders. Thus educators should have basic information about biological factors but focus primarily on how the environmental conditions they may be able to control might affect students' behavior.

With these points in mind, we discuss several biological factors that may contribute to the development of disordered emotions or behavior: genetics, brain injury or dysfunction, malnutrition and allergies, temperament, and physical illness. We cannot discuss the role of every possible biological factor in every type of disorder. Clearly, such things as substance abuse of the mother during pregnancy, infectious diseases, or chronic illnesses *can* contribute to emotional or behavioral problems in children. However, our discussion is brief and focused on representative examples of known or presumed biological causes and disorders in which such factors may play a role.

GENETICS

Children inherit more than physical characteristics from their parents; they also inherit predispositions to certain behavioral characteristics. Not surprisingly, genes have been suggested as causal factors in every kind of emotional or behavioral difficulty, including criminality, hyperactivity, schizophrenia, depression, Tourette's disorder, autism, and anxiety. Research indicates that, indeed, genes have a strong influence on the development of all types of behavior, both desirable and undesirable.

> The first message of behavioral genetic research is that genetic influence on individual differences in behavioral development is usually significant and often substantial. Genetic influence is so ubiquitous and pervasive in behavior that a shift in emphasis is warranted: ask not what is heritable, ask what is not heritable. (Plomin, 1989, p. 108)

The influence of genes is now recognized as so important in human development that scientists have launched the Human Genome Project with the ultimate goal of "mapping" (locating and sequencing) all of the estimated 50,000 to 100,000 human genes. Genes linked to some specific diseases or vulnerabilities have been identified, but gene therapy, in which genes are manipulated, has been "oversold" by some scientists and the news media (Brown, 1995).

Nevertheless, behavioral characteristics are not determined simply by genes. Environmental factors, particularly social learning, play an important role in modifying inherited emotional or behavioral predispositions (Plomin, 1995). At the level of specific behaviors, social learning is nearly always far more important than genetics. Little or no evidence supports the suggestion that specific behaviors are genetically transmitted; however, some type of genetic influence obviously contributes to the major psychiatric disorders of children and adolescents and to many other disorders as well. What is inherited is a predisposition to behave in certain ways, a tendency toward certain types of behavior that may be made stronger or weaker by environmental conditions. The predisposition is created by a very complex process involving multiple genes. Seldom do emotional or behavioral disorders involve a single gene or an identifiable chromosomal anomaly.

The children and youths we are discussing may, however, include some whose emotional or behavioral characteristics are related to a chromosomal irregularity. For example, **fragile X syndrome** (second in prevalence only to **Down syndrome** as a genetic form of mental retardation) is now widely recognized as a factor in mental and behavioral disabilities. Fragile X, in which part of the X chromosome shows variations such as breaks or gaps, appears to be linked to a variety of learning and behavioral disorders—primarily mental retardation, but possibly also to learning disabilities, hyperactivity, and autism (Hagerman & Sobesky, 1989; Santos, 1992).

Genetic factors are suspected in a wide variety of disorders. However, a disorder in which genetic transmission is particularly well recognized is schizophrenia.

Schizophrenia

The onset of schizophrenia occurs only rarely in young children, but onset in middle and late adolescence is not uncommon (Remschmidt, Schulz, Martin, Warnke, & Trott, 1994). In most cases, the first symptoms of schizophrenia are observed in people ranging from 15 to 45 years of age. The features of schizophrenia are similar in children and adults, although onset in childhood may be associated with a severe form of the disorder (Alaghband-Rad et al., 1995; Russell, 1994; Spencer & Campbell, 1994). The major characteristics are delusions, hallucinations, disorganized speech, and thought disorders (see chapter 17 for further discussion).

The exact genetic mechanisms responsible for a predisposition to schizophrenia are still unknown, but research clearly shows an increase in risk for schizophrenia and schizophrenic-like behavior (often called **schizoid** or **schizophrenic spectrum behavior**) in the relatives of schizophrenics (Gottesman, 1991). The closer the genetic relationship between the child and a schizophrenic relative, the higher the risk that the child will develop the condition. Heightened risk cannot be attributed to the social environment or interpersonal factors alone. Figure 7.1 shows the increased level of risk that goes with increasingly close genetic relatedness to a person who has schizophrenia. Having an identical twin who has schizophrenia increases an individual's risk of developing schizophrenia by a factor of 46; having a sibling with schizophrenia carries 10 times the risk of the general population.

Many people misunderstand the implications of increased risk for schizophrenia or other disorders. Does a heightened genetic risk for schizophrenia mean a person will necessarily develop the disorder? Do the genetic factors in schizophrenia mean that prevention is impossible? The answer to both questions is no. "Not all people

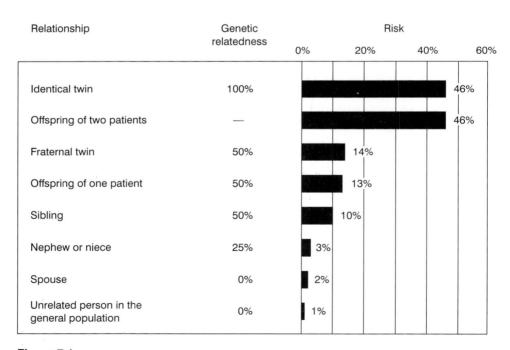

Figure 7.1
Lifetime Risk of Developing Schizophrenia
Source: From "Clues to the Genetics and Neurobiology of Schizophrenia" by S. E. Nicol and I. Gottesman, 1983, *American Scientist, 71,* p. 399. Used with permission.

with the genetic potential to become schizophrenic will actually develop the clinical disorder" (Nicol & Erlenmeyer-Kimling, 1986, p. 33). Plomin (1995) points out that although genetic relatedness increases risk for schizophrenia dramatically, the chance that someone will develop schizophrenia is less than 50 percent even for those at highest genetic risk—those having an identical twin or both parents with schizophrenia. Furthermore, risk factors can be lowered by altering the social environment and avoiding circumstances that might trigger the disorder. The box about genetic factors and their implications summarizes some of the major findings of a leading researcher.

Schizophrenia: Genetic Factors and Their Implications

One of the most common severe mental disorders, schizophrenia strikes about one in every 100 people worldwide. Its victims are likely to suffer delusions, auditory hallucinations (hearing voices), outrageous fears of persecution and suspicions that others can "hear" their thoughts.

"Of all the babies born today, one percent of them will be diagnosed as schizophrenic by the time they reach the age of 55," said [Irving I.] Gottesman, who joined the [University of Virginia] faculty as Commonwealth Professor of Psychology in 1985. "It's a major mental health problem, especially given the fact that it tends to have an early onset. Once it appears, it wipes you out with regard to future education or employability at the level you had before you became ill. It takes you out of the mainstream."

Over the course of a quarter century of research, Mr. Gottesman has found that schizophrenia is "importantly genetic in its origins." Schizophrenics inherit a predisposition—a genetic liability—for the illness, which in turn is set off by some environmental factor, perhaps severe trauma, brain damage, or even drug abuse. In the age-old "nature vs. nurture" debate, schizophrenia takes both sides.

Mr. Gottesman explained that nature's contribution to schizophrenia—the genetic link—was long obscured by the fact that most schizophrenics don't have a near relative who suffers from the condition. Paradoxically, only 10 percent of schizophrenics have a mother or father with the disorder, while in a more typical hereditary disease, such as Huntington's chorea, the victim always has at least one affected parent.

"How could it be that some 90 percent of individuals who are schizophrenic do *not* have a mother or father who is schizophrenic? What on earth kind of genetic disorder is that which does not appear to run vertically through families?" Mr. Gottesman asked rhetorically. "Well, it does run vertically through families, but in an irregular fashion. In Huntington's disease a single gene carries the disease. In schizophrenia we are dealing with a genetic system rather than a single gene that is doing all the work.

"Perhaps the best analogy is that of two short parents who produce tall children. If each parent has genes for height that are not expressed, then by chance one or more of their children could receive all the tall genes from one parent and all the tall genes from the other parent, so a child could have all the characteristics that neither parent has. . . . "

But are genes really the culprit? Since relatives of schizophrenics share the same environment with victims of the disorder, could some kind of contagion be involved? Mr. Gottesman calls that notion naive, and he rules it out by pointing to studies of children who are adopted away from schizophrenic mothers. In one study for instance, 16 percent of the children adopted away from schizophrenic mothers also became ill.

"Because those individuals are not exposed to their chronic schizophrenic parent, they should, on environmental grounds, be free of illness," said Mr. Gottesman. "Instead you find the same, relatively high risk that you see in the children of schizophrenics reared by their sick parents."

Mr. Gottesman . . . is quick to point out that genes rarely work alone to cause schizophrenia. While genetic makeup may weigh heavily against the high-risk individual, environmental factors must be added to tip the scale toward sickness. Those at risk are particularly sensitive to severe psychological trauma. The death of a parent, for example, might cause bereavement and short-term depression in most of us, but it could push someone with a high generic risk into schizophrenia. Brain damage from an auto accident also could precipitate the illness.

But perhaps the most ominous environmental contributor to schizophrenia is drug abuse. Mr. Gottesman warns emphatically that anyone with a genetic predisposition for mental illness should stay away from cocaine, marijuana, LSD, PCP, amphetamines and other hallucinogenic drugs. "What may be simply a bad trip for the person on the street may be a disastrous *Lusitania*-like voyage for the relative of a psychotic," said Mr. Gottesman, adding that even some prescription drugs may have this effect. This warning is "one of the few practical pieces of advice we can give to a relative of a schizophrenic," said the psychologist, who also urges those with a high "genetic liability" to make sure they have adequate health insurance coverage.

Are there times when environmental contributors are the only cause of the illness? Very rarely, said Mr. Gottesman. For the vast majority of victims, the causes of schizophrenia are "multifactorial," a combination of heredity and environment.

Source: From "Schizophrenia: Irving Gottesman Reveals the Genetic Factors." *University of Virginia Alumni News,* 1987, 75(5), pp. 12–14. Used with permission.

Implications of Genetic Factors

A common misperception is that disorders arising from genetic accidents are not treatable, that once the genetic code is set, the related deviant behavior is immutable. But this is not necessarily the case (Gottesman, 1991; Mednick et al., 1986; Plomin, 1995). As with schizophrenia, environmental as well as biological factors are involved in the causation of deviant behavior. When the biochemical mechanisms underlying genetic transmission are discovered, there is hope that effective interventions will be found to prevent or alter the course of behavioral development.

The case of PKU (phenylketonuria, a genetically transmitted metabolic disorder) is perhaps the most dramatic instance in which identification of a genetic disorder has resulted in successful prevention of behavioral disorder (see Guthrie, 1984). The biochemical irregularity caused by the genes that produce PKU can be identified and treated to prevent mental retardation and accompanying behavior problems. If PKU is detected soon after birth and phenylalanine is eliminated from the diet until the child's brain is no longer damaged by abnormal metabolites (i.e., until middle childhood), mental retardation can be prevented. If the child is not treated, he or she may not only have mental retardation but may also exhibit schizoid behavior, hyperactivity, uncontrollable temper tantrums, seizures, and athetoid movements (clumsy movements usually associated with cerebral palsy). Dietary restriction of phenylalanine after the child has acquired mental retardation will not reverse the disability but may help to alleviate the behavior problems (Reed, 1975).

Genetic factors are known to contribute to a variety of behavior disorders, perhaps even to most. In some severe disorders, such as schizophrenia, the level of the genetic contribution is clear, but how the gene system works remains obscure. For most types of emotional or behavioral disorders, the genetic contributions remain unclear and environmental factors appear to be more important. In a few cases, such as PKU, the genetic mechanism is relatively well understood, and effective prevention of behavior disorder is possible.

BRAIN DAMAGE OR DYSFUNCTION

The brain can be traumatized in several different ways before, during, or after birth. Physical insult during an accident or during the birth process may destroy brain tissue. Prolonged high fever, infectious disease, toxic chemicals (such as drugs or poisons taken by the child or by a woman during pregnancy) may also damage the brain. A frequently suspected or known cause of brain damage in children, however, is **hypoxia** (also known as **anoxia**), a seriously reduced supply of oxygen. Hypoxia often occurs during birth but can also occur during accidents or as a result of disease or respiratory disorders later in life.

The brain may function improperly for a variety of reasons. Tissue damage from traumatic injury may cause dysfunction. In the case of traumatic brain injury (TBI), we know that the brain's function has been impaired by documented damage at a specific location or locations. However, the brain may not function properly because of structural anomalies (i.e., malformation of certain parts of the brain) that are present at birth or are part of a disease process or because of a neurochemical imbalance resulting from a disease or drugs. In some cases, scientists do not know exactly why the brain is not working as it should, although it obviously is not. For example, autism has been clearly established as a brain disorder, but we do not yet know exactly what is wrong with the brain of a person who has autism.

A very wide range of emotional or behavioral disorders has been attributed to known or suspected brain damage or dysfunction. Learning disabilities and the related problems of hyperactivity, impulsivity, and inattention have historically been assumed to be caused by brain injury or dysfunction, although the exact nature of the injury or dysfunction has not been demonstrated (Hallahan, Kauffman, & Lloyd, 1996). Subtle brain injury before, during, or shortly after birth is an important contributing cause of serious juvenile delinquency and adult criminality, according to some researchers (Bower, 1995). Nearly every sort of serious emotional or behavioral problem could be hypothesized to be, at some level, a matter of structural or chemical problems of the brain. For purposes of illustration, however, we focus on two disability categories that were made separate special education categories under federal law in 1990: traumatic brain injury and autism.

Traumatic Brain Injury

Synonymous terms for the same general type of neurological damage include **traumatic head injury**, **cerebral trauma**, or **craniocerebral trauma**. However, **traumatic brain injury** (TBI) is the term used in federal laws related to special education. TBI is not a new type of disability, but it was made a separate category for special education because it is an increasingly frequent cause of neurological impairment in children and youths. Furthermore, it presents unique educational problems that have been poorly understood and often mismanaged, and recent medical advances have greatly improved its diagnosis and treatment.

TBI does not include all types of brain damage. The term means the following:

- There is injury to the brain caused by an external force.
- The injury is *not* caused by a degenerative or congenital condition.
- There is a diminished or altered state of consciousness.
- Neurological or neurobehavioral dysfunction results from the injury. (Begali, 1992; Snow & Hooper, 1994)

TBI may involve open head injuries from such causes as a fall, gunshot, assault, vehicular accident, or surgery; there is a penetrating head wound. TBI may also involve closed head injuries, which may be caused by a variety of events including a fall, accident, or abuse such as violent shaking; there is no open head wound, but the brain is damaged by internal compression, stretching, or other shearing motion of neural tissues within the head (cf. Savage & Wolcott, 1994).

The educational definition of TBI focuses on impairments in one or more areas important for learning, such as cognition, language, speech, memory, information processing, attention, reasoning, abstract thinking, judgment, problem solving, perceptual abilities, psychosocial behavior, or physical abilities (Tyler & Colson, 1994). The various **sequelae** (consequences) of TBI create a need for special education; the injury itself is a medical problem.

The effects of TBI depend on a variety of factors, including the part(s) of the brain damaged, the severity of the damage, the age of the individual when the damage occurs, and the medical, psychological, and educational treatment the student receives. The effects may range from very mild to profound and be temporary or permanent (Savage & Wolcott, 1994; Snow & Hooper, 1994). Sometimes all of the effects are immediately apparent, but some effects may not be seen at all, immediately after the injury; some may appear months or even years afterward (Allison, 1992; Mira & Tyler, 1991). About half of the children and youths who experience serious TBI will require special education, and those who return to regular classes will require modifications if they are to be successful (Mira & Tyler, 1991).

As mentioned previously, TBI may have many sequelae, and these may involve various aspects of cognition, memory, attention, perception, emotional states, behavior, and movement. These sequelae may be misattributed to other causes if the brain injury is not diagnosed and understood (Savage & Mishkin, 1994; Tyler & Mira, 1993). Brain injury may be accompanied by a variety of serious emotional and behavioral effects. In many cases, violence and other disturbing behavior cannot be connected to brain damage, and it is important not to attribute such behavior to brain damage in the absence of medical evidence of damage (Allison, 1993). However, we also know that TBI can cause violent aggression, hyperactivity, impulsivity, inattention, and a wide range of other emotional or behavioral problems, depending on just what parts of the brain are damaged. The possible effects of TBI include a long list of other psychosocial problems, some of which we list here (see Deaton & Waaland, 1994):

- inappropriate manners or mannerisms
- failure to understand humor or "read" social situations
- easily tired, frustrated, or angered
- unreasonable fear or anxiety
- irritability
- sudden, exaggerated swings of mood
- depression
- perseveration (getting "stuck" on one thought or behavior)

The emotional and behavioral effects of TBI are determined by more than the physical damage. These effects also depend on the student's age at the time of injury and the social environment before and after the injury occurs (Deaton & Waaland, 1994). Home, community, or school environments that foster misbehavior of any child or youth are known to be associated with increased risk for acquiring TBI. Such environments are extremely likely to make any emotional or behavioral problem resulting from TBI worse. Creating an environment that is conducive to and supportive of appropriate behavior is one of the great challenges of dealing effectively with the sequelae of brain injury (Bergland & Hoffbauer, 1996; Deaton, 1994). Medical treatment usually cannot undo the effects of TBI. Emotional or behavioral problems may be known to have resulted from brain injury, but these problems must be addressed primarily through environmental modifications, primarily through changing other people's demands, expectations, and responses to behavior.

TBI often shatters an individual's sense of self. Recovering one's identity may require a long period of rehabilitation and may be a painstaking process requiring multidisciplinary efforts (Pollack, 1994). Effective education and treatment often require not only classroom behavior management but family therapy, medication, and communication training (Feeney & Urbanczyk, 1994).

Autism

Autism is a rare, severe developmental disorder first described by Kanner (1943). It was initially known as Kanner's Syndrome or early infantile autism. Kanner described the parents of children with autism as being emotionally cold. His observations were seized upon by psychoanalytic theorists, and for decades autism was attributed primarily to the psychopathology of parents (e.g., Bettelheim, 1967). The psychoanalytic view of the cause of autism has been thoroughly discredited, and we now recognize that autism is a disorder caused by brain dysfunction, although the nature of the damage or biochemical irregularity is still a mystery and environmental conditions can make an enormous difference in the behavior of an individual with autism.

The major features of autism are qualitative impairment in social interaction, communication, and symbolic play (we discuss autism and other severe disorders more fully in chapter 17). Children with autism may, for example, avoid eye-to-eye gaze, fail to develop social or emotional reciprocity with their parents or peers, lack spoken language or adopt stereotyped language patterns, be preoccupied with objects or rituals, or adopt stereotyped postures or movement patterns. The onset of the disorder is prior to the age of 3 years. In short, from a very early age children with autism fail to develop normal social behavior and communication. Distinguishing between autism and mental retardation or other severe developmental disorders is often difficult. The behavior of children with autism is usually extremely debilitating, and many of these children are severely disabled throughout their lives.

Speculation about the biological causes of autism has included many hypotheses regarding anomalies of various brain structures and functions and biochemistry (Hertzig & Shapiro, 1990; Klorman, 1995; Schopler & Mesibov, 1987). Some studies using electroencephalography (EEG, a measure of the electrical activity of the brain or "brain waves") have reported differences between normally developing children and those with autism (e.g., Dawson, Klinger, Panagiotides, Lewy, & Castelloe, 1995). However, newer techniques of studying the brain, such as magnetic resonance imaging (MRI), may yield more definitive findings. For example, Hashimoto et al. (1995) used MRI to measure the growth of certain parts of the brain during the critical developmental period for autism. They imaged the brains of infants at risk for developing autism and, over a period of years, continued to use MRI periodically to compare the brain development of those who developed autism and those who did not. This prospective study of brain development let medical researchers see how the development of symptoms of autism was related to brain growth (Courchesne, 1995). Hashimoto et al. (1995) found irregularities in growth rates of the brain stem and cerebellum of individuals who developed autism. The abnormalities suggested damage resulting in underdevelopment of parts of the brain stem and cerebellum that have connections with and affect the function of the **limbic system**, an area of the brain thought to be involved in autism.

Brain damage or dysfunction can produce a wide variety of emotional and behavioral disorders. Brain damage or dysfunction is not the only cause of such disorders, however, and it is important remember that environmental factors can make a significant difference in the effects of brain injury on behavior.

MALNUTRITION AND ALLERGIES

We have known for decades that severe malnutrition can have catastrophic effects on children's cognitive and physical development. Malnutrition is especially devastating to the development of very young children (Brown & Pollitt, 1996; Cravioto & DeLicardie, 1975). It reduces the child's responsiveness to stimulation and produces apathy. The eventual result of serious malnutrition (especially severe protein deficiency) is retardation in brain growth, irreversible brain damage, mental retardation, or some combination of these effects. Apathy, social withdrawal, and school failure are expected long-term outcomes if children are severely malnourished (Ashem & Jones, 1978). Furthermore, it is well recognized that hunger and inadequate nutrition interfere with ability to concentrate on academic and social learning. Thus the concern for children's adequate nutrition in poor families is well justified (Brown & Pollitt, 1996).

The belief that less severe nutritional inadequacies (such as not enough vitamins or minerals) or excesses (such as too much sugar or caffeine) cause children to misbehave has been popular for many years (see Pescara-Kovach & Alexander, 1994; Wolraich, Wilson, & White, 1995). Disorders ranging from hyperactivity to depression to autism to delinquency have been attributed by some to what youngsters eat or do not eat. Hypoglycemia (low blood sugar), vitamin or mineral deficiencies, and allergies can influence behavior, and teachers should be aware of these potential problems (Knapczyk, 1979; McLoughlin & Nall, 1994). Moreover, in rare cases, a specific physiological condition such as PKU (which was discussed earlier in this chapter) may demand dietary restriction to avoid serious consequences. However, the role of specific foods and allergies in causing cognitive, emotional, or behavioral problems has often been exaggerated.

Several investigators have suggested that disordered behavior, especially hyperactivity, is a result of ingesting certain foods (for example, wheat flour, fresh fruits, or sugars) or food additives (for example, colorings or preservatives) or of the absence of certain trace elements in the diet (Boris & Mandel, 1994; Fishbein & Meduski, 1987). Feingold (1975) attracted considerable attention and an avid following when he suggested that children's hyperactivity is often caused by food substances (specifically, salicylates). Such hypotheses have resulted in some parents going to extraordinary lengths to control the diets of their children. However, in many cases diet may be the result, not the cause, of disordered behavior; youngsters whose behavior is deviant may self-select diets that are high or low in food substances thought to be connected with psychopathology (Werry, 1986a). Of course, nutritional factors could be both cause and effect, part of a vicious cycle of poor nutrition and deviant behavior. A youngster whose behavior is problematic might self-select a diet extremely high in "junk food" (i.e., food high in fat, refined sugar, and food additives and low in important nutrients), and this diet might in turn contribute to higher levels of inappropriate behavior.

However, reliable evidence is lacking that hypoglycemia and dietary deficiencies or excesses are causes of emotional or behavioral disorders or learning problems, except in extreme cases (Pescara-Kovach & Alexander, 1994; Silver, 1987; Werry, 1986a; Wolraich et al., 1995). Many of the reports that sugar or some other food substance causes hyperactivity are based on subjective ratings and may be an artifact of parents' expectations.

> Parents' beliefs and expectancies can have a significant effect on how they perceive behavior and how they interact with their children. For example, excited states in children are common with birthday parties and holidays where large sugar intake is likely. Since sugar is commonly ingested and enjoyed by children, variation in their

behavior may be mistakenly correlated with its consumption. In addition, all of the lay publicity suggesting an association between sugar and behavior may prime parents to expect the adverse behavior. This combination could appear very convincing to parents, thus perpetuating their beliefs. (Wolraich et al., 1995, p. 1621)

Although we know that some children are allergic to certain foods and a variety of other substances (e.g., medications, pollens, dust, insect stings), there is little evidence that these allergies are often causes of emotional or behavioral problems. However, teachers, like parents, often prefer the belief that diet is a major factor in causing misbehavior.

What is disturbing is that many teachers continue to think that diet causes learning and behavioral disorders and that these problems can be corrected with a new diet. . . .

The danger inherent in such erroneous beliefs is that teachers and parents will be likely to overlook more obvious reasons why children are not learning and are misbehaving: inappropriate instructional techniques, unmotivating teachers and parents, and inconsistent behavior management strategies. Sometimes it is easier to blame the students for the problems and change their diets than examine and modify instructional and parenting approaches. The best contribution an educator can make is to teach students to eat a well-balanced diet and avoid excess in any type of food (McLoughlin & Nall, 1994, p. 206).

Nutrition and allergies can affect behavior, but there is little evidence that they play a major role in causing emotional or behavioral disorders except in extreme cases. Biases and expectations appear to maintain the superstition that foods and allergies often cause behavioral or emotional problems. Adequate nutrition is crucial; excluding or severely restricting certain food substances seldom is.

TEMPERAMENT

Beginning in the 1960s, researchers began to explore the centuries-old notion of **temperament**. The definition and measurement of temperament and the stability or continuity of temperament across time are matters of considerable controversy (Bates & Wachs, 1994; Garrison & Earls, 1987; Kagan, Gibbons, Johnson, Reznick, & Snidman, 1990; Worobey, 1986). Temperament has been variously defined as "behavioral style," or the *how* rather than the *what* and *how well* of behavior; as the "active and reactive qualities" of infant behavior; and as "measurable behavior" during infancy. It has been measured by questionnaires given to parents or teachers and by direct observation of children's behavior. In spite of differences in the ways researchers define and measure it, we can describe the concept of temperament in general terms: individuals tend to have consistent, predictable reactions to certain types of circumstances or events, and their typical way of responding—their temperament—is partly determined by basic biological processes as well as environmental factors (see Bates & Wachs, 1994; Carey & McDevitt, 1995).

Some of the earliest and most influential research on temperament was done by Thomas, Chess, and Birch (1968), who studied 141 mothers and their infants over a period of years. Thomas suggests that from birth all children exhibit a temperament—a behavioral style. Initial temperament seems to be determined by several factors that operate prenatally, including genetic makeup, the mother's physical status during pregnancy, and the occurrence of perinatal trauma. The point is that infants begin life with an inborn tendency to behave in certain ways. The newborn has a behavioral style that is determined predominantly by biological factors, and how a baby behaves at birth and in the first weeks and months thereafter will influence how others respond. But temperament can be changed by the environment in which the child develops; what the child experiences and how the child is managed may change temperament for better or worse (Bates & Wachs, 1994; Carey & McDevitt, 1995). A difficult temperament may increase the child's risk for emotional or behavioral disorder. However, temperament is an initial behavioral style that may change in interaction with environmental influences. As Thomas et al. (1968) stated in their early work:

> Temperament is not immutable. Like any other characteristic of the organism, its features can undergo a developmental course that will be significantly affected by environmental circumstances. In this respect it is not different from height, weight, intellectual competence, or any other characteristics of the individual. The initially identified pattern of the young child may be relatively unchanged by environmental influences, or it may be reinforced and heightened, diminished, or otherwise modified during the developmental course. . . . (pp. 4–5)
>
> Neither in theory nor in fact would we expect a one-to-one relation to exist between a specific pattern of temperament and the emergence of a behavior problem; temperament, in and of itself, does not produce a behavior disorder. (p. 9)

Based on their longitudinal study, Thomas et al. (1968) described nine categories of temperamental characteristics (see also Garrison & Earls, 1987):

1. Activity level—how much the child moves about during activities such as feeding, bathing, sleeping, and playing

2. Rhythmicity—the regularity or predictability with which the child eats, sleeps, eliminates, and so on

3. Approach or withdrawal—how the child responds initially to new events such as people, places, toys, and foods

4. Adaptability—how quickly the child becomes accustomed to or modifies an initial reaction to new situations or stimuli

5. Intensity of reaction—the amount of energy expended in reacting (positively or negatively) to situations or stimuli

6. Threshold of responsiveness—the amount or intensity of stimulation required to elicit a response from the child

7. Quality of mood—the amount of pleasant, joyful, and friendly behavior compared with unpleasant, crying, and unfriendly behavior exhibited by the child

8. Distractibility—the frequency with which extraneous or irrelevant stimuli interfere with the ongoing behavior of the child in a given situation

9. Attention span and persistence—the length of time a child will spend on a given activity and the tendency to maintain an activity in the face of obstacles to performance

Chess, Thomas, and their colleagues found that children with any kind of temperament might develop emotional or behavioral disorders, depending on the child-rearing practices of their parents and other adults. Children with difficult temperaments, however, were more likely to develop troublesome behavior. For their subjects, a difficult temperament was characterized by irregularity in biological functioning, mostly negative (withdrawing) responses to new stimuli, slow adaptation to changes in the environment, frequent display of negative mood, and a predominance of intense reactions. A difficult temperament may elicit negative responses from a child's caretakers: a baby with a difficult temperament is not easy to care for and may increase parents' irritability, negative mood, and tendency to ignore or punish the child. If infant and parents adopt a pattern of mutual irritation, their negative interactions may increase the probability that the youngster will exhibit inappropriate or undesirable behavior in future years (see also Carey & McDevitt, 1994; Chess & Thomas, 1977). Later longitudinal research by other investigators has also shown that difficult temperament at an early age is predictive of behavior problems in adolescence (Caspi, Henry, McGee, Moffitt, & Silva, 1995). Moreover, easy or positive temperament has been found to be associated with children's resilience in responding to stress (Smith & Prior, 1995).

The concept of difficult temperament has its critics (see Garrison & Earls, 1987). Some suggest that what researchers believe are inborn biological characteristics of infants are merely the subjective interpretations of mothers' reports. That is, "difficult temperament" reflects social perceptions of an infant's behavior and may not be within-the-individual characteristics. A baby is said to have a difficult temperament on the basis of the mother's report rather than on the basis of more objective evaluations; therefore, the mother's perceptions (and the researcher's) are being assessed, rather than a biological characteristic of the baby. Thomas, Chess, and Korn (1982) and others, however, interpret their research as confirming the reality of inborn behavioral characteristics or temperaments that are altered by environmental conditions (see Rutter, 1995).

Carey and McDevitt (1995) note the emerging consensus regarding the interaction of environmental and inborn factors in shaping children's behavior:

1. Environmental effects such as family dysfunction, neighborhood violence, poor schools, and other unfortunate conditions are responsible for a substantial proportion of children's behavioral disorders.

2. Intrinsic factors explain some disorders formerly thought to be caused by the social environment. We now understand, for example, that autism and learning disabilities and, perhaps, other problems such as obesity are caused primarily by

biological processes. These disorders are likely to exist under a wide range of environmental conditions.

3. A poor fit between a child's normal temperament and the values and expectations of the child's caregivers can cause stress leading to emotional or behavioral disorder.

Both environmental and intrinsic, biological factors contribute to emotional or behavioral disorders. Environmental and intrinsic factors combine to shape temperament. Moreover, a mismatch of social environment and the child's behavioral style can exacerbate a difficult temperament. A difficult temperament may increase a child's risk of exhibiting an emotional or behavioral disorder, but the risk may be either heightened further or lowered by the way parents and teachers manage the child's behavior (Kochanska, 1995).

A few researchers have investigated teachers' ratings of children's temperaments in the classroom (see Martin, 1992; Martin et al., 1986; Paget, Nagle, & Martin, 1984; Pullis, 1989). Their general findings are that children do exhibit a consistent behavioral style or temperament in the classroom and that teachers tend to take children's temperaments into account in planning, instruction, and management. Pullis and Cadwell (1985) found that teachers take temperament into consideration in making decisions regarding instruction and behavior management, such as what group situation will best accommodate the student or choosing consequences for behavior. They found no relationship between temperament ratings and decisions regarding students' identification for special education placement.

Three primary temperament characteristics have emerged from teachers' classroom ratings:

■ *Task orientation*, related to the child's ability to stay in seat during working activities, persist on tasks until they are completed, and resist distraction

■ *Adaptability*, related to the child's positive reaction to new stimuli, appropriate modification of behavior when changes occur in routines, and positive response during social interactions

■ *Reactivity*, related to the child's tendency to overreact to stressful circumstances and become very upset when frustrated (Pullis & Cadwell, 1982, 1985)

Pullis (1989) suggests that knowledge of students' temperaments can help teachers manage their own negative feelings about students' behavior, devise accommodations to improve the fit of the classroom to students' temperaments, and find ways to capitalize on students' strengths while helping them compensate for their weaknesses.

Temperament may play a significant role in the development of emotional or behavioral disorders, but it does so only in interaction with environmental conditions. A consistent behavioral disposition or temperament such as irritability or impulsivity, may heighten risk for emotional or behavioral disorders. Research does not indicate that temperament is the direct or exclusive result of biological factors, but it does suggest that students exhibit a consistent behavioral style that teachers recognize and should consider in planning instruction (Martin, 1992).

PHYSICAL ILLNESS

Physical health, emotions, and behavior are connected in complex ways. Old ideas about *psychophysiological disorders*—physical disorders thought to be caused by emotional conflict—have given way to evidence that physical disorders are very seldom, if ever, caused directly by psychopathology but that intense emotions and inappropriate behavior can put someone at risk for physical illness and that physical illness can have serious effects on emotions and behavior.

One's physical well-being can have a profound effect on emotional status and behavior. For example, illness often has the effect of making a person irritable, anxious, or depressed. However, behavior also affects emotions and physical health. For example, engaging in high-risk behavior may increase our anxiety or result in injury or illness, and our behavior when we are ill may slow or speed our treatment or recovery. Illness or injury may affect emotions and behavior directly and immediately, but the after-effects (sequelae) are also important. In short, "not only may children and families experience negative psychological sequelae (e.g., depression) in response to a specific pediatric condition, but behavioral factors have also been demonstrated to be integral in determining the onset, course, and prognosis of many disorders and injuries" (Tarnowski & Brown, 1995, p. 393).

One of the effects of serious injury or illness is often a high level of anxiety about medical treatment (Prins, 1994). Anxiety and depression, including social withdrawal or disrupted peer relationships and schooling, are thus not unusual outcomes of physical illness (Garrison & McQuiston, 1989). However, research clearly shows that no particular psychological response or personality type is associated with physical illness and that psychological problems are not necessarily related to the severity of an injury or illness.

> We have learned that there is no one pattern of psychological response to a specific pediatric illness or injury. Children with the same health problem present with unique patterns of psychological strength and vulnerability. Alternatively, children with vastly different illnesses may evidence marked similarity in their behavioral responding (e.g., withdrawal, disrupted peer relations). Early research in the area of psychological aspects of pediatric disorders attempted to identify "personality" profiles or typical pattern of responding that would characterize children with specific disorders (e.g., asthmatic personality). These attempts were not fruitful. Subsequent research has also taught us that although specific illness and injury variables are important in understanding and conceptualizing a particular case, such variables by themselves often are of little predictive value. (Garrison & McQuiston, 1989, p. 408)

The emotional and behavioral responses of children and youths to physical illness depend on a variety of factors, including family support, coping strategies, and environmental conditions. Educators should understand that a student who is physically ill or injured may have—but will not necessarily have—emotional or behavioral problems as a result. When such emotional or behavioral problems arise, teachers should work with the student's family and health care professionals to address both the physical and emotional or behavioral aspects of the illness.

IMPLICATIONS FOR EDUCATORS

It is erroneous to assume that all emotional or behavioral disorders have a biological origin and that, therefore, all such disorders are best handled by medical intervention. Not only is the tie between many of these disorders and biological causative factors tenuous, but a biological cause may have no direct implications for change in educational methodology. Educators should work with other professionals to obtain the best possible medical care, nutrition, and physical environment for their students. However, educators cannot provide medical intervention, and they have only very limited influence over their students' physical health. Although teachers should be aware of possible biological factors and refer students for evaluation by other professionals when appropriate, they must not allow speculation regarding biological etiologies to excuse them from teaching appropriate behavior—the academic and social skills that will enable students to be happy and successful in everyday environments.

Pharmacological treatment of many emotional and behavioral disorders is becoming more common, systematic, and effective (Campbell & Cueva, 1995a, 1995b; Forness & Kavale, 1988; Gadow & Pomeroy, 1991; Wiener, 1996). Medications can be extremely helpful in controlling some emotional or behavioral disorders. Unfortunately, there appears to be a strong antimedication bias among many educators. Part of this bias may be due to teachers' lack of awareness of the purposes and possible benefits of medications, and to teachers' failure to understand that careful monitoring of classroom behavior is necessary to determine whether the drug is working, should be discontinued, or needs a dosage adjustment to obtain maximum benefits with minimum side effects. Although the teacher is not able to prescribe medications or adjust dosages, the teacher's observations provide critical information for the physician. Teachers should be aware of the major types of drugs that may be prescribed for their students and the possible effects and side effects those drugs may have on classroom behavior and performance. Table 7.1 provides examples of four major types of medication and *some* of their possible effects. The generic (chemical) name is shown in parentheses under the brand or trade name for each example listed.

Table 7.1 provides only a limited amount of information. Teachers should seek additional facts relevant to particular cases. There are many other categories and subcategories of psychotropic drugs, new drugs are constantly being introduced, and the effects and side effects of a given drug may vary greatly depending on the dosage level and the individual. The teacher should consult a nurse, a physician, or professional publications for more detailed information about specific drugs and dosages (e.g., Campbell & Cueva, 1995a, 1995b; DuPaul, Guevremont, & Barkley, 1991; Gadow, 1986; Gadow & Pomeroy, 1991). A student's parents or physician should inform the teacher that the student is taking a particular medication and ask the teacher to monitor its effects on the student's classroom behavior and academic performance. If the teacher is not so informed and is not asked to participate in evaluating the drug's classroom effects but becomes aware that the student is taking a psychotropic medication, he or she should approach the parents or the school nurse about monitoring the way the student is responding to the drug.

Table 7.1
Four Types of Psychotropic Medication and Some Possible Classroom Effects

Class of Drugs	Examples	Possible Classroom Effects
Stimulants	Ritalin (methylphenidate) Dexedrine (dextroamphetamine) Cylert (pemoline)	Increased attention and decreased need for teacher control; effects usually evident within a few hours after ingestion; effects may last for up to 8 hours with time-release capsules; possible side effects include headaches, stomachaches, or increased irritability; too high dosage can decrease learning.
Neuroleptics or Antipsychotics (major tranquilizers)	Thorazine (chlorpromazine) Mellaril (thioridazine) Prolixin (fluphenazine) Haldol (haloperidol) Navane (thiothixene)	Effects usually gradual; decreased aggression or agitation and decreased hallucination within days; increased socialization within 3 to 4 weeks; decreased thought disorder within 2 months; side effects may include tremors, drowsiness, decreased attention.
Antidepressants	Tofranil (imipramine) Prozac (fluoxetine) Wellbutrim (bupropion)	Classroom effects not yet extensively studied; effects may not be seen for 1 to 4 weeks; may increase communication and attention to tasks, decrease disruptiveness; side effects vary widely with drug.
Anticonvulsants	Luminal (phenobarbital) Tegretol (carbamazepine) Dilantin (phenytoin) Mysoline (primidone) Zarontin (ethosuximide) Depaken (valporic acid)	Effects evident in a day or not for weeks, depending on type of seizure and drug; primary objective is decrease in frequency of seizure; side effects may include drowsiness, irritability, hyperactivity, aggression, and impairment of memory or thinking.

SUMMARY

Biological factors have special appeal because all behavior involves biochemical, neurological activity. Among the many biological factors that may contribute to the origins of emotional or behavioral disorders are genetics, brain damage or dysfunction, malnutrition or allergies, temperament, and physical illness.

Genetic factors have been suggested as the causes of nearly every type of disorder. Genetics are known to be involved in causing schizophrenia, but little is known about how the gene system that causes the disorder works. Environmental factors appear to trigger schizophrenia in individuals who are genetically vulnerable. The fact that a disorder has a genetic cause does not mean that the disorder is untreatable.

Brain damage or dysfunction has been suggested as a cause of nearly every type of emotional or behavioral disorder. Traumatic brain injury (TBI) involves known damage to the brain and may cause a wide variety of emotional and behavioral problems. Autism is now recognized as a biological disorder, although neither the exact nature nor the reason for the brain dysfunction are known. In both TBI and autism, environmental conditions can be significant in managing the disorder.

Severe malnutrition has devastating effects on young children's development. However, the popular notion that many emotional or behavioral disorders are caused by diet or allergies has not been supported by a consistent body of research. Teachers should be aware of possible dietary problems and allergies of students, but concern for these possible causes should not distract attention from instructional procedures.

Temperament is a consistent behavioral style or predisposition to respond in certain ways to one's environment. Although temperament may have a biological basis, it is shaped also by environmental factors. Skillful management by parents and teachers can lower the risk of emotional or behavioral disorders associated with difficult temperament.

Physical illness may contribute to emotional or behavioral problems, but emotions and behavior may also contribute to illness. The relationships among physical illness, emotions, and behavior are complex, and there is no simple way of predicting what effect illness will have on emotional status or behavior.

When biological factors contribute to emotional or behavioral disorders, they do not operate in isolation from or independently of environmental (psychological) forces. The most tenable view at this time is that biological and environmental factors interact with one another to cause disorders. It seems reasonable to propose a continuum of biological causes ranging from minor, undetectable, organic faults to profound accidents of nature and a related continuum of emotional or behavioral disorders ranging from mild to profound to which these biological accidents contribute. Implications of biological factors for the day-to-day work of teachers may in some cases be nil, but teachers should be aware of possible biological causes and refer students to other professionals when appropriate. Teachers should be aware of the possible effects and side effects of psychotropic medications and be involved in monitoring drug effects.

Case for Discussion

"She Goes On and On"

Elizabeth (continued)

Sometimes I go on and on when I talk, and people have a hard time understanding what I am talking about. My family is always saying to me "You're going on and on." This is supposed to be a clue to me to stop talking, or that nobody is understanding what I am talking about. My brother says that nobody wants to hear all the things I have to say, but brothers talk that way to sisters all the time.

Actually that was one of the first clues my doctor had as to what was wrong with me. I had lots of problems, but they didn't have a name. My first psychiatrist thought I had attention deficit disorder because I had so much trouble paying attention and getting my work done. But one time when I was going on and on, my mother said that the listener had to share the experience with me to be able to understand what I was talking about, and even then it was hard. My doctor said that was a serious symptom and then he asked if I was hearing voices. When I said yes, he said I needed to be hospitalized for evaluation, and that was a very serious problem. My parents were scared out of their wits.

I still go on and on. I have trouble writing too. I leave words out of sentences, or I don't finish writing a word. Then, of course, the sentences don't make any sense. Sometimes my sentences get really long. I guess I go on and on in writing too. I cannot write more than one or two paragraphs because I get really confused. [This case is taken from Anonymous (1994), p. 589. Other parts of Elizabeth's story are found in chapters 1, 4, and 5.]

Questions About the Case

1. Imagine that Elizabeth is in your tenth-grade class. Would knowing that she has schizophrenia and is taking medication for it make a difference in how you respond to her going on an on? If not, why not? If so, how?

2. As her teacher, what strategies might you try to help Elizabeth learn to converse more normally (i.e., not to go on and on)?

3. If Elizabeth were a student in a regular tenth-grade class, how would you help her classmates respond kindly and helpfully to her when she goes on and on?

PERSONAL REFLECTIONS

Biological Factors

Nirbhay N. Singh, Ph.D., is Professor of Psychiatry and Pediatrics and Director of Research at the Medical College of Virginia in Richmond, Virginia.

What emotional or behavioral disorders have a known biological cause?

There is probably a biological basis for most, if not all, such *disorders*, but not for emotional or behavioral *problems*. Our knowledge of the causal relationship between biological variables and specific disorders is not very sophisticated, but there has been increasing research interest in this area. Basic research has provided us with a reasonable understanding of the biological bases of some disorders, but not of others. The slow progress we have made in identifying markers and, eventually, the biological basis of disorders such as schizophrenia and depression, is probably because these disorders typically have been seen as discrete entities, each with its own causation, symptomology, and course. This narrow view fails to appreciate the fact that disturbances associated with a number of disorders may be indicative of a specific biological dysfunction. Thus, the focus of current research is gradually shifting from investigating the biological basis of discrete disorders to dysfunctions in biological mechanisms that may account for the behavioral and psychological aberrations evident across several disorders. Research on serotonin and catecholamines provide excellent examples of this approach.

Taking the serotonin research as an example, we know that disturbances in central 5–Hydroxytryptophan (5–HT) metabolism were first reported in depression. Subsequently, it was found that disturbances in 5–HT were also associated with other disorders. For example, serotonin is now regarded as being potentially involved in several disorders, including anxiety, obsessive-compulsive behavior, aggression, depression, violence and suicide, and eating disorders. One implication of this research is that eventually we may be able to discover drugs that can selectively correct the biological dysfunctions, irrespective of the emotional or behavioral disorder.

What are the most important signs that a child should be referred for a neurological examination?

There are two types of neurological signs—hard and soft—suggestive of brain damage. Those that provide a clear indication of cerebral dysfunction are known as hard signs and usually can be correlated to other evidence of brain damage, such as scans using computerized tomography, positron emission tomography, and magnetic resonance imaging, or from electroencephalograms. Those that indicate mild and equivocal neurological irregularities are known as soft signs. These irregularities may include poor balance, impaired fine motor coordination, clumsiness, and jerky limb movements.

Conditions indicating a possible need for referral for a neurological examination include developmental delay, headaches, motor disturbances, mood abnormalities, sleep disorders, learning disability, hyperactivity, and a host of behavioral problems that may be organic or psychogenic in origin. Given that the major goals of neurological examination are to determine whether there is an abnormality in function and, if there is, to determine the site of the lesion in one or more areas of the nervous system, it is somewhat questionable whether this information will make any difference in the child's educational or psychological management. Indeed, a teacher can't do much about neurological disorders (such as cerebral palsy and idiopathic seizures) that will have a direct impact on the child's education.

If a student is taking medication, what are the responsibilities of the teacher?

Teachers may find that several of their students are on either psychotropic or anticonvulsant medication, so it behooves them to have some basic knowledge of these and other medications. They should be familiar with the types, dosages, general desired effects, and side effects. Knowing this is important because a drug doesn't affect all children's behavior in the same way, and different dosages of a drug may have different effects on behavior. Knowledge of serious side effects that may impair adaptive behavior, affect, and learning allows teachers to interact appropriately with students who are on medication.

Teachers are a prime source of information about the effects of medication on a student's learning and behavior during school hours. They are responsible for providing such information to the student's doctor, who can use it to change the medication, alter the dosage, or choose an alternative treatment. Teachers should fully participate in any clinical decisions regarding the drug treatment of their students. If they don't, the physician may write a prescription that is not responsive to the student's needs in the classroom. Teachers are often seen by members of a multidisciplinary team as the professional who is in the best position to provide coordination between the doctor, parents, and school regarding a student's treatment.

A student who is taking prescribed medication for an emotional or behavioral disorder may need to take it during school hours. Depending on school policy, teachers may be required to monitor whether the student has either been given the medication by the nurse or has self-administered it. In some cases, teachers are responsible for actually giving the medication to a student. Thus, teachers may be responsible not only for evaluating the effects of medication but also for making sure that the student actually receives it at school.

Under what conditions do you think medication should be considered as a possible treatment for an emotional or behavioral disorder?

Clearly, the answer depends on one's treatment philosophy. My own belief is that a thorough assessment and diagnosis of the emotional or behavioral disorder is essential in determining the treatment of choice. First, if the assessment indicates that we are dealing with a behavior problem that is essentially rooted in faulty learning, a behavioral treatment is indicated and should be tried first. If this fails, then medication may be indicated. Second, if there is a well-established biological basis for the problem, then medication is indicated and should be tried. Indeed, in some cases there is no alternative. For example, at present there is no alternative to medication for delusional disorders. In other cases, where there is some indication that alternative treatment modalities exist, these may be tried before medication. An example would be the treatment of hyperactive behavior, which can often be treated with behavioral procedures either alone or in combination with medication.

The choice of treatment is often made on the basis of immediacy of response, side effects, and maintenance of the treatment effects. For example, we know that a number of cognitive-behavioral treatments can be used to treat depression, but often these take such a long time to show any effects that medication may be the more attractive alternative because of its more rapid response.

Are there other points you would like to make about this topic?

First, I think we are entering an era when there will be a lot of emphasis on the biological bases of behavior and we will see some clinical fruits of this labor within a short time. Our understanding of the basic mechanisms of behavior at the molecular level is changing so rapidly that it is difficult to synthesize all the available research to see what it all means. Nevertheless, when we remove the "noise" from this research, the single most exciting finding is that large clusters of symptoms indicative of various disorders can be traced to dysfunctions within a single biological system. For example, diminished dopamine, serotonin, and noradrenaline metabolism in psychiatric disorders is not disorder-specific but is related to psychopathological dimensions irrespective of psychiatric classification. This means that in the future we may focus more on functions of biological systems instead of present psychiatric classification systems. The clinical implications are that more emphasis will be placed on functional psychopathology and treatment will focus on psychological disturbances rather than on psychiatric symptoms per se. Indeed, psychiatric symptoms are behavioral expressions of psychological dysfunction and not the dysfunction itself. Thus, a visual hallucination is a symptom—a particular perceptual disturbance of the underlying psychological dysfunction—and it is the perceptual disturbance, not the hallucination, that should be the focus of research and treatment efforts. In terms of drug treatment, the implications are clear. Drugs will be chosen for their ability to influence a particular functional system in the brain and, thus, a particular psychological disturbance, irrespective of the psychiatric diagnosis.

Second, I would like to emphasize that medication does not teach the student any new skills; good teachers do. Medication merely acts as a setting event for the occurrence of acceptable behavior. Reducing behavior problems or controlling emotional and behavioral disorders through medication allows the teacher to teach the student appropriate social and academic skills. As far as these disorders are concerned, medication provides symptomatic relief, allowing the student to function more fully at school and at home. Further, medication may relieve the student's symptoms, but it does not remove vulnerability to the disorder; the environmental and constitutional stresses that gave rise to the disorder are not affected by medication.

Third, teachers with a behavioral perspective often do not see any place for medication in controlling the behavior problems of their students. Although I empathize with this view because of my own behavioral bias, I also see it as a very narrow view of behavioral treatment and alternatives. True, the majority of behavior problems can be treated with nonpharmacological methods. However, a small group of children have problems so complex that current behavioral treatments are simply inadequate. For example, some cases of severe self-injury, violence, and suicide attempts, among others, currently cannot be treated with nonpharmacological means. A combination of medication with other treatments often provides the best results. The anti-medication view is a problem of teachers not having adequate knowledge of the efficacy of various treatment modalities because these issues have not been adequately covered in their teacher preparation courses or in-service programs. Current research shows that over 95 percent of teachers would love to have in-service training on medication and its alternatives.

8

Family Factors

As you read this chapter, keep these guiding questions in mind:

- Is the family considered an important source of disordered emotions and behavior?

- How are vulnerability and risk factors related to the development of emotional or behavioral disorders?

- What are the implications of an interactional-transactional model of family influence for families with abused children?

- Why might we need to revise assumptions about the strengths and weaknesses of the traditional family form?

- How could one characterize the most and least desirable types of parental discipline?

- What is a negative reinforcement trap?

- How are coercive family interactions related to the development of antisocial behavior?

- How might parenting practices contribute to child abuse?

- What external influences affect interaction in families?

- How can parents foster school success or school failure?

THE APPEAL OF FAMILY FACTORS AS CAUSAL EXPLANATIONS

All societies consider the family a central factor in early personality development and learning. At least in Western societies, parents have traditionally been held responsible for their children's conduct, usually until they reach late adolescence. When youngsters misbehave, our natural tendency is to blame parental mismanagement or family disintegration. Given the primacy of family relations in children's social development, it is understandable that we have sought the origins of emotional and behavioral disorders in the structure, composition, and interactions of family units. These elements do not, however, provide a straightforward recipe for predicting emotional or behavioral disorders. Like other causal factors, those related to the family are complex and intertwined with other biological and social factors. Our experience of family is influenced by genetic factors as well as by a wide variety of environmental events (Plomin, 1995). We must guard against adopting oversimplifications and facile explanations of "familial determinants" of emotional and behavioral disorders.

> "Familial Determinants" seems to suggest that social scientists have already identified a cookbook of family factors that reliably lead to psychopathology in children. Although it may be an exaggeration to say that social scientists have discovered the recipe for family factors that may lead to child psychopathology, it is probably safe to say that we can now identify the primary "ingredients." (Reitman & Gross, 1995, p. 87)

Family characteristics appear to predict emotional and behavioral development only in complex interactions with other factors, such as socioeconomic status, sources of support outside the family, and the child's age, sex, and temperamental characteristics. The concept of **risk** is important here: the idea that in examining causal factors we are dealing with probabilities and that particular events or conditions may be factors increasing the **probability** that there will be a particular outcome for the child, such as an emotional or behavioral disorder. When several risk factors occur together—for example, poverty, parental antisocial behavior, community violence, and difficult temperament—their effects are not merely additive but multiplicative. That is, two such factors occurring together more than double the probability that a child will develop a disorder; if a third factor is added, the chance of disorder is several times higher yet (Garmezy, 1987).

Rutter's reviews of research on maternal deprivation (1979) and attachment (1995) and Plomin's (1995) review of the role of genetics in children's experiences in the family highlight some of the complexities in family influences. A tempting conclusion, for example, is that separation of the child from one or both parents always works serious mischief with a youngster's psychological and behavioral development. But that conclusion is not valid, because a variety of other circumstances must be taken into account. In an intact family, parental discord may exert a more pernicious influence than parental separation. A good relationship with one parent may sustain a child even in the face of parental discord or separation. The interaction of the child's constitutional or temperamental characteristics with parental behavior may be more important than parental separation or disharmony. In addition, factors outside the home (school, for instance) may lessen or heighten the negative influence of family factors.

For some reason, some children do not succumb to extreme disruption or disintegration of their families (Hetherington & Martin, 1986). Some children are amazingly invulnerable: events or conditions that increase the risk for most youngsters simply do not faze them. We do not know precisely why some children are vulnerable and others invulnerable to negative family influences. A positive, or easy, child temperament (recall our discussion of temperament in chapter 7) and maternal warmth appear to be factors that may heighten resilience (Smith & Prior, 1995), but they may be insufficient to buffer children against psychopathology in violent families (McCloskey, Figueredo, & Koss, 1995). Research also suggests that high cognitive skills, curiosity, enthusiasm, ability to set goals for oneself, and high self-esteem are associated with resilience (Hanson & Carta, 1995).

We know that certain features of family relationships, especially parental deviance and discord, harsh and unpredictable parental discipline, and lack of emotional support, increase children's risk for developing emotional or behavioral disorders. Yet a family environment that creates high risk does not necessarily cause a child to have a disorder. Causation is more complex than that.

Old stereotypes of parents who transmit developmental disorders to their children have yielded to newer research findings. Recall that in chapter 7 we noted that autism is no longer considered a disorder caused by parental rejection. Decades ago, mothers of children with schizophrenia were often thought to be **schizophrenogenic**, especially if they themselves had schizophrenia; they were thought to mother their children in ways that caused them to develop the disorder. The work of Sameroff et al. (1982) confirmed the complex interaction of many variables in the origins of schizophrenia and indicates that parental pathology alone seldom, if ever, accounts for children's problems. Sameroff and his colleagues studied the infants and young children of several hundred mentally ill women and concluded that no simple biological or environmental model can account for the transmission of schizophrenia. In particular, their data appear to refute the notion that schizophrenic mothers cause their children to be mentally ill: "It is our impression from watching our sample of chronic schizophrenics rearing their children for the first few years of life that among their many incompetencies is the incompetence to make their children crazy" (p. 65). Their data indicate that children of parents with schizophrenia are indeed at risk for disordered behavior. However, poor economic circumstance, low social status, unstable family organization, and a parent's prolonged, severe mental disturbance, regardless of the specific diagnosis of schizophrenia, were more notable risk factors than being reared by a parent with schizophrenia. These findings are consistent with more recent research on the risk of developing schizophrenia and other disorders (cf. Gottesman, 1991; Plomin, 1995; Rutter, 1995).

The concept of **heightened risk**, as opposed to a simple cause-effect relationship, is important in all types of disordered behavior, not just schizophrenia. We can best understand risk in terms of a conceptual model of family influence. What happens in families in which risk of emotional or behavioral disorder is high? We can answer this question in general terms, but we cannot make confident predictions of outcomes for individual children for two reasons. First, each child is affected individually by the family environment. "Environmental influences do not operate on a family-by-family basis but rather on an individual-by-individual basis. They are specific to each child rather than general for an entire family" (Plomin, 1989, p. 109). Second, whether life circumstances or environmental conditions are positive or negative for a child, and whether they heighten or reduce the child's risk of emotional or behavioral disorders, depends on the **processes** involved. Processes or mechanisms—not merely the presence of risk variables, but how children *cope* with *degrees* and *patterns* of exposure to those variables—determine how vulnerable or resilient a child will be. Rutter (1990) says the following about how certain stressful life experiences might protect one child against emotional or behavioral disorders but leave another child vulnerable.

> Life involves unavoidable encounters with all manner of stressors and adversities. It is not realistic to suppose that children can be so sheltered that they can avoid such encounters. Rather, protection may lie in the "steeling" qualities that derive from success in coping with the hazards when the exposure is of a type and degree that is manageable in the context of the child's capacities and social situation. This aspect of protection has been little explored up to now in relation to psychosocial hazards, and it warrants further investigation. (p. 203)

We understand little about the processes involved in producing vulnerability and resilience, but a key ingredient for each individual appears to be the pattern, sequence, and intensity of exposure to stressful circumstances. We do know that the accumulation of stressful life events is an important factor in determining how a child will be able to cope. Stressful life events may occur within the family, but they are related to the larger social environment in which the family itself must function as a unit. Therefore, it is important to consider both the interpersonal interactions or transactions that occur between the child and other family members and the external pressures on the family that may affect those interactions.

Whereas the research of 30 years ago tended to focus on the typical style of interaction in families—general processes or overall interactional styles thought to be the basis for the development of child psychopathology—recent research has examined more specific, focused interactions that may contribute to causing emotional or behavioral disorders or intensify them. The empirical evidence increasingly points to social learning as the basis for many emotional and behavioral disorders; research suggests that parental modeling, reinforcement, and punishment of specific types of behavior hold the keys to how families influence children's behavioral development. Dadds (1995) summarized the evidence as follows:

> The evidence . . . shows that family processes that are closely linked to the specific behavioral problems of the child appear to be far more important than more general aspects of the family's style. For each of the disorders reviewed [childhood depression, conduct problems, anxiety, somatic complaints], evidence was clearly supportive of a model in which parents appear to model, prompt, and provide contingent attention to the particular behavioral problem the child has. Parents of aggressive children reward aggression and ignore prosocial behavior; parents of depressed children appear to reward self-denigration and model depressive cognitive style; parents of anxious children appear to model fear and avoidance and reward caution. This is not to say that parents are causing the child's problem, especially not intentionally. Rather, it appears that parents become trapped into a cycle with the child in which the behavioral problem becomes an important, if not dominating, focus for the way in which the family interacts. (p. 84)

Politicians of the late-twentieth century have highlighted "family values," and discussions of family and familial determinants of children's behavior is therefore fraught with possibilities for "sound bite" analyses and highly emotional reactions. Moreover, perspectives on nearly every aspect of the family are embedded in cultural values, which advises caution in drawing conclusions about family and parental characteristics that are deemed "good." Nevertheless, we must begin with a discussion of the question, "What is a family?"

Having considered the definition of family and the effects of family structure, we turn to interaction in families—the interpersonal transactions involved in child management and discipline that may affect children's behavior for good or ill. Families may influence school success or school failure, and we note how they may do so. Families do not exist or function in a vacuum, free of external pressures, and we therefore note also how family interactions may be shaped by external influences, such as poverty and parental employment. Finally, we discuss the implications for educators of what we know about families, especially the families of children and youths with emotional or behavioral disorders. The scope and complexity of family-related research are enormous, and many details of the topic are left untouched in our review.

FAMILY DEFINITION AND STRUCTURE

Although the intact mother-father-children concept of family remains the ideal in mainstream American culture, discrepancies from this ideal are common and increasing in our multicultural society. We may need to revise our traditional assumptions about the strengths and weakness of diverse family forms to fit the realities of contemporary life (Hanson & Carta, 1996; Hetherington & Camara, 1984; Reitman & Gross, 1995). Radke-Yarrow (1990) suggested that function is more important than structure in defining family, that the essential functions of families are to do the following things:

- Provide care and protect children.
- Regulate and control children's behavior.
- Convey knowledge and skills important for understanding and coping with the physical and social worlds.
- Give affective meaning to interactions and relationships.
- Facilitate children's self-understanding.

Hanson and Lynch (1992) propose that regardless of how families define themselves, the key elements of the definition of family are that "the members of the unit see themselves as a family, are affiliated with one another, and are committed to caring for one another" (p. 285). Given these considerations, it may be important to examine whether or to what extent family structure affects children's behavior.

The effects of family size and birth order on behavioral development have been studied extensively, but such elements of family configuration are far outweighed by factors related to divorce and other circumstances resulting in single-parent homes or other nontraditional family structures (cf. Hetherington & Martin, 1986). Family composition or configuration may have an effect on children's behavior (Achenbach et al., 1991), but other factors involving interactions among family members and the social contexts in which they live appear to be far more important contributors to behavior problems. However, we briefly examine the effects of single-parent families and substitute care (e.g., foster care, adoption, care by relatives other than parents) on children's behavior.

Single-Parent Families

A substantial proportion of children are now reared in single-parent families, usually due to divorce but also often due to out-of-wedlock births. Census data from the 1990s indicated that nearly one fourth of U.S. families with children under the age of 18 were headed by single mothers. Many children are being reared by parents who themselves are little more than children, often under adverse environmental conditions and in the context of family discord (Hanson & Carta, 1996). True, many single parents raise their children under adverse conditions, such as poverty or community violence, that are known risk factors. The question we are addressing here, however, is this: Is the presence of only one parent in a family a significant factor in putting children at risk for emotional or behavioral disorders? We begin by considering the effects of divorce on children's behavior.

Divorce is traumatic, not only for parents and children but for extended family and friends as well. The lasting psychological pain and fear felt by many children whose parents divorce are well known (Bolgar, Zweig-Frank, & Paris, 1995; Wallerstein, 1987), along with the increased susceptibility of adolescents of divorced parents to negative peer pressure, even when the family is reconstituted with a stepparent (Steinberg, 1987). Yet the overwhelming finding is that most children adjust to divorce and go on with their lives without developing chronic emotional or behavioral problems. "Most children manifest some disturbances—often a combination of anger, anxiety, depression, dependency, and noncompliance—in the immediate aftermath of divorce; however, most children and adults also recover and adjust to their new life situation by about three years after divorce" (Hetherington & Martin, 1986, p. 340).

How children adjust to divorce depends on a variety of circumstances besides family dissolution, including the child's age when the divorce occurs, the child's level of attachment to the custodial parent and to the noncustodial parent, level of parent conflict prior to and following the divorce, characteristics of the custodial parent, details of custody and visitation rights, behavior of the visiting parent, economic circumstances of the custodial parent, sources of extrafamilial support for members of the partial family, and the child's cognitive and affective characteristics related to coping with stress (see Johnson, 1986). There is no general formula for predicting child psychopathology following divorce, but it is clear that many children and adolescents whose parents are divorced have lower scholastic aptitude, perform less well in school, and have less confidence in their academic abilities than do youngsters from intact families (Watt, Moorehead-Slaughter, Japzon, & Keller, 1990).

Boys in families headed by mothers alone may be at risk for developing aggressive behavior (Vaden-Kiernan, Kalongo, Pearson, & Kellam, 1995). Among the family configurations found by Achenbach et al. (1991) to be significantly related to higher behavior problem ratings of children were: "fewer adults in the household; more unrelated adults in the household; parents who were separated, divorced, or never married to each other" (p. 92). These findings are of concern, but the factors leading to single-parent families may be more important than single-parent configuration itself.

In short, children reared in single-parent families may be at higher risk than those reared in two-parent families, especially boys reared by single mothers. However, being reared in a single-parent family does not appear to play the primary role in family factors that produce children's maladaptive behavior. Far more important are the conditions that often accompany a household headed by a single parent, which is typically the mother. Economic hardship or impoverishment with its attendant deprivations, parental substance abuse or criminality, interpersonal conflict and violence, and lack of parental supervision and nurturing—these factors appear to shape children's behavior more significantly, regardless whether the family contains one parent or two (Baumrind, 1995; Ellwood & Stolberg, 1993). As Rutter (1995) noted:

Early writings on the risks associated with parental divorce and family break-up focused on the role of "loss" because that had received such an emphasis in early writings on attachment. Empirical findings have made clear, however, that the main risks do not stem from loss as such but rather from the discordant and disrupted relationships that tend to precede or follow the loss. . . . Loss is a risk indicator but it is not the major player in most risk mechanisms. (pp. 563-564)

Substitute Care

Children in foster care and those living with relatives who are not their parents appear to be at high risk for emotional or behavioral disorders and school-related problems (Pilowsky, 1995; Smucker, Kauffman, & Ball, 1996; Stein, Raegrant, Ackland, & Avison, 1994). Sheehan's (1993a, 1993b) description of foster care in New York City provides graphic detail about the stresses many foster children and foster parents face.

Some children are placed in substitute care due to the death or incapacitation of their parents, but the great majority—and an increasing percentage—are placed under the care of the child protection system due to their parents' neglect and abuse. Virtually never are children placed in any form of substitute care unless they have suffered trauma that is highly likely to result in at least short-term emotional or behavioral problems (except in the case of adopted infants). Abused children are known to have more behavior problems than those who are not maltreated (Feldman et al., 1995). Yet much remains unknown about why and how children are placed in protective care.

Researchers know astonishingly little about how children fare once they have become identified by child protection caseworkers. Where are they placed when the caseworker decides to remove them from the home? How many placements occur before a permanent home is found? How do these placements vary with the age of the child? What alternatives exist to foster care, and what are their consequences for children? (Thompson & Wilcox, 1995, p. 792)

A major problem in providing substitute care is finding or training caregivers who are highly motivated and skilled in child-rearing (Evans et al., 1994; Moore & Chamberlain, 1994). Many foster parents have little or no training for the task, and few are well trained in dealing with difficult children. Many foster children are placed for short periods in many different foster homes, and the risk for negative behavioral and emotional outcomes appears to increase with the number of different placements (see Smucker et al., 1996). The lack of stability, continuity, attachment, and nurturing that goes with numerous foster placements and unskilled foster parents is likely to promote emotional or behavioral disorders (Clark et al., 1994).

Adoptive families, like biological families, have a variety of structures. The influence of adoptive families on children's emotional and behavioral development can be predicted to parallel the influence of biological families. Controversy sometimes arises regarding the adequacy of adoption by single parents or adoptive families that involve differences in sexual orientation (e.g., gay fathers or lesbian mothers) or differences in the color or ethnicity of children and parents (e.g., Caucasian parents adopting children of color). Here, too, we might expect familial determinants to function as they do in any other family structures. For example, Tasker and Golombok (1995) found that being raised by a lesbian mother did not necessarily cause children to be maladjusted or to become gay or lesbian.

Research clearly suggests that family form by itself has relatively little affect on children's emotional and behavioral development. Although children reared in single-parent families may be at heightened risk, the risk factors appear to be conditions associated with a single-parent family structure, not single parenting itself. Being reared by substitutes for one's biological parents may be associated with heightened risk, but only insofar as abuse, neglect, or other traumatic circumstances affect children before they are removed from their biological parents or after the enter foster care. Far more important than family structure is what happens in the family—the interactions among family members, regardless of how the family is constituted.

FAMILY INTERACTION

When we think of family factors, our tendency is to ask, "What kinds of families produce children with emotional or behavioral disorders?" However, it is also reasonable to ask, "What kinds of families do children with emotional or behavioral disorders produce?" Child developmentalists now realize that children's influence on their parents' behavior is significant in determining family interactions. Researchers found decades ago that undesirable parenting behavior and negative family interactions are in part a reaction of family members to a deviant youngster (e.g., Bell, 1968; Bell & Harper, 1977; Martin, 1981; Patterson, 1982, 1986a, 1986b; Patterson et al., 1992; Sameroff & Chandler, 1975). As Martin (1975) stated:

> At the moment of birth, parent and child begin an interactive drama that will evolve its own unique character and destiny. Affection, joy, antagonism, openness, withdrawal, demands, and acquiescence will be interchanged according to each dyad's own pattern—a pattern that is likely to vary considerably according to circumstances and over time. (p. 463)

In this view of family behavior, interactions and transactions among individuals are the central theme in interpreting developmental data. The data include reinforcement, punishment, imitation, and other teaching transactions consistent with social cognitive theory. Emphasis is on reciprocity of influence from the earliest parent-child interactions and on the pervasiveness of reciprocal influences of parents and children in all subsequent interactions. We examine two issues in this interactional view of family behavior: child management and child abuse.

Child Management

Parental management or discipline comes up as a topic for discussion in children's emotional or behavioral disorders of every description. We shall return to family interactions as potential causal factors in each of the chapters in part 4. Here, we review general findings on parental management of children but focus attention on the role of family interactions in causing the disorder people usually consider first in discussions of family factors: the impulsive, aggressive, acting-out behavior generally known as **conduct disorder**. In fact, we know more about the effects of parental discipline on disruptive, oppositional, aggressive behavior than we do about the effects of parental behavior on children's anxiety, fear, and depression (O'Leary, 1995).

The effects of discipline techniques are complex and not highly predictable without considering both the parents' and the child's general behavioral characteristics and ongoing stress in the family (Campbell, 1995; Rutter, 1995). Nevertheless, we can suggest some general guidelines for discipline that can help parents avoid the types of interactions that research strongly suggests are mistakes, and these principles may hold across all cultural groups. For example, O'Leary (1995) identifies three types of mistakes typically made by mothers of 2- to 4-year-old children: laxness, overreactivity, and verbosity. "Laxness includes giving in, not enforcing rules, and providing positive reinforcement for misbehavior. Overreactivity includes anger, meanness, and irritability. Verbosity involves the propensity to engage in lengthy verbal interactions about misbehavior even when the talking is ineffective" (O'Leary, 1995, p. 12). Parents can be very "nice" to their children but ineffective in discipline because they are unable or unwilling to set consistent, firm, unambiguous limits. These parents may use long, delayed, gentle (but imprudent) reprimands that actually make the child's behavior worse. Others may make the mistake of using harsh reprimands but paying little attention to the child when he or she is behaving well.

Baumrind (1995) reviewed what decades of research on parental discipline in nonabusive middle-class families has shown (see also Campbell, 1995). Researchers describe two primary dimensions of discipline: *responsiveness* (which involves warmth, reciprocity, and attachment) and *demandingness* (involving monitoring, firm control, and positive and negative consequences for behavior). Parents who provide optimal management of their children are both highly responsive and highly demanding; they are highly "invested" in their children. More specifically, parents who discipline most effectively are sensitive to their children's needs, empathic, and attentive. They establish a pattern of mutually positive, reciprocal interactions with their children, and their warmth and reciprocity form the basis for emotional attachment or adult-child bonding. Yet these parents are also demanding of their children. They monitor their children's behavior, providing appropriately close supervision for the child's age. They confront their children's misbehavior directly and firmly rather than attempting to manipulate or coerce their children. They provide unambiguous instructions and demands in a firm but nonhostile manner and consistently follow through with negative but nonabusive consequences for misbehavior. They provide positive reinforcement in the form of praise, approval, encouragement, and other rewards for their children's desirable behavior.

Parental discipline that is both demanding and responsive is sometimes referred to as *authoritative* (as opposed to *authoritarian* discipline, which is demandingness without responsiveness) and is typically found to have the best effects on children's behavioral development. Authoritative discipline balances what is asked of the child with what is offered to the child, and this balance may be the key characteristic of effective parental discipline in various cultures (Abrams, 1995). It may be, in fact, the key to effective discipline by all caretakers of children, but it is not the pattern of interaction typically found in families of children who exhibit antisocial behavior.

The work of Patterson and his colleagues gives insight into the characteristics of interactions in the families of antisocial youngsters (Patterson, 1973, 1980, 1982, 1986a, 1986b; Patterson, Reid, & Dishion, 1992; Patterson et al., 1975). His research group's methods involve direct observation of parents' and children's behavior in the home, revealing an identifiable family pattern. They show that interaction in families with aggressive children is characterized by exchange of negative, hostile behaviors, whereas the interaction in families with nonaggressive children tends to be mutually positive and gratifying for parents and children. In the families with aggressive children, not only do the children behave in ways that are highly irritating and aversive to their parents, but the parents rely primarily on aversive methods (hitting, shouting, threatening, and so forth) to control their children. Thus, children's aggression in the family seems both to produce counteraggression and to be produced by punitive parenting techniques.

Patterson (1980) studied mutually aversive interactions between mothers and children, particularly in families of aggressive children, and found that many of the behaviors are maintained by negative reinforcement. **Negative reinforcement** involves escape from or avoidance of an unpleasant condition, which is rewarding (negatively reinforcing) because it brings relief from psychological or physical pain or anxiety. An example of negative reinforcement in mother-child interactions is shown in Table 8.1. Patterson calls these interactions *negative reinforcement traps* because they set the stage for greater conflict and coercion; each person in the trap tends to reciprocate the other's aversive behavior and to escalate attempts to use coercion—controlling someone by negative reinforcement. Patterson and his colleagues have found that, unlike normal children, problem children tend to increase their disruptive behavior in response to parental punishment. Predictably, therefore, the families of aggressive children seem to foster undesirable child behavior.

In effect, the members of families with aggressive children *train* each other to be aggressive. Although the major training occurs in transactions between an aggressive child and parent(s), it spills over to include siblings. Patterson (1986b) reports that siblings of an aggressive child are no more aggressive toward their parents than are children in families without an aggressive child. Interactions between siblings in families of antisocial youngsters, however, are more aggressive than those in families without an aggressive child. Coercive exchanges between aggressive children and their parents appear to teach siblings to be coercive with each other. Not surprisingly, these children then tend to be more aggressive in other social contexts, such as school. In fact, school conflict and school failure are frequently associated with antisocial behavior at home (cf. Patterson, 1986b; Stevenson-Hinde, Hinde, & Simpson, 1986).

What is the background of these coercive exchanges in families of aggressive children and the negative outcomes for their lives? How do these problems get started? The model emerging from Patterson's research group suggests that they arise from

Table 8.1
Some Reinforcement Traps

	Negative Reinforcement Arrangement		
Neutral Antecedent:	**Time Frame 1**	**Time Frame 2**	**Time Frame 3**
Behavior:	Mother ("clean your room")	Child (whine)	Mother (stops asking)
	Short Term Effect		Long Term Effect
Mother	The pain (child's Whine) stops		Mother will be more likely to give in when child whines
Child	The pain (mother's Nag) stops		Given a messy room, mother less likely to ask him to clean it up in the future
Overall	The room was not cleaned		Child more likely to use whine to turn off future requests to clean room

Explanation: Child's room is messy, an aversive condition for mother. When mother asks child to clean room, child whines. Child's whining is painfully aversive to mother, so mother stops asking or nagging. Mother's nagging is painfully aversive to child, who finds that his whining will stop mother's nagging. In short run, both mother and child escape pain—child stops whining and mother stops nagging—but child's room is not cleaned. In the long run, mother avoids asking child to clean room and child learns to use whining to stop mother's nagging. Both mother and child are negatively reinforced by avoidance of or escape from aversive consequences. However, problem condition (messy room) still exists as potential source of future negative interactions.

Source: From "Mothers: The Unacknowledged Victims" by G. R. Patterson, 1980. *Monographs of the Society for Research in Child Development, 45* (5, Serial no. 186), p. 5. Copyright 1980 by the University of Chicago Press. Reprinted by permission.

"failure by parents to effectively punish garden-variety, coercive behaviors" (Patterson, 1986b, p. 436). The child begins winning battles with the parents, and parents become increasingly punitive but ineffective in responding to coercion. Coercive exchanges escalate in number and intensity, increasing to hundreds per day and progressing from whining, yelling, and temper tantrums to hitting and other forms of physical assault. The child continues to win a high percentage of the battles with parents; parents continue to use ineffective punishment, setting the stage for another round of conflict. And this coercive family process occurs in many cases (but, certainly, not in all cases) in the context of other conditions associated with high risk for psychopathology of both parents and child: social and economic disadvantage, substance abuse, and a variety of other stressors such as parental discord and separation or divorce. During the process, the child receives little or no parental warmth and is often rejected by peers. School failure is another typical concomitant of the process. Understandably, the child usually develops a poor self-image (Patterson & Capaldi, 1990).

Patterson's suggestion that parents of aggressive children do not punish their children effectively does not mean he believes punishment should be the focus of parental discipline. His work does suggest, however, that parents need to set clear limits for children's behavior, provide a warm and loving home environment, provide positive attention and approval for appropriate behavior, and follow through with nonhostile and nonphysical punishment for coercive conduct. Appropriate punishment might consist of withdrawing privileges or restricting the child's activities contingent upon specific types of misbehavior, particularly not minding.

The apparent homeliness of the coercive family process model—its emphasis on ordinary daily interactions rather than more interesting and mysterious unconscious processes—belies its importance. As Patterson (1986b) concluded,

> Perhaps it is curious that a process with such a myriad of effects and outcomes can be initiated by something as ordinary as the level of parents' family-management skills. That, however, is what the general model prompting these studies indicates. Findings from our clinic and the modeling studies also suggest that anger, rejection, poor self-esteem, and perhaps some forms of depression may have their beginnings in the prosaic daily round of parental mismanagement. What is being mismanaged is something as inherently banal as family coercive exchanges. What leads to things getting out of hand may be a relatively simple affair, whereas the process itself, once initiated, may be the stuff of which novels are made. (p. 442)

Patterson and other researchers have shown that the pattern of coercive exchanges characterizing families of antisocial children can be identified early (Loeber, Green, Lahey, Christ, & Frick, 1992; Patterson, 1986b; Patterson et al., 1992; Reid, 1993; Stevenson-Hinde et al., 1986; Waters, Hay, & Richters, 1986). Martin (1981), for example, found indications that mutually uncooperative, coercive styles of mother-child interaction can be identified in some cases by the time the child is 3.5 years old. These and other findings suggest that conduct disordered children are at risk from an early age, partly because they are infants with difficult temperaments and have parents who lack skills in coping with the stress of having a difficult baby (cf. Campbell, 1995; Kazdin, 1991; Patterson, 1986b). The pattern of coercive exchanges is established early and grows more intense and hurtful as the child becomes stronger and more skillful in counterattack as a response to parental irritability or lack of compliance with his or her wishes.

A wealth of research shows a pattern of punishment, negative reinforcement, and coercion in the families of aggressive children. Other research indicates that hostile, inconsistent discipline and family conflict are associated with disordered child behavior (Campbell, 1995; Farrington, 1995; Hetherington & Martin, 1986; Rutter, 1995). Nevertheless, these data do not demonstrate that punitive parents cause their children to become aggressive any more than difficult-to-manage, oppositional, aggressive children cause their parents to become punitive. Fortunately, however, behavioral researchers have demonstrated that many parents can be trained to change their responses to their children to modify the children's aggression (Patterson et al., 1975, 1992; Reid, 1993; Willis et al., 1983).

Child Abuse

We may now know something about how coercive interactions begin and are sustained in families of aggressive children and how parents can make mistakes in discipline (that is, be ineffective or even counterproductive), but we must not forget that "There are probably many routes to becoming a 'good parent' which vary with the personality of both the parents and children and with pressures in the environment with which one must learn to cope" (Becker, 1964, p. 202). When is ineffective child management abusive or neglectful? This question is not easily answered (Haugaard, 1992). Much depends on the developmental level of the child, specific circumstances, professional and legal judgments, and cultural norms. If there is a consensus about how to define *child abuse*, it likely is centered on parental behavior that seriously endangers or delays the normal development of the child (Baumrind, 1995; Cicchetti & Toth, 1995; Janko, 1994).

Given the difficulty in defining *abuse*, it is not surprising that reliable estimates of child abuse and family violence are difficult to find (Cicchetti & Toth, 1995). Nevertheless, without belaboring the issue, we may conclude that family violence and child abuse—physical, psychological, and sexual—are problems of great magnitude; it very likely involves more than a million children per year in the United States (Baumrind, 1995; Cicchetti & Toth, 1995; Haugaard, 1992; Veltkamp & Miller, 1994). In fact, extreme family and community violence may induce **posttraumatic stress disorder** in children, as we discuss in chapter 15 (see Arroyo & Eth, 1995; Yule, 1994). Although abuse of all types is serious and has important sequelae, we focus our discussion here on physical abuse, in part because psychological abuse is much more difficult to define and sexual abuse may not be as pervasive a problem as physical abuse.

> The continuing greater amount of interest in the professional community and general public regarding children who have been sexually abused rather than physically abused seems incorrect, given that many more children are the victims of physical abuse. Part of the difference in interest may be due to the more recent "emergence" of the problem of sexual abuse or a concern that sexually abused children may sustain more serious long- and short-term consequences. Another explanation is that the difference in interest reflects our society's greater abhorrence of those who are sexual with children than of those who beat them. This may reflect our continuing ambivalence about the good or harm that can come from hitting a child, and a deeply rooted belief that children should remain shielded from sexuality. (Haugaard, 1992, p. 105)

Most people give little thought to children's and parents' interactive effects on each other in cases of abuse. Child abuse is often seen as a problem of parental behavior alone, and intervention has often been directed only at changing parents' responses to their children. The **interactional-transactional model** considers abused children's influence on their parents and suggests that intervention deal directly with the abused child's undesirable behavior as well as with the parents' abusive responses (see Parke & Collmer, 1975; Patterson, 1980, 1982; Zirpoli, 1986). This perspective is valuable even when the child is not initially an instigator of abuse but has been drawn into an abusive relationship and is exhibiting inappropriate behavior. Intervention typically needs to be directed toward the entire family and its social context (Baumrind, 1995; Janko, 1994).

One hypothesis about parent-child interaction in child abuse is that their children's responses to punishment inadvertently *teach* parents to become increasingly punitive (recall our prior discussion of how family members may train each other to be aggressive). For example, if the child exhibits behavior that is aversive to the parent (perhaps whining), the parent may punish the child (perhaps by slapping). If the punishment is successful and the child stops the aversive behavior, then the parent is negatively reinforced by the consequence; the parent is, in effect, rewarded by the child's stopping the aversive behavior. The next time the child whines, the parent is more likely to try slapping to get relief from the whining. If at first the child does not stop whining, the parent may slap harder or more often to try to make the child be quiet. Thus the parent's punishment becomes increasingly harsh as a means of dealing with the child's increasingly aversive behavior. Although abusive parents are not usually successful in punishing their child, they continue to escalate punishment. They seem not to understand or be able to use alternative means of control. And although abused children suffer in the bargain, they often hold their own in the battle with their parents; they may "stubbornly" refuse to knuckle under to parental pressure. Parent and child are trapped in a mutually destructive, coercive cycle in which they cause and are caused physical and/or psychological pain (Webster-Stratton, 1985).

The negative reinforcement trap can escalate behavior to the level of abuse. Such a coercive struggle is characteristic of conduct disorder, and the developmental consequences for children are severe (Patterson et al., 1992; Walker, Colvin, & Ramsey, 1995). Moreover, if abuse is transmitted across generations, it is likely through such processes, because children with conduct disorder are likely to become parents with antisocial behavior and poor child management skills. (We discuss the transmission of antisocial behavior across generations in chapter 12.)

The conclusion that the child's behavior is *always* a reciprocal causal factor in an abusive relationship with a parent is not warranted, however. Abusive relationships are extremely varied, both in abusive behaviors and in abused-abuser relations. Sexual abuse in families, for example, takes many forms and may involve incestuous relationships between siblings, parent and child, or other family members (for example, step-parent or grandparent) and child. Because it is a social problem surrounded by many taboos, sexual abuse is a difficult topic for research (Haugaard, 1992; Parker & Parker, 1986). Research does not justify the assumption that children contribute to their sexual abuse, particularly when the abused child is very young. A history of sexual abuse or observation of overt sexual behavior may cause some children to be sexually provocative, which may contribute to their further abuse. However, it would be difficult to make the case that infants and young children initiate their own sexual victimization by their parents or other family members.

Much has been written about the characteristics of abusive parents, and stereotypes abound. One stereotype is that they are socially isolated; another is that they themselves were abused as children; still another is that they are mentally ill. Although all three impressions hold for some cases, none is supported by research as an abusive parent prototype (cf. Baumrind, 1995; Thompson & Wilcox, 1995). Nevertheless, we can point to several psychological characteristics that frequently accompany abusive parenting.

It is generally acknowledged today that few abusive parents are severely or chronically disturbed. A constellation of personality traits frequently found to characterize abusive parents includes deficits in empathy and role-taking, poor impulse control, low self-esteem, and an external locus of control. Abuse by one's own parents is neither a necessary nor a sufficient condition for abusing one's own children. About one-third of abusive parents, however, do claim that they were abused as children. (Baumrind, 1995, p. 80)

Children who are abused by their parents have been shown by research to be at risk for the full range of emotional and behavioral disorders, including both internalizing problems such as depression and externalizing problems such as conduct disorder (Cicchetti & Toth, 1995). Teachers, parents, and peers are all likely to see higher levels of behavior problems in physically abused than in nonmaltreated children (Feldman et al., 1995). The negative effects of abuse may be compounded if the child already has an emotional or behavioral problem (Levendosky, Okun, & Parker, 1995). In devising intervention programs for abused children and youths, it is important to recognize that their behavior may be directly related to family violence and that attempting merely to modify their behavior in school may be insufficient. Teachers, as well as others with responsibility for children's welfare, must report suspected abuse and work toward comprehensive services that meet all of the student's needs.

FAMILY INFLUENCES ON SCHOOL SUCCESS AND FAILURE

The family's contribution to school performance in most cases plays a secondary role, for it is axiomatic that the school is responsible for the child's learning. Parents nevertheless contribute toward or detract from their child's success at school in several ways: their expressed attitudes toward school, academic learning, and teachers; their own competence or lack of success in school; and their disinterest in or reinforcement of appropriate school-related behaviors, such as attending regularly, completing homework, reading, and studying. Gesten, Scher, and Cowen (1978) found that "homes characterized by lack of educational stimulation appear to produce children who are prone to learning problems" (p. 254). Parents and family may also have a significant influence on how children relate to their peers in the community and in school. Poor peer relations in school, especially rejection by peers, is highly predictive of academic problems (DeRosier, Kupersmidt, & Patterson, 1995; Wentzel & Asher, 1995). Consequently, the social training children receive at home may be an important factor in determining school success (Coie, 1990; Patterson et al., 1992).

Parental discipline, parent-school relations, and parent-child relationships play important roles in school success and school failure (Dornbusch, Ritter, Leiderman, Roberts, & Fraleigh, 1987). The authoritative parental discipline described earlier (both responsive and demanding) is likely to support students' achievement (cf. Baumrind, 1995; Campbell, 1995; Rutter, 1995). Hess and Holloway (1984) describe how such discipline and related parental behavior encourages school success:

- Mothers engage in high levels of verbal interaction with their children.

- Parents express clear expectations for achievement.

- Parents maintain a warm and encouraging relationship with their children.

■ Parents use an authoritative style of discipline (controlling, directive, warm, and supportive, not hostile, rigid, or permissive).

■ Parents believe their children can and will learn.

Families in which a coercive process is at work are likely to send students to school unprepared to comply with teachers' instructions, to complete homework assignments, or to relate well to their peers. Unprepared for the demands of school, these students are virtually certain to fail to meet reasonable expectations for academic performance and social interaction (Patterson, 1986b; Patterson et al., 1992; Walker et al., 1995). Parents who are caught up in coercive interactions with their children are not likely to be much involved with their children's schooling; parents who are more involved with education and invest energy in monitoring and facilitating their children's progress at school tend to have youngsters who perform at a higher academic level (Stevenson & Baker, 1987).

EXTERNAL PRESSURES AFFECTING FAMILIES

Family interactions are influenced by external conditions that put stress on parents and children. Poverty, unemployment, underemployment, homelessness, community violence—it is not surprising that these conditions influence the ability of families to cope from day to day, of parents to nurture children, of children to behave well at home and perform well in school (Janko, 1994). Homelessness affects not only entire families but, in some cases, adolescents alienated from their families, sometimes due to external influences that destroyed parent-child bonds (see Schweitzer, Hier, & Terry, 1994).

Poverty is perhaps the most critical problem undermining families today (see Hodgkinson, 1995; Knitzer & Aber, 1995). In the United States in the mid 1990s, more than one child out of every four grows up in poverty, and nearly that many live in "near poverty" (family incomes near the federal definition of poverty). Severe economic hardship is known to be associated with abusive or neglectful parental behavior and children's maladaptive behavior (Achenbach et al., 1991; Bolger, Patterson, Thompson, & Kupersmidt, 1995; Felner et al., 1995; Janko, 1994). Poverty often means that families live in inadequate or dangerous housing (if they are not homeless) in neighborhoods rife with substance abuse and violence. These neighborhood conditions often contribute to parents and children being victimized and to their feelings of inadequacy, depression, and hopelessness (DuRant, Getts, Cadenhead, Emans, & Woods, 1995).

Neighborhoods characterized by low family income, high unemployment, transient populations, high concentrations of children living in single-parent families, and high rates of violence and substance abuse are places in which families are at high risk of dysfunction and disintegration and children are at high risk for psychopathology and school failure (Coulton, Korbin, Su, & Chow, 1995; DuRant et al., 1995; Kupersmidt, Griesler, DeRosier, Patterson, & Davis, 1995; McCloskey,

1995). Violent victimization, whether by family members or others, puts children and youths at risk for emotional and behavioral disorders and school problems of wide variety (Boney-McCoy & Finkelhor, 1995). Furthermore, in communities characterized by danger of victimization, restrictive parenting may be adaptive (Jackson, 1995; Zayas, 1995).

A common misperception of poor families is that the parents typically are unemployed or uninterested in work. Although unemployment and lack of work skills are problems of a substantial percentage of poor parents, the majority of poor parents are workers.

> Contrary to public perception, 57% of all poor children under six live in families where one or both parents work. Eighteen percent of poor families include at least one adult who holds a full-time job and still cannot earn enough income to move out of poverty. The remaining 39% hold part-time jobs. Close to 40% of all poor families with children under six are supported *exclusively* by their own earnings—but these earnings are not sufficient to lift them out of poverty. The significance of these statistics cannot be overstated. The stereotype of poor families, particularly those with young children, is that they sit around and do nothing but have babies. The reality appears to be quite different. (Knitzer & Aber, 1995, p. 174)

We need to be aware of the struggle of poor families to meet daily needs for food, shelter, medical care, and other necessities that most of us take for granted. Parental unemployment is a stressor of enormous proportions, but parental employment that does not pay a decent wage is not far behind in its effects. Employment of both parents places stress on middle-class families and requires extraordinary parental efforts to provide adequate monitoring and nurturing for children, but when such employment does not allow the family to escape poverty the stress is multiplied. Poverty and the social and personal problems stemming from it are issues our society must address more effectively if we wish to reduce family stress and child psychopathology (Freedman, 1993; Knitzer & Aber, 1995).

IMPLICATIONS FOR EDUCATORS

We must begin with a strong cautionary note. In their national survey of behavior problems and competencies of children, Achenbach et al. (1991) found higher ratings on behavior problem scales for children living in homes in which a family member was receiving mental health services. This should not be interpreted to mean that the parents of children who have emotional or behavioral disorders typically have mental health problems. Neither should findings of this type be misinterpreted to indicate that parents typically are the only or primary *cause* of their children's behavior problems. As we have seen, the familial factors in behavior problems are multiple, complex, and interactive.

With what we know about the family's role in children's emotional or behavioral disorders, educators would be foolish to ignore the influence of home conditions on school performance and conduct. Still, blaming parents of troubled students is unjustified. Very good parents can have children with very serious emotional or behavioral disorders. The teacher must realize that the parents of a youngster with an emotional or behavioral disorder have undergone a great deal of disappointment and frustration and that they too would like to see the child's behavior improve, both at home and at school. We find the strongest indicators for family causal contributions to antisocial behavior. However, even for conduct disorder and delinquency, we should not assume that parents are usually the primary cause.

Educators must be careful not to become entangled in the same coercive process that may characterize the antisocial student's family life. Harsh, hostile, verbal or physical punishment at school is likely to function as a new challenge for antisocial students, who may have been trained, albeit inadvertently, by their parents to step up their own aversive behavior in response to punishment. To win the battle with such students, school personnel must employ the same strategies that are recommended for parents—clearly stated expectations for behavior, an emphasis on positive attention for appropriate conduct, and calm, firm, nonhostile, and reasoned punishment for misbehavior (Walker, 1995; Walker et al., 1995). Teachers need to use the same approach to discipline that seems to work best for parents—to be both responsive and demanding. Moreover, it is important not to let the fact that students come from homes that prepare them poorly for learning become an excuse for poor teaching.

For far too long, educators, and many others in our society as well, have not only blamed parents for students' emotional or behavioral difficulties but viewed parents as likely adversaries rather than potential sources of support for their troubled children. More positive views of parents and their role in helping their children is in large measure a result of effective parent advocacy. The organization of the Federation of Families for Children's Mental Health in 1989 brought parents together to advocate more effectively for mental health and special education programs for their children. Parent groups in many states have established resource centers that provide information and guidance for parents who want to become more actively involved in seeing that their children get appropriate education and mental health services (e.g., Jordan, 1995; Jordan, Goldberg, & Goldberg, 1991). The decade of the 1990s is a period of awakening to the strengths of parents and families in fostering the mental health of their children, and we educators will do well to make optimum use of the partnerships we can forge with our students' family members and with others who provide services to families (Hanson & Carta, 1995).

Educators should strengthen families and support students' learning and behavior regardless of the family's structure or patterns of interaction. Hanson and Carta (1996) suggest that teachers must cross professional boundaries and work with other professionals to support families in several ways to do the following things:

- Provide critical positive interactions with students and demonstrate these for parents.
- Find and support the strengths of individual families.
- Help families find and use informal sources of support from friends, neighbors, coworkers, or others in the community.

- Become competent in understanding and valuing cultural differences in families.
- Provide a broad spectrum of coordinated services so that families receive comprehensive, flexible, and usable services that address their needs.

SUMMARY

The family provides the context for early nurturance, so it is not surprising that people tend to look to the family as a likely source of deviant behavior. Family factors do not account for children's disordered behavior, however, except in complex interaction with other factors. Some family factors, notably conflict and coercion, are known to increase a youngster's risk for developing an emotional or behavioral disorder. We do not fully understand why some children are more vulnerable to risk factors than others.

Families are defined by their function more than their structure: they provide protection, regulation, knowledge, affect, and self-understanding to children. Family structure, by itself, appears to contribute relatively little to children's emotional and behavioral problems. Divorce does not usually produce chronic disorders in children, although we can expect temporary negative effects. Children living in single-parent families may be at risk for behavior problems, but we do not know precisely why. When children are cared for by substitutes for their biological parents, any negative effects stem primarily from traumas experienced prior to their separation or from the same types of family interactions that influence children in families with biological parents.

An interactional-transactional model of family influence suggests that children and parents exert reciprocal effects; children affect their parents' behavior as surely as parents affect their children's. Parental discipline is a significant factor in behavioral development. Discipline that is authoritative, characterized by high levels of responsiveness and demandingness, usually produces the best outcomes. Ineffective discipline often involves lax supervision, harshness, and inconsistency.

We can view both conduct disorder and child abuse in terms of the interactions and transactions of parents and their children. In both cases, parent and child become involved in an aversive cycle of negative reinforcement; each escalates behavior that is aversive for the other until someone wins, obtaining reinforcement by getting the other person to withdraw from the battle. The youngster's difficult temperament and the parent's lack of coping skills may contribute to the initial difficulty; the coercive process then grows from nagging, whining, and yelling to more serious and assaultive behavior such as hitting.

Parental behavior, especially style of discipline, verbal interactions with their children, expressed attitudes toward school, expectations that their children will learn, and involvement with the school affect children's school performance and conduct.

External factors such as poverty and employment may have substantial effects on family functioning. Many children grow up in poverty, even if their parents work, and their living conditions put them at risk for a variety of emotional and behavioral disorders.

Educators should be concerned about the family's influence on children's conduct at school, but they must not blame parents for children's misbehavior. School personnel must avoid becoming enmeshed in the same coercive process that antisocial students are probably experiencing at home and should use the same intervention strategies that are recommended for parents. Educators must work with other professionals to obtain comprehensive services for families.

Case for Discussion

"He's Our Son, You Know"

Weird Nick

Earlier in the day I had taken Nick to the principal's office because he had refused to restore the classroom computer password. He was a genius at computers, and it had taken no time at all for him to discover the school password and replace it with one only he knew. He liked the power this action had given him, knowing it had infuriated me. He loved it when people took his bait, as I had, whether it was in the form of a bomb threat, a detailed drawing of a stabbing, or his consistent proclamation that "Satan rules!"

Nick had sat quietly in the principal's office. He looked the part of a Satanic cultist in his black jeans, black shirt, and black shoes. His black hair hung in stringy curls over his pale face. His fingers were busily drawing a pentagram. Was this just the image-building of a middle-school student plagued by self-doubt, or was it really an expression of belief in the occult?

I remembered how Nick seemed to get a special kick out of leaving the school building, forcing support staff to track him visually, walkie-talkies in hand. He knew that leaving the school grounds would necessitate our calling the police, so he would walk the perimeter of the property, running ahead if an adult came too close. All the other kids were afraid of "weird Nick," as they called him. They kept their distance from this tall, powerful loner. And he distanced himself from his family, his classmates, and his teachers, unable to connect with anyone. All of us on the staff shared the concern that someday we would be hearing about Nick on the evening news.

Now his mother sat with me and the principal in my classroom after school, nervously twisting her gloves as if wringing out a rag, staring out the window at the freezing rain and growing darkness. "I just don't know what to do with him. I take him to church with me every chance I get. You know I go to church every day. Why is he doing this to me? He knows that his fascination with Satanism hurts us deeply. Is he going to hurt us? He's our son, you know. What are we supposed to do?"

Questions About the Case

1. If you were Nick's teacher, how would you respond to his mother's obvious distress?
2. Given Nick's pattern of behavior, what focus would you suggest for his school program? That is, what would be your primary concerns and teaching or management strategies?
3. Would you advise Nick's teacher and principal to make special efforts to work with Nick's parents? Why or why not? If so, how?

PERSONAL REFLECTIONS

Family Factors

Dixie Jordan is the parent of a son with an emotional and behavioral disorder, Coordinator of the EBD Project at the PACER Center in Minneapolis (a resource center for parents of children with disabilities), and a founding member of the Federation of Families for Children's Mental Health.

Why do you think there is such a strong tendency to hold parents responsible for their children's emotional or behavioral disorders?

I am the parent of two children, the younger of which has emotional and behavioral problems. When my firstborn and I were out in public, strangers often commented on what a "good" mother I was, to have such an obedient, well-behaved, and compliant child. Frankly, I enjoyed the comments, and really believed that those parents whose children were throwing tantrums and generally demolishing their environments were simply not very skilled in child-rearing. I recall casting my share of reproachful glances in those days and thinking with some arrogance that raising children should be left to those of us who knew how to do it well. Several years later, my second child and I were on the business end of such disdain, and it was a lesson in humility that I shall never forget. Very little that I had learned in the previous 3 years as a parent worked with this child; he was neurologically different, hyperactive, inattentive, and noncompliant even when discipline was consistently applied. His doctors, his neurologist, and finally his teachers referred me to "parenting classes," as though the experiences I had had with my older child were nonexistent; his elementary principal even said that there was nothing wrong that a good spanking wouldn't cure. I expected understanding that this was a very difficult child to raise, but the unspoken message was that I lacked competence in basic parenting skills, the same message that I sent to similarly situated parents just a few years earlier.

Most of us in the world today are parents. The majority of us have children who do not have emotional or behavioral problems. Everything in our experience suggests that when our children are successful and obedient, it is because of our parenting. We are reinforced socially for having a well-behaved child from friends, grandparents, even strangers. It makes sense, then, to attribute less desirable behaviors in children to the failure of their parents to provide appropriate guidance or to set firm limits. Many parents have internalized that sense of responsibility or blame for causing their child's emotional problems, even when they are not able to identify what they might have done or be doing wrong. It is a very difficult attitude to shake, especially when experts themselves cannot seem to agree on causation. With most children, the "cause" of an emotional or behavioral disorder is more likely a complex interplay of multiple factors than "parenting styles," "biology," or "environmental influences" as discrete entities, but it is human nature to latch onto a simple explanation—and inadequate parenting is, indeed, a simple explanation. When systems blame parents for causing their child's emotional or behavioral disorders, the focus is no longer on services to help the child learn better adaptive skills or appropriate behaviors but on rationalizing why such services may not work. When parents feel blamed, their energies shift from focusing on the needs of their child to defending themselves. In either instance, the child is less well served.

Another reason people hold parents responsible for their children's emotional or behavioral disorders is that parents may be under such unrelenting stress from trying to manage their child's behavior that they may resort to inappropriate techniques because of the failure of more conventional methods. A parent whose 8-year-old hyperactive child smashes out his bedroom window while being timed out for another problem may know that tying the child to a chair is not a good way to handle the crisis, but that parent may be out of alternatives. It may not have been the "right" thing for the parent to do, but it is not what was responsible for causing the child's problems in the first place. It would be a mistake to attribute the incidence of abuse or neglect as "causing" most emotional or behavioral disorders without consideration that difficult children are perhaps more likely to be abused due to their noncompliant or otherwise difficult behaviors.

What are the most important things for teachers to understand about being the parent of a child with emotional or behavioral disorders?

Teachers need to try to understand the isolation that many families may feel when raising a child with emotional or behavioral problems. Parents may not have amicable relationships with their extended families or with the neighbors because of their child, and may not have a single person with whom they can freely discuss their child's problems or seek solutions to those problems. They may not have a sitter to watch their child for a few hours in the evening so they can take a break. They may on occasion feel physically threatened by their own child. Raising a child with an emotional or behavioral disorder is hard work—exhausting work—and families in many instances operate as little "islands" in their communities, cut off by their child's behavior from extended families, friends, or community supports.

Parents of children with emotional or behavioral disorders bring with them an historical perspective not only of their child's problems, but perhaps of the failure of other systems to adequately address those problems before the child ever gets into school. By the time their children are enrolled in elementary school, many parents have lost confidence in any system to truly help them. They may be suspicious and distrustful of schools—which, when personalized, leads to suspicion and distrust of teachers. Innocuous comments such as, "What is going on at home with your child?" may be interpreted as, "What are you doing wrong at home with your child?" It can be difficult for teachers to understand that the anger parents sometimes direct toward schools may stem from a frustration with systems in general and not with a specific program or person.

Teachers also need to understand that not all parents will be able to help their child with homework or school activities, especially if homework causes a great deal of stress or anxiety for the child. When the problem gets to be one of providing either academic support or emotional support because providing both is not possible, it may become more important to parents to support the child emotionally and to skip the homework. This should be negotiated with each family and based on the needs and abilities of each child, but the inability to help a child with homework should not be automatically viewed as lack of parental concern or involvement.

What key steps can teachers take in working more effectively with parents who have children with emotional or behavioral disorders?

One of the greatest fears expressed by parents regarding their child's school program is that if they disagree with any part of the program the teachers will take it out on their child. If I were a special education teacher, my first step each year would be to call each parent and let them know that I am interested in their child and need their help in developing a program. I would explain to them that we might not always agree about what to do, but that they could call me and know that I would listen, and that no matter what they said I would never punish any child for the parents' displeasure with the program. As an advocate, I must say that this is the single most important reason—according to the parents I've heard from—that they do not openly disagree with their child's school program, even when they believe it does not meet their child's needs.

A second key to building trust with parents is being honest with them about their child's needs. Parents may opt for a special education program with the expectation that it is for a few weeks or months, while the teacher knows or is at least reasonably sure that the placement may be for a few years, and that the goal of total remediation of academic and behavioral deficits may never be achieved. Many parents, especially of younger children, may not see their child's problems as a disability but as a transitory phase of development. Although that certainly may be true for some children, there are many others for whom an educated guess would be that their problems will be chronic and of long duration. If parents have an understanding of the longitudinal nature of their child's disability, and of the possibility of the long-term need for special education services, they will be less apt to get discouraged or angry when their child continues to need services.

Many parents report that the only time they hear from their child's teacher is when there is trouble at school. It is very important for teachers to communicate regularly with parents. There is no easier nor more effective way to establish a relationship of trust and open communication with families than with frequent (and at least 50-percent positive) communication.

Another suggestion for teachers is to learn to apologize when a mistake has been made. Most parents expect that teachers and other school professionals will make mistakes from time to time in dealing with their child, but it is the wise teacher who is ready with an apology for wrongly accusing or for misunderstanding a situation in which the child was disciplined unfairly.

Most teachers truly do not understand how stressful IEP planning meetings can be for parents. Attention at such meetings is generally focused on the problems a child is having, and parents are nearly always "outnumbered" by professional educators. A common occurrence at such meetings is for the teachers to refer to the parents as "Dad" or "Mom," which many parents report interpreting as denigrating or disrespectful. Careful planning of such meetings with an eye to the comfort and ease of parents can help increase their participation and their sense of power.

Parents are the true experts on their child, and the information they bring, if it can be tapped, can be invaluable in planning an appropriate program. Parents may not be specialists in behavior management, but they know their child across years and across environments, and if they do not know what techniques will work with a particular child they at least know what has *not* worked. It can be helpful for teachers to consider the "honorable intentions" when they are dealing with angry or uncooperative parents. Why are the parents upset? What are they trying to convey (regardless of how inappropriately) about the needs of their child? It is human nature to become defensive, but many such stalemates are resolved by teachers who recognize first that an angry parent is one who is concerned about his or her child's school program; the teacher can then respond to the concern and not the anger. Recognizing honorable intentions, especially in "forced" relationships such as those at IEP planning meetings, can greatly facilitate open communication between parents and teachers.

9

School Factors

As you read this chapter, keep these guiding questions in mind:

- Why should educators consider how the school might contribute to the development of disordered behavior?

- What do we know about the intelligence of students with emotional or behavioral disorders?

- With what academic skill levels should teachers of students with emotional or behavioral disorders be prepared to deal?

- What characteristics of student behavior are most likely to be associated with success in school?

- What behavioral characteristics are most likely to be associated with school failure?

- What is the relationship between school failure and later adjustment?

- How do educators demonstrate insensitivity to students' individual differences, and how might this insensitivity contribute to the development of undesirable conduct?

- What are appropriate expectations for students?

- How might inconsistent management in the classroom produce results similar to those produced by a coercive family process?

- How can one convince students that what they are asked to learn is functional and relevant to their lives?

- How does ineffective instruction in critical academic and social skills contribute to emotional and behavioral problems?

- What reinforcement contingencies relate to student behavior and teacher attention in most classrooms?

- How can teachers use appropriate models to foster desirable classroom behavior?

THE APPEAL OF SCHOOL FACTORS AS CAUSAL EXPLANATIONS

Besides the family, the school is probably the most important socializing influence on children and youths. In our culture, success or failure at school is tantamount to success or failure as a person; school is the occupation of all children and youths in our society—and sometimes it is their preoccupation. Academic success is fundamentally important for social development and postschool opportunity. As nearly any student, teacher, or parent can tell you, certain types of behavior are unacceptable in school. Yet many people, including many educators, seem to be unaware of how the school environment can inadvertently foster the very behavior that teachers, parents, and students find objectionable.

Educators need to scrutinize the role of the school in the development of emotional or behavioral disorders, because the school environment is the causal factor over which teachers and principals have direct control. As we have seen in other chapters, conditions outside the school can influence students' in-school behavior. Some youngsters develop behavior problems before they begin school, but even if a child already has a disorder, educators should consider how the school experience might ameliorate the problem or make it worse. And, because many youngsters do not exhibit emotional or behavioral disorders until after they enter school, educators must recognize the possibility that the school experience could be a significant causal factor.

An ecological approach to understanding behavior includes the assumption that all aspects of a youngster's environment are interconnected; changes in one element of the ecology have implications for the other elements. Success or failure at school affects behavior at home and in the community; effects of school performance ripple outward. Consequently, success at school assumes even greater importance if a youngster's home and community environments are disastrous. Furthermore, pre-referral strategies, required before a student is evaluated for special education, imply that the current classroom environment may be causally related to disordered behavior. Special educators recognize the importance of eliminating possible school contributions to misconduct before labeling the student as having a disability.

Before discussing social-interpersonal behavior and its school and classroom contexts, we must consider the characteristics of students with emotional or behavioral disorders that are relevant to a central mission of the school—academic learning. Intelligence and academic achievement are the two characteristics most closely linked to the way students respond to the expectations and demands of the school.

INTELLIGENCE

Intelligence tests are most reasonably viewed as tests of general learning in areas that are important to academic success. IQ refers only to performance on an intelligence test. IQs are moderately good predictors of how students will perform academically and how they will adapt to the demands of everyday life. Standardized tests are the best single means we have to measure general intelligence, even though performance on a test is not the only indicator of intelligence and may not tap abilities in specific areas that are important in everyday life.

The definition and measurement of intelligence are controversial issues with implications for the definition of giftedness, mental retardation, and other exceptionalities for which special education may be needed (see Hallahan & Kauffman, 1997). Psychologists agree that intelligence is comprised of a variety of abilities, both verbal and nonverbal. Ability to direct and sustain attention, process information, think logically, perceive social circumstances accurately, and understand abstractions, for example, are distinguishable parts of what makes a person "smart." But psychologists continue to debate the merits of the concept of **general intelligence** versus the idea of **multiple intelligences** (e.g., Gardner & Hatch, 1989; Grinder, 1985; Sternberg, 1991), and the debate of these issues is beyond the scope of this book. Goleman (1995) popularized the notion of **emotional intelligence**, which may have particular relevance to children and youths with emotional or behavioral disorders. Later, we discuss emotional intelligence in the context of the social skills children and youths with emotional or behavioral disorders may lack. However, for purposes of the present discussion, we shall assume that intelligence refers to IQ as typically obtained by standardized tests of general intelligence.

Intelligence of Students with Mild or Moderate Disorders

Authorities on emotional and behavioral disorders have traditionally assumed that students with such disorders fall within the normal range of intelligence. If the IQ falls below 70, the student is considered to have mental retardation, even when behavior problems are a major concern. Occasionally, however, students with IQs in the retardation range are said to have emotional or behavioral disorders or learning disabilities rather than mental retardation, on the presumption that emotional or perceptual disorders prevent them from performing up to their true capacity (cf. Hallahan, Kauffman, & Lloyd, 1996).

The average IQ for most students with emotional or behavioral disorders is in the low normal range with a dispersion of scores from the severe mental retardation range to the highly gifted level. Over the past 30 years, numerous studies have yielded the same general finding: average tested IQ for these students is in the low 90s (Bortner & Birch, 1969; Bower, 1981; Duncan, Forness, & Hartsough, 1995; Graubard, 1964, Kauffman et al., 1987; Lyons & Powers, 1963; Motto & Wilkins, 1968; Rubin & Balow, 1978). We have accumulated enough research on these students' intelligence to draw this conclusion: although the majority fall only slightly below average in IQ, a disproportionate number, compared to the normal distribution, score in the dull normal and mild mental retardation range, and relatively few fall in the upper ranges. Research findings suggest a distribution like that in Figure 9.1. The hypothetical curve for most students with emotional or behavioral disorders shows a mean of about 90 to 95 IQ, with more students falling at the lower IQ levels and fewer at the higher levels than in the normal distribution. If this hypothetical

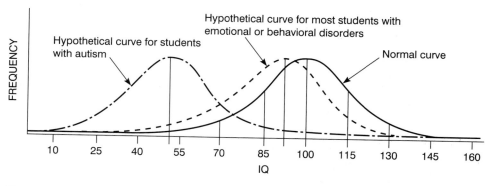

Figure 9.1
Hypothetical Frequency Distributions of IQ for Most Students with Emotional or Behavioral Disorders and Students with Autism as Compared to a Normal Frequency Distribution

distribution of intelligence is correct, then we can expect a greater-than-normal frequency of academic failure and socialization difficulties for these students.

Intelligence of Students with Autism and Schizophrenia

Mental health professionals long suspected that children with autism are not really characterized by mental retardation, even though they function at a retarded level in most areas of development. Kanner's (1943) description of autism strengthened the belief that such children are potentially normal in intelligence. DeMyer (1975) summarized Kanner's reasons for believing that children with autism have normal intelligence.

> The reasons for his belief were the presence of splinter skills, "intelligent" faces, few reports of motor dysfunction, and "refusal" to perform when age-appropriate items from intelligence tests were presented to them. One widely held theory advanced to explain these "facts" was that most if not all autistic . . . children had anatomically normal brains and that relatively high splinter skills were a "true" reflection of their potential intelligence. If the right treatment key could be found, then the seriously delayed verbal intelligence would advance in an accelerated fashion to catch up with the splinter skills and with the norms of the child's chronological age. (pp. 109–110)

Within the past 30 years, data have been accumulated to indicate that the IQs of most children with autism can be reliably determined and that the majority score in the moderate to severe range of mental retardation (DeMyer, 1975; DeMyer et al., 1974; Green, Fein, Joy, & Waterhouse, 1995; Lovaas et al., 1973; Prior & Werry, 1986; Rutter & Schopler, 1987). Only 20 to 25 percent of children with autism have been found to score within the normal range of intelligence; a few have been found to have intelligence in the gifted range. On the basis of available data, the distribution of intelligence for these students is hypothesized as shown in Figure 9.1. The average IQ is probably around 50, with the vast majority of students falling between about 35 and about 70. Nevertheless, we know much more about the nature of the cognitive abilities and disabilities associated with autism today than we did a quarter century ago (Schopler & Mesibov, 1995).

Autism may vary from mild to severe, and the cognitive problems associated with the condition are varied. As Grandin (1995), a highly intelligent and creative adult with autism explains, "Autism is a heterogeneous disorder with subtypes along a continuum ranging from highly verbal classical Kanner's syndrome, to nonverbal regressive/epileptic types with poor receptive speech" (p. 153). Individuals with autism may be particularly adept at some skills, particularly those requiring visuospatial and sensory-motor abilities (Green et al., 1995; see also Sacks, 1995, for extensive case descriptions). The cognitive impairments associated with autism are often severe, but they tend to be problems in specific types of cognitive processes. Green et al. (1995) concluded that "Autistic children have specific impairments in the selectivity and shifting of attention, executive functioning, abstraction of information and reasoning, language (particularly the social aspects), and social cognition" (p. 25).

Although the intelligence of students with schizophrenia is generally higher than that of students with autism, the distribution for students with schizophrenia is probably below that for the general population (Prior & Werry, 1986). If we were to plot a hypothetical distribution for students with schizophrenia, it would approximate the distribution for most students with emotional or behavioral disorders. The cognitive difficulties of these students are primarily problems of attention and information processing—paying attention to the right things, making sense of information, thinking logically, and understanding social relationships (Asarnow, Asamen, Granholm, Sherman, Watkins, & Williams, 1994; Caplan, 1994; Strandburg, Marsh, Brown, Asarnow, & Guthrie, 1994).

Severe emotional or behavioral disorders occur across the entire spectrum of intelligence, but they are most frequently accompanied by a lower than average IQ. Children and youths with autism and schizophrenia tend to have particular problems dealing with cognitive tasks that require social understanding. Severe cognitive and social retardation is associated with poorer prognosis; even with the best available behavioral interventions, it is usually a very long-term, often life-long disability (cf. Asarnow, Tompson, & Goldstein, 1994; Eggers, 1978; Prior & Werry, 1986; Werry, McClellan, Andrews, & Ham, 1994). However, advances in intensive early intervention show promise for ameliorating or even eliminating the behavioral and cognitive deficits of a significant percentage of students with autism (Lovaas, 1987).

Implications of Low IQ

Research clearly suggests that students with emotional or behavioral disorders tend to be lower than normal in IQ and that the most severely disabled students also tend to be the lowest in IQ (DeMyer et al., 1974; Kauffman et al., 1987; Prior & Werry, 1986). The correlation between intelligence and level of disorder does not imply a causal relationship. Even so, the IQs of students with emotional or behavioral disorders appear to be the best single predictor of educational achievement and later adjustment (see Prior & Werry, 1986). DeMyer (1975) and Rutter and Bartak (1973), for example, reported that their subjects' IQs at initial evaluation were good predictors of academic and social skill achievement of children with autism. The predictive power of IQ for less severely disabled students' academic achievement and future social adjustment probably approximates the predictive power of IQ for students in the normal distribution: significant, but far from perfect.

Notwithstanding the bulk of available evidence, we may need to revise the conclusion that general intelligence as indicated by IQ is a good predictor of outcome for students with autism. Unfortunately, some writers have suggested that autism does not typically affect intelligence, although their theories have very little support from scientific evidence (e.g., Biklen, 1990). A procedure called **facilitated communication** (FC) was popularized by Biklen and his colleagues in the early 1990s and touted as a breakthrough in the treatment of autism and other pervasive developmental disorders (e.g., Biklen & Schubert, 1991). Claims were made that with FC children and youths with autism could demonstrate average to gifted intelligence. FC has not stood up to careful scientific scrutiny; the communication in nearly all cases is found to come from the nondisabled "facilitator" who helps the person with a disability type out messages (see Montee, Miltenberger, & Wittrock, 1995; Shane, 1994; Simpson & Myles, 1995). Thus, revision of the concept of autism and of the intellectual abilities of people with it based on FC is unwarranted. However, Lovaas (1987) demonstrated that nearly half of a group of children who received intensive (several hours daily), early (beginning before age 3), behavioral (procedures based on behavioral psychology) intervention for autism tested within normal limits on intelligence measures and were successful in the elementary grades. These findings are a startling contrast to those of most researchers and must await replication by others. Nevertheless, Lovaas's results cannot be dismissed as an anomaly; the research meets rigorous scientific standards and suggests potential major revisions in assumptions about the nature of autism.

ACADEMIC ACHIEVEMENT

Although academic achievement is usually assessed by standardized achievement tests, it is dangerous to place too much confidence in them, because they are not highly accurate measures of academic aptitude, nor highly precise measures of the academic attainment of the individual student. Scores on achievement tests do, however, allow comparisons between the performances of normative and nonnormative groups, which are valuable in assessing and predicting students' school success.

Achievement of Most Students with Emotional or Behavioral Disorders

The academic achievement of disturbed and delinquent students has been studied for many years (Bower, 1981; Graubard, 1964; Kauffman et al., 1987; Motto & Wilkins, 1968; Rubin & Balow, 1978; Silberberg & Silberberg, 1971; Stone & Rowley, 1964; Tamkin, 1960; see also Walker, Colvin, & Ramsey, 1995). Collectively, research leads to the conclusion that most such students are academically deficient even taking into account their mental ages, which are typically slightly below those of their chronological age mates. Although some students with emotional or behavioral disorders work at grade level and a very few are academically advanced, most function a year or more below grade level in most academic areas (see also Epstein, Kinder, & Bursuck, 1989).

Achievement of Students with Pervasive Developmental Disorders

Compared to their age mates, few students with autism and other pervasive developmental disorders are academically proficient. Many require training in self-help skills (toileting, dressing, feeding, bathing, grooming), language, and play skills. The highly intelligent, academically achieving student with autism is a relative rarity; most are severely behind their age mates in academic attainment and require prolonged, directive instruction in a carefully controlled teaching environment to attain functional academic skills (Harris, 1995a, 1995b; Koegel, Rincover, & Egel, 1982; Lovaas, 1987; Schopler, Mesibov, & Hearsey, 1995).

The behavioral characteristics of children diagnosed with schizophrenia tend to persist into adulthood (Howells & Guirguis, 1984; Werry et al., 1994). Although there are few data specific to academic learning, students with schizophrenia might be expected to have problems in academic achievement on the basis of their lower than average IQs, problems with language, attention, perception, and logic, and their deficits in social skills (Prior & Werry, 1986).

Implications of Academic Underachievement

Low achievement and behavior problems go hand in hand; they are highly related risk factors. Figure 9.2 shows data from a study in which children with a greater number of social problems were found to be more likely to have low achievement test scores. In a sample of 1,449 children in grades 2 through 5, Kupersmidt and Patterson (1987) found that about one third of those who had three or more social problems scored below the twenty-fifth percentile on standardized achievement tests; fewer than 10 percent of the children who had no social problems obtained such low achievement scores. Social problems were defined by teacher and peer ratings of aggressive behavior, shy-withdrawn behavior, peer rejection, depression, low self-esteem, low parental involvement in education, and poor grooming and/or personal hygiene.

Figure 9.2
Percentage of Children with Academic Problems as a Function of Social Problems

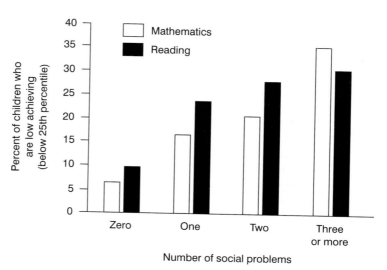

Source: From "Interim Report to the Charlottesville Public Schools on Children at Risk" by J. B. Kupersmidt and C. J. Patterson, 1987, unpublished manuscript, University of Virginia, Charlottesville, Virginia. Reprinted by permission.

In most cases, it is not clear whether disordered behavior causes underachievement or vice versa. Sometimes the weight of evidence may be more on one side of the issue than the other, but in the majority of instances the precise nature of the relationship is elusive. As we will see, there is reason to believe that underachievement and disordered behavior affect each other reciprocally. Disordered behavior apparently makes academic achievement less likely, and underachievement produces social consequences that are likely to foster inappropriate behavior (Bower, 1995; Walker et al., 1995). In any case, we have known for decades that the effects of educational failure on future opportunity should cause alarm for the plight of students with emotional or behavioral disorders.

> Educational attainment and opportunity are linked in many ways. Abundant evidence supports the view that education affects income, occupational choice, social and economic mobility, political participation, social deviance, etc. Indeed, educational attainment is related to opportunity in so many ways that the two terms seem inextricably intertwined in the mind of the layman and in the findings of the social scientist. (Levin, Guthrie, Kleindorfer, & Stout, 1971, p. 14)

Some students with autism and others with pervasive developmental disorders may require an instructional focus on self-care and daily living skills. If they do not achieve these nonacademic skills, they may be consigned to lives of stunted development and continuing dependence.

SOCIAL SKILLS

Interest in the social skills that make people attractive to others and enable them to cope effectively with difficult interpersonal circumstances is many decades if not centuries old. Obviously, people who are considered to have emotional or behavioral disorders lack certain critical social skills. However, it is often not so obvious just what those skills are, and how to teach people the skills they lack is even less apparent.

Walker and his colleagues have defined social skills related to schooling as "a set of competencies that (1) allow an individual to initiate and maintain positive social relationships, (2) contribute to peer acceptance and to satisfactory school adjustment, and (3) allow an individual to cope and adapt effectively with the larger social environment" (1995, p. 227). Thus social skills involve the ability to (1) build social supports and friendships, (2) respond appropriately to the demands of adults and peers, and (3) make adaptations to changes in the social circumstances. Students with emotional or behavioral disorders typically have difficulty in all three areas of social competence. They often do not know how to make and keep friends. They frequently behave in ways that anger and disappoint their teachers and classmates. They find it difficult or impossible to adjust to changing expectations when they move from one social environment to another (cf. Farmer & Hollowell, 1994; Guevremont & Dumas, 1994; Hundert, 1995; Walker, Schwarz, Nippold, Irvin, & Noell, 1994).

A list of the most important social skills encompasses many that are necessary for academic and social success in school. They include such skills as listening to others, taking turns in conversations, greeting others, joining in ongoing activities, giving compliments, expressing anger in socially acceptable ways, offering help to others, following rules, being adequately organized and focused, and doing high-quality work. Knowing what these skills are is important; assessing the extent to which individual students have mastered them is critical in dealing effectively with antisocial behavior (Walker et al., 1995).

Social skills involve not only overt behavior but cognition and affect. Students with deficits in social skills may not only exhibit behavior that is problematic but have problems in thinking about social interactions and developing adaptive, appropriate feelings. Thus, effective social skills training may require not only altering the way students behave toward others but the way they interpret others' behavior and the way they perceive and express their emotional arousal in social circumstances. Striking out at others without provocation may, indeed, be an obvious problem involving social skills. However, the student who hits or threatens others may misinterpret others' behavior as threatening when it is not or be unable to sense and monitor his or her own feelings of anger. Thus assessment of social skills and interventions designed to teach them may need to involve behavioral, cognitive, and affective components (Hundert, 1995; Walker et al., 1994, 1995).

At the heart of social skills is the ability to communicate verbally and nonverbally, to use language competently. In fact, a large percentage of students with emotional or behavioral disorders is known to have language disorders (Sanger, Maag, & Shapera, 1994; Walker, Schwarz, Nippold, Irvin, & Noell, 1994; Warr-Leeper, Wright, & Mack, 1994). Although these students may have problems in any area of language competence (e.g., they may have difficulty with word sounds, word forms, grammar, and so on), they tend to be particularly deficient in **pragmatics**—the practical, social uses of language. Acting-out youngsters may know how to use language very effectively to irritate, intimidate, and coerce others, but they do not have skills in using language effectively for positive, constructive social purposes. A functional analysis of their language skills is likely to indicate that they need to learn to use language to obtain desired consequences in ways that are socially acceptable. Withdrawn students lack the sophisticated language repertoires their normal peers have for engaging others in discourse (Donahue, Cole, & Hartas, 1995). We may conclude that a lack of social skills, especially pragmatic language skills, may underlie many of the behavior problems that are predictive of school failure. Students with emotional or behavioral disorders may need instruction in specific language-based social skills such as these:

- identifying, labeling, and expressing needs, wants, and feelings
- describing and interpreting emotions of oneself and others
- recognizing incipient emotions, providing control over them, and integrating them into appropriate social behavior (Giddan, Bade, Rickenberg, & Ryley, 1995)

BEHAVIOR PREDICTIVE OF SCHOOL SUCCESS AND FAILURE

Intelligence tests were devised in the early twentieth century for predicting children's academic success or failure. Although IQ is not infallible, especially in the individual case, it is a fairly accurate predictor of academic success or failure on a statistical basis. Educational researchers have also become interested in identifying the overt classroom behavioral characteristics associated with academic accomplishment, in the hope that teachers can teach those behaviors. For instance, if attentiveness if found to correlate positively with achievement, then teaching students to pay better attention might improve academic performance. Similarly, if achievement correlates negatively with certain dependence behaviors, then reducing dependency behaviors might be successful. Implicit here is the assumption that the identified behavioral characteristics will have more than a correlational relationship to achievement; there will be a *causal* link between certain overt behaviors and achievement.

The causal relationship between overt classroom behavior and academic success or failure is not entirely clear. Although a frequent strategy of teachers and educational researchers has been to modify behavior (such as task attention) in the hope of improving performance on academic tasks, direct modification of academic skills has proved most effective in preventing failure or remediating deficits (Lloyd, Hallahan, Kauffman, & Keller, 1991). Direct reinforcement of academic performance has in some cases eliminated classroom behavior problems (Hallahan & Kauffman, 1975). Nevertheless, classroom success or failure is determined by more than academic competence; doing the academic work is critical, but it is not the whole story.

Success and failure in school correlate with a variety of academic and social characteristics (McKinney, Mason, Peterson, & Clifford, 1975; Shin, Ramsey, Walker, Stieber, & O'Neill, 1987; Spivack & Swift, 1966, 1977; Swift & Swift, 1968, 1969a, 1969b, 1973; Walker & McConnell, 1988; Walker et al., 1995). Students who are low achieving and socially unsuccessful tend to exhibit the following characteristics:

- Engage in behavior that requires teacher intervention or control, such as teasing, annoying, or interfering with others
- Are overly dependent on the teacher for direction
- Have difficulty paying attention and concentrating
- Offer fewer ideas and bring fewer materials to class than high achievers
- Become upset under pressure
- Do work sloppily and impulsively
- Have low self-confidence; believe they cannot do what is expected
- Are highly opinionated and dogmatic, unreceptive to others' opinions
- Exhibit nervousness and anxiety and/or social withdrawal

High achieving and popular students, on the other hand, exhibit the following characteristics:

- Establish rapport with the teacher, engage in friendly conversation before and after class, and are responsive in class

- Engage in appropriate verbal interaction, asking relevant questions, volunteering, and participating in class discussions

- Do more than the minimum work required, taking care to understand directions and to master all details

- Exhibit originality and reasoning ability, being quick to grasp new concepts and apply them and preparing homework in an interesting way

Walker and McConnell (1988) have devised a 43-item rating scale to identify the social skills deficits related to school failure of elementary age pupils, *The Walker-McConnell Scale of Social Competence and School Adjustment*. It identifies teacher-preferred behavior for success during classroom instruction, peer-preferred behavior, and interpersonal social skills. Teacher-preferred social behavior includes items such as "Shows sympathy for others," "Accepts constructive criticism from peers without becoming angry," "Is sensitive to the needs of others," "Cooperates with peers in group activities or situations," and "Controls temper." Representative items indicating peer-preferred behavior are "Plays or talks with peers for extended periods of time," "Interacts with a number of different peers," "Makes friends easily with other children," "Plays games and activities at recess skillfully," and "Voluntarily provides assistance to peers who require it." Interpersonal social skills related to school adjustment are represented by items such as "Displays independent study skills," "Uses free time appropriately," "Attends to assigned tasks," "Has good work habits," and "Listens carefully to teacher directions and instructions for assignments." The extent to which students do not exhibit these characteristics indicates social deficits that put them at risk for school failure. Friendly, supportive, popular with peers, involved with learning, task-oriented, intelligent, creative, anxious to please—these are characteristics that serve students well in school, but are not the typical characteristics of students with emotional or behavioral disorders.

SCHOOL FAILURE AND LATER ADJUSTMENT

Low IQ and academic failure often foretell difficulty for students. A higher proportion of those with low IQ and achievement than of students with high IQ and achievement will experience adjustment difficulties as adults; those with low IQ are disproportionately represented among those who commit criminal acts (Bower, 1995). A high proportion of schizophrenic and antisocial adults are known to have exhibited low academic achievement as children (Bower, Shellhammer, & Dailey, 1960; Kazdin, 1987; Robins, 1966, 1986; Watt, Stolorow, Lubensky, & McClelland, 1970).

Low IQ and achievement alone do not spell disaster for later adjustment, however. Most youngsters with mild mental retardation, whose achievement may lag behind even their mental ages, do not turn into social misfits, criminals, or institutional residents in adult life; they are considered problems only during their school years (Edgerton, 1984). The same can be said of most youngsters with learning disabilities, whose academic retardation usually marks them as school failures (see Hallahan et al., 1996). Even among children and youths with emotional or behavioral disorders, the prognosis is not necessarily poor just because the student has a low IQ or fails academically.

Follow-back studies, which research the childhoods of adults diagnosed as psychotic, antisocial, or sociopathic through interviews and examination of the records of schools, clinics, and courts, provide adulthood prognoses for youngsters who exhibited certain characteristics (Bower et al., 1960; Robins, 1966, 1986; Watt et al., 1970; see also Garmezy, 1974; Robins, 1974, 1979). In general, these studies reveal that school failure is a part of the pattern identified as **premorbid** (predictive of later mental illness), especially for boys. Premorbid girls are more prone to withdrawal, immaturity, and introversion, whereas premorbid boys are more likely to show underachievement, negativism, and antisocial behavior (Watt et al., 1970; Robins, 1986). Without maladaptive behavior of some sort, however, low intelligence and low achievement in childhood are not highly predictive of disordered behavior in adulthood. School failure, then, cannot be considered by itself to cause adult social failure.

When school failure is accompanied by serious and persistent antisocial behavior—conduct disorder—the risk for mental health problems in adulthood is most grave (Fergusson & Horwood, 1995; Walker et al., 1995). And the earlier the onset and the greater the number of antisocial behaviors, the greater the risk (cf. Kazdin, 1985, 1995; Loeber, 1982; Robins, 1966, 1979, 1986; Shinn et al., 1987; Walker, Shinn, O'Neill, & Ramsey, 1987). Even when conduct disorder is accompanied by low intelligence and low achievement, we must be careful in drawing causal inferences; if a causal connection does exist between achievement and antisocial behavior, however, then it has implications for education.

> It is well known . . . that children with antisocial behavior are usually seriously retarded in academic performance. We do not know at this point whether academic failure usually preceded or followed the onset of antisocial behavior. If experiencing academic failure contributes to the occurrence of antisocial behavior disorders, then it is clear that preventive efforts should include efforts to forestall failure through programs such as those currently endeavoring to improve the IQs and academic success of disadvantaged children either by educating their parents to stimulate them as infants or through a variety of educationally oriented daycare and preschool programs. (Robins, 1974, p. 455)

To reiterate, low IQ and school failure alone are not as highly predictive of adult psychopathology as when they are combined with conduct disorder. The outlook for a youngster is particularly grim when he or she is at once relatively unintelligent, underachieving, and highly aggressive or extremely withdrawn. If conduct disorder is fostered by school failure, then programs to prevent school failure may also contribute to prevention of antisocial behavior.

Intelligence, Achievement, and Antisocial Behavior

Given that antisocial behavior (for example, hostile aggression, theft, incorrigibility, running away from home, truancy, vandalism, sexual misconduct), low intelligence, and low achievement are interrelated in a complex way, it may be important to clarify their apparent interrelationship. Figure 9.3 shows a hypothetical relationship among the three characteristics. The various shaded areas in the diagram represent the approximate (hypothesized) proportions in which various combinations of the three characteristics occur. The diagram illustrates the hypothesis that relatively few youngsters who exhibit antisocial behavior are above average in IQ and achievement (area *A*); most are below average in IQ and achievement (area *D*), and a few are below average in only IQ (area *B*), or only achievement (area *C*). Whereas the majority of underachieving youngsters are low in IQ (areas *D* and *G*), they are usually not antisocial (area *G* is much larger than area *D*). Some youngsters are low in IQ but not achievement (areas *B* and *E*) or vice versa (areas *C* and *F*), but relatively few of these youngsters are antisocial (area *E* is much larger than area *B*, and area *F* is much larger than area *C*).

Keep in mind that additional factors enter the picture to determine the adult outcome for children and youths with a given combination of characteristics. The

Figure 9.3
Hypothetical Relationships
Among Below Average IQ,
Below Average Achievement,
and Antisocial Behavior

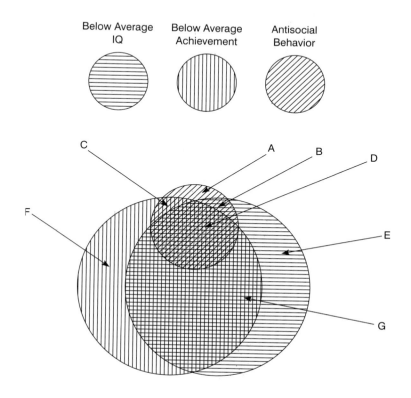

severity of the antisocial behavior, the parents' behavioral characteristics, and perhaps parental socioeconomic circumstances influence the probability that behavior difficulties will persist into adulthood. To the extent that youngsters exhibit many antisocial behaviors in a variety of settings and at high frequency, have parents who are themselves antisocial or abusive, and come from a lower social class, they have a greater chance of being hospitalized as mentally ill or incarcerated as a criminal when they become adults (Bower, 1995; Loeber, 1982; Robins, 1979; Walker et al., 1995). Also, remember that many children and youths who are low in intelligence, low in achievement, high in antisocial behavior, or some combination of these do not exhibit serious behavioral disorders as adults. Any prediction of adult behavior based on childhood behavioral characteristics is subject to substantial error in prediction for the individual case.

THE SCHOOL'S CONTRIBUTION TO EMOTIONAL AND BEHAVIORAL DISORDERS

Below-average intellectual functioning and below expected academic achievement are characteristics of students with emotional or behavioral disorders. Combined with conduct disorder, low intelligence and achievement provide a gloomy forecast for adulthood. Although school failure is not known to cause emotional or behavioral disorders, it frequently accompanies maladaptive behavior and possibly contributes to maladjustment. On the other hand, one could argue that maladaptive behavior makes academic success unlikely and contributes to school failure. Logically, one might take the position that school can contribute to both social difficulties and academic incompetence.

The demands of school and the student's social and academic repertoire probably affect each other reciprocally. For decades, we have known that a circular reaction occurs between the student and the social context of the classroom (Glidewell, 1969; Glidewell, Kantor, Smith, & Stringer, 1966). Students who are healthy, intelligent, upper-middle class, high achieving, high in self-esteem, and adroit in interpersonal skills enter the classroom at a distinct advantage. They are likely to make positive approaches to others, who in turn are likely to respond positively; and these advantaged students will be sensitive to others' responses toward them and able to use their intelligence to further enhance their personal power and social status. Intelligence and achievement beget social acceptability, self-esteem, accurate social perception, and status, all of which in turn induce positive social responses from others and facilitate achievement. This perspective on the student's reciprocal interaction with the social ecology of the classroom is entirely consistent with research (cf. Colvin, Sugai, & Patching, 1993; Hess & Holloway, 1984). Moreover, the same coercive process found in families of antisocial boys (Patterson, 1986a, 1986b) can be found in schools (Walker et al., 1995). Among their peers and in interactions with teachers and administrators, students with conduct disorders may be caught in negative reinforcement traps. Educators (like parents) and classroom peers (like siblings) can become entangled in escalating contests of aversiveness, in which the individual who causes greater pain is the winner, obtaining negative reinforcement and digging in for the next round of conflict.

How the school affects a student's emotional or behavioral development depends, at least to some extent, on his or her characteristics upon entering the educational system. The same type of interaction between the student's temperament and the parents' child-rearing techniques appears to occur between the student's temperament and the school's social and academic demands. The student who is slow to approach others, has irregular work habits, is slow to adapt to new situations, and is predominantly negative in mood is most likely to have difficulty in school, though any temperamental characteristic is susceptible to modification with proper handling (Martin, 1992; Thomas et al., 1968).

The school, like the family and biological factors, does not operate unilaterally to determine students' emotional and behavioral development, but we can identify classroom conditions and teacher reactions to pupil behavior that make behavioral difficulties more likely to occur or that could be changed to reduce the likelihood of acting out and other types of emotional or behavioral problems (Colvin et al., 1993; Gelfand et al., 1986; Kasen, Johnson, & Cohen, 1990; Walker, 1995). The school might contribute to disordered behavior and academic failure in one or more of the following seven ways:

1. Insensitivity to students' individuality
2. Inappropriate expectations for students
3. Inconsistent management of behavior
4. Instruction in nonfunctional and irrelevant skills
5. Ineffective instruction in critical skills
6. Destructive contingencies of reinforcement
7. Undesirable models of school conduct

Besides these, factors such as crowded and deteriorated schools and classrooms are associated with aggression and other problems (McAfee, 1987; Rutter, Maughan, Mortimer, Ouston, & Smith, 1979). The physical conditions under which students are taught will surely affect their behavior for better or worse.

Insensitivity to Students' Individuality

Special educators of all persuasions—psychoanalytic, psychoeducational, humanistic, ecological, and behavioral—recognize the necessity of meeting pupils' individual needs. Some speculate, in fact, that the large proportion of school children identified as having learning and behavioral disorders reflects the refusal of the education system to accommodate individual differences (Reynolds, Wang, & Walberg, 1987; Rubin & Balow, 1971). Although not making reasonable accommodations to individual needs undoubtedly contributes to some students' failures or maladjustment, reasonable requirements for conformity to rules and standards clearly do not account for the failure or deviance of many others. In fact, just the opposite may be the case for some students; they may fail and behave antisocially because reasonable rules and expectations for conformity to standards of achievement and civility are not made clear (cf. Walker, 1995; Walker et al., 1995).

Rigidity and failure to tolerate differences do demand scrutiny, however. By making the same academic and behavioral requirements of each student, schools can force many students who are only slightly different from most into roles of academic failures or social deviants. Through inflexibility and stultifying insistence on sameness, schools can create conditions that inhibit or punish healthy expression of individuality. In an atmosphere of regimentation and repression, many students will respond with resentment, hostility, vandalism, or passive resistance to the system (see Mayer, Nafpaktitis, Butterworth, & Hollingsworth, 1987).

Thus, by squelching individuality and demanding uniformity, schools may contribute to learning and behavioral problems instead of facilitating optimum development. For students unfortunate enough to differ more than slightly from the norm in learning or behavior, the message in some classrooms is clear: "To be yourself is to be bad, inadequate, or unacceptable." These students' self-perceptions are likely to become negative, their perceptions of social situations distorted, and their intellectual efficiency and motivation weakened. They can become caught in a self-perpetuating cycle of conflict and negative influence as described by Long (1974), Glidewell et al. (1966), and Walker et al. (1995) for school environments and by Patterson and his colleagues for family environments (Patterson, 1982, 1986b; Patterson et al., 1992).

Insensitivity to individuals does not, of course, emanate from the school as an abstraction. Administrators, teachers, and other pupils are the people who are sensitive or insensitive to expressions of individuality. School administrators can create a tolerant or a repressive mood in the way they deal with students and in the way they deal with adults. Teachers are primarily responsible for the classroom emotional climate and for how restrictive or permissive, individualized or regimented the student's school day will be. Peers may demand strict conformity regarding dress, speech, or deportment for social acceptance, especially in the higher grades. On the other hand, peers may be an easygoing, open group in which a fellow student can find acceptance even though he or she is quite different from the group.

The effects of school climate may not be as simple as they at first appear, however, as suggested by the study of Kasen et al. (1990). Schools characterized by conflict—deliberate damage to school property and teachers often shouting at students—tended to have more acting-out students. On the other hand, a clear academic focus was associated with lower levels of opposition, conduct problems, and alcohol use. Thus, teachers and administrators who are sensitive to students but have clear and positive expectations for academic performance seem to foster appropriate behavior. We should not assume, however, that a positive and productive school climate is fostered by an emphasis on talking to students about their family and emotional problems; Kasen et al. found this strategy to be associated with higher levels of depressive symptoms in students. Moreover, teachers must not abandon their role as adult authority figures in attempts to develop better relationships with their students: "When teachers who have difficulty in maintaining basic order in the classroom treat pupils as peers, they may worsen an already bad situation" (Kasen et al., 1990, p. 175). A critical key to generally improved student behavior is a clear, consistent plan for school-wide discipline (Walker et al., 1995).

Although there is little experimental evidence to suggest that emotional or behavioral disorders are caused by insensitivity, we can readily find anecdotal and descriptive evidence that insensitivity may be a feature of many students' school experience (Epstein, 1981; Rutter et al., 1979; see also case descriptions in Kauffman et al., 1993). Unfortunately, insensitivity and rigidity are not qualities of school environments that are simply relics of the past. They have always been problematic, and they remain a bane of education. Furthermore, such environments appear to be a breeding ground for antisocial behavior. For example, Mayer et al. (1987) found correlations between vandalism and punitive school environments that did not recognize individual differences. Clarke and her colleagues (1995) found that incorporating student interests into academic tasks without compromising basic academic demands substantially improved the conduct of students.

In classic developmental studies, Thomas and Chess (1984) and Thomas et al. (1968) showed that the growth of emotional or behavioral disorders is accelerated by adults' failure to treat youngsters in accordance with their temperamental individuality. Richard's case (see accompanying vignette) illustrates how the rigidity of the school and the insensitivity of teachers and other students can play a part in creating behavioral problems. In the first grade, Richard had temper tantrums (up to five per day), and the school threatened to force his parents to withdraw him unless both they and Richard undertook psychiatric treatment.

Richard, First Grade

Initially, the tantrums were precipitated whenever Richard objected to stopping what he was doing and moving on to a new activity. As time passed, the number of incidents that would evoke a tantrum increased, especially since the other children had begun to laugh at his crying. Concurrently, he had begun, with much persistence, to ask his teacher that he be taught formal reading. This was not possible inasmuch as the school's educational philosophy emphasized reading readiness procedures in the first grade and the postponement of instruction in formal reading itself to the second or third grade. (Thomas et al., 1968, p. 154)

Richard's behavior greatly improved when his parents placed him in a different school where he was allowed to spend more time than other children on a given activity (such as reading or writing) before shifting to another task and received more instruction in reading, writing, and arithmetic. During the remainder of the first grade and throughout the second and third grades, his tantrums did not recur, because his teachers approved of his persistence in working on his assignments. In the fourth grade, however, his tantrums began again. One of the incidents in his fourth year at school is a particularly clear example of insensitivity on the part of teachers and peers.

Richard, Fourth Grade

Then a poster contest for public school children was announced. The teacher had obtained a specified number of poster papers, selected the children from the class who were to be permitted to enter the contest, and gave them paper. Richard did not get any and, quite innocently, assumed that it would be all right to get his own poster paper. He proceeded to do so and then brought in his finished poster. The teacher interpreted this as insubordination, scolded him for being disobedient, and tore up his poster. The other children laughed, and Richard erupted by flinging his notebook, which hit the teacher on the nose. The teacher reported this to the principal, which made the episode automatically an assault charge with mandatory dismissal of the child. (Thomas et al., 1968, p. 167)

The foregoing discussion is decidedly *not* intended as an indictment of all rules, regulations, or demands for conformity in the classroom or school. Certainly, reasonable rules must be maintained for the safety and well-being of all. No social institution can exist without some requirements of conformity, and one cannot interpret an appeal for tolerance of individual expression to mean that *anything* should be accepted. Nevertheless, insensitivity to students as individuals and needless repression of their uniqueness can contribute to emotional or behavioral problems. Students like to have a piece of the action, and allowing them to participate in self-determination of their classroom lives often results in improved behavior and academic performance (Clarke et al., 1995; Lovitt, 1977; Walker, 1995; Walker et al., 1995).

Inappropriate Expectations for Students

The expectations teachers *do* hold for their students, and the expectations they *should* hold, are continuing sources of controversy in American education. Two facets of the problem of expectations are the effects of what teachers are led to believe about their students (especially the possible biasing effects of diagnostic or administrative labels) and teachers' classroom standards of behavior and academic performance.

The Effects of Labels   Ever since Rosenthal and Jacobson published *Pygmalion in the Classroom* (1968), many educators and critics of education have been concerned that teachers' expectations of students may become self-fulfilling prophecies (Weinstein, Marshall, Sharp, & Botkin, 1987). Dunn's now classic article, "Special Education for the Mildly Retarded—Is Much of It Justifiable?" (1968), which was a rallying point for those opposed to the use of categorical labels in special education, added to the concern that students may fail because they are expected to fail. The labeling controversy continues in the 1990s, with claims that many of the problems of exceptional children originate with and are perpetuated by the labels we use to designate them (cf. Lilly, 1992). Some have assumed that a label, such as *emotionally disturbed*, carries with it an expectation of misbehavior and lower academic performance. The teacher's lower expectation for students labeled *exceptional* will be communicated in subtle ways to the students, and they will indeed fulfill this expectation. Moreover, there is concern for the stigma that goes with receiving a label denoting exceptionality, especially disability. As it happens, students' expectations for themselves may also influence their performance (cf. Rappaport & Rappaport, 1975).

Although we have no reliable experimental data to indicate that teachers' expectations themselves influence students' behavior, it is plausible that teachers do behave differently toward pupils depending on their expectations of them. If teachers have low expectations about a particular pupil, they may then treat that pupil differently than they treat another student about whom they have high expectations. The differences may involve types and difficulty of assignments and instructions, frequency of contact, amount of social praise and criticism, tone of responses to questions, objectivity of evaluation of performance, and other features of teacher behavior. Some differences in teacher behavior may be quite subtle and yet extremely powerful in their effects on students.

In early research on expectancy effects, Meichenbaum, Bowers, and Ross (1969) found that the teacher expectancy effect may be associated with changes in teacher behavior. When teachers were given the expectation that particular students would be potential intellectual bloomers, those students improved significantly more in appropriate classroom behavior and objective measures of academic performance than did control students for whom the expectation was not induced. Measurement of the teachers' behavior showed that they behaved differently toward students for whom the higher expectations were created, significantly increasing positive interactions or significantly decreasing negative interactions with the high expectancy pupils. Meichenbaum et al. (1969) concluded from their data: "It appears one means of modifying behavior of both teachers and pupils is to modify the teacher's perception or label of students' academic potential" (p. 315).

If the hypothesis as to the relationship between teacher expectation and teacher behavior is correct, then it will be important to know whether labels that imply that a student's behavior is deviant carry with them a set of lowered expectations (see Herson, 1974). Studies by Foster, Ysseldyke, and Reese (1975) and Ysseldyke and Foster (1978) provide some evidence that the label *emotionally disturbed* may bias teachers toward an expectation of lower than normal academic performance and poorer than normal social adjustment. Foster et al. (1975) found that undergraduate and graduate special education students rated a normal child (shown on videotape in a variety of situations, including testing and free play) lower in behavior and performance if they were told the child was emotionally disturbed than if they were told the child was normal. Ysseldyke and Foster (1978) found the same biasing effect for the label *learning disabled* as for *emotionally disturbed*. Admittedly, it is dangerous to generalize from these studies, but if *emotionally disturbed* and similar labels do negatively influence teachers' expectations, one might hypothesize this:

> A child is presented to the teacher bearing a deviancy label, and the teacher in turn approaches the child with a mental set based on preconceived expectancies. If the child shows signs of normalcy, these may, to some extent, alter the teacher's preconceived expectancies. This research suggests though that these normal behaviors can be misinterpreted as typical of negatively categorized children. Logic indicates that

an experimenter bias effect may then come into play, with the teacher behaving toward the child in ways consistent with the bias. If the child responds to the bias, he may in turn reinforce the teacher's expectancies. (Foster et al., 1975, p. 473)

Other research suggests that it is not necessarily the diagnostic or categorical label given to a student but the way behavior is characterized that sets teachers' expectations. DeStefano, Gesten, and Cowen (1977) compared the judgments of primary grade teachers and school mental health workers regarding hypothetical children with specific behavioral characteristics. The teachers viewed children with behavior problems as more difficult and less enjoyable to work with and as having a poorer prognosis than did the mental health workers. Coleman and Gilliam (1983) found that regular teachers in an elementary school had more negative attitudes toward students characterized as aggressive than toward those characterized as withdrawn from social contact. Lewin, Nelson, and Tollefson (1983) studied teachers' attitudes toward disruptive students and the changes that might be expected to occur in their attitudes toward disruptive children after they had successfully modified the children's disruptive behavior. They found that teachers carried negative, rejecting attitudes toward disruptive children, and, more importantly, that the teachers' attitudes did not change after they reported success in decreasing the disruptive behavior. Clearly, teachers do tend to view students with emotional or behavioral disorders negatively, particularly if the students are aggressive or disruptive (Johnson & Blankenship, 1984). These negative preconceptions probably carry expectations of negative teacher-pupil interactions and, perhaps, academic failure.

Which label—*emotionally disturbed* or *behaviorally disordered*—carries the more negative connotations for teachers? After studying teachers and teacher trainees' perceptions of students described by these two labels, Feldman et al. (1983) concluded that *behaviorally disordered* is significantly less negative in its meaning for teachers than is *emotionally disturbed*. Pre-service and in-service teachers believed that children labeled *behaviorally disordered* were more teachable, more likely to be successful in a mainstream classroom, and more likely to have a good future than were children described as *emotionally disturbed*. Lloyd, Kauffman, and Gansneder (1987) reported similar findings.

Ultimately, we must face the fact that labels of some type are necessary for communication (Burbach, 1981). They simply cannot be avoided unless we refuse to discuss students's problems (Kauffman, 1989). The issues, then, should be how we understand and use labels and how we work with the larger problem—our perceptions of the people whose characteristics we refer to when we use labels.

> Labels, in and of themselves, are not evil. How they are interpreted by others and by the labeled person determines whether they are harmful or ameliorative. The challenge is to educate society to use labels to arrive at a better understanding of persons with disabilities, to avoid overgeneralizing or stereotyping based on labels, and to see the individuals behind the labels. The challenge is also to help persons with a disability to use their labels as a basis for self-understanding, not as an excuse for failure to learn what they are able, a justification for choosing unacceptable behavior, or a reason to feel unworthy. (Hallahan & Kauffman, 1994, p. 503)

Finally, we note that a popular assumption is that receiving special education services destroys students' self-esteem and social status, regardless of the particular label under which they are served. Research suggests that this assumption may be unfounded for children with learning disabilities and emotional or behavioral disorders. Studies indicate that students receiving special education for learning or behavioral disorders—students receiving these labels—may have lower self-concepts or social status than students without learning or behavioral problems; they have not, however, been found to have lower self-perceptions and status than nonlabeled students who have academic or behavioral problems (Coleman, McHam, & Minnett, 1992; Patterson, Kupersmidt, & Griesler, 1988; Sale & Carey, 1995). Students appear to suffer damage to self-esteem and social status as a consequence of learning and behavior problems, not as a result of being labeled; the label follows the problem, not vice versa (see also Singer, 1988). In fact, a label for their difficulties appears to provide many people with disabilities a sense of relief (e.g., "Finally, I know what my problem is!") and to provide others an understandable reason for differences that, unlabeled, result in social rejection (cf. Hallahan & Kauffman, 1994).

The Effects of Classroom Standards   The research and speculation on effects of teacher bias do not lead logically to the conclusion that simply expecting normal behavior will help students with emotional or behavioral disorders improve. After all, it is quite clear that most such students are lower in tested intelligence, academic achievement, and social adjustment than average students; many are far below their age mates in numerous areas of development, and expecting normal performance from them is unrealistic. Perhaps a discrepancy between the child's ability and adults' expectations about performance contributes directly to the development of disordered behavior (Kirk, 1972). Kirk reasoned that teacher expectations that are too high or too low might contribute to the problem.

Kirk based his concept of discrepancy between potential and expectation on his own clinical observations and on extrapolations from experimental research with animals and children. He noted that experimental psychologists have found aggression, regression, and resignation to be frequent outcomes of frustration. Experimental situations in which animals or children were made to experience frustration caused the subjects to become aggressive in trying to reach their goal, to regress to an immature level of behavior, or to give up. Requiring students to perform in ways they cannot places them in highly frustrating situations; a child may respond by becoming angry and upset; exhibiting silly, irrational, or immature behavior; or simply becoming truant. In fact, students with emotional or behavioral disorders often are motivated by negative reinforcement—by behaving in ways that allow them to escape or avoid expectations for performance (Gunter, Denny, Jack, Shores, Nelson, 1993). Further direct evidence to support Kirk's hypothesis comes from Center, Deitz, and Kaufman (1982), who found that students' disruptive classroom behavior increased when they were given academic tasks that were too difficult for them. Kirk's discrepancy hypothesis is also consistent with research indicating that mothers of depressed children set high criteria for rewards and then reward their children at a very low rate (Cole & Rehm, 1986). If the same high standard–low reward conditions prevail in the classroom, it is reasonable to assume the effect will be the same—the student's depression.

If expectations that are too low become self-fulfilling prophecies and if expectations that are too high are frustrating, depressing, and prompt attempts to avoid them, then what level of expectation will avoid the risk of contributing to development of disordered behavior? Expectations of improvement are always in order—assuming, of course, that the teacher knows the student's current level of academic performance or adequate social behavior and can specify a reasonable level of improvement along a measurable dimension. If pupil and teacher define *reasonable* together, then the expectations should be neither too low nor too high.

Research does not suggest that teachers' expectations and demands are well attuned to students' abilities and characteristics (Gunter et al., 1993). Investigating the standards and expectations of regular and special education teachers for students' academic performance and social-interpersonal behavior, Walker and Rankin (1983) found that teachers' expectations could be described as narrow, intense, and demanding. The typical teacher expressed little tolerance for pupils who could not keep up academically or who exhibited inappropriate social behavior. And teachers consistently saw youngsters' competence in peer relations as less important than academic competence; their expectations centered on behaviors related to academic adjustment. These findings suggest that teachers' expectations may be a significant problem for students with emotional or behavioral disorders, regardless of whether they are in a special or general education class.

Elementary and secondary teachers' expectations and demands appear to be similar. Kerr and Zigmond (1986) studied the behavioral characteristics that high-school teachers considered critical for success and those they considered intolerable; their findings were similar to those of Walker and his associates, who studied elementary teachers' standards and expectations (Hersh & Walker, 1983, Walker & Rankin, 1983). Tables 9.1 and 9.2 list the skills elementary and high-school teachers most often considered critical for success and those they considered intolerable. Note that students with externalizing problems, who act out aggressively or have conduct disorders, are extremely likely to fail to meet teachers' expectations and to violate the teachers' standards of classroom decorum. Walker (1986) also reports that teachers resist placement in their classroom of a student who is at times uncontrollably aggressive, is incontinent, is enuretic, has deficient self-help skills, or is hyperactive. Given teachers' standards and expectations, it should not be surprising that students with emotional or behavioral disorders and their teachers frequently disappoint each other, setting the stage for conflict and coercion.

We should not inappropriately generalize to all teachers, nor assume that high standards and low tolerance for misbehavior are undesirable. Walker (1986) and Kauffman, Lloyd, and McGee (1989) report great variability in teachers' responses to questions about their standards and tolerance; some teachers apparently make few demands and have great tolerance for deviance, and others are just the opposite. Compared to regular classroom teachers, special education teachers may be somewhat more tolerant of misbehavior and judge students' behavior as less deviant (Walker, 1986; Fabre & Walker, 1987; Safran & Safran, 1987). Teachers' expressed

Table 9.1

Skills That Teachers Considered Critical for Success in Regular Classrooms

1. Follows established classroom rules (85)
2. Listens to teacher instructions (84)
3. Can follow teacher-written instructions and directions (81)
4. Complies with teacher commands (78)
5. Does in-class assignments as directed (74)
6. Avoids breaking classroom rule(s) even when encouraged by a peer (67)
7. Produces work of acceptable quality given his/her skill level (67)
8. Has good work habits (e.g., makes efficient use of class time, is organized, stays on task, etc.) (67)
9. Makes her/his assistance needs known in an appropriate manner (64)
10. Copes with failure in an appropriate manner (64)
11. Uses academic tools correctly (63)
12. Uses classroom equipment and materials correctly (62)
13. Attends consistently to assigned tasks (60)
14. Can accept not getting his/her own way (59)
15. Expresses anger appropriately (58)
16. Listens while other students are speaking (56)
17. Observes rules governing movement around the room (53)
18. Behaves appropriately in nonclassroom settings, respects property and the rights of others (53)
19. Is honest with others (52)
20. Improves academic or social behavior in response to teacher feedback (51)
21. Questions rules, directions, or instructions that are not clear to her/him (51)
22. Has independent study skills (51)
23. Responds to requests and directions promptly (51)

Note: Items rated critical for success by 50 percent or more of secondary teachers in the study by Kerr and Zigmond (1986) (percentages indicated in parentheses following items). Items 1, 2, 4, 5, 6, 7, 9, 15, and 18 were nine of the ten items rated critical for success most often by elementary teachers in the study by Hersh and Walker (1983).

tolerance for troublesome behavior may be affected by several factors, including their self-perceived competence, the availability and quality of technical assistance, and the difficulty of the particular group of students they are teaching (Safran & Safran, 1987). Teachers who have higher standards and lower tolerance for disorderly behavior may also provide more effective instruction (Gersten, Walker, & Darch, 1988).

Inconsistent Management of Behavior

A major hypothesis underlying a structured approach to educating students with emotional or behavioral disorders is that a lack of structure or order in their daily lives contributes to their difficulties. When youngsters cannot predict adults' responses to their behavior, they become anxious, confused, and unable to choose

Table 9.2
Problems That Teachers Considered Intolerable in Regular Classrooms

1. Engages in inappropriate sexual behavior (99)
2. Steals (98)
3. Is physically aggressive with others (98)
4. Behaves inappropriately in class when corrected (98)
5. Damages others' property (97)
6. Refuses to obey teacher-imposed classroom rules (97)
7. Disturbs or disrupts the activities of others (96)
8. Is self-abusive (96)
9. Makes lewd or obscene gestures (94)
10. Ignores teacher warnings or reprimands (94)
11. Creates a disturbance during class activities (93)
12. Cheats (93)
13. Is verbally aggressive with others (93)
14. Has tantrums (90)
15. Reacts with defiance to instructions or commands (90)
16. Uses obscene language (89)
17. Is inexcusably late for the beginning of class activities (86)
18. Does not ask permission to use others' property (85)
19. Forces the submission of peers by being dominant (82)
20. Engages in silly, attention-getting behavior (80)
21. Lies (77)
22. Argues and must have the last word in verbal exchanges (76)

Note: Items rated intolerable by 75 percent or more of secondary teachers in the study by Kerr and Zigmond (1986) (percentages indicated in parentheses following items). Items 1, 2, 4, 5, 6, 8, 9, 10, and 14 were the ten items rated intolerable most often by elementary teachers in the study by Hersh and Walker (1983).

appropriate behavioral alternatives. If at one time they are allowed to engage in a certain misbehavior without penalty and at another time are punished for the same misconduct, the unpredictability of the consequences of their behavior encourages them to act inappropriately. If they cannot depend on favorable consequences following good behavior, they have little incentive to perform well.

We find strong support in the child development literature for the contention that inconsistent behavior management fosters disordered behavior (Hetherington & Martin, 1986). If one can extrapolate from the findings that inconsistent parental discipline adversely affects children's behavioral development, then it seems highly likely that inconsistent behavior management techniques in the school will also have negative effects. Capricious, inconsistent discipline in the classroom will contribute nothing toward helping students learn appropriate conduct. School-based studies of antisocial behavior, such as vandalism, also indicate a connection between punitive, inconsistent discipline and problem behavior (Mayer et al., 1987; see also Walker et al., 1995). Even though inconsistent management may not be the root of all behavioral disorders, it obviously contributes to perpetuation of behavioral difficulties.

Instruction in Nonfunctional and Irrelevant Skills

One way the school increases the probability that students will misbehave or be truant is in offering instruction for which pupils have no real or imagined use. Not only does this kind of education fail to engage pupils, it also hinders their social adaptation by wasting their time and substituting trivial information for knowledge that would allow them to pursue rewarding activities.

The problem of making education relevant to students' lives has plagued teachers for a long time. The question is more than whether the teacher or other adults know the instruction to be important for the student's future. To resolve the question, the youngster must be convinced that the learning he or she is asked to do is or will be important. The teacher must convince the student that the instruction is in some ways worthwhile; otherwise the classroom will be merely a place for the pupil to avoid or to disrupt. For some students with a history of school problems, convincing them will require provision of artificial reasons to learn, such as extrinsic rewards for behavior and performance.

Ineffective Instruction in Critical Skills

Social acceptance and positive self-perceptions are greatly enhanced by academic competence and skills in interacting with one's peers and authority figures. Thus, the classroom must be a place in which all class members are learning critical academic skills and the social skills critical for success in general education. Ineffective instruction in either area—academic or social learning—dooms many students to academic or social failure, or both. Nevertheless, many classrooms are not places where students are taught effectively but places where they are left to fend for themselves instructionally, to pick up whatever skills they might acquire through incidental learning or self-discovery.

We cannot overemphasize the importance of academic learning to emotional well-being and behavioral development (cf. Rhode et al., 1992; Walker, 1995). For everyone, not just children and youths, being able to meet everyday expectations is critical to mental health. Faced with constant failure and unfavorable comparisons to peers, nearly anyone will succumb to feelings of frustration, worthlessness, irritability, and rage. Competence on the job is an elixir; incompetence compared to one's peers is an emotional and behavioral poison. The job of students is academic learning, and teachers who are not as effective as they could be in helping students achieve academic competence are contributing to students' emotional and behavioral problems.

Unfortunately, most of general public education in the 1990s has adopted instructional practices that are not effective, especially for students who come to school without the skills that most economically privileged students acquire outside of school. Child-directed, "holistic," "discovery learning" approaches and heterogeneous grouping, for example, are instructional practices virtually certain to fail with students at risk of failure (see Dixon, 1994; Grossen, 1993). Special education classes are also too often places in which effective academic instruction is not provided (Colvin, Greenberg, & Sherman, 1993; Knitzer et al., 1990). Direct instruction is effective in helping students with disabilities acquire academic skills (Bender, 1993; Hallahan et al., 1996; Rosenberg, 1994), and using such instruction could improve the learning of students in both general and special education.

Also unfortunate is the fact that most of general public education in the 1990s has failed to adopt explicit programs for teaching social skills and rewarding desirable behavior. Specific social skills need to be assessed and taught explicitly and systematically to many individuals and groups if they are to learn the basic skills needed for positive interaction with others (Mayer, 1995; Walker et al., 1995). Yet few schools provide such assessment or instruction. Moreover, classrooms need to be places in which desirable conduct is explicitly, frequently, and effectively rewarded (Lloyd & Kauffman, 1995). Yet most classrooms are characterized by very low rates of positive consequences for appropriate behavior (Shores et al., 1993). Popularization of the notion that rewards undermine intrinsic motivation and that positive reinforcement amounts to bribes (e.g., Kohn, 1993) has further impeded the adoption of positive behavioral strategies for managing classroom behavior. However, overwhelming empirical evidence indicates that rewards do not undermine intrinsic motivation (Cameron & Pierce, 1994) and that rewards are essential for effective, positive classroom management, especially of difficult students (Mayer, 1995; Rhode et al., 1992; Walker, 1995; Walker et al., 1995).

Destructive Contingencies of Reinforcement

From the viewpoint of behavioral psychology, the school can contribute to the development of emotional or behavioral disorders in several obvious ways:

- providing positive reinforcement for inappropriate behavior
- failing to provide positive reinforcement for desirable behavior
- providing negative reinforcement for behavior that allows students to avoid their work

The following feature defines positive and negative reinforcement and gives examples of how they may work in a classroom environment (see also Cipani, 1995).

Positive and Negative Reinforcement: A Dynamic Duo

Reinforcement—especially negative reinforcement—is often misunderstood. Many teachers do not understand how positive and negative reinforcement typically work together and how both may be involved in maintaining either desirable or troublesome classroom behavior. In many interactions, students with emotional or behavioral disorders get a double dose of reinforcement, one positive and one negative, and often for the wrong behavior.

Reinforcement, whether positive or negative, is a reward or consequence that makes the behavior it follows more likely to recur. The "reward" may be something one *gets* (i.e., a positive reinforcer) or something one *gets rid of or avoids* (i.e., a negative reinforcer). It may be helpful to think of people looking for work and having signs stating what they want. Some signs might say, "Will work FOR ___." Other signs might say, "Will work TO GET OUT OF ___." Still others might say "Will work FOR ___ AND TO AVOID ___." What someone will work *for* provides positive reinforcement; what someone will work *to get out of or avoid* provides negative reinforcement. Most of us will work for money, and most of us will work to get out of debt or to avoid losing our job. Most of us will work for course credit and, at the same time, work to avoid embarrassment or a bad grade. In fact, in most cases our behavior is motivated by two consequences at once: (1) something we get and (2) something we avoid. We work for money and also to get out of work (the negative reinforcement—escape from work—that we call vacations).

We all experience both positive and negative reinforcement in everyday life, and both types of reinforcement play important roles in motivating our adaptive behavior. However, positive and negative reinforcement become problematic rather than helpful in the classroom or any other environment when they are misused or poorly arranged. Misuse or poor application may be the result of either of two major mistakes:

- *Misidentification.* A teacher may believe that criticisms or reprimands are negative reinforcers that a student will work to avoid, when they are actually positive reinforcers. Being reprimanded is something the student will work to get because of the attention it brings from the teacher and classroom peers (for many of us, attention is something we crave, whether it is criticism or praise; being ignored is what we will work hardest to avoid). A teacher may also fail to see that academic assignments are negative reinforcers for a student who exhibits disruptive classroom behavior: academic work may be something the student will misbehave to get out of. Whatever behavior allows this student to escape from the work will be reinforced; the student will misbehave so that he or she does not have to do the work.

- *Malcontingency.* The contingencies in a classroom are destructive if they result in either positive reinforcement or negative reinforcement for undesirable behavior. Students may learn this: I get lots of attention when I misbehave (positive reinforcement, even if the attention is in the form of intended punishment such as scolding) and, in addition, I get out of my academic work (negative reinforcement).

The dynamic duo of positive and negative reinforcement can be harnessed to give desirable behavior a double boost. Students get a double good deal when the classroom contingencies involving both positive and negative reinforcement are constructive: attention for desirable behavior (positive reinforcement) and little vacations from work (negative reinforcement) as a reward for work done promptly and well.

Ample evidence suggests that in many classrooms, destructive rather than constructive contingencies of reinforcement are in place—appropriate conduct typically goes unrewarded while both positive and negative reinforcement for misconduct is frequent (Gunter et al., 1993; Shores et al., 1993; Strain, Lambert, Kerr, Stagg, & Lenkner, 1983; Webber & Scheuermann, 1991). A great deal of evidence suggests that constructive reinforcement contingencies can be arranged to teach appropriate behavior even to students whose behavior is seriously disordered (Colvin, Sugai, & Patching, 1993; Kerr & Nelson, 1989; Morgan & Jenson, 1988; Webber & Scheuermann, 1991; Walker et al., 1995). In study after study over the past several decades, experimental studies have shown that providing teacher attention during appropriate behavior but withholding it during undesirable behavior results in improvement (see

Kazdin, 1984; Morris, 1985; Nelson, 1981; Sherman & Bushell, 1975; Walker, 1995; Walker et al., 1995; West et al., 1995).

Consider that in many classrooms, contingencies of reinforcement are inadvertently arranged to promote the very behavior the teacher deems undesirable! Strain et al. (1983) corroborated the findings of several previous studies indicating that teachers tend to provide predominantly negative feedback to pupils and seldom reinforce appropriate behavior. The chance that any of the 130 children in their study would receive positive feedback (verbal compliment or gestural approval, such as a pat or hug) following compliance with a teacher's command, demand, or request was only one in 10. In addition, Strain et al. found that the 19 regular class teachers (kindergarten through third grade) they studied gave reinforcement (positive feedback) to poorly adjusted children following noncompliance more often than they gave reinforcement for compliance. And the teachers tended to repeat the commands, demands, and requests more often for poorly adjusted than for well adjusted pupils. Gunter et al. (1993) and Shores et al. (1993) reported similar findings. Given these conditions, which apparently are common in classrooms, it is not surprising that many children's misbehavior becomes a greater problem as they advance through the grades.

The use of constructive consequences for adaptive behavior is consistent with a conceptual model that assumes interactive effects of students' and teachers' responses. An interactional or transactional model suggests that youngsters and adults exert reciprocal influence on each other. It is reasonable to believe that teachers' and problem students' mutual praise and criticism become important factors in the maintenance of behavior, and that mutual hostility could be defused beginning with either teacher or pupil. Polirstok and Greer (1977) trained an eighth-grade girl who was frequently verbally abusive (and who received primarily disapproving, critical comments from her teachers) to increase her approving, complimentary comments to her teachers. In response to what they described as her remarkable socialization and new-found maturity, her teachers reversed their tendency to interact with her in a predominantly negative way. Morgan, Young, and Goldstein (1983) trained three boys with behavioral disorders in elementary school to recruit social reinforcement and assistance from their teachers. The boys were trained to prompt their teachers to offer help on academic tasks, praise their teachers for helping them, and prompt their teachers to give them approval for good behavior and correct work. These studies demonstrated that destructive contingencies of reinforcement are not one-sided; classroom harmony and disharmony are a function of both teacher and student conduct. In the typical educational setting, however, the teacher is responsible for making the first move toward providing positive, constructive consequences for desirable behavior.

Students who have social adjustment problems are usually at odds with their peers as well as their teachers. The same type of mutual hostility and negative reciprocity that characterizes exchanges between some teachers and students also appears in social interactions of rejected students and their peers. Polirstok and her colleagues (Greer & Polirstok, 1982; Polirstok, 1986, 1987; Polirstok & Greer, 1986) report success in teaching adolescents with behavioral problems to serve as tutors for their peers. Both tutors and tutees have benefitted academically from the peer tutoring program. The problem students who served as tutors improved their on-task behavior and engaged in more positive reciprocal responses with their peers. A critical component of the tutoring program is the teacher's awarding points to tutors for giving verbal approval to tutees (Polirstok & Greer, 1986). By initiating reciprocal approval during tutoring, teachers apparently set in motion an interaction style that made the school a much more hospitable environment for everyone. Tutors and tutees exchanged approval; teachers rewarded tutors for their reinforcement of tutees; and tutors and tutees made more academic progress and behaved more appropriately in classes, rewarding teachers for their efforts and setting the stage for continued reciprocity of approval. Polirstok explains the benefits:

> If, as the evidence suggests, problematic adolescents can be taught to earn natural reinforcement in the environment, a unique shaping process between the school and the tutor will ensue. As a result of this shaping process, school life will become more reinforcing for tutors, who, in turn, will improve their academic and social behaviors and, as a consequence, will merit additional reinforcement from the school. (1986, p. 209)

Training students to tutor their peers is not a venture to undertake lightly (Gerber & Kauffman, 1981). Especially when the tutors are students with serious behavioral problems, training and monitoring the tutors require considerable time and effort. Nevertheless, this strategy has demonstrated success in maintaining students with emotional or behavioral disorders in mainstream settings (Polirstok, 1987). Moreover, a skillfully implemented program of peer tutoring could be a key strategy in teaching social skills to all students. Strayhorn, Strain, and Walker (1993) have suggested that peer tutoring be used as a means of teaching students nurturing responses to others, which would help make schools and the larger society kinder and gentler places in which to live.

Abundant empirical evidence shows that students' classroom behavior can be altered by manipulating the contingencies of reinforcement, even when the reinforcement is as natural a part of the classroom as teacher and peer attention. One needs neither a great backlog of classroom observation nor great acumen to see the potential implications of this evidence in the school's contributions to the development of emotional or behavioral disorders. Students whose behavior is a problem often receive abundant attention for misbehavior but little or no attention for appropriate conduct. Even though the attention they receive for misbehavior is often in the form of criticism or punishment, it is still attention and is likely to reinforce whatever they are doing at the time it is dispensed. The effect of attention for misbehavior and nonattention for good deportment is likely to be perpetuation of the miscreant's deeds, regardless of the intentions of the teacher or other adult.

Undesirable Models of School Conduct

Children and youths are great imitators. Much of their learning is the result of watching others and mimicking their behavior. Youngsters are particularly likely to imitate the behavior modeled by people who are socially or physically powerful, attractive, and in command of important reinforcers (Bandura, 1986). Unless the modeling process is carefully controlled, students who act out and disrupt the classroom are likely to gravitate toward other peers who are disruptive (Hallenbeck & Kauffman, 1995). Teachers must find ways to call attention to and reward the appropriate behavior of high-status peers (Walker, 1995; Walker et al., 1995).

Understandably, the examples teachers set strongly influence the way students approach their academic work and the way they behave. Rutter et al. (1979) point out that "pupils are likely to be influenced—either for good or ill—by the models of behavior provided by teachers both in the classroom and elsewhere" (p. 189). Exemplary behavior on the part of the teacher encourages like conduct in pupils; maltreatment by the teacher of any student in the class is very likely to encourage students to treat each other with hostility or disrespect. Teachers whose attitude toward their work is cavalier or who are disorganized may foster similar carelessness and disorganization in their students. Corporal punishment—still used in some schools and classrooms—is a horrid example of aggressive misconduct by adults that may be mimicked by students in their relationships with others (see Evans & Richardson, 1995; Strauss & Brown, 1995).

Peers exert considerable social pressure on students' behavior in school, particularly at the high-school level. Schools in which high-status students either refuse to perform academic tasks or exhibit serious misbehavior with impunity are likely to see the spread of academic failure and social misconduct (Arnold & Brungardt, 1983; Rutter et al., 1979; Walker et al., 1995).

IMPLICATIONS FOR EDUCATORS

The teacher of students with emotional or behavioral disorders must be prepared to work with pupils who are deficient intellectually and academically, as well as deviant in their social behavior, although some of these students are superior intellectually and academically. Teaching these students demands not only the ability to instruct pupils with an extremely wide range of intellectual and academic levels, but also the ability to teach social and other nonacademic behaviors that make scholastic success possible, such as good work habits, attention strategies, and independence. The most crucial tasks of the teacher as a preventive agent are to foster academic success and to lessen the student's antisocial conduct. Academic failure and antisocial behavior predict limited future opportunities and probable future maladjustment.

The most valuable perspective for the teacher is to examine the student's present environment to detect factors that contribute to disordered behavior and those that encourage desirable behavior. The teacher's primary task is to modulate the school environment in ways that will contribute to adaptive, prosocial behavior and academic growth.

Regrettably, many teachers of students with emotional or behavioral disorders are poorly prepared for the task. A national study found that 43 percent of such teachers did not hold permanent certification to teach such students (Clark-Chiarelli & Singer, 1995). As these researchers noted, "we need more teachers to work with these students, and those that we need must be better trained" (p. 165). Moreover, the effectiveness of special education programs was reported by teachers to be undercut by lack of support from administrators and parents. The challenge we face is not just preparing more and better teachers but providing the supports that will facilitate their success and keep them in the field.

SUMMARY

The role of the school in causing emotional or behavioral disorders is a particularly important consideration for educators. In our society, school failure is tantamount to personal failure. The school environment is not only critically important for social development but is the factor over which educators have direct control.

As a group, students with emotional or behavioral disorders score below average on intelligence tests and are academic underachievers. Many of them lack specific social skills. The behavior they exhibit is inimical to school success. Disordered behavior and underachievement appear to influence each other reciprocally; in an individual case, which causes the other is not as important as recognizing that they are interrelated. Academic failure and low intelligence, when combined with antisocial behavior or conduct disorder, portend social adjustment problems in adulthood.

The school may contribute to the development of emotional or behavioral disorders in children in several ways:

- School administrators, teachers, and other pupils may be insensitive to the student's individuality.

- Teachers may hold inappropriate expectations of students.

- Teachers may be inconsistent in managing students' behavior.

- Instruction may be offered in nonfunctional (that is, seemingly irrelevant) skills.

- Ineffective instruction may be offered in skills that are critical for school success.

- School personnel may arrange destructive contingencies of reinforcement.

- Peers and teachers may provide models of undesirable conduct.

Teachers of students with emotional or behavioral disorders must be prepared to teach youngsters who are underachieving and difficult to instruct, and instruction must be provided in both academics and social skills.

Case for Discussion

"You Had Better Get On Them"

Bob Winters

Bob Winters had been prepared to teach preschoolers with disabilities, but he accepted a job teaching a special class of students with mild mental disabilities in a middle school. When he was hired, the principal, Mr. Dudley, had told him, "You're the expert. We'll give you a lot of leeway for making decisions about these students because you're the one who's trained to work with exceptional students. Mr. Arter, the teacher last year, had lots of trouble with these kids. You'll have to come down on them hard."

Bob struggled to develop appropriate instructional programs for his students. Other teachers were coming to him for advice, but he had little or nothing to offer. He ended up assigning lots of worksheets emphasizing basic skills. He tried to keep the kids busy, but as the days and weeks rolled by his class became more and more rowdy, and he felt his classroom control slipping away. The students raced through their assignments and then wandered around the room laughing and joking in small groups and verbally abusing each other. Poor grades did not bother them. In fact, they bragged about getting bad grades and were particularly glad to show off a paper that had the lowest score in the class.

Bob's class became so unruly and noisy that Mr. Dudley occasionally came down the hall to open the classroom door and glare or shout at Bob's students. The students laughed and joked about Mr. Dudley after he left. "He thinks he's bad," one would say, and the others would shake their heads in agreement.

Bob was determined to get tougher. He simply had to get control over this class. He began trying Mr. Dudley's shouted directions. As punishment, he began requiring students to copy pages out of the dictionary, something they seemed to dread. But one Thursday he invoked this punishment when Ronnie disrupted the class as he returned from the restroom. Ronnie grinned impishly and declared, "Okay, I *love* copying the dictionary." He copied more pages than Bob had assigned. But the next day Linwood flatly refused to copy any pages at all, and Bob eventually ordered him to the office.

Eventually, Bob decided to arrange the students' desks facing the classroom walls. Maybe this way they wouldn't distract each other so much and would get more work done, he reasoned. But then they began moving their desks together without permission. They met his reprimands with saucy comments like, "Oh, big man!" and "Yeh, he thinks he's going to do something!" When Gerald jumped out of his seat and ran over to whack Mike playfully on the back of the head, Bob lashed out. "GET YOUR ASS IN THE CHAIR!" he bellowed. Gerald froze. The others stared silently at Bob as he went on, "I don't give a damn what you all want to do. You're going to do as I say." Cathy nudged Linwood, who sat beside her, and they began to giggle. Bob descended on Cathy immediately, shouting, "Go to the office!" With flashing, angry eyes, Cathy stalked out and slammed the door. Her classmates shook their heads and exchanged scowls.

Ten minutes later, Mr. Dudley was at Bob's door. "Mr. Winters, may I see you outside?" As he walked to the door, Bob heard Amber say, "He's going to be in trouble." Bob guessed she was right. [*Note:* This case was adapted from Kauffman, Mostert, Nuttycombe, Trent, & Hallahan (1993).]

Questions About the Case

1. How do Bob's teaching and management strategies illustrate the concepts presented in this chapter? What was Mr. Dudley's role in contributing to the problems with this class?

2. Were you Bob's friend and colleague, what advice would you give him about improving his teaching performance?

3. Where does the responsibility lie for preventing situations like the one depicted here?

PERSONAL REFLECTIONS

School Factors

Valerie Gregory, M.Ed., is principal of Clark Elementary School in Charlottesville, Virginia.

What are the behavioral characteristics that at-risk students exhibit at school?

The behavioral characteristics of these children in school are diverse, but they generally fall into two subgroups—children who tend to direct their behavior outward and children who tend to direct their behavior inward. Children who act out may have temper tantrums or be extremely aggressive with peers and adults. These children seem to operate outside the norms. In the classroom, they find it hard to pay attention; they're fidgety, and they often lack confidence about what they can do. These are children who often interrupt the activities of the classroom and engage in attention-seeking behavior. Their work is usually incomplete, messy, and disorganized. They often don't follow verbal or written directions. Children who tend to direct their behavior inward are often not as noticeable. They may be extremely withdrawn and quiet. A lot of times, teachers don't even realize they're in the classroom because they don't participate in the activities at all. Although children who direct their behavior outward and children who direct their behavior inward seem to be on opposite ends of a spectrum, both types of students are at risk for school failure.

How would you characterize teachers who are likely to have special difficulty with behavior management or have negative effects on children's behavior?

Too often, teachers tend to link achievement with behavior. Teachers really must learn to discern and separate the two. So the first thing teachers may look at is how the child behaves, not what the child may know or how the child may learn. Teachers who are likely to have special difficulty with behavior management usually have an extremely rigid and narrow set of expectations about what a classroom is supposed to be like: every child is supposed to sit behind a desk, pay attention, and raise his or her hand. The teacher may react very negatively toward any child who doesn't meet these norms. Preconceived notions about how a child is going to behave—whether based on comments of other teachers discovered in the child's cumulative records or based on simple prejudice or bias—can be counterproductive. A negative expectation can undermine the teacher's ability to develop sound behavior management strategies for that child. It is really hard for teachers to admit that these preconceived notions exist, but they do exist.

Teachers who do not pay attention to how children learn often have difficulty managing the behavior of their students. Children who already have or are at risk for emotional or behavioral disorders do not necessarily learn in the traditional lecture format. Teachers need to explore the different learning styles of the children in their classes. Also, teachers may rarely call on a child with emotional or behavioral disorders, even for the smallest kinds of things. Whenever that child's name is called, usually right behind it is a "Don't," "Stop," or another negative statement. Rarely is there a positive comment directed to that child. Teachers need to be aware of what they are saying to students in order to influence children's behavior in a positive manner.

Teachers who have difficulty with behavior management also may fall into one of two traps: (1) not considering the circumstances of a child with emotional or behavioral disorders or (2) considering these circumstances to the exclusion of all else. For example, a child who is at risk for or has an emotional or behavioral disorder is rarely provided the luxury of messing up. If this child doesn't do his homework, he has to miss all of his extra activities. The teacher may give little consideration to the circumstances at home that may have prevented this child from completing his work. At the other extreme, some teachers can have too much sympathy for the child's circumstances outside of school. "Poor Johnny, you know, his mom." These teachers provide excuses for Johnny and pat him on the back, but then they don't expect anything else from him. Both of these approaches to behavior management may have negative effects on children's behavior.

What are the things you do as a principal to try to establish a positive and supportive school climate in your school?

I think we need to start with the building itself. The school should project an interesting and warm physical environment. When someone walks into the school, I want him or her to think, "Ah, this is a neat place for learning." I think this is something that everyone in the school has to work on—the principal, the teachers, the students, the parents, the custodial staff, the volunteers.

As a principal, I try to get out of the role of being just an authoritative type of person sitting in the office. When I see students walking in a straight line, I tell them, "I like the way this line looks." Positive reinforcement needs to come from the principal, too. Teachers need this positive reinforcement as well. If I walk into a classroom and I see a teacher helping a child on her or his own time, that teacher needs to know that I noticed. I will stick a little note in the teacher's mailbox and say, "I like what I saw." I also try to encourage teachers to share their ideas with their colleagues. Encouraging the teachers and the students in such ways helps to foster a positive and supportive learning environment.

Along these lines, I have found that it is important to recognize all kinds of successes, not just the As that children earn. This is especially important with children who have or are at risk for emotional or behavioral disorders, because their successes do not always come in the form of excellent grades. We tried something at our school called the BUG (Bring Up a Grade) Roll. Children who bring a grade up, even from F to D, get recognition on this list. We need to recognize even the small increments of progress that our students make.

In order to foster a positive and supportive climate, we also need to contact and involve parents more often. So often, I think, we call parents just to tell them everything that's going wrong. Rarely do principals call and say, "Guess what? Your son got an A on his spelling test!" I try to let parents know some of the good things their children are doing by sending postcards to their homes that praise the children for their successes. Again, looking for those small things, particularly with those children who are at risk, is a key factor. I also believe that the children play a big role in establishing the climate of the school. I try to teach children to be responsible for their school. In this manner, I'm trying to get away from simply imposing and enforcing rules, and instead teach students that it is their responsibility to take care of the school and to create a good classroom environment. I think another real key to success is getting everyone involved in creating such a climate.

What do you think are the most important aspects of a child's experience at school that could contribute to behavior problems?

The first thing that comes to my mind is the way we often teach irrelevant skills very early to students. Often we present tasks as abstract, not applicable to a child's real life. I think we should help children understand the importance of what we are asking them to do.

Another consideration is the way we schedule the school day. We really need to think about how the daily schedule may contribute to kids' problems. We tend to bombard children with instructional tasks the first thing in the morning, leaving very little time for breaks or social interactions. It's a packed day. Maybe we could break it up so that children have the opportunity to perform their best. Also, I think we need to look at how we block off the day with subject matter. Many classrooms are organized around an hour for reading, an hour for math, an hour for science, and so on. This schedule may not always provide the best arrangement for facilitating academic or social learning. An integrated curriculum, in which diverse subject matter is taught in relation to a particular topic, may help stimulate and involve children in learning.

We also need to acknowledge the differences and individual needs of children. Too often, we try to make everybody the same. When a child doesn't fit into that mold, we don't seem to recognize or try to address the differences. I think that we frequently lack differentiation in teaching. We hold the same expectations of everybody. I often tell my teachers when they are giving an assignment or a project, "Don't expect everybody to give a written report." If you're doing something on China, give choices. You may have a child who doesn't write well, but maybe he could build something well. And that should carry as much weight as another child's 10-page report. We need a little more differentiation along that line. Holding the same expectations of all children can set the stage for failure, which may contribute to the behavior problems.

Do you have other reflections on the role of the school?

Today, the school is too often treated as a separate entity in the community, unlike in the past when it was an integral part of the community. We really need to work more on school–community relationships and make each an active part of the other's existence. What happens in the school reflects what happens in the community and vice versa. We need to identify and capitalize on the best features of both in a more integrated way.

10

Cultural Factors

As you read this chapter, keep these guiding questions in mind:

- How do conflicts between cultures create stress for children and youths?

- What steps can educators take to avoid the problems of bias and discrimination against students whose cultures differ from their own?

- Besides family and school, what major cultural factors may contribute to behavioral deviance? Why is it difficult to evaluate the effects of these factors?

- What relationships have been established between TV viewing and children's antisocial and prosocial behavior?

- By what processes do the mass media influence behavior?

- What types of behavior characterize high status peers and youngsters who are rejected by their peers?

- What social skills should we teach youngsters who are rejected by their peers, and how should we teach the skills?

- How would you characterize a neighborhood that provides support for development of children's appropriate social behavior?

- What conclusions can we draw about the effects on behavior of urbanization, ethnicity, and social class?

THE APPEAL OF CULTURAL FACTORS
AS CAUSAL EXPLANATIONS

Neither families nor schools include all the social influences that determine how youngsters behave. Children, families, and teachers are part of a larger culture that molds their behavior. Parents and teachers tend to hold values and set behavioral standards and expectations that are consistent with those of the cultures in which they live and work. Children's attitudes and behavior gravitate toward the cultural norms of their families, peers, and communities. We must therefore evaluate family factors in the context of cultural differences and changes.

> The patterns of parenting associated with adaptive or deviant behavior in children may differ in an inner-city environment, an affluent suburb, or an isolated Virginia mountain hollow, in times of war and peace, economic stability or depression. . . . It may be that results of the studies made in the 1960s will have little relevance for today's changing families and that the findings of current studies will tell us little about American families in the 1990s. (Hetherington & Martin, 1986, p. 333)

Culture involves behavioral expectations, but it is more than that. Banks (1994) suggests that culture has many definitions but that it might be described by six elements: (1) values and behavioral styles, (2) languages and dialects, (3) nonverbal communication, (4) awareness (of one's cultural distinctiveness), (5) frames of reference (normative world views or perspectives), and (6) identification (feeling part of the cultural group). Nations and other large social entities with a shared culture comprise a **macroculture**. Within the larger macroculture are many **microcultures**, smaller groups with unique values, styles, languages, dialects, ways of communicating nonverbally, awareness, frames of reference, and identification. How do we maintain American macroculture and at the same time respect the microcultures that comprise it? The answer is neither obvious nor easy (see Hallahan & Kauffman, 1997, for further discussion of multiculturalism and exceptionality).

We have long viewed our country as a cultural melting pot—an amalgam of various nationalities and cultures. We have come to believe that the diversity of our citizens is something that makes America strong and good. On the other hand, we realize that if we do not make a true alloy of the diverse ingredients of our culture—if we do not amalgamate our diverse elements into a single, uniquely American identity—we can be neither strong nor good as a society. *E pluribus unum* (out of many, one), a slogan stamped on our coins, seems to present an increasing paradox (see Hodgkinson, 1995; Ogbu, 1990). We value cultural diversity; common cultural values hold our society together. The tension between our separateness and our togetherness—our distinctiveness and our oneness—obviously can set the stage for disordered emotions and behavior.

When the child's, family's, or school's values or expectations conflict with other cultural norms, emotional or behavioral development may be adversely affected. To the extent that different cultural forces tug and pull a youngster's behavior in different directions, they create conflicting expectations and increase the probability that he or she will violate cultural norms and be labeled deviant. Comer (1988) notes that "Differences between home and school—whether of class, race, income, or culture—always create potential conflict" (p. 37). It is not surprising, therefore, that researchers have given a great deal of attention to cultural factors that contribute to disordered behavior.

CONFLICTING CULTURAL VALUES AND STANDARDS

It is easy to find examples of conflicting cultural values and standards and the stress they create for children and youths. Television shows, movies, and magazines glamorize the behavior and values of high-status models that are incompatible with the standards of many children's families; youngsters' imitation of these models results in disapproval from parents. Religious groups may proscribe certain behaviors that are normative in the larger community (such as dancing, attending movies, dating, masturbating), and youngsters who conform to these religious teachings may be rejected by peers, stigmatized, or socially isolated, while those who violate the proscriptions may feel extreme guilt. The values children attach to certain possessions or behavior because they are highly regarded by their peers or teachers (such as wearing particular items of clothing or achieving at school) may be incomprehensible to their parents. Differences between parents' and children's values may become the focus of parental nattering.

Children of interracial marriages may have difficulty developing a sense of identity, particularly during adolescence. They may have major problems reconciling their dual racial identifications into a single, personal identity that affirms the positive aspects of each heritage while acknowledging society's ambivalence toward biracial persons (Gibbs, 1987). At the same time, the demographic trends in America are toward a mixing of national, ethnic, and racial categories (Hodgkinson, 1995).

Conflicting cultural influences on behavior are sometimes perverse; the culture provides both inducements for a given type of behavior and severe penalties for engaging in it. This kind of temptation or pressure with one hand and punishment with the other is especially evident in the areas of violent behavior and sexuality. Our society fosters violence through its glorification of high-status, violent models in the mass media, yet seeks severe punishment for youngsters' imitative social aggression. Consider teenage pregnancy—the cultural forces that foster it, and society's responses to it. During the past several decades, sexual mores have changed, so that adolescents now have much greater freedom and added responsibilities for preventing pregnancy. Our society tempts adolescents, offering them freedoms and responsibilities they are not equipped to handle, yet does nothing to help them deal with the freedoms and responsibilities, and in fact punishes them for abusing freedom and behaving irresponsibly. Motion pictures, MTV, and commercials highlight sex appeal and sexual encounters, providing models of behavior that are incompatible with efforts to encourage sexual abstinence and avoid pregnancy. Teenagers often pressure their peers to become sexually active; at the same time, conservative politicians have attempted to restrict sex education and make contraceptives less available to teens. Education for family life and child rearing is often inadequate.

A MULTICULTURAL PERSPECTIVE

Besides the conflicts that differing cultural standards create, children's and adults' own cultural values may bias their perceptions of others. A full discussion of cultural bias in education is far beyond the scope of this chapter, but it is important to note that problems of bias and discrimination carry serious implications for evaluating youngsters' behavior. Ultimately, nearly all behavioral standards and expectations— and therefore nearly all judgments regarding behavioral deviance—are culture-bound; value judgments cannot be entirely culture-free. In our pluralistic society, which values multicultural elements, the central question for educators is whether they have made sufficient allowance in their judgments for behavior that is a function of a child's particular cultural heritage (see Carlson & Stephens, 1986; Council for Children with Behavioral Disorders, 1996). Cultural differences that do not put the youngster at risk in the larger society should be accepted; only values and behaviors that are incompatible with achieving the larger goals of education (self-actualization, independence, and responsibility) should be modified.

Who determines the larger goals of society? We all tend to view our own cultural orientation as the standard against which others should be judged. Because the United States has been dominated by European microcultures, the focus of multicultural concerns has been on non-European minority cultures.

> The United States, like many modern nations, is an aggregate of peoples of many cultural backgrounds. However, the role of culture is most noticeable when any of us view the practices of some other group than our own, and so the study of culture has

generally focused on minorities in the United States and on people of other nations. It is easy for dominant cultural groups to consider themselves as standard and other groups as variations. (Think of the number of people who comment on other people's accents and insist that they themselves do not have one.) (Rogoff & Morelli, 1989, p. 341)

It is not easy to establish rules for applying a multicultural perspective. Teachers and school administrators must make daily decisions as to which standards of conduct represent their personal value systems and which represent justifiable demands for adaptation to the larger society; for example, is it really necessary for students to remove their hats in the classroom? What is "polite" English, and is it necessary that students use it to address adults in school? What values and behaviors are inconsistent with a youngster's success and happiness in society at large? When do the values of a particular culture place a student at risk for school failure? Under what conditions is risk of school failure a fault of the school itself—how it is organized and the demands it makes of students? These and similar questions have no ready answers. They will continue to be part of our struggle for fairness and justice in a multicultural society.

PROBLEMS IN EVALUATING THE EFFECTS OF CULTURAL FACTORS

Besides the family and the school, which are topics of separate chapters, the most frequently researched cultural factors include the mass media, peer group, neighborhood, ethnic origin, social class, religious institutions, urbanization, and health and welfare services. Evaluating the role of these factors in emotional or behavioral disorders is extremely difficult, primarily for two reasons. First, the interrelationships among the many cultural influences are so strong that untangling the effects of most of the individual factors is impossible (see box). Farrington (1986) noted:

> The major problem in drawing conclusions about sociocultural factors in childhood psychopathology is that most possible predisposing factors tend to be interrelated. Children who live in deprived inner-city areas (at least in North America and Great Britain) tend to be from ethnic minorities, tend to have parents with low status, low-paid jobs, or no job at all, and tend to have friends who commit deviant acts. Furthermore, sociocultural factors tend to be related to individual characteristics and to family influences. . . . Children from low-income families tend to have many siblings, which may make peer influence more important relative to parental influence, tend to receive poor nutrition and medical care from conception onwards, and tend to be exposed to lax and erratic child-management practices and to parental conflict, violence, and alcohol abuse. (p. 391)

More recently, Hodgkinson (1995) observed that concern with racial and ethnic differences has diverted our attention from the more pervasive effects of poverty. Although poverty may be correlated with racial or ethnic identities, the best strategy for improving the lives of children who are members of racial or ethnic minorities may be to focus on poverty itself.

To some extent, race diverted our attention from the most urgent issue: *poverty reduces the quality of the lives of all children, regardless of race or ethnicity.* Had we spent the 40 years since the *Brown* [1954 school desegregation] decision systematically seeking to lower the poverty level for *all* American children, we would be in a different, and probably better, condition today. (Hodgkinson, 1995, pp. 178-179)

Second, research related to several of the factors is limited or nearly nonexistent. Religious beliefs and institutions, for example, probably have a strong influence on family life and child behavior, particularly among ethnic families of color (Billingsley & Caldwell, 1991; Ford, 1995; Walton, Ackiss, & Smith, 1991), yet there is little research on the effects of religion on child behavior and family life. Bronfenbrenner, Moen, and Garbarino's (1984) statement remains true: "researchers concerned with the well-being of families and children would do well to attend to the part played by religious institutions within the community, but at present this area remains a scientific terra incognita" (p. 307). Maypole and Anderson (1987) highlight the importance of including the black church in culture-specific intervention programs for African-American youngsters.

Despite these difficulties in understanding cultural factors, available research does suggest relationships between certain cultural characteristics and the development of behavioral deviance. For example, violence in the media and the ready availability of guns, two prominent features of contemporary American culture, are consistently linked to aggressive conduct of children and youths (American Psychological Association, 1993; Walker, Colvin, & Ramsey, 1995). The challenge is to understand and sustain cultural diversity that enhances the human condition while modifying cultural patterns of behavior that are destructive of the human spirit.

Family, School, and Culture: A Tangled Web of Causal Influences

When we think of cultural factors, we think of social institutions—nations, ethnic groups, religions, schools, and families. These and other social institutions are interconnected in ways that defy simple explanations of causal influences on children's behavior. For each possible combination of social institutions, we must ask how one affects the other. To what extent does the nation make its schools, and to what extent do its schools make that nation? To what degree can schools succeed without the support of families, and to what degree can families be successful without schools that teach what their children need to learn? What are the cultural factors other than families and schools that shape children's behavior, and how do families and schools create, enhance, or counteract these other influences? The answers to these questions are neither simple nor obvious, but they are critical to our understanding of the roles of schools and teachers in our society.

The role of schools in American culture—the extent to which schools merely reflect our national character and the extent to which they are responsible for creating it—is frequently a matter for discussion. Perhaps, some suggest, the increasing use of guns in our society is an "American disease" (Morganthau et al., 1992). If it is a "disease" of American culture, then it is no wonder it has invaded our schools. Researchers have found that Southeast Asian refugee families adopting an orientation to certain American values—acquisition of material possessions and pursuit of fun and excitement—have children whose academic performance is lower than that of children from families maintaining traditional Southeast Asian values—persistence, achievement, and family support (Caplan, Choy, & Whitmore, 1992). From one vantage point, then, it appears that schools and teachers face a task at which they cannot succeed unless changes occur in other aspects of social context or culture. "It is clear that the U.S. educational system can work—if the requisite familial and social supports are provided for the students outside school" (Caplan et al., 1992, p. 36).

We cannot, however, ignore the fact that schools and teachers have a special responsibility to influence the families and communities for which they exist—the other parts of our culture that they also reflect. True, parents must be involved with and support the work of teachers if the schools are to succeed. "Yet we cannot expect the family to provide such support alone. Schools must reach out to families and engage them meaningfully in the education of their children" (Caplan et al., 1992, p. 42). And that meaningful engagement can occur only if schools offer instruction that addresses the concerns of families and communities. Delpit (1995) noted that many poor, minority children have been shortchanged by an exclusive focus on "progressive" methods of instruction that cater to the learning of middle-class white students: "I have come to believe that the 'open-classroom movement,' despite its progressive intentions, faded in large part because it was not able to come to terms with the concerns of poor and minority communities" (p. 20).

Many see the role of schools in American culture changing, in large measure because of the increasingly troublesome behavior, attitudes, and social needs of students.

> As the social needs of our students have moved into the classroom, they have consumed the scarce resources allocated to education and have compromised the schools' academic function. The primary role of teachers has become that of parent by proxy; they are expected to transform the attitude and behavior of children, many of whom come to school ill prepared to learn. (Caplan et al., 1992, p. 42)

American culture itself is shaped in significant ways by the distribution of wealth among its citizens, and increasing economic disparities are a troublesome part of American culture. Poverty is a part of American culture that we obviously have not addressed effectively (Hodgkinson, 1995; Knitzer & Aber, 1995). The cultural context of American public schools in the late-twentieth century includes widespread poverty among children and the deterioration of family and other social institutions that previously offered more support for schools. The role of special education for children and youths with emotional or behavioral disorders in this context will likely be a matter for increasingly hot debate.

THE MASS MEDIA

Mass media include printed materials, radio, television, motion pictures, and electronic information now available on the Internet. Societal concern for the effects of mass media on the behavior of children and youths began as long ago as when books and magazines became widely available (Donelson, 1987). A few generations ago, concerns about the effects of radio programs and comic books were frequently expressed. Present controversies rage over the effects of textbooks, pornographic magazines, novels, motion pictures, electronic games, and information available on the World Wide Web on the thinking and behavior of the young. That what people read, see, and hear influences their behavior is hardly questionable, yet relatively little sound research is available to explain how—with the exception of advertising material. Publishers and broadcasters do market research to show the effectiveness of sponsors' ads; they know a lot about what sells and what influences the buying habits of specific segments of their audiences, including children and adolescents. Nevertheless, the influence of the media on youngsters' *social* behavior is often dubious or hotly disputed. Ironically, the same individuals (television network executives) who express confidence in the behavioral effects of television commercials argue that the effects of television violence on children's social behavior is negligible (Eron & Heusmann, 1986).

Today, the effects of television on behavioral development is by far the most serious media issue. Specifically, researchers and policy makers are interested in how watching television may increase children's aggression and their **prosocial behavior** (for example, helping, sharing, cooperation). Research clearly links watching television to increases in aggression, but the link is a statistical probability, not a one-to-one correspondence. Some highly aggressive children do not watch much television, while some children who watch television almost incessantly are not aggressive. Yet television viewing is clearly a contributing factor in *some* children's antisocial conduct, and it is important to understand how television viewing can be involved in causation. One obvious way television violence can facilitate aggressive conduct is observational learning; youngsters imitate what they see. This explanation is probably a gross oversimplification, however, as research now suggests that much more complicated processes are involved.

The most likely explanation of the effects of television viewing fit Bandura's (1986) social cognitive model (see chapter 4). The effects involve reciprocal influence among three components: person variables (thoughts and feelings), the social environment, and behavior. In the case of television violence and aggression, Bandura's triadic reciprocality involves the child's thoughts and feelings about aggression and the television characters who perform it, the child's environment (including school, home, and community), and the child's selection of violent television programs and aggressive responses to problem situations. But general social circumstance—the social ecology in which aggression is exhibited, including friendship patterns and school performance—must also be considered. Eron and Heusmann (1986) summarize reciprocal influences among person variables, environment, and behavior in the social ecology of aggressive children.

> Children who behave aggressively are less popular and, perhaps because their relations with their peers tend to be unsatisfying, watch more TV and view more violence. The violence they see on TV may reassure them that their own behavior is appropriate or teach them new coercive techniques that they then attempt to use in their interactions with others. Thus, they behave more aggressively, which in turn makes them even less popular and drives them back to TV. The evidence supports a similar role for academic failure. Those children who fail in school watch more TV, perhaps because they

find it more satisfying than schoolwork. Thus, they are exposed to more violence and have more opportunity to learn aggressive behavior. Because their intellectual capacities are more limited, the easy aggressive solutions they observe may be incorporated more readily into their behavioral repertoire. In any case, the high frequency of violence viewing isolates them from their peers and gives them less time to work toward academic success. And, of course, any resulting increase in aggression itself diminishes the child's popularity. Thus, the cycle continues with aggression, academic failure, social failure, and TV violence reinforcing each other. (pp. 310–311)

Sprafkin, Gadow, and Abelman (1992) and Gadow and Sprafkin (1993) reviewed decades of research on the effects of television viewing on exceptional children. They found little evidence that watching television programs showing prosocial acts causes children with emotional or behavioral disorders to engage in more appropriate social interaction. Their review also indicated that high levels of television viewing, whether the shows contained much violence or not, have negative effects on children's behavior.

Violent television programs appear to instigate antisocial acts in some cases, to desensitize children to acts of aggression (i.e., make them more apathetic to displays of aggression and less likely to help others), and to perceive their environment as a more aggressive and dangerous place. Although research may not indicate clearly that watching television violence consistently causes children (including those with emotional or behavioral disorders) to be violent, there are good reasons to limit children's television viewing and direct their attention toward more constructive activities. The American Psychological Association (1993) and Walker et al. (1995) conclude that decreasing the violence depicted on television and in movies would help lower the level of violent behavior among children and youths.

The role of the mass media (not just television, but all print, film, and broadcast media) in the development of emotional or behavioral disorders is a concern to those who wish to construct a more prosocial and humane society. For example, teenage suicidal behavior appears to increase following media coverage of teen suicides (Eisenberg, 1984; Hawton, 1986). Motion pictures that glorify violent solutions to problems may add to the effects of television violence. It is difficult to conclude that print materials featuring violence and pornography play any positive role in behavioral development or conduct. Perhaps decreasing portrayal of undesirable behavior and increasing prosocial programming and reporting of prosocial acts would make our culture less self-destructive and more humane. Yet the solution to the media problem is not apparent; censorship is not compatible with the principles of a free society. Personal choice and responsibility in patronage may be the only acceptable way to approach the problem (Sprafkin et al., 1992).

THE PEER GROUP

The peer group is a possible contributing factor to emotional or behavioral disorders in two ways. First, the establishment of positive, reciprocal peer relationships is critical for normal social development. Children who are unable to establish positive relationships with their classmates are at high risk because the peer group is an important link to social learning. Second, some children and youths are enmeshed in a peer group, but the group exerts pressure toward maladaptive patterns of behavior.

Absence of Positive Peer Relationships

Peer relationships are extremely important for behavioral development, especially during middle childhood and early adolescence, yet until the early 1980s, research tended to focus more on family relationships than on socialization to the peer group (Hops, Finch, & McConnell, 1985). We can now identify problematic relations with peers in children as young as 5 years of age, and these problems tend to persist over time (Coie & Dodge, 1983; Loeber, Green, Lahey, Christ, & Frick, 1992). Behavioral characteristics associated with emergence and maintenance of social status in the peer group and relationships between peer status and later behavioral problems are becoming clearer (Coie, Dodge, & Kupersmidt, 1990; Coie & Kupersmidt, 1983; Kupersmidt & Coie, 1987; Maccoby, 1986; Patterson, 1986b; Strain, 1981; Strain, Odom, & McConnell, 1984; Walker et al., 1995).

Research indicates that, in general, high status or social acceptance is associated with helpfulness, friendliness, and conformity to rules—to prosocial interaction with peers and positive attitudes toward others. Low status or social rejection is associated with hostility, disruptiveness, and aggression in the peer group (Guevremont & Dumas, 1994). To complicate matters, aggressive youngsters, compared to nonaggressive, seem more likely to attribute hostile intentions to their peers' behavior; and they are more likely to respond aggressively even when they interpret their peers' intentions as nonhostile (Dodge & Somberg, 1987). Low social status among peers is also associated with academic failure and a variety of problems in later life, including suicide and delinquency (Farrington, 1986, 1995; Gelfand et al., 1986). In fact, poor peer relations, academic incompetence, and low self-esteem are among the primary factors in an empirically derived model of the development of antisocial behavior (Dishion, 1990; Patterson, 1986b; Patterson et al., 1992; Walker et al., 1995).

The evidence that antisocial children and youths are typically in conflict with their peers as well as with adult authorities is overwhelming, as is the evidence that antisocial youngsters tend to gravitate toward deviant peers (Berndt & Keefe, 1995; Dishion, Andrews, & Crosby, 1995). Youngsters who do not learn about cooperation, empathy, and social reciprocity from their peers are at risk for inadequate relationships later in life. They are likely to have problems developing the intimate, enduring friendships that are necessary for adequate adjustment throughout life. Thus the peer group is a critical factor in creating social deviance (see Strayhorn, Strain, & Walker, 1993).

These generalizations do not do justice to the complexity of the research on relationships between social status among peers and children's behavioral characteristics. Social status can be measured using peer nominations, teacher ratings, or direct behavioral observations. Depending on the source of data, different pictures of social acceptance or rejection emerge. Normal or expected behavior in the peer group differs with age and sex, so the same type of behavior can have different implications for peer relations depending on age and sex (Cairns & Cairns, 1986; Maccoby, 1986). The social processes that lead to social rejection may be quite different from those that lead to social isolation or neglect (Coie et al., 1990). The same classroom conditions can produce different effects on social status and friendship patterns for students of different races (Hallinan & Teixeira, 1987; see also Anderson & Webb-Johnson, 1995). And bias in peers' social perceptions can produce different outcomes in terms of social acceptability for two individuals who exhibit similar behavior (Hollinger, 1987).

All sources of information regarding children's social acceptance indicate that better-liked youngsters are those who are considerate, helpful, and able to appeal to group norms or rules without alienating their peers. Social rejection is related to opposite characteristics—violating rules, hyperactivity, disruption, and aggression—although the antisocial behavior that characterizes rejected youngsters changes with age. As children grow older, they tend to exhibit less overt physical aggression. The ways they irritate others, and so become rejected, become more complex, subtle, and verbal. Physical aggression is more often a factor leading to rejection in boys' groups than in girls'.

Social withdrawal is often associated with peer rejection, but the causal relationship is not always clear. Apparently, social withdrawal is not as prominent as aggression in young children's thinking about relations with their peers (Younger & Boyko, 1987). As children grow older, however, withdrawal correlates more closely with rejection, perhaps because rejected children are acquiring a history of unsuccessful attempts to join social groups. This correlation suggests that withdrawal is the result of rejection, a way of dealing with repeated social rebuffs. Youngsters who withdraw following repeated rejection may become the targets of taunts and abuse, perpetuating a cycle of further withdrawal and further rejection.

We know less about the behavior of socially neglected children than about those who are actively rejected, partly because it is difficult to study the characteristics of children who are all but invisible to their peers. Nevertheless, it appears that their peers see them as shy and withdrawn, that they engage in solitary play more frequently than most children, and that they are less aggressive and higher achieving than even popular youngsters (Wentzel & Asher, 1995). Neglected children sometimes appear to exhibit relatively high levels of prosocial behavior and conformity to teacher expectations, but their general lack of assertiveness may result in their peers' not perceiving them as socially competent.

Given that we have identified social skills in which rejected, withdrawn, and neglected youngsters are deficient, programs to teach those skills are logical interventions. Social skills training programs are now readily available (see Walker et al., 1995). Nevertheless, social skills training often yields equivocal results, perhaps in part because training programs are typically implemented poorly or inconsistently (cf. Kavale & Forness, 1995). Moreover, exactly what skills to teach often remains in doubt. The notion that we can easily identify critical social skill deficits without careful assessment is a deceptive oversimplification (Walker et al., 1995). Research increasingly reveals that social competence is much more complex than previously thought. Social competence may relate to the ability to display specific skills in specific situations, but precise identification of skills and exact specifications of performance in given situations are extremely difficult to determine (see Fox, 1987; Weiss-berg & Allen, 1986). Moreover, identifying social skill deficits that *cause* youngsters to have problems with their peers is not always possible; the causes of peer rejection or neglect are typically multiple and complex.

An important aspect of the analysis of peer relations and social skills training, and one that has not always been considered in research, is the development of expectations that bias youngsters' perceptions of their peers' behavior. If, for example, a youngster acquires a reputation among his or her peers, for aggression or for popularity, others respond to this reputation. They expect behavior that is consistent with their attributions of the motives of an individual whose reputation they accept as valid, and they interpret behavioral incidents accordingly. If one child throws a ball that hits another child on the head, peers are likely to interpret the incident in terms of their beliefs about the motives of the child who threw the ball. If the child is popular and does not have a reputation for aggression, they are likely to interpret the incident as an accident; if the child has a reputation for aggression, they are likely to interpret it as aggressive. The reciprocal interaction of biased perceptions and actual behavior must be taken into account in trying to understand why some youngsters are rejected while others who behave similarly are not. Hollinger (1987) summarized this phenomenon:

> Children learn to expect aggressive behavior from peers who have gained a reputation for being aggressive, although the peers may not actually engage in more aggressive behavior. A cyclical pattern develops in which children engage in more aggressive behavior toward peers who have a reputation of being aggressive. Thus aggressive children are both the recipients and instigators of more aggressive behavior than their peers. From the peers' perspective, [their] aggressive behavior is justified as a response to more aggression from the aggressive child. And the hostile attributions of aggressive boys justify their aggressive behavior. In the end, the more aggressive the child, the more likely it is that [he] will attribute hostile intentions in ambiguous situations and consequently get caught in the cycle that maintains aggressive interactions. (p. 23)

Effective social skills interventions must therefore include provisions for dealing with peer group response to the youngster with emotional or behavioral disorders as well as teaching skills that enhance social acceptance (Walker, Schwarz, Nippold, Irvin, & Noell, 1994; Walker et al., 1995). Only when the social ecology of the peer group can be altered to support appropriate behavioral change are social skills likely to result in improved status of the target child. Knowing that a youngster lacks specific social skills necessary for social acceptance and being able to teach those skills is not enough; one must also change the youngster's reputation—the perceptions and attributions of peers.

Negative Peer Pressure

An important causal factor in some emotional or behavioral disorders, especially antisocial behavior and delinquency, is peer pressure. The assumption that students who exhibit antisocial tendencies will observe and imitate the desirable behavior of their regular classroom peers appears to based on myth rather than facts about observational learning (Hallenbeck & Kauffman, 1995). Antisocial students often reject socially skilled models and gravitate toward a deviant peer group (Farmer & Hollowell, 1994; Patterson, Reid, & Dishion, 1992).

Peer pressure toward rejection of academic tasks as well as toward antisocial behavior appears to be a serious problem in many communities (see Banks, 1995; Fridrich & Flannery, 1995). Consider the observations of R. Leon Churchill, Jr., an African-American who, at the time of the following comments, was 33 years of age and the assistant city manager of Charlottesville, Virginia. He recalled that as a boy in school in Williamsburg his good study habits cost him friends. "I remember being teased constantly for getting good grades. . . . One of the major issues that Charlottesville and most schools have to deal with is the gauntlet that African-American males have to run through for achievement" (Zack, 1995, B1, B2). Peer pressure of some African-American students toward academic failure and classroom disruption may involve not wanting to act or be accused of acting "white," but racial and ethnic perceptions are not the only factors in such peer pressure, nor are African-American students the only ones to experience peer pressure toward marginal or failing performance at school. In any ethnic or racial group and in any social stratum, we may find groups of peers who express disdain for those who are studious, high achieving, and tractable.

Teachers must thus be aware of how their efforts to induce and maintain appropriate behavior in their students can be undermined by negative peer pressure. More importantly, teachers need to find ways, perhaps through peer tutoring or other means, to build a peer culture that is supportive of kindness and achievement. Research suggests that this may be accomplished for most students when they are given regular opportunities to learn, with proper training and supervision, to nurture and teach younger children (see Farmer, Stuart, Lorch, & Fields, 1993; Strayhorn et al., 1993).

THE NEIGHBORHOOD AND URBANIZATION

Neighborhood refers not only to residents' social class and the quality of physical surroundings but to the available psychological support systems as well. Separating the neighborhood from other causal factors in social deviance, particularly social class, has proved difficult, if not impossible (Farrington, 1986, 1995). The neighborhood and community may play important roles in the prevention of certain types of highly visible behavioral deviance, such as conduct disorder and juvenile crime (Lorion, Brodsky, Flaherty, & Holland, 1995). For example, a community sense of moral order, social control, safety, and solidarity may be extremely difficult to achieve in a neighborhood in which crime rates are high. Interventions aimed at individuals will probably not succeed because of the lack of neighborhood monitoring and mutual support. Group-oriented, community interventions that promote a shared sense of being able to cope with deviance may be more likely to help prevent juvenile delinquency and crime in high-crime neighborhoods (Lorion et al., 1995; Nietzel & Himelein, 1986).

The belief that city life is not conducive to mental health has persisted for well over a century in spite of lack of evidence that this is the case (cf. Jarvis, 1852). Achenbach and his colleagues (1991), in a national study of behavior problems, found no differences between rural and urban settings in parental ratings of children's behavior problems. However, higher behavior problem ratings were found in areas of intermediate urbanization (i.e., urban areas of less than one million people).

Higher rates of delinquency are sometimes found to occur in urban than in rural areas, but a major difficulty in establishing urban environments as a causal factor in social deviance is that urbanization cannot be easily separated from other factors, such as crowding, quality of housing, community or neighborhood supports, social class, and so on (see Farrington, 1986, 1995). However, it is also clear that family functioning and child rearing are often quite difficult in today's urban environment (Zayas, 1995).

Some people express enthusiasm for the virtues and healing powers of rural retreats and agrarian cultures, but there is not much evidence that they are superior to urban environments in producing mentally healthy and high-achieving children (cf. Herzog & Pittman, 1995; Howley & Howley, 1995). The overriding factors associated with deviance appear to be low socioeconomic status and the breakdown of family and community ties. Recent reports of economic and social conditions in rural America leave no doubt that inner cities are not our only disaster areas for families and children. If rural ever meant "safe," "healthful," or "educationally superior" for children, it is clear that it does not necessarily mean those things in the 1990s (Helge, 1992).

ETHNICITY

Ethnicity has been the focus of much contemporary concern for understanding cultural diversity and forging multicultural education (cf. Banks, 1994; Banks & Banks, 1993; Council for Children with Behavioral Disorders, 1996). Nevertheless, ethnic identity is increasingly difficult for many Americans to define (Hodgkinson, 1995), and we must be careful to separate ethnic influences on behavior from those of other factors such as economic deprivation, social class, the peer group, and so on.

In one of the largest and most carefully controlled studies of prevalence of behavioral problems in children and adolescents, Achenbach and Edelbrock (1981) found very few racial differences. They did, however, find substantial differences in behavioral ratings from different social classes, with children of lower class exhibiting higher problem scores and lower social competence scores than those from higher class. When the effects of social class are controlled, ethnicity apparently has little or no relationship to emotional or behavioral disorders. The risk factors that may appear to accompany ethnicity are probably a function of the poverty of many ethnic minority families (Garmezy, 1987; see also Hodgkinson, 1995).

Ethnicity is often suggested as a factor in juvenile delinquency because studies show higher delinquency rates among black than among white youngsters, but we must question the meaning of differences in rate for at least two reasons. First, discrimination in processing may account for higher official delinquency rates among students of African descent. Second, ethnic origin is difficult or impossible to separate from other causal factors, including family, neighborhood, and social class. Thus, it is not clear that ethnicity is related to delinquency independently of other factors (Farrington, 1986).

Our tendency has been to make sweeping judgments regarding ethnic groups without taking individual backgrounds and experiences into account. This leads to stereotypes based on ethnic identity alone.

> Current research reveals the dominance of a troubling stereotype—that is, one that predicts educational failure for African-Americans and educational excellence for Asian-Americans in studies of educational achievement among African- and Asian-American students. Little differentiation is made either among African-Americans or among Asian-Americans of different cultural, language, immigration, and economic backgrounds. (Slaughter-Defoe, Nakagawa, Takanishi, & Johnson, 1990, p. 373)

We must remember also that ethnic identity does play a part in how youngsters, particularly adolescents, are treated in our society (Ford, 1995; McAdoo, 1990; Peterson & Ishii-Jordan, 1994; Stiffman & Davis, 1990). The issues surrounding ethnicity are complex because the values, standards, and expectations of ethnic groups are shaped not only internally by members of these groups but also by external pressures from the larger macroculture of which they are part. Thus we must be careful in analyses of the effects of ethnicity to separate the influences of ethnic background from the effects of the dominant cultural groups' treatment of other ethnic groups. Given the long history of maltreatment of ethnic groups with relatively little power by the dominant American ethnic groups, we should not be surprised to find that membership in an ethnic minority that has comparatively little political or social power presents barriers to the achievement of academic competence, economic security, and mental health (cf. Stiffman & Davis, 1990).

SOCIAL CLASS AND POVERTY

One ordinarily measures children's social class in terms of parental occupation, with children of laborers and domestic workers representing one of the lower classes and children of professional or managerial workers representing one of the higher classes. Studies (Achenbach & Edelbrock, 1981) and reviews of studies (Farrington, 1986) frequently link behavioral problems, lack of social competence, and delinquency to lower social class. Although lower social class is often associated with psychopathology, the meaning of this finding is controversial. The relationship between social class and specific types of disordered behavior does not hold up as well as the relationship to emotional and behavioral problems in general. Furthermore, family discord and disintegration, low parental intelligence, parental criminality, and deteriorated living conditions seem to be much more influential than parents' occupational prestige in accounting for children's behavior. Although it is true that many parents in low-prestige occupations may be described by the characteristics just cited, it is not clear that low social class in itself is a contributing factor in children's social deviance; social class may be a factor only in the context of these other parental and family characteristics.

Economic disadvantage—poverty, with all its deprivations and stress—is apparently a factor in development of disordered behavior; social class, at least as measured by occupational prestige of parents, probably is not (cf. Delpit, 1995; Hart & Risley, 1995; Hodgkinson, 1995). Merely being poor does not make people inadequate or destroy families or account for children's school failure or emotional and behavioral problems. However, we do know that many of the conditions that often are part of poverty, especially in its extreme, are strong negative influences on children's cognitive and social development: inadequate shelter, food, and clothing; exposure to chaotic living conditions and violence; lack of opportunities to learn from nurturant, attentive adults (Bolger et al., 1995; Felner et al., 1995; Guerra et al., 1995). Nevertheless, poverty itself is the best predictor of school failure, as Hodgkinson (1995) points out:

> If there is one universal finding from educational research, it is that poverty is at the core of most school failures. And this is as true for white children from Appalachia as for black and Hispanic children from inner-city slums. . . .
>
> Consider the issue of relative deprivation. Is a child with dark skin more likely to be disadvantaged in terms of life chances than a child born into poverty? Today, the answer is clearly no; poverty is a more pervasive index of social disadvantage than is minority status.
>
> This emphatically does *not* mean that we can ignore poor minority children; it means that a successful strategy will have to lift the largest number of children out of poverty, regardless of their race. . . .
>
> There is clear evidence from the U.S. Government Accounting Office and from other sources that a number of social programs are effective in mitigating the effects of poverty. Head Start, WIC (Women, Infants, and Children feeding program), AFDC (Aid to Families with Dependent Children), and Upward Bound are programs that reduce the effects of poverty and help reduce the number of America's youngsters who remain in poverty. In addition, the prevention agenda—ensuring that bad things do not happen to young children—is "color blind" in its effectiveness for all poor children. We have at our disposal a set of proven programs for reducing poverty for *all* children from birth to age 18. Why is this agenda not fully implemented? (pp. 176-178)

IMPLICATIONS FOR EDUCATORS

Educators should be aware of how cultural factors may be contributing to their students' emotional or behavioral problems, and of the possibility of cultural bias in evaluating behavioral problems. Recall Farrington's (1986) comments regarding the interrelationships among predisposing sociocultural factors in behavioral deviance. We can seldom untangle the effects of isolated factors from the mix of circumstances and conditions associated with disordered behavior. Nevertheless, research on specific factors that may give rise to disorders has important implications for prevention, especially if intervention can be aimed at improving children's individual circumstances. Strong evidence now suggests a basis for corrective action in many cases; reducing television violence and providing more prosocial television programming, for example, would probably help reduce the level of aggression in our society.

Much could be done to address the needs of children reared under adverse conditions in which their health and safety, not to mention intellectual stimulation and emotional development, are at stake. These kinds of social changes demand large-scale efforts that educators cannot achieve alone; indeed, the politicization of issues regarding the physical and mental health risks of children and youths calls for all Americans to speak out. As Garmezy (1987) and Hodgkinson (1995) have pointed out (see accompanying box), decisions about programs to serve children and youths living in poverty will have enormous consequences for the nation's future.

Of the causal factors discussed in this chapter, the peer relations of rejected and neglected students are perhaps the most important consideration for the daily work of educators. Although we now recognize the great significance of students' poor peer relations, we know relatively little about the most effective means of intervening to improve their status once patterns of maladaptive behavior have become well established. Developing school-based, early interventions for target children and their peers should be a priority for researchers and teachers; these interventions may play an important role in prevention of social adjustment problems (Strayhorn et al., 1993; Walker et al., 1995; Weissberg & Allen, 1986).

The Health and Welfare of Children: How Important Are They in American Culture?

The Children's Defense Fund periodically reports statistics attesting to the plight of America's children, particularly those at greatest risk. In the mid-1980s, the Fund's report suggested that a large percentage of American children were living in poverty and that few citizens seemed to care (see Garmezy, 1987). In 1995, Hodgkinson made the following observations in response to the question, "Who cares about America's children?"

> The answer is: an astonishingly small percentage of the U.S. adult population. The demographic reasons are clear: only about one household in four has a child of school age. My conservative guess is that at least one-third of the U.S. adult population has no daily contact with a child under age 18, and the fraction could be far higher. As the median age of Americans continues to rise and as children become an even smaller percentage of the population—down from 34% in 1970 to 25% projected for 2000—the situation is likely to get even worse. People tend to vote their self-interest, and, as fewer adults have contact with children in their daily lives, there will be even less political support for programs benefiting poor children, most of whom live in central cities and rural areas while most adults live in suburbs.
>
> Even the national leadership of groups that style themselves "pro-life" or "pro-choice" has demonstrated scant concern for the lives of the children who are *already* born. It was 30 January 1995 when the news was released that six million U.S. children under age 6

were living in poverty (up one million between 1987 and 1992) and that three-fourths of these poor children had working parents. None of the six newspapers that I checked carried the story on the front page, and two didn't even mention it. Apparently, the fact that 26% of the nation's future students, workers, voters, parents, and taxpayers have been born into the most debilitating condition of all was not deemed newsworthy. Given such a general lack of interest, it seems unlikely that there will be an increase in concern about or action in response to the amazing facts regarding poverty among America's youth. (Hodgkinson, 1995, p. 178)

SUMMARY

Children, families, and teachers are influenced by the standards and values of the larger cultures in which they live and work. Conflicts between cultures can contribute to youngsters' stress and to their problem behavior. Not only conflicts between different cultures but mixed messages from the same culture can be a negative influence on behavior. Cultures sometimes both encourage and punish certain types of behavior; for example, youngsters may be tempted or encouraged by the media to engage in sexual behavior, yet our society creates penalties for teenage pregnancy.

We must guard against bias and discrimination in our pluralistic, multicultural society. Cultural differences in behavior that do not put the child or youth at risk in the larger society must be accepted. Educators should seek to change only behavior that is incompatible with achievement of the larger goals of education. Clear rules for applying a multicultural perspective are not established, however. Teachers and school administrators must continue to struggle with decisions about what behavior puts a child at risk in society at large.

Besides family and school, cultural factors that influence behavior include mass media, peer group, neighborhood, urbanization, ethnicity, and social class. A major difficulty in assessing most of these and other cultural factors is that they are so intimately intertwined. It is difficult, for example, to untangle the factors of social class, ethnicity, neighborhood, urbanization, and peer groups. Social class, ethnicity, the neighborhood, and urbanization have not been shown to be, in themselves, significant causal factors in emotional and behavioral disorders. They are apparently significant only in the context of economic deprivation and family conflict.

Other cultural factors are more clearly involved in causing disordered behavior. Watching television causes rising levels of aggression among children who are already aggressive. Rejection by peers also increases the upward spiral of aggression among youngsters who are uncooperative, unhelpful, disruptive, and aggressive. In both cases—television violence and peer rejection—youngsters' behavior, their environments (including others' reactions to their behavior) and their perceptions are factors in the development of increasing social deviance.

The literatures on peer relations and social skills training have the clearest and most direct implications for educators. Teachers must be concerned with both the social skills deviant students need and the responses and perceptions of the peer group.

A FINAL NOTE ON CAUSAL FACTORS

When we think about the causes of emotional or behavioral disorders, oversimplification and overgeneralization are great temptations. We are inclined to assume that highly inappropriate behavior is simply a result of inadequate parenting or teaching, physiological problems, or cultural influences. As I hope you understand from reading the four chapters in Part Three, parenting, teaching, physiology, and culture *can* be significant causal factors, but we must be extremely cautious in drawing conclusions about the individual case. Before concluding that a student's undesirable classroom behavior is a result of the teacher's ineptitude or that the child's disorder is caused by poor parenting, we must examine carefully what transpires in the interactions between student and teacher or child and parent. Even if we observe these interactions and find that the adult clearly is behaving toward the child in a less than admirable manner, however, we must be careful not to jump quickly to the conclusion that we have found the root of the problem. A child with a serious emotional or behavioral disorder may be extremely difficult to live with; he or she may be highly effective in frustrating and bringing out the worst in others. Recognizing that causal effects are not so simple or unidirectional as they first appear should help us maintain a reasonable level of humility in evaluating our own work with children and youths and give us caution in placing blame on the other adults who work with them as well.

We know much more today about the origins of emotional or behavioral disorders than we knew 25 or even 10 years ago, but researchers now realize that causal mechanisms are far more complex than previously assumed. At the same time that research is revealing the incredible complexity and interconnectedness of causal factors, it is opening up new possibilities for intervention. Old ideas that the course of psychopathology was set by early life experiences and impervious to intervention have given way to more hopeful attitudes for most disorders.

Case for Discussion

"Where Does She Get These Ideas?"

Teri Leigh

Teri Leigh had been removed from her home when social workers discovered that her mother's boyfriend was sexually abusing her. She and her two little brothers had been placed in separate foster homes. Her school records indicate that she has both learning disabilities and emotional disorders. She has, in fact, been diagnosed as psychotic, but I have not seen any behavior suggesting that she is having visual hallucinations or hearing voices. She is very imaginative, but I have no way of knowing whether some of the things she's reported are actually true. She is generally well behaved, but she seeks affection like a much younger child. Her affection-seeking behavior seems out of character for a 12-year-old, especially because she has a "grown-up" appearance for her age.

Several weeks ago, I taught the basic lesson on pregnancy and childbirth in family life class. A couple of days later, other girls in the class told me that Teri Leigh was claiming to be pregnant. I noticed that she had started bringing baby clothes to school, and there was a lot of secretive talk among Teri Leigh and the other girls. Eventually, Teri Leigh told me she thought she was pregnant. I asked her why she thought so. She explained matter-of-factly that she was probably pregnant because of what her mother's boyfriend had done to her. I explained to her several times that this was impossible because what he had done happened so long ago, but she refused to believe me.

Then I found out that Teri Leigh had given several nude photographs of herself to two high school boys who ride her bus. Lucky for us, the boys gave the pictures directly to the bus driver, who gave them to the principal, Bob Farris. When Bob called Teri Leigh's foster mother, Mrs. Overton, she told him that the pictures had been taken by Teri Leigh's foster sisters. Mrs. Overton claims that she told the girls to tear up the pictures; obviously, they had not obeyed. She refused to discuss the matter with Teri Leigh. She said that is my responsibility. Bob Farris agreed with her. So I made a stab at it.

One day I kept Teri Leigh after school and talked with her for a long time. I told her about how much I love my kids but how much time they take from me, how I have very little time for myself. I also talked to her about AIDS and other sexually transmitted diseases. Unfortunately, Teri Leigh insisted that she wants to get pregnant. And she also insisted, in spite of all the facts I gave her, that she would eventually get pregnant because of her experiences with her mother's boyfriend. I was completely unable to get through to her. What do I do now? I want to help her, but I don't know what to do next. [*Note:* This case was adapted from Kauffman, Mostert, Nuttycombe, Trent, & Hallahan (1993).]

Questions About the Case

1. How might biological, family, school, and cultural influences have contributed to Teri Leigh's behavior?

2. What should Teri Leigh's teacher do next? To whom should she turn for help?

3. What cultural factors make it particularly hard to address the problems of children like Teri Leigh effectively?

PERSONAL REFLECTIONS

Cultural Factors

Bernie Manning, Ed.D., is Deputy Superintendent, Office of School Affairs in the Pittsburgh Public Schools, Pittsburgh, Pennsylvania.

What primary features of African-American cultural values and standards are most important in understanding children's behavior in schools?

For years, educators, diagnosticians, enthnographers, philosophers, sociologists, and psychologists have tried to understand and explain why children—especially those of African-American descent—behave the way they do. Many have failed to examine cultural perspectives, to explore the total Gestalt of the child or the culture the child represents. Sensitivity to variability of values is essential when trying to understand cultural influences. It is important to note that there is some difficulty—albeit, not much—in differentiating between individual and group identity and values of African-Americans. It has been postulated that personal identity includes subordinate factors such as self-esteem, self-worth, and general personality traits; group identity includes racial attitudes and race awareness. I believe that language and music are two really important features of African-American culture and values that are often misunderstood.

Many African-Americans speak standard American English as their primary language, while others speak primarily an African-American dialect that represents a mixture of both African language patterns and American English. African-American students are frequently viewed somewhat differently, too often negatively, because of their language. Language is the characteristic about which others in society first draw negative conclusions, leading to cultural insensitivity. Based upon negative conclusions about their language alone, many children are diagnosed as having mental retardation and speech impairments, or facsimiles thereof.

Music is an element of African-American culture that forms the basis for sustenance; it was originally a depiction of the realities of slavery, a way of providing emotional and psychological relief. The slavery music was highly creative, not imitative. The lyrics were spontaneous and exuberant, with an inimitable style of their own. Their music allowed black workers to blend their physical movement and psychic needs with those of others (Levine, 1977). It provided important outlets for communication, commiseration, and expression. Music is, to the African-American, a definitive means of expression. The expression is different from that of any other ethnic group because of our slavery experiences. For example, gospel music, with its words pertaining to spiritual or godly phenomena, was a means of expression that lent truth to the slaves' insatiable desire to rid themselves of bondage, something they realized only God could accomplish. Music is indeed a feature of the African-American culture.

When African-American children hear "their" type of music and begin to make gyrations that are not particularly accepted by other cultures, this could represent cathartic discourses on power and control. The music allows growing people to exert themselves; it allows them the opportunity to communicate among themselves about themselves and their oppressors. Frequently, the gyrations get interpreted to mean, "These young people are crazy!"

How do you view the effects of social class on children's emotional and behavioral disorders?

Professionals need to understand that their own social class values, attitudes, and behavior play a critical role in interpreting emotional and behavioral patterns of youngsters. Frequently, these factors have a devastating effect on the instructional process, which invariably creates problems of behavior and attitudes in young people. Learning styles, perceptions, interactional styles, behavioral styles, and communication styles vary from class to class. When youngsters cannot or do not conform to certain dominant styles, their disposition attracts a stigma. For example, African-American children place great value on efforts toward achievement; they will argue for recognition of their efforts to complete a task, even though they were unsuccessful (Gilbert & Gay, 1985). When success is not achieved by those youngsters who desire to excel, frustration and anxieties are the result. Before one realizes it, troubling emotional or behavioral patterns can begin to develop. In school, learning is expected to occur in a formal, rather stringent milieu (Gilbert & Gay, 1985). The learning style of many African-American children is relational; in other words, they perform better in a cooperative, informal, and loosely structured environment in which students and professionals work very closely to achieve common goals and there is a dependent relationship. An elitist set of values or principles superimposed on those values, inadvertently or purposely, can cause problems.

Beck and Saxe (1965) suggested that social class is determined primarily by the ability to generalize from the idiographic (individual, concrete) to the nomothetic (universal, abstract). This theory gave rise to the belief that success in any social entity (school, armed forces, church, civic organization) depends on one's understanding of abstract concepts. Emotional or behavioral disorders might be considered from the perspective of the roles played in their development by the family and professionals in the schools—the way concrete and abstract thinking influences the achievement of social objectives. Most people in the upper and middle social classes are oriented toward education; they place great emphasis on acceleration, advancement, socioeconomic status, financial stability, and cultural values. Their abstract understanding of how to attain these concrete goals within the social structure far exceeds that of most people in the lower classes. People of lower class want their children to behave appropriately and excel, but they may not understand the means by which they can accomplish their goals for their children; they value many of the same things as those in the upper classes but not the social system that prevents them from reaching their goals. Unfortunately, teachers may not understand the value system of students and their parents; they may reject it or even deny that it exists.

Alba Ortiz, Ph.D., is Ruben E. Hinojosa Regents Professor in Education, Director of the Office of Bilingual Education, and Associate Dean for Academic Affairs and Research, College of Education, the University of Texas at Austin.

What primary features of Hispanic American cultural values and standards are most important in understanding children's behavior in school?

Many years ago, I worked on a project intended to make curriculum and instructional materials culturally relevant for Mexican-American children. We modified the traditional unit on breakfast foods by using pictures of "typical" Mexican breakfasts that showed Mexican-American children eating chorizo (Mexican sausage) and tortillas in the morning. When we asked parents to review the unit, Mexican-American mothers told us that, because they worked, their children were more likely to eat cold cereal and toast for breakfast. Our intention was to make instruction culturally relevant, but we actually reinforced a stereotype.

Educators must understand that there is no one set of characteristics that can be ascribed to all members of any racial or ethnic group (Ortiz & Yates, 1984). Although incorporating history, heritage, traditions, and lifestyles of diverse cultures into instruction is appropriate, accenting *traditional* aspects of culture may inadvertently reinforce the very stereotypes teachers wish to eliminate. Thus, teachers should also learn as much as possible about student's *contemporary* culture so that learning environments and curricula are compatible with, and build upon, children's daily experiences. A critical analysis of the characteristics of the home and community as they presently exist provides a foundation for curricula that will be relevant to and meet the needs of culturally and linguistically different pupils. This underscores the importance of involving parents and other members of the community in what happens at school. With these cautions about stereotyping, I'll comment on four aspects of Hispanic culture that are particularly important for teachers to understand—language, family relationships, attitude toward authority, and socioeconomic status.

Language is basic to children's sense of security and well-being because it involves communication of basic needs and values. Security and well-being are easily shattered in an environment in which one's native language is not spoken. Bilingual education programs were developed to give children the security, sense of well-being, and identity that are necessary while they learned English as a second language. Equally important, however, is recognition that teachers must adapt curriculum and instruction for language minority students who are proficient in conversational English but who do not yet have the academic and formal language skills necessary to understand textbooks and the language teachers use in formal instruction (Cummins, 1984).

In traditional Hispanic families, the family unit usually consists of the nuclear family (parents and siblings), the extended family (blood relatives and relatives by virtue of religious ceremonies), and close family friends (Ramirez & Castaneda, 1974). All family members, including those in the extended family, participate in childrearing, monitoring of child behavior, and providing feedback to parents as to whether their children are "bien educados" (well educated socially). Children are expected to behave in ways that will not bring shame or embarrassment to their family. Given this, it is not difficult to understand why the family is the most important reference point in decision making. As Hispanics move into less segregated communities, and as they become enculturated as a result of interactions with other cultures, the concept of the traditional family may be modified. For example, as extended members disperse into other communities, physical distance makes it difficult for them to monitor the behavior of children or provide feedback to parents; the influence of the extended family begins to diminish (Ortiz & Yates, 1984).

The emphasis of the Hispanic culture on respect for authority has interesting implications for educators. Parents may perceive educators as experts in academic matters and may therefore choose not to be involved in the schooling process because they fear they will interfere with the experts or because they may not feel they have information and training to make them effective participants in the schooling process. In addition, their own experiences with school may not have been satisfying, so they resist returning to school. These characteristics, along with a lack of English proficiency, may make it difficult for parents to participate meaningfully in decision-making processes associated with special education. Thus, their lack of involvement may actually be a result of their respect for authority or their own feeling of lack of competence rather than a lack of interest in their child's schooling.

Sometimes educators attribute certain characteristics to the student's cultural group when, in reality, these traits are associated with socioeconomic status. Teachers expect children to come to school with a set of experiences that they feel will facilitate learning, including exposure to books, academic orientation, models of success, and educational toys and materials, and interactions of an educational nature with parents. When children have not had such experiences, teachers attribute school problems to the child's having grown up in a "deficient environment" and frequently conclude that they will not be able to help the child because he or she is "culturally deprived" or "culturally disadvantaged." Rather than being deficient or deprived, the child has a wealth of experiences that happen to be different from those of middle-class children. Asking these children to identify with and learn from a curriculum based on experiences that they have not had predisposes them to failure.

What are the most important issues in bilingual special education?

Inappropriate referral is a substantial problem. Many language minority children who are referred have no identifiable disabling condition; they are referred on the basis of race, sex, physical appearance, or socioeconomic status, and the curriculum simply has not been adjusted to meet their needs. We need to prevent inappropriate referrals by making sure that students are provided a school environment conducive to success—one that reflects understanding and acceptance of linguistic and cultural diversity as well as appropriate curriculum and behavior management. Advocacy-oriented assessment, in which testing and other evaluation procedures are focused on providing appropriate instruction rather than merely determining eligibility, is a critical issue.

Consultation and collaboration among teachers and support staff are necessary to make sure that the student with limited English proficiency receives appropriate evaluation and instruction. Lack of trained special educators is a big problem; too few special education teachers have sufficient knowledge of the native languages of students whose primary tongue is not English. Changing the emphasis in instruction to focus on interaction and dialogue is important for many students with limited English proficiency. Finally, offering instruction in students' native language is an important issue. The primary language of instruction should be the language through which the student learns best, and that is usually the language of the student's parents.

Kathleen Wong Shimabukuro, Ph.D., is Director of Admissions at Maryknoll Schools in Honolulu.

What primary features of Asian-American cultural values and standards are most important in understanding children's behavior in schools?

Before responding to this question, it is important to clarify that Asian-American people are not a homogeneous group, but rather a heterogeneous group with origins in the Asian Basin. This includes people from China, Japan, Korea, Taiwan, Vietnam, Southeast Asia, and the Philippines. Although there are many similarities among these different groups, there are at least as many differences. It is also important to point out that Asians who now live in America have entered this country during different time periods and under different circumstances. Those who have recently immigrated to America or have lived primarily among their own people are more likely to maintain and practice traditional cultural

standards and values; those who are descendants of earlier generations who immigrated some time ago and have become integrated into the larger American society are less inclined to hold onto strict, traditional, culture-based standards and values.

Having said this, there are at least five primary features of Asian-American cultural values and standards that I feel are important to understanding children's behavior in schools. One is the sense of honor to the family with which Asian-American children are raised. In the home, children are taught that their actions are a reflection on the family and that, therefore, they should never do anything that might bring shame to the family name. On the other hand, should they do so, they are often made to feel a strong sense of guilt and remorse.

Another feature is the sense of filial piety, or duty to the family, with which Asian-American children are raised. Children are taught that their first obligation is always to the family. Consequently, the needs of the family should always be considered before the needs of others or oneself. Asian-American youngsters with elderly parents or grandparents are expected to assume responsibility for the care of their elders when their elders can no longer provide self-care.

Related to this sense of duty to the family is the belief that the family is responsible for helping its members solve whatever problems they may have. If the problem involves the entire family, then the extended family is looked upon to provide assistance. Sharing one's problems with strangers and seeking outside help has traditionally not been encouraged among Asian-American families.

A fourth feature is the respect that Asian-American children are taught to have for their parents, elders, and other authority figures. From an early age, children are taught to obey, comply with, and unquestioningly accept the authority of their parents, elders, and other authority figures (including teachers). They are taught not to question or discuss concerns with adults but to assume a subordinate, passive, and conforming role. This sign of respect is also demonstrated through body language—children are taught not to make eye contact but to look down and even bow their heads when being spoken to by parents and other adults.

Finally, a fifth feature is the high importance placed upon education, hard work, achievement, and success. Asian-American people have traditionally viewed education as a privilege that should not be taken lightly. They believe that working hard and obtaining a good education will lead to upward mobility, prosperity, and at the same time, bring honor to the family. Consequently, however, children are often pressured and expected to do well in school.

Given these features of Asian-American cultural values and standards, when compared to their non-Asian-American peers, Asian-American children are apt to demonstrate greater levels of obedience, perseverance, conformity, and passivity in school. On the one hand, they are less inclined to speak of difficulties they may be experiencing and less willing to accept offers of help from others. On the other hand, because of the heavy emphasis that is placed on education, achievement, and success, many Asian-American children do experience high levels of stress as they are growing up.

How do you view the effects of the neighborhood and the peer group on children's emotional and behavioral disorders?

For most children, "fitting in" and being like one's peers becomes increasingly important as they get older; failure to "fit in" or "belong" can contribute to a host of emotional and behavioral problems. In the case of the ethnic minority child whose family maintains and practices traditional cultural standards and values, "fitting in" can be particularly difficult if these standards and values vary significantly from those of the neighborhood or peer group.

In one scenario, the child's "differentness" can become the target of peer ridicule. Depending on a variety of factors, the ethnic minority child could respond by: (1) accepting the ridicule with hopes that it will eventually cease and that the peer group will let him/her become a part of the group, (2) attempting to teach the others about his or her cultural group and values and hope that they become more accepting, (3) withdrawing from the peer group and becoming socially isolated if there are no other accepting peer groups, or (4) seeking retaliation.

In a somewhat different scenario, the ethnic minority youngster might not be subject to ridicule but, rather, feel pressured to choose between following the cultural standards and values upheld by his or her family and adopting the norms and values sanctioned by the peer group. Choosing either group over the other could lead to a total separation from the rejected group, including being disowned by the family. On the other hand, an unsuccessful bid to satisfy the demands of both the family and the peer group could lead to alienation from both groups and, in effect, the feeling of "not belonging anywhere."

Bruce A. Ramirez, Ed.D., is Associate Executive Director, Department of Professional Advancement, of The Council for Exceptional Children.

What primary features of American Indian cultural values and standards are most important in understanding children's behavior in schools?

I think the two most important features are the way we look at competition and extended families. Competition for individual gain is a much esteemed value in European-American cultures and often produces conflicts for children and families whose culture stresses cooperation and group attainment. Let me give you some examples. An American Indian child will often resist praise from a teacher or adult if it comes at the expense of praise for his or her peers. Children may not answer a simple question from a teacher for fear of standing out from their peers. They may openly help a classmate who is having difficulty with school work so that he or she will experience success. Young children engaged in a foot race often slow down so that the slower kids can catch up and make the race more even. Teachers' reactions to such behavior range from disappointment to outright punishment. What are we communicating by a negative reaction? What kind of behavior are we reinforcing at a time when education and business are recognizing the importance of peer tutoring, cooperative learning, and group problem solving? Competition is certainly important within native cultures; however, we need to recognize that competition can have very different meaning(s) and that it is not necessary to be considered the best at everything we undertake.

Understanding the extended family and its emphasis on strong ties to relatives beyond the core family unit is extremely important for working with American Indian students. This is especially true now, when the traditional American family is undergoing rapid transformation. You might find Indian children living with grandparents or other family members for extended periods. Family members other than the natural parents may attend school meetings or may be responsible for the child's discipline. In many instances, the response from the schools is to assume, incorrectly, that the parents don't care about their children. Decision-making avenues can become somewhat blurred in extended families, especially if cultural values require that decisions such as placement in a special program or setting be made with the consent of additional family members. Extended family responsibilities sometimes require children and their relatives to be absent from school or work to meet religious, sustenance, or ceremonial responsibilities.

How do you view the effects of urbanization on children's emotional and behavioral disorders?

Urbanization can have detrimental effects on the behavior of students and their families when it disrupts cultural values and traditions. As a result of the Bureau of Indian Affairs relocation program begun in the 1950s, thousands of American Indians have migrated to cities for jobs or job training. The urban experience for far too many Indians, however, has come to mean living in poverty, being unemployed, having substandard housing, and seeing higher rates of infant mortality, alcoholism, and school dropouts. The urban Indian centers now found in virtually all major metropolitan areas are an organized response to the ills that can be associated with urbanization. These centers provide food, clothing, emergency housing, counseling, education, and opportunities for socialization with other Indians from a variety of tribes.

Kenneth D. Gadow, Ph.D., is Professor of Special Education and Professor of Psychiatry at the State University of New York at Stony Brook.

How would you summarize the relationship between behavioral deviance portrayed in the mass media and the behavioral deviance of children in schools?

One of the most commonly held beliefs about children and television is that children are more likely to behave aggressively after watching shows with aggression-laden material than after watching shows with people or cartoon characters engaging in socially constructive interactions. Although laboratory experiments generally support this conclusion, it may come as a surprise to know that many studies of television viewing that are conducted in real-world settings actually show that both aggressive *and* nonaggressive television shows appear to increase aggressive behavior in children. Further, at least half of all studies conducted so far have found the nonaggressive shows to be the most aggression-inducing. This finding is only paradoxical in the sense that it runs contrary to what we have always been told.

If you ask a large number of undergraduate students if they think watching an aggression-laden movie makes them behave more aggressively, they will almost unanimously say, "No." When pressed further about this, some students will say that although they do not act that way, others might. When asked to give examples, it is generally people younger than they, the economically disadvantaged, the poorly supervised, or the emotionally or cognitively impaired. (Interestingly, research does not consistently support the notion that these individuals are at a greater risk for alleged adverse reactions from television viewing.) These same labels can also be applied to many (but certainly not all) children who are labeled emotionally disturbed or behavior disordered by our public schools. To better understand the role of television in the lives of children receiving special education, my colleague Joyce Sprafkin and I conducted a 10-year program of research on this topic, which is reviewed in our book, *Television and the Exceptional Child: A Forgotten Audience* (Sprafkin, Gadow, & Abelman, 1992). Although we found that children with emotional or behavioral disorders prefer aggression-laden television programs, often watch this material, perceive it as realistic, and identify with aggressive characters, as a group they are not necessarily more reactive to this type of television material. Then why are they more likely to behave more aggressively than other children? We believe the answer is to be found in their life experiences interacting with other people, and in some cases, a biological predisposition to respond impulsively. For us, blaming television is the easy way out. More likely causes of violent behavior in our society are poverty, racism, overcrowded living conditions, drug and alcohol abuse, and occasionally biologically-based forms of mental illness. Although we wholeheartedly endorse efforts to limit portrayals of gratuitous violence in the media, we should not be so consumed with this effort as to neglect addressing the true causes of interpersonal aggression.

PART FOUR
Facets of Disordered Behavior

Introduction to Part Four

In the ten preceding chapters, we discussed emotional or behavioral disorders primarily in the general case, with only occasional and brief attention to specific types or categories of disorders. In Part Four, we give more detailed and systematic consideration to several major ways in which emotional or behavioral disorders can be manifested. We revisit earlier questions with which we dealt mostly in the general case, this time giving closer scrutiny to specific types of disorders. For each major type of disorder, we attempt to provide succinct answers to as many of the following questions as possible:

- How is this disorder defined? What is its prevalence?

- What do we know about its causes and its possible prevention?

- What basic strategies are used in its assessment?

- What are the primary approaches to intervention and education?

Although we are able to provide brief answers to these questions for most of the major disorders, we are not able to answer all of the questions for all of the disorders or their subtypes.

Part Four is titled "facets of disordered behavior" to indicate that the types of problems we discuss are merely different sides of what we call emotional or behavioral disorders. As noted in chapter 5, the classification of emotional or behavioral disorders is complex and inevitably produces ambiguous categories. Disorders of all types seem to be interconnected, such that in discussing one type we are by necessity considering several others as well. We noted, for example, that hyperactivity, conduct disorder, and delinquency are interrelated problems. True, one might find a youngster who is hyperactive yet is not considered to have a conduct disorder and has not been designated "delinquent." We occasionally may find a seemingly "pure" case of any given type of disorder, one in which the youngster's problem is apparently neatly limited in character. Nevertheless, these "pure" cases are atypical; in most instances, we find multiple problems, clusters of disorders, behavior that is characteristic of several different facets of what we call emotional or behavioral disorders.

How, then, shall we decide what constitutes a distinctive *facet* of disordered behavior? Clearly, anyone's answer to this question will be in some ways arbitrary. I have chosen to divide this part of the book into seven chapters, partly on the basis of empirical evidence of the way behavioral problems are clustered or factored statistically and partly according to what I believe will facilitate the clearest discussion. I have begun with the disorders that are among the most prevalent: disorders of attention and activity, often referred to as attention deficit disorder (ADD) or attention-deficit hyperactivity disorder (ADHD), and conduct disorders (overt aggression and covert antisocial behavior). I then turn to juvenile delinquency and substance abuse, problems closely related to conduct disorders and attention problems. In the subsequent chapter, I discuss anxiety-withdrawal and a variety of other disorders that do not fit neatly under any other category (fears and phobias, obsessions and compulsions, and disorders involving speaking, eating, eliminating, moving, and sexual behavior). Depression and suicide, which I examine next, are increasingly recognized as serious problems among children and adolescents. Finally, I address the disorders known variously as *psychoses* or pervasive developmental disorders, which are among the least prevalent.

I hope the chapters in Part Four bring you a better understanding of the specific ways in which children and youths can exhibit emotional or behavioral disorders. As you read these chapters, you should be asking yourself how specific disorders are interrelated and how they are distinctive. Here is a sampling of the kinds of questions you might ask:

■ What distinguishes conduct disorder from depression?

■ When we see a youngster who has a conduct disorder, for example, might we also be seeing one who is depressed (that is, might conduct disorder and depression be comorbid conditions)? Could the same set of circumstances give rise to both conduct disorder and depression?

■ To what extent are interventions effective for conduct disorder appropriate or inappropriate for a student who is depressed?

■ How are teenage sexual activity and teenage parenthood linked to delinquency, substance abuse, and other disorders?

■ What do we know about the comorbidity of depression and excessive fears?

■ Under what circumstances are we likely to see a pervasive developmental disorder and hyperactivity or attention deficits in the same person, and when we do what are the implications for teaching?

Questions like these are not easily answered, and my brief discussion of specific disorders cannot do justice to the complexity of these problems and their interconnections.

The serious study of emotional or behavioral disorders calls to mind a statement of C. E. Ayres: "A little inaccuracy saves a world of explanation." Although I have strived for all the accuracy I can bring to the time and space available, I have come to recognize the fact that eliminating every inaccuracy is an insurmountable task; it would require a world more knowledge and explanation than any individual can muster. Contemplating the next seven chapters and the questions they leave poorly answered or not answered at all will, I hope, leave you with a new appreciation of the complexity of emotional or behavioral disorders and their intricate reflection of unique personal identities.

11

Attention and Activity Disorders

As you read this chapter, keep these guiding questions in mind:

■ Why do we not define *hyperactivity* simply as being highly active?

■ What types of behavior are most closely associated with attention-deficit hyperactivity disorder (ADHD)?

■ What biological and psychological causal factors probably contribute to ADHD?

■ Which are the preferred treatments for ADHD—stimulant drugs or behavior modification? Why?

■ Why are students with attention and activity disorders typically unpopular with their peers?

■ What is the relationship between brain damage or dysfunction and disorders of attention and activity?

■ In assessing hyperactivity, what kind of information is most useful for teachers?

■ What behavioral interventions are frequently used to manage hyperactivity and related problems?

■ What general conclusions have been reached regarding the use of self-monitoring to manage off-task behavior and improve academic performance?

■ What steps are generally followed in teaching students to use self-instruction?

DEFINITION AND PREVALENCE

We said in chapter 1 that youngsters with emotional or behavioral disorders often induce negative feelings and behavior in others. Among the many characteristics that are bothersome or irritating to others and induce others to respond negatively are disorders of attention and activity. During the past several decades, individuals with these disorders have been described by a variety of terms, including **hyperactive** and **hyperkinetic**. Severe and chronic problems in regulating attention and activity are now commonly known as **attention-deficit disorder** (ADD) or **attention-deficit hyperactivity disorder** (ADHD). Inability to control one's attention has replaced hyperactivity as the core problem of concern, and the prevailing opinion is that hyperactivity usually, but not always, accompanies attention deficits. The terms ADD, ADHD, and hyperactivity are used interchangeably in many contexts, reflecting much uncertainty in definition (see Hallahan, Kauffman, & Lloyd, 1996).

In this chapter, we refer more often to ADHD than to ADD because we are concerned primarily with children and youths who have attention *and* activity disorders and who have problems that are more severe than most. These youngsters with extreme attention and activity problems are likely to have been categorized as having emotional or behavioral disorders or learning disabilities. However, an increasing number of researchers and clinicians recognize attention-deficit disorder *with* hyperactivity (ADHD) and attention-deficit disorder *without* hyperactivity (ADD) as distinctive subtypes, and many professionals prefer to speak of *ADD and related disorders* (cf. American Psychiatric Association, 1994; Bloomingdale, Swanson, Barkley,

& Satterfield, 1991; Lahey & Carlson, 1991). Youngsters whose attention deficits are accompanied by hyperactivity and impulsivity are more likely to have conduct disorders than are those who show attention deficits and disorganization without hyperactivity. Those who have ADD without hyperactivity are more likely to show sluggishness, drowsiness, social withdrawal, anxiety, and depression (Lahey & Carlson, 1991). Our concern here is with youngsters who have serious social or emotional problems, whether related to hyperactivity or other manifestations of attention deficits, in addition to problems attending to their school work. The varied nature of the social problems of children with disorders of attention and activity is summarized by Whalen and Henker (1991):

> There are two truisms regarding the interpersonal difficulties of children with . . . ADHD. . . . The first is that the vast majority of these youngsters have serious social problems that pervade their everyday lives and spur frequent conflicts and confrontations. The second is that their patterns and styles of social exchange display marked heterogeneity in form as well as intensity. Many hyperactive children show a curious combination of social busyness and clumsiness, frequently initiating contact with others but in a manner perceived as immature, intrusive, or inept. A smaller number of these children show less interpersonal interest, appearing aloof and at times even oblivious as they skirt the periphery of social action. Still other hyperactive youngsters are highly aggressive, but even in this realm, heterogeneity is the rule rather than the exception. Some may engage in aggressive acts that appear planned, instrumental, and at times even hostile. For others, aggression seems to be more explosive than exploitative, linked to emotional volatility and difficulties dealing with frustration. (p. 231)

Disorders of attention and activity are among the most prevalent emotional or behavioral disorders of children and youths—if you believe that such disorders exist. They are also among the most controversial disorders. The terminology used to describe them has changed during the past decade: "'Hyperactivity' and 'short attention span' have become 'attention deficit-hyperactivity disorder' and 'attention deficit disorder'" (Bateman, 1992, p. 29). Like learning disability, ADHD is seen by some people as a real and serious handicap and by others as an attempt to legitimize teachers' or parents' inadequacies or as "a fancy excuse for getting undeserved special consideration" (Bateman, 1992, p. 29). Good teaching and good discipline at home and school would, according to some skeptics, resolve the problem of ADHD in all but a small percentage of cases (e.g., Armstrong, 1995). Others see ADD and ADHD as true developmental disabilities for which there is no cure (e.g., Neuwirth, 1994). Professional disagreement and public confusion are found at almost every point of research and practice (Fletcher, Morris, & Francis, 1991; Fowler, 1992; Neuwirth, 1994).

We discuss ADD and ADHD under the assumption that they *do* exist and that a consensus among professionals regarding their nature and treatment is gradually emerging. Contrary to much popular opinion, the emerging consensus is that ADHD is neither a minor problem nor a temporary characteristic of childhood that is typically outgrown (Barkley, 1990; Braswell & Bloomquist, 1991; DuPaul, Guevremont, & Barkley, 1991; DuPaul & Stoner, 1994; Whalen & Henker, 1991).

Most definitions of ADHD suggest that it is a developmental disorder of attention and activity, is evident relatively early in life (before the age of 7 or 8 years), persists throughout the life span, involves both academic and social skills, and is frequently accompanied by other disorders. The Professional Group for ADD and Related Disorders, representing leading researchers and clinicians in the field of developmental disorders, formulated the following educational description:

> The condition "attention deficit disorder" refers to a developmental disorder involving one or more of the basic cognitive processes related to orienting, focusing or maintaining attention, resulting in a marked degree of inadequate attention to academic and social tasks. The disorder may include verbal or motor impulsivity and excessive non-task related activities such as fidgeting or restlessness. The inattentive behavior of ADD most commonly has onset in early childhood, remains inappropriate for age, and persists throughout development. (Bloomingdale et al., 1991, p. 3)

DuPaul, Guevremont, and Barkley (1991) suggest that cognitive deficits are now seen as central to the definition of ADHD. That is, the basic problems of children with ADHD are primarily inattention, impulsivity, and deficits in rule-governed behavior, not the restlessness or squirminess that often have been the focus of adults' concern.

> The emphasis previously given to the overactivity or motor restlessness of these children was somewhat misplaced, as it seems to be their attentional, cognitive, and conduct problems that lead them into chronic conflict with their social environment and cause them to be referred for treatment. (DuPaul, Guevremont, & Barkley, 1991, p. 115)

In addition, ADHD appears to involve problems of motivation—individuals with this disorder often do not do what they know how to do (Barkley, 1990).

The difficulties in focusing and sustaining attention, controlling impulsive action, and showing appropriate motivation that characterize ADHD can make a person with the disorder—regardless of his or her age—a trial for parents, siblings, teachers, classroom peers, or coworkers. Hyperactive, distractible, impulsive youngsters upset their parents and siblings because they are difficult to live with at home; at school they often drive their teachers to discomposure. They are often unpopular with their peers; they do not typically make charming playmates or helpful workmates (Grenell, Glass, & Katz, 1987; Guevremont & Dumas, 1994; Whalen & Henker, 1991). Incessant movement, impulsiveness, noisiness, irritability, destructiveness, unpredictability, flightiness, and other similar characteristics of students with ADHD are not endearing to anyone—parents, siblings, teachers, and schoolmates included. The following description illustrates how unpleasant a child with ADHD can be to those around him.

> A hyperactive child's mother might report that he has difficulty remembering not to trail his dirty hand along the clean wall as he runs from the front door to the kitchen. His peers may find that he spontaneously changes the rules while playing Monopoly or soccer. His teacher notes that he asks what he is supposed to do immediately after detailed instructions were presented to the entire class. He may make warbling noises or other strange sounds that inadvertently disturb anyone nearby. He may seem to have more than his share of accidents—knocking over the "tower" his classmates are erecting, spilling his cranberry juice on the linen tablecloth, or tripping over the television cord while retrieving the family cat, thereby disconnecting the set in the middle of the Superbowl game.

A hyperactive child is all too frequently "in trouble"—with his peers, his teachers, his family, his community. His social faux pas do not seem to stem from negativism and maliciousness. In fact, he is often quite surprised when his behaviors elicit anger and rejection from others. (Whalen, 1983, pp. 151–152)

The types of behavior problems that bring youngsters with ADHD to the attention of psychologists and teachers are further illustrated in Figure 11.1. Note that problems in school are the symptoms most clearly associated with differences between hyperactive and nonreferred children. Teachers need to be aware of the developmental aspects of attention and understand what distinguishes the student with ADHD from one who exhibits normal levels of inattention and impulsivity. We frequently see a high level of seemingly undirected activity, short attention span, and impulsive behavior in normally developing young children. As children grow older, however, they gradually become better able to direct their activity into socially constructive channels, to pay attention for longer periods and more efficiently, and to consider alternatives before responding. Thus, only when attentional skills, impulse control, and motoric activity level are markedly discrepant from those expected at a particular age is the child's behavior considered to require intervention.

Children with ADHD stand out from their age peers, often from an early age (DuPaul & Stoner, 1994). Moreover, the characteristics of ADHD are not typically subtle; they tend to be "in your face" behaviors that make most of the child's peers and most adults want to exclude the child from their environment or resort to "in your face" reprisals. In fact, it is becoming more and more apparent that ADHD is frequently a component of other disorders.

Relationship to Other Disorders

Disorders of attention and activity are very frequently seen in children and youths with a wide variety of other disorders (DuPaul & Stoner, 1994). Nearly all teachers, parents, and clinicians agree that many youngsters with other types of emotional or behavioral disorders—conduct disorders or autism, for example—have difficulty controlling their attention to academic and social tasks and are impulsive. In combination with other developmental problems such as conduct disorders or juvenile delinquency, ADHD greatly increases the risk of school failure and severity of symptoms (Kolko, 1994; Moffitt, 1990). Nearly all researchers who recognize that disorders of attention and activity exist conclude that although ADHD is a separate, distinctive disorder in its own right, there is great overlap between ADHD and other diagnostic categories (Lynskey & Fergusson, 1995; Schachar & Tannock, 1995; Stormont-Spurgin & Zentall, 1995). Whether ADD or ADHD should become a separate category under federal law (IDEA) and regulations has been a matter for hot debate.

Whether there are unique features of ADHD and, if so, where the boundaries between ADHD and other disorders should be drawn are points of considerable controversy. Most expert opinion is that a significant percentage (perhaps about 30 percent) of the children with ADD have not been served under any category of spe-

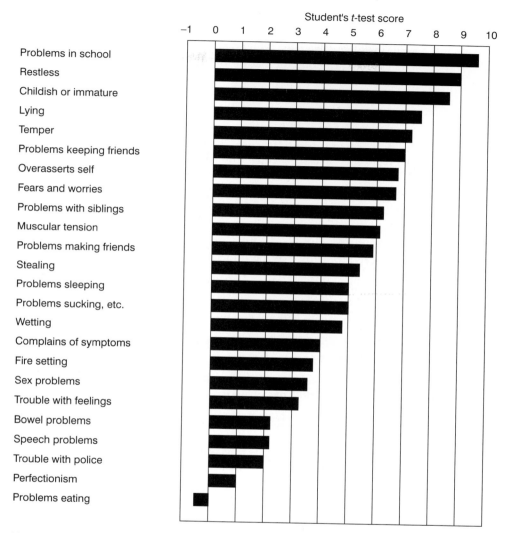

Note: Student's *t* test refers to a test of statistical significance. Significant at the 5% level means that differences as large or larger than approximately 2.0 could be expected to occur less than 5% of the time purely by chance. Thus, in common parlance, differences represented by a *t* score greater than 2.0 are probably reliable (i.e., true) differences.

Figure 11.1

Symptoms in Clinic versus Control Patients

Source: From C. K. Conners & K. C. Wells, *Hyperkinetic children: A neuropsychosocial approach,* p. 28. Copyright ©1986 by Sage Publications, Inc. Reprinted by permission of Sage Publications, Inc.

cial education and that a high percentage (perhaps 50 to 70 percent) of those with specific learning disabilities or "serious emotional disturbance" (emotional or behavioral disorders) also have ADD (cf. Bloomingdale et al., 1991; Fletcher et al., 1991). The confusion about the nature of ADD and its relationship to other disorders is heightened by the fact that the children referred for mental health services often are those with extreme ADD, with or without hyperactivity:

> We warn those professionals working with children with ADD that the evidence suggests that ADD occurs along a continuum and that children referred to child psychiatric centers appear to represent the extreme of that continuum; as such, they are not representative of all children with ADD. (Epstein, Shaywitz, Shaywitz, & Woolston, 1991, p. 85)

Children and youths with emotional or behavioral disorders typically have difficulty in relating to their peers, often being actively rejected by peers because of their inappropriate social behavior. Although many children with attention deficits do not have problems with peers, some are rejected. If they have extreme attention deficits, their peer problems may be understandable: "ADD children seem to desire friendships and have the skills to initiate them, but due to inattention and impulsivity they fail to spontaneously utilize their skills to maintain friendships" (Bloomingdale et al., 1991, p. 13).

We may conclude the following things:

- Many children and youths with ADD will not be found to have emotional or behavioral disorders.

- A sizable percentage of those with extreme ADD or ADHD will be identified as having emotional or behavioral disorders.

- Many of those receiving special education because of other emotional or behavioral disorders will have ADD or ADHD.

- Learning disabilities may accompany any combination of ADD, ADHD, and emotional or behavioral disorders.

We might speculate that the relationships among the populations of individuals having ADD, ADHD, emotional or behavioral disorders (EBD), and learning disabilities (LD) are approximately those shown in Figure 11.2. All cases of ADHD are included in the population with ADD, but not all cases of ADD involve hyperactivity (ADHD). EBD and LD may occur alone or in combination with each other and with either ADD or ADHD.

Prevalence

Controversy regarding definition makes the prevalence of a disorder extremely hard to estimate, as we noted in chapter 2. Most authorities estimate the prevalence of ADHD at about 3 to 5 percent of the school-age population (DuPaul & Stoner, 1994), making it one of the most common disorders of children and youths. Among those referred for ADD and related disorders, boys outnumber girls by three or more to one.

Figure 11.2
Hypothetical Relationships among the Populations Having Attention Deficit Disorder (ADD), Attention-Deficit Hyperactivity Disorder (ADHD), Emotional or Behavioral Disorders (EBD), and Learning Disabilities (LD)

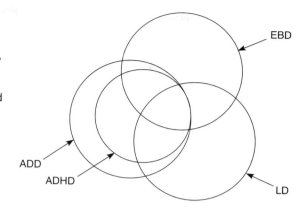

CAUSAL FACTORS AND PREVENTION

Historically, brain dysfunction has been the presumed cause of what is now known as ADD or ADHD (Hallahan et al., 1996). Today, researchers are investigating biological causes through more sophisticated anatomical and physiological tests involving blood flow to the brain, neurotransmitters, and so on (e.g., electrical potentials in brain tissue, magnetic resonance imaging; see Hynd et al., 1991; Klorman et al., 1991; Neuwirth, 1994). As yet, no reliable evidence shows what neurological problem is the basis of ADHD, although many researchers suspect an underlying biological cause of most cases (DuPaul & Stoner, 1994).

Various food substances (e.g., dyes, sugars, preservatives), environmental toxins (e.g., lead), and allergens have been suggested as causes of hyperactivity and related disorders (see chapter 7). None of these has been demonstrated to be a frequent cause of ADHD, although evidence does suggest that such factors may be a cause in a very small number of cases. Claims that foods or toxins or allergies are *frequent* causes are not substantiated by credible research (Barkley, 1990; DuPaul, Guevremont, & Barkley, 1991; McLoughlin & Nall, 1994; Wolraich et al., 1995).

Genetic factors appear to increase risk for ADHD, although the genetics of the disorder are very poorly understood. We do know that ADHD is more common among the biological relatives of children who have the disorder than in the general population, suggesting that ADHD is genetically organized in some way (Alberts-Corush, Firestone, & Goodman, 1986). It is plausible that genetic factors may give some individuals a predisposition toward attention problems and impulse control and that it leads to ADHD in combination with other biological or psychological factors (DuPaul, Guevremont, & Barkley, 1991).

A difficult temperament—an inborn behavioral style characterized by irritability, high activity level, short attention span, distractibility, and so on (see chapter 7)—has been suggested as a possible starting point for ADHD. Children with ADHD are often identifiable as toddlers or preschoolers (DuPaul, Guevremont, & Barkley, 1991). Temperamentally, they fit the description of the "difficult child." They are children who "in the early preschool years show a mixture of problems in attention, impulse control, noncompliance, and aggression" (Campbell et al., 1986, p. 232). Yet temperament alone does not explain all the problems of these youngsters.

In short, evidence does not clearly and consistently link any particular biological factor to ADHD. It is plausible, however, that biological factors are involved in most cases, but precisely what they are and how they operate remain unknown (Neuwirth, 1994).

Hypothesized psychological causes of ADHD range from psychoanalytic explanations to those involving social learning theory. For instance, numerous studies of modeling and imitation illustrate how children *could* acquire deviant behavior patterns through observation of frenetically active parents or siblings. The literature is replete with examples of how children's inappropriate behavior *can* be manipulated by social attention, suggesting that parents and teachers *could* inadvertently teach youngsters to behave in the manner that characterizes ADHD (see Kazdin, 1984; Ross & Ross, 1982). Nevertheless, research has not demonstrated that ADHD is primarily a matter of undesirable social learning, and therefore it is inappropriate for us to lay responsibility for the creation of ADHD on parents or teachers (Barkley, 1985, 1990; Braswell & Bloomquist, 1991; DuPaul, Guevremont, & Barkley, 1991; Neuwirth, 1994).

To summarize what we know about causes, we do not know exactly why children have ADHD. There does not appear to be a single cause. In the vast majority of cases, we suspect that neurological or genetic factors launch the child toward ADHD and that these factors in combination with other influences in the child's physical and social environment produce the inattentive or hyperactive behavior.

We know more about how to control the problems related to this disorder once it has appeared than we know about its origins, so prevention is largely a matter of intervening in the families and classrooms of youngsters who are difficult to manage. Effective primary prevention—keeping ADHD from emerging during the child's development—would require knowledge of neurology and genetics that we do not have, in addition to training in child care and management that would eliminate possible environmental causes. Secondary prevention—reduction and management of problems that have emerged—is the most feasible approach.

Much of the responsibility for secondary prevention falls upon educators, who must manage the child's behavior in school and provide instructional programs that will foster academic success and social adjustment (Hallahan et al., 1996). ADHD appears to be a persistent set of problems that follows children into adolescence and adulthood (Campbell & Werry, 1986; DuPaul & Stoner, 1994). It interferes with academic achievement and peer relations. Lack of achievement, feelings of failure, social isolation or rejection, and low motivation make for high rates of socially inappropriate behavior. The student with ADHD becomes trapped in a self-perpetuating pattern of negative self-perceptions, inappropriate behavior, and negative interactions with others. Prevention of later and more serious difficulties depends on breaking this cycle.

ASSESSMENT

The clinical assessment of ADHD by a psychologist or psychiatrist and the educational assessment of ADHD by teachers or other school personnel may differ considerably. Clinicians will likely be interested primarily in determining whether the child meets certain diagnostic criteria; teachers will be more interested in devising a plan for management of classroom behavior and instruction. Although the characteristics of ADHD may be noticed by parents or others before the child enters school, it is often not until the child is confronted by the demands of the classroom that someone— usually a teacher—becomes aware of the seriousness of the child's problems. In the context of school, ADHD often becomes intolerable and the child's behavior is perceived as provoking a crisis. Children with ADHD often exhibit social behavior about which teachers are understandably upset. However, teachers' concerns about their students' academic performance are those that apparently most often lead them to refer students for special education (Lloyd, Kauffman, Landrum, & Roe, 1991). Many pupils with ADHD present both behavioral and academic concerns.

The primary means of assessment of ADHD that have usefulness in school settings are teacher and peer rating scales, direct observation, and interviews (DuPaul & Stoner, 1994; Montague, McKinney, & Hocutt, 1994). A wide variety of rating scales have been used, some intended to be specific to ADHD and others the broader, more inclusive scales described in chapter 5. The value of any of these scales is that they allow someone to organize and quantify teachers' and peers' perceptions of the student's academic and social behavior. These perceptions are important, but they may not correspond well to direct observation of the student's behavior.

One of the problems in assessing ADHD is determining whether the youngster shows problems related to attention deficits, aggression, or both. Attention deficit or ADD is distinguished by disrupting the classroom, exhibiting problems in daily academic performance, being unprepared for class, not having required materials, and so on. These problems may or may not be accompanied by aggressive behavior or other indications of additional emotional or behavioral disorders. The distinction may be important in judging the seriousness of the student's problems and designing an intervention plan.

Direct observation of the youngster's behavior in various school settings—classroom, playground, lunchroom, hallways—and careful daily records (as opposed to teacher ratings) of academic performance are critical aspects of assessment. These can pinpoint the behavioral aspects of the problem of ADHD and serve as an objective measure of the effectiveness of interventions. Both objective records of behavior and performance, and subjective judgments regarding the nature and acceptability of the student's behavior and performance are important in managing ADHD.

INTERVENTION AND EDUCATION

In most cases, ADHD involves a cluster of related behavioral characteristics, including problems in regulating attention, motivation, hyperactivity, and socially inappropriate responses. Consequently, many different intervention techniques have been tried in both home and classroom settings. The two most common and successful approaches have been medication and training parents and teachers how to manage the student's behavior. The vast majority of cases require multiple interventions involving both parents and teachers (Barkley, 1990; Blackman, Westervelt, Stevenson, & Welch, 1991; DuPaul & Stoner, 1994; DuPaul, Stoner, Tilly, & Putnam, 1991).

Medication

No method of dealing with ADHD has been so controversial as medication. The medications usually given are psychostimulants such as Ritalin (methylphenidate), Dexedrine (dextroamphetamine), or Cylert (pemoline) (Campbell & Cueva, 1995a; Gadow & Pomeroy, 1991). Opponents of medication have described the drugs' possible negative side effects, unknown long-term effects on growth and health, possible negative effects on perceptions of personal responsibility and self-control, and possibility of encouraging drug abuse. The statements of some of the opponents of medication have been unfounded and hysterical; others have been thoughtful, cautious, and based on reliable evidence that stimulant drugs are not a panacea and do, like all medications, carry risks as well as benefits (Fowler, 1992; Weiss & Hechtman, 1993; Whalen & Henker, 1991).

Research now clearly indicates that the right dosage of the right drug results in remarkable improvement in behavior and *facilitates* learning (makes the student more teachable) in about 90 percent of youngsters with ADHD (DuPaul & Stoner, 1994; Gadow & Pomeroy, 1991; Neuwirth, 1994). It is important to recognize that higher than optimal dosage may impair learning rather than facilitate it, that a medication may not have effects on all of the youngster's problem behaviors (e.g., it may improve hyperactivity but have little or no effect on aggression), and that the effects of medication may be different in different settings (e.g., more improvement in school than at home). Children with other disorders in addition to ADHD, such as anxiety or depression, may not respond well to stimulant drugs (Tannock, Ickowicz, & Schachar, 1995).

The effects of stimulant drugs are typically apparent within 30 minutes after a child takes a dose, and the effects usually last for only 3 to 4 hours (unless given in a sustained-release capsule), meaning that behavior may change within school hours and that a missed dose may be noticeable. Although proper administration of a stimulant drug may help to improve a youngster's social interactions with peers and adults, the effects on social cognition and interpersonal relationships is not well understood (Whalen & Henker, 1991).

Apparently, many teachers who recognize the potential value of drugs in treating a variety of emotional and behavioral disorders, including ADHD, feel that they should be more involved in the decision to use or discontinue medication, and feel a need for more information and training regarding medication issues (Epstein, Singh, Luebke, & Stout, 1991). Certainly, teachers should offer parents and physicians their observations about the effects (or noneffects) and side effects of medications on the behavior and learning of a medicated student who is in their class. Although there are alternatives to medication in a substantial percentage of cases—and these alternatives should be tried first—stimulant drugs in combination with other interventions are often very helpful in dealing with ADHD. When reasonable precautions are taken in their use and the dosage and effects are carefully monitored, stimulant drugs are an apparently safe and sane way of augmenting parents' and teachers' other strategies for managing ADHD (DuPaul & Stoner, 1994; Neuwirth, 1994; Whalen & Henker, 1991).

Parent Training

Medication alone is not sufficient to bring the behavior of children with ADHD under control, and parents typically have serious difficulty managing these children at home. Consequently, systematic training of parents in behavior management skills is an approach frequently used by psychologists who serve children with ADHD and their families (Barkley, 1990). The objective of this training is not to cure or eliminate ADHD but "to learn methods of coping with and compensating for this ongoing learning and behavioral disability" (Anastopoulos, DuPaul, & Barkley, 1991). The training is organized around principles of behavioral psychology and involves teaching parents to interact more positively with their children during ordinary activities, avoiding the coercive interactions that are hallmarks of families with aggressive and hyperactive children and adolescents (DuPaul, Guevremont, & Barkley, 1991; for other examples of behavioral training for parents, see Patterson et al., 1975; Patterson & Forgatch, 1987). The procedures parents are taught to use may include a token reinforcement system for encouraging appropriate behavior, and response cost (withdrawing rewards) or time out (brief social isolation) for misbehavior. Ultimately, parents may be taught techniques for managing behavior in public places and generalizing the training to new problems and settings. This type of training is not possible with all parents, nor is it always successful when parents are receptive to it. However, it has been used successfully with many parents. The psychologist working with parents will typically involve teachers as well in a behavior management plan, as little change is likely in school unless similar behavior management procedures are used in the classroom.

Teacher Training

The problems of students with ADHD are usually most evident in the classroom. "The school setting taxes the child with ADHD in precisely those areas where he or she has the greatest deficits—sustained attention, impulse control, and compliance" (DuPaul, Guevremont, & Barkley, 1991, p. 130). Behavior modification and cognitive strategy training are the two most widely recommended approaches to managing the problems of ADHD (Barkley, 1990; Braswell & Bloomquist, 1991; DuPaul & Stoner, 1994). Teachers must be trained in how to use these approaches if they are to have a reasonable chance of success; they are not intuitive methods or ones that every teacher learns.

Behavior Modification   *Behavior modification* is the application of principles of learning, primarily the principle that behavior is affected by its consequences. Behavior modification is not likely to be successful unless the person who is trying to use it both understands the principles that make it work and is attuned to the student's individual characteristics and preferences. It is a powerful tool—but a good one only in the hands of a perceptive and sensitive teacher (Alberto & Troutman, 1995; Kauffman et al., 1993; Walker, 1995).

Behavior modification is not a foolproof method of controlling problems of ADHD or any other emotional or behavioral disorder, but research has demonstrated that noisy, destructive, disruptive, and inattentive behavior can usually be changed for the better by controlling the contingencies of reinforcement (Walker, 1995; Walker et al., 1995). Like medication or any other intervention, behavior modification can be abused and misused. Even when it is used skillfully, it can have unanticipated or undesirable outcomes, and it will not necessarily make a student with ADHD appear normal (Abikoff & Gittelman, 1984).

Modifying the behavior of a youngster with ADHD ordinarily means making certain that rewarding consequences follow desirable behavior and that either no consequences or punishing consequences follow undesirable behavior. As is true with parents, rearranging consequences to support desirable behavior and punish undesirable behavior may be as simple as shifting attention from inappropriate to appropriate behavior. More powerful consequences such as *token reinforcement*, *response cost*, and *time out* may be needed as well. In many cases it is helpful to make the contingencies of reinforcement and punishment more explicit by writing a *contingency contract* (see chapter 12). In addition to the procedures used in the classroom, the parents may be involved in a home–school behavior modification program in which behavior at school earns the pupil rewards provided by the parents at home (see Hallahan et al., 1996). The emphasis must be on positive consequences for appropriate behavior, but prudent negative consequences for misbehavior may be necessary (DuPaul, Stoner, Tilly, & Putnam, 1991; Etscheidt & Ayllon, 1987; Rosen, O'Leary, Joyce, Conway, & Pfiffner, 1984; see also chapter 12).

DuPaul, Stoner, Tilly, and Putnam (1991) describe Jason, a 7-year-old with ADHD who was being considered for special education placement or referral to a pediatrician for possible medication. His classroom teacher and a school psychologist designed a behavior modification strategy that incorporated token reinforcers (e.g., checkmarks or points given for appropriate behavior and accumulated on a card or chart) that could be exchanged for preferred activities or tangible rewards (backup reinforcers). The tokens were given for specific desirable behaviors (e.g., paying attention to work, completing assignments, accuracy), and the effects of the token system were evaluated by periodic teacher ratings and daily observations of on-task behavior and work completion and accuracy. The percentage of his classroom seatwork that Jason completed and the percentage of completed work that was correct during several different conditions is shown in Figure 11.3. When the token system was in effect, Jason completed a much higher percentage of his work correctly than under baseline conditions (when the token system was not used, as shown for days 1–5 and 16–18 in Figure 11.3). Beginning on day 11, a response cost contingency was added to token reinforcement, meaning that Jason lost a token when he was engaged in off-task behavior. Combining token reinforcement and response cost produced better results than token reinforcement alone. The teacher returned to baseline conditions on days 16, 17, and 18 to test whether the token system was actually causing the changes in Jason's performance. Teacher ratings and observations of on-task behavior showed changes similar to those depicted in Figure 11.3.

Figure 11.3 demonstrates that dramatic improvement occurred during Jason's seatwork time. This improvement did not generalize to other times; he continued to

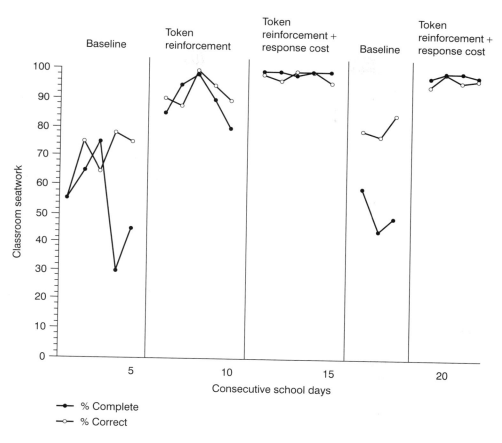

Figure 11.3

Classroom Performance Data During Behavior Change Program

Source: From G. J. DuPaul, G. Stoner, W. D. Tilly, & D. Putnam (1991). Interventions for attention problems. In G. Stoner, M. R. Shinn, & H. M. Walker (Eds.), *Interventions for achievement and behavior problems*. Silver Spring, MD: National Association of School Psychologists, p. 696. Used with permission.

be disruptive and inattentive during other classroom activities, and it was necessary to implement behavior modification procedures during other periods as well. Although the token reinforcement system was gradually changed to less time-consuming and more natural strategies during the course of the school year, it was also necessary to use additional intervention strategies, including medication and parent training in behavioral strategies (DuPaul, Stoner, Tilly, & Putnam, 1991).

Cognitive Strategy Training   The interventions falling under the general rubric of cognitive training or cognitive strategy training include self-instruction, self-monitoring, self-reinforcement, and cognitive-interpersonal problem solving. All have the goal of helping individuals become more aware of their responses to academic tasks and social problems and actively engage in the control of their own responses.

We describe just two strategies—self-instruction and self-monitoring—because they are the most widely used in classroom settings. However, other strategies that involve students cognitively and actively in their self-management, such as goal setting, are also valuable in working with ADHD (Lyman, 1984; Maher, 1987).

Self-instruction involves teaching students to talk to themselves about what they are doing and what they should do. Teaching students to use label stimuli and to rehearse the instructions or tasks they have been given appears to have merit as an instructional strategy in many cases. For example, a student may be told to verbalize each arithmetic problem or its operation sign while working a problem, to say each letter of a word aloud while writing it, or to rehearse a reading passage before reading it aloud to the teacher (Lovitt, 1977). However, this method of managing attention problems has its limits (O'Leary, 1980). Verbal self-instruction can be a cumbersome procedure and is, at least for some students, no better than direct instruction by the teacher (Hallahan, Lloyd, Kauffman, & Loper, 1983).

Typically, self-instruction training requires a series of steps in which verbal control of behavior is first modeled by an adult, then imitated by the student, and finally used independently by the student. On a given task or in a given social situation, the adult first performs the task or response while verbalizing thoughts about the task requirements or social circumstance. The adult may talk about relevant stimuli or cues, planning a response, performing as expected, coping with feelings, and evaluating performance. Then the adult and student might run through the task or response to the social situation together, with the student "shadowing" the adult's verbal and nonverbal behavior. Eventually, the student tries it alone while verbalizing aloud, and finally with subvocal self-instruction. Teaching students to use their own language to regulate behavior has been a successful approach with some impulsive children and youths in academic or social situations. Telling impulsive students to slow down and be careful before responding may not work, yet if these same students can be taught to tell *themselves* in some way to stop and think before they respond, they might improve their behavior considerably.

Self-monitoring has been widely used for helping students who have difficulty staying on task in the classroom, particularly during independent seatwork time. A tape recorder is used to produce tones (prerecorded to sound at random intervals ranging from 10 to 90 seconds, with an average interval of about 45 seconds) that cue the student to ask, "Was I . . . [usually, paying attention]?" and self-record the response on a form. This simple procedure has been found effective in increasing the on-task behavior of many students, ranging from children as young as 5 years to adolescents, who have ADHD and a variety of other disorders. Variations on the procedure have been used to improve academic productivity, accuracy of work, and social behavior (Lloyd, Hallahan, Kauffman, & Keller, 1991; Lloyd, Landrum, & Hallahan, 1991). Research on self-monitoring has led to the following general conclusions:

1. Self-monitoring procedures are simple and straightforward, but they cannot be implemented without preparing the students. Brief training is necessary, in which the teacher talks with the student about the nature of off-task and appropriate behavior, explains the procedure, role-plays the procedure, and has the student practice.

2. Self-monitoring of on-task behavior increases time on task in most cases.

3. Self-monitoring of on-task behavior also typically increases academic productivity.

4. Improvement in on-task behavior and performance usually lasts for several months after the procedure is discontinued.

5. The beneficial effects of self-monitoring are usually achieved without the use of backup reinforcers; extrinsic rewards, such as tokens or treats for improved behavior, are seldom necessary.

6. The tape-recorded tones (cues) prompting self-monitoring are a necessary part of the initial training procedure and implementation, although they can usually be discontinued after a period of successful self-monitoring.

7. Students' self-recording—marking answers to their self-questioning—is a necessary element of initial training and implementation, but can be discontinued after a period of successful self-monitoring.

8. Accuracy in self-monitoring is not critically important; some students will be in close agreement with the teacher's assessment of their on-task behavior, but others will not be.

9. The cuing tones and other aspects of the procedure are usually minimally disruptive to other students in the class.

Figure 11.4 shows a recording form used by two adolescents with behavioral disorders who were taught by their teacher to self-monitor several of their inappropriate off-task behaviors during seatwork (talking out without permission, telling off-task stories, humming or singing, and playing with objects) (McManus, 1985). When these students heard the tape-recorded tone, they made a slash through the symbol representing any target behavior they had exhibited during the previous interval. Some of the effects of their self-monitoring are shown in Figure 11.5.

Notwithstanding the enthusiasm with which development of cognitive strategies was greeted and the many reports of their success in dealing with a wide variety of problems, they have not produced the generalized changes in behavior and cognition in ADHD that researchers and others had hoped for (Abikoff, 1991). Cognitive training in all its various forms clearly is not a panacea for the problems presented by disorders of attention and activity. Moreover, cognitive training is not as simple as it might first appear. The teacher who wishes to use any of the techniques effectively must understand their theoretical basis and carefully construct procedures to fit the individual case (Harris et al., 1985; Meichenbaum, 1983; Rooney & Hallahan, 1985).

A Perspective on Intervention

Nearly every type of intervention that has been used with any kind of troublesome behavior has been tried with ADHD (cf. Barkley, 1990; Neuwirth, 1994; Ross & Ross, 1982). Perhaps that in itself is a commentary on the seriousness with which adults approach the problem. Psychotherapy, providing an optimal level of sensory stimulation, biofeedback, relaxation training, dietary control—you name it, and it

Name _____   Date _____

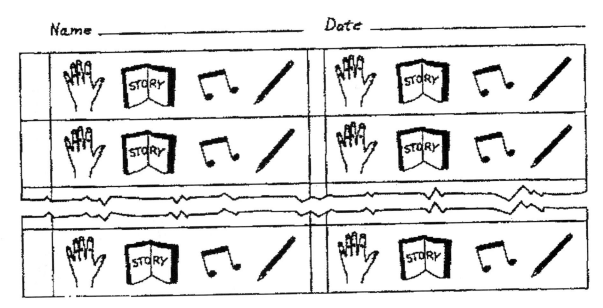

Figure 11.4

Sample Recording Form for Off-Task Behaviors (Note: Upon hearing the cue (tone) to self-monitor, students marked a slash through the symbol(s) describing their behavior: hand = talking out; book = telling off-task stories; musical notes = humming or singing; pencil = playing with objects. Each line of four symbols represents one self-monitoring interval.)
Source: From "Modification of Adolescent Students' Off-Task Behaviors Using Self-Monitoring Procedures" by M. McManus, 1985, unpublished manuscript, University of Virginia, Charlottesville. Reprinted by permission.

has probably been experimented with or even touted as a breakthrough, a revolutionary treatment, or an outright cure.

The lure of the idea that we should be able to find a way to "fix" this common and perplexing malady of children and youths is strong, perhaps irresistible. Over the past several decades, various intervention strategies have been devised by leading scholars and researchers, investigated with initial excitement, adopted widely, and endorsed enthusiastically by many as a solution, if not the cure, for the problems we now call ADD and related disorders, or ADHD. Each strategy eventually has been found not to be the "fix." This initial overenthusiasm for an intervention—one said to be so powerful that the developmental disorder disappears—and the eventual disappointment it leads to has been the history of our approach to every developmental disability, including mental retardation, autism, cerebral palsy, and other developmental disorders. Leading researchers now suggest that ADHD is, indeed, a developmental disability for which we have no cure, and we are not likely to find one soon (Barkley, 1990, 1991; DuPaul & Stoner, 1994). Recognition of the fact that we have no cure for ADHD should not deter us from seeking and implementing the most effective interventions possible. We do have interventions and approaches to

Figure 11.5
A Record of Off-Task Behavior of
Two Students with Behavioral
Disorders

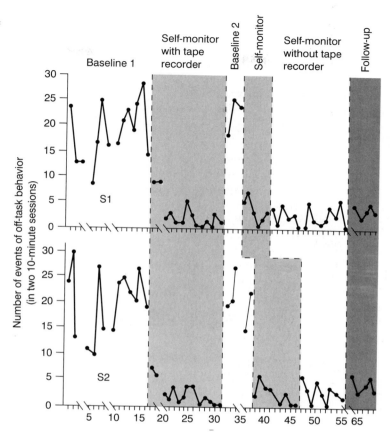

Source: From "Modification of Adolescent Students' Off-Task Behaviors Using Self-Monitoring
Procedures" by M. McManus, 1985, unpublished manuscript, University of Virginia, Charlottesville.
Reprinted by permission.

education that will help us reach important goals. Given our present level of understanding, our goal should not be to eliminate the disability known as ADHD but to manage it as effectively as possible, recognizing that it is a chronic, disabling condition. Barkley (1991) suggests that management of the condition without the expectation of cure has advantages in that it:

(1) reduces the severity of the behavioral symptoms as much as possible; (2) attempts to preclude or diminish the risks for secondary problems developing over time from these primary symptoms; (3) provides periodic reintervention as required to manage crises that emerge with the changing developmental demands made on the disabled child; (4) better prepares the primary caregivers and other family members for the raising of a behaviorally handicapped child; and (5) prevents or diminishes the likelihood of deterioration in the adjustment of other family members as a consequence of the presence of the handicapped ADHD child within that family. (p. x)

SUMMARY

ADD (attention-deficit disorder) and ADHD (attention-deficit hyperactivity disorder) are now the most widely used terms for disorders of attention and activity. There is still considerable controversy and confusion regarding terminology and definition. However, most definitions suggest that ADD (or ADHD) is a developmental disorder of attention and activity level that is evident before the age of 7 or 8 years, persists throughout the life span, involves both academic and social problems, and is frequently accompanied by other disorders. The core problems of concern are regulation of attention, cognition, motivation, and social behavior. ADD, ADHD, learning disabilities, and emotional and behavioral disorders are overlapping, interrelated categories. Approximately 3 to 5 percent of the school-age population is believed to have ADD or ADHD, with boys greatly outnumbering girls.

Brain injury or dysfunction has long been suspected as a cause of ADD and related disorders. Many other biological causes, including food substances, environmental toxins, genetic factors, and temperament have been researched. Various psychological causes have also been suggested, but as yet research does not clearly and reliably point to any specific biological or environmental cause. Leading researchers suggest that poorly understood neurological factors instigate the problem, which is then exacerbated by a variety of factors in the physical and social environment. Prevention of ADD and related disorders consists primarily of managing problems once they are evident.

Assessment for teaching and assessment for clinical treatment may differ considerably. School personnel are interested primarily in assessment that helps them design an intervention program. Teacher and peer rating scales and direct observation of troublesome behavior in various school settings are most useful to educators.

The most widely used and successful approaches to intervention and education with ADD and related disorders are medication with psychostimulant drugs, parent training, and teacher training in behavior modification and cognitive strategies. Medication is very controversial, but research clearly indicates its value when it is properly managed and alternative approaches have not been successful. Medication cannot teach skills or resolve all problems, but it can make the youngster more teachable. Parent training typically involves instruction in behavior management skills and may need to be articulated with a school program. Teacher training usually involves implementing behavior modification (e.g., token reinforcement, response cost, contingency contracts) or cognitive training strategies (e.g., self-instruction or self-monitoring). It may be important to articulate classroom behavior modification with a home-school program involving contingencies managed by parents.

Nearly every known type of intervention has been suggested and attempted with ADD and related disorders. None has provided a cure. The goal of intervention should be to manage the youngster's problems as successfully as possible, realizing that a cure is not available and that coping strategies for parents and teachers are important for dealing with this chronic, disabling condition.

Case for Discussion

"If He Touches Me or My Stuff One More Time . . . !"

John

When other kids start telling you, "If he touches me or my stuff one more time, I'm going to kill him!" you know you have a problem. John is a seventh grader who bugs his peers until they scream. He makes me want to scream too. He's been screamed at a lot, but that hasn't changed his behavior.

John reminds me of a fast-moving mink, poking his nose in and out of hollow logs hunting for mice. He's always on the hunt. But he's doing more than hunting. He's looking for the next moment of excitement, aggravation, or distraction. John is always in motion, squirming, tapping, twitching, and darting. He is unable to keep his hands to himself. If he is not bopping someone on the head as he passes by, then he forces attention from the other seventh-grade students in his class by knocking their books and lunch bags to the floor, where they become great soccer toys as he kicks them down the hall. There is a permanent red ring around his mouth where he habitually sucks on his lips and licks his perpetually chapped skin.

John knows that at the age of 13 he should be able to quiet down for his teacher. Many days, he tries to sit still at his desk and "behave himself." But the moment he sees the small printed words page after page in his textbook, or numbers, symbols, and letters all jumbled up together on the math review, he blows up, scattering his papers as they fly off the desk. Often, as he escapes the room, he is the target of jokes as he trips over himself in his haste. For although he moves with lightning speed, it is not with grace or agility.

In private moments, John sadly tells me how hard it is to feel so jittery all the time, how hard it is to concentrate. He hates the way little kids in elementary school tower over him and especially how his younger brother is stronger, taller, better looking, and more athletic than he thinks he will ever be. The other day he said to me, "I'm always the bad one. Why can't I be the good one sometimes? Mrs. Armand, Why am I this way?" I wanted to tell him, "You *know* how to behave better. *Just DO it!*"

Questions About the Case

1. How is John's behavior typical or atypical of students with ADHD?

2. What do you think Mrs. Armand should have said in response to John's questions?

3. What strategies would you recommend for improving John's relationships with his peers?

Unique Characteristic(s) or Need(s)	Present Level(s) of Performance	Special Education, Related Services, and Modifications	Annual Goal(s)	Objective(s) (Including Procedures, Criteria, and Schedule)
John violates other students' personal space and property.	John currently annoys other students by aggressively touching them and their belongings without permission at least 5 times per day.	1. Use response cost with daily point sheet (i.e., John begins the day with n points and one is taken away each time he touches inappropriately). 2. Offer praise and rewards for each day John reaches the goal of having n points left at end of day. 3. Arrange seating near teacher or teacher assistant 4. Monitor hall behavior to observe and record touching 5. Model, role-play, and have John rehearse other, socially acceptable ways to obtain and retain peer attention	John will touch other students and their property only with their permission and in an appropriate manner as judged by teachers and peers.	John will decrease his inappropriate touching of other students and their belongings as judged by teacher observation and student reports and recorded daily on a log kept by the teacher: a. within 4 weeks to less than 3 times per day for at least 5 consecutive days; b. within 8 weeks to less than 3 times per week for at least 2 consecutive weeks; c. within 12 weeks to 0 (i.e., touch only appropriately and with permission for at least 10 consecutive days).

PERSONAL REFLECTIONS

Attention and Activity Disorders

Peggy Metzger, M.Ed., teaches third grade at Greenbrier Elementary School in Charlottesville, Virginia.

Briefly describe the school and class in which you teach.

The school has a high percentage of children from across the city receiving special education services; of the approximately 250 pupils, about 50 receive special education services. The fact that our school is small is nice, but we are really overloaded with children who need special education services. As a result, we have two self-contained classes for children with emotional or behavioral disorders, two self-contained classes for children with learning disabilities, one self-contained class for children with moderate mental retardation, plus speech and resource classes. I have 23 students in my regular third-grade class. It is a very bright group, according to their scores on the Iowa Test of Basic Skills; their composite scores were all in the fourth-grade range. Although this is a bright group, I do have several students who have attention and activity problems.

Think of a particular child in your classroom who has attention and activity problems. How did this child behave at first in your class?

Kenny had no inhibition and no impulse control. He ran everywhere he went—in the hallway or from one end of the classroom to the other. As he ran, he would always drag his hand along the wall. He seemed to have to be touching the wall everywhere he went, something that can be irritating and can also be funny. One time a teacher was standing in her doorway, and when he ran by—dragging his hand, of course—he tickled her in her ribs. They both seemed quite surprised! I had a beanbag chair

in the back of the classroom, and throughout the day he would unpredictably get up and jump into it. In reading groups, he kicked other people. He always wanted to be first—first to read, first to be in line, first in everything.

Although these behaviors were fairly overt, Kenny also engaged in behaviors that were more irritating than physical. He constantly asked, "Why?" No matter what I said, he would ask, "Why?" And he was very whiny. With the combination of activeness and whininess, Kenny was usually in trouble.

What did you explore as possible causes of his attention and activity problems?

Kenny had lived with his father, a Vietnam veteran, for several years before being moved to his mother's house. During his time with his father, he had participated in his father's counseling sessions for flashbacks and nightmares about the war. Kenny began performing poorly in school during this time, and his father decided to send him to live with his mother. Yet his mother, who also had a 2-year-old daughter, was not prepared for Kenny's arrival. The whole move was chaotic. I don't know that these situations caused his attention and activity problems, but they may have contributed to them.

How did he get along with the other children in the class?

As you might expect, Kenny had trouble getting along with his peers. He made fun of others, especially a child in the class who had a physical disability. When Kenny began making fun of the handicapped child, the other students were shocked and appalled. They wanted nothing to do with him at first. In time, they came to realize that Kenny had problems, and then they became more tolerant of him.

What were the most successful strategies you found for working with him?

My prior years of experience in teaching students with emotional or behavioral disorders really helped me here. When working with children with emotional or behavioral problems, especially children with attention and activity problems, I think it's important to be consistent with rules and then with leveling consequences for breaking such rules. This is where being in a small school with a cohesive faculty really helps. Everyone in my school is consistent about enforcing the rules, so Kenny got the same message from every adult.

Along with consistent rules and consequences for adhering to them, it was also important for Kenny to have a consistent routine he could count on in the classroom. My schedule was predictable; he knew the sequence of activities that was coming each day.

In the classroom, Kenny responded well to praise and tangible reinforcers, such as candy or pencils. Being positive with him and using reinforcers for his appropriate behavior was much more effective than emphasizing negative consequences. He seemed to shrug off punishment.

I also found that it was important to involve his mother in Kenny's behavior management. His mother really wanted him to do well in school, and she tried to back up the management system I used in school. We talked often, and I think our contact indicated to Kenny that we were supportive of one another.

One strategy that was helpful for academic tasks was peer tutoring. I had a group of very strong, very capable students, and I would often pair Kenny with another student. They then worked together on the task. This worked very nicely because the arrangement helped Kenny not only with his academic work but with his social behavior as well. The student with whom Kenny was working modeled appropriate social behavior, which Kenny tended to imitate.

How do the children with disorders of attention and activity that you teach in a regular class differ from those you taught in a special education class?

I don't think that they are very different. The children in regular classes with attention and activity problems are much like students you would find in special classes. I think that the children with attention and activity problems who are still in regular classrooms are there because they have had teachers who are willing to work with them. So much depends on who identifies the student for special education and on their level of tolerance for behaviors associated with attention and activity problems.

Are there other things that you would like to say about teaching children with disorders of attention and activity?

Although I think it's true that most children who have attention and activity problems display types of behavior that are similar along some dimensions, I also think it's important to look at each child individually. I've described only one student—Kenny. I could just as easily have talked about any of the other four children in my classroom who have problems of attention and activity. I could have described the behaviors they display, the causes of their problem behavior, and the strategies that are helpful. What I would have described would have been different for each one. Their circumstances, their behaviors, their strengths and weaknesses are different, and they require different reactions. There is no substitute for focusing on the individual child.

12
Conduct Disorder: Overt Aggression

As you read this chapter, keep these guiding questions in mind:

- What distinguishes the aggressive antisocial youngster from one who is developing normally?

- What do we know about the prevalence of conduct disorder?

- How might conduct disorder be classified into subtypes, and which subtype carries the worst prognosis?

- How is aggression a multicultural issue?

- How is conduct disorder likely to be exhibited in school, and why is it such a serious problem?

- According to social learning theory, how is aggression learned?

- What environmental conditions are associated with high risk for conduct disorder?

- What personal, family, school, and peer factors place a youngster at risk for conduct disorder, and how do these factors combine to pass conduct disorder from one generation to the next?

- What steps might be taken to prevent conduct disorder?

- What should be included in the assessment of conduct disorder?

- What are the major features of social learning interventions in conduct disorder?

- How is punishment defined, and why is it a dangerous and controversial but common approach to dealing with aggression?

- When punishment is necessary, what guidelines should one follow?

- What are the phases in the acting-out behavior cycle, and on which phases should intervention be concentrated?

- What are the components of a pre-correction intervention?

- How is pre-correction related to the acting-out behavior cycle?

- How might schoolwide discipline lower school violence?

DEFINITION, PREVALENCE, AND CLASSIFICATION

Definition

Normally developing children and adolescents occasionally exhibit antisocial behavior of various descriptions. They may throw temper tantrums, fight with their siblings or peers, cheat, lie, be physically cruel to animals or to other people, refuse to obey their parents, or destroy their own or others' possessions. Normally developing youngsters do not, however, perform antisocial acts in most social contexts, nor with such frequency as to become pariahs among their peers or excessively burdensome to their parents and teachers.

A child or youth who has a conduct disorder exhibits a persistent pattern of antisocial behavior that significantly impairs everyday functioning at home or school or that leads others to conclude that the youngster is unmanageable (Kazdin, 1991, 1994; Walker, 1995; Walker, Colvin, & Ramsey, 1995). Many of these children are known as bullies (Tattum & Lane, 1989). Kazdin (1993) summarized the essential features of the disorder:

> The overriding feature of conduct disorder is a persistent pattern of behavior in which the rights of others and age-appropriate social norms are violated. Isolated acts of physical aggression, destruction of property, stealing, and fire setting are sufficiently severe to warrant concern and attention in their own right. Although these behaviors may occur in isolation, several of these are likely to appear together as a constellation or syndrome. (p. 293)

The children about whom we are concerned here perform noxious behaviors at a much higher rate and at a much later age than normally developing children. A youngster with aggressive conduct disorder may match the noxious behaviors of the normally developing child two-to-one or more, and whereas the normally developing child exhibits social aggression at a decreasing rate as he or she grows older, the youngster with conduct disorder usually does not (Patterson et al., 1975). Table 12.1 lists fourteen noxious behaviors that aggressive and normally developing youngsters exhibit. Patterson and his colleagues identified the behaviors and typical rates of occurrence through many hours of naturalistic observation in the homes of families with socially aggressive and nonaggressive children. Note the marked differences between rates of aggressive behaviors in aggressive and nonaggressive children. According to the data in Table 12.1, an aggressive child can be expected to be noncompliant about every 10 minutes, as well as to hit and to tease about every half hour; a nonaggressive child, on the other hand, might be expected to be noncompliant once in 20 minutes, to tease once in about 50 minutes, and to hit once in a couple of hours. While this list is certainly not exhaustive, it does represent the most common means by which children inflict suffering on others.

The case of Don (in the box) illustrates the type of behavior extremely socially aggressive young children exhibit at home and at school. Don's interactions with his family are characterized by coercive exchanges. Without effective intervention to break the coercive cycle at home and at school, Don seems virtually certain to experience a high rate of failure in school and continuing conflict in the community.

Don

When I met him, he was 6½ years of age. . . . A trim four-footer, he had a sleazy look about him, like a postcard carried too long in a hip pocket. He sat in the reception room, slouched down in the chair and coolly looked me over as I approached. . . . The violence of his temper outbursts was frightening and seemed to be triggered by relatively minor provocations. At school, a simple request to turn in his homework, a mild rebuke, or a suggestion that he had erred in his work could lead to shouted obscenities, overturned desks, or attacks on the other children with a pencil held as a dagger. The observers commented that in the home he ruled whatever territory he occupied. . . .

Table 12.1

Noxious Behaviors and Average Time between Occurrences in Aggressive and Nonaggressive Children

Noxious Behavior	Description	Average Number of Minutes between Occurrences[a]	
		Aggressive Children	Nonaggressive Children
Disapproval	Disapproving of another's behavior by words or gestures	7	12
Negativism	Stating something neutral in content but in negative tone of voice	9	41
Noncompliance	Not doing what is requested	11	20
Yell	Shouting, yelling, or talking loudly; if carried on for sufficient time it becomes extremely unpleasant	18	54
Tease	Teasing that produces displeasure, disapproval, or disruption of current activity of person being teased	20	51
High rate activity	Activity that is aversive to others if carried on for a long period (e.g., running in the house or jumping up and down)	23	71
Negative physical act	Attacking or attempting to attack another with enough intensity to potentially inflict pain (e.g., biting, kicking, slapping, hitting, spanking, throwing, grabbing)	24	108
Whine	Saying something in a slurring, nasal, high-pitched, or falsetto voice	28	26
Destructive	Destroying, damaging, or trying to damage or destroy any object	33	156
Humiliation	Making fun of, shaming, or embarrassing another intentionally	50	100
Cry	Any type of crying	52	455
Negative command	Commanding another to do something and demanding immediate compliance, plus threatening aversive consequences (explicitly or implicitly) if compliance not immediate; also directing sarcasm or humiliation at another	120	500
Dependent	Requesting help with task the child is capable of doing himself (e.g., a 16-year-old boy asking his mother to comb his hair)	149	370
Ignore	Appearing to recognize that someone has directed behavior toward oneself but not responding in an active fashion	185	244

Source: Adapted from "A Social Learning Approach to Family Intervention," by G. R. Patterson, J. B. Reid, R. R. Jones, and R. E. Conger. In *Families with Aggressive Children,* Vol. 1 (p. 5), 1975, Eugene, OR: Castalia. Reprinted by permission.

During the intervals when he was absent from home, telephone calls would often mark his progress through the neighborhood; e.g., he left school two hours early, stole candy from a store, and appropriated a toy from a neighborhood child.

No baby-sitter would brave this storm center, so the parents had long ago given up the idea of a private life, movies, or weekends together. Both parents worked. The mother (not yet 30 and physically attractive) looked as if she was in the throes of a severe illness. The family physician provided medication for her chronic depression and accompanying fatigue. Work was a reprieve from her morning and afternoon bouts with her son, Don. . . . Typically, her day began at 7:00 a.m., rousing him from his wet sheets (which she changed), then scolding until he went sullenly to his tub. Once there, she washed and dried him as if he were an infant or visiting royalty.

He often dawdled while dressing, which produced a stream of prompts and commands from his mother. Suggested items of clothing were refused; this led to bitter exchanges with the now thoroughly exasperated mother. He emphasized their disagreements by kicking the door and throwing things around the room. Through all of this the mother hovered about, helping to get him dressed. She alternately cajoled and scolded, wheedled and glared.

She stood in attendance while he dined. Not only did she serve, but she finally fed him whenever he deigned to open his mouth. Through it all ran a steady cacophony of yells, cries, and arguments about whether his mother had any right to force these unreasonable requests upon him. The mother alternated between patient and antagonistic answers to his arguments and threats. At one point, she brought a stick from behind the refrigerator door. Her menacing demeanor left little doubt that she regularly employed this weapon. In the face of this ultimate threat, Don showed temporary compliance and moved forward in his glacial progress toward leaving for school.

In the afternoon Don returned from school to pick up the morning refrain. His 4-year-old brother was also available as a partner. The latter (a Machiavellian of considerable stature) knew when to probe, when to attack, and when to withdraw with tearful protestations to the protection afforded by his parents. For example, as Don sat eating his ice cream (with his fingers), the younger brother surreptitiously slipped a more efficient spoon into the mess and ran triumphantly down the hall to hide behind the door in his bedroom. Don ran shrieking after him, grabbed the door, and repeatedly slammed it into his younger brother. The screams brought both parents to the scene. The father listened for a moment to their shouted claims and counterclaims. After a brief pause, he simply began to slap both children. With that, the mother turned, walked quietly back into the kitchen and sat staring out the window.

Later the family was to go for a ride in the car. Both parents began shouting commands. In the rush of the moment, they often overlapped in their targets; e.g., the mother said, "Don, wash your face right now," while the father ordered, "Put on your jacket, Don. Hurry up now." A steady stream of commands was given as they moved toward the car. The children moved at their own pace, largely ignoring both parents.

During the day, the observers noted periods where the interactions seemed warm and positive. For example, on numerous occasions one parent would read to the children, who would often sit for long periods of time entranced with the story. At these times they seemed to be the prototypical loving family unit. (Patterson, 1982, pp. 294–295, used with permission)

The *DSM-IV* criteria for diagnosing conduct disorder include a list of 15 characteristics under four headings:

- Aggression to people and animals: e.g., bullying, threatening, forcing sex on someone

- Destruction of property: e.g., setting fires or destroying others' property in some other way

- Deceitfulness or theft: e.g., breaking and entering, shoplifting

- Serious violations of rules: e.g., running away, staying out late without parental permission, often being truant

To be diagnosed with conduct disorder, a youngster under the age of 18 needs to have exhibited 3 or more of the 15 characteristics during the past 12 months, with at least 1 having been shown during the past 6 months. Another criterion is that the behavior must cause significant impairment in social, academic, or job-related functioning. Moreover, *DSM-IV* notes that the behavioral characteristics are not a realistic reaction to the immediate environment—for example, not a response to living in a war-ravaged country or in a threatening, impoverished, high-crime neighborhood in which the behavior is necessary for survival (American Psychiatric Association, 1994; see also Richters & Cicchetti, 1993).

Conduct disorder must be judged with reference to chronological age. Ordinarily, children tend to exhibit less overt aggression as they grow older. Compared to nonaggressive youngsters, children and youths with aggressive conduct disorder typically show age-inappropriate aggression from an earlier age, develop a larger repertoire of aggressive acts, exhibit aggression across a wider range of social situations, and persist in aggressive behavior for a longer time (Patterson et al., 1992; Walker et al., 1995). A significant percentage of children and adolescents with conduct disorder showed, in earlier years, the characteristics of oppositional defiant disorder. That is, they showed a pattern of negativistic, hostile, and defiant behavior uncharacteristic of normally developing children of the same age. Representative characteristics include having frequent temper tantrums and often arguing with adults, refusing to obey adults, deliberately annoying other people, and acting angry and resentful (American Psychiatric Association, 1994).

Conduct disorder is often comorbid with other disorders. It is classified in *DSM-IV* under the same general heading as attention-deficit/hyperactivity disorder (ADHD), that is, under *attention-deficit and disruptive behavior disorders*. Oppositional defiant disorder, ADHD, and conduct disorder are known to be closely linked, although having one of these disorders does not necessarily mean that a youngster will have the other. Conduct disorder often occurs along with a variety of other disorders, including depression and attention-deficit/hyperactivity disorder (Kazdin, 1995; Kovacs & Pollock, 1995; Loeber et al., 1995; Reynolds, 1992; Stark et al., 1995).

Prevalence

Estimates of the prevalence of conduct disorder range from 6 to 16 percent of boys and 2 to 9 percent of girls under age 18 (American Psychiatric Association, 1994; Institute of Medicine, 1989). The preponderance of boys with conduct disorder may reflect a combination of biological susceptibilities and socialization processes involving social roles, models, expectations, and reinforcement. Boys with conduct disorder tend to exhibit fighting, stealing, vandalism, and other overtly aggressive, disruptive behavior; girls are more likely to exhibit lying, truancy, running away, substance abuse, prostitution, and other less overtly aggressive behavior. The consensus among researchers is not only that the problem affects at least the officially estimated percentage of children and youths but also that the prevalence is increasing. Moreover, the severity of the disorder is perceived as increasing.

Classification

One way of classifying conduct disorder is by age of onset. *DSM-IV* distinguishes between childhood-onset (before age 10 years) and adolescent-onset (characteristics not observed prior to age 10) types (American Psychiatric Association, 1994). Researchers have frequently found that children with early onset of conduct disorder and delinquency typically show more severe impairment and have a poorer prognosis than those with later onset (see Patterson et al., 1992; Dinitz, Scarpitti, & Reckless, 1962; Walker, 1995). *DSM-IV* also notes that conduct disorder may be classified as mild (resulting in only minor harm to others), moderate, or severe (causing considerable harm to others).

Conduct disorder may also be classified as *undersocialized* or *socialized* (Quay, 1986a, 1986b). *Undersocialized conduct disorder* includes characteristics such as hyperactivity, impulsiveness, irritability, stubbornness, demandingness, arguing, teasing, poor peer relations, loudness, threatening and attacking others, cruelty, fighting, showing off, bragging, swearing, blaming others, sassiness, and disobedience. *Socialized conduct disorder* is characterized by more covert antisocial acts such as negativism, lying, destructiveness, stealing, setting fires, associating with bad companions, belonging to a gang, running away, truancy, and abuse of alcohol or other drugs. However, some youngsters are described as *versatile* because they show both overt and covert forms of antisocial conduct (Loeber & Schmaling, 1985a, 1985b). In this chapter, we focus on overtly aggressive and versatile forms of conduct disorder; covert antisocial behavior is discussed in chapter 13. However, as we shall see, antisocial behavior of all types is closely linked to delinquency and substance abuse. Much of the discussion in this chapter provides a foundation for our consideration in chapters 13 and 14 of covert antisocial behavior and delinquency.

Undersocialized aggressive conduct disorder is closely associated with violent behavior. The level of violence in our society, especially among youths, is a widespread concern, especially to educators and others concerned with children's development (cf. American Psychological Association, 1993; Eron et al., 1994; Furlong &

Morrison, 1994; Walker et al., 1995). Our discussion in this chapter thus addresses both conduct disorder and the problem of violence among children and youths, including school violence.

AGGRESSION AND VIOLENCE IN SOCIAL CONTEXT

"Aggression and America have long been intimate companions" (Goldstein, Carr, Davidson, & Wehr, 1981). Aggression is not new to American children, their homes and families, or their schools. Even cursory examination of *Children and Youth in America* (Bremner, 1970, 1971) and other similar sources quickly reveals that coercion, violence, and brutality have been practiced by and toward children and youths since the founding of this nation. Recognizing the historical presence of violence does not in any way, however, reduce the crisis proportions of aggression in the present-day lives of American children. Both violent adult crime and violent juvenile delinquency have increased dramatically during the past few decades (Eron, Gentry, & Schlegel, 1994). Through the media, children are exposed to brutal acts of aggression at a rate unprecedented in the history of civilization (Eron & Heusmann, 1986; Sprafkin et al., 1992). Assaultive behavior, disruptiveness, and property destruction in schools have grown commonplace. Violence and weapons in schools are problems now apparent in small towns as well as in big cities, in small schools as well as in big ones, and in affluent as well as in poor schools.

Aggression as a Multicultural Issue

Aggression and violence are multicultural issues in that all subcultural groups in America are affected and stereotypes regarding cultural minorities are common. African-American and Latino cultures are frequently miscast as tolerant of violence (Hammond & Yung, 1994; Soriano, 1994). Violence among Native American and Asian/Pacific Island American youths is poorly understood (Chen & True, 1994; Yung & Hammond, 1994). Particularly vulnerable populations of youths are often overlooked in discussion of violence, including children with disabilities (Levey & Lagos, 1994), girls and young women (Sorenson & Bowie, 1994), and lesbian, gay, and bisexual youths (D'Augelli & Dark, 1994). Without ignoring the special vulnerabilities and needs of any group of youths, it is important to recognize the commonalities of sociocultural conditions and needs for nurturing among all children and youths regardless of color or ethnic background. Hill et al. (1994) noted that "the developmental mandates of all youth during adolescence are similar. But the resources for achieving developmental milestones are significantly fewer for economically disadvantaged ethnic minority youth, particularly in inner cities and particularly if they have not had the opportunity to internalize the values of their own ethnic culture that can protect against violence" (p. 86).

Intervention programs designed for particular groups of aggressive students, such as African-American males, have been suggested (e.g., Hudley & Graham, 1995; Middleton & Cartledge, 1995). However, Hudley and Graham (1995) concluded that "although it has been asserted that African-American children have distinct learning styles and preferred modes of instruction, in truth the data in support of these assertions are scant" (p. 193). Cultural sensitivity and multicultural competence are important, but they are no substitute for effective interventions that transcend ethnic and gender identity. Regardless of color, ethnicity, gender, and other personal characteristics, children and youths are placed at risk by common factors such as poverty, family disruption, abuse, neglect, racism, poor schools, lack of employment opportunities, and other social blights. Likewise, the most effective remedies for these risk factors and the protective factors that increase children's resilience are essentially the same across all cultural groups.

Aggression in the Context of School

General education teachers must be prepared to deal with aggression, for it is likely that at least one of their students will be highly disruptive, destructive, or assaultive toward other students or the teacher. Teachers of students with emotional or behavioral disorders must be ready to handle an especially large dose of aggression, for conduct disorder is one of the most common forms of exasperating deportment and psychopathology that brings students into special education. The prospective special education teacher who expects most students to be withdrawn or who believes that students with conduct disorder will quickly learn to reciprocate a kindly social demeanor will be shocked. Without effective means for controlling aggression, the teacher of students with emotional or behavioral disorders must develop a superhuman tolerance for interpersonal nastiness.

Observations in schools and studies of school records suggest that we may expect classroom behaviors similar to those in Table 12.1 from aggressive youngsters (Walker et al., 1995). These behaviors are frequently accompanied by academic failure. Not surprisingly, students who exhibit aggressive conduct disorder are often rejected by their peers and perceive their peers as hostile toward them. When children exhibit aggressive antisocial behavior and academic failure beginning in the early grades, the prognosis is particularly grim, unless effective early intervention is provided (Walker, Shinn, O'Neill, & Ramsey, 1987).

The high rates of antisocial behavior and the significant impairment of everyday functioning of youngsters with undersocialized aggressive conduct disorder do not bode well for their futures. Such youngsters tend to exhibit a relatively stable pattern of aggressive behavior over time; their problems do not tend to dissipate, but to continue into adulthood (Kazdin, 1991, 1995; Olweus, 1979; Patterson et al., 1992; Robins, 1986). Consequently, the prognosis for later adjustment is poor, and the pattern of antisocial conduct is often transmitted over generations. Because aggressive antisocial behavior tends to keep people in contact with mental health and criminal justice systems, and because the behavior inflicts considerable suffering on victims of physical assault and property loss, the cost to society is enormous. Although for boys a history of serious antisocial conduct before age 15 increases the chances of externalizing psychopathology (aggression, criminal behavior, alcohol and drug abuse) in adulthood, for girls this kind of childhood history increases the probability of adulthood externalizing disorders and internalizing disorders (depression, phobias) as well (Robins, 1986). "Clearly, no other disorder of childhood and adolescence is so widespread and disruptive of the lives of those who suffer it and the lives of others" (Quay, 1986b, p. 64). Thus, finding effective interventions for conduct disorder is a priority among social scientists and educators (Eron et al., 1994; Walker et al., 1995). Antisocial behavior, especially when it is characterized by violent aggression, is rightfully a critical concern of all teachers, but especially of special educators who teach students with emotional or behavioral disorders.

CAUSAL FACTORS AND PREVENTION

Aggression has historically been an object of study for scientists in many disciplines, and many alternative explanations have been offered for it. Psychoanalytic theories, drive theories, and simple conditioning theories have not led to effective intervention strategies, and they have been largely discounted by alternative explanations based on scientific research (cf. Pepler & Slaby, 1994). Biological and social learning theories are supported by more reliable evidence.

Although genetic and other biological factors apparently contribute to the most severe cases of conduct disorder, their role in milder cases of aggression is not clear; in both severe and mild forms of conduct disorder, the social environment obviously contributes to the problem (cf. Wells & Forehand, 1985; Webster-Stratton & Dahl, 1995). Sociobiology is an intriguing and controversial topic (Wright, 1995a, 1995b), but it has little to offer developmental psychologists who are seeking more immediate causes of aggression (Hinde, 1986). In fact, decades of research by numerous scientists strongly suggest that an individual's social environment is a powerful regulator of neurobiological processes and behavior; social learning may be the most important determinant of aggression and prosocial behavior (Bandura, 1973; Pepler & Slaby, 1994).

Among the several psychological explanations of aggression, one that stands out as most clearly supported by careful, systematic, scientific research is the *social learning theory* (Pepler & Slaby, 1994). Particularly relevant to our discussion here is the coercive process model constructed after decades of research by Gerald Patterson and his colleagues (e.g., Patterson et al., 1992). Consequently, we focus on these social learning explanations for aggression and its prevention. We first summarize the general findings of social learning research, and then we highlight personal, family, school, peer group, and other cultural factors and review Patterson's model of the coercive process that produces and sustains aggression.

General Conclusions from Social Learning Research

A social learning (or social cognitive) analysis of aggression includes three major controlling influences: the environmental conditions that set the occasion for behavior or that reinforce or punish it, the behavior itself, and cognitive/affective (person) variables (Bandura, 1973, 1986; see Chapter 4). Whether or not a person exhibits aggressive behavior depends on the reciprocal effects of these three factors and the individual's social history. Social learning theory suggests that aggression is learned through the direct consequences of aggressive and nonaggressive acts and through observation of aggression and its consequences. Research in social learning supports several generalizations about how aggression is learned and maintained (see Bandura, 1973; Goldstein, 1983a, 1983b; Patterson, 1986a, 1986b; Patterson et al., 1992; Pepler & Slaby, 1994; Walker et al., 1995):

- Children learn many aggressive responses by observing models or examples. The models may be family members, members of the child's subculture (friends, acquaintances, peers, and adults in the community), or individuals portrayed in the mass media (including real and fictional, human and nonhuman).

- Children are more likely to imitate aggressive models when the models are of high social status and when they see that the models receive reinforcement (positive consequences or rewards) or do not receive punishment for their aggression.

- Children learn aggressive behavior when, given opportunities to practice aggressive responses, they experience either no aversive consequences or succeed in obtaining rewards by harming or overcoming their victims.

- Aggression is more likely to occur when children experience aversive conditions, perhaps physical assault, verbal threats, taunts, or insults or by decreases in or termination of positive reinforcement. Children may learn through observation and/or practice that they can obtain rewarding consequences by engaging in aggressive behavior. The probability of aggression under such circumstances is especially high when alternative (appropriate) means of obtaining reinforcement are not readily available or have not been learned, and when aggression is sanctioned by social authorities.

- Factors that maintain aggression include three types of reinforcement: *external reinforcement* (tangible rewards, social status rewards, removal of aversive conditions, expressions of injury or suffering by the victim), *vicarious reinforcement* (gratification obtained by observing others gain rewards through aggression), and *self-reinforcement* (self-congratulation or increased self-esteem following successful aggression).

- Aggression may be perpetuated by cognitive processes that justify hostile action: comparing one's deeds advantageously to more horrific deeds of others, appealing to higher principles (such as protection of self or others), placing responsibility on others (the familiar "I didn't start it" and "he made me do it" ploys), and dehumanizing the victims (perhaps with demeaning labels such as *nerd, dweeb, trash, pig, drooler*).

- Punishment may also serve to heighten or maintain aggression when it causes pain, when there are no positive alternatives to the punished response, when punishment is delayed or inconsistent, or when punishment provides a model of aggressive behavior. When counterattack against the punisher seems likely to succeed, punishment maintains aggression. The adult who punishes a child by striking out not only causes pain, which increases the probability of aggression, but provides a model of aggression as well.

A social learning analysis of aggression generates testable predictions about environmental conditions that foster aggressive behavior. Research over several decades has led to the following empirically confirmed predictions about the genesis of aggression:

- Viewing televised aggression will increase aggressive behavior, especially in males and in children who have a history of aggressiveness.

- Delinquent subcultures, such as deviant peer groups or street gangs, will maintain aggressive behavior in their members by modeling and reinforcing aggression.

- Families of aggressive children are characterized by high rates of aggression on the part of all members, by coercive exchanges between the aggressive child and other family members, and by parents' inconsistent, punitive control techniques and lack of supervision.

- Aggression begets aggression. When one person presents an aversive condition for another (hitting, yelling, whining), the affronted individual is likely to reply by presenting a negative condition of his or her own, resulting in a coercive process. The coercive interaction will continue until one individual withdraws his or her aversive condition, providing negative reinforcement (escape from aversive stimulation) for the victor.

Family, school, and cultural factors involving social learning were discussed in previous chapters. These factors undoubtedly play a major role in the development of aggressive conduct disorders. By providing models of aggression and supplying reinforcement for aggressive behavior, families, schools, and the larger society teach youngsters (albeit inadvertently) to behave aggressively. This insidious teaching process is most effective for youngsters who are already predisposed to aggressive behavior by their biological endowment and/or their previous social learning. And the process is maintained by reciprocity of effects among the behavior, the social environment, and the child's cognitive and affective characteristics. The teaching/learning process involved in aggression includes reciprocal effects such as these:

- The social environment provides aversive conditions (noxious stimuli), including social disadvantage, academic failure, peer rejection, and rejection by parents and other adults.

- The youngster perceives the social environment as both threatening and likely to reward aggression.

- The youngster's behavior is noxious to others, who attempt to control it by threats and punitive responses.

- ■ The youngster develops low self-concept and identifies himself or herself in primarily negative terms.

- ■ In coercive bouts, the youngster is frequently successful in overcoming others by being more aversive or persistent, thereby obtaining reinforcement for aggression and confirming his or her perceptions of the social environment as threatening and controlled by aggressive behavior.

All of these factors contribute to the development of antisocial behavior and, over time, cement it into a pattern very resistant to change. Patterson et al. (1992) depict the major causal factors that contribute to antisocial behavior as shown in Figure 12.1. We next examine major contributing factors and how they are interrelated in a coercive process.

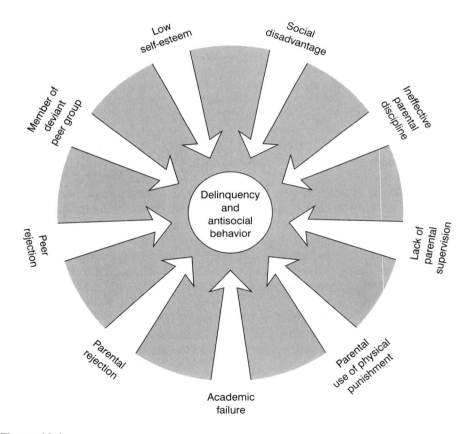

Figure 12.1
The Causal Wheel
Source: From *Antisocial Boys* by Gerald R. Patterson, John B. Reid, and Thomas J. Dishion. Copyright ©1992 by Castalia Publishing Company. Reprinted by permission.

Personal Factors

As discussed in chapter 7, children are born with dispositions or temperaments that, although modifiable, tend to be fairly consistent over a period of years (see Caspi et al., 1995; Smith & Prior, 1995). Many children with difficult, irritable temperaments are at risk for developing antisocial behavior. Their difficult temperaments as infants may evolve through social interaction with their caretakers into high rates of noncompliance and oppositional behavior in the early childhood years. These children are likely to develop low self-esteem and depressed affect as well as to have major problems in peer relations and academic achievement. In short, they may begin life with personal attributes that make social rejection likely, and these characteristics may be exacerbated by cycles of negative interaction with caretakers, peers, and teachers. Although demographic factors such as low socioeconomic status and family factors such as parental substance abuse are important, the personal characteristics of attention problems and, especially, fighting are predictive of the early onset of conduct disorder in boys (Loeber et al., 1995).

Family Factors

The families of antisocial children tend to be characterized by antisocial or criminal behavior of parents and siblings. Often, the homes and family relationships are chaotic and unsupportive of normal social development (Campbell, 1995; Lavigueur, Tremblay, & Saucier, 1995; Patterson et al., 1992). There are often many children in the family. The families are often broken by divorce or abandonment and characterized by high levels of interpersonal conflict. Parental monitoring of children's behavior tends to be lax or almost nonexistent, and discipline tends to be unpredictable but harsh. Often there are multigenerations living together, and grandparents or other relatives living in the home also typically lack childrearing skills. As discussed in chapter 8, the children and parents often become enmeshed in a coercive cycle of interaction in which parent and child increase the pain they cause the other until one party "wins." We should be careful not to assume that *all* families of antisocial children can be so characterized. However, these are the *typical* family characteristics of children who are antisocial.

School Factors

Most antisocial students experience academic failure and rejection by peers and adults in school. In many cases, they attend schools that are in deteriorated or crowded buildings. The discipline they experience in school is often little better than the parental discipline they experience at home—highly punitive, erratic, escalating, with little or no attention to their nonaggressive behavior or efforts to achieve. The academic work they are given is often not consistent with their achievement level or relevant to their eventual employment, forcing them to face failure and boredom every day they attend school (Jones & Jones, 1995; Walker et al., 1995). As for family factors, we must be careful not to accuse *all* teachers and school administrators of failing to teach and manage difficult students well. However, the typical school experience of antisocial students is highly negative, contributing to further maladjustment, as discussed in chapter 9.

Peer Group and Other Cultural Factors

From an early age, normally developing peers tend to reject their peers who are highly aggressive and disruptive of play and school activities (Guevremont & Dumas, 1994). Antisocial students may achieve high status among a subgroup of peers, but they are likely to be rejected by most. To achieve some sense of competence and belonging, antisocial children and youths often gravitate toward a deviant peer group. Especially given poor parental monitoring and other family risk factors and academic failure, adolescents are likely to identify with deviant peers and be drawn into delinquency, substance abuse, and antisocial behavior that limits their opportunities for further education, employment, and development of positive and stable social relationships.

As discussed in chapter 10, many cultural factors increase the risk that children will adopt antisocial patterns of behavior. Besides the peer group, neighborhoods with high rates of poverty, unemployment, violence, substandard housing and social opportunities, and other negative social conditions and media portrayals contribute to the growth and maintenance of aggression and violence.

The growth, development, and perpetuation of antisocial behavior is pictured in Figure 12.2. Patterson et al. (1992) describe the stages of growth of the "vile weed" of antisocial behavior. Their coercive model begins in stage one with the contextual variables shown in the ground: difficult child temperament, stressors such as poverty and family conflict, poor discipline and monitoring by parents and grandparents, and parental antisocial behavior and substance abuse. This social context is very likely to produce an antisocial child with low self-esteem. In the next stage, school failure, parental rejection, peer rejection, and depression all contribute to one another and further strengthen the child's antisocial tendencies. In stage three, the youngster becomes oriented toward antisocial peers and becomes engaged in delinquency and substance abuse. Now the youth has become enmeshed in social relationships and behavioral patterns that often lead to the final stage in which the antisocial youth becomes an antisocial adult who is unable to hold a job and is at high risk for incarceration or other institutionalization and a disrupted marriage. Clearly, any offspring of someone in stage four in this model is highly likely to drop into similar ground (social context) and grow through the same stages. So antisocial behavior is passed from one generation to the next.

Prevention

The foregoing discussion suggests that we know quite a bit about the social contexts in which antisocial behavior grows most readily, and, indeed, we do. Rigorous research during the past 2 decades has yielded a bonanza of evidence about community, family, school, peer, and personal characteristics that place children and youths

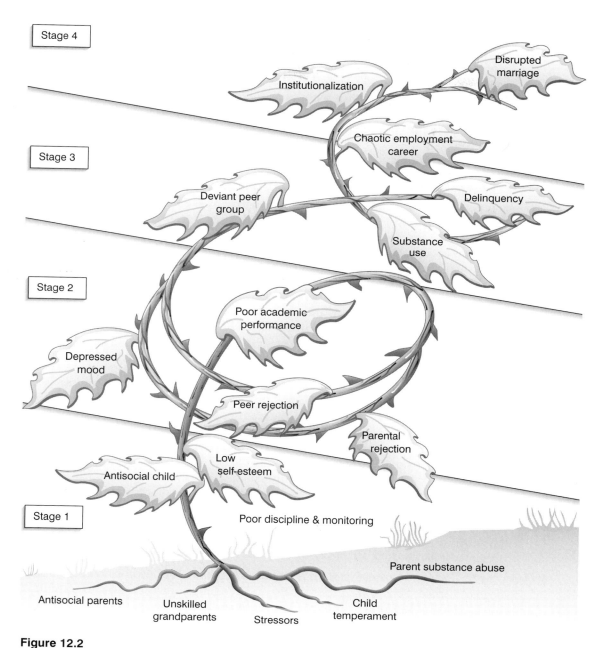

Figure 12.2

The Vile Weed: Stages in the Coercion Model

Source: From *Antisocial Boys* by Gerald R. Patterson, John B. Reid, and Thomas J. Dishion. Copyright ©1992 by Castalia Publishing Company. Reprinted by permission.

at high risk of adopting antisocial behavior patterns. In fact, we can now make recommendations regarding the prevention of aggressive behavior with considerable confidence, based on research like that we have just reviewed (Biglan, 1995; Kauffman, 1994b; Mayer, 1995; Walker et al., 1995). However, as Biglan (1995) noted, "It is ironic that we have such high rates of serious antisocial behavior at the same time that the behavioral sciences are making so much progress in understanding and intervening in the contextual conditions that contribute to the development of antisocial behavior" (p. 479). Clearly we need to address antisocial behavior at all levels of prevention: primary (to prevent serious antisocial behavior from emerging as an established pattern), secondary (to remediate or ameliorate antisocial behavior once it is established), and tertiary (to accommodate or attenuate the negative effects of antisocial behavior that is unlikely to be changed). Walker et al. (1995) describe primary prevention as a feasible goal only for children 8 years old or younger; early intervention is essential.

Many members of our society, including professional practitioners in education and related disciplines as well as politicians and policy makers, have been reluctant to take the steps that we have good reason to believe would prevent or attenuate antisocial behavior. Although all may agree that the level of antisocial behavior and violence in our society is unacceptable, many are opposed to the coherent, sustained, and costly programs of government at all levels that are necessary to address the problem effectively. The steps research suggests we should take might be summarized as follows (see Kauffman, 1994b):

1. *Provide effective consequences to deter aggression.* Antisocial behavior is less likely to recur if it is followed by consequences that are nonviolent but immediate, certain, and proportional to the seriousness of the offense. Violence as a means of controlling aggression engenders counteraggression, setting the stage for further coercion. Aggression is reduced in the long term if the consequences are swift, assured, and restrictive of personal preferences rather than harsh or physically painful. Antisocial children and youths are typically punished capriciously and severely; the consequences of their behavior are often random, harsh, and unfair, cementing the pattern of counteraggression. The belief that harsher punishment is more effective is a deeply ingrained superstition. If teachers, parents, and others dealing with antisocial behavior learn to use effective nonviolent consequences, then the level of violence in our society will decline.

2. *Teach nonaggressive responses to problems.* Aggressive behavior is, to a significant degree, learned. So is nonaggressive behavior. Teaching youngsters how to solve personal conflicts and other problems nonaggressively is not easy, nor will teaching nonaggression help them solve all problems. A school curriculum including nonaggressive conflict resolution and problem solving could lower the level of violence, but that effect would be multiplied many times were the media, community leaders, and high-profile role models to join forces with educators in teaching that nonviolence is a better way.

3. *Stop aggression early—before it takes root.* Aggression begets aggression, particularly when it is successful in obtaining desired ends and when it has become well

practiced. Aggression often escalates from relatively minor belligerence to appalling acts of violence, and nonviolent consequences are more effective when applied early in the sequence. We need intervention that is early in two ways: first, early in that we intervene with young children; second, early in that we intervene from first instances of antisocial behavior, the earliest behaviors in a chain of aggressive interactions.

4. *Restrict access to the instruments of aggression.* Aggressors use the most efficient tools available to damage their targets. True, some will aggress with whatever tools are available. The more important truth is that having more efficient weapons (e.g., guns) enables aggressors to accomplish violent ends with less immediate risk to themselves and to escalate the level of violence easily. More effective restriction of access to the most efficient tools of aggression would help to check the rise in violence—restrictions on the manufacture, distribution, and possession of both the tools themselves and of the parts that make the most efficient weapons of violence operable.

5. *Restrain and reform public displays of aggression.* The behavior one observes affects one's own thinking and overt behavior. Much of the fare marketed by the entertainment industry is saturated with aggressive acts, desensitizes observers to aggression and its consequences, and disinhibits expressions of aggression. Reducing the amount and type of aggression purveyed to the public as entertainment and requiring that the realistic consequences of aggression be depicted would contribute to the goal of a less violent society. Sports figures who eschew violence could add immeasurably to this effect.

6. *Correct the conditions of everyday life that foster aggression.* People tend to be more aggressive when they are deprived of basic necessities, experience aversive conditions, or perceive that there is no path to their legitimate goals other than aggression. Poverty and its attendant deprivations and aversive conditions affect an enormous proportion of American children and youths, and these conditions of everyday life provide fertile ground for aggressive conduct. Social programs that address poverty, unemployment, and related social inequities would help to remove the conditions that breed aggression. Opportunities for supervised recreation offer alternatives to antisocial behavior. A reasonably supportive society cannot abolish poverty or remove all of life's dangers, but it can keep many children from living in abject fear, misery, and hopelessness. We must have more effective social programs of government, the private sector, local communities, religious groups, families, and individuals.

7. *Offer more effective instruction and more attractive educational options in public schools.* Achieving academic success and engaging in study that they see as interesting and useful in their lives reduces the likelihood that youngsters will behave aggressively. By adopting instructional methods known to produce superior results—putting instruction on a solid scientific footing—schools could ensure that more students achieve success in the basic skills needed to pursue any educational option. By offering highly differentiated curricula, school systems could help more students find options that interest them and prepare them for life after high school.

The basic features of effective early identification and prevention programs are becoming increasingly clear (cf. Biglan, 1995; Blechman, Prinz, & Dumas, 1995;

Coie et al., 1993; Kazdin, 1995; Kingston & Prior, 1995; Mayer, 1995; Tremblay et al., 1995). Although preventive efforts may have a significant effect if implemented in only one social context (e.g., school or family), they will have maximum effect only if implemented as a coherent package of interventions involving multiple facets of the problem. This knowledge should not deter educators or any other professionals from implementing preventive practices immediately, regardless of what happens in spheres outside their immediate responsibility or direct influence.

Most important for educators is understanding how instruction is a key tool for prevention (cf. Kauffman et al., 1993). In a review of research on the effects of instructional variables on problem behavior, Munk and Repp (1994) found that such seemingly mundane procedures as giving students more choice over instructional tasks, varying types of tasks, increasing the pace of instruction, interspersing preferred (high-probability) and nonpreferred (low-probability) tasks, reducing task difficulty and errors have been found effective in reducing problem behavior. In short, being confronted daily, if not hourly, by academic and social tasks at which they are failures is known to contribute directly to students' tendency to exhibit antisocial behavior (Blechman et al., 1995; Mayer, 1995). Many antisocial students do not know how to do the academic tasks and do not have the social coping skills to be successful in the typical classroom, and each failure increases the probability of future antisocial responses to problems.

One way of averting problems through proactive planning and instructional analysis is called *pre-correction* (Colvin, Sugai, & Patching, 1993; Walker et al., 1995). A pre-correction analysis is a systematic way of looking at problem behavior to find ways of preventing a behavioral mistake from occurring. Emphasis is placed on intervening early—*before the problem behavior occurs, not after*. Pre-correction and other instructional procedures represent a shift in focus from the consequences of behavior to its antecedents. Certainly, consequences are important in managing antisocial behavior as well as other types of emotional or behavioral disorders. However, prevention requires attention to the contexts or conditions that make problem behavior less likely to occur in the first place. We return to these strategies in our discussion of intervention, but we list here the steps in a pre-correction strategy as described by Walker et al. (1995):

Step 1   Identify the context and the likely problem behavior.

Step 2   Specify the expected behavior.

Step 3   Systematically modify the context.

Step 4   Conduct behavioral rehearsals.

Step 5   Provide strong reinforcement for expected behaviors.

Step 6   Prompt expected behaviors.

Step 7   Monitor the plan. (pp. 176-178)

The most effective approaches to school-based prevention of antisocial behavior are *proactive and instructive*—planning ways to avoid failure and coercive struggles regarding both academic and social behavior and actively teaching students more adaptive, competent ways of behaving. Antisocial behavior should prompt teachers to ask what prosocial skills the student needs to learn as a replacement for aggression and to devise an explicit *instructional* strategy for teaching those skills.

ASSESSMENT

The antisocial behavior characterizing conduct disorder is included on nearly all behavior problem checklists and behavior rating scales. Moreover, a variety of instruments have been designed specifically to measure the antisocial behavior of children and adolescents through self-reports or ratings of parents, teachers, or peers (Kazdin, 1993). These measures of antisocial behavior are often helpful, but they must always be supplemented by direct observation of the children or youths in several different settings to obtain more precise information about the problem.

In chapter 5, we discussed screening and identification instruments that might be used to select students for further study or confirm the existence of a problem requiring intervention. The instruments and practices described in chapters 5 and 6 apply to the assessment of conduct disorder. Kazdin (1993) suggested several considerations in the assessment of conduct disorder that build upon our prior discussion, and these may be summarized as follows:

- A student with conduct disorder is likely to show dysfunctions in diverse domains other than antisocial behavior (e.g., hyperactivity, academic failure, problems at home and school). Multidimensional rating scales (e.g., the *Child Behavior Checklist*) are likely to tap these various problems without necessitating the use of many different instruments. Sometimes it is appropriate to use particular items or groups of items from such instruments to focus on an individual's particular problems.

- Assessment of prosocial skills is critical. The goal of assessment and intervention is not merely to demonstrate a reduction in antisocial behavior but to show that antisocial behavior has been replaced by positive social interaction.

- Comparisons of the student's behavior to norms is important. In judging the severity of problems and the outcomes of intervention, we must know how the student's behavior compares to that of peers of the same age and sex. Most standardized rating scales provide such norms.

- The student's behavior must be assessed in social context. That is, we must assess also the family characteristics and classroom environments that may be contributing to the problem. Intervention and assessment usually need to include more than the student's behavior.

- Periodic or ongoing assessment is required to monitor progress and, if necessary, redesign intervention.

Walker et al. (1995) and Cartledge and Milburn (1995) describe methods of assessing social skills (see also Walker et al., 1983). These skills include behaviors like listening, greeting others, joining in with peers in play groups, using self-control, expressing anger of disagreeing with others appropriately, and so on. It is important not only to assess such social skills systematically and accurately but to assess the effects of attempts to improve such skills and the way students use them in everyday circumstances and whether they improve the students' social standing in the peer group.

Another aspect of assessment is *functional analysis*—finding out what purpose the student's behavior serves, what consequences, gains, or benefits it provides (see Mayer, 1995; O'Neill et al., 1990). A functional analysis can provide guidance for making alterations in the environment (e.g., tasks, commands, reinforcement) that will prevent or ameliorate problems. Munk and Repp (1994) provide a series of assessment questions related to instructional variables that might affect problem behavior, suggest how a functional analysis related to the questions might be carried out, and offer actions that might be taken based on the findings. Table 12.2 shows the kinds of questions, functional analysis procedures, and actions that might be used to examine the effects of student choice of tasks and task variation. Munk and Repp provide similar guidelines for examining the pace of instruction, interspersal of preferred and nonpreferred activities, and task difficulty. Researchers are increasingly finding that assessment of instructional procedures is a key component of preventing and ameliorating antisocial behavior in school.

As mentioned in our discussion of prevention, pre-correction strategies are based on the premise that assessment of the context in which antisocial behavior is likely to occur will help teachers find ways of short-circuiting misbehavior and coercive struggles. Ultimately, assessment is of little value unless it suggests the variables that could be changed to alter antisocial behavior (Walker et al., 1995).

INTERVENTION AND EDUCATION

Prediction and social control of violent behavior are among the most controversial and critical issues involving American youths (Eron et al., 1994; O'Donnell, 1995; Sautter, 1995; Tate et al., 1995; Walker et al., 1995). A variety of conceptual approaches, ranging from psychodynamic therapies to behavioral interventions to biological treatments, has been suggested during the past century. Kazdin (1995) notes that parent management training, problem-solving training, family therapy based on systems theory and behaviorism, and treatments addressing multiple social systems (family, school, community) as well as the individual are among the most promising approaches. Interventions based on social learning principles (e.g., Patterson et al., 1992) have generally been more successful than those based on other conceptual models (cf. Kazdin, 1994; Walker, 1995; Walker et al., 1995; Webster-Stratton & Dahl, 1995). Furthermore, a social learning approach offers the most direct, practical, and reliable implications for the work of teachers. Consequently, we confine discussion here to interventions based on social learning concepts.

Table 12.2

Assessment of Instructional Variables

Instructional Variable	Assessment Question	Functional Assessment	Action
Student choice of tasks	1. Does student or teacher select most activities? 2. Does student have identifiable preferences for tasks or activities 3. Does maladaptive behavior occur more often when teacher assigns tasks? 4. Does student express a preference for alternative tasks when stimuli are presented by the teacher? 5. Does maladaptive behavior result in a change in tasks or activities? Is the student allowed to select an alternative task? 6. If allowed to select tasks, does the student select one or two tasks, or several tasks?	1. Select several tasks available in classroom. 2. Test two conditions—Condition A, in which teacher assigns all tasks, and Condition B, in which the student is allowed to select from the tasks previously assigned. 3. Record occurrences of maladaptive behavior under Conditions A and B.	If Condition B (student choice of tasks) produces decreased maladaptive behavior, provide opportunities for student choice. If maladaptive behavior does not vary between conditions, assess other variables.
Task variation	1. How many tasks are available within 5, 10, 15, 30, and 60 minutes of instruction? 2. Does maladaptive behavior increase as time on a single task increases? 3. Does the student stop the assigned task and begin other activities during an instructional period? 4. Does the student display less maladaptive behavior during brief tasks?	1. Select several tasks commonly used during instruction. 2. Implement Condition A—instruct student to perform a single task for normal amounts of time before switching to another task. 3. Implement Condition B—instruct student on each task for shorter periods of time and rotate tasks continually. 4. Record occurrences of maladaptive behavior under Conditions A and B.	If Condition B (task variation) produces reduced rates of maladaptive behavior, continue task variation. If maladaptive behavior does not vary between conditions, assess other variables.

Source: From "The Relationship Between Instructional Variables and Problem Behavior: A review" by Dennis D. Munk and Alan C. Repp. *Exceptional Children*, 1994, p. 397. Copyright © 1994 by the Council for Exceptional Children. Reprinted by permission.

Major Features of Social Learning Interventions

A *social learning approach* to the control of aggression includes three primary components: specific behavioral objectives, strategies for changing behavior by altering the social environment, and precise measurement of behavioral change (Carr, 1981a). These components allow us to judge the outcome of intervention quantitatively as well as qualitatively against an objective goal. Behavior change techniques are employed by those who have the most continuous contact with the aggressive child and the greatest amount of control over his or her immediate environment—usually parents, siblings, teachers, or peers, as opposed to therapists who see the youngster infrequently and work in highly artificial or contrived settings. The focus is on modifying the social environment to reduce aggression primarily by teaching prosocial behavior, including cognitive and affective dispositions as well as directly observable behavior.

Social learning interventions sometimes appear quite simple, but the apparent simplicity is deceptive, because it is often necessary to make subtle adjustments in technique to make them work. An exquisite sensitivity to human communication is necessary to become a virtuoso in the humane and effective application of behavior principles. The range of possible techniques for an individual case is extensive, calling for a high degree of creativity to formulate an effective and ethical plan of action.

School-based social learning interventions designed to reduce aggression may include a very wide variety of strategies or procedures (see Sprick & Howard, 1995). Walker (1995) discusses 12 intervention techniques for managing the acting-out student, providing guidelines for correct application, special issues, and advantages and disadvantages of each. These 12 techniques (and others) may be used individually or in combination. The following thumbnail sketches of the 12 techniques provide a beginning point for understanding how effective interventions for conduct disorder may be constructed.

■ *Rules*—clear, explicit statements defining the teacher's expectations for classroom conduct. Clarity of expectations is a hallmark of corrective or therapeutic environments for students with conduct disorder. A few clear rules let students know how they should behave and what is prohibited; they are important guidelines for classroom conduct and teacher behavior as well. Positively stated rules, which should predominate, guide the teacher's praise, approval, and other forms of positive reinforcement. Negatively stated rules, which should be kept to a minimum, guide the teacher's use of punishment.

■ *Teacher praise*—positive verbal, physical, gestural, or other affective indications of approval. Teacher praise for desirable, nonaggressive student conduct is one of the key ingredients in successful behavior management. Many teachers neglect this aspect of instruction or use praise too sparingly or unskillfully. Yet it is perhaps the most important element in a program of positive reinforcement. Moreover, rules alone are much less effective than rules combined with frequent, skillful teacher praise for following the rules.

■ *Positive reinforcement*—presentation of a rewarding consequence that increases the future probability or strength of the behavior it follows. Such consequences

can be extremely varied in form.
to be most effective, praise and othe
given (a) *immediately* following appro
enthusiasm, (d) with *eye contact* from the
the behavior that earned the reward, (f) in w
pation for obtaining them, and (g) in great
forcers are given that can be exchanged later fo
(much like any other economic exchange or moneta
of positive reinforcement requires differential respondi
ior. That is, the desired behavior is to be reinforced; un
be ignored (not reinforced). The basic idea of positive reinfo
ple; its skillful implementation is not, especially with difficult a

■ *Verbal feedback*—information about the appropriateness or inappr
   academic or social behavior. Teachers' responses to students' academic
   and conduct—the content, emotional tone, and timing of what they say
   reaction to students' behavior—are crucial factors in how students learn to
   Giving clear feedback, keeping it primarily positive, steering clear of argume
   and finding the most effective pace and timing are critical issues. Using verb
   feedback effectively requires much experience, training, and reflection.

■ *Stimulus change*—alteration of antecedent events or conditions that set the stage
   for behavior. Sometimes antecedents can be changed easily, resulting in a marked
   decrease in problem behavior. For example, making instructions or assignments
   shorter and clearer may result in greatly improved levels of compliance. Presenting tasks or commands in a different way may also defuse resistance to them.
   Increasing attention is being given to the effects of the context in which aggression occurs, and modification of the context is often found to be both feasible
   and effective in reducing aggression.

■ *Contingency contract*—a written performance agreement between a student and
   teacher (or parents, or both teacher and parents), specifying roles, expectations,
   and consequences. Contracts must be written with the student's age and intelligence in mind. They should be simple, straightforward statements. Successful
   contracts are clearly written, emphasize the positive consequences for appropriate conduct, specify fair consequences to which all parties agree, and are strictly
   adhered to by the adults who sign the document. Contracts are not generally
   successful if they are used as the only or primary intervention strategy. They are
   useful primarily for individuals and carefully delimited problem behaviors.

■ *Modeling plus reinforcing imitation*—showing or demonstrating the desired
   behavior and providing positive reinforcement for matching responses. Learning
   through watching models and imitating them—*observational learning*—is a basic
   social learning process. The models may be adults or peers, but it is critical that
   the student who is to learn more appropriate behavior be taught whom to
   watch, what to look for, and what to match; models without explicit instruction
   are not typically effective in remediating academic or social problems (see Hal-

ing and reinforcement often must
teacher, and procedures must be
imstances the improved behavior

beginning with behavior the stu-
ing successive approximations of
identifying and reinforcing small
ires very careful attention to the
ioral goal. It also requires ignor-
vard the goal. As is true of posi-
skillful implementation is not.

hich the skills taught are those
ositive social interactions, (b)
, and (c) cope effectively with
ig along with authority figures
variety of activities, and solv-
ways. They involve both skill
formance deficits (the student
s training program must not
onstration and practice of the
...iich they are needed to avoid

Rhode, Jenson, and Reavis (1992) suggest that
r forms of positive reinforcement should be
opriate behavior, (b) *frequently*, (c) with
teacher, (e) after or with *description* of
ays that build excitement and *antici-*
ariety. Sometimes, "token" rein-
r desired objects or privileges
y system). The effective use
g to the student's behav-
desirable behavior is to
orcement is very sim-
ntisocial students.

opriateness of
erformance
and do in
ehave.
its,

353

_gg_... and aggressive behavior.

- *Self-monitoring and self-control training*—consistent tracking, recording, and evaluating of specific behaviors of one's own with the intention of changing those behaviors. These procedures many involve not only keeping track of one's own behavior but prompting oneself or applying consequences to oneself. These procedures require explicit training and rehearsal as well as motivation to use them. As discussed in chapter 11, self-monitoring is a strategy frequently used with students who have attention-deficit hyperactivity disorder (ADHD). Self-monitoring may be an inappropriate strategy for serious aggressive behavior and for students who do not have the cognitive awareness or social maturity to carry out the procedures.

- *Timeout*—the removal, for a specified period of time and contingent upon a specific misbehavior, a student's opportunity to obtain positive reinforcement. Timeout may involve removing a student from the group or classroom, although that is not always necessary (e.g., it may involve the teacher's turning away and refusing to respond or a time during which the student cannot earn points or other rewards). Timeout should be reserved for serious behavior problems. Like any punishment procedure, it is easily misunderstood, misused, and abused. Used knowledgeably, skillfully, and in combination with other positive procedures, it is an important nonviolent tool for reducing aggressive behavior.

- *Response cost*—the removal of a previously earned reward or reinforcer (or a portion thereof) contingent upon a specific misbehavior. Response cost is a "fine" or penalty incurred for each instance of an inappropriate behavior. Minutes of recess, free time, or access to another preferred activity or points toward earning a reinforcing item or activity may be lost for each misbehavior. Like any other punishment procedure, response cost is subject to misunderstanding and misuse. Moreover, it is ineffective in the absence of strong program of positive reinforcement. However, of all types of punishment procedures, it is probably the least likely to engender strong emotional side effects and resistance.

The Uses and Misuses of Punishment

Many educators in the United States appear to be extremely regressive in their attitudes toward corporal punishment and other highly punitive approaches to child discipline (e.g., Evans & Richardson, 1995; Hyman, 1995). Indeed, numerous studies have confirmed the low rates of positive reinforcement for appropriate behavior and high rates of aversive conditions for students in typical American classrooms, as discussed in chapter 9. In reaction to excessive and ineffective punishment, some have advocated a ban on all manner of punishment, arguing that positive measures alone are sufficient and punishment in any form is unethical. Research does not support a complete abandonment of punishment as a means of child management, but it does suggest great care in the use of punishment procedures.

Although teaching appropriate behavior is important in social learning interventions, some behaviors may require punishment because they are intolerable or dangerous and unresponsive to alternative positive interventions (cf. Axelrod & Apsche, 1983; Kazdin, 1991; Walker, 1995; Walker et al., 1995). It may be difficult or impossible to establish adequate classroom control, particularly with students who have learning and behavior problems, without using negative consequences for misbehavior in addition to positive reinforcement of appropriate conduct. Judicious use of negative consequences for misconduct can even enhance the effectiveness of positive consequences (Pfiffner & O'Leary, 1987; Pfiffner, Rosen, & O'Leary, 1985).

We must be extremely careful in the use of punishment, however, because ill-timed, vengeful, and capricious punishment, especially in the absence of incentives for appropriate behavior, provides a vicious example for youngsters and encourages their further misbehavior. Harsh punishment provokes counteraggression and coercion. Punishment is a seductive, easily abused approach to controlling behavior. Harsh punishment has an immediate effect; because it frequently results in immediate cessation of the individual's irritating or inappropriate behavior, it provides powerful negative reinforcement for the punisher. Thus it is often the beginning point of a coercive style of interaction in which the punished and the punisher vie for the dubious honor of winning an aversive contest. And because people mistakenly believe that punishment makes the individual suffer, physical punishment is frequently thought to be more effective than milder forms. These dangers, misconceptions, and abuses of punishment appear to underlie the coercive relationships that characterize families of aggressive antisocial children (cf. Patterson et al., 1992). Consequently, it is critical to carefully consider punishment in educational settings to avoid having the school become another battleground for aversive control.

A pervasive misconception about punishment is that it requires inflicting physical pain, psychological trauma, or social embarrassment. None of these is required; punishment can be defined as any consequence that results in a decline in the rate or strength of the punished behavior. Thus a mild, quiet reprimand, temporary withdrawal of attention, or loss of a small privilege may often be effective punishment. For persistent and serious misbehavior, stronger punishment may be necessary, but mild forms of social punishment such as restrictions or loss of rewards are most effective if the youngster's environment also provides many opportunities for positive reinforcement of appropriate behavior.

The social learning literature clearly supports the assertion that punishment, if carefully and appropriately administered, is a humane and effective tool for controlling serious misbehavior (cf. Axelrod & Apsche, 1983; Bandura, 1973; Braaten et al., 1988; Kauffman, Boland, Hopkins, & Birnbrauer, 1980; Polsgrove, 1983; Walker, 1995; Walker et al., 1995). Effective punishment may actually be necessary to rear a nonaggressive, socialized child (Patterson, 1982; Patterson et al., 1992), but clumsy, vindictive, or malicious punishment is the teacher's or parent's downfall. We must first give attention to what types of behavior may be legitimately punished, as noted in the following box.

Punishment: What Are the Priority Behaviors?

Braaten, Simpson, Rosell, and Reilly (1988) proposed criteria dividing disturbing behaviors into five priority levels for deciding whether punishment is warranted.

- *Low priority* behaviors include those that are annoying, but not harmful to others, and those that may impede goal achievement. Examples include teasing, disrupting, and various other off-task behaviors that do not substantially interfere with class routine.

- *Mild priority* behaviors frequently interfere with or prohibit achievement of adaptive goals, involve minor property damage, and result in minor injury to self or others. Examples include defiance or off-task behaviors, defacing desktops, pushing, poking, or other provocative behaviors. These behaviors require teacher intervention.

- *Moderate priority* behaviors interfere repeatedly and significantly with achievement of adaptive goals or with other members of the class and may require the involvement of support staff, administrators, and parents. Examples include fighting, avoidance of schoolwork, throwing objects or engaging in other behaviors likely to result in injury, exaggerated temper outbursts, and abuse of staff.

- *High priority* behaviors are characterized by a generalized alienation or agitation that is excessively disruptive to self and others. These are behaviors that have persisted despite interventions by teachers, support staff, administrators, and parents, and they may require use of nontraditional interventions. Examples vary from physical assault to the ritualistic behaviors of autism. (p. 80)

- *Urgent priority* behaviors involve extreme risk and may require immediate, expert intervention. Examples include life-threatening and potentially injurious behaviors.

Before using punishment procedures, educators must be sure that a strong program of teaching and positive consequences for appropriate behavior is in place, and they must carefully consider the types of behavior that are priorities for punishment. Teachers should study the use of punishment procedures in depth before implementing them in the classroom. Following are general guidelines for humane and effective punishment:

- Punishment should be reserved for serious misbehavior that is associated with significant impairment of the youngster's social relationships and behaviors that positive strategies alone have failed to control.

- Punishment should be instituted only in the context of ongoing behavior management and instructional programs that emphasize positive consequences for appropriate conduct and achievement.

- Punishment should be used only by people who are warm and loving toward the individual when his or her behavior is acceptable and who offer ample positive reinforcement for nonaggressive behavior.

- Punishment should be administered matter-of-factly, without anger, threats, or moralizing.

- Punishment should be fair, consistent, and immediate. If the youngster is able to understand descriptions of the contingency, punishment should be applied only to behavior that he or she has been warned is punishable. In short, punishment should be predictable and swift, not capricious or delayed.

- Punishment should be of reasonable intensity. Relatively minor misbehavior should evoke only mild punishment, and more serious offenses or problems should generally result in stronger punishment.

- Whenever possible, punishment should involve response cost (loss of privileges or rewards or withdrawal of attention) rather than aversives.

- Whenever possible, punishment should be related to the misbehavior, enabling the youngster to make restitution and/or practice a more adaptive alternate behavior.

- Punishment should be discontinued if it is not quickly apparent that it is effective. Unlike positive reinforcement, which may not have an immediate effect on behavior, effective punishment usually results in an almost immediate decline in misbehavior. It is better not to punish than to punish ineffectively, as ineffective punishment may merely increase the individual's tolerance for aversive consequences. Punishment will not necessarily be more effective if it becomes harsher or more intense; using a different type of punishment, making the punishment more immediate, or making the punishment more consistent may make it more effective.

- There should be written guidelines for using specific punishment procedures. All concerned parties—students, parents, teachers, and school administrators—should know what punishment procedures will be used. Before implementing specific punishment procedures, especially those involving time out or other aversive consequences, they should be approved by school authorities.

As we have discussed, children and youths with conduct disorder have typically experienced lax monitoring and inconsistent, harsh punishment with little positive reinforcement for appropriate behavior. Their discipline has typically contributed to their conduct disorder, not because it has included punishment *per se*, but because it has included too little positive reinforcement for the right kind of behavior and punishment that is not appropriate. Effective intervention in conduct disorder may often require punishment, but punishment of a different character and in a different context than that which the youngster has experienced previously.

The Acting-Out Behavior Cycle and Pre-Correction

Social learning interventions are increasingly focused on stepping in early to prevent the escalation of aggression and the "blow-ups" in which it often terminates. Perhaps the clearest exposition of this approach is provided by Walker et al. (1995), who describe the phases children and youths typically go through in a cycle of acting-out behavior. Figure 12.3 is a graphic depiction of the seven phases, and Table 12.3 is a summary of characteristic behaviors associated with each phase.

A highly significant feature of the acting-out cycle described by Walker et al. (1995) is that it begins with a *calm* phase in which the student is behaving in ways that are expected and appropriate. The student is cooperative, compliant, and task-oriented. Most students with conduct disorder exhibit appropriate behavior at least some of the time, but this behavior is typically ignored by teachers. Major emphasis should be placed on recognizing and showing approval of students in the calm phase.

Unresolved problems, either problems in school or outside of school, may *trigger* the first stage in moving toward a major blow-up. At this point, teachers may avert further escalation if they recognize the triggering events or conditions and move quickly to help the student resolve the problems.

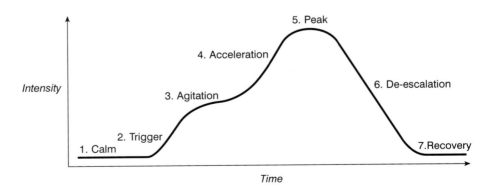

Figure 12.3
Phases of Acting-Out Behavior
Source: From *Managing Acting-Out Behavior* by Geoffrey Colvin. Copyright ©1992 by Behavior Associates. Reprinted by permission.

If triggering problems are not resolved, the student may move into a state of *agitation*, in which overall behavior is unfocused and off-task. If the teacher recognizes indications of agitation, further escalation of aggressive behavior may be prevented by altering teacher proximity, engaging the student in alternative activities, involving the student in a plan of self-management, or using other strategies designed to help the student avoid a blow-up.

Agitation may lead to *acceleration*, a phase in which the student engages the teacher in a coercive struggle. Acceleration is characterized by attempts to draw the teacher into arguments or demand teacher attention through noncompliant, highly disruptive, abusive, or destructive behavior. At this point, it is extremely important for the teacher to avoid getting drawn in, to use crisis-prevention strategies to extricate himself or herself from the struggle. By the time the student gets to this point, it is very difficult to de-escalate the behavior. Clear consequences for such behavior need to be established and communicated to the student beforehand so that at this point the teacher can deliver the needed information to the student matter-of-factly and allow the student a few seconds to make a decision (e.g., "Roger, you must stop throwing stuff around now, or I will call the principal. Take a couple of seconds to decide."). Prompt and unequivocal follow-through in applying the consequence is extremely important.

In the *peak* phase, the student's behavior is out of control. It may be necessary to call the police or the student's parents or remove the student from the classroom or school. Preparation for such out-of-control behavior is essential so that the involved adults are as calm, systematic, and effective as possible in preventing injury or damage and the de-escalation phase can be entered as quickly as possible. Frequent out-of-control behavior should be a prompt to educators to examine the environment and school work for conditions that need to be changed.

During *de-escalation* following a peak phase, the student typically is beginning to disengage from the struggle and is in a confused state. Behavior may range from withdrawal, to denial and blaming others for what happened, to wanting to "make up," to responsiveness to directions and willingness to engage in simple tasks. It is important to take measures to help the student cool down, restore the environment as much as possible (e.g., pick up books and chairs, clean up mess), and get back to routine activities. This is not yet the time to talk to the student about his or her behavior. Debriefing at this point in the cycle is likely to be counterproductive; the student is likely to be reluctant to talk at all or may not be able to think clearly about the incident, what led to it, and how similar problems might be avoided.

Finally, the student enters a *recovery* phase in which there is eagerness for busy work and a semblance of ordinary classwork but still a reluctance to discuss what happened. It is important to provide strong reinforcement for normal routines and to avoid negotiations about the negative consequences that may have been applied to the serious misbehavior. However, it is very important at this point to *debrief* the student, to review what led up to the problem and what alternative behaviors the student might have chosen. Any effort of the student to problem-solve should be acknowledged, and the student should be helped to devise a step-by-step plan for avoiding repetitions of the blow-up. The student needs reassurance that he or she can succeed and avoid such out-of-control incidents with help.

Table 12.3
Summary of the Acting-Out Cycle

Phase One: Calm

1. On-task behavior
2. Following of rules and expectations
3. Responsiveness to praise
4. Initiation of behavior
5. Goal-orientedness

Phase Two: Triggers

School-Based

1. Conflicts
   a. Denial of something they need
   b. Something negative is inflicted
2. Changes in routine
3. Provocations
4. Pressure
5. Ineffective problem solving
6. Errors
7. Corrections

Nonschool-Based

1. Dysfunctional homes
2. Health problems
3. Nutrition
4. Sleep
5. Substance abuse
6. Gangs

Phase Three: Agitation

Increases in Behavior

1. Darting eyes
2. Nonconversational language
3. Busy hands
4. Moving in and out of groups
5. Off-task, then on-task behavior

Decreases in Behavior

1. Staring into space
2. Subdued language
3. Contained hands
4. Withdrawal from groups

Phase Four: Acceleration

1. Questioning and arguing
2. Noncompliance and defiance
3. Off-task behavior
4. Provocation of others
5. Compliance with accompanying inappropriate behaviors

Source: From *Antisocial Behavior in School: Strategies and Best Practices* by Hill M. Walker, Geoffrey Colvin, and Elizabeth Ramsey. Copyright ©1995 by Brooks/Cole. Reprinted by permission.

Table 12.3 (continued)

6. Criterion problems
7. Whining and crying
8. Avoidance and escape
9. Threats and intimidation
10. Verbal abuse
11. Destruction of property
12. Serious behavior in general

Phase Five: Peak

1. Serious destruction of property
2. Assault
3. Self-abuse
4. Severe tantrums
5. Hyperventilation

Phase Six: De-Escalation

1. Confusion
2. Reconciliation
3. Withdrawal
4. Denial
5. Blaming others
6. Responsiveness to directions
7. Responsiveness to manipulative or mechanical tasks
8. Avoidance of discussion (unless there is occasion to blame others)

Phase Seven: Recovery

1. Eagerness for independent work or activity
2. Subdued behavior in group work
3. Subdued behavior in class discussions
4. Defensive behavior
5. Avoidance of debriefing

Educators often place a great deal of emphasis on phases four and five of the acting-out behavior cycle, virtually ignoring the first three phases, particularly phase one (calm). Walker et al. (1995) note that this is counterproductive. The opposite emphasis is recommended by decades of research: focus attention on the earlier phases of the cycle, on attention to and reinforcement of calm behavior, removing or ameliorating triggers, and intervening early and nonthreateningly when students begin showing signs of agitation. One systematic way of focusing attention and effort on earlier phases of the cycle is the pre-correction plan described by Colvin, Sugai, and Patching (1993) and Walker et al., (1995). Strong reinforcement for appropriate behavior is important, but pre-correction begins with examination of the context in which misbehavior is likely and how conditions might be altered and instructional (as opposed to correctional) procedures might be used to prevent the misbehavior from occurring—how triggers and agitation can be avoided. Figure 12.4 shows a pre-correction checklist and plan devised by a fifth-grade teacher.

In chapter 8, we quoted Patterson's (1986b) observation that many of the characteristics of conduct disorder emerge from "the prosaic daily round of parental mismanagement . . . something as inherently banal as family coercive exchanges. What leads to things getting out of hand may be a relatively simple affair, whereas the process itself, once initiated, may be the stuff of which novels are made" (p. 442). It is highly probable that a similar process characterizes the emergence of conduct disorder in school. Astute teachers perceive the potential for triggers and agitation and move quickly and positively to help students learn to avoid them, not just to deal appropriately with the early stages of acting out. Thus many of the most effective interventions, especially those related to pre-correction, are characterized by expert management of the most ordinary events.

School Violence and Schoolwide Discipline

There is strong consensus among those who study schools and behavioral deviance that the problems of student misconduct have increased enormously in seriousness and pervasiveness during the past 2 decades. "Public school personnel are having to manage problem student behavior at ever-increasing levels of intensity and severity. Behavioral episodes are occurring routinely that would have been unthinkable several decades ago" (Walker et al., 1995, p. 149). Such episodes will not be managed well or lessened without a coherent schoolwide plan of behavior management in addition to strategies designed for individuals and classroom groups.

In many schools today, especially middle schools, students are concerned about the violent behavior of their peers. The popular press (e.g., Moyers, 1995), general education publications (e.g., Sautter, 1995), and television reports frequently highlight the problem of violence in and around schools. Teaching peace and conflict-resolution skills has been suggested as an effective strategy for reducing violence (e.g., Lantieri, 1995), and perhaps such instruction can contribute to safer, less violent schools. However, it is possible that the most effective approach to school violence is focused primarily on the more ordinary, routine interactions that characterize

Figure 12.4
Pre-Correction Checklist and Plan for Dominic

PRE-CORRECTION CHECKLIST AND PLAN

Teacher: *Sarah Endow*
Student: *Dominic Smith*
Date: *11/15/94*

☐ 1. Context

Students enter classroom immediately after recess.

Students shouting, laughing, and pushing before complying with teacher directions.

☐ 2. Expected behavior

Enter the room quietly, go to desks, begin task, keep hands to self.

☐ 3. Context modification

Teacher meets students at door, has them wait, and then go to desks to begin entry tasks.

☐ 4. Behavior rehearsal

Teacher reminds students just before recess of expected behaviors. Ask Dominic to tell what expected behaviors are.

☐ 5. Strong reinforcement

Students are told that if they cooperate with teacher requests, they will have additional breaks and 5 extra minutes for recess.

☐ 6. Prompts

Teacher gives signals at the door to be quiet and points to activity on chalkboard. Teacher says "hush" to noisy students and praises students who are beginning work.

☐ 7. Monitoring plan

Teacher uses a watch to measure how long it takes for all students to get on-task and counts how many students begin their tasks immediately (within 10 seconds).

Source: From *Antisocial Behavior in School: Strategies and Best Practices* by Hill M. Walker, Geoffrey Colvin, and Elizabeth Ramsey. Copyright © 1995 by Brooks/Cole. Reprinted by permission.

classrooms and other school environments and that are natural extensions or refinements of basic educational practices rather than special curricula. In fact, schoolwide discipline plans may fit the definition of universal interventions that help to prevent severe disorders (see Coie et al., 1993).

An important concept in the prevention of violence is that violent acts, like the more mundane acts of aggression that characterize conduct disorder, typically follow a pattern of escalating conflict. The most effective strategies for controlling school violence, therefore, are those that modify the conditions under which lower levels of aggressive acts are most likely to occur, deal quickly and nonviolently with the earliest indications that aggressive behavior is on an escalating path, and organize the school staff to support consistent, schoolwide implementation of discipline procedures. With a good schoolwide plan, the entire school staff functions as a team to set clear behavioral expectations, establish a positive school climate in which desirable behavior is frequently recognized and reinforced, monitor student behavior continuously, apply consistent and planned consequences for unacceptable behavior, provide collegial support, and maintain clear communication about both behavioral expectations and problem incidents (see Walker et al., 1995). The following box illustrates one middle schools' coherent, schoolwide response to violence—a school in which students had previously organized protests against the violence of their peers and the lack of the school's control of aggressive behavior. The "Caught you!" strategy described in the newspaper article, one way of increasing attention to students' prosocial behavior, is only one aspect of the schoolwide plan to lower the level of aggressive behavior.

Buford Kids Get Caught Doing Good

"Caught you!"

Those words, often associated with dread by mischievous adolescents, could now mean the proverbial free lunch for students at Buford Middle School in Charlottesville.

The school, the site of protests last spring condemning attacks by students upon other students, has embarked on a program to reward students for the good they do.

Students who are spotted doing something nice for another student or someone else in the school are greeted by a teacher or another adult with "Hey, caught you!" said Marty Bass, an instructional coordinator at Buford.

Each act of kindness is then recorded on a slip of paper that is placed in a box for a drawing each Thursday. Winners of the drawing, each representing their grade, receive a free submarine sandwich from Domino's Pizza. The slips for all the students cited that week are displayed on a bulletin board in the cafeteria. . . .

The idea for the program, "Caught Doin' Good," was that of Paula Dufault, a resource teacher. . . . "It's based on positive actions, politeness, manners, helping others," Dufault said, "I guess being civil." (Denery, 1994, pp. B1-B2)

Much of the problem of antisocial behavior in schools is in the form of bullying—coercion, intimidation, and threats that often start as mean-spirited teasing and progress to extortion and physical attack. Bullying is now recognized as a serious problem in the schools of many nations throughout the world (cf. Olweus, 1991; Tattum & Herbert, 1990; Tattum & Lane, 1989; Walker et al., 1995). It is a serious problem that is often a precursor to school violence. Antisocial students are typically the bullies, not the victims, although they sometimes suffer the same fate as those they bully. Any student who is particularly passive, submissive, or provocative is a potential victim of bullies. Effective intervention in bullying typically requires a schoolwide, if not communitywide, effort, as well as individual intervention, as much of the bullying occurs outside the presence of any one adult. The general features of effective anti-bullying interventions include the following (see Olweus, 1991; Walker et al., 1995 for further discussion):

- A school climate characterized by a warm, positive, supportive school atmosphere in which adults set clear and firm limits on unacceptable behavior

- Nonhostile, nonphysical sanctions applied immediately and consistently to violations of behavioral expectations

- Continuous monitoring and surveillance of student activities in and around the school

- Adult mediation of student interactions and assumption of authority to stop bullying when it is observed

- Discussion of the issue of bullying with bullies, victims, parents, and neutral students (nonparticipants) to clarify school values, expectations, procedures, and consequences

We would like to think that all schools are responsible for all children and that no child should be excluded from a school because of his or her disability. However, some students with severe conduct disorder are disabled in ways that make their inclusion in regular classrooms and neighborhood schools inadvisable on ethical grounds, if not a mockery of social justice (see Kauffman, Lloyd, Baker, & Riedel, 1995). Violent behavior cannot and must not be tolerated in schools if nonviolent students and their teachers are to maintain a viable social and instructional environment. In the epilogue of their book on antisocial behavior in school, Walker et al. (1995) put it this way:

> Many middle schools and high schools are held hostage by a relatively small group of antisocial, potentially violent students. They poison the schooling atmosphere for everyone. Such students need caring adults in their lives, but they must be held accountable for their actions and evicted from schooling if they pose threats to the safety of other students and school staff. In our view, students who choose to bring weapons to school, who physically intimidate and assault others, and who attempt to hold the school hostage through use of terror tactics forfeit their rights of access to that setting. Such students should also experience the full force of available legal sanctions for these forms of behavior. (p. 386)

SUMMARY

Conduct disorder is characterized by persistent antisocial behavior that violates the rights of others as well as age-appropriate social norms. It includes aggression to people and animals, destruction of property, deceitfulness and theft, and serious violation of rules. We distinguish youngsters with conduct disorder from those who are developing normally by their higher rates of noxious behaviors and by the persistence of such conduct beyond the age at which most children have adopted less aggressive behavior. Conduct disorder is often comorbid with other disorders. It is one of the most prevalent psychopathological disorders of childhood and youth, estimated to affect 6 to 16 percent of males and 2 to 9 percent of females under the age of 18. Conduct disorder may be classified by age of onset, and those with early onset (before age 10) typically show more serious impairment and have a worse prognosis. Other subtypes include overt aggressive (undersocialized); covert antisocial (socialized), such as theft, lying, and arson; and versatile (socialized and undersocialized).

Aggressive behavior has long been a common phenomenon in American culture, but aggression and violence have become a much greater concern in schools during the past 2 decades. Aggression and violence are multicultural issues, although most contributing factors and interventions appear to apply equally across all subgroups. Both general and special education teachers must be prepared to deal with aggressive behavior of students.

Many contributing causes of aggression have been identified, but social learning theory provides the best supported and most useful conceptualizations for educators. We know that aggression may be learned through processes of modeling, reinforcement of aggression, and ineffective punishment. The risk of aggressive behavior is increased by a wide variety of personal, family, school, peer, and other cultural factors. These factors are often combined in a coercive process leading to aggressive behavior that is passed from one generation to the next.

Steps likely to be effective in preventing conduct disorder include consequences that deter aggression, instruction in nonaggressive responses to problems, early intervention, restriction of the tools of aggression, restraint of public displays of aggression, correction of everyday living conditions, and more effective and attractive school options. A proactive, instructional approach to prevention is of greatest value to educators.

A variety of rating scales are of value in assessing conduct disorder, but direct observation of behavior in various settings must supplement the ratings. Assessment requires evaluation of a variety of domains, including both academic and social problems and behavior at home and at school. Assessment must include prosocial skills as well as social deficits. Ongoing assessment to monitor progress is essential. Social skills must be assessed to guide instruction. Functional assessment of behavior to determine what consequences, gains, or benefits it provides the student will help guide intervention.

Interventions based on social learning are the most reliable and useful for teachers. These may include strategies such as rules, teacher praise, positive reinforcement, verbal feedback, stimulus change, contingency contracts, modeling and reinforcement of imitation, shaping, systematic social skills instruction, self-monitoring and self-control training, timeout, and response cost. Particular care must be taken in the use of punishment, as it is seductive and easily misused. The focus must be on positive strategies. The concepts of the acting-out cycle and pre-correction help keep the focus of intervention on positive strategies applied early in the sequence. The acting-out cycle includes the phases calm, trigger, agitation, acceleration, peak, de-escalation, and recovery. Greatest emphasis should be placed on intervention in the first three phases of the cycle. Pre-correction plans help to keep the focus on earlier phases in the cycle. Schoolwide discipline plans may help decrease the level of violence in schools by focusing efforts on positive attention to appropriate behavior, clear expectations and monitoring of student behavior, staff communication and support, and consistent consequences for unacceptable behavior.

Case for Discussion

"A Field Day with 'Baby Huey'"
David

The other boys called David "Baby Huey." Huge, awkward, and mean, he lunged after them, hoping that maybe this time his swinging bookbag might actually make contact with a vulnerable part of at least one of them. They were almost always too quick for his bulk, which infuriated him even more. Flailing out at them always triggered his hyperventilation, and as he gasped for breath he would start to whine and whisper to himself—how he hated them, how he hated the stupid teachers, too, how he hated everyone. He was convinced that he was being persecuted, the only one being wronged. He was a loner, an object of bullying by his sixth-grade peers who obtained endless entertainment by observing his helpless rage.

David tested in the very superior range of intellectual ability, but his severe coping limitations did not allow him to rationally analyze the antecedents or consequences of his behaviors. Real and imagined incidents of physical and verbal harassment by classmates merged in his mind. His psychological suffering was overtaking his ability to perform even simple academic tasks, and he was slipping a year or more below grade level in all subjects. He always had an excuse: "This is baby work, I ain't that stupid!" I found this kind of comment one of the most frustrating aspects of working with David. And, as you might guess, reactions of this type caused his classmates to torment him with even more vigor.

I learned that David's facial contortions signified his irrational thoughts. They were signals that he was about to run—in his case, lumber determinedly—out of range of adults who, in his opinion, were just a bunch of incompetent fools. His "running" was typically a beeline for the classroom door, then down the hall and out onto the school grounds where he skulked behind vehicles. Sometimes when we followed him, he picked up desks, chairs, and other large objects, hurling them like toys and cursing profusely. In the school parking lot, he would gather the largest gravel he could find to use as projectiles against anyone who came too close.

Our late September field day was one more disaster in David's life. I knew it would be an opportunity for his peers to have a field day teasing him. It didn't take long for events to unfold. Within 30 minutes, four teachers brought David back into the building after he tried to pummel a smaller boy for "looking" at him. David hadn't done any serious damage to the smaller kid, thanks to the quick intervention of the staff. But in the bargain David slapped, kicked, scratched, and spit in the faces of the teachers. So, David was suspended for 2 days.

Now I sat in the principal's office with David's angry mother. She objected to his suspension, claiming that he was only defending himself against his peers, who were the real problem. "What I want to know, Mr. Kunckle, is what are you going to do about those boys who are always teasing him and upsetting him? Those are the kids who ought to be suspended."

Questions About the Case

1. In what way is David atypical of antisocial boys, given what we know about such boys and bullying?
2. If you were Mr. Kunckle, would you focus your efforts on David or the peers who tease him? Why? What would be the primary features of your intervention?
3. What do you think Mr. Kunckle should say to David's mother?

Unique Characteristic(s) or Need(s)	Present Level(s) of Performance	Special Education, Related Services, and Modifications	Annual Goal(s)	Objective(s) (Including Procedures, Criteria, and Schedule)
David is unable to ignore or respond appropriately to teasing and consistently retaliates by using profanity, verbal and physical threats, and physical attacks.	David currently engages in at least three verbal or physical confrontations with his peers daily when being teased.	*Note:* The following are to be provided in the context of a program to reduce teasing by peers. 1. Provide a social skills training program with special emphasis on instruction, role-playing, and rehearsal to teach effective responses to teasing. 2. Negotiate a behavioral contract providing positive consequences for David's responses to teasing. 3. Provide counseling with trained school staff to discuss David's relationship-building skills.	David will respond to teasing in appropriate, non-violent ways.	1. The teacher will keep a daily log of David's physical attacks on others. As shown by the teacher's log, David's attacks on peers in response to teasing will decrease to: a. less than 3 times per week (within 2 months) b. less than 3 times in 4 weeks (within 4 months) c. no attacks during the last 2 months of the current school year 2. By the end of the current school year, David will respond appropriately to teasing by his peers by ignoring, leaving the situation, using nonthreatening requests to stop, or other appropriate behavior as documented by the teacher's observations and anecdotal records.

PERSONAL REFLECTIONS

Aggressive Conduct Disorder

Michele H. Cornett, B.A., teaches a self-contained classroom for students with behavioral disorders in Fayette County, Kentucky, and is a graduate student in special education at the University of Kentucky.

Briefly describe the school and class in which you teach.

My class is in a public inner-city elementary school with grades 1–5. The students in my unit come from elementary schools throughout the county.

How would you describe the antisocial behavior of the students you teach?

The students I teach could be classified as having undersocialized conduct disorder. They are extremely impulsive, argumentative with peers, and sometimes physically aggressive. They are impulsive in both academic and social behavior; they don't think before they respond. If I ask them a question, they reply immediately without thinking their answer through. They're impulsive because they lack problem-solving strategies and thus can't resolve conflict in a positive way. They're threatened by authority that tries to dominate them. This is the reason most of my students end up in my classroom. The teachers they had prior to me would demand that things be done their way. Some of these teachers were inconsistent in their management strategies; their classrooms were unpredictable. When their environment is unpredictable, these students respond inappropriately due to frustration and the unfairness of the situation. Too often, power struggles resulted in the student being suspended, which also reinforced the teacher's inconsistent management techniques.

Peer relations are another big problem. I've observed that the greatest conflict occurs among students similar in age (1 or 2 years difference). Peer-related problems that I see include teasing, falsely accusing others, irritability, and cruelty.

Teasing usually revolves around the clothes children wear, where children live and shop, comments about family members, and intelligence. Teasing usually occurs in unstructured settings like recess and lunch.

Falsely accusing others is another problem that occurs in my room. Accusations are typically related to students taking materials that belong to others or blaming others for materials of mine which have been damaged.

I see irritability in my classroom, often when students have had a bad morning at home and their attitude carries over to school. I also notice it sometimes when I give a student a consequence and others try to make him or her feel better or give encouragement to take the consequence appropriately. Many times, the children I teach reject others' encouragement or kindness because they are angry with themselves.

Cruelty is another common characteristic of my students. Their cruelty is usually in the form of teasing with regard to specific situations. I had a girl in my class whose mother was dying of cancer, and one boy in the class brought it up just to upset her. He seemed to have no regard for her feelings at all. However, he does not have a good relationship with his own mother and does not regard women in general very highly.

Physical aggression is another type of antisocial behavior that I see in my classroom. It doesn't occur very often (fewer than 10 times a year, I'd guess). It usually occurs during unstructured times and is triggered by competition and verbal confrontation between peers.

Think of a particular child you have taught. How did the child behave at first in your classroom?

The student I think of first is a first-grade boy I taught. He lived in a housing project with his mother, her boyfriend, and two sisters. He was considered unmanageable at his previous school and spent many hours in the principal's office for out-of-control behavior.

When he came to me, we had the typical "honeymoon" period of 2 or 3 days. One day during his first week he received three consequences, which meant he had to go to in-school suspension for 30 minutes. He refused to go, and I didn't physically guide him to the in-school suspension room. When a student refuses to take a consequence, I administer the next consequence on the continuum. He refused this consequence as well and ended up being put on a home-parent program which meant he was removed from the school by security (which happens if the parent cannot come to get the student) and taken home. While we were waiting for security, he proceeded to knock over chairs and desks, jumped on the furniture, said he wasn't going home, and began to take things off the wall and throw them to the floor. When the officer came, the student refused to go with him, and eventually the officer physically carried him to the car. He resisted every step of the way. This scenario occurred twice within the same week.

This child also had a lot of more minor behavior problems, including excessive noise making (puttering noises), not following directions, and talking out. After being in my classroom for a few weeks, these behaviors disappeared.

What did you explore as possible causes of his overt aggressive behavior problems?

In my opinion, two major factors contributed to his behavior problems. The first was his home environment; the housing project where he lived was known for its high crime rate. Kids grow up tough there, just in order to survive, and this carried over into his school life. When confronted with conflict, he reacted as he would in his neighborhood, not being able to see school as a safe place. It was almost an "I'm going to get you before you get me" attitude. The other factor that led to his self-contained placement was the "unfairness" of his previous placement. He felt his teachers were the enemy because they would say one thing and do another. In my opinion, they were inconsistent in their management techniques. They would not go the extra mile to keep him in a resource room. It was easier to pass the buck to someone else and get him out of their room. He realized he had beaten their system, and so did they. When a student obtains that much control, it is impossible for the teacher to regain authority in the classroom.

How did he get along with the other children in the class?

When he first came to our school, he had a hard time making friends. He was younger than most of the other students, so he had little in common with them. He also isolated himself by the strange noises he made and his out-of-control behavior when he had to be sent out of the classroom. The other kids just thought he was weird and were also afraid of him. They also got upset when I had to take time away from working with them in order to deal with his behavior. When he finally realized that we would follow through with our management system, his behavior problems decreased and the other students began including him in their conversations and at recess.

What did you find were the most successful strategies in working with him?

My classroom management system contains many components. I feel it's the combination of these components that allows my general management system to control almost all of my students' behavior problems. The first component is a token economy in which students earn points when they are following the rules. Initially, students are reinforced frequently, and then reinforcement is faded so that students are under stimulus control. Students who make their behavior goals are able to trade in their points daily for a variety of reinforcers.

The second component is a phase system. There are five phases in which students gain more privileges as their behavior improves. Students gain classroom privileges in addition to access to the regular classroom or resource room. They are moved up or back one phase according to their performance over 3-week intervals for phases 1 to 3 and after 6 weeks for phase 4. Students at phase 5 have as much access to the regular classroom as deemed appropriate by me, in consultation with the regular classroom teacher.

The third component is a list of consequences to be applied when students break the rules. Students take a cool-off for every rule they break. This means they put their heads down wherever they are for about 10 to 15 seconds. When a student breaks a rule three times, my continuum of consequences is implemented. My system includes a warning, head down 5 minutes, head down 10 minutes, in-school suspension for 30 minutes, being sent to the office, and being sent home. Physical aggression toward someone else and disrespect warrant a more serious consequence instead of a cool-off.

The fourth component is appropriate academic programming. Monitoring and assessment of academic skills and correct placement of students into instructional groups plays a big part in how successful students will feel and be in a self-contained classroom. The classroom must be motivating, and instruction must be fast-paced and exciting all the time. If the academics are not motivating and students do not feel successful, you will have a hard time making your consequences effective.

Do you have other thoughts about teaching aggressive children?

Create an environment that is nurturing, consistent, and fair—and also highly academically oriented—and you will rarely have to design individual management strategies for children. Children who are enjoying school do not want to be removed from it. Initially, you may have to go through your entire list of consequences, but if you've created a positive atmosphere, then you and your students will enjoy coming to school every day.

13

Conduct Disorder:
Covert Antisocial Behavior

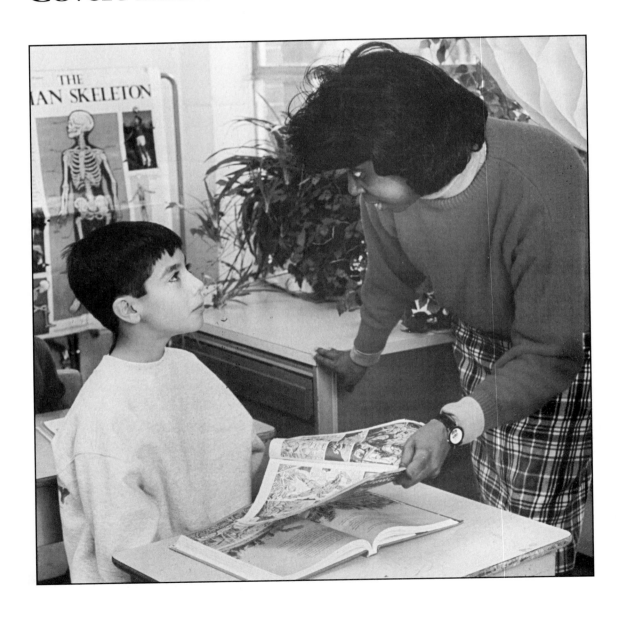

As you read this chapter, keep these guiding questions in mind:

■ If we conceptualize overt and covert antisocial behavior as different ends of a single dimension or continuum, what type of behavior is shared by both?

■ What specific covert antisocial behaviors are typically thought to be "masculine," and what types are considered "feminine"?

■ What family process characteristics may distinguish youngsters with covert antisocial behavior?

■ What type of prevention programs are particularly relevant for children with covert antisocial behavior?

■ What special problems does one encounter in assessing covert antisocial behavior?

■ Why is intervention in the families of stealers particularly difficult?

■ What guidelines for management of theft should school personnel follow?

■ Why is children's lying a major concern of parents and teachers?

■ What are the probable risk factors in firesetting by children and youths?

■ How do successful programs to decrease school vandalism differ from the usual response to increased violence and destructiveness in schools?

■ What general suggestions can one offer for decreasing truancy?

DEFINITION AND PREVALENCE OF COVERT ANTISOCIAL BEHAVIOR

As we saw in chapter 12, antisocial behavior may involve overt acts, such as physical and verbal aggression, covert acts, such as stealing, lying, and firesetting, or both overt and covert forms of disordered conduct. Loeber and Schmaling (1985a) suggest that overt and covert antisocial behavior may represent different ends of a single behavioral dimension, with noncompliance—sassy, negative, persistent disobedience—as the most common or keystone characteristic of both extremes (see also Loeber et al., 1993; Patterson, Reid, & Dishion, 1992). Figure 13.1 depicts this conceptualization of overt and covert forms of conduct disorder.

Awareness of different forms of conduct disorder has existed for decades, but reliable empirical evidence of the different forms emerged from large-scale studies in the 1980s (Loeber & Schmaling, 1985a, 1985b; Quay 1986b). These studies are based on statistical probabilities; thus, a particular child is not necessarily characterized by behavior at one end of the continuum shown in Figure 13.1. As noted in chapter 12, some children are versatile in their antisocial conduct, showing both overt and covert forms. Youngsters who show versatile antisocial behavior generally have more severe problems, and their prognosis is usually poorer compared to those who exhibit only one type of antisocial behavior (Kazdin, 1995; Loeber & Schmaling, 1985a; Loeber et al., 1993). Versatility is a matter of degree; some individuals are much more versatile or exclusive in their antisocial conduct than others. Conduct disorder of both types is often difficult to distinguish from other disorders, especially

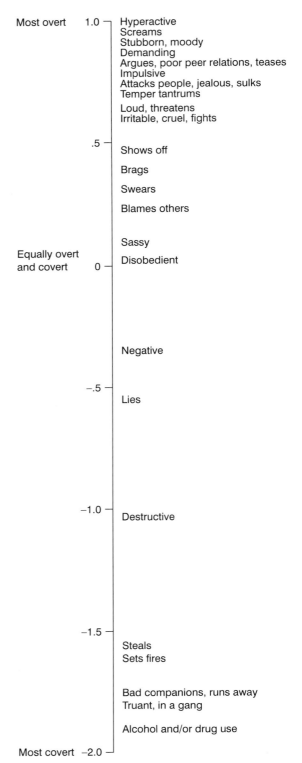

Figure 13.1

Overt and Covert Behaviors in One Dimension

Source: From "Empirical Evidence for Overt and Covert Patterns of Antisocial Conduct Problems: A Meta-analysis" by R. Loeber and K. B. Schmaling, 1985, *Journal of Abnormal Child Psychology, 13,* p. 347. Copyright by Plenum Publishing Corp. Reprinted by permission.

juvenile delinquency. In fact, the socialized (covert) form typically involves delinquent activities, often with bad companions or gangs and often involving alcohol or other drug use. *Delinquency* is a legal term, however, and connotes behavior that is the topic of chapter 14. The focus of this chapter is the other covert antisocial behavior problems listed on the lower, arithmetically negative area of the scale shown in figure 13.1.

As you know, conduct disorder is one of the most common and serious behavior problems of children and youths, with prevalence estimates ranging from 4 to 10 percent of the child population. The prevalence of each subtype of conduct disorder has not been estimated precisely. Robins (1986) indicates that conduct disorders are on the increase for both boys and girls, but boys and girls have tended to exhibit somewhat different patterns of antisocial misconduct. In Robins's research, relatively more "masculine" antisocial behaviors included vandalism, fighting, and stealing, whereas lying, running away, and substance abuse were typed as more "feminine." Four school-related problems (truancy, expulsion, underachievement, and discipline) clustered together for both males and females. Vandalism, lying, and stealing clustered together for girls, but not for boys (Robins, 1986); that is, girls who vandalized, lied, or stole tended to do all three, whereas boys tended to perform antisocial acts in different patterns (vandalism with fighting and substance abuse, lying with truancy and underachievement, and stealing with running away).

CAUSAL FACTORS AND PREVENTION

In general, the same causal factors seem to underlie covert aggression and aggressive antisocial conduct, as we saw in chapter 12. The contextual variables and determinants found by Patterson et al. (1992) are shown in Figure 13.2. The personal, family, and social contexts are the background for poor behavior management skills of the parents, who are unskilled in monitoring and disciplining their children and fail to use positive reinforcement and problems solving in family interactions. The outcome is social incompetence and antisocial behavior of the child. To be sure, this inadequacy in childrearing on the part of parents is not *always* the cause of antisocial behavior, either overt or covert. However, it is characteristic of the environments of the great majority of children and youths who exhibit antisocial behavior.

In some studies comparing overt to covert antisocial children, families of those who exhibited covert antisocial behavior are characterized by lower rates of aversive, coercive behavior on the part of parents and children and less supervision or monitoring on the part of parents. Other studies, however, have found no differences between overtly and covertly antisocial youngsters on family process variables such as parental rejection. A fairly consistent finding is that youngsters with versatile antisocial behavior come from the most disturbed families in which childrearing practices are the most inadequate (Loeber & Schmaling, 1985a; Patterson et al., 1992).

Prevention of covert antisocial behavior in many ways parallels prevention of overt aggression. Character training or moral education seems particularly relevant

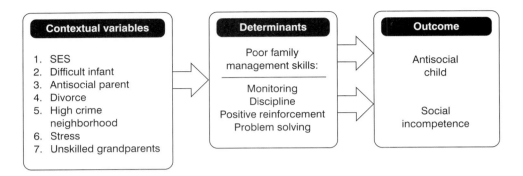

Figure 13.2
The Effect of Context on Child Adjustment
Source: From *Antisocial Boys* by Gerald R. Patterson, John B. Reid, and Thomas J. Dishion. Copyright ©1992 by Castalia Publishing Company. Reprinted by permission.

to prevention of stealing, lying, vandalism, and so on. A few studies indicate that deficits in moral reasoning are associated with conduct problems and peer conformity among delinquents (Bear & Richards, 1981; Gibbs, Arnold, Ahlborn, & Chessman, 1984; Krouse, 1982; Sigman, Ungerer, & Russell, 1983). The effects of typical moral and character education, however, have been nil or very slight (Zimmerman, 1983). Moral behavior often does not match moral judgment: children and youths, as well as adults, often do wrong even though they know what is right. Moral behavior tends to be controlled at least as much by situational factors as by moral or character traits; youngsters are honest or altruistic at some times and in some situations but not in others (Walker, de Vries, & Trevethan, 1987). Teachers' talk about classroom conventions, procedures, and moral issues has little effect on children's reasoning about morals (Blumenfeld, Pintrich, & Hamilton, 1987). For schools to have much influence in teaching prosocial values, they must develop coherent and pervasive programs of character education that include discussion, role playing, and social-skills training to help students recognize moral dilemmas, adopt moral values, and select moral behavioral alternatives (Edelman & Goldstein, 1981). This training may be particularly important for students with emotional or behavioral disorders (Blakeney & Blakeney, 1991; Walker et al., 1995; Zionts, 1985).

ASSESSMENT

As with prevention, assessment of covert antisocial conduct disorder seems to parallel assessment of overt aggression. A particularly difficult problem, however, is direct observation of behavior; the behavior is, by definition, not usually observed first-hand by educators or other responsible adults. Often, the antisocial deed is not discovered until long after it is committed, and even then there may be doubts as to who was responsible (see Sprick & Howard, 1995, regarding assessment and intervention for problems such as stealing and vandalism). Although extremely serious, the behavior may occur at a relatively low rate compared to overt acts of aggression; thus, comparison of baseline rates to treatment may require lengthy evaluation. Assessment can therefore involve long periods of observation, and research may employ self-reports of acts such as stealing, lying, truancy, and vandalism. Laboratory assessment suggests that covert antisocial behavior, including stealing and property destruction as opposed to overt physical and verbal aggression, distinguishes specific subgroups of children with emotional and behavioral disorders (Hinshaw, Simmel, & Heller, 1995).

INTERVENTION AND EDUCATION

Because of similarities in the nature and causes of the problems, intervention and education in overt and covert forms of conduct disorder share many features, along with important differences (cf. Walker et al., 1995). "The treatment of covert antisocial acts such as theft is necessarily more complicated than that of overt antisocial acts because the covert acts are less easily detected and defined, and consequences therefore cannot as quickly and consistently be applied" (Loeber & Schmaling, 1985b, p. 333). Consequently the particular problems as well as the approaches to intervention may differ somewhat for specific types of covert antisocial acts. Families of children who steal, more often than families of aggressive children who do not steal, are extremely difficult treatment targets (Patterson, 1982; Patterson et al., 1992). Sometimes family therapy or parent discipline training is simply infeasible or ineffective. Vandalism is often a particular problem in schools, and some intervention programs may therefore be primarily school-based. Firesetting may be only tangentially related to school programs, but schools may be targets of arson by students with academic difficulties. Truancy is by definition an educational problem, although it is associated with delinquency, and programs to encourage school attendance may involve both the school and other community agencies.

Stealing

A common behavior problem that parents of young children report is that they do not recognize and respect the property rights of others. Many young children simply take what they want when they see it, without regard for ownership; in short, they steal. If this behavior persists beyond the age of 5 or 6 years, the child may become known as a stealer and get into trouble with peers and adults. The most useful analyses of the origins and management of stealing come from a behavioral or social learning perspective (Miller & Prinz, 1991; Sprick & Howard, 1995).

In an early case study, Wetzel (1966) found that he could modify a disturbed boy's compulsive stealing by means of behavior modification principles. Reid and Patterson and their associates (Loeber et al., 1983; Moore et al., 1979; Patterson, 1982; Patterson et al., 1975; Reid & Hendricks, 1973; Reid & Patterson, 1976) have systematically researched the characteristics and behavior modification of aggressive children who steal. Their subjects were primarily predelinquent children referred for treatment of social aggression; about half were also in trouble because of stealing. Reid and Hendricks (1973) found that children who stole exhibited a lower rate of positive-friendly behaviors at home than did nonstealers or nonreferred children. In turn, stealers also exhibited a higher rate of negative-coercive acts than nonreferred children. Compared to aggressive children who did not steal, however, stealers showed a *lower* rate of negative-coercive acts. In all three groups (nonreferred, stealers, and nonstealers), the fathers interacted less than mothers with their families, but there were no significant differences in the interaction of fathers in the three groups. Mothers of stealers exhibited a lower rate of positive-friendly interaction than mothers of nonstealers or nonreferred children. The rate of negative-coercive acts of mothers of stealers fell between the rates of nonreferred children and others of nonstealers. These generalizations emerged:

- Stealers exhibited lower rates of observable out-of-control (negative-coercive and antisocial) behavior than aggressive children who did not steal.

- Families of stealers demonstrated lower rates of both positive-friendly and negative-coercive behaviors than families of aggressive children who did not steal.

- The differences in positive-friendly and negative-coercive behavior rates were due almost completely to the mothers' behavior.

Reid and Hendricks (1973) also found that stealers did not respond as well as nonstealers to treatment based on social learning theory. They base their speculation on the nature of the child's behavior and the nature of the family's social interaction. Many stealers appear to exhibit high rates of antisocial behavior only away from home or at home when no observers are present. Many stealers are likely to confine their antisocial behavior to settings outside the home, disturbing the community rather than their parents by their theft and leaving their parents with little motivation to work on the problem. Parents of stealers tend to blame the stealing on someone else, thus refusing to recognize the problem and failing to follow through on intervention plans (see Patterson, 1982; Patterson et al., 1975; Reid & Patterson, 1976).

Families of stealers appear to be loosely structured and characterized by lack of parental supervision or emotional attachment to the children (Patterson, 1982; Reid & Patterson, 1976). The stealer may, therefore, learn that taking others' possessions is acceptable behavior, that no one will care what he or she takes, and that no adverse consequences will follow theft. The child who learns to steal may be motivated to seek stimulation and reinforcement outside the family.

Despite the difficult and destructive family interaction patterns of stealers, relatively successful behavioral interventions have been devised. Patterson et al. (1975) believe a behavioral antistealing program has several essential components. Before instituting the actual antistealing program, however, one must resolve a fundamental problem—parental definition of stealing. Parents of stealers are usually hesitant to accuse the child of theft and are loath to take disciplinary action. Because they are unlikely to observe the child in the act of taking something, the parents feel obliged to accept their child's explanation for how something came into his or her possession. Many parents blindly accept the child's claims of finding, borrowing, trading, winning, or receiving as payment whatever item was stolen. When their child is accused by teachers, peers, or police, parents of stealers argue that the child is being unjustly attacked. By blaming others—making it somebody else's problem—the parents avoid having to deal with the problem themselves. Even when the behavior occurs at home, parents often do not adequately define *stealing*. Some parents consider it theft to take food from the refrigerator without specific permission, while others view all family possessions as common property. The value of an item is also an issue, as many parents of stealers cannot bring themselves to apply consequences for stealing something they consider to be worth very little.

As Patterson et al. (1975) point out, the first step in dealing with theft is to recognize that the child is in difficulty because he or she steals more than other children of the same age, may steal valuable objects, and has been labeled by others as a thief. The antitheft strategy must include steps to help the child stop being accused of theft and being viewed with suspicion. The child will not lose the stigma associated with the label until he or she learns to avoid even the appearance of wrongdoing.

Patterson et al. (1975) (see also Patterson et al., 1992) promote the following strategy to help the family deal with theft:

1. Agree to define *stealing* as the child's possession of anything that does not belong to him or her or taking anything he or she does not own.

2. Only the parents decide whether a theft has occurred. They may base their judgment on either their own observation or on the report of a reliable informant.

3. When it is determined that the child has stolen, the parents state that, according to the rules, the child has taken the item, and then apply the consequences. The parents must not shame or counsel the child at the time they discover the theft and apply the consequences, but they are encouraged to discuss the theft with him or her other at another time.

4. Every instance of stealing must receive consequences.

5. Parents are advised to keep their eyes open and ask about "new" property rather than use detective tactics such as searching the child's room or clothing.

6. Consequences for stealing are either a specified interval of useful work or a period of "grounding" or restriction. Stealing more expensive items receives more severe consequences. Harsh consequences, such as humiliation or beating, are prohibited.

7. No positive reinforcement is given for periods of nonstealing, because it is impossible to know that successful covert stealing has not occurred.

8. The program should stay in effect at least 6 months following the last episode of stealing.

If the child steals both at home and at school, parents and teachers must implement consistent antitheft programs in both environments. Effective and early management of stealing is particularly important; the younger the age at which children begin stealing and the longer they persist, the more likely they are to become chronic stealers and adjudicated delinquents (Loeber et al., 1993). In general, the more severe the conduct disorder, the less likely it is that intervention will be successful (Webster-Stratton & Dahl, 1995). Management of stealing at school can present legal problems, particularly with older students, and the school must avoid illegal searches and seizures. The following feature provides general guidelines for managing stealing in school.

Dealing with Stealing: General Guidelines for School Personnel

Stevens (1980) reports that the child does have some rights to privacy in the dignity of his body and his place of residence. Similarly, Trosch, Williams, and Devore (1982) maintain that the fourth amendment of the United States Constitution protects children in school from unreasonable searches conducted by teachers or administrators without first establishing probable cause. Defining probable cause is not easy; however, known facts and tips from reliable sources are admissible in the courts. Teachers and school officials are often in a better position than parents to identify, interpret, and record the totality of circumstances necessary to establish probable cause (Trosch et al., 1982). Teachers can observe children from hour to hour on a daily basis and in relationship to other children. A student's individual actions, such as unusual secretiveness, departures from normal schedules or travel patterns, possession of questionable items, and instances of lying or other "rule-breaking" behaviors, may provide the documentation necessary for establishing probable cause for searches in schools not in violation of the child's Fourth Amendment rights.

In addition to those guidelines offered for dealing with instances of theft, common sense suggests the following approach may be considered with regard to theft detection:

1. Clearly state rules and authority to search a child's possessions based upon establishment of probable cause, particularly for older children and youths;
2. Carefully observe and monitor the behavior of all children and record instances of unusual behavior;
3. Refrain from being a "detective" and indiscriminately searching a child's possessions;
4. Ask children about unusual behavior or possession of questionable objects. . . .

Only by clearly establishing rules, and firmly and fairly enforcing those rules within an atmosphere of loving concern and respect for the child, can parents and teachers hope to eliminate stealing behavior in children.

Source: From "Children's Stealing: A Review of Theft-control Procedures for Parents and Teachers" by R. L. M Williams, 1985, *Remedial and Special Education, 6*(2), pp. 21–22. Used with permission.

Lying

Parents and teachers consistently rate lying as a serious problem behavior of childhood, yet there has been little research on the subject (Stokes & Osnes, 1991; Stouthamer-Loeber & Loeber, 1986). Developmental changes clearly occur in the understanding of lies and liars (Peterson, Peterson, & Seeto, 1983; Rotenberg, 1991), but the relationship of these changes to the development of pathological lying is not understood. Apparently, children often lie in attempts to escape punishment. Adults consider lying a serious problem not only because it is an attempt at concealment, but also because it is associated with other antisocial behavior such as stealing and truancy. In the classroom, lying and cheating are functionally similar behaviors.

As one might expect, lying is related to the same sort of family process variables, especially lack of parental monitoring or supervision, that characterize stealing (Stouthamer-Loeber & Loeber, 1986). Although lying is a serious problem and may be a steppingstone to the development of other conduct problems (Loeber et al., 1993), only a small body of research is available to guide intervention. However, "the cornerstone of effective management of honest behavior is the monitoring of work in progress and its subsequent verbal and written products to accurately identify occurrences of lying and cheating" (Stokes & Osnes, 1991, p. 619). In addition to careful monitoring, providing reinforcement for honest behavior and punishment of lying and cheating is necessary. It is important to determine whether the student can discriminate truth from nontruth, to find the probable reason for the student's telling untruths (e.g., to avoid consequences or work), and to avoid getting caught up in arguments about the veracity of what the student has said (see Sprick & Howard, 1995).

Firesetting

The fires that children set frequently cause injury, loss of life, and property damage. In fact, youthful arsonists account for more than half of all set fires. The United States has the highest arson rate in the world, and arson has been the fastest growing crime (Wooden & Berkey, 1984). "Few problem behaviors provoke as much anxiety in the community because of the possible harm to life, safety, and property" (Koles & Jenson, 1985).

Although firesetting has been a behavior of scientific interest for more than 150 years (Wooden & Berkey, 1984), we still do not understand the causes and management of this behavior in children. Fanciful psychodynamic explanations that connect firesetting to sexual excitement have only recently begun to give way to conceptualizations grounded in reliable empirical evidence (Quinsey, Chaplin, & Upfold, 1989). Kolko and Kazdin (1986) propose a social learning model for conceptualizing risk factors of fire play and firesetting that consists of three primary factors: learning experiences and cues, personal repertoires (cognitive, behavioral, and motivational), and parent and family influences and stressors. Kolko and Kazdin note that children learn attitudes and behaviors from early experiences, such as watching parents or older siblings working or playing with fire. Children of firefighters, furnace stokers, smokers, and adults who otherwise model behavior dealing with fire may be more likely to set fires.

We see interest in fire and playing with fire in a high percentage of young children. The ready availability of incendiary materials to children who are interested in fire and observe models who set or manage fires may set the stage for firesetting. Another major factor, however, is the personal repertoires that may heighten the risk of firesetting. Children may be more likely to set fires if any of the following are true:

- They do not understand the danger of fire or the importance of fire safety.

- They do not have the necessary social skills to obtain gratification in appropriate ways.

- They engage in other antisocial behaviors.

- They are motivated by anger and revenge.

Finally, stressful life events, parental psychopathology, and lack of parental supervision, monitoring, and involvement can increase the chances that a child will set fires (Kolko & Kazdin, 1989). Whatever the explanation of the behavior, it is clear that firesetting by preschoolers is associated with serious psychopathology in the child, the family, or both (Hanson et al., 1995).

Although research does not clearly distinguish different types of firesetters, all fires obviously are not set under the same conditions or for the same reasons. Some fires are set accidentally by children playing with matches or lighters, some by angry children who are seeking revenge but do not understand the awful consequences, others by delinquents who know full well the consequences of arson and are seeking to conceal another crime they have committed, some in response to deviant peer pressure, some in attempts to injure the firesetters themselves, and still others by youngsters whose behavior is related to anxiety and obsessions or compulsions (see Sakheim & Osborn, 1994; Swaffer & Hollin, 1995).

Most school-age youngsters who set fires have a history of school failure and multiple behavior problems (Rasanen, Hirvenoja, Hakko, & Vaisanen, 1995; Wooden & Berkey, 1984). Schools are sometimes their targets, so educators are among the many who have an interest in identifying and treating firesetters. At this point, however, we can make few research-based recommendations for intervention or prevention. Both intervention and prevention will probably require efforts similar to those suggested for managing other covert antisocial behaviors such as stealing, vandalism, and truancy (cf. Forehand, Wierson, Frame, Kempton, & Armistead, 1991; Kolko & Kazdin, 1986).

Vandalism

Deliberate destruction of school property costs hundreds of millions of dollars each year, and vandalism in other community settings results in much higher costs. Destructiveness and violence against people are often linked, and both are on the increase (Walker et al., 1995). The typical response of school administrators and justice officials to violence and vandalism is to tighten security measures and provide harsher punishment. Unfortunately, punitive measures may only aggravate the problems (Mayer et al., 1987; Mayer & Sulzer-Azaroff, 1991).

Vandalism in schools appears to be, at least in part, a response to aversive environments (cf. Kasen, Johnson, & Cohen, 1990; Mayer, 1995; Mayer & Butterworth, 1981; Mayer, Butterworth, Nafpaktitis, & Sulzer-Azaroff, 1983; Mayer & Sulzer-Azaroff, 1991; Mayer et al., 1987). More specifically, students tend to be disruptive and destructive when school rules are vague, discipline is punitive, punishment is rigidly applied regardless of students' individual differences, relationships between students and school personnel are impersonal, and the school curriculum is mismatched with students' interests and abilities, and when students receive little recognition for appropriate conduct or achievement. Decreasing the aversiveness of the school environment by adjusting school rules, teachers' expectations, and consequences for desirable and undesirable behavior might be more effective in preventing vandalism than increasing security and making punishment more severe.

Mayer et al. (1983) provide evidence of the effectiveness of a positive approach to dealing with disruption and destruction in schools. They worked with students and school personnel in 18 junior high schools over a 3-year period to try to prevent school vandalism and improve discipline by emphasizing positive management rather than sterner punishment. The intervention consisted of workshops to train school personnel in behavioral strategies. The effort was to establish a positive rather than a punitive atmosphere in the schools. The cooperation of community citizens and students was enlisted by focusing on campus improvement projects and activities such as neighborhood walks to inform people of the school's efforts to stop vandalism. The program achieved significant increases in teachers' positive behavior (such as praise for appropriate student conduct) and significant reductions in students' vandalism and off-task behavior. In fact, Mayer and his colleagues have found that this type of program helped decrease the average cost of vandalism in 23 elementary and junior high schools by 73.5 percent (Mayer et al., 1987; Mayer & Sulzer-Azaroff, 1991; see Sprick & Howard, 1995 for additional interventions).

Truancy

Truancy becomes a greater problem in higher grades, and it is a major factor in school failure and delinquency. Attendance at school certainly does not guarantee academic success, but chronic unexcused absence virtually assures failure. Frequent truancy is serious not only because of probable school failure but because chronic truants are at risk for later unemployment or employment failure, criminal convictions, substance abuse, and a variety of other difficulties (Dangelo, Weinberger, & Feldman, 1995; Farrington, 1995; Walker et al., 1995). Dissatisfaction with school programs and failure to attend school regularly are important signals that the student may drop out (Edgar, 1987; Edgar & Siegel, 1995).

The traditional approach of attendance officers counseling truants has not been remarkably successful. One of the key factors in reducing truancy is offering instructional programs that engage the interests and meet the needs of students who have emotional and behavioral difficulties (cf. Edgar & Siegel, 1995). Moreover, we have known for many years that behavioral strategies can be highly effective in reducing truancy. Copeland et al. (1974) found that truants from an elementary school improved their attendance when the school principal stopped by their classrooms to compliment them on their presence. Working with older children and adolescents, Tharp and Wetzel (1969) improved school attendance by making participation in certain events or interaction with certain individuals in the community contingent on attendance. The contingencies of reinforcement were often administered with the aid of *natural mediators*, people living in the community who could control the young-ster's access to rewards and could themselves be rewarding to the child or youth, as in the case of Cowboy Gaines (see box).

Case #98

Cowboy Gaines operated a riding stable on the outskirts of the city. Cowboy and his plumpish, fortyish wife were warm, homespun people, and they enjoyed the role of coun-selors to mixed-up youths. Cowboy himself was full of rustic figures of speech, and he dispensed his rough and ready ranch philosophy generously. Cowboy and his wife, Irma, proved to be highly effective mediators.

Case #98 was an extraordinarily truant seventh grader who was powerfully attracted to animals, especially horses. There was no adult person with whom he had a positive relationship.

The Behavior Analyst asked Cowboy and Irma if they would help with Billy, and they at once agreed. The arrangement was simple. Billy could earn time at Cowboy's stable by staying in school. Billy was allowed to ride the horses in return for attending to minor chores when he was not riding.

Billy responded perfectly and thereafter never missed an hour of school. Cowboy and Irma had a little trouble with him at first because the undersized boy complained in smart-alec terms when he felt he wasn't getting enough riding. Cowboy gave him a few bits of rough advice and Irma was obliged to become a disciplinarian. Billy sulked and made plain his displeasure, but the horses and riding were too important to give up. (Tharp & Wetzel, 1969, pp. 95–96)

MacDonald, Gallimore, and MacDonald (1970) compared similar contingencies to more traditional attendance counseling and found the contingency arrangements superior in increasing the attendance of ninth-, tenth-, and twelfth-grade pupils. Lawrence, Litynsky, and D'Lugoff (1982) reduced truancy dramatically using behav-ioral interventions and counseling in a special day school. Students earned points for school attendance and appropriate behavior, and they could exchange the points for a variety of activities and treats during special recreation periods.

The problem of truancy is not new, and neither are the most effective approaches to reducing it. Clearly, interventions based on social learning principles continue to produce better results than other approaches (see Guevremont, 1991; Kerr, Nelson, & Lambert, 1987). An effective approach to truancy of students with emotional or behavioral disorders will likely include most or all of the features described in the accompanying box.

Suggestions for Dealing with Behaviorally Disordered Adolescents' Truancy

Increase satisfaction obtained by school attendance:

- Reduce academic demands on the student to increase the likelihood of success.

- Monitor and intervene in peer relations to reduce peer tensions.

- Provide more frequent social reinforcement for completed work.

- Frequently communicate successful school experiences to parents.

- Encourage parents to equate favorable reports with special after-school and weekend activities.

- Encourage parents to send the student to bed at a reasonable time.

- Engage the student in frequent conferences with the teacher, in which concerns about the school program can be openly expressed.

Decrease satisfaction obtained by being absent from school:

- Have someone make a home visit immediately if the student does not come to school.

- If the student is ill, send home the day's schoolwork.

- If the student is not ill, but is at home, escort the student to school (accompanied by parents if possible).

- If the student is not willing to be escorted to school, impose prearranged sanctions such as removing television privileges for the day or decreasing allowance.

Actively teach skills that enhance ability to benefit from school attendance:

- Provide small group activities designed to develop social skills.

- Include special interest areas in which the student is highly motivated in the academic program (shop, art, athletics).

(Schloss, Kane, & Miller, 1981, p. 178)

SUMMARY

Covert antisocial behavior consists of acts such as stealing, lying, firesetting, vandalism, and truancy. Overt and covert antisocial behavior may represent different ends of a continuum, with noncompliance as the keystone behavior or common origin of both extremes.

Researchers note sex differences in antisocial behavior. Vandalism, fighting, and stealing are typed as "masculine," while lying, substance abuse, and running away are considered "feminine." Four school-related problems (truancy, expulsion, underachievement, and discipline) characterize both boys and girls with conduct disorders.

In general, the same types of causal factors seem to underlie overt and covert forms of conduct disorder. Some studies indicate, however, that families of youngsters who steal and exhibit other covert forms of antisocial behavior are characterized by lower rates of aversive, coercive behavior and lower rates of parental supervision and monitoring. A particularly relevant preventive strategy for covert antisocial behavior is moral education or character training, although typical moral education seems ineffective, suggesting the need for comprehensive, pervasive programs.

Because the acts are usually unobserved and are performed at relatively low rates, assessment of covert antisocial conduct disorder presents special problems and often involves self-reports in addition to other measures. Intervention and education for youngsters with covert antisocial problems are similar to those for overt aggression but are more complicated because covert acts are harder to detect and the consequences often cannot be applied immediately and consistently. Specific covert behaviors may thus require special treatment.

Families of stealers differ from families of aggressive youngsters who do not steal, showing less parental supervision and involvement with their children. Intervention in families of stealers is often particularly difficult because the parents do not recognize or do not want to be bothered with the problem. Effective management of stealing includes careful supervision of the child and consistent, appropriate punishment of all instances of stealing. When theft-management procedures are implemented in schools, care must be taken not to violate students' constitutional rights.

Lying is considered a major child behavior problem because it is often part of other covert antisocial behavior. There is little research on lying and few guidelines for handling it.

Firesetting is a growing and dangerous problem among children and youths. There is little understanding of the causes of firesetting behavior and little research for managing it. A social learning model suggests that early learning experiences, personal repertoires (cognitive, behavioral, and motivational), and parent and family influences and stressors may put children at risk for firesetting. Research to distinguish different types of firesetters is needed.

Rising rates of violence and destructiveness in schools are typically met by tightening security measures and applying more punitive discipline, but these measures may be counterproductive. Vandalism may represent a response to an aversive school environment. Programs to make the school environment less aversive for students by increasing positive attention to appropriate conduct, making the school curriculum more relevant, and improving school discipline practices have dramatically reduced school vandalism.

Chronic truancy virtually ensures school failure and is associated with a variety of negative outcomes in adulthood. Traditional counseling approaches have not been very effective. Behavioral interventions that make school attendance more rewarding and nonattendance less attractive have been successful with many truants.

Case for Discussion

"He Needs to Be Around Real Men"

Edward

"Edward is a thief and a liar and I hate him and if he doesn't stop, I'm going to make him stop myself! I'll get that sucker if you don't, you wait and see!" The angry student stormed out of the room, leaving me no recourse as the school principal but to try to intervene before Edward's bus left for dismissal. I called Edward into my office before he could exit the building and get lost among the hundreds of students en route to their buses.

"Edward, here we go again. I need you to empty your pockets and your bookbag. You've been accused of taking another CD." As the stolen CD appeared, Edward sputtered about how he thought the student had given it to him and this was all a big misunderstanding. He was quite familiar with the search routine. It never seemed to embarrass him very much, and he continued to be incredulous that people no longer accepted his explanations for how this item or that item ended up in his possession. He wanted what he wanted, and he took it when he chose.

In elementary school, Edward's stealing was limited to small, fairly inexpensive items. But in middle school his pilfering extended to expensive software, jewelry, and clothing. A new dimension to "taking what he wanted" arose as Edward reached puberty. Female classmates became an additional attraction for Edward's grasping. He found it inconceivable that a girl could or would demand that he leave her alone. He liked to touch their hair, not to mention other parts of their anatomies. He liked to sit close. He liked writing suggestive and intimidating notes. He did not like hearing that parents were ready to prosecute for sexual harassment, threatening letters, and stalking. Lately, to Edward's outrage and dismay, he discovered that students were breaking into his locker and, in retaliation, taking everything they found there.

Edward's foster mother called to say that if we didn't do something soon to help Edward, she was considering sending him to a military school. She revealed that Edward had broken into her locked bedroom and was discovered in her lingerie stimulating himself. This disclosure of "the family secret" that Edward had been stealing and wearing her clothing was yet another puzzle piece tying his stealing, lying, and sexual difficulties together. Gulping air in her anxiety, she revealed that she was worried that Edward's behavior would not end there, and she admitted that she was increasingly afraid of her large, strong, 15-year-old foster son. When I questioned her about putting him in a private school, she shared her opinion that the military school she had investigated was just what he needed. She was adamant that he had no appropriate role models in a public middle school. "He needs to be around big, strong, disciplined 'real' men. That's really all he needs to get straightened out. Besides, what can you really do for him in this school to stop his stealing and pestering the girls?"

Questions About the Case

1. How would you describe Edward's behavior on the overt-covert continuum shown on page 376?

2. What factors do you think are the most likely causes of Edward's behavior problems?

3. How should the principal respond to Edward's having the CD he was accused of stealing? What should she and Edward's teachers do to try to stop his stealing?

4. What strategies do you think the principal should tell Edward's foster mother will be used in the public school?

Unique Characteristic(s) or Need(s)	Present Level(s) of Performance	Special Education, Related Services, and Modifications	Annual Goal(s)	Objective(s) (Including Procedures, Criteria, and Schedule)
Edward steals without any indication of remorse or desire to change.	Edward is accused by peers of stealing three to five times a month.	1. A response cost contingency for stealing with punishment being proportional to the value of the item(s) stolen. 2. Close observation by all school personnel of Edward's belongings and demand for explanation of ownership of any questionable item. 3. Counseling with school psychologist or comparable personnel regarding social skills, moral judgment, and property rights.	Edward will not steal from others at school.	Reports of Edward's stealing and instances of finding Edward with items of uncertain ownership will decrease such that teachers and the principal will have recorded fewer than 5 during the next 3 months and none for the remainder of the school year.

PERSONAL REFLECTIONS

Covert Conduct Disorder

Susan Isaacs, B.S., formerly taught a self-contained class for high-school students with emotional or behavioral disorders in Lexington, Kentucky. She is now a resource specialist for students with emotional and behavioral disorders in the Fayette County Public Schools.

Briefly describe the school and class in which you taught.

I taught in a large district high school that served approximately 1,500 students. In my self-contained classroom there were 10 students ranging in age from 14 to 18. As is true in many cases, my students were assigned to the self-contained classroom for the entire school day. The students could earn the privilege of taking mainstream classes as we noted progress in their social competencies.

How would you describe the covertly antisocial behavior of the students you taught?

In 10 years of teaching students with emotional or behavioral disorders, I have learned that by the time they reach adolescence the covert behaviors they exhibit are refined to perfection. As a teacher of academics, I have often been frustrated that students who have difficulty reading or doing simple math problems can manifest so much imagination in their covert antisocial behaviors. Although they may not master three-digit multiplication, they can create elaborate ways to steal money from their classmates. They cannot decode a two-syllable word, but they can make up a detailed lie to avoid unpleasant consequences. They cannot pass a civics test, but they can present a well-prepared defense shifting blame from themselves to others as if they were in a court of law.

Lying, cheating, and stealing made up the most common covert antisocial behaviors displayed in my classroom. These problems would have been easier to address if the behaviors had occurred in isolation. However, I found that stealing often leads to lying, which goes hand-in-hand with cheating. The problems caused by these covert antisocial behaviors are not restricted to the classroom, as evidenced by the number of court-appointed social workers or probation officers who check up on these young offenders. Although stealing occasionally happens at school, the more serious problems occur in the community. The offenses of my students ranged from stealing food and cigarettes from local convenience stores to charges such as shoplifting and auto theft. Many of my students spent several school days each year in the juvenile detention center for crimes such as these. Students who commit more serious crimes are often removed from the community for a period of time. This is very frustrating, as students may enroll in and be withdrawn from a program several times over the course of a school year.

Students who steal at school are usually unpopular, but they are famous. Word travels quickly among students and teachers when a thief has been identified in school. A student who has been labeled a thief must bear this burden for many years to come. An incident involving one of my female students is a good illustration. The girl was a very good freshman basketball player. Her uncle, who had been a district star and had played professional basketball, had helped coach her. She was very excited to be following in his footsteps. When I asked the coach about her trying out for the team,

391

he said that he would like to have her play but couldn't allow it because of her reputation. She was the prime suspect in a series of thefts of clothing and jewelry from the locker room during practice. Even though this had occurred when she was in junior high school, it followed her into senior high.

When stealing occurs in the classroom, people usually accuse the person who is known to have had problems with stealing in the past. Sometimes this person is the guilty party, but not always. Having a reputed thief in the classroom will occasionally give license to other students to steal, knowing blame will be cast on the most logical suspect. They appear to do this without feeling any guilt in their attempt to avoid detection.

In order to reduce stealing in the classroom, I had strict guidelines as to which items were appropriate for school. Walkman radios, cassette tapes, expensive coats, and gold jewelry are all items that I judged did not belong in a school. In an effort to reduce stealing, we closely observed students who were out of their assigned area, and we questioned any suspicious activity. If a student repeatedly stole in the classroom, I devised a plan for searching students to make sure that they were not stealing. Initially, the students were searched daily (in the privacy of the principal's office to reduce embarrassment). After several weeks of demonstrating that they were not carrying stolen property, the interval between searches was gradually lengthened.

I am disheartened to realize that the number of students who think that stealing is an acceptable behavior seems to increase each year. One student told me that he obtained a new bicycle from his neighbor because the neighbor left it in his yard. When I pointed out that he had stolen the bicycle, he reasoned that the neighbor should not have left it outside. It did not occur to this young man that he had done anything wrong. He felt that his neighbor's failure to safeguard his bicycle excused his act of thievery. He equated it with finding money that some unknown person had lost on the street.

Attitudes such as these evidence the need for ongoing social skills training. I addressed this with an hour each day of direct teaching of social skills in addition to the informal training that occurred throughout the day. This reinforced any training they received at home, and offset some of the attitudes and examples they were exposed to by their peers. For those students who either received no training at home or were exposed to extremely poor role models at home, my lessons might have been their only appropriate social training. Through sessions on empathy and moral reasoning, we attempted to teach the students to consider the feelings of others before they act. In addition, we demonstrated our thought process by verbally expressing our thoughts when we were faced with a moral dilemma. Students seemed to respond well to this kind of training at school. Whether this behavior generalized to the home or community was difficult to assess.

I'd like you to describe a particular student you have taught. How did this student behave at first in your classroom? How did the student get along with the other children in the class? What were your most successful strategies in working with this student?

I'll describe a student who was placed in my classroom from another self-contained high school class. The transfer was made because he was skipping many classes and seemed to be the ring leader of students looking to form a gang. It was thought that the move to an out-of-district school would eliminate his status as a leader or member of this group. He was sullen and quiet in the classroom for several weeks. Other students did not relate or interact with him. Some students appeared to be in awe of him, while others were afraid and kept their distance. He was often truant and rarely turned in assignments. However, he displayed very few inappropriate behaviors in the classroom. By refusing to discuss anything about his schoolwork or behavior, he remained extremely uncommunicative.

After several weeks passed, he gradually gained status with other students in the classroom. This change was not due to any change in his behavior toward the other students. It was brought about by rumors and subtle references to his gang activities. The stories of gang fights and drunken brawls were only rumors, but they became fodder for the imaginations of his classmates. This youngster was able to manipulate the situation and change his status in the classroom from outcast to hero. This transformation happened so smoothly that it almost went undetected.

While we were reviewing the social and school history of this student, it became clear to us that he was experienced in displaying behaviors that caused teachers to report him as sneaky and difficult to catch in misbehavior. Other teachers also noted that he found ways to blame others for his inappropriate behavior.

The fact that he was so practiced at covert kinds of behaviors led me to believe that he thought he could bring a gun to school and not be caught. He showed the gun to the other students with confidence that they would not report him. After the gun had been taken from him, the students reported that he had been concealing the gun for several hours. Later, he said that he found the gun at his bus stop and was afraid to turn it in. His parents told school officials that they were sure the gun had been found at the bus stop and that their son was telling the truth.

When the incident was reported to the principal and to school security, they immediately suspended the student. A meeting was held to determine the best course of action. The decision was that I would press criminal charges against him by filing a petition in juvenile court. Charges must be brought by the person who witnesses an incident in order for an arrest to be made. We also recommended that the student be placed in an alternative school for a period of time to receive some intensive counseling. We developed a plan for the student to be searched on a regular basis while he attended the alternative school. It was determined that if the student completed both his sentence for the criminal charge and the program at the alterna-tive school he would be allowed to return to our high school.

The strategies we developed seemed to be successful. He served 25 days in juvenile detention and made progress at the alternative school. After attending there for several months, he decided that he would remain there to earn the credits needed for graduation.

Are there other things that you would like to say about teaching children with covert antisocial behavior?

Working with students who display covert antisocial behavior is often very frustrating. It is difficult to plan adequate intervention strategies because the behaviors are hard to observe or measure. They happen so infrequently or are detected so late that reinforcement procedures are almost impossible to implement.

It is also frustrating that when we discuss issues such as lying or stealing, students act as if they are unaware that these behaviors are considered wrong or undesirable. In the environment from which some of these students come, these undesirable behaviors may seem necessary for survival.

As the number of students identified as having behavior disorders increases, I am convinced that teachers of these students must make social skills instruction a major part of the curriculum. The real task is to teach students that acceptable behavior can allow them to meet the same goals they achieve through antisocial behavior. If our students are ever to be successful as employees and law-abiding citizens, we must address these problems with them at a very early age.

14

Delinquency, Substance Abuse, and Early Sexual Activity

As you read this chapter, keep these guiding questions in mind:

- What makes juvenile delinquency difficult to define precisely?

- What is the difference between a status offense and an index crime?

- What are the similarities and differences between conduct disorder and delinquency?

- What types of delinquency and delinquents can be described?

- What are the primary contributing factors to delinquency?

- What is necessary for an effective delinquency prevention program?

- What arguments support the view that most or all incarcerated youngsters have disabilities and need special education?

- Why is it often extremely difficult to assess delinquents' educational needs?

- What makes effective intervention in juvenile delinquency especially difficult?

- What options are available under the juvenile justice system, and which options are recommended?

- What characterizes schools' typical responses to delinquent behavior, and how might they better approach the problem?

- What are the features of a good special education program in a corrections facility, and why is it so difficult to achieve these features?

- What is the relationship between street gangs and delinquency?

- How are causes and prevention of street gangs similar to the causes and prevention of delinquency?

- Which substances do children and youths most commonly abuse, and why are they not the focus of most concern about drugs?

- What are the primary causes and prevention strategies related to substance abuse?

- What can educators do to help prevent and manage substance abuse?

- What are the primary reasons for concern about early sexual activity?

Juvenile delinquency is hard to define precisely, because it has various legal meanings, as well as meanings that connote individual perceptions or personal evaluations of behavior. Behavior that some adults perceive to be intolerable or highly inappropriate is sometimes mistakenly called delinquent, although it is not prohibited by law. Strictly speaking, *delinquency* is a legal term that denotes violation of the law. However, delinquency is often a part of a constellation of deviant behaviors. "For adolescents, these deviant behaviors include alcohol abuse, illicit drug use, academic problems, precocious sexual involvement, frequency of various sexual activities, deviant attitudes, and delinquent behavior" (Newcomb & Richardson, 1995, p. 415). We discuss substance abuse in this chapter because for juveniles it involves law-violating behavior as well as high psychological and physiological risks and is often part of a pattern of other delinquent conduct. We also discuss early sexual activity in this chapter because it is often associated with delinquent behavior or substance use.

JUVENILE DELINQUENCY

Definition

When someone who is not legally an adult (someone who is a juvenile) commits an act that could result in apprehension by police, he or she is said to have committed a *delinquent* act. Because many delinquent acts do not result in arrests, the extent of juvenile delinquency is difficult to determine. Some laws are vague or loosely worded, so that *delinquency* is not clearly defined. Some acts are illegal if committed by a juvenile but not if they are committed by an adult (such as buying or drinking alcoholic beverages). Other delinquent acts are clearly criminal; they are considered morally wrong and punishable by law regardless of the age of the person who commits them. The following cases illustrate instances in which juveniles were accused of offenses that are criminal, whether committed by juveniles or adults.

V. K.

V.K., a teenager serving a 15-year sentence for the second-degree murder of a 16-year-old classmate, will not have her sentence reduced. She was a 15-year-old senior when she became involved in a knife fight with another student at a school bus stop. Testimony in her trial indicated that dozens of students and adults stood by without intervening as the two fought. The girl who was stabbed bled to death from a wound in her neck, one of several she received in the fight.

Seven-year-old Murderer

An 8-year-old boy is charged with murder in a house fire that killed a 66-year-old woman. The boy, who was 7 at the time of the fire, is the youngest person ever charged with murder in this state. He is also charged with arson in two other fires in which there were no injuries.

"Scarface"

The child, nicknamed "Scarface" because of the cuts and scars on his face, was 10 years old, only 5 feet tall, and weighed just 90 pounds. His spindly legs barely touched the floor as he sat in detention, waiting for his court-appointed lawyer. He was accused of molesting a 10-year-old girl on the school grounds while one of his friends held her down. The judge released him into the custody of his parents. Over the next 10 weeks, he was arrested five more times—more times than any other juvenile in Washington, D.C. in that year. His other arrests were for holding up and robbing two men, threatening a woman with an iron pipe, participating in a brawl, illegally entering a car, and roughing up a woman and snatching her purse.

Teaon

He had just turned 14 when he raped and sodomized a woman who lived in his apartment building. After shoving her into a closet, Teaon stole her car and fled the scene. Ordinarily, given his age, his case would have been handled in a juvenile court. But under a recently enacted Virginia law, Teaon's case went to an adult court and he was sentenced to 10 years in an adult prison. If Governor George Allen and some state legislators have their way, Teaon will be only the first of many juveniles tried and sentenced as adults for violent crimes.

Not all delinquent behavior is so clearly illegal or criminal as that in these cases. Many aggressive children's behavior just skirts legal delinquency. Much of the behavior of delinquents, including incarcerated youths and those at risk of incarceration, is irritating, threatening, or disruptive, but not delinquent in a legal sense. Delinquent behavior is behavior that may bring juveniles into contact with law enforcement.

It is important that we distinguish between delinquent behavior and official delinquency. Any act that has legal constraints on its occurrence may be considered delinquent behavior. Juveniles may commit **index crimes,** crimes that are illegal regardless of a person's age and that include the full range of criminal offenses from misdemeanors to first-degree murder. Common index crimes committed by juveniles are vandalism, shoplifting and various other forms of theft such as auto theft and armed robbery, and assault.

Other illegal behavior may be against the law only because of the offender's age. Acts that are illegal only when committed by a minor are called **status offenses.** Status offenses include truancy, running away from home, buying or possessing alcoholic beverages, and sexual promiscuity. They also include a variety of ill-defined behaviors described by labels such as *incorrigible, unmanageable,* or *beyond parental control.* Status offenses are a grab-bag category that can be abused in determining whether a child is a juvenile delinquent; it is a category that encompasses serious misdeeds but which adult authorities can expand to include mere suspicion or the appearance of misconduct (Blackburn, 1993).

The differences between official delinquency and delinquent behavior are significant. Surveys in which children and adolescents report whether they engage in specific delinquent acts indicate that the vast majority (80 to 90 percent) have done so. Self-reports appear to be by far the best way to estimate the true extent of delinquent behavior (Siegel & Senna, 1994). Self-reported delinquent behavior does not correlate with social class or race. Only about 20 percent of all minors are at some time officially delinquent; in a given year, approximately 3 percent of all American children are adjudicated (Siegel & Senna, 1994). We find a disproportionate number of official delinquents among lower socioeconomic classes and ethnic minorities (Goldstein, 1991; Leone, Walter, & Wolford, 1990). The older the child or youth whose delinquent behavior is discovered, the more likely he or she is to become an official delinquent due to society's preference for dealing with younger children in more informal ways.

Delinquent behavior, conduct disorder, and official delinquency are overlapping phenomena. A youngster with conduct disorder of either the overt or covert variety may or may not engage in delinquent behavior and may or may not become an official delinquent. Kazdin (1994) draws the distinctions and describes the similarities clearly:

Official contact with police is unlikely to take place or to be recorded for young children. Delinquent acts in early and middle childhood usually are dealt with informally rather than officially. On the other hand, conduct disorder may be identified and brought to attention early, as the child's behavior comes into conflict on a daily basis with parent and teacher expectations. Youth who are identified as meeting criteria for conduct disorder are not necessarily defined as delinquent. Similarly, delinquent youth, adjudicated by the courts, would not necessarily be considered as having conduct disorder. The youth may have committed crimes (homicide, selling of narcotics, prostitution) on one or more occasions but not be regarded as impaired, emotionally disturbed, or functioning poorly in the context of everyday life. Although the distinction can be drawn, many of the behaviors that make up conduct disorder and delinquency overlap and fall under the general rubric of antisocial behavior. (p. 344)

Because delinquency and antisocial behavior are closely linked, we do not repeat here our discussion from chapters 12 and 13 of the conduct disorders that may lead to delinquency. Rather, we focus here on delinquent behavior, official delinquency, and the implications for education.

Types of Delinquents

Researchers have attempted to delineate homogeneous groups of delinquents based on behavioral characteristics, types of offenses, and membership in subcultural groups. Achenbach (1982a) and Quay (1975, 1986a) suggest subtypes of the delinquent population similar to those they have found for nondelinquent disturbed children. Achenbach (1982b) discusses three major subtypes:

- *Socialized-subcultural delinquents*, who tend to be lower in IQ and socioeconomic status, experience less parental rejection than the other types. They relate socially to bad companions, engage in gang activities, and maintain their social status among their delinquent peers by their illegal behavior.

- *Unsocialized-psychopathic delinquents* are aggressive, assaultive individuals who tend to feel persecuted and respond poorly to praise or punishment. They tend to be irritable, defiant, explosive, and extremely insensitive to other people's feelings.

- *Disturbed-neurotic delinquents* are overly sensitive, shy, and worried, and unhappy with themselves and their lives.

It may be more helpful to distinguish between those who commit one or a few delinquent acts versus those who are serious, repeat offenders, especially those who commit violent crimes against persons. Some have argued that, because a majority of adolescents commit delinquent acts, the differences between those who are convicted and those who are not are largely a reflection of police or court biases, but "this view can be firmly rejected" (Farrington, 1995, p. 956). Farrington argues that the correspondence between official arrest records and self-reports of delinquent and criminal acts, plus the ability of self-reports to predict future convictions, indicates that both self-reports and convictions are valid measures that distinguish the worst offenders. This view is supported by the finding that prior arrest for a violent crime and a history of family violence and criminality are the best predictors (e.g., better than prior gang involvement or heavy alcohol and drug use) of a youth's likelihood of committing a violent crime (Lattimore, Visher, & Linster, 1995).

Another useful way of thinking about different types of delinquents is the age at which they commit their first offense. Prior research has indicated that the prognosis for those who begin a delinquent pattern of behavior before the age of 12 is much worse than for those who are "late starters" (Dinitz, Scarpitti, & Reckless, 1962). Bryant et al. (1995) studied 5- to 17-year-old delinquent children and youths with emotional and behavioral disorders, finding that minor offending (offense not adjudicated or status offense) was correlated with age and parental incarceration and that major offending (index crime) was correlated with age, sibling incarceration, and running away. These data appear to be consistent with the observation that more serious delinquent behavior is associated with a coercive family process that trains children in antisocial behavior from an early age (Patterson et al., 1992).

Prevalence of Delinquency

Statistics regarding juvenile delinquency clearly show that most children and youths commit at least one delinquent act. But because authorities do not detect most illegal acts, "hidden" delinquency remains a major problem. About half the juveniles who become official delinquents are adjudicated for only one offense before they become adults. Juveniles who commit repeated offenses (*recidivists*) account for the majority of official delinquency. Recidivists commit more serious offenses, begin performing delinquent acts at an earlier age (usually before they are 12 years old), and tend to continue their antisocial behavior as adults (Farrington, 1995; Tolan, 1987; Tolan & Thomas, 1995). Males commit most juvenile offenses, particularly serious crimes against people and property. Females may be increasingly involved in major offenses, but males still far outnumber females in official delinquency statistics (Siegel & Senna, 1994).

The peak ages for juvenile delinquency are 15 to 17 years, after which delinquency rates decline. In fact, national statistics have shown a decreasing overall crime rate in the 1990s but a large increase in crimes committee by juveniles. All sources of information indicate that official delinquency and delinquent behavior have become more prevalent, violent, and destructive during the past 20 years; the rate of violent crime committed by children and youths has soared (Kinnear, 1995; see the most recent reports available from the Federal Bureau of Investigation published by the U. S. Government Printing Office, *Crime in the United States: Uniform Crime Reports*). Homicide is the second leading cause of death among children and youths under the age of 21 (O'Donnell, 1995). Orientation to drugs and delinquency related to drugs, especially alcohol abuse, are pervasive concerns of parents, educators, and other adults.

Causal Factors and Prevention

The nature of delinquency is not just law-violating behavior but also the responses of adult authority to it (Farrington, 1995; Goldstein, 1990; Lundman, 1993; Sampson & Laub, 1993). Incarceration and other forms of punishment have failed to control delinquency. Many socio-cultural factors, including our society's failure to control access to firearms, contribute to delinquency (O'Donnell, 1995). The problem is not merely a surge in young people's criminal behavior, but adult responses that tend to exacerbate rather than reduce delinquency. The scope of the problem is great, and the issues in delinquency have complex legal, moral, psychological, and sociological implications. Criminologists have constructed a variety of theories of crime that include social-environmental, biological, familial, and personal causal factors (see Blackburn, 1993; Siegel & Senna, 1994). We focus here on explanations of the origins of delinquency having greatest implications for educators.

Longitudinal research in England and New Zealand, as well as the United States, has led to remarkably consistent findings and hypotheses about the risk factors for delinquency and for suggestions for prevention (see Farrington, 1995; Lundman, 1993; Sampson & Laub, 1993; see also Bower, 1995). Research consistently reveals that the following characteristics put preadolescents at high risk for later delinquency:

- Antisocial behavior or conduct disorder, including especially aggressive behavior and stealing
- Hyperactivity, impulsivity, and problems in paying attention
- Low intelligence and academic achievement
- A family history of criminality and family conflict
- Poverty, large family size, densely populated neighborhood, poor housing
- Lax parental supervision and harsh, authoritarian discipline

Researchers have formed hypotheses about how these and related factors work in leading to delinquency. For example, Sampson and Laub (1993) state that

> We believe that the causes of crime across the life course are rooted not in race, and not simply in drugs, gangs, and guns—today's policy obsessions—but rather in structural disadvantage, weakened informal social bonds to family, school, and work, and the disruption of social relations between individuals and institutions that provide social capital. (p. 255)

Farrington (1995) summarized his explanation as follows:

> Children from poorer families may be likely to offend because they are less able to achieve their goals legally and because they value some goals (e.g., excitement) especially highly. Children with low intelligence . . . because they tend to fail in school and hence cannot achieve their goals legally. Impulsive children, and those with a poor ability to manipulate abstract concepts . . . because they do not give sufficient consideration and weight to the possible consequences of offending. Also, children with low intelligence and high impulsivity are less able to build up internal inhibitions against offending.
>
>   Children who are exposed to poor parental child rearing behaviour, disharmony or separation may be more likely to offend because they do not build up internal inhibitions against socially disapproved behaviour, while children from criminal families and those with delinquent friends tend to build up anti-establishment attitudes and the belief that offending is justifiable. The whole process is self-perpetuating, in that poverty, low intelligence, and early school failure lead to truancy and a lack of educational qualifications, which in turn lead to low status jobs and periods of unemployment, both of which make it harder to achieve goals legitimately. (p. 949)

As we saw in chapter 12, the parents of youngsters with conduct disorder typically do not monitor their children's behavior appropriately. Fridrich and Flannery (1995) found that parental monitoring and susceptibility to antisocial peer influence characterized early adolescent delinquents regardless of their ethnicity. In addition to family conflict, lack of parental monitoring appears to be a critical factor in allowing affiliation with antisocial peers to move adolescents toward delinquency. All of these risk factors appear to be what Patterson et al. (1992) have called "a concatenation of actions and reactions"—a series of interconnected, interdependent events and conditions leading through several stages to a criminal career. These stages and their defining characteristics, as described by Patterson et al. (1992), are shown in Figure 14.1. Not only the stages and their descriptions but the coercive process involving the exchange of mutually aversive reactions are depicted by the wavelike "His Reaction-Their Reaction" sequence. You may recall from the discussion in chapter 12 that this "my turn-your turn" sequence is part and parcel of the acting-out cycle that we see in school. Patterson et al. (1992) see it as the essence of the coercive process leading to antisocial behavior and, left unchecked, eventually to a criminal career.

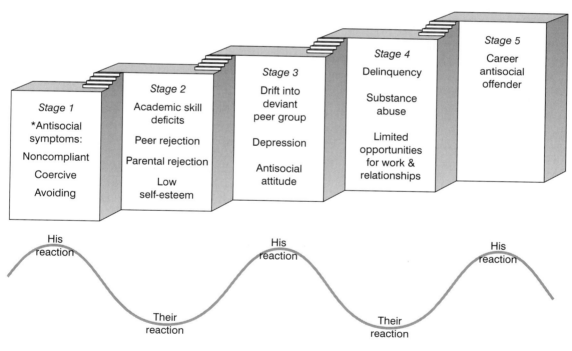

*The defining characteristics for that stage.

Figure 14.1
A Concatenation of Actions and Reactions
Source: From *Antisocial Boys* by Gerald R. Patterson, John B. Reid, and Thomas J. Dishion. Copyright ©1992 by Castalia Publishing Company. Reprinted by permission.

Given these risk factors, can we predict with a high degree of accuracy which students who experience them will become delinquent? More specifically, can we make accurate enough predictions to warrant specific prevention efforts? Farrington (1995) and Sampson and Laub (1993) argue that we can; Lundman (1993) argues that we cannot and that we should abandon at least the *traditional* delinquency-prevention efforts and focus on more effective intervention for youths who have been apprehended for delinquent acts (as we discuss later). Those who argue for prevention programs suggest that they be aimed at relieving many of the disadvantageous conditions of life associated with delinquency—employment, poverty, poor housing, ineffective parental discipline, family and community disintegration, and school failure. However, currently popular approaches rely primarily on incapacitation by incarceration—earlier, more adult-like, harsher, and longer punishment. Research shows that these strategies are ineffective, at least for youths who have not committed index crimes against other people (Lundman, 1993). Popular as they may be with social policy makers, these punitive approaches are seen by many researchers as counterproductive.

> As we write this book, a generation of adolescent and adult offenders are being locked up and are at risk of being permanently cut off from society. These offenders are being relegated to the structural role of the "dangerous, criminal class" . . . with the promise of a future life course that is very bleak indeed. We question the wisdom and foundation of such a devastating and costly crime policy. (Sampson & Laub, 1993, p. 256)

Delinquency, Disabling Conditions, and Need for Special Education

Educating juvenile delinquents presents difficult problems for public schools and correctional institutions because of unclear definitions of disabling conditions (McIntyre, 1993; Nelson et al., 1987; Wolford, 1983). Are juvenile delinquents disabled and, therefore, included under the Individuals with Disabilities Education Act (IDEA—Public Law 94–142)? We might contend that most or all *incarcerated* delinquents logically fall into the IDEA category of "seriously emotionally disturbed." But the current federal definition specifically excludes youngsters who are "socially maladjusted but not seriously emotionally disturbed." Delinquent behavior may be said to reflect social maladjustment rather than emotional disturbance, and juvenile delinquents are, therefore, often excluded under IDEA unless they have mental retardation, learning disabilities, physical or sensory impairments, or mental illness as determined by a psychiatrist (see Leone et al., 1991; McIntyre, 1993; Murphy, 1986b; Nelson, 1987; Wood, 1987b).

Researchers have consistently found that disabilities are common in delinquents, with learning disability the most prevalent disabling condition (Jarvelin et al., 1995; Murphy, 1986b; Nelson et al., 1987; Siegel & Senna, 1994). Nevertheless, the fact that a child or youth has been adjudicated and assigned to a correctional institution is apparently not in itself considered an indication that he or she is disabled or in need of special education (Gilliam & Scott, 1987; McIntyre, 1993). It requires curious turns of logic, however, to conclude that many incarcerated youths do *not* have emotional or behavioral disorders and are *not* entitled to special education under the law. If behavioral disorders include both overt and covert antisocial behavior (socialized and undersocialized conduct disorder as described by Kazdin, 1994, Quay, 1986a, 1986b, and others), then finding incarcerated youths who do *not* have behavioral disorders is a logical impossibility (except, of course, children or youths who are held unjustly).

We know that conduct disorder is very frequently accompanied by emotional or behavioral disorders of other types (Kazdin, 1994; Pullis, 1991; Webster-Stratton & Dahl, 1995). If higher levels of delinquent conduct indicate higher levels of psychopathology, and if youths who commit more frequent and more serious delinquent acts are more likely to be incarcerated, then the argument that all or nearly all incarcerated youths are disabled is supported. Finally, if behavioral disorders are *not* defined as disabling conditions under the law, then logically indefensible distinctions are drawn between emotional disturbance and social maladjustment, as we discussed in chapter 1. Wolf, Braukman, and Ramp (1987) concluded that "evidence and consensus are growing that delinquent behavior, especially when persistent and serious, may often be part of a durable, significantly handicapping condition that is composed of multiple antisocial and dysfunctional behaviors, and that sometimes appears to be familially transmitted" (p. 350).

Assessment of Delinquents' Educational Needs

Delinquents' disruptive behavior and bravado can make them inaccessible or uncooperative, or successful in covering up their academic deficits. However, the assessment of their educational needs does not differ in any essential way from the assessment of other students' needs; evaluation should focus directly to the skills in which instruction is to be offered (cf. Howell, 1985, 1987; Howell, Fox, & Morehead, 1993; Merrell, 1994). Because many delinquents have cognitive and academic deficits in addition to social and vocational skills deficits, their assessment must often be multifaceted. Assessment must often be done hurriedly and without relevant background information because delinquents are often in detention centers or special facilities where student populations are transient, educational records are unavailable, and communication with other agencies is difficult. Finally, because there is little agreement as to what are the most important skills for delinquents—social, academic, or vocational—the focus of assessment is often questionable.

Intervention in Juvenile Delinquency

Juvenile delinquency—antisocial behavior that crosses the line into the illegal or criminal—presents one of the most difficult challenges for effective intervention. There are no easy or sure-fire solutions for any facet of the problem of delinquency, and the issues in treating violent juvenile delinquents are particularly complex (Tate, Reppucci, & Mulvey, 1995). Achenbach (1975) notes that society's attempts to deal with juvenile delinquency are characterized by a recurrent pattern of enthusiasm for proposed solutions that have no solid foundation in research, followed by failure to win enough support for the new ideas to make them fulfill the hopes they arouse. Other writers also comment on the cyclic history of interventions and the failures of our legal system and other social structures to deal with the problems of crime and violence, including delinquency of minors (Lundman, 1993; Silberman, 1978; Spergel, 1995). The 1990s are a period of pessimism regarding government social programs and enthusiasm for harsher punishment (cf. Baker, 1996). Although an exclusive reliance on harsher punishment is clearly inadvisable on scientific grounds (cf. Tate et al., 1995), some have argued that we need to lower our typical expectations when working with persistent antisocial behavior, understanding that human behavior of this type is very hard to change and that many objectives short of a "cure" are worthy (Etzioni, 1994).

Effective intervention, like prevention, must include the astute, persistent, multi-faceted efforts of a variety of individuals and agencies. We make brief mention here of intervention in families and the juvenile court and corrections systems but concentrate attention on schooling.

Families   Make no mistake about this: Parents who are loving, nurturing, and skilled in childrearing can have delinquent children, but neglectful parents with poor discipline skills are far more likely than parents with good skills to have delinquent children. The typical parents of chronic delinquents do not monitor and nurture their children closely. They punish aggressive, delinquent behavior unpredictably, harshly, and ineffectively. They often show little concern when their children offend the community by stealing or fighting outside the home. As long as they do not have to deal with the misbehavior, they tend not to see their children as a serious problem. Within the home, they show little motivation to change their own behavior to decrease the coercion and violence that characterize their interactions with their children (cf. Dishion, 1990; Patterson, 1982, 1986b; Patterson et al., 1992).

Intervention in the families of chronic offenders is extremely difficult. Changing long-standing patterns of coercion may be impossible in families where parents are unmotivated and have few cognitive and social skills. Patterson and his colleagues report success in significantly reducing aggressive behavior and stealing in many families of aggressive children; however, the long-term outcome for stealers and chronic adolescent delinquents is guarded. Although delinquent behavior may be significantly reduced during behavioral intervention, research does not show that the improvement will persist after treatment is terminated (Patterson et al., 1992). Follow-up of juvenile offenders who were placed in group homes that used a *teaching-family method* (a behaviorally-oriented program designed to provide an appropriate family atmosphere) also shows that behavioral improvement during treatment is not maintained (Kirigin, Braukman, Atwater, & Wolf, 1982; Wolf et al., 1987). At this time, there appears to be no effective substitute for a family social system that has failed—at least when the criterion for effectiveness is "cure" or permanent behavioral change that requires no further treatment. Wolf et al., (1987) have suggested that serious delinquency should be considered a social disability requiring long-term supportive environments. Unless effective childrearing skills can be taught to the parents of a delinquent youth, effective long-term intervention in this disability may require placing the youth with a foster or surrogate family in which trained parents provide appropriate behavioral controls, models, and supports throughout adolescence and into adulthood.

Juvenile Courts and Corrections   Juvenile courts were instituted in the United States around 1900 to offer more humane treatment of juvenile offenders than the nineteenth-century reform schools had provided. Judges were empowered to use their discretion in determining the consequences of a child's misconduct, with the idea that the judge would consider the case carefully and then act as a wise father in its disposition. Although the intent was good, the institution has become mired in an overload of cases. Judges are often not "wise fathers," and the rights of children—if children are considered to have constitutional rights equal to those of all other citizens—have been blatantly abridged (Kittrie, 1971; Siegel & Senna, 1994; Silberman, 1978). Consequently, the juvenile court system and the question of children's rights have come under close scrutiny (see Bazemore & Umbreit, 1995; Snarr, 1987; Warboys & Shauffer, 1990; Wood, 1987).

Although we frequently hear proposals for drastic reform, the juvenile court system is likely to remain as it is for a considerable time. A sizable proportion of children and youths will make appearances before a juvenile court during their school years, and teachers could profit from familiarity with the court's workings (see Siegel & Senna, 1994; Silberman, 1978; Snarr, 1987; Wolford, 1987). Whatever the failures in the social systems of families and schools, one can find equal disasters in the procedures and institutions devised by lawyers and judges.

Under the juvenile justice system, juvenile court judges have wide discretion in handling cases. They may release juveniles to the custody of their parents, refer youngsters to social service agencies, or assign them to a variety of correctional programs ranging from probation to restitution to wilderness-challenge experiences or boot camps to community attention homes to state detention centers. The effectiveness of the various juvenile justice and corrections options are widely and hotly debated (see Siegel & Senna, 1994). However, most researchers conclude that harsher punishment is counterproductive in the vast majority of cases, contrary to the opinions of many holding political office.

Lundman (1993) argues persuasively for community-based intervention for all juveniles who have committed property crimes, reserving incarceration or other institutional treatment only for those who have committed index crimes against persons (nearly everyone agrees that juveniles who commit violent crimes against people must be placed in correctional facilities for some period of time). Lundman (1993) suggests *diversion* should be the standard juvenile justice response to minor property offenses and other relatively nonserious delinquency (see also Siegel & Senna, 1994). *Diversion* means that the juvenile is referred for services (e.g., family services, counseling) rather than sent to juvenile court. For moderately delinquent juveniles who are convicted of index crimes against property, Lundman recommends probation as the first and most frequent sentencing option. He also recommends abandoning efforts to scare delinquents straight through prison visits, informational seminars, and so on. Community-based interventions, including intensive monitoring and supervision, are the best approaches for most chronic property offenders, Lundman concludes.

When should the legal system treat a child or youth charged with a serious crime as an adult? This was one of the questions about Teaon, whose case we summarized earlier. The rights of children and their treatment under the adult system of justice versus juvenile justice are crucial matters of moral and scientific judgment (Tate et al., 1995). Given the present court and corrections systems and their options for dealing with adult criminals and juvenile delinquents, it perhaps makes little difference whether a young person encounters the adult world of justice or is "sheltered" by typical juvenile justice in which rehabilitation is often nonexistent. In any case, the trend in many states is toward trying and sentencing younger juveniles as adults, at least if they commit violent crimes (Baker, 1996).

Schooling   A substantial proportion of all juvenile crime occurs in school buildings or on school grounds (Siegel & Senna, 1994). Students and teachers frequently observe delinquent behavior in the classroom, in other areas of the school, and on the way to and from school, as reported in the descriptions of Scarface and V.K. earlier in this chapter. Many of the delinquent behaviors result in psychological trauma for victims and observers, costly damage to school property, total disruption of instruction, serious injury, or death. Each month during the academic year, thousands of teachers and millions of children in America's schools are assaulted or otherwise victimized. Theft, assault, drug and alcohol abuse, extortion, sexual promiscuity, and vandalism occur all too frequently, not just in deteriorated inner-city schools but in affluent suburban and rural communities as well.

Punishment and increased focus on security are schools' usual responses to delinquent behavior. The typical punishment (detention) or exclusion (office referral, suspension, disciplinary transfer, or expulsion) is usually ineffective in reducing the problem behavior and improving the student's academic progress. In short, the typical school's response to disruptive behavior is woefully inadequate and does little more than maintain a semblance of order and prevent total abandonment of its traditional programs (Mayer et al., 1987; Walker et al., 1995). In chapter 12, we discussed schoolwide discipline and positive, nonpunitive procedures designed to reduce antisocial behavior. Those strategies apply also to delinquent behavior in school.

One approach to dealing with problems of students at risk for a variety of undesirable outcomes (e.g., dropping out, delinquency) is the establishment of alternative schools. In a review of research, Cox, Davidson, and Bynum (1995) found that alternative schools have had a small overall positive effect on school performance, attitude toward school, and self-esteem, but not on delinquency. Alternative programs that target specific populations, such as those at risk for delinquency or low achievers, generally produced larger positive effects than those with open admissions.

Providing appropriate education for children and youths who are in jails or other detention facilities presents enormous problems. Implementing the essential components of an effective correctional education program and applying them to individual students, especially to those who have other disabling conditions in addition to emotional and behavioral disabilities, is extremely difficult. These are important components that Nelson, Rutherford, and Wolford (1987) mention:

- Functional assessments of the deficits and learning needs of disabled offenders

- A functional curriculum (that is, one that meets a student's individual needs)

- Vocational training opportunities specifically tailored to the needs of disabled persons

- Transition services that effectively link the correctional education program to a student's previous educational program, as well as to the educational and human services needed to support the disabled offender following incarceration

- A comprehensive system for providing a full range of educational and related services to offenders with disabilities

- Effective training in correctional special education to improve skills of educators currently serving disabled offenders and develop skills of preservice special educators (pp. 14–15)

Education of children and youths with disabilities in detention is governed by the same federal laws and regulations as education of youngsters in public schools (Leone et al., 1991). Those in detention facilities are guaranteed all the procedural protections and requirements for nonbiased individualized assessment, individualized education programs, and so on afforded under IDEA and related laws and regulations (Leone, Price, & Vitolo, 1986; Wood, 1987). Ideally, therefore, assessment of students in detention is functionally related to an appropriate curriculum (Howell, 1987), and the instruction of students is data-based and prepares them with critical life skills (Fredericks & Evans, 1987; Leone, 1985; McIntyre, 1993). Nevertheless, incarcerated children and youths often do not receive assessment and education. Given these difficulties summarized by Leone et al. (1986) and Nelson (1987), it is not surprising that many delinquent youngsters' needs are not met.

- Criminal justice officials and the public often take the attitude that delinquent and criminal young people are not entitled to the same educational opportunities as law-abiding citizens.

- Some psychologists, psychiatrists, and educators take the position that many incarcerated youths are not disabled.

- There is a shortage of qualified personnel to staff good special education programs in correction facilities.

- Some of the provisions of IDEA, such as regulations requiring education in the least restrictive environment and parental involvement in educational planning, are particularly difficult to implement in correction facilities.

- The student population of correctional facilities is transient, making educational assessment and planning especially difficult.

- Interagency cooperation and understanding are often limited, which hampers obtaining student records, designating responsibility for specific services, and working out transition from detention to community.

- Administrators of correction facilities often consider security and institutional rules more important than education.

- Funds for educational programs in correction facilities are limited.

Street Gangs

An increasing problem related to delinquency is gang activities. There is no doubt that gangs have proliferated across the United States during the 1980s and 1990s, that a thousand or more cities and towns now have problems with gangs, and that gang violence has increased (cf. Goldstein & Glick, 1994; Klein, 1995; Spergel, 1995). However, misconceptions about gangs and gang activities abound, and misunderstandings are often created or perpetuated by distorted media coverage, misinformed professionals, or both (Klein, 1995). Among the most egregious misimpressions is that most youth street gangs are organized to distribute drugs. Drug involvement by street gangs has increased, but the drug trade is not the primary activity of most street gangs.

Gangs have been an object of serious study for several decades, and we must be satisfied to summarize only a small part of the extensive and complex literature on gangs that is most relevant to educators. The definition of *gang* is difficult and controversial. Suffice to say that there are many different kinds of gangs organized for different purposes. There are motorcycle gangs, skinhead racist gangs, drug gangs, and a variety of others. We are concerned here primarily with what are known as *street gangs*, which Klein (1995) defines as aggregations of youths who recognize themselves as a group and are oriented toward delinquent acts. It is important to recognize that some gang members are not delinquents, and some delinquents are not gang members.

Gang membership is a means of obtaining affiliation, protection, excitement, and money, objects, or substances that members desire. The two characteristics that most clearly set an aggregation of youths apart as a gang are (1) commitment to a criminal orientation and (2) self-recognition as a gang, as signified by special vocabulary, clothing, signs, colors, and graffiti marking territory (Klein, 1995). Gang members are overwhelmingly male, mostly adolescent, and predominantly homogeneous groups of ethnic minorities. Minority groups differ in the nature or focus of their gang activities (Klein, 1995; Spergel, 1995). However, increases in younger and older members, female members, and white supremacist gangs are being seen in the 1990s. The typical gang member exhibits one or more of the following characteristics, according to Klein (1995).

■ A notable set of personal deficiencies—perhaps difficulty in school, low self-esteem, lower impulse control, inadequate social skills, a deficit in useful adult contacts.

■ A notable tendency toward defiance, aggressiveness, fighting, and pride in physical prowess.

■ A greater-than-normal desire for status, identity, and companionship that can be at least partly satisfied by joining a special group like a gang.

■ A boring, uninvolved lifestyle, in which the occasional excitement of gang exploits or rumored exploits provides a welcome respite. (p. 76)

Street gangs spend most of their time just "hanging out" together. Contrary to popular perception, researchers who have spent decades studying street gangs portray them as inactive most of the time.

> Street gangs through the years have done nothing more often than they have done something exciting. Their customary activities are sleeping, eating, and hanging around. Criminal acts are a minority of the activities they engage in, and violent acts are a minority of those. We must remember that despite the drama and lethality of gang violence, its prevalence does not deserve using the label *violent gang*. This only

feeds a stereotype that needs no help from scholars. To repeat, most gang members' behavior is not criminal, and most gang members' crimes are not violent. And of course, most violent people are not gang members, so it's not very useful to define gangs in terms of violent crime alone. (Klein, 1995, pp. 28-29)

A variety of causal models have been constructed to explain the formation and maintenance of gangs. Figure 14.2 depicts the model constructed by Klein (1995) after decades of studying gangs. A major feature of his explanation is that gangs are, in part, a phenomenon fostered by social and economic conditions that create an

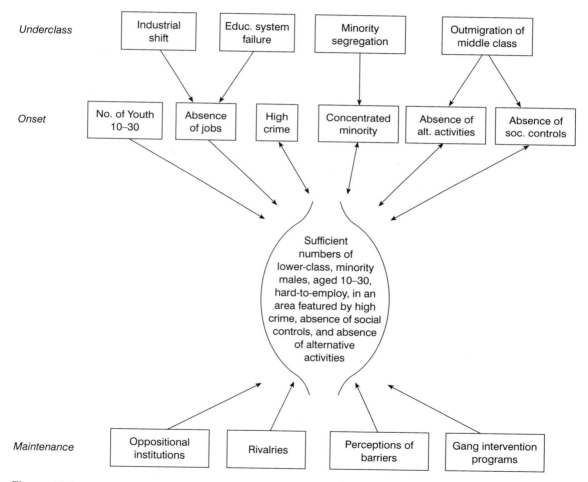

Figure 14.2
The Structural Variables Model for the Emergence of Gang Cities
Source: From *The American Street Gang: Its Nature, Prevalence, and Control* by Malcolm W. Klein.
Copyright ©1995 by Oxford University Press. Reprinted by permission.

underclass. The underclass is created by industrial withdrawal from an area (typically an inner city area), creating an absence of jobs. The failure of the education system further contributes to joblessness in the area. Segregation of ethnic minorities also plays a role, as do other forms of racism. Opportunities for individuals in the middle class to migrate out of the depressed area result in the absence of alternative social and employment-related activities and the absence of social controls provided by important vibrant, active institutions that are necessary to maintain the social fabric. Churches, children's service agencies, business clubs, and so on suffer the loss of talented leaders, and many of those left in the community have poor skills in parental discipline and few practical skills in maintaining community organizations that control social behavior. The onset of gang organizations is fostered by these conditions and a high number of youths between 10 and 30 years of age; gang behavior then exacerbates crime, minority segregation, and other negative community conditions. Gangs are maintained, in Klein's opinion, by things that threaten members, legitimize the need for the gang, and increase the cohesiveness of the group. These maintaining factors include institutions that oppose the gangs (e.g., police); gang rivalries that threaten personal safety, possessions, or status; perceived barriers to alternatives to gang membership and activities; and gang intervention programs that inadvertently strengthen the gang's cohesion, for example, attempts to use the gang structure to redirect members toward noncriminal activities.

Interventions designed to reduce gang membership and gang-related delinquent behavior are matters of considerable controversy, and to date no intervention approach has been shown to be very effective (Goldstein & Glick, 1994; Klein, 1995). Programs typically have lacked intensity and comprehensiveness or relied primarily on punitive measures (e.g., a crackdown by law enforcement) or other approaches that exacerbate the problem (see bottom line, Figure 14.2). Goldstein and Glick (1994) describe efforts to turn gangs toward prosocial purposes through aggression replacement training (ART), a program to teach social skills, moral reasoning, anger control, and alternative responses to aggression. Initial evaluations of their efforts are encouraging, but it is clear that ART alone is unlikely to be sufficient. Truly effective programs to stem the tide of gangs and gang violence would require an unlikely scenario, given the political climate of the 1990s; they would need to include massive and sustained efforts to reduce poverty, provide job training and well-paid jobs for youths in the underclass, provide decent housing in inner cities, rebuild and reform deteriorated schools and their instructional programs, and a variety of other strategies designed to bring economic opportunity and reduce racism and other social blights (cf. Klein, 1995; Siegel & Senna, 1994; Spergel, 1995).

Many schools, Klein (1995) observes, are running scared, approaching the gang problem primarily through scare tactics, tightened security, and punitive measures, often with the help of law enforcement. Although school safety is an important, legitimate concern, schools should put their primary efforts into positive schoolwide discipline plans and restructured programs designed to meet more of the social and educational needs of students (Mayer, 1995; Spergel, 1995; Walker et al., 1995). In their obsession with collegebound youths, schools fail to provide the work-oriented high school programs that keep youths in school and help them find employment (Edgar & Siegel, 1995; Spergel, 1995). Schools could play a major role in gang reduction if they focused on positive discipline, effective instruction and remediation, a differentiated curriculum with courses leading directly to the world of work for those who are not headed for college, coordination of efforts with other community agencies, and an array of extracurricular activities designed to attract all students into meaningful alternatives.

SUBSTANCE ABUSE

We use the term *substance abuse* rather than *drug abuse* because not all abused chemicals are drugs. Abused substances other than drugs include gasoline, cleaning fluids, glue, and other chemicals that can cause psychological effects. The substances under discussion here are those deliberately used to induce physiological or psychological effects (or both) for other than therapeutic purposes. *Abuse* usually is defined as use that contributes to health risks, disruption of psychological functioning, adverse social consequences, or some combination of these.

As Newcomb and Richardson (1995) note, substance abuse disorders cannot exist without the availability of the substance and a willing user. Many substances are readily available and many people are willing or anxious to use or abuse them. These facts imbue much of the discussion of substance abuse with a moralistic tone (the notion that substance abusers are simply evil or weak-willed) and encourage the assumption that interdiction of supply will be effective in reducing use and abuse.

Definition and Prevalence

The definition of *substance abuse* is clouded by controversy regarding specific criteria, changing social attitudes, and political use of the issue (Bukstein, 1995). What is the difference between experimentation and abuse? Does a single episode of use by a child or adolescent constitute abuse? At what level of use should an adolescent be considered to have a substance abuse disorder? It is clear that most adolescents take or use substances but that only a minority of them (perhaps 6 to 10 percent of users) become chronic abusers (Newcomb & Richardson, 1995). Adolescent substance abuse is in many ways similar to substance abuse in adulthood, but it is not exactly the same. Many adolescents who use or abuse substances do not become adults with substance abuse disorders.

The topic of drug use is especially prone to distortion of fact and hysterical rhetoric because the definition of adolescent substance abuse is anchored in cultural tradition, social fad, and political positioning as well as scientific evidence. Moreover, controversy regarding definition makes many prevalence figures suspect. Nevertheless, nearly all authorities on the topic agree that substance use and abuse are alarmingly high among American children and youths and that effective measures to reduce both use and abuse of substances are needed.

A common misperception is that substance abuse has to do primarily with illegal drugs such as cocaine, marijuana, and heroin, or with illicit use of prescription medications such as barbiturates, but as Werry (1986b) notes, *"alcohol and tobacco are, as ever, the real drug problem"* (p. 228). Alcohol and tobacco are the largest problems because they are readily available to adults, they are advertised for sale, most people view their use by adults as socially acceptable, and children usually receive their first exposure to and first experiment with these substances in the home. The earlier the child's first experience with alcohol and tobacco, the more likely he or she will become a regular user. Early use of alcohol and tobacco, as well as other substances, correlates with family problems, low socioeconomic status, and school failure. Because the negative health consequences of alcohol and tobacco are staggering, Werry (1986b) suggests that "it seems wisest to concentrate on preventing children and young people from starting smoking and drinking, not overtargeting the high-risk but numerically small group of illicit drug users" (p. 228). Indeed, the most common cause of death among teenagers in the United States is auto accidents while driving under the influence of alcohol, and disease caused by smoking cigarettes is the leading mortality factor among the general population of the United States (Newcomb & Richardson, 1995). Thus, the "war on drugs" has, so far, not been focused on what likely should be its primary targets.

Another common misperception is that substance abuse is disproportionately a problem of ethnic minorities. This mistaken impression is likely an artifact of data collection procedures and intervention programs. "We may conclude that, nationwide, there are no real differences in overall patterns of use as a function of ethnicity. Nonetheless, ethnic minorities (particularly African Americans and Hispanics) are currently far *more* likely than other adolescent groups to be targeted for attention from law enforcement officials as a function of drug involvement" (Newcomb & Richardson, 1995, p. 414).

Some youngsters, primarily adolescents 15 years or older, do abuse substances other than alcohol and tobacco. Table 14.1 lists major drugs of abuse (some of which are prescribed for therapeutic purposes), along with the most typical effects of drug intoxication and withdrawal. As mentioned earlier, the substances that become popular or receive intensive media attention in any given period of time are highly variable and affected by fads and other social phenomena. For example, in the mid-1990s, Ritalin (methylphenidate, a stimulant commonly prescribed for attention deficit disorders) became a popular drug of abuse, and national media attention heightened concern about its prescription and control. In addition to those listed in Table 14.1, people may abuse many other preparations, including *designer drugs,* new concoctions made up in illegal laboratories and represented as well-known drugs or touted to produce euphoria. The street names of various drugs are very numerous, and new names are constantly being invented (see Kaminer, 1994, pp. 227-228 and Wodarski & Feit, 1995, pp. 40-43 for examples). The adolescent substance abuser who becomes a substance abusing adult typically abuses multiple substances.

The emotional and behavioral problems associated with substance abuse include both the effects produced by using the substance and the effects of abstinence after a period of use (i.e., withdrawal). Terms commonly used in discussion of substance use include the following:

- *Intoxication* indicates symptoms of a toxic amount of substance in the bloodstream (enough to have physiological and/or psychological effects).

- *Tolerance* refers to physiological adaptation to a substance such that an increasing amount is required to produce the same effects; tolerance typically increases with repeated usage and decreases after a period of abstinence.

Table 14.1

Major Drugs of Abuse and Their Prominent Effects

Drug Class	Representative Drugs	Prominent Effects	
		Intoxication	Withdrawal
Depressants	alcohol phenobarbital Valium Quaalude	relaxation sedation drowsiness irritability	tremulousness fever hallucinations psychological dependence
Marijuana	cigarettes (joints) hashish (resin)	relaxation sleepiness poor concentration confusion anxiety distortion of perception	psychological distress
Stimulants	amphetamines cocaine nicotine caffeine phencyclidine (PCP)	pupil dilation restlessness loss of appetite paranoia hallucinations	mental and physical depression fatigue

Hallucinogens	lysergic-acid-
	  diethylamide (LSD)
	mescaline
	psilocybin
	cannabis (marijuana)
	scopolamine
		pupil dilation
		disturbed attention
		hallucinations
		altered body concept
		distortions of time
		  perception
		emotional fluctuations
			inconsistent evi-
			dence—little or
			none noted

Inhalants	aerosols glue paint thinner cleaning fluid	exhilaration confusion loss of balance drowsiness depression hallucinations frequent coughing	inconsistent
Narcotics	morphine Darvon methadone codeine Dilaudid	analgesia slurred speech drowsiness constricted pupils poor coordination	fever vomiting cramps sweating "goose flesh" chills irritability runny nose tearing

Source: From *Strategies for Managing Behavior Problems in the Classroom,* 2nd ed. (p. 348) by M. M. Kerr and C. M. Nelson, 1989, Columbus, OH: Merrill/Macmillan. Copyright 1989 by Merrill/Macmillan. Reprinted with permission.

- *Addiction* indicates compulsive use of a substance and that obtaining and using the substance has become a central concern and pattern of behavior.

- *Dependence* refers to need to continue using a substance to avoid physical or emotional discomfort or both.

- *Withdrawal* designates physical and/or emotional discomfort associated with a period of abstinence.

An important feature of advanced substance abuse is its insidious onset, progressing through various stages. A substance abuser rarely becomes a habitual user immediately; rather, experimentation, perhaps under peer pressure, is followed by occasional social or recreational use, then use in certain circumstances or situations (perhaps to relax after a stressful event, to stay awake to perform a demanding task, or to sleep). Situational use may intensify and become part of daily routine; eventually, the substance can become the individual's central focus. Clearly, substance use and abuse does not always progress to the obsessive-dependent, addiction stage (Newcomb & Richardson, 1995). However, teachers and other adults should be aware of the danger signals of the transitions from experimentation to social-recreational and to situational-circumstantial use. Teachers may first observe changes in social behavior and academic performance at the point of transition to situational use.

An additional concern regarding substance abuse since the 1980s is contracting the human immunodeficiency virus (HIV) through unprotected sex or the use of contaminated needles for intravenous injection of drugs (Allison et al., 1990; Kaminer, 1994; Ross, 1994; Wodarski & Feit, 1995). The probability of sexual activity, including sexual intercourse without a condom, is greatly increased by the use of alcohol and other substances that alter mood and cognitive control. Adolescents who are runaways, homeless, or substance abusers are a particularly high-risk group for sexual promiscuity and for contracting HIV.

It is difficult to estimate the extent of substance abuse among children and adolescents. Students with emotional or behavioral disorders are at higher risk than the general population of students (Genaux, Morgan, & Friedman, 1995; Morgan, 1993). The level of use and abuse of specific substances by adolescents reflects adult patterns and is affected by fads, social attitudes, and prohibitions (Bukstein, 1995; Newcomb & Richardson, 1995; see also box "Coke Is It?"). Use of hallucinogenic drugs was lower in the 1980s than in the previous two decades, but in the 1980s cocaine became a major concern and marijuana use, which in previous decades caused much alarm and sometimes resulted in legal penalties of absurd proportions, was considered comparatively safe (cf. Miksic, 1987). Beginning in the mid-1980s, there was a steady decrease in the use of most illicit drugs (Bukstein, 1995). The trends or fads that will appear during the next decade are impossible to predict.

Coke Is It? Changing Social Attitudes Toward Substances

The Coke you sit down with today is still basically Priestly's carbon dioxide-in-water mix. There have been only one or two small changes. When in 1888 a pharmacist in Atlanta, Georgia, bottled a variant of Priestly's water as something he called "Coca-Cola," he was so proud of the medicinal pedigree that he marked it as a mouthwash and gargle, guaranteed, in company advertising of the time, to "whiten the teeth, cleanse the mouth, and cure tender and bleeding gums." That was useful, but apparently of limited attraction. In time the gargle angle was dropped, and drinking the water, carbon dioxide, and sugar concoction was encouraged instead. There were still judicious amounts of cocaine poured in. To us that might seem excessive, especially as it was designed as a beverage for all the family, but this was before the first food and drug acts of the U.S. Brandy was common in children's tonic, morphine was available in many places without prescription, and by the end of the century a brand-new powder pick-me-up was being sold over the counter by an aspirin company: this was heroin. In that pharmacological flurry a little crushed coca leaf was not to be remarked upon. In 1903 it was dropped, though, with labels of that date noting "Cocaine Removed." (Bodanis, 1986, pp. 72–73)

Causal Factors and Prevention

A variety of theories have been said to explain adolescent substance abuse, including models that view it as a disease (metabolic or genetic abnormality), a moral issue (lack of will power), a spiritual problem (needing the help of a higher power), or a psychological disorder (learned maladaptive behavior or intrapsychic conflicts) (Bukstein, 1995; Newcomb & Richardson, 1995). Most researchers have concluded that no single cause has been or is likely to be found and that substance abuse has multiple causes. The focus is on assessing factors that heighten risk or tend to protect against risk.

Family factors known to increase risk are poor and inconsistent parental discipline, family conflict, and lack of emotional bonding of family members. Family members may provide models of substance abuse and introduce children to the use of substances. Undoubtedly, genetic factors contribute risk, perhaps by making some individuals more susceptible to the physiological and psychological effects of drugs (Newcomb & Richardson, 1995).

Socialization to a deviant peer group may play a major role in substance abuse, as may media exposure to substance use and abuse. All aspects of the culture in which the youngster is embedded may have a substantial influence on initiation to substances use (Kaminer, 1994).

Community conditions of joblessness and deteriorated living conditions are also risk factors. Certainly, substance abuse is no stranger to middle-class and upscale communities. Still, the lack of socioeconomic opportunity, hopelessness, crowding, and violence that characterize many poor urban communities are very significant risk factors (Bukstein, 1995).

Age of onset of substance use is a known risk factor. The earlier the age at which a youngster has his or her first experience with substance use, the greater the risk of later abuse.

Substance abuse disorders often occur with a variety of other disorders or psychiatric illnesses. Externalizing behavior problems (aggression and other characteristics of conduct disorder) are especially likely to increase risk (Lewinsohn et al., 1995; Steele et al., 1995). The polysubstance abuser typically has multiple disorders, all of which are intertwined and need to be addressed. It is important to note the reciprocal influences of substance use and other disorders. Some disorders, such as schizophrenia and depression, may be precipitated by substance use. A variety of disorders may both contribute to substance abuse and be exacerbated by substance abuse.

Protective factors include not only the opposite of family characteristics associated with high risk but personality characteristics, perhaps extending from early temperament, such as low anger and aggression, school achievement, compliance, and responsibility (Brook et al., 1995). Social and cultural influences such as peer support and societal disapproval can help influence children and youths to avoid substance use during adolescence, or at least delay the age at which they have their first experience with substance use. Communities in which there are jobs and alternative activities to substance abuse are also protective.

Bukstein (1995) notes that a variety of targets for prevention have been suggested, including prevention of use (especially early onset of use), abuse, the consequences of use, and the risk factors associated with use and abuse. Prevention can also be aimed at increasing the protective factors that lower risk. The most effective prevention efforts we can devise will address all of these concerns. Moreover, prevention strategies should encompass and be matched with all risk factors, including peer-related factors, individual factors (e.g., poor academic and social skills, conduct disorder), family factors (e.g., parental discipline), biological factors (e.g., use of medications), and community factors (e.g., socioeconomic conditions). General recommendations for prevention strategies are that they should be developmentally appropriate, focused on high-risk populations, comprehensive (address multiple risk factors), coordinated with changes in social policies in the community, and long-term.

Most relevant for discussion here are the skills-based interventions that comprise educational efforts to prevent adolescent substance abuse—interventions aimed at helping students understand the effects and consequences of substance use and abuse. Bukstein (1995) discusses curricula designed to help students learn a variety of skills that allow them to do the following things:

- resist peer pressure
- change attitudes, values, and behavioral norms related to substance use
- recognize and resist adult influences toward substance use
- use problem-solving strategies such as self-control, stress management, and appropriate assertiveness
- set goals and improve self-esteem
- communicate more effectively (see also Morgan, 1993)

Prevention is preferable to intervention after substance abuse has become a reality, but if it is to be effective it must be intensive, comprehensive, sustained, and focused on high-risk youths in high-risk neighborhoods, especially on improving the social and economic conditions in the communities of youths at highest risk.

The latter issue is likely the most important and is certainly the most costly and socially controversial. Not to recognize the importance and impact of socioeconomic conditions on the escalation of substance experimentation to hard-core use, abuse, dependency, and severe negative consequences is to put a bandaid on cancer. Prevention does not involve doing a little, but doing a lot to produce the greatest effect possible on the many risk factors for adolescent substance use or abuse. (Bukstein, 1995, p. 199)

Bukstein's conclusion rings true with others' observations on the pervasive negative effects of poverty and its consequences (e.g., Hodgkinson, 1995; Knitzer & Aber, 1995). Unfortunately, public sentiment and social policy in the United States in the mid-1990s appear headed toward less willingness to support effective prevention programs of the type Bukstein (1995) recommends.

Intervention and Education

A wide range of intervention approaches and combinations of treatments are employed in treating adolescent substance abuse. Traditional methods include 12-step programs such as those suggested by Alcoholics Anonymous and Narcotics Anonymous. Group therapy, family therapy (either single families or groups of families), cognitive-behavior modification, and psychopharmacological treatment are alternatives frequently employed. Family involvement and programs that are consistent with cultural traditions are critical features of prevention and intervention efforts (Bukstein, 1995; Maypole & Anderson, 1987; Ross, 1994). Some programs provide a comprehensive approach to prevention and intervention involving the entire spectrum of intervention agents: schools, peer groups, families, the media, communities, law enforcement, and the business sector (e.g., Wodarski & Feit, 1995). It is important that treatment be designed for the individual case and that careful consideration be given to inpatient versus outpatient treatment (Bukstein, 1995; Newcomb & Richardson, 1995).

Our primary concern here is educational intervention. One important feature of successful substance abuse education programs is getting accurate and useful information into the hands of teachers, parents, and students in an accessible, abbreviated form. Table 14.2 is an example of the type and amount of information that can be made available. Information alone does not necessarily change behavior, and it is therefore necessary to take more specific action. Miksic (1987) outlines the major actions in a successful substance abuse education program:

1. Establish a clear, well-defined policy for teachers and students spelling out how teachers and administrators will deal with apparent or substantiated drug use or possession.

2. Encourage teachers to establish a basic drug education curriculum for their grade levels—keeping it simple, brief, and nonjudgmental and emphasizing the teachers' concern for the students' physical and psychological welfare.

3. Help teachers increase their awareness of local drug problems and community service agencies.

Table 14.2
Drug Information Guide

Drug Used	Alcohol	Cocaine	Depressants
	(beer, wine, liquor)	(coke, rock, crack, base)	Barbiturates, Sedatives, Tranquilizers, (downers, tranks, ludes, reds, Valium, yellow jackets, alcohol)
Physical Symptoms	Intoxication, slurred speech, unsteady walk, relaxation, relaxed inhibitions, impaired coordination, slowed reflexes.	Brief intense euphoria, elevated blood pressure & heart rate, restlessness, excitement, feeling of well-being followed by depression.	Depressed breathing and heartbeat, intoxication, drowsiness, uncoordinated movements.
Look for	Smell of alcohol on clothes or breath, intoxicated behavior, hangover, glazed eyes.	Glass vials, glass pipe, white crystalline powder, razor blades, syringes, needle marks.	Capsules and pills, confused behavior, longer periods of sleep, slurred speech.
Dangers	Addiction, accidents as result of impaired ability and judgment, overdose when mixed with other depressants, heart and liver damage.	Addiction, heart attack, seizures, lung damage, severe depression, paranoia (see Stimulants).	Possible overdose, especially in combination w/alcohol, muscle rigidity, addiction, withdrawal & overdose require medical treatment

Seven POSSIBLE Symptoms of Drug Involvement
1. Change in school or work attendance or performance.
2. Alteration of personal appearance.
3. Mood swings or attitude changes.

Source: Drug Information Guide. Promotional Slideguide Corp., 33 Rockwell Place, Brooklyn, NY 11217. Used with permission.

Hallucinogens	Inhalants	Marijuana	Narcotics	Stimulants
(acid, LSD, PCP, MDMA, Ecstasy, psilocybin mush-rooms, peyote)	(gas, aerosols, glue, nitrites, Rush, White out)	(pot, dope, grass, weed, herb, hash, joint)	Heroin (junk, dope, Black tar, China white), Demerol, Dilau-did (D's). Mor-phine, Codeine	(speed, uppers, crank, Bam, black beauties, crystal, dexies, caffeine, nicotine, cocaine, amphetamines)
Altered mood and perceptions, focus on detail, anxiety, panic, nausea, synaes-thesia (ex: smell colors, see sounds)	Nausea, dizzi-ness, headaches, lack of coordina-tion and control.	Altered percep-tions, red eyes, dry mouth, reduced concentration and coordination, euphoria, laugh-ing, hunger.	Euphoria, drow-siness, insensiti-vity to pain, nau-sea, vomiting, watery eyes, runny nose (see Depressants).	Alertness, talkative-ness, wakefulness, increased blood pressure, loss of appetite, mood elevation.
Capsules, tablets, "microdots," blot-ter squares.	Odor of sub-stance on clothing and breath, intoxi-cation, drowsi-ness, poor mus-cular control.	Rolling papers, pipes, dried plant material, odor of burnt hemp rope, roach clips.	Needle marks on arms, nee-dles, syringes, spoons, pin-point pupils, cold moist skin.	Pills and capsules, loss of sleep and appetite, irritability or anxiety, weight loss, hyperactivity.
Unpredictable behavior, emo-tional instability, violent behavior (with PCP).	Unconsciousness, suffocation, nau-sea and vomiting, damage to brain and central ner-vous system, sud-den death.	Panic reaction, impaired short term memory, addiction.	Addiction, lethargy, weight loss, contamina-tion from unster-ile needles (hepatitis, AIDS), acciden-tal overdose.	Fatigue leading to exhaustion, addic-tion, paranoia, depression, confu-sion, possibly hallucinations

4. Withdrawal from responsibilities/family contacts.
5. Association with drug-using peers.
6. Unusual patterns of behavior.
7. Defensive attitude concerning drugs.

4. Provide an atmosphere in which the teacher can develop the skills and sensitivity for resolving classroom and individual problems and for leading group discussions about topics such as adolescent development and drug use.

5. Develop an intervention program that involves families as well as students by offering both one-to-one and group counseling and by utilizing community resources such as community counseling centers and drop-in centers within the school. (A drop-in center could be staffed by an education counselor with some training in drug abuse counseling.)

6. Try to get teachers to review their role perceptions. If they feel their jobs are basically unfulfilling and that they are unable to empathize with students and deal with affective as well as cognitive training, this may lead to constructive career reorientation.

7. Develop peer-group approaches with positive role models for group or individual support (see Wodarski & Feit, 1995 for extensive peer-oriented instructional activities).

8. Promote understanding of the emotional structure and perceptions that often accompany drug use. Many drug-using students feel they are incompetent and unreasonably rejected by adults and peers. They need a sympathetic approach rather than a disciplinary and judgmental attitude that confirms their belief that teachers and administrators are only concerned about keeping order, not about helping students. (See Kerr, Nelson, & Lambert, 1987; Wodarski & Feit, 1995)

Teachers need to know how to manage suspected substance abuse episodes and suspected intoxication or withdrawal crises in school. Their role is to manage and refer students appropriately, not to become investigators or counselors. Although educators must be aware of indications of substance abuse, they should not automatically assume that certain physical or psychological symptoms are the result of intoxication or withdrawal. Referral to counselors or medical personnel is appropriate to determine the cause. A clear school policy regarding detection and management helps teachers and administrators respond correctly to suspected abuse and crisis situations. In the event of an emotional-behavioral crisis, the teacher should remain calm and nonconfrontational; safety is more important than demonstrating disciplinary control (Miksic, 1987).

EARLY SEXUAL ACTIVITY AND TEEN PARENTHOOD

Delinquency, substance abuse, and sexual activity are often linked. Sexual activity itself may be defined as a juvenile status offense, but some juveniles commit index sex crimes such as rape, sodomy, or molestation (see Morenz & Becker, 1995). However, most early sexual intercourse is a concern because it is associated with a high risk of teenage pregnancy and premature parental responsibility, contracting sexually transmitted diseases (STDs), and a wide variety of psychological and health risks (Botvin,

Schinke, & Orlandi, 1995). Sexual intercourse itself is of much less concern when it is engaged in by an 18-year-old than by a 13-year-old; the level of concern is inversely proportional to the age of the child or youth (cf. Gordon & Schroeder, 1995).

Adolescents with psychological problems are at particularly high risk for contracting acquired immunodeficiency syndrome (AIDS) and other STDs through casual sexual encounters, which are often are linked with substance abuse (Genius & Genius, 1995; Rolf & Johnson, 1990). Sexual activity of young teenagers is also associated with social and emotional maladjustment and inadequate childcare skills (Thomas & Rickel, 1995). Many adolescents have distorted perceptions of their own high-risk behavior, seeing having sex as relatively low in risk and high in benefit for them (Siegel et al., 1994). Students with emotional or behavioral disorders tend to have distorted ideas about sexual behavior that puts them at high risk of contracting AIDS (Singh et al., 1994). Teenage pregnancy and parenthood present enormous problems for young people, particularly those who may already be penalized by our society's responses to ethnicity (Benson & Torpy, 1995; Lewis, 1990; McAdoo, 1990; McGowan & Kohn, 1990). The problems encountered by the children of teenage mothers and fathers are often overwhelming (Scott-Jones, 1993).

The sexual behavior of teens may be motivated by a variety of factors other than physiological urges. The social and psychological conditions that encourage early sexual activity are many and complex; they include the family and cultural factors we discussed in Part Three. The sexual activity of some teenagers has been initiated by their sexual abuse by older individuals, and they may suffer long-term psychological stress or dysfunction as a result (Gordon & Schroeder, 1995; Polunsy & Follette, 1995). Many sexually active teenagers appear to be seeking a sense of belonging, emotional closeness, or importance that they are unable to achieve in other ways. They may romanticize parenthood, believing that their child will give them the love they have not found from others. Some appear to be addicted to sex and "love" (Griffin-Shelley, 1994). Whatever the cause of their behavior, the psychological and physical risks are grave for young teenagers. The realities and personal costs of teenage parenthood—to the teenagers and to their children—are staggering.

> The physical fact that the adolescent has reproduced in no way indicates readiness to rear children (i.e., to care for and facilitate a child's growth and development). Most teenage parents have yet to develop a sense of their identity and life goals. Early introduction to parenthood interrupts their development. (Lewis, 1990, p. 209)

> Perhaps the most striking finding is the utter poverty of the lives of most of those whom we studied [pregnant teenagers living in the inner city]. . . . What was not expected was that so many of the respondents' lives would be equally devoid of other instrumental, social, and emotional resources. The fact that these young women generally depend on a very small circle of intimates to meet all of their support needs and are quite satisfied with the limited help they receive, suggests that they lead rather narrow, constricted lives and have few aspirations for anything better. (McGowan & Kohn, 1990, p. 203)

The facts of teenage sexual activity and parenthood are often assumed to imply a need for education about sexuality, family life, and parenting (Scott-Jones, 1993).

However, education and other interventions designed to decrease teen sexual activity have yet to demonstrate their effectiveness. Benson and Torpy (1995) studied the sexual behavior of students in grades six through eight in Chicago schools, finding that none of the following variables were related to loss of virginity: church attendance, religious affiliation, school grade point average, type of housing, marital status of the child's natural parents, self-esteem, knowledge related to sex education, or school attendance. They concluded that current school-based efforts to reduce sexual activity and pregnancy among young teenagers are unlikely to be effective. Research on how to lower the prevalence of early sexual activity has lagged behind research on the prevention of substance abuse (Botvin et al., 1995).

Because early sexual activity and premature parenthood are often accompanied by emotional or behavioral disorders of both teenagers and their children, special educators are often involved in planning and implementing the curriculum. In addition, special educators must work with other professionals who provide supportive services to families and children in distress.

SUMMARY

Juvenile delinquency is a legal term indicating violation of the law by an individual who is not yet an adult. Acts that are illegal only if committed by a minor are *status offenses*; *index crimes* are illegal regardless of the individual's age. The vast majority of youngsters commit delinquent acts; a small percentage are apprehended. Delinquent children and youths often have other emotional or behavioral disorders, especially conduct disorder. However, not all delinquents are identified as having conduct disorder; not all youngsters with conduct disorder are delinquents. Several subtypes of delinquents (socialized-subcultural, unsocialized psychopathic, and neurotic-disturbed) have been identified, but the most important distinctions are probably between those who commit few delinquent acts and those who are chronic offenders, especially those who repeat violent offenses against persons.

About 20 percent of all children and youths are at some time officially delinquent, and about 3 percent are adjudicated each year. About half of all official delinquents commit only one offense before reaching adulthood. Recidivists account for the majority of official delinquency. Peak ages for juvenile delinquency are 15–17 years. Most adjudicated delinquents are male. Juvenile crime and delinquency have become more frequent and more violent in recent years.

Causal factors in delinquency are numerous and include antisocial behavior, hyperactivity and impulsivity, low intelligence and school achievement, family conflict and criminality, poverty, and poor parental discipline. Delinquency appears to grow from environmental disadvantages, weakened social bonds (to family, school, and work), and disrupted social relationships between youths and social institutions in the community. Effective prevention would have to address all of the conditions that increase risk of delinquency.

We might logically take the position that very nearly all incarcerated delinquents have emotional or behavioral disorders requiring special education. Assessment of delinquents' educational needs is extremely difficult because of the behavioral characteristics of delinquents and the social agencies that serve them.

Intervention in delinquency, if it is to be successful, must involve families, juvenile justice, schools, and communities. Parents need training to monitor and discipline their children more effectively. Juvenile justice may involve a variety of strategies ranging from diversion to incarceration. The recommendations of researchers are typically for interventions keeping all but violent offenders in the community. Schools typically respond to disruptive and delinquent behavior with heightened punishment and a focus on security, but schoolwide discipline and emphasis on attention to appropriate behavior is more successful. Education in the corrections system should include functional assessment of students' needs, a curriculum that teaches important life skills, vocational training, supportive transition back to the community, and a full range of educational and related services from collaborating agencies.

Street gangs are an increasing problem in many cities, but misperceptions of these gangs are common. *Street gangs* are aggregations of youths who define themselves as a group and are committed to a criminal orientation. Most do not have drug distribution as a primary focus, and most of gang members' time is spent doing noncriminal and nonviolent acts. Gang members typically have notable personal deficiencies, are antisocial, desire status and companionship, and lead mostly boring lives. The causes and approaches to prevention of gangs are similar to those for delinquency, and many of the same intervention strategies apply, especially addressing problems of poverty and joblessness. However, gangs are maintained by perceived external threats and interventions that strengthen their cohesiveness. Many schools are running scared and approach gangs in ways that are counterproductive. A particular educational need is a differentiated curriculum that includes programs for noncollegebound youths.

Substance abuse is not easy to define. However, a substance may be considered abused when it is deliberately used to induce physiological or psychological effects (or both) for other than therapeutic purposes and when its use contributes to health risks, impaired psychological functioning, adverse social consequences, or some combination of these. The most pervasive substance abuse problems involve alcohol and tobacco. Substance abuse typically progresses through several stages, from experimentation, to social-recreational use, to circumstantial-situational use, which may become intensified and lead to obsessional dependency. Teachers are most likely to observe the first indications of substance use during the transition from experimentation to social-recreational or to circumstantial-situational use. The causes of substance abuse are varied and include family, peer, community, and biological factors. Substance abuse is often accompanied by other disorders. Effective prevention programs are expensive, multifaceted, and controversial. Intervention in substance abuse must be designed for the individual case. School-based interventions require clear school policies regarding drugs, systematic efforts to provide information, referral to other agencies, and involvement of families and peers.

Early sexual activity is of concern primarily because of the risk of pregnancy, sexually transmitted diseases, and psychological and health problems. The sexual activity of juveniles may be motivated by a variety of factors, but the risk of negative consequences is always high. Teachers may be involved in educational programs, but current school-based intervention programs may be ineffective.

Case for Discussion

"Everybody's So Uptight!"

Christy

Sitting in the detention center girl's unit, Christy knows how to put on the perfect "poor, pitiful, woe-is-me" look. Her blonde hair flips from side to side as she dramatically massages her temples. The tears well up just to the brim of her large, blue eyes, but they never quite fall over. This reminds me how she handles her deepest emotions: she puts on a good show but never admits her role in any problem, and what you see is a facade. This time she's been sent to us, once again, for hitting her mother. Far from remorseful, she slouches in the chair across from me, adamant that she was justified in hitting her mom. "The bitch was snooping in my room!"

At 16, Christy believes that if she wants to smoke a little marijuana now and then, or even party with the gang with a keg bought by her 30-year-old boyfriend, those behaviors should be her own choice. Besides, she says, "I'm not pregnant anymore, so what's the harm in having a little fun while you are young? Everybody is being so god-damned uptight!"

Christy protested similarly when she got picked up for running away. She needed the break, she said, from "that old, fat bitch. What's the big deal? I was planning to come back eventually, anyway." And the time before that, when she had the fender-bender? Well, the fact that she had no driver's license was no big deal, she explained. "A lot of people a lot worse than me do it all the time."

Christy laughs when she discusses the fact that she is the only resident in years to be dismissed from the local probation house for girls without successfully completing the program. She brags that she knew all along that no one would break her. In her opinion, our special education program doesn't work either. She is critical of the rules, and she knows the teachers can't force her to do anything she doesn't want to do. The solution, as Christy sees it, is simply this: "Everybody needs to get off my back and leave me the hell alone!" Christy has no plans for what she will be doing in 2 years, once she finishes her high school coursework (if she does).

So, now, there she sits, putting on her pitiful act, blaming the social studies teacher for her outburst because he criticized her for coming late to class once again.

Questions About the Case

1. How are Christy's behavior patterns typical of youths known as juvenile delinquents?

2. What agencies should be involved in working with Christy? What role should each play?

3. Describe the primary features of a good educational program for Christy. What are the predictable difficulties in implementing such a program in a detention center? What predictable difficulties might we encounter implementing the program in a public school?

Unique Characteristic(s) or Need(s)	Present Level(s) of Performance	Special Education, Related Services, and Modifications	Annual Goal(s)	Objective(s) (Including Procedures, Criteria, and Schedule)
Christy is disobedient and defiant with authority figures.	Christy refuses to follow school rules on a daily basis, with a minimum of 3 confrontations with adults per day about rule violations.	1. Maintain consistent, school-wide discipline program. 2. Use chart to record progress in getting to classes on time, following classroom routines, and following teachers' directions; provide positive reinforcement for improvement. 3. Provide counseling with a psychologist in the context of a trusted peer group.	Christy will follow school and classroom rules, routines, and procedures.	As judged by teacher reports, Christy will: 1. within 3 weeks, enter all her classes on time daily 2. within 6 weeks, enter classes on time and follow all classroom routines daily 3. within 9 weeks, enter classes on time, follow classroom routines, and obey all teacher directions without arguing daily.

PERSONAL REFLECTIONS

Delinquency and Substance Abuse

Nan Mary Gordon, M.Ed., has taught a self-contained class for high-school students with emotional and behavioral disorders in Lexington, Kentucky.

How would you describe the academic needs of most of the delinquents you teach?

Most of the delinquents that I have taught have had one thing in common: in spite of widely varied academic abilities, most arrive functioning below grade level. Is this deficit the reason they have behavior problems, or have their behavior problems caused them to fall behind? This is certainly a major question, but it has to be approached in a practical way. For me, as a classroom teacher of teenagers, it is really a moot point. They are here, needing to be taught, and their personal histories cannot be changed.

My students generally are not in school because it can prepare them for life. Some attend because they are not yet 16, others because they are under a court order to attend. To some, school offers a safe haven from a poor home environment; for others, it has become their only way to put off full-time employment. Whatever their individual reasons, they rarely come to school because education is intrinsically motivating. For an educator, this can present a challenge that is sometimes rewarding, sometimes frustrating.

Many of my students arrive hesitantly, regarding me as the enemy. For them, I must make education as positive and interesting as possible. The curriculum must be adapted to meet their needs so that they can see a relationship between school and their future. These students cannot adapt to fit an academic program; rather, the program must be adapted to fit their needs. They need attention in three specific academic areas.

1. *Life-Skills Math.* Many do not know the basic math facts. Trying to teach these to older stu-

dents is difficult. They are bored with the same old information and don't see that it will help them. Ratios, decimals, and fractions have little place in their lives. Instead, learning how to measure for cooking or building, how to write checks and balance accounts, and how to use a calculator seems to have more value for them.

2. *Language Arts.* My students are generally unenthusiastic readers. Many have poor reading skills and seem to have retained little that they have encountered about writing a sentence. Most consider reading a chore, not a pleasant experience or leisure activity. To overcome this, I have had success with reading aloud to them. I allow my students to get relaxed—only having to stay awake and remain quiet. Before each reading, we review orally what has happened thus far, and afterward we discuss what I've just read. The students can't wait for "novel time" and are always eager to learn what the next book will be. To encourage writing, I've cut silly headlines from sensational papers. Students pick one and write a story to go with it. Then we edit their stories together and put them into a newspaper format on the computer. For this, my students read, write, spell, and type with zeal.

3. *Content Areas.* Because a great deal of reading is involved in science and social studies, these areas must be made as real as is possible with experiments, speakers, movies, and field trips. Also, when students can see an actual connection with their lives, they are more likely to retain the information.

One of the most difficult obstacles to overcome is the lack of teaching materials. Finding materials that are of interest to delinquent teens—and at the same time cover the recommended curriculum and are on a level commensurate with their academic ability—is very difficult. These students respond best when academics are taught through real-life applications.

Another consideration in teaching delinquent students is their poor attendance. No matter how good your materials, no matter how much time you spend designing wonderful lesson plans, no matter your personal enthusiasm, if the students don't show up for school, you can't teach them.

To meet the needs of delinquent students, you must be positive, enthusiastic, and professional. You need to search out materials that present information in an interesting, realistic, down-to-earth way. You must motivate students to attend. And you must have in place a system of behavior checks and balances (expectancies/rewards/consequences) so that they are always aware of what is expected from them, what they will get out of it, and what will happen when they do not comply with expectations.

To what extent have you found social skills training to be important for the youths you teach?

I have found that social skills training for delinquent students takes two forms. Each is not only important but necessary to the success of the program. The first is a behavior-management system consisting of rules, reinforcing agents, and consequences. The system must be taught and retaught, as well as consistently applied to students in the school situation. The second area is direct instruction of social skills, such as training in empathy, anger control, resisting substance abuse, and dealing with conflict and aggression. Much of this is taught through modeling and role-playing.

Perhaps the most challenging aspect of social skills training with the students in our school is accepting the fact that most of them live in a world totally alien to what we as teachers know. The code by which they have been raised is generally unknown to us. To try to teach these students morals, principles, and ideals that are acceptable to our world may be to make them unable to survive in their own. In order to overcome this chasm, we must not judge or denigrate their ways but add to their repertoire from our own. We hope this will enable them to exist in whatever section of society they find themselves.

I was involved for a year in a unique program written by four other teachers and me. We first taught students a unit on empathy. Next, student participants made several visits to a daycare center for Alzheimer patients, where the students ate lunch with individuals and gave a presentation for them. For many of our students, this was their first experience in being "useful" or able to give of their talents and abilities to others. The overall reaction from our students and the day care clients was very positive. The program has been written up and presented both nationally and internationally.

A major difference found between teens with emotional or behavioral disorders and other teens is the lack of acceptable or appropriate social skills. This deficit needs to be addressed with behavior-management systems and with actual social skills training to enable our students to lead productive lives in society.

What advice would you offer to teachers in regular public schools who work with students who are likely to become delinquents?

A talk with teachers of at-risk students in regular public schools would need to include several ideas:

1. It is important to explain the necessity of being very consistent with such students. These students particularly need to have definite boundaries and to know what the expectations and consequences are—and that they will not change.

2. They also need to know that teachers are aware of them as learners. A few minutes of positive attention given early on for appropriate behavior may alleviate the later need for large expenditures of time for disciplining.

3. Another tactic for working with these students is to remove them physically as much as possible from other "active" students. If there is no one to perform for, then there is less chance of their acting out.

4. Another need is for frequent feedback from teachers. These students may need to be

shown both academic and conduct grades—often, and on a regular basis.

5. It is also important to set high expectations for these students, and to make them aware of what these goals are. Many times students live up to what is expected of them. Whether this has a negative connotation or a positive one is determined by the teacher.

6. One other idea that is more often used by special educators than by general educators is parent contact. Give parents the chance to support the school. Let students see that there is the opportunity for a supportive relationship between home and school.

7. As a last idea, I would suggest that emphasis be put on positive ideas and communications with students. So often we educators become lost in paperwork and begin to see chewing gum as a major school problem. Let's save our concern for drug and alcohol abuse, truancy, dropout rates, teenage pregnancy, teen suicide rates. Our outlook can affect how students view teachers and their school experience.

What are the most important things a teacher can do to help students who have begun to abuse substances?

When I suspect that a student is using drugs or alcohol, I try to approach him or her individually to talk. Some students will be very open about the abuse (either defensively or proudly), while others will refuse to admit there is reason for concern. My involvement is as a support or resource person. In my social skills, health, and science classes, I introduce units on substance abuse. In these, I try not to lecture or be judgmental. Rather, I attempt to offer factual information in a straightforward manner. I also give suggestions about resources available for help. If students are willing to talk, I try to get them to talk about why they are becoming involved with alcohol or drugs. Their reasons vary from being unhappy at home or frustrated at school to losing a partner in a relationship. If the problem continues, I discuss my concerns with the school psychologist, who is sometimes able to intervene. If

not, then we tell others involved with the student of our suspicions. This includes parents, social workers, and probation officers. If the student is actually intoxicated at school, I call the parent or guardian and send the student home.

Schools in my county are starting "student assistance teams." These are groups of administrators and teachers in each school trained to work with students who are substance abusers. These people act as mentors, advisors, and sounding boards, as well as referring students to other agencies for help.

What are the most common behavior problems that you must deal with in your classroom?

I see a variety of behaviors, just as in any classroom. This variety is magnified, however, when the students in the class have emotional or behavioral disorders. Management systems help, but these are adolescents, many of whom have been in special classes since early elementary grades. Their behavior patterns have been in place for years.

One of the symptoms exhibited by many of my students, and one that leads to a variety of problem behaviors, is low self-esteem. Because they have never developed a respect for themselves, neither have they learned to respect others. This is evidenced by students' disrespect for authority and authority figures. Teachers, parents, and law enforcement officials are examples of people that my students do not want to deal with. One way they manifest this is by refusing to follow directions; another is by making inappropriate verbal comments to adults. Students are also likely to get into difficulty through their disrespectful nonverbal actions. My students often set unrealistic goals for themselves; then, when they fail to reach them, they consider it proof that they are failures. This is the sort of mindset that students often have about completing school and getting preparation for future employment. They want more than a fast-food future, but they see themselves as unable to achieve any better. This leads to confusion and acting out as a release for the frustration they feel. All of these difficulties and more are contributing factors to one of our biggest problems—school dropouts.

Other behaviors sometimes exhibited by my students are stealing, cheating, lying, and being physically rough with each other. These are typically the behaviors of newer students, who have not yet "bought into" the behavior-management system.

My students tend to have poor attendance, because many do not want to be in school. Frequently, those who do show up for school do not stay all day. This results in more failure. One of my main goals is to get students to stay on task during class and to complete the assignments they are given.

15

Anxiety and Related Disorders

As you read this chapter, keep these guiding questions in mind:

- How is anxiety related to a variety of emotional and behavioral disorders?

- Under what conditions should educators and others be concerned when a youngster exhibits behavior characteristic of anxiety?

- What are the most likely causes of anxiety disorders?

- What are the most effective intervention strategies in anxiety disorders, including school phobia?

- What kinds of obsessive-compulsive behavior are most often seen in children and adolescents?

- What do we know about posttraumatic stress disorder in children and youths?

- What is Tourette's disorder, and how is it related to other disorders?

- What is the role of anxiety in selective mutism, and how is it best treated?

- What are the most common eating disorders, and what role does anxiety play in them?

- What are the most common elimination disorders, and how might they be involved in school problems?

- How are sexual problems defined, and what is a teacher's role in addressing them?

- What role can the peer group play in effective intervention in social isolation?

- What strategies are most effective in helping adolescents overcome social withdrawal and social ineptitude?

Chapters 11 through 14 dealt mostly with problems that fall under the general dimension of *externalizing disorders*. This chapter turns to problems designated generally as *internalizing*. Although the broad band classification *internalizing* is well established in empirical studies of behavioral dimensions, most of the specific categories and disorders that fall under it are not. In short, there is more confusion and controversy over terminology and classification for internalizing problems than for externalizing problems. Grouping internalizing problems for discussion therefore presents unavoidable difficulties.

Anxiety, social withdrawal, and other internalizing behavior problems often occur together (Last, 1992; Tankersley, 1992). Eating disorders and reluctant speech may both involve specific fears or anxieties, stereotyped movement disorders may involve obsessions or compulsions or both, and so on. Anxiety is a frequent component of other disorders, and anxiety disorders of all types may be comorbid with a variety of other disorders. "In general, it is important to keep in mind that comorbidity is the rule—not the exception in abnormal child psychology" (Rabian & Silverman, 1995, p. 236). Other writers have also had great difficulty in grouping internalizing disorders for discussion (Quay & La Greca, 1986; Werry, 1994), and confusion about the classification of anxiety-related disorders has been apparent in the various revisions of the American Psychiatric Association's diagnostic criteria (Rabian & Silverman, 1995).

The relationships among the various problems related to anxiety and other internalizing problems are for the most part tenuous, and because they are so varied and loosely related we will not attempt to summarize definition, prevalence, causal factors, prevention, assessment, intervention, or education for the general case or for all specific disorders. The problems we discuss are representative of those most frequently described in the literature. We begin with anxiety disorders because they are the broadest category; anxiety appears to be a significant component of all the others.

ANXIETY DISORDERS

Anxiety—the distress, tension, or uneasiness that goes with fears and worries—is part of the normal development of young children (Stevenson-Hinde & Shouldice, 1995). At birth, infants have a fear of falling and of loud noise; fear of other stimuli (strange persons, objects, situations) ordinarily develops during the first few months. These fears probably have survival value, and they are considered normal and adaptive, not deviant. As children grow into the middle childhood years, they develop additional fears, especially about imaginary creatures or events (Morris & Kratochwill, 1983, 1991; Siegel & Ridley-Johnson, 1985). Unless the fears become excessive or debilitative and prevent the child from engaging in normal social interaction, sleep, school attendance, or exploring the environment, they are not maladaptive. Indeed, a child who has no fears at all is not only highly unusual, but also likely to be hurt or killed because of inappropriate brashness.

Children's anxieties or fears may be mild and short-lived enough that they do not seriously interfere with social growth. In fact, "study of the *prevalence of anxiety* in childhood has focused on subclinical fears and school phobia" (Strauss, 1993, p. 240). Most studies show that about 7 or 8 percent of children experience intense anxieties at some time, although not all of these anxieties require clinical intervention (see Anderson, 1994). When fear unnecessarily restricts the child's activity, however, intervention is called for. A child or youth may be in a chronic state of anxiety about a broad range of things, in which case he or she may be described as having a generalized anxiety disorder. However, a youngster may also have a more specific anxiety. It may be an extreme, irrational fear that is out of proportion to reality and leads to automatic avoidance of the feared situation, which is often called a **phobia**. The child showing extreme anxiety and social withdrawal (often labeled *neurosis* in psychodynamic literature) has traditionally been assumed to be more disturbed and to have a worse prognosis for adult adjustment than the hostile, acting-out child with an externalizing disorder. Research does not bear out this assumption.

Characteristics associated with anxiety and withdrawal are usually more transitory and amenable to treatment than those associated with conduct disorder, and anxiety does not put a child at risk for later development of schizophrenia or other major psychiatric disorder in adulthood (Klein & Last, 1989; Quay & La Greca, 1986; Robins, 1966, 1986). Compared to their awareness of peers' aggressive and disruptive behavior, children's awareness of their peers' anxiety and withdrawal is not as keen or as early to develop (Safran, 1995). Anxiety-withdrawal in its typical form is not, then, the greatest concern to knowledgeable professionals who work with children and youths who have emotional or behavioral disorders. Nevertheless, in their extreme forms, anxiety and related disorders *do* result in serious impairment of functioning. Extreme social isolation, extreme and persistent anxiety, and persistent extreme fears, for example, can seriously endanger social and personal development and demand effective intervention. Moreover, anxiety is frequently comorbid with depression, conduct disorder, learning disabilities, and other disorders (see Last, 1992; Newcomer, Barenbaum, & Pearson, 1995; Rabian & Silverman, 1995).

Quay and La Greca (1986) estimate that *persistent* anxiety may characterize 2 percent of the child population and that about 5 percent may be affected by such behavior problems at one time or another. Anxiety may be part of the problems of 20 to 30 percent of youngsters referred to clinics for treatment of behavioral disorders. The prevalence of anxious-withdrawn behavior appears to be approximately the same as that of conduct disorder, placing it among the most common emotional or behavioral disorders of childhood (Anderson & Werry, 1994). Boys and girls are referred for these problems in about equal percentages, but these are only rough estimates, because there have been no extensive studies of prevalence in children.

Evidence suggests that much anxiety is learned but that biological factors also may contribute to anxiety disorders. Humans learn fears in a variety of ways (see Herbert, 1994; Morris & Kratochwill, 1983; Siegel & Ridley-Johnson, 1985, for detailed analyses of fear acquisition). Infants and young children especially may learn fear through classical or respondent conditioning. If an already fright-producing stimulus is paired with another object or event, the child may come to fear that object or event. Comments, remonstrations, and other verbal communications of parents (especially the mother) and other adults about objects, activities, places, persons, or situations induce fearfulness in children who have acquired language skills. Adults' and other children's nonverbal behavior can also have a powerful influence on a child's learning fear. A child who is overly fearful of dogs may have acquired the fear in one or a combination of ways: a dog may have frightened the child by barking or growling, jumping, knocking the child down, biting, and so on; the parents or someone else may have warned the child in an emotional way about the dangers of dogs, or the child may have heard people talk about a dog's meanness and dangerousness; the child may have seen a parent, sibling, or other child (or someone in a movie or on television) attacked by or frightened by dogs.

In addition to social learning, anxiety appears in some cases to be affected by physiological factors (Harden et al., 1995). Anxiety disorders of various types tend to run in families, and it is suspected that genetic or other physiological factors may be involved in the origins of these disorders as well as social learning. However, "at the present time, causes of anxiety and phobic disorders in childhood are not well understood and appear to be multifaceted" (Rabian & Silverman, 1995, p. 248).

Some children develop fears or phobias about separation, and leaving home or their parents may be extremely traumatic for them, even leaving for a short time. Some are extremely anxious about going to school. School phobia may more appropriately be called "social phobia" in some cases, as it is a fear of the social interactions that are an expected part of school attendance. Of course, a student may have extreme anxiety about both separation from home or parents and social interaction in school. Rabian and Silverman (1995) describe the case of Jerry.

Jerry

Jerry is a 9-year-old boy who was referred to a childhood anxiety program by the school psychologist because of repeated absences from school. Jerry's parents reported that he is very fearful of school and cries almost every morning when preparing for that setting. In particular, Jerry, an only child, complains to his parents about how uncomfortable he feels around other children. Both in and out of school, Jerry has few friends and avoids participation in group activities whenever he can. In addition, Jerry's parents indicated that he is a "worry wart," who is almost constantly seeking reassurance from others about his abilities and performance. Although Jerry had experienced these problems for some time, they became problematic (repeated absences from school) only recently. (p. 247)

Social learning principles can help resolve both children's and adults' excessive or irrational anxieties and fears. Three approaches, which can be used in combination, have been particularly successful: modeling, desensitization, and self-control training. With these techniques, clinicians have helped children and youths overcome a wide array of fears and phobias (see Kendall & Gosch, 1994; March, 1995; Morris & Kratochwill, 1983; Siegel & Ridley-Johnson, 1985). Teachers may be asked to assist in implementing these procedures in school settings. Medications to reduce anxiety may be helpful in addition (Campbell & Cueva, 1995b).

Having fearful children watch movies in which other youngsters are having fun (at a party or playing games) while approaching the feared object without hesitation (for example, the youngsters in the movie may be handling dogs or snakes while playing) reduces fear in the observers and makes them more willing to approach the thing they fear. Having individuals with phobias watch several different peer models unanxiously approach several different feared objects and showing films that display the actual feared object (rather than a replica) have increased the effectiveness of this method of fear reduction. Positive reinforcement of the fearful person's approach to the feared object adds to the fear-reducing effects of watching models. Filmed modeling procedures have been highly effective in preventing children from acquiring maladaptive fears of medical and dental procedures as well as in dealing with children who have already become fearful (King, Hamilton, & Murphy, 1983).

Procedures variously referred to as **systematic desensitization**, **reciprocal inhibition**, and **counterconditioning** have also been effective in lowering fears of children and adults. The central feature of these procedures involves the individual's gradual and repeated exposure to the fear-provoking stimuli (either in real life—*in vivo*—or in purposeful fantasy of them) while the person remains unanxious and perhaps engaged in an activity that is incompatible with or inhibits anxiety (such as eating a favorite treat or relaxing comfortably in a chair). The gradual approach to the feared object, repeated exposure to it, and maintenance of an unanxious state during exposure are thought to weaken the conditioned or learned bond between the object and the fear response it elicits (cf. Rabian & Silverman, 1995; Wolpe, 1975).

In self-control training, fearful individuals learn to talk through a variety of techniques for managing anxiety. They may learn relaxation, self-reinforcement, self-punishment, self-instruction, visual imagery, or problem-solving strategies. The trainer might help the individual develop mental images that represent calm or pleasant feelings that are incompatible with anxiety and that the subject can recall when he or she encounters anxiety-provoking circumstances.

Interventions based on behavior principles have been quite successful in remediating the problem of school phobia (King, Ollendick, & Tonge, 1995). Specific techniques vary from case to case, but general procedures include one or more of the following:

- desensitization of the child's fear through role-playing or in vivo approximations of attending school for an entire day

- reinforcement for attending school even for a brief period, gradually lengthening the time the child is required to stay in school

- matter-of-fact parental statements that the child will go back to school, avoiding lengthy or emotional discussion

- removal of reinforcers for staying home (such as being allowed to watch television, play a favorite game, stay close to mother, or engage in other pleasurable activities)

King et al. (1983) suggest that many maladaptive fears in the school setting are preventable. Prevention would involve desensitizing young children to school by introducing future teachers, school routines, play activities, and so on. Transitions to middle school and senior high school similarly can be made less anxiety-provoking by preparing students for their new environments and new expectations. Although many schools attempt to provide orientation experiences, they are often not carefully planned. Individual students may need to learn coping skills to deal with irrational thoughts and to learn adaptive behavior (such as asking a teacher or peer for assistance) through modeling, rehearsal, feedback, and reinforcement.

OBSESSIVE-COMPULSIVE DISORDERS

Obsessions are repetitive, persistent, intrusive impulses, images, or thoughts about something, not worries about real-life problems. *Compulsions* are repetitive, stereotyped acts the individual feels he or she must perform to ward off a dreaded event, although these acts are not really able to prevent it. Both obsessions and compulsions may be part of ritualistic behavior by which an individual attempts to reduce anxiety. When such behavior causes marked distress, is inordinately time-consuming, or interferes with a person's routine functioning in home, school, or job, it is considered an obsessive-compulsive disorder (OCD). Children with OCD often do not understand that their behavior is excessive and unreasonable, although adults with OCD typically do (American Psychiatric Association, 1994).

OCD affects perhaps as many as 1 in 200 children and adolescents, making it a relatively rare disorder (Johnston & March, 1992). It may involve many types of ritualistic thoughts or behaviors such as these

- washing, checking, or other repetitive motor behavior
- cognitive compulsions consisting of words, phrases, prayers, sequence of numbers, or other forms of counting
- obsessional slowness, taking excessive time to complete simple, everyday tasks
- doubts and questions that elevate anxiety

Many children and adolescents with this disorder are not diagnosed, in part because they are often secretive about their obsessional thoughts or rituals. However, OCD can result in significant impairment in social and academic impairment. Johnston and March (1992) describe a case in point.

> Betsy, an 11-year-old girl, was referred to our clinic by a local psychologist. During the initial telephone contact, Betsy's mother explained that their situation seemed desperate, as Betsy had been unable to attend school for the 2 preceding weeks. Her mother explained that Betsy repeatedly dressed and undressed and then dressed again, over and over, and was unable to stop until she was nearly exhausted. (p. 118)

Betsy's dressing rituals had begun 7 months earlier. Psychodynamic therapy was ineffective, and her symptoms worsened. Her school work suffered, and her teachers reported that she was not turning in homework and completing assignments. When her parents asked her why she was having trouble, she was evasive but eventually said that it was because "she had to read each sentence three times, 'just the right way'" (Johnston & March, 1992, p. 119). After more probing by her mother, Betsy admitted that she thought if she did not "get it right" her parents would get hurt. Later, Betsy began repeating phrases and sentences and performing other rituals, including washing her hands up to 30 times a day to avoid contracting AIDS.

The most effective interventions are based on social learning principles, particularly strategies employed for reduction of anxiety (March, 1995; Milby & Weber, 1991). Medications to reduce anxiety may also be helpful (Campbell & Cueva, 1995b; Johnston & March, 1992; Quintana & Birmaher, 1995). Teachers may play an important role in detecting OCD, especially when the student is secretive about thoughts or rituals and careful observation and questioning are necessary to discover why the student is having socialization or academic difficulties. Special educators may be expected to assist in intervention by implementing features of anxiety-reduction procedures in the classroom.

POSTTRAUMATIC STRESS DISORDER

Posttraumatic stress disorder (PTSD) refers to prolonged, recurrent emotional and behavioral reactions following exposure to an extremely traumatic event involving threatened death or serious injury to oneself or others. The person's response at the time of experiencing the event must include intense fear, helplessness, or horror (children may show disorganized or agitated behavior). PTSD is characterized by persistent cognitive, perceptual, emotional, or behavioral problems related to the event. For example, people with PTSD may reexperience the traumatic event in a variety of ways, such as through recurrent and intrusive thoughts, images, or dreams. They may avoid stimuli associated with the event or experience a general emotional numbing or unresponsiveness. Their symptoms may also include increased arousal (e.g., difficulty sleeping or concentrating) (see American Psychiatric Association, 1994).

Until relatively recently, children's delayed emotional and behavioral reactions to extreme stress were largely ignored. PTSD was seldom studied unless the traumatic stress occurred in adulthood. Since the mid-1980s, however, mental health workers have recognized that extremely traumatic experiences can cause delayed emotional or behavioral disorders in children as well as adults (American Psychiatric Association, 1994; Terr, 1995; Yule, 1994). By the mid-1990s, it was well recognized that extreme stress or life-threatening experiences can produce not only depression, anxiety, fears, and other reactions in children but also can result in PTSD. Yule (1994) notes the historical neglect of posttraumatic stress in children:

> The form of PTSD varies according to the age of the child, and, sadly, the internal distress often goes unrecognized for long periods by parents and teachers. Indeed, one of the reasons that there was doubt as to whether PTSD occurred in children was that few investigators had asked the children themselves how they were affected. (p. 223)

At this time, relatively little is known about PTSD in children. However, Terr (1995) concludes that four characteristics are common to extreme childhood trauma:

- visualized or otherwise repeatedly perceived memories of the trauma
- repetitive behaviors that may be similar to obsessions or compulsions
- fears linked specifically to the traumatic event
- altered attitudes toward people, life, or the future, reflecting feelings of vulnerability

There is tremendous variation in the way individuals respond to a given traumatic event. However, researchers are finding that accidents, wars, natural disasters such as earthquakes or hurricanes, and the domestic and community violence commonly experienced in contemporary urban life may often produce PTSD in children and adolescents (see, for example, Arroyo & Eth, 1995; Horowitz, Weine, & Jekel, 1995; Shaw, Applegate, & Schorr, 1996). Treatment of these disorders may involve a variety of approaches, such as group discussion and support activities, crisis counseling, and individual treatment to reduce anxiety and improve coping strategies. Prevention involves not only efforts to reduce accidents and violence but also planning for the traumas that are likely if not inevitable (Yule, 1994).

Events producing PTSD may occur in school or the community. Regardless of the location at which the traumatic event occurs, the student with PTSD is likely to have serious problems in school. Anxiety and related responses to the trauma may make it very difficult for the student to concentrate on academic work or engage in typical social activities. Consequently, it is important that teachers be aware of the indicators of possible PTSD, refer students for evaluation, and participate in efforts to reduce anxiety to manageable levels.

STEREOTYPED MOVEMENT DISORDERS

Stereotyped movements are involuntary, repetitive, persistent, and nonfunctional acts over which the individual can exert at least some voluntary control under some circumstances but not total control in all circumstances. Stereotyped movements include self-stimulation and self-injury, as we discuss in chapter 17. However, they may also include repetitive movements related to obsessions or compulsions (Werry, 1986c).

Most stereotyped movements that are not labeled self-stimulation or self-injury are referred to as **tics**. Tics that involve only the facial muscles and last only a short time are common; nearly one fourth of all children will at some time during their development display this kind of tic, and it is best to ignore them. Tics involving the entire head, neck, and shoulders, however, typically require intervention. Tics may be vocal as well as motor; the individual may make a variety of noises or repeat words or word sounds, with or without accompanying motor tics.

Chronic motor tics that last more than a year and involve at least three muscle groups simultaneously are more serious than those involving fewer muscles or lasting a shorter time. There are a variety of tic disorders, but the most severe variety and the one on which most research has been done is **Tourette's disorder** or **Tourette's syndrome** (TS) (Spencer et al., 1995). *DSM-IV* defines TS as a disorder with onset before age 18 years in which the person has both multiple motor and one or more verbal tics occurring many times a day (usually in clusters) nearly every day or intermittently for more than a year (American Psychiatric Association, 1994). TS occurs in about 4 or 5 individuals per 10,000, across diverse racial and ethnic groups, and about 1.5 to 3 times more often in males than in females.

In the 1990s, TS has become a focus for much research on obsessive-compulsive and anxiety disorders. Because it has been so misunderstood until recently, TS has carried extraordinary social stigma. The symptoms of TS may be very mild and not readily apparent to the casual observer. However, a person with severe symptoms may find that others respond with fear, ridicule, or hostility to their bizarre behavior (e.g., twitching, grunting, shouting obscenities or words inappropriate to the circumstances). The diagnosis of TS in two high-profile athletes (baseball player Jim Eisenreich and basketball player Mohmoud Abdul-Rauf, formerly Chris Jackson), the brilliant writing of neurologist Oliver Sacks for the popular press (see "A Surgeon's Life" in Sacks, 1995, the story of a surgeon and pilot with TS), and the work of the Tourette Syndrome Association have done much to dispel ignorance, discrimination, and cruelty shown toward children and adults with TS.

We now know that TS is a neurological disorder, although the cause and precisely what is wrong neurologically are not known. TS is a multifaceted problem with social and emotional as well as neurological features (Coffey et al., 1995; Kerbeshian & Burd, 1994; Linet, 1995). It may have a genetic component. It can vary greatly in severity and nature of symptoms, and it is often a comorbid condition with a variety of other disorders, especially attention-deficit hyperactivity disorder (ADHD) and obsessive-compulsive disorder (OCD). In fact, some researchers suggest that TS is a specific form of attentional or obsessive-compulsive disorder. Some symptoms of TS may involve tic-like ritualistic behavior (e.g., stereotyped touching or arrangement of objects, repetition of words or phrases). In some cases, the person with TS has difficulty inhibiting aggression, and TS can be mistaken for or comorbid with conduct disorder (Riddle et al., 1988). The symptoms of TS may become more severe under specific conditions, especially with the experience of anxiety, trauma, or social stress (Silva et al., 1995).

TS is becoming better understood as diagnosis becomes more accurate and research reveals more about its nature and treatment. The most effective treatments are cognitive-behavioral therapies and medications or a combination of the two (March, 1995). Many individuals with TS do not like the side effects of neuroleptics and other medications that may be prescribed to attenuate their symptoms. Management of tics by other means, including allowing them to occur under many circumstances and educating others to understand and accept them, are often preferred strategies. The report of Kane (1994) gives us a small window into the experience of one person with TS:

> I experienced TS onset 19 years ago, at age 7. My first symptom was head jerking, and subsequent (primarily simple tic) symptoms included facial tics, extremity tics, vocal tics (e.g., squeaking, grunting), and touching tics. From ages 11 to 13 I was prescribed haloperidol, but eventually, because of side effects, I was prescribed clonidine. One year later, clonidine was deemed ineffective and all medication was discontinued. (p. 805)

Kane (1994) goes on to describe his bodily sensations involving TS, which read in part:

> Perhaps the best description for the sensory state of TS is a somatic hyperattention: It is not as itch-like as it is an enduring somatosensory bombardment. I experience the TS state as one of keen bodily awareness, or a continual consciousness of muscle, joint, and skin sensations. . . . If all tics are suppressed, virtually all of my joints and muscles begin to demand my attention. The TS state heightens to a stiffening feeling, such that my skin feels like a hardened casing and my joints feel as though they are becoming rigid. The intensity rises until it becomes so unpleasant and distracting that tics must be executed (with a compulsion that rivals the scratching of a severe itch).
>
> The reason that tics are only marginally effective in providing relief, however, is that unlike scratching an itch, tics do not make the hyperattention go away. Tics merely reset the TS state temporarily back to a baseline. Thus, tics are not themselves pleasant, but they do provide a temporary respite from the persistent hyperawareness. (p. 806)

The experience of TS, like the experience of any other disorder, is highly individualized. However, the attentional and obsessive-compulsive aspects of TS appear to be common themes in people's first-person accounts.

Special educators are likely to encounter students with TS because it is often comorbid with other disorders and because misunderstanding of TS often leads to stigma and social rejection or isolation. Effective intervention often requires involvement of the family and school as well as the student with TS (Riddle et al., 1988). A major aspect of the educator's role is understanding and communicating to others the nature of TS, ignoring the tics that cannot be controlled, and focusing on the student's capabilities.

SELECTIVE MUTISM

Children who are extremely reluctant to speak, although they know how to converse normally, are said to exhibit *selective mutism*—they choose to speak only to a certain individual or small groups of people and refuse to talk to all others. These children present a puzzling behavior problem to teachers (Dow et al., 1995; Hultquist, 1995).

Because the selectively mute youngster does not need to acquire normal speech but merely to learn to use speech under ordinary circumstances, remediation is often considerably easier than that of the mute or echolalic child. The selectively mute child is, at least to some degree, socially withdrawn, although he or she may be withdrawn only from adults or only from peers. Selective mutism may sometimes be a response to trauma or abuse (Jacobsen, 1995), but it appears to be a result of social anxiety in most cases, a specific fear of talking to certain individuals or groups of people (Black & Uhde, 1995). The causes of selective mutism are apparently diverse, however, and many children who exhibit this behavior have multiple behavior problems and dysfunctional families (Cunningham, Cataldo, Mallion, & Keyes, 1984; Hultquist, 1995). Nevertheless, parents may often assist in the assessment and treatment of selective mutism (Schill & Kratochwill, 1996). Psychopharmacological treatment may be an important adjunct of other interventions (Campbell & Cueva, 1995b).

As with other fears, social learning principles have been the basis for the most successful approaches to selective mutism. Strategies involve alteration of the demands or conditions under which the child is expected to speak, desensitization to the fear of speaking, and reinforcement for gradual approximations of speaking freely to the person(s) in whose presence the child has been mute. Selective mutism can be an extraordinarily challenging problem for teachers. It is important to work with other professionals, especially speech-language pathologists and those involved with the student's family. It is also important to implement a nonpunitive, behavioral approach to encouraging speech in the classroom and to realize that in many cases successful intervention requires long-term treatment (Dow et al., 1995; Harris, 1996; Hultquist, 1995).

EATING DISORDERS

Eating disorders receive much attention in the press, because the nation's affluence makes food a wastable commodity and because of the near obsession many people—particularly of high social status—have with slenderness (Boodman, 1995a; Mizes, 1995; Rodin, Striegel-Moore, & Silberstein, 1990; Siegel & Smith, 1991). Among eating disorders, **anorexia nervosa** (or simply *anorexia*), **bulimia** (sometimes called *bulimarexia* or *bulimia nervosa*), and obesity garner the most attention. These disorders are primarily, but not exclusively, problems of females, especially adolescent girls.

Anorexia (literally, loss of appetite) is a misnomer, for those with the disorder do not report absence of hunger, and the problem is clearly a refusal to eat a proper diet. Individuals with anorexia are obsessively concerned with losing weight and extremely anxious about getting fat. They starve themselves down to an abnormally low weight, often exercising compulsively as well as severely restricting caloric intake. They endanger their health, sometimes dying of self-starvation. Anorexia occurs most often in females (by a ratio of about ten to one), usually in the early adolescent to young adult age range.

Bulimia involves binge eating followed by behavior designed to offset the food intake, such as self-induced vomiting, using laxatives or enemas, or extra exercise. People with bulimia often try to keep their eating binges and related behavior a secret. They often feel depressed and unable to control their eating habits.

Despite public fascination with anorexia and bulimia and the relatively high estimates of prevalence of these disorders among high school and college females, we have relatively little understanding of the causes or effective treatment, especially when the onset of these disorders is in childhood (Lask & Bryant-Waugh, 1993). Researchers now recognize that the problems are multidimensional and require multimodal treatment approaches. The cultural ideal of thinness may be a factor in precipitating some cases of eating disorders (Adams et al., 1993). Family conflicts about eating and difficulty in communicating with other family members are known to be associated with adolescents' maladaptive attitudes toward food and eating (Eme & Danielak, 1995; Mueller et al., 1995). However, genetic predisposition to eating problems is increasingly recognized by researchers (Mizes, 1995). Behavioral analyses of causes and behavioral or cognitive-behavioral interventions have been encouraging in the short run, but long-term follow-up evaluations indicate the need for more comprehensive assessment and treatment approaches (Mizes, 1995). Effective intervention requires consideration of the eating behaviors themselves and the thoughts and feelings associated with anorexia and bulimia, plus the social environment in which the patterns have developed and are maintained.

Other eating disorders include **pica** (eating inedible substances such as paint, hair, cloth, or dirt), **rumination** (self-induced vomiting, which usually begins in infancy), highly exclusive food preferences, and obesity (Foreyt & Kondo, 1985; Johnson & Hinkle, 1993; Siegel & Smith, 1991; Werry, 1986c). These problems severely limit a child's social acceptability and endanger health.

Childhood and adolescent obesity is a growing problem in most Western cultures and carries significant health risks, usually results in a poor self-image, often contributes to poor social relations, and tends to persist into adulthood (Boodman, 1995a; Johnson & Hinkle, 1993). Obese children often pay a heavy price in social rejection or neglect. Although causes of obesity include genetic, physiological, and environmental factors, "the basic problem is a negative imbalance between calorific intake and energy expenditure, resulting in the storage of fat in adipose cells" (Spence, 1986, p. 447). Successful management of obesity therefore requires not only changing eating habits but increasing physical activity (Johnson & Hinkle, 1993). Obesity has often been thought to be caused by learning undesirable eating patterns, and poor nutritional habits undoubtedly play a critical role. However, the discovery in 1995 of a gene that controls obesity in mice spurred public perceptions that morbid obesity in humans is often caused by genetic factors (Weiss, 1995). It is important to remember that avoidance of obesity requires a combination of proper diet and exercise—a regimen harder for some than for others but possible for nearly everyone. Jose Caro, Chairman of the Department of Medicine at Thomas Jefferson Medical College, is quoted as saying, "Obesity is a disease . . . but it is exacerbated by a social and cultural environment that encourages consumption while minimizing physical exertion" (Weiss, 1996, p. 11).

Specific fear of obesity, but without all the characteristics of anorexia or bulimia, has been described by Pugliese, Lifshitz, Grad, Fort, and Marks-Katz (1983). They found that some children and youths restrict their caloric intake because of a specific fear of obesity and its alleged consequences, such as physical unattractiveness, poor health, and shortened life span. These children showed retardation in growth and delayed puberty as a result of their extremely limited diets but resumed normal eating patterns and recovered normal growth and sexual development following nutritional and psychiatric counseling. Mueller et al. (1995) noted that both those who are concerned about undereating and those concerned about overeating had poorer family relationships, lower self-concept, and lower levels of exercise compared to adolescents who did not have concerns about eating.

McCarthy (1990) notes that severe eating disorders, especially anorexia and bulimia, are related to societal influence.

> In countries in which food is scarce, most persons do not have the luxury of overeating to the point of obesity, or gaining attention through refusing to eat. In countries such as India and Sri Lanka, where food is scarce and obesity has traditionally been highly valued as a sign of wealth, extremely low rates of anorexia nervosa are manifested. Both obesity and anorexia nervosa are most common in more affluent countries of the Western hemisphere. (Leon & Dinklage, 1983, p. 271)

Special educators will often deal with students who have eating disorders. These disorders are not to be addressed by special educators alone, and teachers should not independently assume responsibility for eating problems. Students with anorexia and other eating disorders may display high levels of anxious or obsessive-compulsive behavior in the classroom. The role of special education in such disorders is to provide instruction and support for proper nutrition as needed and to work with other disciplines in managing students' food intake (Tate, 1993).

ELIMINATION DISORDERS

Attitudes toward toileting vary widely among cultures and within social groups. In Western culture, toilet training is considered very important and is generally begun at a young age. Although the extreme practice of beginning toilet training in the first few weeks of life is ill-advised, behavioral research shows that most children can be taught by 16 or 18 months (see O'Leary & Wilson, 1975). When children continue to wet or soil themselves after the age of 5 or 6 years, they are considered to have a problem that demands intervention. **Enuresis** may be either diurnal (wetting during waking hours) or nocturnal (bedwetting). About twice as many boys as girls are enuretic, and 2 or 3 percent of children are enuretic at age 14. At the time they begin first grade, approximately 13 to 20 percent of children are enuretic. **Encopresis**, or soiling, usually occurs during the day and is a rarer problem than enuresis.

Toilet training is usually a gradual process, and stress and illness have an effect on bowel and bladder control. Thus, the younger the child and the more stressful the circumstances, the more one can expect accidents to occur. Enuresis and encopresis are not matters of infrequent accidents; the child has a chronic problem, after the age at which children are expected to be continent of urine and feces, in retaining urine or feces and releasing it only in the toilet (Siegel, 1992; Siegel & Smith, 1991).

Psychodynamic ideas attribute enuresis and encopresis to underlying emotional conflicts, usually conflicts involving the family. Although these psychodynamic ideas are not supported by reliable evidence, family factors obviously play an important role if the family is inconsistent or unreasonable in toilet training. At the least, wetting and soiling can sour parent-child relationships regardless of the cause of the problem. Not many parents can face these problems with complete equanimity, and rare is the child who is completely unaffected by adults' reactions to misplaced excrement. Thus one must recognize that negative feelings about the problem often run high in families of children with elimination disorders. Treatment must be planned to avoid further parental anger and abuse of the child.

Enuresis is seldom the child's only problem; the child with enuresis often has other difficulties—perhaps stealing, overeating, or underachievement (cf. Siegel & Smith, 1991; Vivian, Fischel, & Liebert, 1986). Nearly all children with encopresis have multiple problems, often of a severe nature. Diurnal enuresis and encopresis at school are intolerable problems for teachers and result in peer rejection (cf. Walker & Rankin, 1983). Understandably, most youngsters with elimination disorders have low self-esteem.

In a few cases, elimination disorders have physiological causes that can be corrected by surgery or medication, but the vast majority of cases have no known anatomical defect, and medication is not particularly helpful. These disorders are in the vast majority of cases a matter of failure to learn how to control the bladder or bowel, and the effective methods of treating them involve habit training or practice. Intervention may thus involve training the child in urine retention, rapid awakening, and practice in toileting as well as reward for appropriate toileting or mild punishment for wetting. For many children, a urine alarm system in the bed or pants has successfully eliminated enuresis (cf. Mountjoy, Ruben, & Bradford, 1984; Taylor & Turner, 1975).

Although many approaches to enuresis have been tried and many behavioral techniques have been highly successful, no single approach has been successful for every child, and combinations of techniques are often used. Encopresis is sometimes treated by training children in biofeedback so that they learn to control their sphincters more deliberately. Those who soil themselves may be required to clean themselves rather than receive solicitous attention and cleaning from an adult. Selecting a successful technique depends on careful assessment of the individual case (Siegel, 1992; Siegel & Smith, 1991).

Special educators who work with students having more severe disorders are particularly likely to encounter those who have elimination disorders. These disorders can be extremely troublesome in school, making students unwelcome to adults and peers alike and becoming the central issue in behavior management. Special educators need to work with professionals from other disciplines, particularly psychology and social work, to address the problems created by elimination disorders in the classroom.

SEXUAL PROBLEMS

A wide variety of sexual behavior is of concern to parents, teachers, and other adults who manage children and youths (Graziano & Dorta, 1995; Rekers, 1985; Werry, 1986c; Zucker & Bradley, 1995). Promiscuous sexual conduct is often thought to connote moral misjudgment, and promiscuity is often involved in delinquency. Teenage pregnancy is a serious problem for teenagers and their children, as discussed in chapter 14. Dating and related heterosexual relationships are of great concern to teens and their adult caretakers. Sexual relationships and sexual behavior can be sources of enormous anxiety and obsessive-compulsive behavior for children and teens. Scarcely anyone condones exhibitionism, sadomasochism, incest, prostitution, fetishism, and sexual relations involving children, and these behaviors usually carry serious social penalties. American social mores do not condone all sex practices—some sexual behavior is clearly taboo. However, most people now recognize the wide variety of normal sexual expression that is a matter of preference or biological determination. Graziano and Dorta (1995) noted types of behavior that brings children and youths to therapy:

> Intense, excessive, and inappropriate masturbation (e.g., public), cross-sex dressing and other behavior, sexual promiscuity in young adolescents, homosexuality, and paraphilia (bizarre/perverted sexual behavior) are examples of sex-related child/youth problems treated in behavior therapy. Unlike most of the others listed, homosexuality in children is defined as a problem based largely on parents' personal values and whether the child or adolescent feels the homosexual urges are threatening. (pp. 174-175)

Autoerotic activity is not inherently maladaptive, although it is viewed as undesirable or prohibited by some religious groups. When carried to excess or done publicly, sexual self-stimulation is considered disordered behavior by nearly everyone. Although many or most teachers have observed children masturbating publicly, little research has been done on the problem of children's public masturbation, perhaps because masturbation has for so long been looked upon as evil (Hare, 1962; Stribling, 1842) and is still condemned by some religions.

Classifying gender-related behavior of any kind as a *disorder* raises serious questions of cultural bias and discrimination. The consensus is that *some* forms of sexual expression are deviant and should be prevented—incest, sexual sadism or masochism, and public masturbation, for example. Today, however, many people feel there is nothing deviant about other sex-related behaviors, such as preference for clothing styles, stereotypical masculine or feminine mannerisms, and homosexuality. Clothing styles and accepted sex roles have changed dramatically since about 1970. *Androgyny* (having the characteristics of both sexes) is apparent in many fashions and in role models. Problems related to sexual preference may be seen as primarily a matter of cultural or personal intolerance, so we must be sensitive to the possibility of cultural and personal bias in judging sex-related behavior, just as we must be aware of personal biases toward racial and ethnic identity. Nevertheless, *DSM-IV* defines *gender identity disorder* in which children or youths have a strong and persistent identification with the other sex (American Psychiatric Association, 1994). In children, gender identity disorder may be manifested by insistent desire to be the opposite sex, strong preference for or insistence on dressing like the other sex or adopting the opposite sex role, strong preference for playmates of the other sex, and persistent wishes to have the physical features of the opposite sex. If such characteristics cause significant distress or impairment of social functioning, then they may be considered a disorder (see Gordon & Schroeder, 1995; Zucker & Bradley, 1995).

Sexual behavior that involves intimidation, harassment, and other forms of aggression are, as noted in prior chapters, more accurately associated with conduct disorder and delinquency. However, many individuals who exhibit sexual aggression may experience high levels of anxiety as a comorbid condition.

Special educators, especially those who deal with adolescents, are certain to be confronted by students' sexual behavior and knowledge (or lack of it) that are of great concern. Maintaining an open mind about sexual preferences and alternative modes of sexual expression is important; so is an understanding of pathological behavior and the necessity of addressing it. Teachers must be ready to work with psychologists, psychiatrists, social workers, and other professionals in identifying and managing deviant sexual behavior (see Soutter, 1996).

SOCIAL ISOLATION AND INEPTITUDE

Social isolation may result from excessive behavior, such as hyperactivity or aggression, that drives others away, or it may result from deficiencies in behavior, such as lack of social initiative. Some socially isolated youngsters lack social approach skills, such as looking at, initiating conversation with, asking to play with, and appropriately touching their peers or adults. Usually, they also lack responsiveness to others' initiations of social contact. Others may be neglected by their peers for reasons that are not well understood. However, rejected, socially isolated children do not engage in the *social reciprocity* (exchange of mutual and equitable reinforcement between pairs of individuals) that is characteristic of normal social development. The isolated or neglected student usually lacks specific social skills for making and keeping friends and may be rejected by peers (see Asher & Coie, 1990; Wentzel & Asher, 1995).

Social isolation is not an all-or-nothing problem. All children and youths sometimes exhibit withdrawn behavior and are socially inept. This behavior may occur with any degree of severity, ranging along a continuum from a normal social reticence in new situations to the profound isolation of psychosis. In nearly any classroom, from preschool through adulthood, however, some individuals are distinguished by their lack of social interaction. Their social isolation is often accompanied by immature or inadequate behavior that makes them targets of ridicule or taunts. They are friendless loners who are apparently unable to avail themselves of the joy and satisfaction of social reciprocity. Unless their behavior and that of their peers can be changed, they are likely to remain isolated from close and frequent human contact and the attendant developmental advantages afforded by social interaction. Their prognosis, then, is not good without intensive intervention (McEvoy & Odom, 1987).

Causal Factors and Prevention

Social learning theory predicts that some children, particularly those who have not been taught appropriate social interaction skills and those who have been punished for attempts at social interaction, will be withdrawn. A mildly or moderately withdrawn youngster is likely to be anxious and have a low self-concept, but the conclusion that anxiety and low self-concept cause withdrawal and social isolation is not justifiable. It is more plausible that anxiety and low self-concept result from the child's lack of social competence.

Parental overrestrictiveness or social incompetence, lack of opportunity for social learning, and early rebuffs in social interaction with peers may contribute to a child's learning to play in isolation from others and to avoid social contact (Campbell, 1995). Parents who are socially obtuse are likely to have children whose social skills are not well developed, probably because socially awkward parents provide models of undesirable behavior and are unable to teach their children the skills that will help them become socially attractive (Putallaz & Heflin, 1990). Aversive social experiences, including abuse by parents or siblings, may indeed produce anxious children who have little self-confidence and evaluate themselves negatively. Anxiety and self-derogation may thereafter contribute to reticence in social situations and help to perpetuate social incompetence. Nevertheless, the child's temperamental characteristics, in combination with early socialization experiences and the nature of the current social environment, probably account for the development of social isolation (Kochanska, 1995). The social learning view of isolate behavior, which focuses on the factors of reinforcement, punishment, and imitation, carries direct implications for intervention and suggests ways to remediate isolation by teaching social skills (Cartledge & Milburn, 1995; Hops et al., 1985; Hundert, 1995; McConnell, 1987). Effective prevention of social isolation, however, involves more than teaching youngsters how to approach and respond to others; it requires arranging a social environment that is conducive to positive interactions.

Assessment

The definition of *social isolation* includes active rejection by peers or neglect of peers (Wentzel & Asher, 1995). Measurement of rejection and acceptance frequently includes use of a questionnaire or sociometric game that asks youngsters to choose or nominate classmates for various roles. Students may be asked to indicate which of their peers they would most like to play, sit, work, or party with, and with whom they would least like to interact. The results of this procedure are then analyzed to see which individuals have high social status in the group (to whom many peers are attracted), those who are isolates (not chosen as playfellows or workmates by anyone), and those who are rejected (with whom peers want to avoid social contact). More precise measurement of social interaction may be obtained by direct daily observation and recording of behavior. We can thus define *social isolates* as children who have a markedly lower number of social interactions than do their peers.

Sociometric status and direct measurement of social interactions, though both valuable in assessment, do not necessarily reveal what causes a youngster to experience social isolation. A student could, for example, have a relatively high rate of positive social interaction and still be a relative social isolate; his or her interactions might involve relatively few peers and be characterized by a superficial or artificial quality (Hundert, 1995; Walker, Colvin, & Ramsey, 1995). Consequently, assessment should also include teacher ratings and self-reports. Thus, adequate measurement of social skills or social isolation requires attention to the *rate* of interactive behaviors, *qualitative* aspects of social interaction, and children's *perceptions* of social status (see Cartledge & Milburn, 1995).

As social skills research becomes more sophisticated, the nuances of appropriate social interaction become more difficult to capture. Much of our knowledge about the nature of children's social skills is superficial. Children's social *intentions* (*why* as well as *what* they do) may be an important area to research; we may need to assess their pragmatic reasons for interacting with peers in specified ways to fully understand social isolation and social acceptance.

Intervention and Education

One approach to the problem of withdrawal is to try to improve the youngster's self-concept, on the assumption that this will result in a tendency to engage more often in social interactions. We can encourage children to express their feelings about their behavior and social relationships in play therapy or in therapeutic conversations with a warm, accepting adult. As they come to feel accepted and able to express their feelings openly, their self-concepts will presumably become more positive. The incidence of positive social interactions should then increase as well. Attempts to remediate social isolation without teaching specific social skills or manipulating the social environment are usually ineffectual, however. Few data show that self-concept can be improved without first improving behavior. If youngsters' appraisals of their own behavior are unrealistic, then bringing self-perceptions into line with reality is, to be sure, a worthy goal. If youngsters are indeed socially isolated, then attempting to convince them of their social adequacy without first helping them learn the skills for social reciprocity may be misleading. After their behavior has been improved, however, there is a foundation for improving self-image.

Arranging appropriate environmental conditions helps teach socially isolated youngsters to reciprocate positive behavior with their peers. Situations that are conducive to social interaction, that contain toys or equipment that promote social play, bring the isolated youngster into proximity with others who have social interaction skills or who require social interaction from the target child. Specific intervention strategies based on social learning principles include these:

- reinforcing social interaction (perhaps with praise, points, or tokens)
- providing peer models of social interaction
- providing training (models, instruction, rehearsal, and feedback) in specific social skills
- enlisting peer confederates to initiate social interactions and reinforce appropriate social responses

Of course, all four strategies may be used together, and experimental research shows the effectiveness of these procedures in modifying certain behaviors (Hops et al., 1985; Hundert, 1995; McConnell, 1987; Walker, Schwarz et al., 1994). A well tested intervention program for increasing withdrawn children's social interactions in kindergarten through third grade—PEERS (Procedures for Establishing Effective Relationship Skills)—includes this combination of strategies (Hops et al., 1978).

Social learning strategies for defining, measuring, and changing disabled youngsters' deficient social behavior show great promise. Nevertheless, current social skills training methods do not adequately address the problems of producing behavioral changes that actually make disabled children and youths more socially acceptable, that generalize across a variety of social situations, and that are maintained after intervention is terminated. As Strain et al. (1984) note, social skills involve *reciprocity*—an exchange of behavior between two people. Interventions that focus exclusively on changing the isolated individual's behavior miss that vital aspect of social adaptation—social interaction. The goal of intervention must be to help the socially isolated individual become enmeshed or entrapped in positive, reciprocal, self-perpetuating social exchanges, which can be done only by carefully choosing the target skills. One must select target skills with these questions in mind:

- Are the particular social behaviors likely to be maintained after intervention is terminated?
- Are the skills likely to generalize across different settings (such as in different areas of the school and during different types of activities)?
- Do the target skills relate to peers' social behavior, so that peer behavior prompts and reinforces performance of the skill (that is, are the skills part of naturally occurring, positive social interactions)?

If these questions generate affirmative answers, then social skills training is more likely to last (McConnell, 1987).

Perhaps the most promising approach is peer-mediated intervention that includes both the isolated youngster's behavior and that of peers. Twardosz, Nordquist, Simon, and Botkin (1983) and Sainato, Maheady, and Shook (1986) experimented with this approach. Twardosz et al. encouraged preschoolers and their teachers to engage in games and group activities in which affectionate behavior is demonstrated naturally. Socially isolated children were not singled out for treatment, but their social interaction increased following participation in the group affection activities. For example, 5-year-old Matthew had been diagnosed at various times as having learning disabilities, brain injury, and exhibiting autistic-like behavior. His peculiar and inappropriate behaviors caused his peers to avoid him. He did not like being touched and resisted other children's approaches with statements such as "I hate you," "Get away from me," and "Don't look." The intervention with group affection activities, conducted for 10 minutes each day, consisted of gradually more intimate and extended physical contact between Matthew and his peers and included nine other children and two teachers. Children were encouraged but not required to participate. The activities began with shaking hands and saying hello and progressed to clasping arms, hugging, and tickling. The affection training dramatically increased Matthew's interaction with his peers.

Sainato et al. (1986) explored the effects of serving as a classroom manager on the social interaction of withdrawn kindergartners. For example, a manager's "job" might consist of leading or directing the class in highly preferred activities such as directing the feeding of the class guinea pig, collecting milk money and taking lunch count, ringing the bell for clean-up time, and handing out the "keys" to the barber shop and shoe store areas. As class managers, the withdrawn children made more positive social initiations to their peers during free-play time, received more positive and fewer negative social bids from their peers, and were chosen more often as best friends by their peers.

Some children and youths are not social isolates but still do not fit in well with their peers and are hampered by inadequate social sensitivity or ineptness in delicate social situations. Children whose previous social experience is at odds with the majority of their peers, adolescents making their first approaches to members of the opposite sex, and adolescents interviewing for their first jobs are often quite tactless or unskilled in the social graces demanded for acceptance. Some individuals have irritating personal habits that detract from social adequacy. The results of social ineptitude may be negative self-image, anxiety, and withdrawal.

One can often eliminate or avoid bungling social behaviors by teaching important social cues and appropriate responses. Offering group and individual counseling, showing the youngster videotaped replays of his or her own behavior, modeling appropriate behavior, and providing guided practice (or some combination of these strategies) have been used to teach social skills (see Cartledge & Milburn, 1995; Hundert, 1995; Walker, Schwarz et al., 1994, for reviews). A social learning view of the origin and remediation of interpersonal ineptness is clearly a functional view for the special educator, for it implies that direct instruction is most effective.

The design of intervention strategies depends partly on the age of the student and the nature of the student's relationship to peers. Older students with a long history of socialization difficulties and victimization by peers may need a safe haven, such as a special school or class, in which to learn new skills. Pauline is an example.

Pauline

Pauline entered the school bedraggled. Tall and slender, she hobbled in more like a wounded crow than a graceful swan. This was Pauline's first day in a special school for students with emotional and behavioral difficulties. She was now 14 years old.

For the past 3 years in secondary school her life had been a story of daily trauma. Due to her height, she had very quickly become the butt of jokes among her peer group. The jokes led to bullying—verbal taunts and eventually physical attacks. Teachers tried to intervene, but always the hunting pack of students would seek out its prey, and Pauline would again fall victim to abuse from her peers.

Pauline changed from being an outward-going student of average ability, always eager to contribute in class. She became withdrawn, pale, shoulders hunched, frightened to speak or to be spoken to for fear of ridicule. When teachers unaware of the peer pressure she was suffering, urged her to play a more active role in class, she became distraught. School was no longer a safe place; Pauline began to play truant. When her parents discovered this, they forced her to attend school daily by taking her there themselves. This caused Pauline physical distress to the extent that she would vomit. Her peer group turned on her even more, barring her from entering the bathroom when she needed to be sick (pretending, if a teacher passed by, to be helping her).

Pauline's emotional state did not cause her to display aggressive behavior, but it certainly reflected a disturbed child who found her whole school environment disturbing and alien. Such was her mental state that she began to underachieve in all lessons. There were suggestions from teachers that she had specific learning difficulties. She was certainly suffering from curriculum malnourishment. The curriculum diet she was receiving was failing to give her any sustenance. She was failing to thrive in her school environment, merely existing as a lonely, hyper-anxious, vulnerable child. She had lost her dignity.

At the instigation of the educational psychologist, an alternative placement was sought in a special school for students with emotional and behavioral difficulties. As the weeks passed in the special school, Pauline began to make contact with the teachers. She would never speak in class, but after a lesson ended, she would hang around to discuss some point with the teacher. Teachers were soon convinced that she did not have any significant learning difficulty.

Her attendance was good. Gradually, the dreadful pallor began to fade; her eyes lost some of their traumatized glare. She eventually shared with the school counsellor the extent of her personal pain and anguish over the previous three years. She described it as "a daily nightmare." She had found the secondary school of 1,500 students totally disorientating. Once her peer group abandoned her, she described herself as "floating in a sea of people," none of whom she recognized, or who recognized her.

In the small special school of 40 students, Pauline found peace. She learned to trust again—first adults, and then fellow students. She became an active participant in classroom learning experiences, no longer the peripheral onlooker. Her capacity to care for others became clear, and she befriended many isolated individuals.

Her time at the special school was short. She left at the age of 16, and not all problems had been solved by far. Three years of lost education cannot be regained in two. New situations or change still caused Pauline anxiety. But when she left the school, she had a renewed sense of self-worth. This "restrictive environment" had been her safe haven; it had given her back her dignity. (Carpenter & Bovair, 1996, pp. 6–8)

SUMMARY

Grouping anxiety and related disorders for discussion is problematic because the disorders are loosely interrelated. Subcategories of anxiety disorders are not well defined, and anxiety disorders are frequently comorbid with a variety of other disorders.

Anxiety—uneasiness, fears, and worries—is part of normal development. However, extreme anxiety and fears (phobias) can be seriously debilitating. Anxiety disorders are generally more transient and are associated with lower risk for adulthood psychiatric disorder than are behaviors related to externalizing disorders. Excessive anxiety may characterize 2 to 5 percent of the child population and 20 to 30 percent of youngsters referred to clinics for behavior problems. Boys and girls are affected about equally. Anxiety disorders appear to have both social and biological causes and to be most amenable to social learning approaches to intervention, sometimes combined with medication.

Anxiety appears to play a significant role in a variety of related disorders. Obsessive-compulsive disorder involves ritualistic thinking or behavior intended to ward off feared events. It may take many forms and is potentially a serious detriment to school attendance and performance. Posttraumatic stress disorder (PTSD) is now recognized as a disorder of children and adolescents as well as adults. The anxiety and other problems associated with PTSD can seriously impede students' progress in school. Stereotyped movement disorders include *Tourette's syndrome* (TS), a disorder involving multiple motor and vocal tics and now recognized as a neurological problem. TS is often comorbid with other disorders and appears to be particularly closely associated with anxiety, attention disorders, and obsessive-compulsive disorders. *Selective mutism* is extreme, persistent anxiety about speaking in the presence of certain individuals. Intervention is typically designed to reduce anxiety in situations demanding speech. *Eating disorders* include anorexia, bulimia, and obesity, which often involve anxiety about food, eating, and body weight. *Elimination disorders* include enuresis and encopresis. These disorders are extremely problematic in school settings and must be resolved if children are to develop normal peer relations. *Sexual problems* are difficult to define due to societal attitudes toward sexual behavior. However, some types of sexual behavior, such as public masturbation, incest, and masochism, are clearly taboo.

Socially isolated children and youths do not have the social approach and response skills necessary to develop reciprocally reinforcing relationships. They may lack these skills because of inappropriate models of social behavior at home, inadequate instruction or opportunity to practice social skills, or other circumstances that inhibit social development. Intervention and prevention call for teaching social skills that are assumed important for social development, but there is a great deal of controversy concerning which are the most appropriate skills and the most effective instructional methods. In general, social skills training involves modeling, rehearsal, guided practice, and feedback, either for individual students or for groups. Peer-mediated interventions that alter both the socially isolated youngster's behaviors and those of peers in naturally occurring interactions may be the most effective strategies.

Case for Discussion

"Mirror, Mirror . . . "

Lisa

Lisa was fascinated with her reflection. If she happened to glance into a mirror or catch her image in a pane of glass, she stopped dead in her tracks. Like a moth attracted to the porch light, she would flutter her hands through her hair, totally self-absorbed. She placed no time limit on this narcissistic behavior and was often drawn back to her school routine only if I or another teacher intervened by moving her physically away from the looking glass.

When Lisa failed to make it to my fourth-grade class after lunch or recess, we could almost always track her down by the sound of her gentle singing in the girl's bathroom. Her voice was soft and clear, lilting and childlike in its innocence. She exhibited natural talent in both singing and dancing. Unfortunately, she would perform at any opportunity, which put off many classmates who might otherwise have appreciated her talents. Lisa readily agreed that she was quite an actress and stated emphatically that she wanted to be a star someday.

Lisa was conscientious though anxious about her academic work. She got good grades in and always completed all of her homework assignments, but her dependence on teachers' reassurances caused others to perceive her as "slow." Her frequent questioning and requests for my assistance, coupled with her bizarre "on-stage" performances, alienated her from her peers. Her peers' reactions caused her to alternate between sorrow and anger, and she often cried or made inappropriate comments to those with whom she had most wanted to be friends.

One day I had my class working in cooperative learning groups on math story problems. Lisa insisted on asking for my help rather than working with her group, and I could tell they were getting a little put out with her for coming to me all the time. I told her gently but firmly, "Lisa, you're supposed to work with your group on that. If you don't understand, ask one of the other students in your group."

Apparently Lisa tried to do what I told her, but in a manner that caused some of her peers to lash out at her. According to Naomi, one of the other girls in her group, "Lisa kept going, like, 'How do you know that's the way to do it? Are you *sure* that's right?' and then Kevin goes, 'Oh, shut up, Lisa! Why don't you just go fix your hair?' and then she runs over to look at her hair in the window and when she comes back Shirley goes, 'Oh, Lisa, you are sooo stuuupid!' and then she just ran out crying."

I found Lisa huddled under the school secretary's desk.

Questions About the Case

1. How would you describe the nature of Lisa's emotional and behavioral difficulties?

2. In what social skills do you think Lisa needs instruction most? Why? How would you teach those skills?

3. What social and academic difficulties do you see ahead for Lisa if her problems are not addressed effectively?

Unique Characteristic(s) or Need(s)	Present Level(s) of Performance	Special Education, Related Services, and Modifications	Annual Goal(s)	Objective(s) (Including Procedures, Criteria, and Schedule)
Lisa demonstrates inappropriately dependent behavior under normal school circumstances; fails to work independently when she can.	Lisa repeatedly asks for unnecessary assistance from her teacher on a daily basis, on average about 15 times per day.	1. Teach Lisa to discriminate necessary from unnecessary requests for assistance. 2. Encourage Lisa to re-read written directions before asking for help. 3. Ask Lisa to repeat oral directions when first delivered so that she does not ask for clarification. 4. Both the teacher and Lisa will record Lisa's unnecessary requests for assistance; plot data on a graph to monitor progress; provide rewards for improved performance.	Lisa will complete her assignments independently with minimal teacher assistance.	According to the teacher's and Lisa's self-recorded observations, Lisa will decrease inappropriate requests for teacher assistance to: a. 8 or fewer per day on average within 3 weeks b. 4 or fewer per day for at least 3 consecutive weeks within 3 months c. 1 or fewer per day for at least 4 consecutive weeks within 6 months

PERSONAL REFLECTIONS

Anxiety and Related Disorders

Jill Hahn-Jakulski, M.A., teaches middle school students with emotional and behavioral disorders in Herndon, Virginia.

Describe the school in which you teach and your role as a crisis teacher.

Herndon Center is a small, middle-school special education program in Fairfax County, Virginia, for students whose primary handicapping condition is significant emotional or behavioral disabilities. We currently serve 56 students. Academic classes in the Center have an average of 6 to 9 students. Each teacher has an instructional assistant. Elective classes include music therapy, art therapy, work awareness and transition (WAT), keyboarding, and technology. The Center is co-located with a regular middle school so that the educational experience can be as "normalized" as possible, providing mainstreaming opportunities into the middle school for those students for which it is appropriate. The expectation is that all students share the main cafeteria (5 different lunch periods), which adds opportunities for social interaction. In addition to the teaching staff, the Center also has a principal, crisis resolution teacher, psychologist, social worker, part-time guidance counselor, secretary, and health awareness monitor.

I work as the crisis resolution teacher (CRT) for the Center. The rationale for my position is that I am able to take the necessary amount of time to help students work through emotional turmoil so that they can return successfully to their classes. My room, known as the "quiet room," is centrally located in our small facility, making me very accessible to everyone. Students as well as teachers tend to view me as their primary resource and support in dealing with students who are demonstrating emotional and behavioral difficulties, which has shown how vital the CRT position can be in a program like ours.

Students are able to refer themselves to the quiet room when they feel a need for a time-out from their immediate environment or additional adult assistance in dealing with something that is upsetting to them. When the quiet room and my skills are used in this manner, I feel very good because the students are developing their ability to advocate for themselves and seek appropriate resolutions to their problems. Used in this way, students view the quiet room as a very positive and helpful environment. Students can also be referred to the quiet room by adults when they are engaging in inappropriate behaviors or are not responsive to adult cues.

Because aggressive and sometimes dangerous behaviors are often exhibited by the students, I carry a walky-talky, making verbal contact with me possible at all times. I frequently go into classrooms to mediate or remedy potentially volatile situations, provide proximity support, or direct students to the quiet room as a result of their actions. Their feelings for me aside, when referred to the quiet room against their wishes, students tend to view the resource negatively because they become so consumed with their own feelings of anger, sadness, or perception of unfairness and are unable to accept the logical cause-and-effect relationship between behavior and consequences.

Think of a particular student who exhibits severe anxiety. How did this student behave in the classroom at the beginning of the school year?

Sarah is a 14-year-old, eighth-grade student who, when I met her for the first time a year and a half ago, presented as an extremely timid, frightened little girl with few social skills. She was with her now-divorced parents, who are extremely limited in their cognitive and social capabilities. All three of them were at school for our summer open house. Because Herndon Center was a brand new school, we went "all out" at the open house—serving, among other things, fancy finger foods and cocktail shrimp. Sarah and her parents sat at an otherwise empty table, each with two plates of food—one with a little of everything, and another with nothing but shrimp, piled high enough that pieces tumbled to the floor as they carried them to their table. When the three of them were finished with that, they returned to the hors d'oeuvres area so they could each create a plate of deserts. They left only after wrapping in napkins handfuls of shrimp, which they placed in the two females' purses for safe-keeping.

During the initial days of school, I quickly learned that not only did Sarah have poor social skills, she was the most anxiety-stricken, self-conscious child I had ever met, with limited coping skills. Sarah was the sort of child who had pretty features, but because of the way that she carried herself she looked more homely than not. As she walked in her hunched-over posture, she frequently gazed left and right, not trusting her environment, adults, or peers to ensure her comfort and safety. When uncomfortable with a situation, she held one hand to the side of her face as if to shield herself from reality, as if to say, "If I don't see it, it isn't there, and I don't have to deal with it."

Coming from a home where little modeling or guidance was available for a blossoming teenager, Sarah quickly developed new interests in middle school—boys, makeup, socializing with peers, and so on—which seemed to ease her anxieties somewhat. Because she was so consumed with what were, to her, new and exciting facets of teenage life, she initially began to develop appropriate friendships with male and female peers and to exhibit disturbing signs of anxiety less frequently. However, her peers soon learned that Sarah was limited in her ability to function in what, to them, were routine social experiences. This resulted in Sarah's being left out and singled out with increasing frequency. By the fourth week of school, her anxieties were more evident than ever—the hunched-over posture, shielding herself from reality with her hand, and more.

Almost every event in her life that was not routine and rehearsed seemed to produce anxiety for Sarah. She became anxious about things that are trivial to most kids and needed constant supervision, guidance, and reassurance from the adults she trusted. Upon entering school, she often immediately sought out specific adults to discuss her worries or problems. These preoccupations included such things as her hairstyle, peers' perception of her, parental decisions, personal abilities, routine activities, and so on. Despite lengthy, concrete discussions, she had extreme difficulty dealing with daily events. She perseverated on everything that bothered her, unable to focus on what should have been priorities. Despite continual reassurance from adults, she was often lost in these thoughts and worries for hours at a time.

How did Sarah get along with and respond to peers?

As the school year progressed, Sarah maintained few stable friendships. In attempts to demonstrate an understanding for her uniqueness, peers tolerated Sarah and were less critical of her than they would have been in most circumstances. However, most who interacted with her did so with reluctance. Sarah tended to either be extremely possessive with peers or extremely volatile. She sought out those who were popular or pretty and would almost bow down to them in greeting when they would pass in the hall. She appeared mesmerized by them and took anything they said to her very seriously. She was elated when they simply said hello to her. Male peers were less tolerant of her, however. Sarah had extremely poor relationships with some, which frequently resulted in yelling, cursing, and threats of violence (by Sarah). So overcome by her emotions, she would sometimes actually hit them. Her self-consciousness and fragility were so evident that she could be manipulated by the boys, and Sarah would react accordingly. Unfortunately, because she wanted so desperately to be liked and popular, Sarah was on several occasions found in potentially compromising positions with boys.

Through time Sarah seems to have accepted the fact that she has few friends. She prefers to be by herself, when not with the few she trusts, and avoids interaction. Sarah has become her own best friend. She is no longer overly solicitous with her peers, although she is very reactive to positive or negative attention. Although she continues to try to shield herself from everyday situations that make her anxious, Sarah has made tremendous progress in that she is now responsive to short, intense adult intervention and makes courageous attempts to accept and follow through with her responsibilities as a student and a person. Sarah is a survivor, and probably always will be.

What strategies have you found most helpful in working with Sarah?

Through my experiences with Sarah, I have learned that I can often not completely satisfy her, no matter what I say or do, unless I allow her to literally avoid those situations that make her uncomfortable. If permitted to do so, she would sit and "explain" her problems to me all day, avoiding her responsibilities as a student. I am empathetic but demanding with Sarah.

Regardless of the situation, when I assess her needs I try to be as consistent as possible so that she is familiar with procedures. I first determine whether I think she can be quickly redirected and manage herself in class. Whenever possible, I attend to her needs while still in the classroom or in the hallway so she is unable to remove herself from the what or who that is causing her anxiety. I have been more successful in helping her regain focus when we talk in a location that is easily accessible to people rather than in my room or another secluded area where she can escape or becomes much less resilient. I validate her feelings while emphasizing the reality of the situation and her options, focusing on priorities. I am careful not to let her avoid the real problem; she is a master at manipulating conversations to further avoid facing her anxieties! Finally, taking into consideration all mitigating factors, I reiterate the immediate expectations of her as a student.

It is always my goal to help Sarah internalize the strategies and skills she needs to grow and develop socially. With the intensity of her anxiety, however, progress is very slow. Sarah's life is like a rollercoaster—many ups and downs. Although she at times demonstrates improvement, she is not consistent and progress sometimes seems nonexistent. Therefore, my colleagues and I continue to provide stability and consistency for Sarah, feeling the pain of her anxieties with her every day, every step of the way.

16

Depression and Suicidal Behavior

As you read this chapter, keep these guiding questions in mind:

- How does the federal definition of "seriously emotionally disturbed" include internalizing disorders and depression?

- To what extent is childhood depression like depression in adults?

- What are mood disorders, and how are they related to depression?

- What are the primary indications that a child or youth is depressed?

- How do comorbidity and the episodic nature of mood disorders complicate the assessment of depression?

- What are the major risk factors for depression?

- How might parents contribute to their children's depression, and how might children contribute to the parents' depressed feelings?

- What are the major theories or models of depression that guide intervention?

- Why is it difficult to define suicide and to estimate its prevalence?

- What is *parasuicide*, and why is attempted suicide hard to define?

- What is the relationship between age, gender, ethnicity, and suicide rates?

- What environmental factors are most clearly related to an elevated risk of suicidal behavior?

- Why are problems of false positives and false negatives so difficult to resolve in identifying students who are at risk for suicide?

- What risk factors indicate that an adolescent may be planning to attempt suicide?

- How can teachers help reduce suicide risk, and how should they manage students following a suicide threat or attempt?

One of the five distinguishing characteristics of children defined in federal regulations as having serious emotional disturbance is "a general, pervasive mood of unhappiness or depression" (see chapter 1). Just which youngsters federal officials meant to identify by this characteristic is not clear (cf. Duncan, Forness, & Hartsough, 1995; Forness, 1988). A general, pervasive mood of unhappiness or depression is more narrow and restrictive than the broad-band behavioral dimension *internalizing*, yet it does not correspond exactly with other, narrower dimensions, such as social withdrawal (see chapters 5 and 15). Neither is it consistent with the clinical criteria for major depressive episode but approximates a less severe condition referred to by clinicians as **dysthymia**. However, "depression and depressive (mood) disorders in children and adolescents may be viewed as prototypic internalizing disorders. Depression as a psychological disorder is replete with symptom characteristics that are internal to the individual" (Reynolds, 1992, p. 151). A reasonable conclusion is that the federal definition of seriously emotionally disturbed should be interpreted to include a wide range of internalizing disorders such as anxiety-withdrawal and clinical depression.

Depression has been relatively neglected in special education research, yet its close relationship to a variety of other disorders and to academic and social difficulties is now clear. It is recognized as an important disorder of childhood and adolescence that increases in prevalence with age, often coexists with other disorders, and is associated with long-term risks of mental illness and suicide (Pataki & Carlson, 1995). The relationship between depression and suicidal behavior—a concern of all educators, but especially those who work with psychologically disturbed students— makes these important related topics (Reynolds, 1992; Stark, 1990).

DEPRESSION

Definition and Prevalence

Depression has only recently become a topic of serious study in child psychopathology. Childhood depression has been a controversial topic for several decades. Controversy continues regarding its definition, assessment, and treatment. Traditional psychoanalytic theory suggests that depression cannot occur in childhood because psychological self-representation is not sufficiently developed. Some scholars suggest that children's depression is "masked" by other symptoms—expressed indirectly through symptoms such as enuresis, temper tantrums, hyperactivity, learning disabilities, truancy, and so on. However, most researchers now agree that depression in childhood parallels adult depression in many ways, but the specific types of behavior the depressed person exhibits will be developmentally age appropriate (Reynolds, 1992; Stark et al., 1995). Both children and adults can thus be characterized by depressed mood and loss of interest in productive activity, but adults may develop problems around work and marriage, while children may have academic problems and exhibit a variety of inappropriate conduct such as aggression, stealing, social withdrawal, and so forth.

The assumption that depression in childhood is similar to depression in adulthood is evident in *DSM-IV* (American Psychiatric Association, 1994). Depression is not listed among the disorders that are usually first diagnosed in infancy, childhood, or adolescence, but special notes on depression in children are included under the section on adults' mood disorders. To some extent, however, the assumption that depression is the same phenomenon in children and adults may be misleading (Rutter, 1991). We must remember that children are not merely scaled-down versions of adults, that childhood depression may be accompanied by other disorders (attention-deficit hyperactivity disorder, conduct disorder, anxiety disorders, learning disabilities, school failure, and so on), and that children's limited experience and cognitive capacity may give them perceptions of depression that differ from adults'.

Childhood depression was at one time looked upon as just a normal part of human development, an idea we now realize is erroneous. After the abnormality of childhood depression had been recognized, it was seen by some as the underlying problem behind all other childhood disorders, another view that clearly is not tenable (Reynolds, 1992). If aggression, hyperactivity, noncompliance, learning disabilities, school failure, and other problems of nearly any sort are all attributed to underlying depression in the absence of core features of depressed behavior (depressed mood, loss of interest in most or all normal activities), then depression becomes meaningless as a concept and diagnostic category. A more defensible perspective is that childhood depression is a serious disorder in its own right that may or may not be accompanied by other maladaptive behavior or be comorbid with other disorders.

Depression is part of a larger category of *mood disorders* delineated in *DSM-IV*. One's mood may be elevated or depressed, and mood disorders may involve different levels of severity of symptoms in both directions (or toward both poles). Depressed mood is characterized by **dysphoria**, feelings of unhappiness or unwellness not consistent with one's circumstances. In children and adolescents, dysphoria may be shown as irritability as well as by unhappiness. Elevated mood is characterized by the opposite—**euphoria**, a feeling of extraordinary and often unrealistic happiness or wellness. Dysphoric mood or irritability that lasts for a protracted period of time (a year or more for children and adolescents) but does not reach an intense level is called **dysthymia**. Euphoria and frenetic activity are known as **mania**. Some mood disorders are **unipolar**, such as depressive disorder in which mood varies between normal and extreme dysphoria (depression) or normal and extreme euphoria (mania). Others are **bipolar**, in which mood swings from one extreme to the other (*bipolar* has largely replaced earlier terminology, *manic-depressive*).

Although *DSM-IV* sets out detailed diagnostic criteria for the clinical diagnosis of various mood disorders in adults and makes notes regarding diagnosis in children and adolescents, considerable uncertainty remains about just how these criteria should apply to children and adolescents. The same general characteristics apply to adults and children, but the exact characterization of these disorders in children awaits much more research. Generally speaking, the symptoms one looks for in depression and related mood disorders in children and adolescents include the following:

- Anhedonia (inability to experience pleasure in all or nearly all activities)
- Depressed mood or general irritability
- Disturbance of appetite and significant weight gain or loss
- Disturbance of sleep (insomnia or hypersomnia)
- Psychomotor agitation or retardation
- Loss of energy, feelings of fatigue
- Feelings of worthlessness, self-reproach, excessive or inappropriate guilt, or hopelessness
- Diminished ability to think or concentrate, or indecisiveness
- Ideas of suicide, suicide threats or attempts, recurrent thoughts of death

These symptoms indicate depression only if several are exhibited over a protracted period of time and if they are not temporary, reasonable responses to life circumstances (e.g., a death in the family, as a consequence of which we would expect several symptoms associated with depression during a period of grieving). Stark et al. (1995) illustrate with the description of depression in a 10-year-old boy.

Bryan

Bryan is a 10-year-old boy who manifests many of the signs of childhood depression. He expresses sadness, social withdrawal, disinterest in sports, and increasing complaints of stomach aches. Over the past 10 weeks, Bryan has become increasingly disinterested in his studies. Although he continues to display excellent scores on standardized achievement tests, he has been receiving failing grades in many subject areas. His grades began deteriorating immediately after his father and mother separated. The separation resulted after a protracted period of conflict between his parents that ultimately included both verbal and physical aggression. During the interval that immediately preceded the separation, the parents admit to being preoccupied and had little inclination to interact with Bryan. Both parents have experienced depression in the past, and Bryan's mother is currently involved in therapy and receiving antidepressants. Bryan believes that he is at fault for his parents' separation and that there is little hope for a reconciliation between his parents. Although his father visits him on a weekly basis, Bryan is afraid that each visit is the last and that he will never see his father again. (Stark et al., 1995, p. 277)

Depression and other mood disorders tend to be episodic and of long duration. People tend to have repeated bouts with depression and related disorders, and those who have a major episode are at high risk for more (Harrington, 1993). Children and adolescents with long-standing depression (2 years or longer) have been found to have more significant impairments and greater anxiety, lower self-esteem, and to show more acting-out behavior (Dubois et al., 1995). Depressive behavior may result in peer rejection, particularly if it is exhibited under conditions of low stress and there is no apparent reason for depressive behavior (Little & Garber, 1995).

Unipolar depressive disorders affect a substantial percentage of children and adolescents, perhaps 2 to 5 percent. In prepubescent children, the prevalence of these disorders is about the same in boys and girls, but the female–male ratio widens beginning in early adolescence to become 2:1 in adulthood (Stark et al., 1995). Although there is still considerable uncertainty about the definition and diagnosis of many mood disorders, bipolar disorder is increasingly diagnosed in adolescents with major mental health problems and recognized as a topic needing research (Kafantaris, 1995). Also, the comorbidity of depressive disorders with other disorders, particularly conduct disorder and attention-deficit hyperactivity disorder, is increasingly recognized (Kovacs & Pollock, 1995; Reynolds, 1992; Stark et al., 1995).

Assessment

The diagnosis of depression and other mood disorders in children and adolescents is generally left to psychologists or psychiatrists. However, educators can play a key role in aiding the assessment of these disorders. Competent assessment requires a multimodal approach in which several sources of information are tapped: self-reports, parental reports, peer nominations, observation, and clinical interviews (Curry & Craighead, 1993; Kaslow & Rehm, 1991; Reynolds, 1992). A substantial number of devices are available for assessing depression, including rating scales and structured interviews (Merrell, 1994). However, the most important contribution of teachers to assessment may be careful observation of students' behavior that may reflect depression.

The types of behavior indicating possible depression include four categories of problems: affective, cognitive, motivational, and physiological. We may expect the depressed student to show depressed affect, to act unusually sad, lonely, and apathetic. Cognitive characteristics may include negative comments about oneself that indicate low self-esteem, excessive guilt, and pessimism. Depressed students often avoid demanding tasks and social experiences, show little interest in normal activities, and seem not to be motivated by ordinary or special consequences. Finally, depressed students often have physical complaints of fatigue or illness or problems in sleeping or eating. If a student exhibits such characteristics frequently for a period of weeks, the teacher should consider the possibility that the student is suffering from a mood disorder and refer him or her for evaluation. However, it is important not to overlook the possibility that other behaviors, such as general irritability or acting out, are also sometimes signs of depression, especially in children and adolescents. Difficulty in expressing anger appropriately is one characteristic associated with depression (Kashani et al., 1995), so a student's behavior might be thought mistakenly to reflect an externalizing disorder.

Comorbidity of depression with other disorders sometimes makes assessment particularly difficult, as does the episodic nature of mood disorders and the fact that an individual can have more than one mood disorder. If the student exhibits conduct disorder or attention-deficit hyperactivity disorder, for example, it may be easy to overlook indications of depression. When an individual is recovering a more normal mood after a depressive episode, it is easy to assume that the depression was not serious or that the risk of another episode is nil. If the student has a dysthymic disorder but is going through a major depressive episode, the low-grade depression may be misinterpreted as normal.

Causal Factors and Prevention

In most cases, we do not know exactly what causes depression. Some cases are evidently *endogenous* (a response to unknown genetic, biochemical, or other biological factors); other cases are apparently *reactive* (a response to environmental events, such as death of a loved one or academic failure). Predictably, child abuse, parental psychopathology, and family conflict and disorganization are frequently linked to children's depression. Rutter (1991) provides the following perspective on the question of cause:

> The concept of "cause" involves not one question but many. . . . For example, there is the "who" question; that is, the explanation for why Person A becomes depressed but Person B does not. Then there is the "when" question, that is, why Person A becomes depressed in this circumstance but not that one, or at this time but not that one. Alternatively, the "cause" question may be put in "how many" terms; that is, why do more 18-year-olds than 8-year-olds become depressed, or why does depression seem to be more prevalent now than it was a generation ago . . .? (p. 292)

Evidence is accumulating that there is a significant correlation between parents' depression and a variety of problems in their children, including depression (Kaslow & Rehm, 1991; Reynolds, 1992; Snyder & Huntley, 1990; Stark et al., 1995). This relationship undoubtedly reflects genetic influences on behavior. However, the fact that depression runs in families may reflect family interactions as well. Depressed parents may provide models of depressed behavior (which their children imitate), reinforce depressive behaviors in their children, or create a home environment that is conducive to depression (by setting unreasonable expectations, providing few rewards for achievement or initiative, emphasizing punishment, or providing non-contingent rewards and punishments). Depressed mothers are known to lack parenting skills, which could account for at least some of their children's behavioral and affective problems.

Substance abuse is often associated with depression. Depressed delinquents have been found more often to have a substance abuse disorder, along with other emotional and behavioral problems, than those who are not depressed (Riggs et al., 1995). Lewinsohn, Gotlib, and Seeley (1995) found that risk for both major depressive disorder and substance abuse disorder was elevated by current depressive symptoms, internalizing behavior problems (e.g., anxiety), poor coping (problem solving) skills, interpersonal conflict with parents, dissatisfaction with school grades, and externalizing behavior problems.

Educators should give special attention to the ways a student's depression may affect and be affected by school performance. Depression appears to be associated with lowered performance on some cognitive tasks, lowered self-esteem, lowered social competence, deficits in self-control, and a depressive attributional style in which children tend to believe that bad outcomes are a result of their own unmodifiable and global inadequacies (Gladstone & Kaslow, 1995; Reynolds, 1992; Stark, 1990). There is an inverse relationship between depressive symptoms and problem solving abilities: better problem solvers tend to show fewer depressive symptoms (Goodman, Gravitt, & Kaslow, 1995). These findings suggest that school failure and depression may be reciprocal causal factors: depression makes the student less competent and less confident, both academically and socially; failing academically and socially makes the student feel and act more depressed, and reinforces the attribution of failure to unalterable personal characteristics (Patterson & Capaldi, 1990). Depression and failure may thus become a vicious cycle that is hard to break. Evidence to date suggests that this cycle may often be a part of conduct disorder and, to a lesser extent, learning disabilities (Newcomer, Barenbaum, & Pearson, 1995).

Preventing depression is important because childhood depression, at least in its severe and chronic form, is linked to adult maladjustment and sometimes to suicidal behavior (Harrington, 1993). An accumulation of major stressful life events is an important factor in some youngsters' depression and suicide (Johnson, 1986; see also Goodman et al., 1995). However, more typical daily hassles can also put adolescents at risk for depression (Lewinsohn et al., 1995). Primary prevention may therefore involve efforts to reduce all manner of stressful life events for all children, but such broad-based, unfocused efforts are unlikely to receive much political or fiscal support. There is a better chance for support and success if efforts focus on relieving stress for abused and neglected youngsters and others whose lives are obviously extremely stressful. Another approach to primary prevention, somewhat more focused and feasible, is parenting training for depressed parents (Harris & Ammerman, 1987). Secondary and third-level prevention are still more focused and feasible, giving depressed youngsters behavioral or cognitive-behavioral training in overcoming their specific difficulties. This training is preventive in that it keeps the child's current situation from worsening and may forestall the development of long-term negative outcomes and recurrent episodes of depression.

Intervention and Education

Antidepressant drugs are often prescribed for childhood depression, although there has been inadequate research on their effectiveness and the side effects can be problematic (Campbell & Cueva, 1955b; Quintana & Birmaher, 1995; Reynolds, 1992). When medications are prescribed, teachers need to carefully monitor the effects on behavior and learning. As is the case in nearly every type of disorder, successful intervention requires collaborative, multimodal treatment involving a variety of professionals.

Teachers are most likely to be directly involved in interventions that are behavioral or cognitive-behavioral (Maag & Forness, 1991). These interventions are based on theories of depression that highlight the roles of social skills, productive and pleasurable activity, causal attributions, cognitive assertions, and self-control (see Kaslow & Rehm, 1991; Reynolds, 1992; Stark et al., 1995). Following are capsule summaries of four theories or models of depression and the focus of intervention strategies related to them:

■ Depressed individuals often appear to lack the social skills necessary to obtain reinforcement from their social environments. People may also become depressed because many of their primary activities, such as work, play, school, or homemaking, result in very little reinforcement. Consequently, they engage in fewer activities and obtain even less pleasure from them. Programs based on this theory teach social skills to help increase the depressed person's participation in a variety of pleasurable and rewarding activities.

■ Another theory is that depression is a form of learned helplessness. Depressed people have learned to attribute failure to highly predictable, global, internal factors. They do not seem to recognize that they are not responsible for all negative events or that they can change what will happen to them. Intervention therefore consists of strategies for changing the depressed person's causal attributions of success and failure.

■ A cognitive theory of depression suggests that depressed people have adopted a negative bias in their thinking and view themselves, the rest of the world, and the future in predominantly negative terms. They distort reality to make it conform to negative patterns of thinking that developed early in life. Intervention based on a cognitive theory consists of behavioral activities and cognitive exercises for changing the person's characteristically negative behavior and belief system.

■ Intervention may be based on a theory of self-control deficits. According to this theory, a depressed person has deficits in self-monitoring, self-evaluation, and self-reinforcement. He or she selectively attends to negative events and their immediate consequences, sets criteria for self-evaluation that are too stringent, makes inaccurate attributions of responsibility for his or her behavior, does not engage in enough self-reinforcement, and engages in too much self-criticism and self-punishment. Intervention consists of training in self-monitoring, self-evaluation, and self-reinforcement to make the person's interpretation of and response to events more realistic and gratifying.

Kaslow and Rehm (1985) provide case studies of children for whom various intervention strategies were chosen. Their descriptions of Jack, Yvette, Sandra, and Don provide a glimpse of the kinds of difficulties for which four types of intervention are appropriate. Jack's major problems appear to center around low levels of activity, partly because of social skills deficits. Consequently, his treatment consisted of programs to get him engaged in pleasurable, age-appropriate activities and teach him social skills that would help him relate to his peers. Yvette appears to have adopted an attributional style in which she blames herself for all kinds of misfortune, so her therapy focused on attribution retraining. Sandra was given cognitive therapy to help correct her distorted thinking about herself, and Don received self-control training to help him adopt more realistic goals and reinforce himself for reasonable accomplishments.

Behavioral Strategies: Jack

Jack, a nine-year-old male, was brought to the clinic by his parents. Data obtained at the initial evaluation revealed that Jack was feeling sad and lonely, he felt isolated from his peers, he did not enjoy any in-school activities, and he was not involved in much activity after school. Further, Jack stated that he was hesitant to approach other children and was reluctant to assert himself. Jack was a good student in school, although he was not feeling interested in his school work. No suicidal ideation was present. (Kaslow and Rehm, 1985, p. 622)

Helplessness Strategies: Yvette

Yvette, a 12-year-old female, was referred for a psychological evaluation by her pediatrician. She had recently been diagnosed as having juvenile onset diabetes and was feeling sad, helpless, and hopeless, was blaming herself for her physical problems, and was feeling like everything that went bad was her fault. She did not want to try to do anything at school or with her peers because she felt that nothing would turn out well for her. (Kaslow and Rehm, 1985, pp. 626–627)

Cognitive Strategies: Sandra

Sandra, a 13-year-old female, was referred for treatment by her school counselor. Her teachers were concerned that, despite the fact that she was performing adequately at school, she frequently made self-deprecatory comments. At the initial interview, Sandra acknowledged feeling sad. She stated that she did not like anything about herself—not her brains, her looks, or her personality. She felt as if things would never get better for her and that she was in a dark tunnel and there was no light at the end. When queried, she admitted to having thoughts about killing herself; however, she claimed that she would not do that because she did not have enough courage. (Kaslow and Rehm, 1985, p. 629)

Self-Control Strategies: Don

Don, an 11-year-old, was brought to the clinic by his mother who was concerned about his continued sad mood, which appeared to be in response to marital tension. Although Don was typically an above-average student, he was not doing well in school. He did not like doing anything anymore, and he spent his free time at home watching TV or napping. He frequently complained of stomachaches, which had no known etiology. At the interview, Don said very little, he appeared hypoactive, and he complained of feeling tired all of the time. He denied feeling sad. He did say that nothing good ever happened in his life, and he felt that he never got praised for anything he did. He stated the reason for staying at home was that he used to want to be a football player, but since he did not make his junior high school team, he had given up. (Kaslow and Rehm, 1985, p. 633)

Source: These four cases are from "Conceptualization, Assessment, and Treatment of Depression in Children" by Nadine J. Kaslow and Lynn P. Rehm, in P. H. Bornstein and Alan E. Kazdin (Eds.), *Handbook of Clinical Behavior Therapy with Children*. ©1985 by The Dorsey Press, Homewood, IL. Reprinted by permission.

Kaslow and Rehm (1991) outlined a general decision-making model for approaching the treatment of depression. First, if a student appears to be depressed, it is important to ask whether there are associated disorders. If so, then interventions should be implemented to address them first, as depression might be relieved if the other disorders are ameliorated; if not, then intervention for depression is necessary. In designing interventions for depression, Kaslow and Rehm suggest assessing the student's problems in the following order and providing intervention if significant problems of that type are found:

1. deficiencies in social skills
2. low activity level
3. distorted self-monitoring
4. low self-esteem
5. depressive attributional style
6. low self-reinforcement

In their schema, the priority for assessment and intervention is social skills and the second target for intervention is activity level. Teachers can be extremely helpful, if not the key players, in implementing both of these strategies.

SUICIDAL BEHAVIOR

Definition and Prevalence

The definition of *completed suicide* is straightforward: to kill oneself intentionally. However, determining that a death was a suicide is often difficult because the circumstances, particularly the intentions of the deceased, are in question. However, estimates of the prevalence of deaths ruled as suicide are reliable (Shaffer & Hicks, 1994). Suicide is socially stigmatizing, so the label *suicide* is likely to be avoided if death can be attributed to accident. Accidents are the leading cause of death among adolescents in the 15 to 24 age bracket, and many researchers suspect that, in this age group, many deaths attributed to accident are disguised or misreported suicides (e.g., Guetzloe, 1991; Hawton, 1986; Poland, 1989). Others have found little support for underreporting (Shaffer & Hicks, 1994).

The term **parasuicide** sometimes refers to unsuccessful or uncompleted suicidal behavior. *Attempted suicide* is difficult to define because studies often differ in distinctions between suicidal gestures (suicidal behavior that is interpreted as not "serious" in intent), thoughts of suicide, threats of suicide, and self-inflicted injury requiring medical treatment. There is no precise, commonly accepted definition of *suicide attempt* (Shaffer & Hicks, 1994).

Regardless how we define them, suicide and suicide attempts of adolescents, and to a lesser extent younger children, have increased dramatically during the past several decades (cf. Shaffer & Hicks, 1994). Only accidents and homicides are more often the cause of death among youths between the ages of 15 and 24. Suicidal behavior among children and adolescents is a major public health problem, not only in this country but in many countries of the world (cf. Kerfoot, Harrington, & Dyer, 1995; Marttunen et al., 1995; Shaffer & Hicks, 1994). Adolescent males have a higher suicide rate than females, and this sex difference becomes more marked with age. Among older adolescents and young adults, parasuicides are more common for females than for males. Among children the sex difference is reversed, with suicide attempts more common for boys than for girls. In the U.S., until recently black males have had significantly lower suicide rates than white males; rates for Native American youths are higher than rates for whites (Wyche & Rotheram-Borus, 1990). However, suicide rates for black males have increased markedly since 1986, and it may no longer be accurate to say that black males are at lower risk of suicide than white males (Shaffer, Gould, & Hicks, 1994). Suicide rates are higher for married than for unmarried teenagers. Suicide methods appear to relate to the availability of means; firearms are more commonly used in the U.S. than in most other countries (Hawton, 1986).

Although suicide is rarely reported in children under 10 years and is relatively infrequent even in prepubertal children (Shaffer & Hicks, 1994; Smith, 1992), we do occasionally encounter reports of suicide attempts and successful suicides of very young children (e.g., Rosenthal & Rosenthal, 1984). However, rising suicidal behavior among young people and the high rate at which children and youths kill or attempt to kill themselves are alarming. "It appears . . . that by late adolescence, teenagers' tendency toward self-destructiveness has mushroomed from a rare event to a phenomenon that is at least passingly considered by most teens and is acted on by 1 out of 12 of them" (Smith, 1992, p. 257). Greater understanding of the causes and more effective prevention programs must be priorities. We also need better means of dealing with suicidal individuals after an attempted suicide, and with survivors after a completed suicide.

Causal Factors and Prevention

Most authorities agree that biological and nonbiological factors interact in complex ways in the causation of suicide and depression. There appear to be genetic and other physiological contributions to depressive behavior, as noted earlier, and these factors may increase risk for suicidal behavior as well. However, educators focus primarily on the environmental factors involved. The many complex factors that contribute to children's and adolescents' suicidal behavior include major psychiatric problems, feelings of hopelessness, impulsivity, naive concepts of death, substance abuse, social isolation, abuse and neglect by parents, family conflict and disorganization, a family history of suicide and parasuicide, and cultural factors, including stress caused by the educational system and attention to suicide in the mass media. Youths with emotional or behavioral disorders, especially those who use alcohol or illicit drugs, are at particularly high risk of suicidal behavior (Bryant et al., 1995).

The common thread among all causal factors, Sheras (1983) feels, is that suicidal individuals believe they have little impact on the world around them: "They have no means of gaining acknowledgement of their very existence. In short, they feel invisible" (p. 774). They often do not know that help is available for dealing with their problems, believing that no one cares and that they must deal with their problems alone. Gulp, Clyman, and Culp (1995) studied 220 students in grades 6 through 12. Nearly half of those who reported feelings of depression did not ask for help, most often because they did not know about services available to them in the school or, if they did, believed they had to take care of their problems by themselves. Feelings of loneliness and, especially, hopelessness appear to be among the best predictors of suicidal thoughts and intentions (Levy, Jurkovic, & Spirito, 1995).

Hopelessness has long been recognized as a primary characteristic of the thinking of those prone to suicide (Dwyer & Kreitman, 1984; Kazdin, French, Unis, Esveldt-Dawson, & Sherick, 1983; Pfeffer, 1984). Hopelessness and intent to commit suicide correlate more highly than depression and suicide intent. Apparently, all individuals who feel hopeless are depressed, but not all who are depressed feel hopeless. Those who feel hopeless are convinced that things will not get better, cannot get better, so they might as well give up hope. Hopelessness may represent the final stage of depression that tends to precede suicidal intent, the stage at which an individual concludes that suicide is justified (Dwyer & Kreitman, 1984; Guetzloe, 1989; Sheras, 1983). Hopelessness and alienation justify the act of ultimate withdrawal from the world.

Many children and adolescents who commit suicide or parasuicide have a history of emotional or behavioral disorders and school failure (Bryant et al., 1995; Guetzloe, 1991; Miller, 1994; Rotheram, 1987). In fact, school performance of adolescents who show suicidal behavior is almost uniformly poor, and a large proportion of teenagers' suicides and parasuicides occurs in the spring months, when school problems (grades, graduation, college admission) are highlighted.

Other factors increasing the likelihood of suicide attempts include high levels of stress related to parents (e.g., having been physically hurt by a parent, running away, living apart from both parents), sexuality (e.g., concerns regarding pregnancy, sexually transmitted diseases, and pressure to become sexually active), police contacts, and lack of adult support outside the home (Wagner, Cole, & Schwartzman, 1995). Some have suspected that social stress related to homosexuality is a factor in suicide, but research has found no reliable connection between sexual orientation and suicide (Shaffer et al., 1995). Unsurprisingly, suicidal behavior appears to be learned, at least in part, through observation of the behavior of others in family and social contexts. Families that do not form emotional bonds and parents whose discipline style is chaotic are also factors increasing risk for suicidal behavior (Bush & Pargament, 1995). Outbreaks of suicide attempts are particularly likely to occur in institutional settings and psychiatric hospitals, probably partly as a result of imitation or competitive bids for attention and status.

Ordinarily, we think of depression as the primary disorder associated with suicidal behavior. However, the role of aggressive behavior is increasingly recognized. Apter et al. (1995) found that aggression may be as important as depression in some kinds of suicidal behavior of adolescents. They hypothesized that there may be two kinds of suicidal behavior in adolescence: one reflecting the wish to die, which is related primarily to depression; another reflecting the wish not to be here for a time, which is associated with poor impulse control, aggressive behavior, and conduct disorder.

Primary suicide prevention presents enormous problems of identifying individuals who are at risk, because in any attempt to make predictions, the number of false positives is extremely high and the consequences of false negatives are extremely severe. Because only a relatively small percentage of the population commits or attempts suicide, and because suicidal and nonsuicidal individuals have many common characteristics, any general screening procedure turns up many false positives—individuals who are not actually at high risk. But the consequence of identifying as "not at risk" those who are in fact likely to attempt or commit suicide (the false negatives) are obviously grim. Consequently, most primary prevention programs are aimed at entire school populations.

Eisenberg (1984) believes there are three major preventive measures:

1. limiting access to devices often used in impulsive self-destruction (as through enacting effective gun control)

2. limiting the publicity given to suicides, because extensive publicity is almost always followed by a sharp increase in suicidal acts

3. improving early detection of depression in children and youths

So far, American society has not made guns any less accessible, has placed no controls on publicity about suicides, and has done virtually nothing to improve early detection and intervention in childhood and adolescent depression.

Assessment

Suicidal behavior is not always preceded by recognizable signals, although some characteristics and circumstances are danger signals for which educators and other adults should be on the lookout. Adults' and peers' awareness of indications that a child or youth might be at risk for suicidal behavior is an important aspect of assessing the general school population (Guetzloe, 1989, 1991; Poland, 1989; Underwood, 1987). These are some indications of risk in the general school population:

- sudden changes in usual behavior or affect
- serious academic, social, or disciplinary problems at school
- family or home problems, including parental separation or divorce or child abuse
- disturbed or disrupted peer relations, including peer rejection and breakup of romantic relationships
- health problems, such as insomnia, loss of appetite, sudden weight change, and so on
- substance abuse
- giving away possessions or talk of not being present in the future
- talk of suicide or presence of a suicide plan
- situational crisis such as death of a family member or close friend, pregnancy or abortion, legal arrest, loss of employment of self or family member

Part of any assessment of risk involves systematic evaluation of the characteristics of individuals who are thought to be at higher than usual risk. A personal characteristic associated with most suicides, parasuicides, and thoughts of suicide is depression, so it is important to assess depression. However, depression may be accompanied by aggressive behavior, conduct disorder, or a variety of other problems.

Rotheram (1987) suggests procedures for evaluating imminent danger of suicide. These consist of an initial 10-minute interview in which statistically based risk factors are considered: male sex, past attempts with methods other than ingestion, more than one previous attempt, history of antisocial behavior, close friend or family member committed suicide, frequent drug and alcohol use, depression, incompatible social environment. If five or more of these indicators are present, then the youngster is judged to be potentially in imminent danger of suicide; if two or more are present, or if it is found that the youth has current ideas or plans of suicide, the next step in evaluation is recommended. The second phase requires about 20 to 30 minutes and evaluates the youngster's ability to behave in a nonsuicidal manner as demonstrated in four ways:

- ability to make a written promise not to engage in suicidal behavior for a specified period of time, such as 2 weeks
- ability to deliver compliments to self and others, which is inconsistent with a pessimistic and hopeless outlook

- capacity to assess feelings by rating own feelings, including those associated with emotional discomfort and suicidal ideation

- capacity to plan ahead for suicidal situations, including specific steps for coping with threatening circumstances

Rotheram (1987) notes that "In practice, most youths are able to accomplish all of the tasks outlined or none of them. Failure to perform these tasks is a behavioral indication of imminent danger: coping skills to ward off suicidal tendencies are not available" (p. 108).

Intervention and Education

Sheras (1983) suggested three general considerations for responding to the suicidal child or adolescent. They remain sound recommendations. Adults should do the following things:

- Take all suicide threats and attempts seriously.

- Seek to reestablish communication.

- Provide emotional support or sustenance that relieves alienation.

Although dealing adequately with the problem of suicidal behavior requires a complex, multifaceted effort, the general notion is that the suicidal individual must be helped to establish and maintain as many points of contact as possible with significant others, including adults and peers. The child or adolescent must be shown unself-destructive ways to solve problems and get attention from others. Teachers can aid in suicide preventions by realizing that they can identify students who are at risk; school systems can play a part in prevention by providing curricula that acquaint students with others' experience of normal physical and social development (Guetzloe, 1991; Poland, 1989; Underwood, 1987).

The educator's role in intervention is primarily to provide information about suicide and refer students who appear at risk to other professionals. A comprehensive program of suicide awareness and prevention has several parts: administrative guidelines specifying school policy, faculty inservice to obtain support of teachers and provide them with basic information and skills in dealing with students, and curricular programs for students (Underwood, 1987). In addition, hotlines, peer counseling, and programs designed to reduce and manage stress may be implemented (Guetzloe, 1989). Figure 16.1 shows a wallet-sized card that is printed on both sides and folds in the middle. Prepared by a guidance counselor, it addresses adolescents in plain language, without technical jargon, but is also appropriate for adults. Its convenient size makes it more likely to be kept and used than would a sheet of paper.

Managing children and adolescents following their suicide attempts or threats is the joint responsibility of counselors or other mental health personnel and teachers. Although teachers should not attempt to offer counseling or therapy themselves, they can provide critical support by encouraging students and families to obtain help

MYTHS AND FACTS ABOUT SUICIDE

- It is a **myth** that talking to someone about suicidal feelings will cause them to commit suicide.
  Fact: Asking someone about their suicidal feelings may make the person feel relieved that someone finally recognized their emotional pain.

- It is a **myth** that all suicidal people want to die and there is nothing that can be done about it.
  Fact: Most suicidal people are ambivalent, that is, part of them is saying: **"I want to live."**

- It is a **myth** that people who talk about committing suicide never actually do it.
  Fact: When someone talks about committing suicide, he/she may be giving a warning that should not be ignored by others who hear such comments.

- It is a **myth** that there is a "typical" type of person who commits suicide.
  Fact: The potential for suicide exists in all of us. There is no "typical" type of suicidal person.

- It is a **myth** that suicide occurs without warning.
  Fact: Many people, including adolescents, give warning of their suicidal intent.

LIFELINES

St. Clare's Hospital Department of Consultation & Education

ADOLESCENT SUICIDE

WHY?

The suicidal person feels a tremendous sense of loneliness, isolation, helplessness and hopelessness. For the young person these feelings may be caused by family conflicts, a divorce or separation, the death of a parent, the break-up of a romance, the move to a new school or pressure to succeed at school.

Suicidal people feel that they can no longer cope with their problems and that suicide may be the only way out. Most people think about suicide at some point in their life. Most people find that these thoughts are temporary and that things do get better. Suicide is a needless and permanent solution to short-term problems.

Figure 16.1
St. Clare's "Lifelines" Card
Source: The author gratefully acknowledges John Kalafat, Ph.D., Department of Education, St. Clare's Riverside Medical Center, Denville, NJ 07834, for giving permission to reproduce the card.

SOME SIGNS OF SUICIDE

Often people who are contemplating ending their lives will give signs or signals of their intent. One sign alone does not mean that a person is suicidal. Several signs at one time, however, may mean that the person is seeking help. A few of these signs are:

- Verbal suicide threats.
- Previous suicide attempts.
- Personality changes (unusual withdrawal, aggression or moodiness).
- Depression (changes in normal appetite, sleep disturbances, sudden drop in school performance, etc.)
- Final arrangements (making a will, giving away prized possessions.)

When you suspect that a friend or a family member may be suicidal, you may become nervous and anxious. This is a normal feeling. It may help if you remember the following:

WHAT NOT TO DO

Do not allow yourself to be sworn to secrecy by the suicidal person. You may lose a friendship but you may save a life.

Do not leave the person alone if you believe the risk for suicide is immediate.

Do not act shocked at what the person tells you.

Do not counsel the person yourself.

Do not debate whether suicide is right or wrong. This may make the person feel more guilty.

WHAT TO DO

Believe or trust your suspicions that the person may be self-destructive.

Communicate your concern for the well-being of the person. Be an active listener and show your support.

Be direct. Talk openly and freely and ask direct questions about the person's intentions. Try to determine if the person has a plan for suicide (how, where, when). The more detailed the plan, the greater the risk.

Get professional help. Encourage the person to seek help from a school counselor, minister, or someone who would know what else to do. If the person resists, you should get help for them anyway.

MORRIS COUNTY
24 HOUR CRISIS PHONE LINES

Contact Morris/Passaic	831-1870
St. Clare's Hospital	625-0280
Morristown Memorial Hospital	540-5045
Pequannock Valley Mental Health Center	
	839-0770

HOSPITAL EMERGENCY SERVICES

St.Clare's Hospital	625-6063
Morristown Memorial Hospital	540-5004
Dover General Hospital	989-3200
Chilton Memorial Hospital	831-5000

POISON CONTROL CENTER
800-962-1253

LOCAL POLICE
Inside cover of phone directory or 911.

Figure 16.1,
continued

from qualified counselors or therapists. Teachers can also help by reducing unnecessary stress on students and being willing and empathic listeners.

Schools need to work out plans for dealing with the aftermath of a student's suicide. The plan should be suited to the needs of students and faculty of the particular school, but the procedures must be designed to avoid contagion. Peers of the student who died may be at risk for emulating the suicide, especially if they were close friends or were depressed at the time of the suicide.

School-based intervention and prevention programs can inadvertently increase suicide risk. By focusing too much attention on suicide, particularly if suicidal behavior is glamorized or glorified, students may be more rather than less inclined to engage in this behavior. If the program dispenses information that is not simple, factual, and practical, it is not likely to decrease suicide risk. And if school personnel and professionals in community agencies are not able and willing to follow through with appropriate support and services to students who seek help for themselves and their friends, the information provided in an educational program will be useless or worse.

SUMMARY

The federal definition of *seriously emotionally disturbed* suggests that youngsters with internalizing problems, including depression, should be eligible for special education, although the definition describes depression and related disorders ambiguously. Childhood depression has only recently become a topic of serious research. Consensus is emerging that depression is a major disorder of childhood that parallels adult depression in many respects, but particular behaviors exhibited in response to depressed affect will be developmentally age-appropriate. Both adults and children who are depressed experience depressed moods and lose interest in productive activity. Depressed children may exhibit a variety of inappropriate behavior, and depression is often comorbid with other conditions.

Depression is part of the larger category of mood disorders, which includes unipolar and bipolar disorders involving elevated or depressed mood. Indications of depression include anhedonia, depressed mood or irritability, disturbances of sleep or appetite, psychomotor agitation or retardation, loss of energy or fatigue, feelings of self-derogation or hopelessness, difficulty thinking or concentrating, and suicidal ideation or attempts. Several of these symptoms are exhibited for a protracted period and are not a reasonable response to life events. Prevalence of depression is higher among older adolescents than young children, and girls are more affected at older ages. Depression may be found in 2 to 5 percent of the child population.

Assessment of depression must be multifaceted and should include self-reports, parental reports, peer nominations, observations, and clinical interviews. The judgments of teachers should not be overlooked. Teachers should be on the lookout for four categories of problems: affective, cognitive, motivational, and physiological.

Some cases of depression clearly result from unknown biological factors, but the causal factors in most cases are indeterminable. In some cases, depression represents a reaction to stressful or traumatic environmental events. We find significant correlations between parents' depression and problems of their children, including depression. Educators should give special attention to how depression and school failure can be reciprocal causal factors. Prevention of depression is important because severe, chronic depression is associated with adult maladjustment and suicidal behavior. Prevention may involve reducing stress, training in parenting, or teaching specific cognitive or behavioral skills.

Antidepressant drugs may be useful in some cases of depression, but their effects and side effects should be monitored carefully. Interventions are based on theories that attribute depression to inadequate social skills, maladaptive thought patterns, and lack of self-control. Selecting intervention strategies depends on analyzing the depressed individual's specific cognitive and social characteristics. Teachers can play a major role in teaching social skills and engaging students in higher levels of productive activities as well as assisting in other approaches.

Suicide and suicidal behavior (parasuicide) of children and youths, especially of adolescents and young adults, have increased dramatically in the past several decades. Factors increasing the risk of suicidal behavior include biological and environmental factors, especially a history of difficulty or failure in school, stress related to family dysfunction or abuse, substance abuse, family members or acquaintances who have completed suicide, depression and feelings of hopelessness, and aggressive behavior.

Prevention of suicide is extremely difficult because of the problems associated with false positives and false negatives. Prevention programs are typically aimed at entire school populations and consist of guidelines for teaching, inservice for teachers, and instructional programs for students and parents. Assessment of suicide risk involves recognizing danger signals and evaluating the individual's sense of hopelessness. Evaluation of statistically based risk factors and the student's ability to perform specific coping tasks are required to determine whether a suicide attempt is imminent.

Teachers and other adults should take all suicide threats and attempts seriously, seek to reestablish communication with students who feel alienated and help them establish as many points of contact as possible with significant others, and provide emotional sustenance and support. Schools should have a plan for follow-up intervention when a suicide occurs but must be careful in implementing prevention and intervention programs so that suicide risk is not inadvertently increased.

Case for Discussion

"Tell My Friends to Visit Me" Katherine

I knew that Lyle Byrd was exhausted as she walked into the teacher's lounge yesterday after a long day with Katherine.

"It's like being sucked into a black hole!" she reported to those of us trying to get ready to go home. "She sucks every ounce of energy out of me. She uses up her share of my attention and then she takes all the other students' shares as well. But I don't dare ignore her! What in the world do I do now?"

Lyle's dilemma was created by Katherine's self-destructive behavior. All appeared to be going well with Katherine, but then we discovered that at home Katherine had slashed her arms and wrists with a razor. Katherine appeared to be making friends in school, then turned them away by her bizarre dress, actions, and comments. When Katherine felt someone else was receiving too much attention, she would bully her way onto the social scene by some outrageous act or statement that demanded a response from her peers and any available adult. Two weeks ago, for example, one of Katherine's classmates, 13-year-old Jackie, was receiving considerable attention because she had begun dating a 18-year-old—"an older man," in her words. Katherine then reported that she was pregnant and began feigning morning sickness. We were able to establish within a few days that she wasn't pregnant, but not without a huge bonanza of attention for Katherine.

And today Katherine had brought her amazing school performances to a climax at 1:30 by announcing to me, the principal, that she had just consumed dozens of pills, which, of course, necessitated her immediate hospitalization. You can't hear a student report that she has swallowed a life-threatening bunch of pills and not take it seriously unless you are *absolutely certain* that it's a hoax. Katherine had been out of our sight just enough to make her claim plausible, especially in the light of her previous wrist-slashing.

As the school principal, I went to the hospital to await the arrival of her mother. Katherine had taken some pills all right, though we'll never know for certain how many of what kind. To be on the safe side, the hospital staff had suctioned her stomach and was keeping her under observation, at least overnight.

Her mother and I sat quietly on the hospital bed watching the tears stream down Katherine's face when she realized that none of her classmates would be coming to fawn over her. Her desperate attempt to seize center stage was playing itself out in this lonely, silent room with starched linens that held little comfort or warmth through the night. Katherine's mother stared out the window with tired eyes, knowing that this was not yet the culminating act that would turn Katherine's life around. With twisted emotions wrenching her heart, she gave thanks that Katherine would live into her fourteenth year. She turned to kiss her daughter's forehead. Their parting words were unforgettable.

"I'll see you in the morning, sweetie. I have to go do my night shift now."

"Hey, Mom, make sure you call my friends and tell them to come see me."

Questions About the Case

1. Given what you know about adolescent suicide, how should Lyle and her colleagues respond to Katherine's suicidal behavior?

2. What clues in this case do you find, if any, suggesting that Katherine is depressed?

3. Were you Lyle Byrd, on what would you focus Katherine's instruction?

Unique Characteristic(s) or Need(s)	Present Level(s) of Performance	Special Education, Related Services, and Modifications	Annual Goal(s)	Objective(s) (Including Procedures, Criteria, and Schedule)
Katherine seeks attention through dangerous and inappropriate activities.	Katherine engages in extremely inappropriate, attention-seeking behavior, such as self-injury, suicidal behavior, or bizarre behavior, at least 5 times per school week.	Focus on social skills training and positive reinforcement of appropriate attention-seeking, including: 1. daily point sheets with individual academic and social goals 2. social skills training with emphasis on how to express emotions appropriately and how to make and keep friends 3. planned ignoring of inappropriate behavior that is not self-threatening, combined with increasing attention to approximations of appropriate language, dress, and social interaction	Katherine will seek positive attention from others in ways that are emotionally and physically safe.	1. Within 3 months, school personnel will have received no reports of Katherine's self-injury or suicide threats for at least 10 consecutive school days. 2. Within 6 months, Katherine will engage in appropriate, positive attention-getting behaviors at least 3 days per week for 4 consecutive weeks as judged by teachers' anecdotal reports. 3. By the end of the school year, Katherine will engage in only appropriate, positive attention-getting behaviors while at school as reported by school personnel.

PERSONAL REFLECTIONS

Depression and Suicide

Kathleen McGee-Benton, Ph.D., teaches high-school students with severe emotional and behavioral disorders in Ohio.

The literature suggests that teachers often miss signs of depression in children. What are the most important things for teachers to be aware of in recognizing depression in children and adolescents?

The signs of depression are easy for teachers to overlook because a quietly depressed student is less likely to obtain teacher attention than the overt, acting-out student. So, it's very important that teachers get to know each student on an individual basis. Once a rapport is developed, subtle changes can be observed more easily. Three things teachers should be aware of and look for in depressed students are a sense of hopelessness, helplessness, and haplessness.

Hopelessness can be revealed in many different ways, but typically a student will express the feeling that life is hopeless. Life is seen in distinctly black-and-white terms; unfortunately, for this child, life is very black. This student may accept the blame for things that truly were beyond his or her control. Another typical response is the melancholy "I don't care" attitude (which is much different than the angry "I don't care" of the aggressive student). When this attitude gets to the point that the student does not care about a prized possession (a CD or skateboard) or a significant event (spring break or the prom), the problem is serious and demands immediate attention.

Helplessness is the feeling that no matter what you do, even if you try your hardest, the result is worthless. Life for this student is beyond personal control. These feelings are likely to be expressed when preparing for an upcoming event and may be as seemingly insignificant as "Why should I bother to take my math book home? I'll just get all of the problems wrong anyway." A student who is feeling helpless can be very resistant to a teacher's suggestion to "Just *try* to do something." On the other hand this student may verbalize willingness to try but then not be able to comply.

Haplessness is the inability to feel pleasure or satisfaction. A student with these feelings is likely to express these thoughts in terms of never being good at anything. This student will forget the *A* on last week's quiz because this week's quiz grade was lower than expected, and that could be a *B*. Key things to watch for in all three cases are the expression of finality and the all-or-none syndrome.

In my last example, finality is expressed in the idea that this is the final grade and the only one that counts. If a student can't remember that there were other quizzes or that there will be more, the problem is more serious. All-or-none is expressed similarly. Often, severely depressed people experiencing a particularly depressive episode will not be able to recall times in their lives when they were happy. If they are reminded of happier times, they will be able to rationalize the event in some way or might tell you that they were merely "acting happy."

In working with depressed students, what strategies have you found to be most successful?

Teachers must learn to look for and listen for the little gestures and comments made by students. One comment or gesture does not diagnose a person as depressed, but a record of these observations can assist the teacher in recognizing a pattern of behavior. Once a pattern has been recognized, dealing with the depressed behavior is necessary.

Developing a sense of rapport with the student is essential to working with those who are depressed. The student must respect and trust you. This does not mean that the teacher-student relationship must be abandoned; in fact I believe that this is not advisable at all, but rather the teacher-student relationship must be solidified so that the student can depend on you as a significant, responsible adult. Along with the rapport, the student must feel some success of accomplishment. Teachers are instrumental in assuring that each student attains a degree of success before moving on to the next level of difficulty. When problems are encountered, the teacher should be willing to work with the student through a solution. Problem-solving strategies should be taught and practiced in more routine situations so that when the student enters a depressive episode, the necessary skills are available and the teacher-student problem-solving team is comfortable working together.

Prevention is the key, but the teacher cannot eliminate potentially depressing events from occurring; therefore, it is inadvisable to try to prevent all depressing events. The key to prevention is to teach the student to prevent depressing events from becoming all-consuming. Identifying positive aspects about self and others is an essential skill. Taught initially during "up" times, the skill can transfer to looking for good in a bad situation. Both problem solving and positives are ideally taught when the student is not incapacitated by depression. During a depressive episode, the teaching strategies will be different.

Lowering expectations because a student is depressed may do more harm than good. First, it reinforces the feelings of inadequacy. This becomes a self-fulfilling prophecy and enables the student's hopelessness. Second, it teaches the student that acting depressed will make life easier in some respects; it is negative reinforcement (removing something aversive—work, contingent upon the behavior, acting depressed). Instead, different expectations and assignments may be made. Being line leader, caring for the class pet, or running an errand may be acceptable responsibilities in which the teacher

"needs" the student. All responsibilities should be closely monitored and should in no way positively reinforce the depressed behavior. They must be normal classroom responsibilities taken "in turn."

As a classroom teacher, what behavior related to depression do you find most difficult to deal with?

The behavior of administrators and school counselors who act as if the depressed student has the plague or respond by saying that the student is in special education—and, therefore, my problem—are the most difficult behaviors that I must deal with. Parents who are insensitive or uncaring are also difficulties in this area, and being told to "Keep your nose out of our business!" can make dealing with the depressed student more difficult than necessary.

One of the most difficult aspects of dealing with depressed behavior is the apathy it produces. A depressed student in the classroom is usually quite content to sit quietly. When aggressive, acting-out students are in the same room, the teacher can be tempted to put off dealing with the depressed student. I have seen many depressed students praised for sitting quietly and some actually dismissed from programs because their behavior was under control! Apathetic behavior is often confused for an easy-going nature and held up as an example for others to emulate. Unfortunately, as a high-school teacher I often see the depressed student back in the program in worse shape than before. By this time, the student has learned to be depressed and has actually been rewarded for displaying depressed, apathetic behavior!

This type of student is not capable of caring or making a decision. These skills must be taught. Getting to know this type of student is extremely difficult. The student's most frequent response is, "I don't care" or "It doesn't matter." These responses tend to build a barrier between the student and her or his real desires. Sometimes decisions must be made by the teacher. At times, I have made what seemed to be the poorer of the two choices for a student in the hope that the student would reject my choice and express his or her own opinion. This technique will sometimes work, but the student may feel that I did this out of spite. Praise for expressing an opinion and for really caring about something will usually temper this reaction. Sometimes after I make a decision that the student didn't care to make, I can see the anger or hurt building inside. Discussion will usually lead to blaming me for the anger, but again I remind them that they really do care and that is a good thing. Finally, if the student would like to alter my decision, I allow it. In the end, praise for really caring and expressing an opinion are administered. But sometimes when a student can't express an opinion I respond with a lighthearted, "We'll work on how to express opinions appropriately later" and watch for the student's reaction. Then I've gained insight into at least something that the student cares about.

As a teacher, what are the most important things you think you can do to help prevent suicide of your students?

Letting students know that I am here to help them with their problems and that there is no problem that cannot be worked through is the most important idea I can present to my students. I try to help them understand that problems are a part of life, and working through them is what is important. I also let them know that there are many solutions to problems and that sometimes I need assistance to help them.

Unfortunately, what works for the average student in relation to suicide prevention education may be detrimental to students who are depressed and possibly suicidal. Learning about the signs of suicide and talking about suicide have actually caused students with emotional or behavioral disorders to contemplate their own suicide, and have left them feeling depressed about previously "workable" problems. These sessions were conducted by well-intentioned counselors, mental health professionals, and psychology teachers. On the other hand, reading *Romeo and Juliet*—required reading in many high-school curriculums and on the poor-choice list by many suicide experts—can be made into a lesson about "everything Romeo and Juliet had to live for," and it may be better suicide prevention for these students. In either case, great care must be taken to achieve closure on a positive note each day, not just at the end of the unit, and careful monitoring of student reactions to the subject matter is extremely important.

If you are working with an individual student who is contemplating suicide, you should first assess the immediate risk. Any indication of suicide must be taken seriously, but suicidal intentions with well thought out plans and an accessible means are much more serious. These may require immediate hospitalization. If the danger is not as definite, a plan or contract for living can be discussed. Discussions usually begin with the perceived cause of the suicidal behavior. Usually, a list of grievances is easy to elicit. Some of these will be well beyond the control of the student or the teacher. From the list, the teacher and student must choose one or two items that the student can do something about. Small steps that ensure success and are easy to measure must be established, and a review session scheduled. Parents and other professionals must be notified of this plan and may be helpful in writing it.

The classroom teacher must ask for assistance at the slightest feeling of discomfort or being in over her or his head. However, because the special education teacher is likely to be the professional who has the greatest experience with the student, he or she may be asked to continue to participate, sometimes in a major role, even though school counselors and mental health professionals are involved.

17

Schizophrenia and Pervasive Developmental Disorders

As you read this chapter, keep these guiding questions in mind:

- What does "psychotic" mean, and how might schizophrenia and autism fit or not fit a definition?

- Why is autism being discussed here when it is not included in the federal category of "serious emotional disturbance?"

- What are the signs or symptoms of schizophrenia, and how might they be mistaken for other disorders in children?

- How would you characterize autism, and what is the prognosis for a child with this disorder?

- On what problems does a good educational program for children with autism focus?

- Why is a full range of educational interventions required for students with schizophrenia and autism?

- What are the major trends in intervention in the communication disorders of children with autism?

- What are the primary causes of and interventions for stereotypies?

We have already sketched major features of schizophrenia and autism, primarily in chapters 5 and 7. This chapter briefly recaps information regarding the nature and causes of these severe disorders but focuses primarily on the educational implications of several characteristics common to many individuals who have psychotic disorders or pervasive developmental disorders.

Schizophrenia is explicitly included in the federal category *seriously emotionally disturbed*, as discussed in chapter 1. Schizophrenia is typically referred to as a psychotic disorder (cf. American Psychiatric Association, 1994), and autism and other pervasive developmental disabilities have often been called *psychoses* as well. However, the term *psychotic* has had many definitions, none of which is universally accepted. The narrowest definition of *psychotic* includes childhood schizophrenia but not autism; the broadest definition includes both.

> The narrowest definition of *psychotic* is restricted to delusions or prominent hallucinations, with the hallucinations occurring in the absence of insight into their pathological nature. A slightly less restrictive definition would also include prominent hallucinations that the individual realizes are hallucinatory experiences. Broader still is a definition that also includes other positive symptoms of Schizophrenia (i.e., disorganized speech, grossly disorganized or catatonic behavior). (American Psychiatric Association, 1994, p. 273)

Besides autism, pervasive developmental disorders include **Asperger's disorder** (much like autism but without significant delays in cognition and language), **Rett's disorder** (normal development for 5 months to 4 years, followed by regression and retardation), and **childhood disintegrative disorder** (normal development for at least 2 and up to 10 years, followed by significant loss of skills) (see American Psychiatric Association, 1994). Because these additional disorders are rare and their characteristics overlap considerably with autism, the only pervasive developmental disorder we discuss under a separate heading is autism.

Much controversy has surrounded the inclusion of autism in special education categories. As noted in chapter 1, autism has been excluded from the category *seriously emotionally disturbed* and has been made a separate category of its own under federal special education regulations. Nevertheless, we discuss autism in this book because children and youths with autism typically exhibit behaviors that are severely problematic and may be considered emotional or behavioral disorders in their own right (e.g., mutism, extreme self-stimulation or self-injury). An important point about the emotional and behavioral problems associated with both autism and schizophrenia is that they are now recognized as having their origins primarily in biological factors, as noted in chapter 7.

We first discuss schizophrenia and autism under separate headings, and then we turn our attention to behavior often seen in youngsters with severe disabilities, regardless of their diagnostic labels: socialization problems, communication disorders, and **stereotypy**, especially self-stimulation and self-injury. Behavior of these types is severely debilitating and often presents persistent challenges to teachers and others who work with children and youths who have schizophrenia, autism, severe mental retardation, or other severe developmental disabilities.

SCHIZOPHRENIA

Definition and Prevalence

Schizophrenia is a disorder in which people usually have two or more of the following symptoms:

- delusions
- hallucinations
- disorganized speech (e.g., they may frequently get "derailed" or be incoherent)
- grossly disorganized or **catatonic** behavior
- negative symptoms such as lack of affect, inability to think logically, or inability to make decisions (cf. American Psychiatric Association, 1994)

The definition is not simple. "Schizophrenia is a complex, multifaceted disorder (or group of disorders), which has escaped precise definition after almost a century of study" (Russell, 1994, p. 631). Defining schizophrenia in children is even more problematic than defining it in adults (the usual age of onset is between ages 18 and 40 years) because children usually have more difficulty explaining themselves. Nevertheless, "There is no longer any question that schizophrenia can be reliably diagnosed in children using the same criteria used with adults" (Asarnow & Asarnow, 1994, p. 595).

Schizophrenia affects about 1 in 100 adults, but it is increasingly rare with ages lower than 18. Delusional thinking is rare in children, but sometimes young children are convinced of the reality of their fantasies or the delusions of other people (Simonds & Glenn, 1976). They may engage in wild fantasies during play, and these fantasies may interfere with their socialization or academic learning. The case of Wanda (see box) illustrates the extent to which children with schizophrenia can become caught up in their fantasies. Wanda was diagnosed with childhood schizophrenia and reported having auditory hallucinations, hearing buildings and other objects talk to her. Excessive fantasies can make a student very difficult to teach, if not inaccessible to teaching. Note the frustration of Wanda's teacher.

Wanda

I was aware, of course, that emotionally disturbed children sometimes have wild fantasies, but I was not prepared for Wanda. Wanda was 11 years old when I met her. She had a tested IQ of about 160, but it didn't do her much good except, perhaps, to enrich her fantasy life. I was never able to find a topic of conversation, an area of the curriculum, a place, or a time that was free of her bizarre imaginings. She had fantasies about jeans—she "wore" special 40-pocket and 100-pocket jeans with zippers in the front and drew stylized pictures of them. She had fantasies about the president and the governor and crucifixes and *The Pit and the Pendulum*, doctors, nurses, swimming pools, toilets, injections, physical examinations . . ., moles (she had one on her arm that was a microphone into which she talked and one on her leg that was a thermostat controlling her body temperature). . . . [T]here was no end.

When she engaged in her fantasies, Wanda got a peculiar, fixed grin on her face, her eyes became glazed, she giggled, and she talked (often apparently to herself) in a high-pitched squeaky voice. Frequently, she drew pictures with captions representing fantasied objects and activities. Sometimes she engaged in other bizarre behaviors, such as flattening herself on the floor or wall, kissing it, caressing it, and talking to it. It was impossible to teach Wanda or to have a rational conversation with her while she was fantasizing, and she was "in" fantasy most of the time. It was impossible to predict when, during times of lucidity and reality-oriented behavior, she would suddenly enter her fantasy world again. (Patton, Blackbourn, Kauffman, & Brown, 1991, pp. 29–30)

Table 17.1 shows examples of the hallucinations, delusions, and thought disorders seen in children. The hallucinations and delusions take a wide variety of forms. The delusions of children and adolescents frequently have sexual or religious content. Children having delusions and hallucinations are not always diagnosed as having schizophrenia. They may be diagnosed as having bipolar disorder (Isaac, 1995), or they may have comorbid disorders, such as schizophrenia along with conduct disorder or ADHD. In many cases, the diagnosis is difficult because the onset is insidious—slow, perhaps beginning with conduct problems, anxiety disorders, or ADHD. Symptom patterns may go unrecognized or be confused (Asarnow, Tompson, & Goldstein, 1994; Russell, 1994). Some children who are diagnosed with autism or

Table 17.1
Examples of Psychotic Symptoms

Hallucinations

Unrelated to affective state

A 7-year-old boy stated "everything is talking, the walls, the furniture, I just know they're talking."

Command

An 11-year-old boy heard both "good" and "bad" voices. The bad voices tell him to hit others and that they will kill the good voices if he does not obey. The "good" voices say things like "help your mom with dinner."

Conversing

An 8-year-old boy stated "I can hear the devil talk—God interrupts him and the devil says 'shut up to God.' God and the devil are always fighting."

Religious

An 11-year-old boy heard God's voice saying "Sorry D., but I can't help you now, I am helping someone else." He also reported hearing Jesus and the devil.

Persecutory

A 9-year-old boy reported voices calling him bad names, and threatening that if he doesn't do what he is told something bad will happen to him.

Commenting

An 8-year-old girl reported an angel saying things like, "You didn't cry today" and "You've been a very nice girl today."

Visual

A 9-year-old girl reported "If I stare at the wall I see monsters coming toward me. If I stop staring, they'll come faster."

Tactile

An 5-year-old boy felt snakes and spiders on his back (and was so convincing he was taken to the emergency room by his parents).

Somatic

An 8-year-old girl reported feeling an angel, babies, and devil inside her arm, and that she could feel them fighting.

Source: From "The Clinical Presentation of Childhood-Onset Schizophrenia" by A. T. Russell, 1994, *Schizophrenia Bulletin, 20*, pp. 634-635.

Delusions

Bizarre

A 7-year-old boy believed that there were "memory boxes" in his head and body and reported that he could broadcast his thoughts from his memory boxes with a special computer using radar tracking.

Persecutory

A girl believed that the "evil one" was trying to poison her orange juice.

Somatic

One 7-year-old boy believed that there were boy and girl spirits living inside his head: "They're squishing on the whole inside, they're touching the walls, the skin."

Reference

An 8-year-old girl believed that people outside of her house were staring and pointing at her trying to send her a message to come outside. She also believed that people on the TV were talking to her because they used the word "you."

Grandiose

An 11-year-old boy had the firm belief that he was "different" and able to kill people. He felt that when "God zooms through me [him]" he became very strong and developed big muscles.

Thought Disorder

"I used to have a Mexican dream. I was watching TV in the family room. I disappeared outside of this world and then I was in a closet. Sounds like a vacuum dream. It's a Mexican dream. When I was close to that dream earth, I was turning upside down. I don't like to turn upside down. Sometimes I have Mexican dreams and vacuum dreams. It's real hard to scream in dreams."

other pervasive developmental disorders are later diagnosed as having schizophrenia. Most children with schizophrenia never lose their symptoms completely, though some do. "The majority of children with a schizophrenic disorder show continuing schizophrenia as they progress into adolescence and adulthood" (Asarnow & Asarnow, 1994, p. 595).

Causes and Prevention

As discussed in chapter 7, the causes of schizophrenia are known to be in large measure biological, but the exact biological mechanisms responsible for the illness are not known (Asarnow, Asamen et al., 1994; Gottesman, 1991). Genetic factors are known to play a critical role, but which genes are involved and how they work is not understood. It is quite likely that schizophrenia is not a single disease entity but a cluster of highly similar disorders in the same way that cancer is not a single disease. The same causal factors seem to operate whether schizophrenia is first diagnosed in childhood or adulthood. "Many neurobehavioral impairments observed in adults with schizophrenia can be detected in children with a schizophrenic disorder" (Asarnow & Asarnow, 1995, p. 595).

We know that in the vast majority of cases, if not all, biological and environmental factors work together to cause schizophrenia. Families in which the parents exhibit deviant behavior may contribute to the development of schizophrenia (Rosenbaum et al., 1994). Primary prevention consists of assessing genetic risks and avoiding behavior that may trigger schizophrenia in vulnerable persons, especially substance abuse and extreme stress (Gottesman, 1987). Secondary prevention consists mainly of psychopharmacological treatment and structured environments in which symptoms can be managed most effectively.

Education and Related Interventions

Educational intervention for children and youths with schizophrenia is nearly impossible to describe because the symptoms and educational needs of these students vary so greatly. We are safe in saying that education will be only one of several interventions, as pharmacological treatment and social work with the family will be critical as well. When special education is necessary, it appears that a highly structured, individualized program provides a feeling of safety and allows the student to keep symptoms in check as much as possible.

The outcomes for children and youths with schizophrenia are extremely variable. A substantial proportion of these students do not make a good overall adjustment as they progress into adulthood. Some cases, however, turn out quite well, as characterized by Bill (recall also the case of Elizabeth, introduced in chapter 1).

Bill

Bill's difficulties began during infancy. He was described as a colicky baby who was in constant motion and prone to head banging. During early childhood he required constant supervision because of his high activity level, unpredictable behavior, and tendencies toward destructive behavior such as hurting family pets and lighting fires. Because of delayed visual-motor functioning, Bill was placed in a school for children with learning disabilities at 6 years of age.

Bill's behavior became increasingly bizarre. He began to defecate and urinate in odd places, would scratch and hit himself, and threw himself against the walls crying. He became preoccupied with germs, death, and sex, and would panic if separated from his mother. At roughly 8 years of age, Bill's language became illogical and difficult to follow and tended to drift to morbid themes. At home and at school Bill acted as if he was hallucinating. During one episode he claimed that blood was oozing from the walls and floors and frantically attempted to tear them apart. He began playing with knives, talked of killing himself, and jumped off a high roof. Bill showed increasing signs of depression, spent his time lying on the sofa, and talked about hating himself.

Concerns about suicidal behavior and deteriorating behavior led to Bill's psychiatric hospitalization. A trial of haloperidol was initiated and his behavior stabilized with the combination of medication and the structured inpatient treatment program. After roughly 2 months of inpatient care, Bill returned home, where he received outpatient therapy, continued on haloperidol, and attended a school program with a highly structured behavioral program and considerable individual attention. His special education classroom contained eight students, and classroom work was supplemented with daily individual tutoring.

Until age 13, Bill continued to be described as highly anxious and as sometimes disorganized, out of touch with reality, bizarre, and silly. He showed persistent problems with attention, unpredictable mood changes, impulsivity, and daydreaming. These difficulties were most apparent during unstructured times, and the structure of the behavioral program appeared to help him control his behavior. Despite his difficulties, Bill was described as likable, popular with classmates and teachers, intelligent, and curious.

Bill showed gradual but steady improvement. At age 15 he was taken off haloperidol with no adverse effects. He transferred to his neighborhood high school, received A's and B's in his classes, and was described as a boy who "liked to study and apply himself." He developed a group of friends and became active in sports and school activities. At the final interview, when Bill was 17 years old, he was described as a popular high school senior, editor of the school newspaper, and a member of the soccer team. The summer before his senior year, he had held a responsible job working in his father's business. There were no signs of schizophrenia or other psychiatric disorder, and Bill was preparing for college the following year. (Rosenbaum et al., 1994, pp. 610-611)

Schizophrenia is nearly always treated with antipsychotic drugs (neuroleptics), such as Haldol (haloperidol) or Mellaril (thioridazine), which are designed to reduce hallucinations and other symptoms (see Table 7.1). "Children with schizophrenia show a positive treatment response to some of the same pharmacologic treatments that have demonstrated efficacy with adults with schizophrenia" (Asarnow & Asarnow, 1995, p. 595). However, these drugs do not work well for all children and youths (or adults), and they may have serious side effects (Campbell & Cueva, 1995b).

In summary, schizophrenia is a rare and disabling disorder of childhood. The onset is often insidious and confused with other disorders. Intervention nearly always involves psychopharmacology, along with social and educational interventions. A structured, individualized educational program is often necessary. With appropriate intervention, some children and youths with schizophrenia lose many or most of their symptoms.

AUTISM

Definition and Prevalence

The symptoms of autism are first observed during the child's first 3 years; autism is distinguished by its early onset. The primary definition of autism is detailed in the extensive criteria listed in *DSM-IV* (American Psychiatric Association, 1994). However, Harris (1995a) summarizes the essential features: "Although the subtle details of the diagnosis continue to be debated, the basic symptoms of autism remain consistent. These symptoms fall under three broad headings: social, communication, and behavior" (p. 305). The symptoms may range from mild to severe. Children with autism differ greatly in their specific abilities and disabilities; autism is something one may have in degrees, just as people may have varying degrees of conduct disorder, cerebral palsy, mental retardation or any other special ability or disabling condition.

Impairment of social relatedness to others is a prime characteristic of autism. Parents of children with autism often notice that their babies or toddlers do not respond normally to being picked up or cuddled. They may show little or no interest in other people but be preoccupied with objects. They may not learn to play normally. These characteristics persist and prevent the child from developing attachments to their parents (Buitelaar, 1995) or friendships with their peers. Some children with autism, but not all, improve somewhat as they progress through later childhood and adolescence in their ability to relate to other people. However, even those who do improve may seem unable to catch the nuances of social relationships or comprehend many ordinary social meanings. They may remain distant and unable to develop intimate relationships.

Autism also involves impairments in verbal and nonverbal communication. A substantial proportion of children with autism, perhaps half, have no functional language. Autism may often involve failure to establish normal eye-to-face gaze or inability to "read" the emotions and intentions expressed by people's eyes and other facial features (Arbelle et al., 1994; Baroncohen et al., 1995), and children with autism may lack facial expressions that communicate their feelings effectively or accurately. Those who do develop speech typically show abnormalities in intonation, rate, volume, and content of their oral language. Their speech may sound like that of a "robot," or they may exhibit *echolalia*, a parroting of what they hear. They may reverse pronouns (e.g., confuse "you" and "I," or refer to themselves as "he" or "she" rather than "I" or "me"). The pragmatics of language—using language as a tool for social interaction—is particularly difficult for most people with autism. Those who do acquire the mechanics of language, especially those who are older and higher functioning, may have considerable difficulty using language appropriately because they are unaware of the reactions of their listeners. For example, they may not realize that the people they are talking to are not interested in all the details of stock quotes that they have committed to memory.

Stereotyped, ritualistic behavior is a common feature of autism. So is aggression directed at others and self-injury. In fact, the behavior problems associated with autism are legion. As Schopler and Mesibov (1994) noted,

> The behavior difficulties in autism are not as easy [as communication difficulties] to characterize or describe. They can be simply humorous and trivial deviations from what we generally expect to see in others, such as enjoying the click of an automobile turn signal or loving to watch the rhythm of a garbage truck picking up its cargo. Characteristic behaviors also can be more extreme—even devastating—such as the self-injurious, destructive behaviors that sometimes dominate the lives of these children and their families. Between these two extremes are a wide range of behavior problems that emerge from frustration over problems with communication, interactions, and understanding. (p. 3)

More extreme behavior problems are generally linked to more severe disabilities in children with autism and mental retardation (Emerson & Bromley, 1995). Self-stimulation and self-injury may be caused by a variety of physiological and social factors and used to communicate a variety of wants or needs (e.g., "Pay attention to me," "Let me out of here," "There's nothing to do," "There's too much to do"; see Dunlap, Robbins, & Kern, 1994; Repp & Deitz, 1990). The interrelationships among the social, communication, and behavioral characteristics are critically important for conceptualizing autism and designing effective, humane interventions.

Autism occurs in about 0.4 or 0.5 percent of the child population, more often in boys than in girls. It is not a phenomenon of American culture; children with autism are found among children around the world. It may occur across the entire range of intelligence, although the majority of children with autism test below the criterion for mental retardation (70) and relatively few score above average. Besides mental retardation, autism may be comorbid with a variety of other disabilities such as learning disabilities, epilepsy, or conduct disorder.

Some people with autism have provided descriptions of their experiences, and these can help us understand more about the nature of this disorder as well (e.g., Grandin, 1995; see also Sacks, 1995). It is important to recognize that individuals with autism and other pervasive developmental disabilities experience anxiety, stress, and the other internal states that all of us share as human beings (Groden et al., 1994). Volkmar and Cohen (1985) reported the case of Tony W., whose account helps us understand more immediately the necessity of treating people with autism as we ourselves would like to be treated.

Tony W. was initially referred for evaluation at the age of 26 months. At the age of 22 years, he wrote of his experiences as a child and youth. He was then working, living alone, and had a few superficial friendships. His IQ was 93. The accompanying feature presents excerpts from his description of his experiences as a child and youth and shows that his cognitive, affective, and social problems have persisted into adulthood.

Notes on the Personal Experience of Autism

I was living in a world of daydreaming and Fear revolving aboud my self I had no care about Human feelings or other people. I was afraid of everything! I was terrified to go in the water swimming, (and of) loud noises; in the dark I had severe, repetitive Nightmares and occasionally hearing electronic noises with nightmares. I would wake up so terrified and disoriented I wasnt able to Find my way out of the room for a few miniuts. I felt like I was being draged to Hell. I was afraid of simple things such as going into the shower, getting my nails cliped, soap in my eyes, rides in the carnival—except the Spook house I love it, I allso like Hellish envirments such as spookhouses at the Carnival, Halloween, and movies—horror. I daydreamed a lot and tried to actvly communicate and get into that world. I rember Yale Child Study Ctr. I ignored the doctors and did my own thing such as make something and played or idolize it not caring that anybody was in the room. I was also very hat(e)full and sneakey. I struggled and breathed hard because I wanted to kill the gunia pig; as soon as the examiner turned her back I killed it. I hated my mother becaus she try to stop me from being in my world and doing what I liked; so I stoped and as soon as she turn her back I went at it agen. I was very Rebellious and sneaky and distructive. I would plot to kill my mother and destroy the world. Evil thing astonished me such as an H.Bomb. I loved cartoons and their envirments. I also (had) a very warp sence of humor and learn(ed) perveted thing(s) verry quickly; I used to lash out of controll and repeat sick, perverted Phrases as well as telling people violent, wild, untrue things to impress them.

In school I learned somethings verry quickly but other were beyond learning comprehenshion. I used to disrupt the whole class and love to drive the teachers nuts. . . .

After I left (this school) The physical problems continued The list gets longer. I lived with my father and the(n) saw the so call(ed) normal, sick teenage world. I was 14. I set my will (to) be normal like everybody else. (I) look(ed) up to people in school and did what they did to be accepted and put (up) more of a show to hide the problems and be Normal. I force(d) my self to Know all the top rock groups, smoke pot, and drink and (tried to) have a girl friend. This was the 9th grade and 10th. I constantly got in trouble in school and did som(e) real crazy things to be cool. Like everybody else I thought I was normal. Most of it was a failure. More people hated me then ever. My interests were destroyed becouse I thought they wernt normal. Things were going bad at home. My Father and I were not getting along becouse of trouble in school. I wasn't getting along with No one. I got my (drivers) license and tryed to impress people at school and girls by driving like a nut. IN tenth grade I quit school and worked washing cars and work(ed) many other Jobs too. I was verry depressed and Hyper at work. I got along with my boss at all my Jobs. I tend to get lazy and had trouble getting along with other people. So in (an) effort to keep my Jobs I avoided many people. I found It a lot easeyer to get along with older people and FEARED People my age because of school. I went to the army and got in lots of Fights with people. So I got discarged (discharged). I allso have great Troub(l)e getting thing(s) organized and missunderstand allmost everything. I worked a few more Jobs and hung around w/some Crazy people I knew from school and got drunk a lot and did distructive things, Magnified Fears and Peronia on pot. I never got Fired from a job. My problems havn't changed at ALL from early childhood. I was Just able to Function. And it still (is) the same today—1983. Plus more physical problems in 1982 knowing that NONE of these problems are gone but only sepressed (suppressed) by Physcatric (Psychiatric) treatment. Then (I) insisted on their was a medical problem but IT programed that Medical Help was a cop out and after (I) Find out more truth about lie and rebelling and hating its and doubting it. And then all the childhood problems and physical problems starting eating me like a cancer. I then felt The medical help in one of the only hopes for my well being and (that of) Approx. 500,000+ Autistic kids.

Source: From "The Experience of Infantile Autism: A First-person Account by Tony W." by F. R. Volk-mar and D. J. Cohen, 1985, *Journal of Autism and Developmental Disorders, 15*, pp. 47–54. Copy-right ©1985 by Plenum Publishing Corp. Reprinted by permission.

Causes and Prevention

The causes of autism remain mostly unknown. We do know that the blame heaped upon parents by psychoanalytic interpretations of the disorder was unwarranted, a horrid consequence of the arrogant disregard of scientific methodology. As noted in chapter 7, there is a consensus among scientific researchers that autism is a brain dis-order, probably having multiple causes, none of which is very well understood (Har-ris, 1995a; Marcus & Schopler, 1993; Schopler & Mesibov, 1987). Various neuro-chemicals and brain structures have been researched for many years, yet no definitive findings have emerged for a single cause—only hypotheses that seem partially sup-ported in some cases. We do know that genetics plays a role in the disorder. One bit of evidence that genes are important is that identical twins are far more likely than fraternal twins to be concordant for autism (i.e., both to have the disorder). A rea-sonable guess, given the range of symptoms and associated conditions, is that autism has no single cause.

The only primary, physiological prevention strategies are genetic counseling and prenatal care, but these are not very specific because so little is understood about the biology of autism. Secondary prevention consists of early identification and interven-tion. Early intervention involves treatment of family problems as well as treatment of the child with autism. As we have noted, the effect of a child with disabilities on the family varies enormously from one family to another. Having a child with autism can be a very stressful experience for parents and siblings. The child with autism may precipitate family problems, but family discord or disorganization may affect the out-comes for the child. "These two factors may intertwine, with family dysfunction heightening the child's needs, and the child's behavior problems intensifying family difficulties" (Harris, 1994, p. 161). Educational programs may play an important role in secondary prevention, as we discuss later.

Education and Related Interventions

Educational work with children who have autism must be both early and intense, and it must be focused on helping children overcome their greatest disability: inability to communicate effectively. True, these children have social and behavioral problems that need attention as well. However, it is increasingly clear that communication skills are at the heart of the disability of autism. Communication skills are essential for estab-lishing and maintaining social relatedness. Moreover, many of the behavior problems associated with autism may represent socially unacceptable attempts to communicate with others. Communication disorders are not peculiar to autism but are a common problem among children with a wide range of developmental disabilities, hence our later discussion of communication disorders under a separate heading.

In addition to the focus on communication, many children and youths with autism need intensive instruction in daily living skills (Bondy & Frost, 1995; Harris, 1995a, 1995b; Schopler, Mesibov, & Hearsey, 1995). Effective instruction in both language and other functional daily living skills requires a highly structured, directive approach that uses basic principles of behavioral psychology as the basis for analyzing tasks and teaching procedures. The principles and techniques most often employed successfully include positive and negative reinforcement, modeling and imitation training, shaping, prompting, extinction, and a variety of punishment procedures, as we discuss later under the heading of socialization problems (see Schreibman, 1994).

However, emphasis is increasingly on using these behavioral principles and techniques in "natural" settings and in "natural" interactions. Researchers are constantly seeking to make better instructional use of the natural interactions by which children normally learn language and other social skills. For example, at the preschool level, the emphasis is on natural interactions with normal peers in regular classrooms (e.g., Bondy & Frost, 1995; Strain, Danko, & Kohler, 1995). At the elementary level, children with autism have sometimes been included in cooperative learning groups with their normal peers in regular classrooms (e.g., Dugan et al., 1995). Educators are looking for ways to help students with autism learn at any age, including the teen years, the skills of self-management (e.g., Koegel, Frea, & Surratt, 1994; Newman et al., 1995).

In part because of the emphasis on finding more natural ways of teaching children with autism, an increasing percentage of such students are being taught in neighborhood schools and general education classrooms, especially at younger ages (cf. Bondy & Frost, 1995; Dunlap, Robbins, & Kern, 1994; Strain et al., 1995). Still, the majority of students with autism are not taught in regular classrooms. Although there is wide variation from state to state, data from the U.S. Department of Education (1995) showed that, for the school year 1992–93, about half of all students with autism were taught primarily in separate classes, although many of these students no doubt spent part of their school day with normal peers. About 10 percent were educated primarily in regular classrooms and about 10 percent primarily in resource rooms. Nearly 28 percent were placed in special public or private day schools, and about 4 percent were in residential, hospital, or homebound placements.

Understanding the parental role in autism has resulted in recruiting parents as therapeutic agents in many treatment programs (e.g., Bondy & Frost, 1995; Butera & Haywood, 1995; Charlop et al., 1991; Harris, 1994; Lovaas, 1987; Simpson & Zionts, 1992). If early intervention is to have the intensive, pervasive character that makes it effective, then family involvement is essential. Without parental participation in training, children with autism are unlikely to acquire and maintain the functional communication and daily living skills they need for social development and eventual independence. Siblings may also play an important role in developing and sustaining the social learning of children with autism. For example, Strain and Danko (1995) used a social skills training program, originally developed for the preschool classroom, to teach parents and other caretakers how to increase the positive social interactions of children 3 to 5 years of age with their preschool-age siblings who had autism.

Psychopharmacological interventions in autism consist of a wide variety of experimental drugs, including *neuroleptics* (antipsychotic drugs) such as Haldol (haloperidol) and stimulants such as Ritalin (methylphenidate) (Campbell & Cueva, 1995a). Although these medications may give symptomatic relief in some cases (e.g., reducing self-injurious behavior or hyperactivity), responses to the drugs are idiosyncratic; the effects tend to be unpredictable and depend on individual sensitivities. Even when drugs are helpful, behavior management and instruction by parents and teachers are still critical; medications may sometimes make the individual more tractable or teachable, but they are not sufficient themselves to address the disorder.

In summary, education and related interventions for students with autism must be early, intensive, highly structured, and involve families, if they are to be most effective. Early, intensive intervention may produce remarkable gains in many young children with autism, although no intervention yet can claim universal success in enabling children with autism to overcome their disabilities (Harris, 1995a, 1995b; Lovaas, 1987). Education is increasingly focused on using natural interactions to teach students in natural environments, including regular classrooms. All interventions must address problems in socialization, communication disorders, and stereotypy.

SOCIALIZATION PROBLEMS

As we have noted, socialization depends to a great extent on competence in communication. However, children and youths with schizophrenia or pervasive developmental disorders may fail to develop other social skills besides language. Their odd, unresponsive, and rejecting patterns of behavior may disable them in learning to play with, befriend, and be befriended by others.

One social skill in which many children with autism have difficulty is *eye gaze*. Failure to establish eye contact with others makes children with autism seem to look "through" or "beyond" other people or to appear "out of it." Rather than focus on others' faces, they often rely on peripheral vision and quick, furtive glances to interpret social cues. This gaze aversion makes adults feel ill-at-ease and shut out. Failing to look at people's faces could also be one reason these children have difficulty interpreting others' emotions and learning communication skills (Baroncohen et al., 1995). Infants and toddlers with autism may have great difficulty learning to imitate adults in part because they do not look at their faces and eyes like normally developing infants and young children do. Because gaze aversion is obviously a disturbing and debilitating social behavior, one of the first steps in teaching children who avert their gaze must be to establish appropriate eye contact. Methods for overcoming averted gaze include games that require looking at another person, prompts, imitating the child's behavior, and reinforcement for eye contact (see Bondy & Frost, 1995; Butera & Haywood, 1995; Koegel et al., 1982).

Many children with pervasive developmental disorders have extreme problems with social skills of nearly every type. "Children with autism often have to be taught in considerable detail all of the complexities of social interactions such as how to play a game with another child, how to express affection, to wait one's turn, to console another child who is crying, or to initiate a play interaction" (Harris, 1995b, p. 312). Many critical social skills cannot be taught one-on-one by an adult teacher or with a group of other equally unskilled children, so it is not surprising that most intervention requires interaction with normally developing peers. Peers may be trained to serve as models, to initiate interactions, and to respond appropriately to the student with autism in home, classroom, or community settings (see Pierce & Schreibman, 1995; Strain & Danko, 1995; Strain et al., 1995).

As discussed previously, students with schizophrenia and pervasive developmental disorders exhibit a wide range of emotional and behavioral problems and often have comorbid disorders. Consequently, the full range of interventions used with disorders discussed in other chapters, including attention-deficit disorder, hyperactivity, conduct disorder, depression, and so on may be needed.

COMMUNICATION DISORDERS

Teaching children with autism and other pervasive developmental disorders to use communication effectively is one of the greatest challenges in their education. Enormous progress has been made since the 1960s, when the first systematic attempts were made, in teaching language to children with autism.

Educational programs of the 1960s and 1970s used an operant conditioning approach to teach, step-by-step, approximations of functional language. The child's responses at each step in the sequence were rewarded, typically with praise, hugs, and food given by the teacher immediately following the child's performance of the desired behavior. For example, at the earliest step in the sequence, a child might be reinforced for establishing eye contact with the teacher. The next step might be making any vocalization while looking at the teacher, next making a vocalization approximating a sound made by the teacher, then imitating words spoken by the teacher, and finally replying to the teacher's questions. Of course, this description is a great simplification of the procedures that were employed, but through such methods nonverbal children were taught basic oral language skills (Koegel, Rincover, & Egel, 1982).

A disappointing outcome of early language training was that few of the children acquired truly useful or functional language, even after intensive and prolonged training. Their speech tended to have a mechanical quality, and they often did not learn to use their language for many social purposes. A current trend in language intervention is emphasis on pragmatics (making language more functional in social interaction) and motivating children to communicate (Koegel & Koegel, 1995). Instead of training children to imitate words in isolation or to use syntactically and grammatically correct forms, we might train them to use language to obtain a desired result. For example, the child might be taught to say, "I want juice" (or a simplified form: "juice" or "want juice") in order to get a drink of juice. Increasingly, language intervention in autism involves structuring opportunities to use language in natural settings (Sigafoos, Kerr, Roberts, & Couzens, 1994). For example, the teacher may set up opportunities for children to make requests by using a missing item strategy (e.g., give the child a coloring book but not crayons, prompting a request for the crayons), interrupting a chain of behavior (e.g., stopping the child on her way out to play, prompting a request to go out), or delaying assistance with tasks (e.g., waiting to help a child put on his coat until he asks for assistance). This approach is compatible with today's emphasis on inclusion of children with autism in regular preschool and elementary school programs (Harris, 1995b).

People with autism have special difficulty understanding the communication of social and emotional meanings (Happe, 1994; Happe & Frith, 1995; Sigman, 1994). They may not be able to form a coherent picture of social contexts, use social imagination, accurately attribute mental states or feelings to others, or understand jokes, pretense, lies, or figures of speech. In fact, the core disability in autism may be an absence of a "theory of mind," the inability to understand the existence of subjective mental states (e.g., beliefs, desires, intentions) and the way these help people explain and make sense of behavior (Happe, 1994; Happe & Frith, 1995). Language intervention, then, might focus on helping children with autism understand more about how language is used to communicate about subjective mental states as well as more object-centered social interactions.

Some children with autism do not acquire truly functional oral language under an operant training regimen, and training is extremely time-consuming in the face of slow progress. For these children, alternatives to speech, such as sign language or augmentative communication systems may be necessary (Harris, 1995b). Augmentative and alternative communication includes systems in which people use pictures, picture boards, signing, or computerized systems to "talk." Researchers are attempting to make it more likely that children who use alternative communication will talk about the same kinds of things other youngsters talk about (see Marvin, Beukelman, Brockhaus, & Kast, 1994). It is important to train users of alternative communication systems to understand the pragmatics of language. Whether communication is through speech or other language systems, the primary purpose of training is social interaction.

Autism and other severe developmental disabilities are developmental puzzles that many people would like to solve, for obvious reasons. Progress comes slowly through careful, programmatic research. Claims of "breakthrough" interventions are almost always misleading and disappointing. In the early 1990s, there were claims of the discovery of normal or extraordinary intelligence and communicative ability in children and adults with autism using a procedure called "facilitated communication" (e.g., Biklen, 1990; Biklen & Schubert, 1991). However, by the mid-1990s, researchers had accumulated overwhelming evidence that facilitated communication is not a reliable and efficient means of communication except, perhaps, in extremely rare cases (e.g., Crews et al., 1995; Mesibov, 1995; Montee, Miltenberger, & Wittrock, 1995; Shane, 1994; Siegel, 1995; Simpson & Myles, 1995). In the vast majority of cases, research has shown that facilitated communication is a complete hoax in which the facilitator, not the person with a developmental disability, does the communicating. When not an outright fraud, facilitated communication has been found to be a very limited, inefficient means of communication except, perhaps, in extremely rare cases.

The language training procedures based on operant conditioning applied to natural language contexts has not led to dramatic breakthroughs or a "cure." However, reliable research over a period of decades now supports their use as highly effective in helping children with autism learn to communicate more effectively (e.g., Koegel & Koegel, 1995; Koegel, O'Dell, & Koegel, 1987; Koegel, Rincover, & Egel, 1982; Lovaas, 1987).

STEREOTYPY

Children and adults with severe emotional, behavioral, or cognitive disabilities may engage in persistent, repetitive, seemingly meaningless behavior. Their stereotypical patterns of behavior, or *stereotypy*, may or may not result in serious self-injury. Often, it seems to serve the primary or sole purpose of providing sensory feedback, and it is therefore called self-stimulation. We briefly discuss both noninjurious self-stimulation and self-injury.

Self-Stimulation

Self-stimulation can take an almost infinite variety of forms, such as staring blankly into space, body rocking, hand flapping, eye rubbing, lip licking, or repeating the same vocalization over and over. The listing in Table 17.2 illustrates the diversity of self-stimulation that a given individual may exhibit (see also Koegel & Koegel, 1990). Depending on the *topography* (particular movements) of self-stimulation and the rate or intensity, it can result in physical injury; for example, eye rubbing at a high rate and pressure.

Self-stimulation is apparently a way to obtain self-reinforcing or self-perpetuating sensory feedback. It is not likely to stop for long, unless demands for other incompatible responses are made or it is actively suppressed. This appears to be true of some self-stimulatory behavior (such as nail biting) of ordinary people. As Sroufe, Steucher, and Stutzer (1973) suggest, we could probably find some form of self-stimulation in everyone's behavior, varying only in subtlety, social appropriateness, and rate. It is a pervasive characteristic of normally developing infants, and nearly everyone engages in higher rates of self-stimulatory behavior when bored or tired. Thus, like most behaviors, self-stimulation is considered normal or pathological depending on its social context, intensity, and rate.

High rates of self-stimulation sometimes require highly intrusive, directive intervention procedures, because students are unlikely to learn academic or social tasks when engaged in such behavior. Many procedures have been researched, among them using self-stimulation or alternative sensory stimulation as a reinforcer for appropriate behavior and a variety of punishing consequences (see Charlop, Kurtz,

Table 17.2

Complete List of Self-stimulatory Responses for Subject 1 and Subject 2

Subject 1
1. Eye crossing
2. Finger manipulations (moving the hands with continuous flexion and extension)
3. Repetitive vocalizations (excluding recognizable words)
4. Feet contortions (tight sustained flexions)
5. Leg contortions (tight sustained flexions)
6. Rhythmic manipulation of objects (repeatedly rubbing, rotating, or tapping objects with fingers)
7. Grimacing (corners of mouth drawn out and down, revealing the upper set of teeth)
8. Staring or gazing (a fixed glassy-eyed look lasting more than 3 seconds)
9. Hands repetitively rubbing mouth
10. Hands repetitively rubbing face
11. Mouthing of objects (holding nonedible objects in contact with the mouth)
12. Locking hands behind head
13. Hands pressing on or twisting ears

Subject 2
1. Staring or gazing (a fixed glassy-eyed look lasting more than 3 seconds)
2. Grimacing (corners of mouth drawn out and down, revealing the upper set of teeth)
3. Hand waving vertically or horizontally with fingers outstretched in front of eyes
4. Hands vigorously and repetitively rubbing eyes
5. Hands vigorously and repetitively rubbing nose
6. Hands vigorously and repetitively rubbing mouth
7. Hands vigorously and repetitively rubbing ears
8. Hands vigorously and repetitively rubbing hair
9. Hands vigorously and repetitively rubbing clothes
10. Hands vigorously and repetitively rubbing objects
11. Hand flapping in air
12. Hand wringing (hands alternately rubbing and clutching each other)
13. Finger contortions (tight sustained flexions)
14. Tapping fingers against part of body or an object
15. Tapping whole hand against part of body or object
16. Mouthing of objects (holding nonedible objects in contact with the mouth)
17. Rocking (moving the trunk at the hips rhythmically back and forth or from side to side)
18. Head weaving (moving head from side to side in a figure-eight pattern)
19. Body contortions (sustained flexions or extensions of the torso)
20. Repetitive vocalizations (excluding recognizable words)
21. Teeth clicking (audibly and rapidly closing teeth together)
22. Tongue rolling and clicking
23. Audible saliva swishing in mouth
24. Repetitive tapping feet on floor
25. Repetitive tapping toes inside shoes (visible through canvas tennis shoes)
26. Leg contortions (tight sustained flexions)
27. Repetitive knocking knees against each other
28. Repetitive knocking ankles against each other
29. Tensing legs and suspending feet off the ground
30. Head shaking (rapid small movements from side to side)
31. Tensing whole body and shaking

Source: From "Increasing Spontaneous Play by Suppressing Self-stimulation in Autistic Children" by R. L. Koegel, P. B. Firestone, K. W. Kramme, and G. Dunlap, 1974, *Journal of Applied Behavior Analysis*, 7, p. 523. Copyright 1974 by Society for the Experimental Analysis of Behavior, Inc. Reprinted by permission.

& Casey, 1990). As we learn more about the nature of self-stimulation and related behavior, we are coming to understand that the context in which it occurs (e.g., highly structured tasks or relatively unstructured recreation) has much to do with the success of the procedures used to control it (Haring & Kennedy, 1990). Research by Koegel and Koegel (1990) suggests that teaching some children and youths with autism a self-management procedure—recognizing their self-stimulation and reinforcing themselves for abstaining from it—may be highly effective.

The best method of controlling self-stimulation varies according to the individual. Intervention is not always justified; for some, reducing self-stimulation may serve no therapeutic purpose. When self-stimulation does not result in physical injury or deformity, interfere significantly with learning, or prevent participation in normal activities, then intervention may not be justified (O'Brien, 1981). Whether to intervene depends on the topography, rate, duration, and typical social consequences of the behavior.

Self-Injury

Some youngsters injure themselves repeatedly and deliberately in the most brutal fashion. We find this kind of *self-injurious behavior* (SIB) in some individuals with severe mental retardation, but it is a characteristic often associated with multiple disabilities—for example, mental retardation *and* autism or schizophrenia *and* another disorder. Very rarely does an individual with SIB have well-developed oral language. Most people who show SIB of the type we are discussing here are either mute or have very limited language abilities. In fact, one frequent approach to SIB is to try to figure out what function such behavior has, what it communicates, what noninjurious consequences it produces (e.g., attention or escape from adults' demands).

Nevertheless, some children and youths with normal intelligence and language skills deliberately injure themselves without the intent of killing themselves. The prevalence of such behavior may be as high as 2 to 3 percent of adolescents (Garrison et al., 1993). Such behavior may include "skin cutting, skin burning, self-hitting, interfering with wound healing, severe skin scratching, hair pulling and bone breaking" (Garrison et al., 1993 p. 343). As noted in chapter 14, such behavior is closely associated with depression and thoughts of suicide.

Whatever their causes or functions, the atavistic (primitive) behaviors known as SIB take a variety of forms, but left unchecked, they share the consequence of bodily injury. Without physical restraint, or effective intervention, there is risk that the youngster will permanently disfigure, incapacitate, or kill himself or herself.

The deviant aspects of SIB are its rate, intensity, and persistence. Perhaps 10 percent of young, nondisabled children under the age of 5 years occasionally engage in some form of self-injurious behavior (cf. Zirpoli & Lloyd, 1987). It is considered normal, for example, for young children in fits of temper to bang their heads or hit themselves. Deviant self-injury, however, occurs so frequently and is of such intensity and duration that the youngster cannot develop normal social relationships or learn self-care skills and is in danger of becoming even more severely disabled.

Psychodynamic, biological, and social learning etiologies of self-injury have been suggested. Psychoanalytic formulations of the causes of SIB cannot be scientifically confirmed and offer no effective treatment (see Lovaas, 1982; Schroeder, Schroeder, Rojahn, & Mulick, 1981). Evidence indicates that SIB could in some cases be a result of deficiencies in biochemicals required for normal brain functioning, inadequate development of the central nervous system, early experiences of pain and isolation, sensory problems, insensitivity to pain, or the body's ability to produce opiate-like substances in response to pain or injury. But no single biological explanation is now supported by research (Iwata, Zarcone, Vollmer, & Smith, 1994; Oliver, 1995).

Biological factors need not, and probably do not, operate independently of social factors in causing SIB. Perhaps in many cases biological factors cause initial self-injury, but social learning factors exacerbate and maintain the problem. Self-injury, like other types of behavior, may be reinforced by social attention. This notion has important implications for intervention, as it suggests ways of teaching alternatives to self-injury.

Some children appear to use SIB as a means of getting adults to withdraw demands for performance, which the children experience as aversive. When presented with a task that demands their attention and performance, these children begin to injure themselves; the demands are then withdrawn. The social interaction and attention involved in teaching and learning is reinforcing for some children, and withdrawal of attention contingent upon SIB is, for some, an effective extinction or punishment procedure. The same type of interaction and attention is apparently aversive for other children, and withdrawal of attention contingent upon SIB is negatively reinforcing for them; it makes the problem worse instead of better (see Oliver, 1995).

The assessment of self-injury is at once straightforward and complex. It is straightforward in that assessment involves direct observation and measurement: self-injurious behaviors should be defined, observed, and recorded daily in the different environments in which they occur. It is complex in that the causes are not well understood, and care must be taken to assess possible biological and subtle environmental causes (see Iwata et al., 1994; Lerman et al., 1994). Possible biological causes include genetic anomalies and factors such as ear infections and sensory deficits. SIB may occur more often in some environments than in others, and a change in environmental conditions (such as demands for performance) may dramatically alter the problem (Iwata et al., 1990; Repp & Deitz, 1990). It is thus important to assess the quality of the youngster's surroundings and social environment as well as the behavior itself, and it is particularly important to assess the social consequences of SIB (see Belcher, 1995).

Many different approaches to reducing SIB have been tried. No approach has been entirely successful, although some show much better results than others. Among the least successful have been various forms of psychotherapy, "sensory-integration therapy," and "gentle teaching," approaches that are nonaversive (i.e., do not involve punishment) but are supported by very little scientific evidence that they reduce SIB. The most effective nonaversive strategies yet devised involve functional analysis (to find the purpose the behavior serves) and arranging an environment in which alternative behaviors are taught or SIB is less likely to occur. For example, Vollmer, Marcus, and Ringdahl (1995) found that if the self-injury of young children was maintained by the negative reinforcement of escaping from tasks (i.e., when they did their SIB, they didn't have to do something), then short, noncontingent "breaks" from required activities reduced their SIB. SIB is an extremely complex problem requiring extraordinarily careful, precise research and intervention. The emphases of research and practice in the 1990s are on functional analysis, nonaversive procedures, and pharmacological treatments (cf. Oliver, 1995).

Some have suggested that all behavior problems are resolvable without the use of punishment or aversive consequences (e.g., LaVigna & Donnellan, 1986). However, nonaversive approaches are not always successful, and in some cases punishing consequences (e.g., electric shock or time out) have been quickly and highly effective in reducing self-injury (see Iwata et al., 1994; Linsheid et al., 1990; Schreibman, 1994). Controversy continues regarding the use of aversives, partly because *aversive* and *successful treatment* are difficult to define. Although everyone agrees that the use of nonaversive interventions is preferable, not everyone agrees that aversive interventions should be strictly and totally prohibited. Some argue that aversive interventions should be kept to a minimum and be used only under very strict controls but that a full range of treatment options should be available (Gerhardt, Holmes, Alessandri, & Goodman, 1991).

SUMMARY

In the federal category *serious emotional disturbance*, schizophrenia is explicitly included and autism is excluded (it is a separate category under IDEA). However, both are rare, severe disorders of children and youths in which emotional and behavioral disorders are manifested. Schizophrenia is a major psychiatric disorder falling under the category of "psychotic disorders." Autism is one of several pervasive developmental disorders. Both autism and schizophrenia may occur with other disorders.

Symptoms of schizophrenia include hallucinations, delusions, and grossly aberrant behavior or thinking. It affects about 1 in 100 adults. It is unusual in individuals under 18 years of age, especially in preteens. The onset is often insidious and may be confused with other disorders. However, schizophrenia seems to be essentially the same disorder in children and adults. The causes appear to be primarily biological, although they are not well understood. Effective education is usually highly structured and individualized. Psychopharmacological treatment is essential. Some children with schizophrenia recover, although many make little improvement and continue to have major symptoms in adulthood.

Autism is defined by the early onset (before age 3 years) of severe problems in socialization, communication, and behavior. It occurs across the entire range of intelligence, although most children with autism show mental retardation. Children with autism are severely impaired in building social relationships and in verbal and nonverbal communication, and they often exhibit stereotyped patterns of behavior. Autism affects about one half of one percent of children under the age of 3 years, more boys than girls. Its causes are known to be brain dysfunction, but the nature of the dysfunction is not known. Educational intervention focuses on building communication skills, daily living skills, and management of inappropriate behavior, and programs increasingly emphasize education involving interaction with normal peers. Early, intensive intervention produces good outcomes for some children with autism, but many continue to have serious disabilities throughout adolescence and adulthood.

The socialization problems of children and youths with schizophrenia and pervasive developmental disorders are extremely varied. Bizarre behavior, problems with eye-to-face gaze, and lack of understanding of social interactions are characteristics associated with autism. Schizophrenia may be comorbid with a wide variety of other disorders, such as conduct disorder, ADHD, or depression. A full range of intervention strategies is needed to address the socialization problems of these children and youths.

Communication disorders are a central feature of autism. About half of children with autism have no functional oral language. Interventions now focus on naturalistic applications of operant conditioning principles in communication training. Some children with autism need to rely on alternative means of communication such as signing.

Stereotypy consists of repetitive, stereotyped acts that seem to provide reinforcing sensory feedback. Stereotypies may be merely self-stimulatory or self-injurious. Self-stimulation may interfere with learning. The best method of control depends on its topography and function. Self-injurious behavior appears to have multiple causes, both biological and social. It may serve the function of getting attention from others or allowing the individual to escape from demands. Current trends in research and intervention emphasize functional analysis, nonaversive procedures, and psychopharmacological treatment.

Case for Discussion

"It's Cool. The Pain Doesn't Faze Me"

Shaun

Bam! Bam! Bam! Bam! Bam! The sound of a head being bashed against a concrete block wall is unforgettable. I makes my head hurt just to hear this hollow sound, like a hard green mellon or squash being thumped against a wall.

"Shaun's in the quiet room again."

"How long has he been at it?"

"Only a minute or two. I told him I'd give him a few moments to see if he could calm down. He's not hitting hard yet. He started getting really agitated when I tried to put the shirt behind his head as a cushion. I seemed to make it worse. He was just barely banging before I went in."

BAM! BAM! BAM! BAM! BAM!

"Gotta go."

"Shaun, I know you say that banging your head makes you feel better, but you are really using some force now that you were not using before. The back of your head is very red and I am worried it is going to start bleeding like last time. We don't want to put our hands on you, but you need to understand that if you keep hurting your head we have to try to stop you. Let's see if you can make a good choice here."

"Get away! I don't care. Leave me alone!"

BAM! BAM! BAM!

Shaun has been a head-banger throughout the fourth, fifth, and sixth grades. His angry outbursts are frequently heard echoing down the hall of the special education center, starting with the slammed door, the hiss of textbooks being slid across the floor, and the rising verbal barrage detailing how stupid his teacher is to cause all of this. Shaun knew that when he behaved this way he was to come to the "quiet room," and he had learned, after many trials, that his behavior would determine what would happen next. On many days, he could satisfy his obsession for repetitive motion when he was upset with paper-ripping, turning notebook paper into confetti as he calmed himself enough to think through the events that had precipitated his loss of control. But at other times it was not so easy, and Shaun would start the head-pounding as if in a trance. His eyes would glaze as he seemed to melt into an internal chant of rage. Later, he would explain.

"It feels good. The pain doesn't really faze me until later."

On rare occasions, he would cut his fingers, squeezing them to make them bleed more and more until someone intervened physically to stop him. He resented being stopped, claiming that his behavior was no big deal and that he liked to bleed.

"It's cool," as he described it.

Questions About the Case

1. What are the primary hypotheses we might make about why Shaun bangs his head?

2. What alternative intervention procedures might be used to reduce Shaun's self-injury?

3. How might you proceed in completing a functional analysis of Shaun's head-banging?

Unique Characteristic(s) or Need(s)	Present Level(s) of Performance	Special Education, Related Services, and Modifications	Annual Goal(s)	Objective(s) (Including Procedures, Criteria, and Schedule)
Shaun engages in self-injurious behavior when stressed or angry.	Shaun head-bangs forcefully when highly upset at least 3 times a month, requiring that he be physically restrained.	1. Use authorized physical restraint to prevent self-harm. 2. Provide training in anger management techniques. 3. Use functional analysis to identify and teach alternative responses to frustration.	Shaun will stop headbanging and use appropriate language to describe his feelings.	1. Within 2 months, Shaun will not bang his head when he is frustrated or restrained. 2. Within 2 months, when Shaun is upset he will talk appropriately with adults about his feelings.

PERSONAL REFLECTIONS

Schizophrenia and Pervasive Developmental Disorders

Rosmarie Contini McGuinness, M.Ed. is the Program Specialist for Autism for the Fairfax County Public Schools.

Briefly describe the kinds of students you serve in your program.

In our school division of approximately 143,000 students, we have a full continuum of program options for students with autism and other complex disabilities. My primary responsibility is to coordinate programs for students with autism between the ages of 5 and 22 who are in 33 self-contained classes. These students range from those who are included for at least part of the day in regular classes to those whose behavior is very challenging to manage in any setting. Some show stereotyped behavior patterns, such as repetitive hand movements, while others exhibit the inherent rigidity of autism through their reliance on routines. Most of the students in this program are boys. We have about four boys for each girl, which reflects the sex differences typically found in autism. The abilities of these students, like their behavior, are extremely varied, ranging from those who need to learn basic self-care and communication skills to those who achieve academically in a similar manner to their peers. Most of our classes are grouped by age and instructional level. The older students generally are involved in school programs related to transition to work.

How would you describe one of the classes in your program for younger students?

I'll tell you about one of our classes for children 5 to 7 years old. All six of the students in this class are boys. They're taught by a teacher and two assistants. Our activities include a mix of individual and group work. The high adult–student ratio allows us to work on specific skills with individual students

or in groups of two students at a time. Group activities may include snack, morning circle, aerobics, physical education, recess, and some academics.

What were the typical behaviors of these students at the beginning of the school year?

Three of our students provide good examples. Billy came to us from a noncategorical preschool program. He was nonverbal and had a very limited attention span. He communicated through high-pitched screaming, which may have been due to frustration, lack of ability to communicate verbally, or attention seeking. Fred was able to attend to activities, but only those of his own choosing. Alan was not toilet trained, and his food preferences were very selective. These children are atypical compared to their nondisabled peers but fairly typical of young children identified as having autism or other pervasive developmental disorders. Students with autism are a diverse group, and a student's behavior can change markedly over a period of a year.

Do you see real progress in these children's abilities in your program?

Oh, definitely! Some make more rapid progress than others, but we are making progress with all of the students. All of the students in the class I've been describing can now sit at a table or desk and work for a specific amount of time on an instructional activity. They are learning skills at the kindergarten level, learning to recognize the letters of the alphabet and numbers. They're learning to communicate. Their problem behaviors have diminished markedly. We include our students in regular classes as much as possible, and one of the students from this class is going into a regular first grade for part of the day and doing nicely there in academics with some modifications. Two others from this class are going to a regular kindergarten for part of the day.

What teaching procedures have you found most helpful in working with these students?

The procedures we use would be described by most people as basic behavior modification techniques. Our program is highly structured. We depend on routines, expectations of success with whatever activity the student is given, and rewards for appropriate behavior and achievement. We use reinforcers such as crackers, stickers, marbles, and choice of preferred activities. We focus on intensive instruction in the skills the students need most. For nearly all of our young students, this means focusing on language. We use augmentative communication systems (for example, picture boards) for students who are currently nonverbal or require a means of assisting with communication.

Some of our other students are mainstreamed for most of the day in regular classes. A few of these students need only occasional help from support staff. They may need modifications of their academic work, such as shorter assignments, alternative directions from the teacher, or cuing to stay on task. Our goal is to provide effective instruction that is as normal as possible, but for many children with autism this means a highly structured program with external reinforcement to keep them focused on task and moving through the curriculum.

What is the relationship between the autism program and programs for students with other disabilities?

We are more concerned about programming for students' instructional needs than grouping students by diagnostic labels. A few students who carry a label of *emotional disability* have done well in the autism program. However, when the autism program no longer meets the needs of a child, other programs and resources are considered, including general education. Special education is about designing appropriate education for each individual student, not making students fit programs or grouping them by diagnostic labels.

Is there anything else you would like to say about the students you serve?

Yes. In reading about students with autism and other pervasive developmental disabilities, it is easy to get the impression that these children present only problems. However, these children bring much joy to the lives of their parents and families, and it is delightful and rewarding to work with them. We must not fail to see the positive aspects of these children's characteristics.

PART FIVE
Implications: A Beginning Point

Introduction to Part Five

To this point, we have concentrated on the characteristics of emotional or behavioral disorders. We turn now to the role of teachers in the amelioration or resolution of these problems. What can teachers do to help students with emotional or behavioral disorders? What might they expect as outcomes of their work? With what basic assumptions should one approach the tasks of teaching and managing these students in school? What teaching and management strategies are most likely to be successful? These and related questions are logical extensions of what we have discussed in prior chapters, but their answers demand more space than a single chapter—or a single book. My comments in the final chapter are therefore only a preface or brief orientation to educational methodology, based primarily on my understanding of the research findings I have summarized in the other sections of the book.

My purpose in this final chapter is to sketch what I consider to be a conceptual or philosophical foundation for educating children and youths with emotional or behavioral disorders. To the extent that my sketching is successful, you will be able to describe the essence of my views of good teaching after you have read chapter 18. I suggest that as teachers we must begin by examining our expectations, not only of the students we teach but of ourselves and others who live and work with these students. Within the context of our expectations, we must try to make sense of causal factors and our role in them. As professional educators, we also have an obligation to accomplish these tasks:

- Define and measure each student's behavior precisely enough to monitor progress and communicate that progress clearly to others.
- Design appropriate and corrective experiences for students.
- Communicate effectively with students about their behavior.
- Teach students self-control through modeling and direct instruction.

I offer a synopsis of my views on teaching because I feel it is important that every professional educator work out a basic philosophy regarding what teachers can and should do to help students with emotional or behavioral disorders. I do not mean to suggest that when you have done so you will stop questioning yourself and others. Although I have written a statement revealing something of my own philosophical orientation to teaching, I do not consider it final or immutable. It is by necessity a tentative statement, open to revision as I learn more about teaching and about students with special problems. As I suggested in my introduction to Part One, I hope that reading this book will launch you on an adventure of self-questioning. I also hope that you will question the discernment of my comments in Part Five in the light of what you have experienced first-hand and what you have read, not only in this book but in many other sources as well. Ultimately, my hope is that you will work toward articulating your own views on teaching particularly challenging students and that your self-questioning adventure will never stop.

18

A Personal Statement

As you read this chapter, keep these guiding questions in mind:

- What should I expect of myself as a teacher?

- How do I determine what is reasonable to expect of my students?

- What causal factors should I be most concerned about, and what is my role as a teacher?

- How should I define and measure the behavior of my students?

- How might I conceptualize my major goals for students?

- What roles do communication, directness, and honesty play in effective education for students with emotional or behavioral disorders?

- How are modeling and self-control related to my tasks as a teacher?

- Why must instruction be the primary concern of teachers of students with emotional or behavioral disorders?

- What does the past tell us about the future?

SETTING EXPECTATIONS

What we expect of our students and ourselves is a critical factor in our choice of educational strategies, and our expectations determine in part what we and our students achieve. Furthermore, our expectations greatly influence how we evaluate what we and our students accomplish. Setting appropriate expectations is not only important but surprisingly difficult—if we take the task seriously. Unfortunately, the past decade may be remembered as an era of hollow slogans and trite pronouncements regarding educators' expectations. "All children can learn," for example, may be recalled as a particularly popular but banal phrase that was very seldom followed by important questions regarding what all children can learn or at what rate, to what degree of proficiency, with what allocation of resources, or for what purpose (Kauffman & Hallahan, 1993). Likewise, holding "the same high expectations for all students" may be remembered as a gross oversimplification that ignores the need to recognize students' individual differences (Kauffman, Mostert, Nuttycombe, Trent, & Hallahan, 1993). Setting appropriate expectations for others and ourselves requires considerable reflection on what we know about human development and learning, the nature of each student's problems, and our own limitations and biases. Let us hope that the next decade brings a more serious and reflective attitude toward what we should anticipate from ourselves and others.

Educators are sometimes impulsive in setting their expectations for students, neglecting the questions that might help them establish a constructive and realistic foundation for teaching and its evaluation. The special educator working with students who have emotional or behavioral disorders must begin with the same questions that every teacher must ask before designing a behavior management plan:

- Could this problem be a result of inappropriate curriculum or teaching strategies?

- What do I demand and prohibit—and what should I?

- Why do certain behaviors bother me, and what should I do about them?
- Is the behavior I am concerned about developmentally significant?
- Should I focus on a behavioral excess or a deficiency?
- Will resolution of this problem solve any others?

A reflective approach demands much additional self-questioning to arrive at academic and behavioral expectations that do not sell the student short, set the student up for failure, or impose improper personal or cultural biases (Kauffman et al., 1993).

Teachers are sometimes acculturated during their training or by others in the school system to expect too little or too much of themselves and other adults who live and work with children. The primary objectives of some teachers seem to be survival and self-serving behavior, with little apparent concern for their role in improving the achievement and social behavior of their students. They accept little responsibility for their students' failure, expecting of themselves only that they "put in their time." They typically get what they expect and leave the world no better than they found it. Other teachers see themselves as martyrs or saviors, sacrificing nearly all other personal desires for the sake of their students. Their students' failure becomes their personal failure, and they expect to achieve a "cure" that will make their students "normal." They seldom get what they expect, and they tend to leave education—often prematurely—embittered by human failure.

Predictably, those who expect too little of themselves tend to excuse the abuse, neglect, and incompetence of other adults; those who expect too much of themselves are often disparaging of others who are unable or unwilling to measure up to their extraordinary personal standards of goodness. Finding a level of expectation for oneself and others that facilitates personal growth, fosters hope and persistence in the face of failure, and allows one to develop supportive relationships with parents and other teachers is no small accomplishment. These are particularly daunting tasks for the many teachers who begin teaching students with emotional or behavioral disorders without adequate training (see Clark-Chiarelli & Singer, 1995; Lloyd & Kauffman, 1995).

UNDERSTANDING CAUSAL FACTORS AND THE ROLE OF THE TEACHER

The first or ultimate causes of emotional or behavioral disorders almost always remain unknown. A realistic and productive approach is to consider contributing factors that may interact to cause disorder. Contributing factors may be predisposing or precipitating; both increase the probability that a disorder will occur under given circumstances. Precipitating factors may trigger a maladaptive response, given a set of predisposing variables. An important task of the teacher is to identify the contributing factors that account for the student's current emotional or behavioral status. We know that a variety of biological factors are important, but experience—including the experience a teacher can provide in school—is not only at least equally as important as biology but a factor the teacher can do something about. As Hart and Risley (1995) noted:

> The fundamental consensus among scientists has not changed: Experience and heredity contribute about equally to human functioning. Of course in the human species, genetics contributes both to the general competence of parents and children and to specific social behaviors of parenting and childing that influence the experience children receive. But beyond the contribution of genetics, all societies assume that experience can be enhanced and supplemented to improve the competencies of children and that those competencies will become part of the inheritance they pass on to their children. (p. xvi)

The primary focus of the special educator's concern must be on the contributing factors that the teacher can alter. Factors over which the teacher has no control may determine how children or youths are approached initially, but the teacher is called upon to begin working with specific pupils after disorders have appeared. The special educator has two primary responsibilities: first, to make sure that he or she does no further disservice to the student; and second, to manipulate the student's present environment to foster development of more appropriate behavior in spite of unalterable past and present circumstances. Emphasis must be on the present and future, not the past. And although other environments may be important, the teacher's focus must be on the classroom environment. Certainly teachers may profitably extend their influence beyond the classroom, perhaps working with parents to improve the home environment or using community resources for the child's benefit. But talk of influence beyond the classroom, including such high-sounding phrases as *ecological management* and *wraparound services*, is patent nonsense until the teacher has demonstrated that he or she can make the classroom environment conducive to improved behavior.

This is not to say that collaboration of school personnel with families and communities is unimportant. Comer's (1988) observations on working with troubled schools are timely: "We realized that no single group—parents, teachers, administrators, students—was at fault. We recognized that no single intervention—curriculum change, behavior modification method, physical environment improvement—would make a significant and sustained difference" (p. 38). Yet we must recognize that many teachers work under conditions in which administrators and consultants do not facilitate home–school or community–school ties. Teachers are often on their own, and the individual contribution they can make outside the classroom is limited.

The stance of the special educator, therefore, must be that behavior is predictable and controllable; in the case of disordered behavior, enough controlling factors can be found and changed in the classroom to produce a therapeutic result in that context. We cannot change the past, and the teacher alone cannot alter many of the contributing factors operating in the present. Educators must have faith that the proper classroom environment alone *can* make a difference in the student's life, even if nothing else can be altered. We must also hope that more than classroom environment can be changed, and we must work toward that end. But we cannot escape our responsibility for implementing best practices in the classroom or atone for our "implementational sins" by pointing the finger at other factors such as the structure of education or the lack of comprehensive, integrated, collaborative services (cf. Kauffman, 1994a).

DEFINING AND MEASURING BEHAVIOR

I agree with the suggestion of Forness, Sinclair, and Russell (1984) that teachers must have the primary role in determining students' eligibility for special education and deciding how children and youths will be served. Teachers' tolerance for and knowledge of individual students' behavior in the context of their classrooms must become the ultimate criteria for deciding which students need special help and where a student can be educated appropriately (Gerber, 1988; see also Kauffman et al., 1995a).

Defining and classifying emotional or behavioral disorders are persistent problems—enigmas that appear always to defy a truly satisfactory resolution. The intractibility of defining and classifying youngsters' *disorders* does not, fortunately, preclude useful definition and measurement of behavior. The teacher can define and measure precisely the behaviors that bring children and youths into conflict with others and are self-defeating. Indeed, the teacher who cannot or will not pinpoint and measure the relevant behaviors of the students he or she is teaching is probably not going to be very effective. As we have seen in previous chapters, students are considered to need help primarily because they exhibit behavioral excesses or deficiencies. Not to define precisely and to measure these behavioral excesses and deficiencies, then, is a fundamental error; it is akin to the malpractice of a nurse who decides not to measure vital signs (heart rate, respiration rate, temperature, and blood pressure), perhaps arguing that he or she is too busy, that subjective estimates of vital signs are quite adequate, that vital signs are only superficial estimates of the patient's health, or that vital signs do not signify the nature of the underlying pathology. The teaching profession is dedicated to the task of changing behavior demonstrably for the better. What can one say, then, of educational practice that does not include precise definition and reliable measurement of the behavior change induced by the teacher's methodology? *It is indefensible*. Measurement need not be sophisticated to be extremely valuable. Vance's story illustrates this type of definition and measurement (see box).

The technology of behavioral definition and measurement is readily available to teachers (e.g., Alberto & Troutman, 1995; Cooper et al., 1987; Kerr & Nelson, 1989). With relatively little investment of effort, the teacher can learn behavior-measurement techniques and teach them to students. When students know how to define and measure their own behavior and the responses of those with whom they live, two additional benefits accrue:

- The teacher is relieved of some of the mechanical aspects of teaching.

- The students have an opportunity to gain an extra degree of control over their own environments.

My suggestion is not that every behavior of every student should be measured or that the teacher should become preoccupied with measurement to the exclusion of other crucial concerns (Kauffman et al., 1993). Teaching is much more than measurement. A mechanical approach to teaching that excludes affective concerns is no more justifiable than an approach that neglects cognitive and behavioral goals. If the student's most important behavioral characteristics are not monitored, however, then it will be almost impossible for the teacher to communicate anything of substance about the student's progress to the youngster or to anyone else.

Vance

Vance was placed in Ms. Sullivan's class in mid-February. His progress in a self-contained classroom for the behavior disordered called for placement in the least restrictive environment, specifically the regular classroom. Ms. Sullivan is the type of teacher who provides a lot of structure for her students. She gives very clear directions, has rules for her classroom that she reviews with all the children and, most important, she provides consequences when students either follow or disobey those rules. She has a schedule that sets a brisk pace for instruction and activities throughout the school day. She is the type of teacher that multidisciplinary teams love to have as a resource for [behaviorally disordered] student placement. Vance was placed in her class for this reason. Vance is a very impulsive student who acts without thinking. He blurts out answers in class, speaks out of turn, and frequently jumps at answers before considering what might be the best response. Of course, he has many other problems, but Ms. Sullivan can tolerate his impulsiveness the least, and thus it is the first target for intervention. Ms. Sullivan has also determined when this problem is worst—during reading group instruction, when she simply can't tolerate interruptions. During this 20-minute period, she has counted Vance's interruptions and found that they occur about every two minutes (median number of interruptions: 12).

Source: From "Methods of Instruction" by G. J. Williams, 1987, in *Assessing and Managing Behavior Disabilities*, N. G. Haring, Ed., pp. 287–288. Seattle: University of Washington Press. Used with permission.

The importance of behavioral measurement is demonstrated so clearly and frequently that one is prompted to ask why many teachers still do not measure their pupil's behavior. Measurement has probably been neglected for at least these reasons:

- There has been a strong bias among some special educators in support of theoretical models that do not include direct measurement of behavior and, in fact, include the presumption that measurable responses are unimportant or a superficial aspect of psychopathology.

- Parents have placidly accepted less than adequate evidence of teachers' effectiveness as the best that the education profession can offer.

- Many teachers are still uninformed about the value of direct measurement of behavior or are untutored in the appropriate methodology.

■ Some teachers are incompetent and negligent.

■ Although measurement of behavior is invaluable for precise assessment of therapeutic effects, measurement is often not a prerequisite for behavioral change.

■ Informal and subjective estimates of students' behavioral status, which include anecdotal records and statements such as "She is much improved this week" without any objective data to back up the claim, give the impression that more precise measurement is unnecessary.

Admittedly, some qualitative or affective aspects of pupil's behavior and teachers' methodology cannot be measured directly, and these affective variables may be extremely important. I do not mean to imply that one should ignore everything that cannot be measured. But for a teacher of students with emotional or behavioral disorders not to ask "Exactly what is it this student does or does not do that is causing a problem?" and then not set about measuring the behavior in question as objectively and precisely as possible is unconscionable. Without direct measurement of behavior, the teacher risks being misled by subjective impressions of the student's responses and the effects of instructional and behavioral management techniques. It is reasonable to expect that the teacher show objective and precise evidence of pupils' behavioral change as well as describe the quality of his or her relationship to students in more subjective and affective terms.

HELPING STUDENTS EXPERIENCE
WORK, PLAY, LOVE, AND FUN

It does not take great wisdom to see that children and youths with emotional or behavioral disorders often do not do productive work or know how to play, give and receive love, and have fun. Yet these four experiences—work, play, love, and fun— are nearly the essence of satisfying and meaningful existence. Education of these students requires a curriculum that brings these essential experiences into sharp focus. This is not to imply that a curriculum must try to teach these experiences directly; in fact, someone who wishes to teach a youngster how to work, play, love, or have fun must have a curriculum with a content of useful specific skills, but the skills in themselves do not constitute essential life experiences. The vapid antics of "fun-seekers" and the desperate "play" of professional athletes illustrate the difficulty in apprehending fun and play through concentrated effort alone. Relations among events—the structure of experience as well as events themselves—teach a person to work, play, love, and enjoy.

The teacher's primary task is to structure or order the environment for the pupil in such a way that work is accomplished, play is learned, love is felt, and fun is enjoyed—by the student and the teacher. The teacher does not provide structure and order by allowing the student complete freedom to choose what to do. Youngsters with emotional or behavioral disorders are in difficulty because they make unguided and unfortunate choices about how to conduct themselves. One must make value judgments as to what a student should learn. Hobbs (1974, p. 156) writes, "A child simply must know how to read, write, spell, and do arithmetic, and it is good for him to know how to hit a ball, to play a guitar, to scull a canoe, . . . and to travel by bus across town." The teacher must have confidence in his or her own judgment about what is good for the youngster to learn and how the student should behave, or effective structuring of the student's environment is impossible. This does not mean the teacher should determine every skill the pupil learns or every way of behaving. The point is not to make students mindlessly conform to ridiculous behavioral standards but to require a reasonable standard of conduct and learning that will allow them greater personal choice and fulfillment in a free society.

In addition to the value judgments and difficult decisions one must make about what to teach, questions remain about how to best arrange the teaching environment. Two fundamental principles guide the organization of an effective teaching environment: choosing tasks that are appropriate for the pupil (tasks that are at the right level and at which the student can usually succeed) and arranging appropriate consequences for performance. One does not learn work, play, love, and fun through failure, but through success and mastery. We do not learn pride, dignity, self-worth, and other attributes of good mental health by having our wishes immediately gratified, but by struggling to overcome difficulties, meeting requirements, and finding that our own efforts will achieve desired goals.

We cannot depend on our students to learn by some magical, mysterious, internally guided process; their learning will be assured only by a skillful and sensitive adult who makes the expectations for their behavior appropriately difficult. Hobbs (1974) describes the appropriate level of expectation as the "Principle of Just Manageable Difficulties." The "J.M.D. Principle" is that people are most well adjusted or in the best mental health when they choose for themselves problems or tasks that are just about, but not quite, insurmountable.

> Part of the art of choosing difficulties is to select those that are indeed just manageable. If the difficulties chosen are too easy, life is boring; if they are too hard, life is defeating. The trick is to choose trouble for oneself in the direction of what he would like to become at a level of difficulty close to the edge of his competence. When one achieves this fine tuning of his life, he will know zest and joy and deep fulfillment. (Hobbs, 1974, p. 165)

The teacher's task is to choose at first just manageable tasks for students and then gradually allow them to set their own goals as they become attuned to their true capabilities and desires.

Ample evidence indicates that the order in which events are structured has a profound influence on students' learning—specifically, that making highly preferred events (play) contingent or dependent upon less preferred events (such as work) improves the individual's work performance (cf. Bandura, 1986; Walker, 1995; Walker et al., 1995). The expectation "work before play (or pay)" is a fundamental principle of behavior modification. An environment in which rewards and privileges (beyond those that are everyone's right) are gratis is stultifying. "Earning your way," on the other hand, builds self-esteem. Rothman (1970), who worked with disturbed and delinquent girls in New York City, comments on the value of work and pay:

> If I had my way, all children would work and be paid for the work they do. If the work of children is to learn, then children should be paid for learning. Money is a powerful motivator. I daresay that truancy might decrease and that more children would learn, even those children who have been relegated to the substratum of the nonachiever, if they were paid for services rendered. Someday, I would like a fund to pay girls for increasing their reading and arithmetic skills. Supposing I could say to a girl, "You increased your reading from fourth grade to fifth. You have earned five dollars." How great! If only we could do it. (p. 211)

It *can* be done, if not with money, then with special privileges, goods, or services that are meaningful to the child. The fundamental principle underlying a token economy is payment of a fair wage for work. Rothman (1970) also notes one of the usual outcomes of work: "Pride—an essential personal ingredient. All the girls who work find it" (p. 232).

I will not be so presumptuous as to try to define play, love, or fun; a definition of *work*—purposeful and necessary expenditure of effort to achieve a desired goal—is daring enough. For the emotionally healthy individual, work, play, love, and fun are inextricably intertwined; and for someone with emotional or behavioral disabilities, they are unrelated or unattainable. When a youngster's emotions and behavior have become disordered, the most effective strategy for restoring a "vital balance" or "zest, joy, and deep fulfillment" is to provide appropriate work and consistent consequences for performance. Play, love, and fun are likely to follow the experience of accomplishing a valued task and earning a reward by one's own labor. To work is to build a sound basis for self-esteem.

COMMUNICATING DIRECTLY AND HONESTLY

Some advocates of a structured approach and some behavior-modification enthusiasts imply that consistent consequences for behavior alone will be enough to bring about therapeutic change. Teaching is more than just providing a structured relationship among events, however. How the environment is arranged may be as important as the structure itself in determining the outcome for the student.

How one listens and talks to students will have an effect on their perceptions and their responses to other environmental events. In describing the consequences of behavior, for example, the teacher can emphasize either the positive or the negative aspects of an arrangement. A teacher may say, "You may not go to recess until your math is finished." Another teacher might phrase it, "You may go to recess as soon as you finish your math." Both teachers have described the response–consequence relationship and both statements are equally correct, but the second draws attention to the positive consequences of appropriate performance and the first to the negative results of nonperformance. Each statement may affect the student differently. Nonverbal communication, too, is important and should be consistent with what is said.

To be therapeutic, teachers must listen, talk, and act in ways that communicate respect, caring, and confidence, both in themselves and in their students.

It does not follow that the teacher must always communicate approval or positive regard for the student's behavior. In fact, the teacher must communicate disapproval with great clarity. We cannot expect a youngster to learn to behave appropriately if we respond to all behavior with approval or equanimity. Candor, including honest appraisal of inappropriate behavior, will serve the teacher well. Consistent follow-through with positive and negative consequences for desirable and undesirable behavior, combined with extremely clear communication of expectations, will be successful in managing most behavior problems. Recall Vance and his teacher, Ms. Sullivan. Ms. Sullivan was assisted by a consulting teacher, Mr. Nottingham. Together, they decided to implement a nonseclusionary time-out procedure for Vance's interruptions. Vance would be sent to a chair outside the reading group for 3 minutes when he interrupted; there he would be ignored. When he was behaving appropriately, he would be praised, especially for waiting to be called on before talking. Continuing Vance's story, we can see the kind of directness, honesty, and consistency in applying consequences that serves all teachers well.

Follow-Through With Vance

Having decided upon this plan of action, on Tuesday morning, Ms. Sullivan called Vance aside. She carefully told him what the target behavior was, "Vance, every time you interrupt our reading group by talking out when you haven't been called on, you are going to have to sit in this chair [she points to a chair next to the reading group area] for three minutes. At the end of the three-minute period, I will tell you to come back and join the group. In order to come back, though, you must be sitting quietly. If you are talking, or bugging other students, you will have to stay in time out until you are quiet. Every time you talk out, you will have to sit there for three minutes."

And so reading group instruction began. Ms. Sullivan was pleased when after about seven or eight minutes, she noted that Vance was obviously attempting to control his talk-outs. After about 12 minutes, however, Vance did blurt out, "Johnny, quit looking at me that way!" Ms. Sullivan immediately told Vance, "Vance, you can't talk out like that in class. Go to that chair until I tell you to return to the group." Well, Vance didn't want to go—that was obvious from the look on his face—but slowly, he got up and went to sit in the chair. Ms. Sullivan went on with the group activity, not even looking in Vance's direction. She remembered what Mr. Nottingham had said about not paying attention to the student in time out. To Ms. Sullivan's surprise, Vance sat quietly the entire three minutes. She made sure to actively engage all the other students' attention during that time so they wouldn't be tempted to look in Vance's direction. At the end of three minutes, she said, "Vance, you're sitting quietly, you may return to the group." Vance walked to his seat, sat down, and participated in the group activity. Ms. Sullivan, remembering what Mr. Nottingham had said, praised him soon thereafter for sitting quietly and (most importantly) for waiting to be called on before talking. That day, Vance spoke out inappropriately only twice. The number of his inappropriate interruptions remained between one and three for the rest of the week.

Source: From "Methods of Instruction" by G. J. Williams, 1987, in *Assessing and Managing Behavior Disabilities*, N. G. Haring, Ed., pp. 287–288. Seattle: University of Washington Press. Used with permission.

Communication is a two-way affair, and teachers will not be successful unless they learn to listen skillfully, to watch students' behavior with understanding, and to interpret accurately the relation between children's verbal and nonverbal behavior. Youngsters who do not believe they are being listened to will go to extreme lengths to make themselves understood, often getting into additional trouble by their efforts to establish communication.

Directness in talking to children and youths facilitates communication. Many teachers and parents tend to be tentative, noncommittal, and obfuscatory in their conversations with youngsters, perhaps out of fear of rejecting or being rejected, or perhaps from the misguided notion that to help youngsters who have emotional or behavioral disorders one must never direct them (cf. O'Leary, 1995). These youngsters do not profit from having to guess about adults' wishes or intentions. A few, in fact, will improve their behavior almost immediately if the teacher merely states clearly, forthrightly, and unequivocally how they are to behave.

Students with emotional or behavioral disorders are sure to test the teacher's honesty. Honesty is more than candor in expressing opinions and reporting facts accurately. Students want to know whether teachers are as good as their word. A teacher who makes idle threats or fails to deliver positive and negative consequences as promised will surely run afoul of his or her students.

MODELING AND TEACHING SELF-CONTROL

There is overwhelming evidence that children learn much through observing others' behavior (Bandura, 1986). Teachers whose own behavior is not exemplary may corrupt rather than help students, regardless of their finesse with other teaching strategies. To be blunt, teaching students with emotional or behavioral disorders is not an appropriate job for social misfits or the psychologically unstable. Imitating the teacher should lead to behavioral improvement, not to maladaptive conduct. These statements should not be taken to mean that the teacher must be a model of perfection. The expectation of perfection in oneself or others is itself maladaptive, a problem that the teacher will need to help many students with emotional or behavioral disorders overcome. Being able to accept imperfections in oneself and others and to cope constructively with one's own and others' failures are among the emotional and behavioral characteristics that the teacher must demonstrate. Hobbs (1966) sums up the kind of model a teacher (in this example a teacher-counselor in Project Re-ED) should provide:

> But most of all a teacher-counselor is a decent adult; educated, well trained; able to give and receive affection, to live relaxed, and to be firm; a person with private resources for the nourishment and refreshment of his own life; not an itinerant worker but a professional through and through; a person with a sense of the significance of time, of the usefulness of today and the promise of tomorrow; a person of hope, quiet confidence, and joy; one who has committed himself to children and to the proposition that children who are emotionally disturbed can be helped by the process of re-education. (pp. 106–107)

A teacher of students with emotional or behavioral disorders should be a model of self-control. Not only should one model self-control; one should also teach through direct instruction. Every pupil, those with emotional or behavioral disorders included, should be allowed free choice and self-determination, for appropriate self-guidance is both inherent in the concept of individual rights and inimical to the loss of control that characterizes disordered behavior. This statement does not mean that students should always be allowed to behave as they will without interference or that the teacher is always wrong to require a pupil to behave willy-nilly. Students should be allowed to choose for themselves how they will behave except when they choose to behave in ways that are self-defeating, ways that clearly are not in their best interests, or in ways that violate the rights of others. The teacher's role should be to structure the classroom environment so that the student is aware of options, can exercise choice in as many areas of behavior as possible, and is tutored in and rewarded for appropriate decisions. Students should be taught cognitive behavior-modification techniques, such as self-instruction, rehearsal, and guided practice, to make them as self-sufficient as possible in controlling their own behavior. External control may be required at first to humanize the pupil, but the task of truly humanistic education is not completed until control is internalized to the greatest extent possible.

INSTRUCTION: REFOCUSING ON THE BUSINESS OF EDUCATION

One of the most important lessons we have learned during the past 3 decades as educators of students with emotional or behavioral disorders is that academic instruction must not be ignored or even made secondary. The observation that the education of these students too often relegates academic instruction to a secondary concern and focuses on control or containment of misbehavior (Knitzer et al., 1990) is a serious indictment that must not be allowed to characterize our work.

We must refocus our efforts on instruction for two reasons. First, academic achievement is so fundamental to emotional and social adjustment that it is foolish not to make it a capstone of educational intervention. Enhancing their academic achievement is the single most reliable way of improving students' self-appraisal and social competence. Second, managing or modifying students' behavior is best approached, at least by teachers, as an instructional problem (see discussion of precorrection by Colvin et al., 1993, and Walker et al., 1995). This means placing more emphasis on the antecedents of problems, the settings or contexts in which behavior problems predictably occur. It means thinking of social or emotional problems much as one would think of problems in teaching reading or math or any another academic subject. It means paying very careful attention to specifying precisely the behavior that is expected, modifying the contexts in which misbehavior happens, and rehearsing and prompting expected behavior. Strong reinforcement for desirable behavior is important, but it will be maximally effective only if the other instructional components are well implemented (Walker et al., 1995).

REMEMBERING THE PAST WHEN THINKING ABOUT THE FUTURE

Textbooks often end with speculation about the future. I have chosen instead to comment on the past because I believe the best prediction of future developments derives from analysis of past events. In the past, we have seen an ebb and flow of concern for the plight of students with emotional or behavioral disorders and periods of progress and regression in effective intervention. Professionals have expressed enthusiasm for new methods, and disillusionment when the solution turned out to be less than final. A solely legal-bureaucratic approach to fulfilling society's obligation to disabled students has failed in the past and shows no particular promise for the future. IDEA (P.L. 94–142) and its successors may set forth legal standards and promises, but these can easily be circumvented. Effective and humane education of students with disabilities has always depended on the individual actions of competent, caring teachers, and this will be the case in the future regardless of legal mandates or prohibitions.

The issues today parallel those of the last century, though the potential for helping students with emotional or behavioral disorders is greater today than it was then because of our broader base of knowledge and experience. We have reason, then, for guarded optimism. Quick and easy cures are unlikely, but as long as people care and go beyond caring to search diligently for answers to the questions of how youngsters come to have emotional or behavioral disorders and how they can be helped to develop appropriate behavior, we can have confidence that periods of progress will outweigh periods of regression.

Glossary

Adjustment disorders   Maladaptive reactions to an identifiable and stressful life event or circumstance. Includes impairment of social/occupational functioning. Maladaptive behavior is expected to change when stress is removed.

Affective disorders   *See* Mood disorders.

Amnesia   Chronic or severe inability to remember; loss of memory that is general or more than temporary.

Anorexia nervosa   Severe self-starvation and marked weight loss that may be life threatening; occurs most often in adolescent girls.

Anoxia; Hypoxia   Deprivation of oxygen for a long enough time to result in brain trauma.

Anxiety disorders   Disorders in which anxiety is the primary feature. Anxiety may focus on specific situations, such as separation or social contact with strangers, or it may be generalized and pervasive.

Anxiety-withdrawal   Behavior characterized by anxiety, feelings of inadequacy, embarrassment, shyness, and withdrawal from social contact.

Asperger's disorder   Impairment of social behavior (e.g., eye-to-eye gaze, facial expression, peer relationships, sharing of experience, social reciprocity) and restricted, repetitive, stereotyped patterns of behavior or interests but without significant delay in language or cognitive development.

Athetoid movement   Involuntary, jerky, writhing movements (especially of the fingers and wrists) associated with athetoid cerebral palsy.

Attention-deficit and disruptive behavior disorders   Includes attention-deficit hyperactivity disorder, conduct disorder, oppositional defiant disorder, and disruptive behavior disorder.

Attention-deficit disorder (ADD)   Inability to direct or sustain attention such that the child has academic and social disabilities. *See also* Attention-deficit hyperactivity disorder.

Attention-deficit hyperactivity disorder (ADHD)   A disorder that includes inattention, impulsivity, and hyperactivity, beginning before age 7 years and of sufficient severity and persistence to result in impairment in two or more settings (e.g., home and school) in social, academic, or occupational functioning; may be primarily hyperactive-impulsive type or primarily inattentive type.

Attentional strategies   Use of verbal labeling, rehearsal, self-instruction, or other techniques to improve a child's ability to attend efficiently to appropriate stimuli.

Autism; Autistic   *See* Autistic disorder.

Autistic disorder   A pervasive developmental disorder with onset before age 3 years in which there is qualitative impairment of social interaction and communication and restricted, repetitive, stereotyped patterns of behavior, interests, and activities.

Aversive conditioning   A form of punishment; presenting an aversive (painful or unpleasant) consequence following a behavior to reduce the frequency of probability of its recurrence.

Behavioral model   Assumptions that emotional or behavioral disorders result primarily from inappropriate learning and that the most effective preventive actions and therapeutic interventions involve controlling the child's environment so as to teach appropriate responses.

Behavior modification   Systematic control of environmental events, especially of consequences, to produce specific changes in observable responses. May include reinforcement, punishment, modeling, self-instruction, desensitization, guided practice, or any other technique for strengthening or eliminating a particular response.

Biological model   Assumptions that emotional or behavioral disorders result primarily from dysfunction of the central nervous system (because of brain lesions, neurochemical irregularities, or genetic defects) and that the most effective preventive actions and therapeutic interventions involve prevention or correction of such biological defects.

Bipolar disorder   Major mood disorder characterized by both manic and depressive episodes. *See also* Depression, Manic.

Brain syndrome   *See* Organic brain syndrome.

Bulimia   Recurrent episodes of binge eating followed by purging (by vomiting or enemas) or other compensatory behavior (e.g., fasting or excessive exercise) intended to prevent weight gain, accompanied by preoccupation with body shape or weight.

Catatonic   Behavior characterized by muscular rigidity and mental stupor, sometimes alternating with periods of extreme excitement; unable to move or interact normally; "frozen" posture or affect.

Catharsis   Cleansing; in psychoanalytic theory, the notion that it is therapeutic to express one's feelings freely under certain conditions (e.g., that aggressive drive can be reduced by free expression of aggression in a safe way, such as hitting a punching bag or doll).

Cerebral palsy   A developmental disability resulting from brain damage before, during, or soon after birth and having as a primary feature weakness or paralysis of the extremities. Often accompanied by mental retardation, sensory deficiencies, and/or behavioral disorders.

Character disorder   Acting-out, aggressive behavior with little or no indication of associated anxiety or guilt.

Childhood disintegrative disorder   Normal development followed by significant loss, after age 2 years but before age 10 years, of previously acquired social, language, self-care, or play skills with qualitative impairment in social interaction or communication and stereotyped behavior.

Childhood psychosis   Used to denote a wide range of severe and profound disorders of children, including autism, schizophrenia, and symbiotic psychosis.

Choreoathetoid movement   Involuntary, purposeless, uncontrolled movement characteristic of some types of neurological disorders.

Comorbid condition   A condition or disorder occurring simultaneously with another.

Comorbidity   Two or more disorders occurring together, as in comorbidity of depression and conduct disorder.

Conceptual model   A theory; in emotional or behavioral disorders, a set of assumptions regarding the origins and nature of the problem and the nature of therapeutic mechanisms; a set of assumptions guiding research and practice.

Conduct disorder; Conduct problem   Repetitive, persistent pattern of behavior violating basic rights of others or age-appropriate social norms or rules, including aggression toward people and animals, destruction of property, deceitfulness or theft, and serious violation of family or school rules; onset may be in childhood or adolescence and severity may range from mild to severe.

Contingency contract   In behavior modification, a written agreement between a child and adult(s) specifying the consequences for specific behavior.

Counterconditioning   Behavior therapy that teaches, by means of classical and operant conditioning, adaptive responses that are incompatible with maladaptive responses.

Countertheorists   *See* Humanistic education.

Cyclothymia; Cyclothymic disorder   Fluctuation of mood alternating between depression and mania but with symptoms not severe enough to be considered bipolar disorder. *See also* Bipolar disorder; Depression; Manic.

Delusion   Abnormal mental state in which something is falsely believed.

Delusional disorder   Disorder characterized by nonbizarre (i.e., potentially true) delusions without schizophrenia.

Depression; Depressive episode   Depressed mood and loss of interest or pleasure in nearly all normal activities; episode lasting for at least 2 weeks.

Desensitization; Systematic desensitization   Elimination of fears or phobias by gradually subjecting the fearful individual to successively more anxiety-provoking stimuli (real or imagined), while the individual remains relaxed and free of fear.

Developmental disorders   Disorders apparently caused by the child's failure to develop at a normal rate or according to the usual sequence.

Distractibility   Inability to direct and sustain attention to the appropriate or relevant stimuli in a given situation. *See also* Selective attention.

Down syndrome   A genetic defect in which the child is born with an extra chromosome (number 21 in the 22 pairs; hence, trisomy 21) in each cell; a syndrome associated with mental retardation.

DSM   *Diagnostic and Statistical Manual of the American Psychiatric Association*; editions designated by roman numerals, as *DSM-IV* for fourth edition. Revised third edition is referred to as *DSM-III-R*.

Dynamic psychiatry   The study of emotional processes, mental mechanisms, and their origins; study of evolution, progression, or regression in human behavior and its motivation. Distinguished from *descriptive psychiatry*, in which focus is on static clinical patterns, symptoms, and classification.

Dysphoria   General feeling of unhappiness or unwellness, especially when disproportionate to its cause or inappropriate to one's life circumstances. Opposite of *euphoria*.

Dysthymia   Feeling of depressed mood on most days for at least 2 years, but not of the severity required for diagnosis of major depressive episode or clinical depression.

Echolalia; Echolalic   The parroting repetition of words or phrases either immediately after they are heard or later; usually observed only in individuals with schizophrenia or autism.

Ecobehavioral analysis   A procedure in which naturally occurring, functional events are identified and employed to improve instruction and behavior management.

Ecological model   Assumptions that emotional or behavioral disorders result primarily from flaws in a complex social system in which various elements of the system (e.g., child, school, family, church, community) are highly interdependent, and that the most effective preventive actions and therapeutic interventions involve changes in the entire social system.

Educateur   An individual broadly trained to enhance social development of children and youth in various community contexts; someone trained in education and related disciplines to intervene in the social ecology of troubled children and youths.

Ego   The conscious mind; in Freudian psychology, the volitional aspect of behavior.

Ego psychology   Psychological theories or models emphasizing the ego.

Elective mutism   *See* Selective mutism.

Electroencephalogram (EEG)   A graphic record of changes in the electrical potential of the brain; used in neurological and psychiatric research.

Emotional intelligence   Adeptness in assessing and managing emotions, including skills in awareness of one's own emotions, recognition of others' emotional states, regulation of one's own emotions and motivation, and management of interpersonal relationships.

Emotional lability   Unstable or rapidly shifting emotional states.

Encephalitis   Inflammation of the brain, usually as a result of infection and often accompanied by behavioral manifestations such as lethargy.

Encopresis   Incontinence of feces, which may consist of passing feces into the clothing or bed at regular intervals or leaking mucus and feces into the clothing or bed almost continuously.

Endogenous depression   Depression apparently precipitated by biological factors rather than adverse environmental circumstances.

Enuresis; Enuretic   Incontinence of urine, which may be diurnal (wetting oneself during the day) or nocturnal (bedwetting).

Epilepsy   Recurrent abnormal electrical discharges in the brain that cause seizures. A person is not considered to have epilepsy unless repeated seizures occur.

Ethology   Scientific comparative study of animal and human behavior, especially study of the development of human character.

Eugenics   Belief that human qualities can be improved through selective mating; a science dealing with improving inherited characteristics of a race or breed.

Facilitated communication   A procedure said to allow persons who are unable to communicate through speech to communicate by using a keyboard. A "facilitator" assists communication by giving emotional and physical support as the disabled person types.

Feeding disorder of infancy or early childhood
Feeding disturbance, occurring before age 6 years, characterized by persistent failure to eat adequately and gain weight, not due to gastrointestinal or other general medical conditions.

Follow-back studies   Studies in which adults with a given disorder are "followed back" in an attempt to find the antecedents of their condition in their medical, educational, or social histories.

Fragile X syndrome   A genetic disorder, associated primarily with mental retardation but also a variety of other mental or behavioral problems, in which part of the X chromosome shows variations, such as breaks or gaps.

Frustration-aggression hypothesis   Hypothesis that frustration always produces aggression and that aggression is always the result of frustration.

Functional analysis   Assessment of behavior in which the purpose is to determine the purposes, goals, or function of behavior.

General intelligence   The totality of skills and knowledge that enable a person to solve problems and meet social expectations; the theory that intelligence consists of general problem solving abilities rather than abilities to perform specific tasks.

Holistic education   An approach emphasizing individuals' construction of their own realities based on personal experience and rejecting traditional analytic and quantitative views of reality.

Humanistic education   Education suggested by "countertheorists" who call for radical school reform and/or greater self-determination by the child; education in which freedom, openness, innovation, self-direction, and self-evaluation by students and mutual sharing between students and teachers are practiced.

Hyperactivity; Hyperactive   High level of motor activity accompanied by socially inappropriate behavior, often including conduct disorder, distractibility, and impulsivity.

Hyperkinesis   Excessive motor activity.

Hyperthyroidism   Enlargement of and excessive secretion of hormones from the thyroid gland that may result in nervousness, weakness, and restless overactivity.

Hypoglycemia   Abnormally low level of blood sugar that may produce behavioral symptoms such as irritability, fretfulness, confusion, negativism, or aggression; may be associated with diabetes.

Hypomanic   *See* Manic.

Hypoxia   Severely reduced supply of oxygen. *See* Anoxia.

Immaturity-inadequacy   Disorder characterized by social incompetence, passivity, daydreaming, and behavior typical of younger children.

Impulsivity   Tendency to react quickly and inappropriately to a situation rather than take time to consider alternatives and choose carefully.

Incidence   The rate of occurrence (as new cases) of a specific disorder in a given population during a given period of time (e.g., 25 per 1,000 per year).

Incontinence; Incontinent   The release of urine or feces at inappropriate times or places; lack of control of bladder or bowel function.

Index crime   An act that is illegal regardless of the person's age; crimes for which the FBI keeps records, including the range from misdemeanors to murder.

Individuals with Disabilities Education Act (IDEA)   The federal special education law, enacted in 1990, that amended the Education for All Handicapped Children Act of 1975 (which was also known as Public Law 94–142).

Induction approach   Use of reasoning, explanation, modeling, and expressions of love and concern in discipline, especially in teaching or enforcing moral standards.

Infantile autism   *See* Autistic disorder.

Interactional-transactional model   Assumptions that emotional or behavioral disorders result primarily from the mutual influence of the child and other people on each other and that the most effective preventive actions and therapeutic interventions involve changing the nature of interactions and transactions between the child and others.

Intervention   Method or strategy used in treatment of an emotional or behavioral disorder.

Intrapsychic; Intrapsychic causal factors   Having to do with the mind; in the mind itself; conflict or disequilibrium between parts of the mind (in psychoanalytic theory, the id, ego, and superego); especially conflict in the unconscious.

Kanner's syndrome   Early infantile autism (originally described by Leo Kanner in 1943). *See also* Autistic disorder.

Life space interview (LSI)   Therapeutic way of talking with disturbed children about their behavior; a set of techniques for managing behavior by means of therapeutic communication.

Locus of control   Belief that one's behavior is under internal or external control. Individuals have an *internal* locus to the extent that they believe they are responsible for their actions; an *external* locus to the extent that they believe chance or others' actions determine their behavior.

Macroculture   A nation or other large social entity with a shared culture.

Mania   Excessive excitement or enthusiasm, usually centered on a particular activity or object.

Manic; Manic episode   Persistently elevated, expansive, or irritable mood; episode of such mood lasting at least 1 week.

Megavitamin therapy   Administration of extremely large doses of vitamins in the hope of improving or curing behavior disorders.

Metacognition; Metacognitive   Thinking about thinking; awareness and analysis of one's thought processes; controlling one's cognitive processes.

Microculture   A smaller group existing within a larger cultural group and having unique values, style, language, dialect, ways of communicating nonverbally, awareness, frame of reference, and identification.

Minimal brain dysfunction; Minimal brain damage   Term applied to children who exhibit behavioral characteristics (e.g., hyperactivity, distractibility) thought to be associated with brain damage, in the absence of other evidence that their brains have been damaged.

Minimal cerebral dysfunction   *See* Minimal brain dysfunction.

Modeling   Providing an example to imitate; behavior modification technique in which a clear model of the desired behavior is provided (typically, reinforcement is given for imitation of the model).

Mood disorders   Disorders of emotion that color outlook on life. Usually characterized by either elation or depression. May be episodic or chronic, manic or depressive.

Moral therapy; Moral treatment   Treatment provided in the late-eighteenth and early-nineteenth centuries characterized by humane and kindly care, therapeutic activity, and consistent consequences for behavior.

Multiaxial assessment   A system used in DSM-IV in which the client is rated on five axes: clinical disorders; personality disorders or mental retardation; general medical conditions; psychosocial and environmental problems; global assessment of functioning.

Multiple intelligences   Highly specific types of problem-solving abilities (e.g., analytical, synthetic, and practical abilities) or intelligence in specific areas (e.g., linguistic, musical, spatial, interpersonal, intrapersonal, bodily-kinesthetic, or logical-mathematical); the theory that persons do not have a general intelligence but specific intelligences in various areas of performance

Negative reinforcement   Withdrawal or postponement of a negative reinforcer (aversive event or stimulus) contingent upon a behavior, which increases the probability that the behavior will be repeated.

Neologism   A coined word that is meaningless to others; meaningless word in the speech of a person with a psychotic disorder or pervasive developmental disorder.

Neuroleptics   Antipsychotic drugs; drugs that suppress or prevent symptoms of psychosis; major tranquilizers.

Neurosis; Neurotic behavior   Emotional or behavioral disorder characterized by emotional conflict but not loss of contact with reality.

Operant conditioning   Changing behavior by altering its consequences; altering the future probability of a response by providing reinforcement or punishment as a consequence.

Oppositional defiant disorder   A pattern of negativistic, hostile, and defiant behavior that is unusual for the individual's age and developmental level, lasting at least 6 months and often characterized by fits of temper, arguing with adults, refusing to comply with adults' requests or rules, deliberately annoying others, and resulting in significant impairment of social, academic, or occupational functioning.

Organic brain syndrome; Organic psychosis   Disorder caused by brain damage.

Organicity   Behavioral indications of brain damage or organic defects.

Organic mental disorders   Disorders caused by transient or permanent brain dysfunction, often resulting from anoxia, ingestion of drugs or other toxic substances, or injury to brain tissue.

Orthomolecular therapy   Administration of chemical substances, vitamins, or drugs on the assumption that they will correct a basic chemical or molecular error that causes emotional or behavioral disorders.

Overcorrection   Set of procedures designed to "overcorrect" behavioral errors; may be *positive practice* overcorrection (requiring the individual to practice a more adaptive or appropriate form of behavior) or *restitution* overcorrection (requiring the individual to restore the environment to a condition better than its status before the misbehavior occurred).

Overselective attention   *See* Selective attention.

Parasuicide   Attempted suicide.

Permissive approach to education   Allowing children to behave as they wish within broad or loosely defined limits, on the assumptions that it is therapeutic to allow them to "act out" their feelings (unless they endanger someone) and that the teacher must be permissive to build a sound relationship with children; derived mostly from psychoanalytic theory.

Personality disorders   Deeply ingrained, inflexible, maladaptive patterns of relating to, perceiving, and thinking about the environment and oneself that impair adaptive functioning or cause subject distress.

Personality problem   Disorder characterized by neurotic behavior, depression, and withdrawal.

Person variables   Thoughts, feelings, and perceptions; private events or states.

Pervasive developmental disorder   Distortion of or lag in all or most areas of development, as in autism. *See also* Rett's disorder; Asperger's disorder; childhood disintegrative disorder.

Phenomenological model   Assumptions that emotional or behavioral disorders result primarily from inadequate or distorted conscious experience with life events and that the most effective preventive actions and therapeutic interventions involve helping individuals examine their conscious experience of the world.

Phobia   Irrational and debilitating fear.

Pica   Persistent eating of nonnutritional substances (e.g., paint, plaster, cloth).

Play therapy   Therapeutic treatment in which the child's play is used as the theme for communication between therapist and child.

Positive practice   *See* Overcorrection.

Positive reinforcement   Presentation of a positive reinforcer (reward) contingent upon a behavior, which increases the probability that the behavior will be repeated.

Postencephalitic behavior syndrome   Abnormal behavior following encephalitis (inflammation of the brain).

Posttraumatic stress disorder   Disorder in which after experiencing a highly traumatic event the individual persistently reexperiences the event, avoids stimuli associated with the event, becomes generally unresponsive, or has persistent symptoms of arousal (e.g., hypervigilant, irritable, difficulty concentrating, difficulty sleeping), resulting in significant impairment of everyday functioning.

Pre-correction   The strategy of anticipating and avoiding misbehavior by identifying and modifying the context in which it is likely to occur; using proactive procedures to teach desired behavior rather than focusing on correction of misbehavior.

Premorbid; Premorbid personality   Condition or personality characteristics predictive of later onset of illness or disorder.

Prevalence   The total number of individuals with a specific disorder in a given population (e.g. 2 percent).

Primary process thinking   Psychoanalytic concept that disorganized or primitive thought or activity represents direct expression of unconscious mental processes; distinguished from *secondary* process (rational, logical) thinking.

Prosocial behavior   Behavior that facilitates or maintains positive social contacts; desirable or appropriate social behavior.

Pseudoretardation   Level of functioning associated with mental retardation that increases to normal level of functioning when environmental factors are changed; falsely diagnosed mental retardation.

Psychoactive substance use disorders   Disorders involving abuse of mood-altering substances (e.g., alcohol or other drugs).

Psychoanalytic model   Assumptions that emotional or behavioral disorders result primarily from unconscious conflicts and that the most effective preventive actions and therapeutic interventions involve uncovering and understanding unconscious motivations.

Psychodynamic model　*See* Psychoanalytic model.

Psychoeducational　Approach to education that takes into account psychodynamic concepts such as unconscious motivation but focuses intervention on the "ego processes" by which the child gains insight into his or her behavior.

Psychoneurosis; Psychoneurotic　*See* Neurosis.

Psychopath; Psychopathic　An individual who exhibits mostly amoral or antisocial behavior and is usually impulsive, irresponsible, and self-gratifying without consideration for others. Also called *sociopath* or *sociopathic*.

Psychopathology　Mental illness; in psychiatry, the study of significant causes and development of mental illness; more generally, emotional or behavioral disorder.

Psychophysiological　Physical disorder thought to be caused by psychological (emotional) conflict.

Psychosexual disorder　Disorders involving sexual functioning or sex-typed behavior.

Psychosomatic; Psychosomaticization　*See* Psychophysiological.

Psychotherapy　Any type of treatment relying primarily on verbal and nonverbal communication between patient and therapist rather than on medical procedures; not typically defined to include behavior modification; typically administered by a psychiatrist or clinical psychologist.

Psychotic disorder; Psychotic behavior　Emotional or behavioral disorder characterized by major departure from normal patterns of acting, thinking, and feeling (schizophrenia is an example). *See also* Schizophrenic disorder, Substance-induced psychotic disorder.

Punishment　Consequences that reduce future probability of a behavior; may be *response cost* (removal of a valued object or commodity) or *aversive conditioning* (presentation of an aversive stimulus such as a slap or electric shock).

Reactive attachment disorder of infancy or early childhood　Markedly disturbed and developmentally inappropriate social behavior beginning before age 5 years and assumed to be caused by neglect of the child's basic emotional and physical needs or by repeated changes in primary caregiver (e.g., frequent changes in foster placement).

Reactive depression　Depression apparently precipitated by a specific event; depression that is a reaction to adverse circumstances.

Reactive disorders　Emotional or behavioral disorders apparently caused by reaction to stressful circumstances.

Reciprocal inhibition　*See* Desensitization.

Reinforcement　Presenting or removing stimuli following a behavior to increase its future probability. *Positive reinforcement* refers to presenting positive stimuli (rewards); *negative reinforcement* refers to removing negative stimuli (punishers) contingent on a response. Both positive and negative reinforcement increase rate or strength of the response.

Respondent behavior　An elicited response; reflexive behavior elicited automatically by presenting a stimulus (e.g., pupillary contraction elicited by shining a light in the eye).

Respondent conditioning　Process by which a previously neutral stimulus comes to elicit a respondent behavior after the neutral stimulus has been paired with presentation of another stimulus (an unconditioned stimulus that already elicits a response) on one or more trials.

Response cost　Punishment technique consisting of taking away a valued object or commodity contingent on a behavior; a fine; making an inappropriate response "cost" something to the misbehaving child.

Response topography　The particular movements that comprise a response; how the response looks to an observer, as opposed to the effect of the response on the environment.

Restitution　*See* Overcorrection.

Rett's disorder　Apparently normal development through at least age 5 months, followed by deceleration of head growth between ages 5 months and 48 months, loss of psychomotor skills, and severe impairment of expressive and receptive language; usually associated with severe mental retardation.

Risk　The chance or probability that a specified outcome or set of outcomes will occur; a risk factor is an event or condition increasing the probability of a specified outcome.

Rumination (Mercyism)　Regurgitation with loss of weight or failure to thrive.

Schizoaffective disorder　An episode of mood disorder concurrent with schizophrenia.

Schizoid; Schizophrenic spectrum behavior   *See* Schizophreniform disorder.

Schizophrenia   *See* Schizophrenic disorder.

Schizophrenic disorder   Psychotic disorder characterized by distortion of thinking, abnormal perception, and bizarre behavior and emotions lasting at least 6 months.

Schizophreniform disorder   Behavior like that seen in schizophrenia but not as long in duration or accompanied by decline in functioning. *See also* Schizophrenic disorder.

School phobia   Fear of going to school, usually accompanied by indications of anxiety about attendance, such as abdominal pain, nausea, or other physical complaints just before leaving for school in the morning.

Selective attention   Ability to direct and sustain one's attention to the appropriate and relevant stimuli in a given situation. Disorders of selective attention include *underselective* attention (inability to focus attention only on relevant stimuli or to disregard irrelevant stimuli) and *overselective* attention (inability to attend to all the relevant stimuli or tendency to focus on an irrelevant stimulus).

Selective mutism   Consistent failure to speak in specific social circumstances in which speaking is expected, such as school (and in spite of speaking in other situations, e.g., home), not due to lack of knowledge of or ability to use language.

Self-instruction   Telling oneself what to do or how to perform; technique for teaching children self-control or how to improve their performance by talking to themselves about what they are doing.

Self-stimulation   Any repetitive, stereotyped activity that seems only to provide sensory feedback.

Sensitization approach   Use of harsh punishment, threats, and overpowering force in discipline, especially in teaching or enforcing moral standards.

Separation anxiety disorder   Developmentally inappropriate and excessive anxiety about separation from home or those to whom the individual is attached lasting at least 4 weeks, beginning before the age of 18 years, and causing significant distress or impairment of social or academic functioning.

Sequela   Something that follows; a consequence; the lingering effect of an injury or disease (pl. *sequelae*).

Socialized delinquency; Subcultural delinquency   Delinquent behavior in the context of an anti-social peer group.

Social learning theory   Assumptions that antecedent or setting events (e.g., models, instructions), consequences (rewards and punishments), and cognitive processes (perceiving, thinking, feeling) influence behavior; includes features of behavioral model or behavior modification with additional consideration of cognitive factors.

Sociological model   Approximate equivalent of *Ecological model*.

Sociopath; Sociopathic   *See* Psychopath.

Soft neurological signs   Behavioral indications, such as incoordination, distractibility, impulsivity, perceptual problems, and certain patterns of nerve reflexes, that may occur in individuals who are not brain damaged as well as in those who are; signs that an individual may be brain damaged, but that cannot be said to indicate the certainty of brain damage.

Somatic   Physical; of or relating to the body.

Somatoform disorders   Physical symptoms suggesting a physical disorder, in the absence of demonstrable organic findings to explain the symptoms.

Status offense   An act that is illegal only if committed by a minor (e.g., buying or drinking alcohol).

Stereotype   A simplified, standardized concept or image with particular meaning in describing a group; a routine or persistently repeated behavior.

Stereotypic behavior   Persistent repetition of speech or motor activity.

Stereotypic movement disorder   Repetitive, seemingly driven, nonfunctional motor behavior that markedly interferes with normal activities or results in self-inflicted injury requiring medical treatment.

Stereotypy   A persistent, repetitive behavior or vocalization associated with self-stimulation, self-injury, or tic.

Strauss syndrome   Group of emotional and behavioral characteristics, including hyperactivity, distractibility, impulsivity, perceptual disturbances, no family history of mental retardation, and medical history suggestive of brain damage; named after Alfred A. Strauss.

Structured approach to education   Making the classroom environment highly predictable by providing clear directions for behavior, firm expectations that students will behave as directed, and consistent consequences for behavior. Assumes that children lack order and predictability in everyday life and will learn self-control in a highly structured (predictable) environment; derives primarily from learning theory.

Substance-induced psychotic disorder Delusions or hallucinations caused by intoxication with or withdrawal of drugs or other substances.

Systematic desensitization *See* Desensitization.

Target assessment Definition and direct measurement (counting) of behaviors that are considered to be a problem (as opposed to administering psychological tests designed to measure behavioral traits or mental characteristics).

Temperament Inborn emotional or behavioral style, including general level of activity, regularity or predictability, approach or withdrawal, adaptability, intensity of reaction, responsiveness, mood, distractibility, and persistence.

Therapeutic milieu Total treatment setting that is therapeutic; environment that includes attention to therapeutic value of both physical and social surroundings.

Tic Sudden, rapid, recurrent, nonrhythmic, stereotyped movement or vocalization.

Tic disorder Stereotyped movement disorder in which there is disregulation of gross motor movement; recurrent, involuntary, repetitive, rapid, purposeless movement; may be transient or chronic.

Time out Technically, time out from positive reinforcement; interval during which reinforcement (rewards) cannot be earned. In classroom practice, usually a brief period of social isolation during which the child cannot receive attention or earn rewards.

Token economy; Token reinforcement; Token system System of behavior modification in which tangible or "token" reinforcers, such as points, plastic chips, metal washers, poker chips, or play money are given as rewards and later exchanged for "backup" reinforcers that have value in themselves (e.g., food, trinkets, play time, books); a miniature economic system used to foster desirable behavior.

Topography *See* Response topography.

Tourette's disorder Multiple motor and vocal tics occurring many times daily (not necessarily together), with onset before age 18 years and causing marked distress or significant impairment of social or occupational functioning.

Tourette's syndrome *See* Tourette's disorder.

Transference Unconscious redirection of feelings toward a different person (e.g., responding to teacher as if to parent); in psychoanalytic theory, responding to the therapist as if to another person, usually a parent.

Traumatic brain injury Injury to the brain caused by an external force, not caused by a degenerative or congenital condition, and resulting in a diminished or altered state of consciousness and neurological or neurobehavioral dysfunction.

Underselective attention *See* Selective attention.

Unsocialized aggression Unbridled aggressive behavior characterized by hostility, impulsivity, and alienation.

Vicarious extinction Extinction of a fear response by watching someone else engage in an anxiety-provoking activity without apparent fear; loss of fear (or other response) by observing others' behavior.

Vicarious reinforcement Reinforcement obtained by watching someone else obtain reinforcers (rewards) for a particular response.

References

Abikoff, H. (1991). Cognitive training in ADHD children: Less to it than meets the eye. *Journal of Learning Disabilities, 24,* 205–209.

Abikoff, H., & Gittelman, R. (1984). Does behavior therapy normalize the classroom behavior of hyperactive children? *Archives of General Psychiatry, 41,* 449–454.

Abrams, L. A. (1995). Strengthening the fabric of child and family policies: Interweaving the threads of research. In D. Baumrind, *Child maltreatment and optimal caregiving in social contexts* (pp. 101–116). New York: Garland.

Achenbach, T. M. (1975). The historical context of treatment for delinquent and maladjusted children: Past, present, and future. *Behavioral Disorders, 1*(1), 3–14.

Achenbach, T. M. (1982a). Assessment and taxonomy of children's behavior disorders. In B. B. Lahey & A. E. Kazdin (Eds.), *Advances in clinical child psychology* (Vol. 5, pp. 2–38). New York: Plenum.

Achenbach, T. M. (1982b). *Developmental psychopathology* (2nd ed.). New York: Ronald Press.

Achenbach, T. M. (1985). *Assessment and taxonomy of child and adolescent psychopathology.* Beverly Hills, CA: Sage.

Achenbach, T. M. (1991). *Manual for the Child Behavior Checklist/4-18 and 1991 profile.* Burlington, VT: University of Vermont, Department of Psychiatry.

Achenbach, T. M., & Edelbrock, C. S. (1981). Behavior problems and competencies reported by parents of normal and disturbed children aged four through sixteen. *Monographs of the Society for Research in Child Development, 46* (1, Serial No. 188).

Achenbach, T. M., & Edelbrock, C. S. (1983). Taxonomic issues in child psychopathology. In T. H. Ollendick & M. Hersen (Eds.), *Handbook of child psychopathology* (pp. 65–93). New York: Plenum.

Achenbach, T. M., & Edelbrock, C. S. (1984). *Child behavior checklist—teacher's report.* Burlington, VT: University Associates in Psychiatry.

Achenbach, T. M., & Edelbrock, C. S. (1989). Diagnostic, taxonomic, and assessment issues. In T. H. Ollendick & M. Hersen (Eds.), *Handbook of child psychopathology* (2nd ed., pp. 53–69). New York: Plenum.

Achenbach, T. M., Howell, C. T., Quay, H. C., & Conners, C. K. (1991). National survey of problems and competencies among four- to sixteen-year-olds. *Monographs of the Society for Research in Child Development, 56*(3), Serial No. 225.

Ack, M. (1970). Some principles of education for the emotionally disturbed. In P. A. Gallagher & L. L. Edwards (Eds.), *Educating the emotionally disturbed: Theory to practice* (pp. 1–17). Lawrence, KS: University of Kansas.

Ackerson, L. (1942). *Children's behavior problems.* Chicago: University of Chicago Press.

Adams, P. J., Katz, R. C., Beauchamp, K., Cohen, E., & Zavis, D. (1993). Body dissatisfaction, eating disorders, and depression: A developmental perspective. *Journal of Child and Family Studies, 2,* 37–46.

Adler, J., Wingert, P., Wright, L., Houston, P., Manly, H., & Cohen, A. D. (1992, February 17). Hey, I'm terrific!. *Newsweek, 119*(7), 46–51.

Aichorn, A. (1935). *Wayward youth.* New York: Viking Press.

Alaghband-Rad, J., McKenna, K., Gordon, C. T., Albus, K., Hamburger, S. D., Rumsey, J. M.,

Frazier, J. A., Lenane, M. C., & Rapoport, J. L. (1995). Childhood-onset schizophrenia: The severity of premorbid course. *Journal of the American Academy of Child and Adolescent Psychiatry, 34,* 1273–1283.

Alberto, P., & Troutman, A. (1995). *Applied behavior analysis for teachers* (4th ed.). Columbus, OH: Merrill/Macmillan.

Alberts-Corush, J., Firestone, P., & Goodman, J. T. (1986). Attention and impulsivity characteristics of the biological and adoptive parents of hyperactive and normal control children. *American Journal of Orthopsychiatry, 56,* 413–423.

Alexander, F. G., & Selsnick, S. T. (1966). *The history of psychiatry: An evaluation of psychiatric thought from prehistoric times to the present.* New York: Harper & Row.

Allison, K., Leone, P. E., & Spero, E. R. (1990). Drug and alcohol use among adolescents: Social context and competence. In P. E. Leone (Ed.), *Understanding troubled and troubling youth* (pp. 173–193). Newbury Park, CA: Sage.

Allison, M. (1992). The effects of neurologic injury on the maturing brain. *Headlines, 3*(5), 2–10.

Allison, M. (1993). Exploring the link between violence and brain injury. *Headlines, 4*(2), 12–15.

American Psychiatric Association. (1994). *Diagnostic and statistical manual of mental disorders* (4th ed.). Washington, DC: Author.

American Psychological Association. (1993). *Violence and youth: Psychology's response. Volume I: Summary report of the American Psychological Association Commission on Violence and Youth.* Washington, DC: Author.

Anastopoulos, A. D., DuPaul, G. J., & Barkley, R. A. (1991). Stimulant medication and parent training therapies for attention deficit-hyperactivity disorder. *Journal of Learning Disabilities, 24,* 210–218.

Anderson, J., & Werry, J. S. (1994). Emotional and behavioral problems. In I. B. Pless (Ed.), *The epidemiology of childhood disorders* (pp. 304–338). New York: Oxford University Press.

Anderson, J. C. (1994). Epidemiological issues. In T. H. Ollendick, N. J. King, & W. Yule (Eds.), *International handbook of phobic and anxiety disorders in children and adolescents* (pp. 43-65). New York: Plenum.

Anderson, M. G., & Webb-Johnson, G. (1995). Cultural contexts, the seriously emotionally disturbed classification, and African American learners. In B. A. Ford, F. E. Obiakor, & J. M. Patton (Eds.), *Effective education of African American exceptional learners: New perspectives* (pp. 151–187). Austin, TX: Pro-Ed.

Anonymous. (1994). First person account: Schizophrenia with childhood onset. *Schizophrenia Bulletin, 20,* 587–590.

Apter, A., Gothelf, D., Orbach, I., Weizman, R., Ratzoni, G., Hareven, D., & Tyano, S. (1995). Correlation of suicidal and violent behavior in different diagnostic categories in hospitalized adolescent patients. *Journal of the American Academy of Child and Adolescent Psychiatry, 34,* 912–918.

Apter, S. J., & Conoley, J. C. (1984). *Childhood behavior disorders and emotional disturbance.* Englewood Cliffs, NJ: Prentice-Hall.

Arbelle, S., Sigman, M. D., & Kasari, G. (1994). Compliance with parental prohibition in autistic children. *Journal of Autism and Developmental Disorders, 24,* 693–702.

Armstrong, M. I., & Evans, M. E. (1992). Three intensive community-based programs for children and youth with serious emotional disturbance and their families. *Journal of Child and Family Studies, 1,*, 61–74.

Armstrong, T. (1995). ADD: Does it really exist? *Phi Delta Kappan, 77,* 424–428.

Arnold, E. H., & O'Leary, S. G. (1995). The effect of child negative affect on maternal discipline behavior. *Journal of Abnormal Child Psychology, 23,* 585–595.

Arnold, W. R. & Brungardt, T. M. (1983). *Juvenile misconduct and delinquency.* Boston: Houghton Mifflin.

Arroyo, W., & Eth, S. (1995). Assessment following violence-witnessing trauma. In E. Peled, P. G. Jaffe, & J. L. Edelson (Eds.), *Ending the cycle of violence: Community responses to children of battered women* (pp. 27–42). Thousand Oaks, CA: Sage.

Artiles, A. J., & Trent, S. C. (1994). Overrepresentation of minority students in special education: A continuing debate. *Journal of Special Education, 27,* 383–409.

Asarnow, J. R., Tompson, M. C., & Goldstein, M. J. (1994). Childhood-onset schizophrenia: A follow-up study. *Schizophrenia Bulletin, 20,* 599–617.

Asarnow, R. F., Asamen, J., Granholm, E., Sherman, T., Watkins, J. M., & Williams, M. E. (1994). Cognitive/neuropsychological studies of children with a schizophrenic disorders. *Schizophrenia Bulletin, 20*, 647–669.

Asarnow, R. F., & Asarnow, J. R. (1994). Childhood-onset schizophrenia: Editors' introduction. *Schizophrenia Bulletin, 20*, 591–597.

Ashem, B., & Jones, M. D. (1978). Deleterious effects of chronic undernutrition on cognitive abilities. *Journal of Child Psychology and Psychiatry, 19*, 23–31.

Asher, S. R., & Coie, J. D. (Eds.). (1990). *Peer rejection in childhood*. New York: Cambridge University Press.

Axelrod, S., & Apsche, J. (Eds.). (1983). *The effects of punishment on human behavior*. New York: Academic Press.

Axline, V. (1947). *Play therapy*. Boston: Houghton Mifflin.

Baker, E. M., & Stullken, E. H. (1938). American research studies concerning the "behavior" type of exceptional child. *Journal of Exceptional Children, 4*, 36–45.

Baker, H. J. (1934). Common problems in the education of the normal and the handicapped. *Exceptional Children, 1*, 39–40.

Baker, P. (1996, January 16). Virginia joins movement to get tough on violent youths. *The Washington Post*, B1, B4.

Balthazar, E., & Stevens, H. (1975). *The emotionally disturbed mentally retarded*. Englewood Cliffs, NJ: Prentice-Hall.

Bandura, A. (1973). *Aggression: A social learning analysis*. Englewood Cliffs, NJ: Prentice-Hall.

Bandura, A. (1977). *Social learning theory*. Englewood Cliffs, NJ: Prentice-Hall.

Bandura, A. (1978). The self-system in reciprocal determinism. *American Psychologist, 33*, 344–358.

Bandura, A. (1986). *Social foundations of thought and action: A social cognitive theory*. Englewood Cliffs, NJ: Prentice-Hall.

Bandura, A. (1995). Comments on the crusade against the causal efficacy of human thought. *Journal of Behavior Therapy and Experimental Psychiatry, 26*, 179–190.

Banks, J. A. (1993). *Introduction to multicultural education*. Boston: Allyn & Bacon.

Banks, J. A. (1994). *Multiethnic education: Theory and practice* (3rd ed.). Boston: Allyn & Bacon.

Banks, J. A. (1995). The historical reconstruction of knowledge about race: Implications for transformative teaching. *Educational Researcher, 24*(2), 15–25.

Banks, J. A., & Banks, C. A. (Eds.). (1993). *Multicultural education: Issues and perspectives* (2nd ed.). Boston: Allyn & Bacon.

Barker, R. G. (1968). *Ecological psychology: Concepts and methods for studying the environment of human behavior*. Palo Alto, CA: Stanford University Press.

Barker, R. G., & Wright, H. F. (1949). Psychological ecology and the problem of psychosocial development. *Child Development, 20*, 131–143.

Barker, R. G., & Wright, H. F. (1954). *Midwest and its children*. Evanston, IL: Row, Peterson.

Barkley, R. A. (1985). Attention deficit disorder. In P. H. Bornstein & A. E. Kazdin (Eds.), *Handbook of clinical behavior therapy with children* (pp. 158–217). Homewood, IL: Dorsey Press.

Barkley, R. A. (1990). *Attention-deficit hyperactivity disorder: A handbook for diagnosis and treatment*. New York: Guilford Press.

Barkley, R. A. (1991). Foreword. In L. Braswell & M. L. Bloomquist, *Cognitive-behavioral therapy with ADHD children: Child, family, and school interventions* (pp. vii–xii). New York: Guilford Press.

Baroncohen, S., Campbell, R., Karmiloff-Smith, A., Grant, J., & Walker, J. (1995). Are children with autism blind to the mentalistic significance of the eyes? *British Journal of Developmental Psychology, 13*, 379–398.

Barrett, R. P. (Ed.) (1986). *Severe behavior disorders in the mentally retarded*. New York: Plenum.

Barrios, B. A. (1993). Direct observation. In T. H. Ollendick & M. Hersen (Eds.), *Handbook of child and adolescent assessment* (pp. 140–164). New York: Pergamon.

Bateman, B. D. (1992). Learning disabilities: The changing landscape. *Journal of Learning Disabilities, 25*, 29–36.

Bateman, B. D. (1994). Who, how, and where: Special education's issues in perpetuity. *The Journal of Special Education, 27*, 509–520.

Bateman, B. D. (1996). *Better IEPs* (2nd ed.). Longmont, CO: Sopris West.

Bateman, B. D., & Chard, D. J. (1995). Legal demands and constraints on placement decisions.

In J. M. Kauffman, J. W. Lloyd, D. P. Hallahan, & T. A. Astuto (Eds.), *Issues in educational placement: Students with emotional and behavioral disorders* (pp. 285–316). Hillsdale, NJ: Erlbaum.

Bateman, B. D., & Herr, C. L. (1981). Law and special education. In J. M. Kauffman & D. P. Hallahan (Eds.), *Handbook of special education* (pp. 330–360). Englewood Cliffs, NJ: Prentice-Hall.

Bates, J. E., & Wachs, T. D. (Eds.). (1994). *Temperament: Individual differences at the interface of biology and behavior*. Washington, DC: American Psychological Association.

Baumeister, A. A., Kupstas, F., & Klindworth, L. M. (1990). New morbidity: Implication for prevention of children's disabilities. *Exceptionality, 1,* 1–16.

Baumrind, D. (1995). *Child maltreatment and optimal caregiving in social contexts*. New York: Garland.

Bazemore, S. G., & Umbreit, M. (1995). Rethinking the sanctioning function of juvenile court: Retributive or restorative responses to youth crime. *Crime and Delinquency, 41,* 296–316.

Bear, G. G., & Richards, H. C. (1981). Moral reasoning and conduct problems in the classroom. *Journal of Educational Psychology, 73,* 664–670.

Beare, P. L. (1991). Philosophy, instructional methodology, training, and goals of teachers of the behaviorally disordered. *Behavioral Disorders, 16,* 211–218.

Beck, J. M., & Saxe, R. W. (Eds.) (1965). *Teaching the culturally disadvantaged pupil*. Springfield, IL: Charles C. Thomas.

Beck, S. J. (1995). Behavioral assessment. In M. Hersen & R. T. Ammerman (Eds.), *Advanced abnormal child psychology* (pp. 157–170). Hillsdale, NJ: Erlbaum.

Becker, W. C. (1964). Consequences of different kinds of parental discipline. In M. L. Hoffman & L. W. Hoffman (Eds.), *Review of child development research* (Vol. 1, pp. 169–208). New York: Russell Sage Foundation.

Beers, C. W. (1908). *A mind that found itself: An autobiography*. New York: Longmans, Green.

Begali, V. (1992). *Head injury in children and adolescents* (2nd ed.). Brandon, VT: Clinical Psychology Publishing Company.

Belcher, T. L. (1995). Behavioral treatment vs. behavioral control: A case study. *Journal of Developmental and Physical Disabilities, 7,* 235–241.

Bell, R. Q. (1968). A reinterpretation of the direction of effects in studies of socialization. *Psychological Review, 75,* 81–95.

Bell, R. Q., & Harper, L. V. (1977). *Child effects on adults*. Hillsdale, NJ: Erlbaum.

Bender, L. (1948). Genesis of hostility in children. *American Journal of Psychiatry, 105,* 241–245.

Bender, L. (1956). Childhood schizophrenia—Its recognition, description, and treatment. *American Journal of Orthopsychiatry, 26,* 499–506.

Bender, L. (1969). The nature of childhood psychosis. In J. G. Howells (Ed.), *Modern perspectives in international child psychiatry*. New York: Brunner/Mazel.

Bender, R. (1993). What makes a pull-out program work? *Effective School Practices, 12*(1), 16–19.

Benson, M. D., & Torpy, E. J. (1995). Sexual behavior in junior-high-school students. *Obstetrics and Gynecology, 85,* 279–284.

Bergland, M., & Hoffbauer, D. (1996). New opportunities for students with traumatic brain injuries. *Teaching Exceptional Children, 28*(2), 54–56.

Bergman, P., & Escalona, S. (1949). Unusual sensitivities in very young children. *Psychoanalytic Study of the Child, 3–4,* 333–352.

Berkowitz, P. H. (1967). Public schools in treatment centers: An evaluation. In P. H. Berkowitz & E. P. Rothman (Eds.), *Public education for disturbed children in New York City* (pp. 182–196). Springfield, IL: Charles C. Thomas.

Berkowitz, P. H. (1974). Pearl H. Berkowitz. In J. M. Kauffman & C. D. Lewis (Eds.), *Teaching children with behavior disorders: Personal perspectives* (pp. 24–49). Columbus, OH: Merrill.

Berkowitz, P. H., & Rothman, E. P. (1960). *The disturbed child: Recognition and psychoeducational therapy in the classroom*. New York: New York University Press.

Berkowitz, P. H., & Rothman, E. P. (1967a). Educating disturbed children in New York City: An historical overview. In P. H. Berkowitz & E. P. Rothman (Eds.), *Public education for disturbed children in New York City* (pp. 5–19). Springfield, IL: Charles C. Thomas.

Berkowitz, P. H., & Rothman, E. P. (Eds.). (1967b). *Public education for disturbed children in New York City*. Springfield, IL: Charles C. Thomas.

Berndt, T. J., & Keefe, K. (1995). Friends' influence on adolescents' adjustment to school. *Child Development, 66,* 1312–1329.

Berry, C. S. (1936). The exceptional child in regular classes. *Exceptional Children, 3,* 15–16.

Bettelheim, B. (1950). *Love is not enough.* New York: Macmillan.

Bettelheim, B. (1961). The decision to fail. *The School Review, 69,* 389–412.

Bettelheim, B. (1967). *The empty fortress.* New York: Free Press.

Bettelheim, B. (1970). Listening to children. In P. A. Gallagher & L. L. Edwards (Eds.), *Educating the emotionally disturbed: Theory to practice* (pp. 36–56). Lawrence: University of Kansas.

Bettelheim, B., & Sylvester, E. (1948). A therapeutic milieu. *American Journal of Orthopsychiatry, 18,* 191–206.

Biglan, A. (1995). Translating what we know about the context of antisocial behavior into lower prevalence of such behavior. *Journal of Applied Behavior Analysis, 28,* 479–492.

Biklen, D. (1990). Communication unbound: Autism and praxis. *Harvard Educational Review, 60,* 291–314.

Biklen, D., & Schubert, A. (1991). New words: The communication of students with autism. *Remedial and Special Education, 12*(6), 46–57.

Billingsley, A., & Caldwell, C. H. (1991). The church, the family and the school in the African-American community. *Journal of Negro Education, 60,* 427–440.

Black, B., & Uhde, T. W. (1995). Psychiatric characteristics of children with selective mutism. *Journal of the Academy of Child and Adolescent Psychiatry, 34,* 847-856.

Blackburn, R. (1993). *The psychology of criminal conduct: Theory, research, and practice.* New York: Wiley.

Blackman, J. A., Westervelt, V. D., Stevenson, R., & Welch, A. (1991). Management of preschool children with attention deficit-hyperactivity disorder. *Topics in Early Childhood Special Education, 11*(2), 91–104.

Blair, R. J. (1992. Application of the life-impact curriculum. *Journal of Emotional and Behavioral Problems, 1*(2), 16–21.

Blanton, S. (1925). The function of the mental hygiene clinic in schools and colleges. *New Republic, 122,* 93–101.

Blatt, B. (1975). Toward an understanding of people with special needs. In J. M. Kauffman & J. S. Payne (Eds.), *Mental retardation: Introduction and personal perspectives* (pp. 388–427). Columbus, OH: Merrill.

Blatt, B., & Kaplan, F. (1966). *Christmas in purgatory: A photographic essay on mental retardation.* Boston: Allyn & Bacon.

Blechman, E. A., Prinz, R. J., & Dumas, J. E. (1995). Coping, competence, and aggression prevention: I. Developmental model. *Applied and Preventive Psychology, 4,* 211–232.

Bloomingdale, L., Swanson, J. M., Barkley, R. A., & Satterfield, J. (1991, March). *Response to the ADD notice of inquiry by the Professional Group for ADD and Related Disorders (PGARD).* Scarsdale, NY: PGARD.

Blumenfeld, P. C., Pintrich, P. R., & Hamilton, V. L. (1987). Teacher talk and students' reasoning about morals, conventions, and achievement. *Child Development, 58,* 1389–1401.

Bockoven, J. S. (1956). Moral treatment in American psychiatry. *Journal of Nervous and Mental Disease, 124,* 167–194, 292–321.

Bockoven, J. S. (1972). *Moral treatment in community mental health.* New York: Springer.

Bodanis, D. (1986). *The secret house.* New York: Simon & Shuster.

Bolgar, R., Zweig-Frank, H., & Paris, J. (1995). Childhood antecedents of interpersonal problems in young adult children of divorce. *Journal of the American Academy of Child and Adolescent Psychiatry, 34,* 143–150.

Bolger, K. E., Patterson, C. J., Thompson, W. W., & Kupersmidt, J. B. (1995). Psychosocial adjustment among children experiencing persistent and intermittent family economic hardship. *Child Development, 66,* 1107–1129.

Bondy, A. S., & Frost, L. A. (1995). Educational approaches in preschool: Behavior techniques in a public school setting. In E. Schopler & G. B. Mesibov (Eds.), *Learning and cognition in autism* (pp. 311–333). New York: Plenum.

Boney-McCoy, S., & Finkelhor, D. (1995). Psychosocial sequelae of violent victimization in a national youth sample. *Journal of Consulting and Clinical Psychology, 63,* 726–736.

Boodman, S. G. (1995a, June 13). Researchers study obesity in children. *The Washington Post Health,* pp. 10, 13, 15.

Boodman, S. G. (1995b, December 11). Stressed for success: Youths face enormous pressures, yet most are happy. *The Washington Post*, pp. A1, A16–A17.

Boris, M., & Mandel, F. S. (1994). Foods and additives are common causes of the attention deficit hyperactive disorder in children. *Annals of Allergy, 72,* 462–468.

Bortner, M., & Birch, H. G. (1969). Patterns of intellectual ability in emotionally disturbed and brain-damaged children. *Journal of Special Education, 3,* 351–369.

Botvin, G. J., Schinke, S., & Orlandi, M. A. (1995). School-based health promotion: Substance abuse and sexual behavior. *Applied and Preventive Psychology, 4,* 167–184.

Bower, B. (1995). Criminal intellects: Researchers look at why lawbreakers often brandish low IQs. *Science News, 147,* 232–233, 239.

Bower, E. M. (1960). *Early identification of emotionally handicapped children in school.* Springfield, IL: Charles C. Thomas.

Bower, E. M. (Ed.). (1980). *The handicapped in literature. A psychosocial perspective.* Denver: Love.

Bower, E. M. (1981). *Early identification of emotionally handicapped children in school* (3rd ed.). Springfield, IL: Charles C. Thomas.

Bower, E. M. (1982). Defining emotional disturbance: Public policy and research. *Psychology in the Schools, 19,* 55–60.

Bower, E. M., & Lambert, N. M. (1962). *A process for in-school screening of children with emotional handicaps.* Princeton, NJ: Educational Testing Service.

Bower, E. M., Shellhammer, T. A., & Daily, J. M. (1960). School characteristics of male adolescents who later became schizophrenic. *American Journal of Orthopsychiatry, 30,* 712–729.

Braaten, S. R. (1982). A model for the differential assessment and placement of emotionally disturbed students in special education programs. In M. M. Noel & N. G. Haring (Eds.), *Progress or change: Issues in educating the emotionally disturbed: Vol. 1. Identification and program planning* (pp. 61–94). Seattle: University of Washington.

Braaten, S. R. (1985). Adolescent needs and behavior in the schools: Current and historical perspectives. In S. R. Braaten, R. B. Rutherford, & W. Evans (Eds.), *Programming for adolescents with behavioral disorders* (Vol. 2, pp. 1–10). Reston, VA: Council for Children with Behavioral Disorders.

Braaten, S. R., Kauffman, J. M., Braaten, B., Polsgrove, L., & Nelson, C. M. (1988). The regular education initiative: Patent medicine for behavioral disorders. *Exceptional Children, 55,* 21–28.

Braaten, S. R., Simpson, R., Rosell, J., & Reilly, T. (1988). Using punishment with exceptional children: A dilemma for educators. *Teaching Exceptional Children, 20*(2), 79–81.

Brandenburg, N. A., Friedman, R. M., & Silver, S. E. (1990). The epidemiology of childhood psychiatric disorders: Prevalence findings from recent studies. *Journal of the American Academy of Child and Adolescent Psychiatry, 29,* 76–83.

Braswell, L., & Bloomquist, M. L. (1991). *Cognitive-behavioral therapy with ADHD children: Child, family, and school interventions.* New York: Guilford Press.

Bremner, R. H. (Ed.). (1970). *Children and youth in America: A documentary history: Vol 1. 1600–1865.* Cambridge, MA: Harvard University Press.

Bremner, R. H. (Ed.). (1971). *Children and youth in America: A documentary history: Vol. 2. 1866–1932.* Cambridge, MA: Harvard University Press.

Brigham, A. (1845). Schools in lunatic asylums. *American Journal of Insanity, 1,* 326–340.

Brigham, A. (1847). The moral treatment of insanity. *American Journal of Insanity, 4,* 1–15.

Brigham, A. (1848). Schools and asylums for the idiotic and imbecile. *American Journal of Insanity, 5,* 19–33.

Bronfenbrenner, U., Moen, P., & Garbarino, J. (1984). Child, family, and community. In R. D. Parke (Ed.), *Review of child development research* (Vol. 7, pp. 283–328). Chicago: University of Chicago Press.

Brook, J. S., Whiteman, M., Cohen, P., Shapiro, J., & Balka, E. (1995). Longitudinally predicting late adolescent and young adult drug use: Childhood and adolescent precursors. *Journal of the American Academy of Child and Adolescent Psychiatry, 34,* 1230–1238.

Brown, D. (1995, December 8). Researchers, journalists "oversold" gene therapy: NIH advisers cite nearly uniform failure. *The Washington Post*, pp. A1, A22.

Brown, F. (1943). A practical program for early detection of atypical children. *Exceptional Children, 10,* 3–7.

Brown, J. L., & Pollitt, E. (1996). Malnutrition, poverty, and intellectual development. *Scientific American, 274*(2), 38–43.

Brown, L. L. (1987). Assessing socioemotional development. In D. D. Hammill (Ed.), *Assessing the abilities and instructional needs of students* (pp. 504–609). Austin, TX: Pro-Ed.

Brown, L. L., & Hammill, D. D. (1990). *Behavior rating profile: An ecological approach to behavioral assessment* (2nd ed.). Austin, TX: Pro-Ed.

Bryant, E. S., Garrison, C. Z., Valois, R. F., Rivard, J. C., & Hinkle, K. T. (1995). Suicidal behavior among youth with severe emotional disturbance. *Journal of Child and Family Studies, 4*, 429–443.

Bryant, E. S., Rivard, J. C., Addy, C. L., Hinkle, K. T., Cowan, T. M., & Wright, G. (1995). Correlates of major and minor offending among youth with severe emotional disturbance. *Journal of Emotional and Behavioral Disorders, 3*, 76–84.

Buitelaar, J. K. (1995). Attachment and social withdrawal in autism—Hypotheses and findings. *Behaviour, 132*, 319–350.

Bukstein, O. G. (1995). *Adolescent substance abuse: Assessment, prevention, and treatment*. New York: Wiley.

Burbach, H. J. (1981). The labeling process: A sociological analysis. In J. M. Kauffman & D. P. Hallahan (Eds.), *Handbook of special education* (pp. 361–377). Englewood Cliffs, NJ: Prentice-Hall.

Burke, D. (1972). Countertheoretical interventions in emotional disturbance. In W. C. Rhodes & M. L. Tracy (Eds.), *A study of child variance: Vol. 2. Interventions* (pp. 573–657). Ann Arbor: University of Michigan.

Bush, E. G., & Pargament, K. I. (1995). A quantitative and qualitative analysis of suicidal preadolescent children and their families. *Child Psychiatry and Human Development, 25*, 241–252.

Butera, G., & Haywood, H. C. (1995). Cognitive education of young children with autism: An application of Bright Start. In E. Schopler & G. B. Mesibov (Eds.), *Learning and cognition in autism* (pp. 269–292). New York: Plenum.

Cairns, R. B., & Cairns, B. D. (1986). The developmental-interactional view of social behavior: Four issues of adolescent aggression. In D. Olweus, J. Block, & M. Radke-Yarrow (Eds.), *Development of antisocial and prosocial behavior: Research, theories, and issues* (pp. 315–342). New York: Academic Press.

Cameron, J., & Pierce, W. D. (1994). Reinforcement, reward, and intrinsic motivation: A meta-analysis. *Review of Educational Research, 64*, 363–423.

Campbell, M., & Cueva, J. E. (1995a). Psychopharmacology in child and adolescent psychiatry: A review of the past seven years. Part I. *Journal of the American Academy of Child and Adolescent Psychiatry, 34*, 1124–1132.

Campbell, M., & Cueva, J. E. (1995b). Psychopharmacology in child and adolescent psychiatry: A review of the past seven years. Part II. *Journal of the American Academy of Child and Adolescent Psychiatry, 34*, 1262–1272.

Campbell, S. B. (1983). Developmental perspectives in child psychopathology. In T. H. Ollendick & M. Hersen (Eds.), *Handbook of child psychopathology* (pp. 13–40). New York: Plenum.

Campbell, S. B. (1995). Behavior problems in preschool children: A review of recent research. *Journal of Child Psychology and Psychiatry, 36*, 113–149.

Campbell, S. B., Breaux, A. M., Ewing, L. J., & Szumowski, E. K. (1986). Correlates and predictors of hyperactivity and aggression: A longitudinal study of parent-referred problem preschoolers. *Journal of Abnormal Child Psychology, 14*, 217–234.

Caplan, N., Choy, M. H., & Whitmore, J. K. (1992, February). Indochinese refugee families and academic achievement. *Scientific American, 266*(2), 36–42.

Caplan, R. (1994). Communication deficits in childhood schizophrenia spectrum disorders. *Schizophrenia Bulletin, 20*, 671–683.

Caplan, R. B. (1969). *Psychiatry and the community in nineteenth century America*. New York: Basic Books.

Carey, W. B., & McDevitt, S. C. (1995). *Coping with children's temperament: A guide for professionals*. New York: Basic Books.

Carlson, E. T., & Dain, N. (1960). The psychotherapy that was moral treatment. *American Journal of Psychiatry, 117*, 519–524.

Carlson, P. E., & Stephens, T. M. (1986). Cultural bias and identification of behaviorally disordered children. *Behavioral Disorders, 11*, 191–199.

Carnine, D. (1993, December 8). Facts, not fads. *Education Week*, pp. 40.

Carpenter, B., & Bovair, K. (1996). Learning with dignity: Educational opportunities for students with emotional and behavioral difficulties. *Canadian Journal of Special Education, 11*(1), 6–16.

Carr, E. G. (1981). Contingency management. In A. P. Goldstein, E. G. Carr, & W. S. Davidson (Eds.), *In response to aggression* (pp. 1–65). New York: Pergamon.

Cartledge, G., & Milburn, J. F. (Eds.). (1995). *Teaching social skills to children: Innovative approaches* (3rd ed.). Boston: Allyn & Bacon.

Caspi, A., Henry, B., McGee, R. O., Moffitt, T. E., & Silva, P. A. (1995). Temperamental origins of child and adolescent behavior problems: From age three to age fifteen. *Child Development, 66*, 55–68.

Center, D. B., Deitz, S. M., & Kaufman, M. E. (1982). Student ability, task difficulty, and inappropriate classroom behavior: A study of children with behavior disorders. *Behavior Modification, 6*, 355–374.

Center, D. B., & Obringer, J. (1987). A search for variables affecting underidentification of behaviorally disordered students. *Behavioral Disorders, 12*, 147–169.

Charlop, M. H., Kurtz, P. F., & Casey, F. G. (1990). Using aberrant behaviors as reinforcers for autistic children. *Journal of Applied Behavior Analysis, 23*, 163–181.

Charlop, M. H., Schreibman, L., & Kurtz, P. F. (1991). Childhood autism. In T. R. Kratochwill & R. J. Morris (Eds.), *The practice of child therapy* (2nd ed., pp. 257–297). New York: Pergamon.

Chen, S. A., & True, R. H. (1994). Asian/Pacific Island Americans. In L. D. Eron, J. H. Gentry, & P. Schlegel (Eds.), *Reason to hope: A psychosocial perspective on violence and youth* (pp. 145–162). Washington, DC: American Psychological Association.

Chesapeake Institute. (1994, September). *National agenda for achieving better results for children and youth with serious emotional disturbance*. Washington, DC: Author.

Chess, S., & Thomas, A. (1977). Temperamental individuality from childhood to adolescence. *Journal of the American Academy of Child Psychiatry, 16*, 218–226.

Christoffel, K. K. (1994). Intentional injuries: Homicide and violence. In I. B. Pless (Ed.), *The*

epidemiology of childhood disorders (pp. 392–411). New York: Oxford University Press.

Cicchetti, D., & Toth, S. L. (1995). A developmental psychopathology perspective on child abuse and neglect. *Journal of the American Academy of Child and Adolescent Psychiatry, 34*, 541–565.

Cipani, E. (1991). Behavior analysis and emotional disturbance. *Journal of Developmental and Physical Disabilities, 3*, 289–308.

Cipani, E. C. (1995). Be aware of negative reinforcement. *Teaching Exceptional Children, 27*(4), 36–40.

Clark, H. B., & Clarke, R. T. (1996). Research on the wraparound process and individualized services for children with multiple-system needs. *Journal of Child and Family Studies, 5*, 1–5.

Clark, H. B., Prange, M. E., Lee, B., Boyd, A., McDonald, B. A., & Stewart, E. S. (1994). Improving adjustment outcomes for foster children with emotional and behavioral disorders: Early findings from a controlled study of individualized services. *Journal of Emotional and Behavioral Disorders, 2*, 207–218.

Clark-Chiarelli, N., & Singer, J. D. (1995). Teachers of students with emotional or behavioral disorders: Who they are and how they view their jobs. In J. M. Kauffman, J. W. Lloyd, D. P. Hallahan, & T. A. Astuto (Eds.), *Issues in educational placement: Students with emotional and behavioral disorders* (pp. 145–168). Hillsdale, NJ: Erlbaum.

Clarke, R. T., Schaefer, M., Burchard, J. D., & Welkowitz, J. W. (1992). Wrapping community-based mental health services around children with a severe behavioral disorder: An evaluation of Project Wraparound. *Journal of Child and Family Studies, 1*, 241–261.

Clarke, S., Dunlap, G., Foster-Johnson, L., Childs, K. E., Wilson, D., White, R., & Vera, A. (1995). Improving the conduct of students with behavioral disorders by incorporating student interests into curricular activities. *Behavioral Disorders, 20*, 221–237.

Cline, D. H. (1990). A legal analysis of policy initiatives to exclude handicapped/disruptive students from special education. *Behavioral Disorders, 15*, 159–173.

Coffey, B. J., Miguel, E. C., Savage, C. R., & Rauch, S. L. (1994). Tourette's disorder and related problems: A review and update. *Harvard Review of Psychiatry, 2*, 121–132.

Coie, J. D. (1990). Toward a theory of peer rejection. In S. R. Asher & J. D. Coie (Eds.), *Peer rejection in childhood* (pp. 365–401). New York: Cambridge University Press.

Coie, J. D., & Dodge, K. A. (1983). Continuities and changes in children's social status: A five-year longitudinal study. *Merrill-Palmer Quarterly, 29,* 261–282.

Coie, J. D., Dodge, K. A., & Kupersmidt, J. (1990). Peer group behavior and social status. In S. R. Asher & J. D. Coie (Eds.), *Peer rejection in childhood* (pp. 17–59). New York: Cambridge University Press.

Coie, J. D., & Kupersmidt, J. B. (1983). A behavioral analysis of emerging social status in boys' groups. *Child Development, 54,* 1400–1416.

Coie, J. D., Watt, N. F., West, S. G., Hawkins, J. D., Asarnow, J. R., Markman, H. J., Ramey, S. L., Shure, M. B., & Long, B. (1993). The science of prevention: A conceptual framework and some directions for a national research program. *American Psychologist, 48,* 1013–1022.

Cole, D. A. & Rehm, L. P. (1986). Family interaction patterns and childhood depression. *Journal of Abnormal Child Psychology, 14,* 297–314.

Coleman, J. M., McHam, L. A., & Minnett, A. M. (1992). Similarities in the social competencies of learning disabled and low-achieving elementary school children. *Journal of Learning Disabilities, 25,* 671–677.

Coleman, M. C., & Gilliam, J. E. (1983). Disturbing behaviors in the classroom: A survey of teacher attitudes. *Journal of Special Education, 17,* 121–129.

Colvin, G., Greenberg, S., & Sherman, R. (1993). The forgotten variable: Improving academic skills for students with serious emotional disturbance. *Effective School Practices, 12*(1), 20–25.

Colvin, G., Sugai, G., & Patching, B. (1993). Precorrection: An instructional approach for managing predictable problem behaviors. *Intervention in School and Clinic, 28,* 143–150.

Comer, J. P. (1988). Is "parenting" essential to good teaching? *NEA Today, 6*(6), 34–40.

Conners, C. K., & Wells, K. C. (1986). *Hyperkinetic children: A neuropsychological approach.* Beverly Hills, CA: Sage.

Cooper, J. O., Heron, T. E., & Heward, W. L. (1987). *Applied behavior analysis.* Columbus, OH: Merrill/Macmillan.

Copeland, R. E., Brown, R. E., & Hall, R. V. (1974). The effects of principal-implemented techniques on the behavior of pupils. *Journal of Applied Behavior Analysis, 7,* 77–86.

Cossairt, A., Marlowe, M., Stellern, J., & Jacobs, J. (1985). Biofeedback assessment of behaviorally disordered students' stress levels and performance with a parent present during academic tasks. *Journal of Child and Adolescent Psychotherapy, 2,* 197–200.

Coulton, C. J., Korbin, J. E., Su, M., & Chow, J. (1995). Community level factors and child maltreatment rates. *Child Development, 66,* 1262–1276.

Council for Children with Behavioral Disorders (1989). Best assessment practices for students with behavioral disorders: Accommodation to cultural diversity and individual differences. *Behavioral Disorders, 14,* 263–278.

Council for Children with Behavioral Disorders. (1996). Guidelines for providing appropriate services to culturally diverse youngsters with emotional and/or behavioral disorders: Report of the Task Force of the CCBD Ad Hoc Committee on Ethnic and Multicultural Concerns. *Behavioral Disorders, 21,* 137–144.

Council for Children with Behavioral Disorders, Executive Committee. (1987). Position paper on definition and identification of students with behavioral disorders. *Behavioral Disorders, 13,* 9–19.

Courchesne, E. (1995). New evidence of cerebellar and brainstem hypoplasia in autistic infants, children and adolescents: The MR imaging study by Hashimoto and colleagues. *Journal of Autism and Developmental Disorders, 25,* 19–22.

Cox, S. M., Davidson, W. S., & Bynum, T. S. (1995). A metaanalytic assessment of delinquency-related outcomes of alternative education programs. *Crime and Delinquency, 41,* 219–234.

Cravioto, J., & DeLicardie, E. R. (1975). Environmental and nutritional deprivation in children with learning disabilities. In W. M. Cruickshank & D. P. Hallahan (Eds.), *Perceptual and learning disabilities in children: Vol. 2. Research and theory* (pp. 3–102). Syracuse, NY: Syracuse University Press.

Crews, W. D., Sanders, E. C., Hensley, L. G., Johnson, Y. M., Bonaventura, S., & Rhodes, R. D.

(1995). An evaluation of facilitated communication in a group of nonverbal individuals with mental retardation. *Journal of Autism and Developmental Disorders, 25,* 205–213.

Crissy, M. S. (1975). Mental retardation: Past, present, and future. *American Psychologist, 30,* 800–808.

Cruickshank, W. M. (1975). The learning environment. In W. M. Cruickshank & D. P. Hallahan (Eds.), *Perceptual and learning disabilities in children: Vol. 1. Psychoeducational practices* (pp. 227–277). Syracuse, NY: Syracuse University Press.

Cruickshank, W. M., Bentzen, F., Ratzeburg, F., & Tannhauser, M. A. (1961). *A teaching method for brain-injured and hyperactive children.* Syracuse, NY: Syracuse University Press.

Cruickshank, W. M., Paul, J. L., & Junkala, J. B. (1969). *Misfits in the public schools.* Syracuse, NY: Syracuse University Press.

Csapo, M. (1987). Anorexia nervosa and bulimia. *British Columbia Journal of Special Education, 11,* 251–288.

Cullinan, D., & Epstein, M. H. (1979). Administrative definitions of behavior disorders: Status and directions. In F. H. Wood & K. C. Lakin (Eds.), *Disturbing, disordered, or disturbed? Perspectives on the definition of problem behavior in educational settings* (pp. 17–28). Minneapolis: Advanced Training Institute, Department of Psychoeducational Studies, University of Minnesota.

Cullinan, D., & Epstein, M. H. (1985). Adjustment problems of mildly handicapped and nonhandicapped students. *Remedial and Special Education, 6*(2), 5–11.

Cullinan, D., Epstein, M. H., & Kauffman, J. M. (1982). The behavioral model and children's behavior disorders: Foundations and evaluation. In R. L. McDowell, G. W. Adamson, & F. H. Wood (Eds.), *Teaching emotionally disturbed children* (pp. 15–46). Boston: Little, Brown.

Cullinan, D., Epstein, M. H., & Kauffman, J. M. (1984). Teachers' ratings of students behaviors: What constitutes behavior disorder in schools? *Behavioral Disorders, 10,* 9–19.

Cullinan, D., Epstein, M. H., & Lloyd, J. W. (1991). Evaluation of conceptual models of behavior disorders. *Behavioral Disorders, 16,* 148–157.

Cummins, J. (1984). *Bilingualism and special education: Issues in assessment and pedagogy.* Clevedon, Avon, England: Multilingual Matters.

Cunningham, C. E., Cataldo, M. F., Mallion, C., & Keyes, J. B. (1984). A review and controlled single case evaluation of behavioral approaches to the management of elective mutism. *Child and Family Behavior Therapy, 5*(4), 25–49.

Curry, J. F., & Craighead, W. E. (1993). Depression. In T. H. Ollendick & M. Hersen (Eds.), *Handbook of child and adolescent assessment* (pp. 251–268). New York: Pergamon.

Dadds, M. R. (1995). *Families, children, and the development of dysfunction.* Thousand Oaks, CA: Sage.

Dain, N., & Carlson, E. T. (1960). Milieu therapy in the nineteenth century: Patient care at the Friend's Asylum, Frankford, Pennsylvania, 1817–1861. *Journal of Nervous and Mental Disease, 131,* 277–290.

Daly, P. M. (1985). The educateur: An atypical childcare worker. *Behavioral Disorders, 11,* 35–41.

Dangelo, L. L., Weinberger, D. A., & Feldman, S. S. (1995). Like father, like son: Predicting male adolescents' adjustment from parents' distress and self-restraint. *Developmental Psychopathology, 31,* 883–896.

D'Augelli, A. R., & Dark, L. J. (1994). Lesbian, gay, and bisexual youths. In L. D. Eron, J. H. Gentry, & P. Schlegel (Eds.), *Reason to hope: A psychosocial perspective on violence and youth* (pp. 177–196). Washington, DC: American Psychological Association.

Davids, L. (1975). Therapeutic approaches to children in residential treatment: Changes from the mid-1950s to the mid-1970s. *American Psychologist, 84,* 161–164.

Dawson, G., Klinger, L. G., Panagiotides, H., Lewy, A., & Castelloe, P. (1995). Subgroups of autistic children based on social behavior display distinct patterns of brain activity. *Journal of Abnormal Child Psychology, 23,* 569–583.

Deaton, A. V. (1994). Changing the behaviors of students with acquired brain injury. In R. C. Savage & G. F. Wolcott (Eds.), *Educational dimensions of acquired brain injury* (pp. 257–276). Austin, TX: Pro-Ed.

Deaton, A. V., & Waaland, P. (1994). Psychosocial effects of acquired brain injury. In R. C. Savage

& G. F. Wolcott (Eds.), *Educational dimensions of acquired brain injury* (pp. 239–255). Austin, TX: Pro-Ed.

Delpit, L. (1995). *Other people's children: Cultural conflict in the classroom*. New York: New Press.

Dembinski, R. J., Schultz, E. W., & Walton, W. T. (1982). Curriculum intervention with the emotionally disturbed student: A psychoeducational perspective. In R. L. McDowell, G. W. Adamson, & F. H. Wood (Eds.), *Teaching emotionally disturbed children* (pp. 206–234). Boston: Little, Brown.

DeMyer, M. K. (1975). The nature of neuropsychological disability in autistic children. *Journal of Autism and Childhood Schizophrenia, 5,* 109–128.

DeMyer, M. K., Barton, S., Alpern, G. D., Kimberlin, C., Allen, J., & Steele, R. (1974). The measured intelligence of autistic children. *Journal of Autism and Childhood Schizophrenia, 4,* 42–60.

Denery, J. (1994, October 22). Buford kids get caught doing good. *The Charlottesville Daily Progress,* pp. B1, B2.

Dennison, G. (1969). *The lives of children*. New York: Random House.

Denny, R. K., Gunter, P. L., Shores, R. E., & Campbell, C. R. (1995). Educational placements of students with emotional and behavioral disorders: What do they indicate? In J. M. Kauffman, J. W. Lloyd, D. P. Hallahan, & T. A. Astuto (Eds.), *Issues in educational placement: Students with emotional and behavioral disorders* (pp. 119–144). Hillsdale, NJ: Erlbaum.

Deno, S. L. (1985). Curriculum-based measurement: The emerging alternative. *Exceptional Children, 52,* 219–232.

Deno, S. L. (1987). Curriculum-based measurement. *Teaching Exceptional Children, 20,* 41–42.

DeRosier, M. E., Kupersmidt, J. B., & Patterson, C. J. (1995). Children's academic and behavioral adjustment as a function of the chronicity and proximity of peer rejection. *Child Development, 65,* 1799–1813. DesLauriers, A. M., & Carlson, C. F. (1969). *Your child is asleep: Early infantile autism*. Homewood, IL: Dorsey Press.

Despert, J. L. (1965). *The emotionally disturbed child—Then and now*. New York: Brunner.

Despert, J. L. (1968). *Schizophrenia in children*. New York: Brunner.

DeStefano, M. A., Gesten, E. L., & Cowen, E. L. (1977). Teachers' views of the treatability of children's school adjustment problems. *Journal of Special Education, 11,* 275–280. Deutsch, A. (1948). *The shame of the states*. New York: Harcourt, Brace, & World.

Devany, J., Rincover, A., & Lovaas, O. I. (1981). Teaching speech to nonverbal children. In J. M. Kauffman & D. P. Hallahan (Eds.), *Handbook of special education* (pp. 512–529). Englewood Cliffs, NJ: Prentice-Hall.

Diamond, S. C. (1993). Special education and the great god, inclusion. *Beyond Behavior, 4*(2), 3–6.

Dinitz, S., Scarpitti, F. R., & Reckless, W. C. (1962). Delinquency vulnerability: A cross group and longitudinal analysis. *American Sociological Review, 27,* 515–517. Dishion, T. J. (1990). The peer context of troublesome child and adolescent behavior. In P. E. Leone (Ed.), *Understanding troubled and troubling youth* (pp. 128–153). Newbury Park, CA: Sage.

Dishion, T. J., Andrews, D. W., & Crosby, L. (1995). Antisocial boys and their friends in early adolescence: Relationship characteristics, quality, and interactional process. *Child Development, 66,* 139–151.

Dishion, T. J., Loeber, R., Stouthamer-Loeber, M., & Patterson, G. R. (1984). Skill deficits and male adolescent delinquency. *Journal of Abnormal Child Psychology, 12,* 37–54.

Dixon, B. (1994). What's worse: An evil conspiracy or a very bad accident? *Effective School Practices, 12*(4), 10–23.

Dodge, K. A., & Somberg, D. R. (1987). Hostile attributional biases among aggressive boys are exacerbated under conditions of threats to self. *Child Development, 58,* 213–224.

Dokecki, P. R., Strain, B. A., Bernal, J. J., Brown, C. S., & Robinson, M. E. (1975). Low-income and minority groups. In N. Hobbs (Ed.), *Issues in the classification of children* (Vol. 1, pp. 312–348). San Francisco: Jossey-Bass.

Doll, E. A. (1967). Trends and problems in the education of the mentally retarded: 1900–1940. *American Journal of Mental Deficiency, 72,* 175–183.

Donahue, M., Cole, D., & Hartas, D. (1994). Links between language disorders and emotional/behavioral disorders. *Education and Treatment of Children, 17,* 244–254.

Donelson, K. (1987). Six statements/questions from the censors. *Phi Delta Kappan, 69,* 208–214.

Dornbusch, S. M., Ritter, P. L., Leiderman, P. H., Roberts, D. F., & Fraleigh, M. J. (1987). The relation of parent style to adolescent school performance. *Child Development, 58,* 1244–1257.

Dow, S. P., Sonies, B. C., Scheib, D., Moss, S. E., & Leonard, H. L. (1995). Practical guidelines for the assessment and treatment of selective mutism. *Journal of the American Academy of Child and Adolescent Psychiatry, 34,* 836–846.

Dubois, D. L., Felner, R. D., Bartels, C. L., & Silverman, M. M. (1995). Stability of self-reported depressive symptoms in a community sample of children and adolescents. *Journal of Clinical Child Psychology, 24,* 386–396.

Duchnowski, A., Berg, K., & Kutash, K. (1995). Parent participation in and perception of placement decisions. In J. M. Kauffman, J. W. Lloyd, D. P. Hallahan, & T. A. Astuto (Eds.), *Issues in educational placement: Students with emotional and behavioral disorders* (pp. 183–195). Hillsdale, NJ: Erlbaum.

Dugan, E., Kamps, D., Leonard, B., Watkins, N., Rheinberger, A., & Stackhaus, J. (1995). Effects of cooperative learning groups during social studies for students with autism and fourth-grade peers. *Journal of Applied Behavior Analysis, 28,* 175–188.

Duncan, B. B., Forness, S. R., & Hartsough, C. (1995). Students identified as seriously emotionally disturbed in day treatment: Cognitive, psychiatric, and special education characteristics. *Behavioral Disorders, 20,* 238–252.

Dunlap, G., dePerczel, M., Clarke, S., Wilson, D., Wright, S., White, R., & Gomez, A. (1994). Choice making to promote adaptive behavior for students with emotional and behavioral challenges. *Journal of Applied Behavior Analysis, 27,* 505–518.

Dunlap, G., Kern, L., dePerczel, M., Clarke, S., Wilson, D., Childs, K. E., White, R., & Falk, G. D. (1993). Functional analysis of classroom variables for students with emotional and behavioral disorders. *Behavioral Disorders, 18,* 275–291.

Dunlap, G., Robbins, F. R., & Kern, L. (1994). Some characteristics of nonaversive intervention for severe behavior problems. In E. Schopler & G. B. Mesibov (Eds.) *Behavioral issues in autism* (pp. 227–245) New York: Plenum.

Dunn, L. M. (1968). Special education for the mildly retarded—Is much of it justifiable? *Exceptional Children, 35,* 5–22.

DuPaul, G. J., Guevremont, D. C., & Barkley, R. A. (1991). Attention-deficit hyperactivity disorder. In T. R. Kratochwill & R. J. Morris (Eds.), *The practice of child therapy* (2nd ed., pp. 115–144). New York: Pergamon.

DuPaul, G. J., & Stoner, G. (1994). *ADHD in the schools: Assessment and intervention strategies.* New York: Guilford Press.

DuPaul, G. J., Stoner, G., Tilly, W. D., & Putnam, D. (1991). Interventions for attention problems. In G. Stoner, M. R. Shinn, & H. M. Walker (Eds.), *Interventions for achievement and behavior problems* (pp. 685–713). Silver Spring, MD: National Association of School Psychologists.

DuRant, R. H., Getts, A., Cadenhead, C., Emans, S. J., & Woods, E. R. (1995). Exposure to violence and victimization and depression, hopelessness, and purpose in life among adolescents living in and around public housing. *Developmental and Behavioral Pediatrics, 16,* 233–237.

Dwyer, J. A. T., & Kreitman, N. (1984). Hopelessness, depression, and suicidal intent. *British Journal of Psychiatry, 144,* 127–133.

Edelman, E. M., & Goldstein, A. P. (1981). Moral education. In A. P. Goldstein, E. G. Carr, W. S. Davidson, & P. Wehr (Eds.), *In response to aggression* (pp. 253–315). New York: Pergamon.

Edgar, E. B. (1987). Secondary programs in special education: Are many of them justifiable? *Exceptional Children, 53,* 555–561.

Edgar, E., & Siegel, S. (1995). Postsecondary scenarios for troubled and troubling youth. In J. M. Kauffman, J. W. Lloyd, D. P. Hallahan, & T. A. Astuto (Eds.), *Issues in educational placement: Students with emotional and behavioral disorders* (pp. 251–283). Hillsdale, NJ: Erlbaum.

Edgar, E. G., Webb, S. L., & Maddox, M. (1987). Issues in transition: Transfer of youth from correctional facilities to public schools. In C. M. Nelson, R. B. Rutherford, & B. I. Wolford (Eds.), *Special education in the criminal justice system* (pp. 251–272). Columbus, OH: Merrill/Macmillan.

Edgerton, R. B. (1984). Mental retardation: An anthropologist's changing view. In B. Blatt & R. J. Morris (Eds.). *Perspectives in special education: Personal orientations* (pp. 125–156). Glenview, IL: Scott, Foresman.

Eggers, C. (1978). Course and prognosis of childhood schizophrenia. *Journal of Autism and Childhood Schizophrenia, 8,* 21–36.

Eggleston, C. (1987). Correctional special education: Our rich history. In C. M. Nelson, R. B. Rutherford, & B. I. Wolford (Eds.), *Special education in the criminal justice system* (pp. 19–23). Columbus, OH: Merrill/Macmillan.

Eiduson, B. T., Eiduson, S., & Geller, E. (1962). Biochemistry, genetics, and the nature-nurture problem. *American Psychologist, 119,* 342–350.

Eisenberg, L. (1984). The epidemiology of suicide in adolescents. *Pediatric Annals, 13,* 47–54.

Eissler, K. R. (1949). *Searchlights on delinquency.* New York: International Universities Press.

Ellwood, M. S., & Stolberg, A. L. (1993). The effects of family composition, family health, parenting behavior and environmental stress on children's divorce adjustment. *Journal of Child and Family Studies, 2,* 23–36.

Elmquist, D. L. (1991). School-based alcohol and other drug prevention programs: Guidelines for the special educator. *Intervention in School and Clinic, 27,* 10–19.

Eme, R. F., & Danielak, M. H. (1995). Comparison of fathers of daughters with and without maladaptive eating attitudes. *Journal of Emotional and Behavioral Disorders, 3,* 40–45.

Emerson, E., & Bromley, J. (1995). The form and function of challenging behavior. *Journal of Intellectual Disability Research, 39,* 388–398.

Emery, R. E., Binkoff, J. A., Houts, A. C., & Carr, E. G. (1983). Children as independent variables: Some clinical implications of child effects. *Behavior Therapy, 14,* 398–412.

Epperson, S. E., Mondi, L., Graff, J. L., & Towle, L. H. (1995, October 2). The EQ factor. *Time, 146*(14), pp. 60–68.

Epstein, J. L. (1981). *The quality of school life.* Lexington, MA: D. C. Heath.

Epstein, M. A., Shaywitz, S. E., Shaywitz, B. A., & Woolston, J. L. (1991). The boundaries of attention deficit disorder. *Journal of Learning Disabilities, 24,* 78–86.

Epstein, M. H., Cullinan, D., & Polloway, E. A. (1986). Patterns of maladjustment among the mentally retarded. *American Journal of Mental Deficiency, 91,* 127–134.

Epstein, M. H., Kauffman, J. M., & Cullinan, D. (1985). Patterns of maladjustment among the behaviorally disordered: II. Boys aged 6–11, boys aged 12–18, girls aged 6–11, and girls aged 12–18. *Behavioral Disorders, 10,* 125–135.

Epstein, M. H., Kinder, D., & Bursuck, B. (1989). The academic status of adolescents with behavioral disorders. *Behavioral Disorders, 14,* 157–165.

Epstein, M. H., Singh, N. N., Luebke, J., & Stout, C. E. (1991). Psychopharmacological intervention. II: Teacher perceptions of psychotropic medication for students with learning disabilities. *Journal of Learning Disabilities, 24,* 477–483.

Epstein, M. J., Cullinan, D., & Sabatino, D. A. (1977). State definitions of behavior disorders. *Journal of Special Education, 11,* 417–425.

Eron, L. D., Gentry, J. H., & Schlegel, P. (Eds.). (1994). *Reason to hope: A psychosocial perspective on violence and youth.* Washington, DC: American Psychological Association.

Eron, L. D., & Huesmann, L. R. (1986). The role of television in the development of prosocial and antisocial behavior. In D. Olweus, J. Block, & M. Radke-Yarrow (Eds.), *Development of antisocial and prosocial behavior: Research, theories, and issues* (pp. 285–314). New York: Academic Press.

Esquirol, E. (1845). *Mental maladies: A treatise on insanity* (E. K. Hunt, Trans.). Philadelphia: Lea & Blanchard.

Etscheidt, M. A., & Ayllon, T. (1987). Contingent exercise to decrease hyperactivity: *Journal of Child and Adolescent Psychotherapy, 4,* 192–198.

Etzioni, A. (1994, July). Incorrigible: Bringing social hope and political rhetoric into instructive contact with what it means to be human. *Atlantic Monthly, 274,* pp. 14–16.

Evans, E. D., & Richardson, R. C. (1995). Corporal punishment: What teachers should know. *Teaching Exceptional Children, 27*(2), 33–36.

Evans, M. E., Armstrong, M. I., Dollard, N., Kuppinger, A. D., Huz, S., & Wood, V. M. (1994). Development and evaluation of treatment foster care and family-centered intensive case management in New York. *Journal of Emotional and Behavioral Disorders, 2,* 228–239.

Fabre, T. R., & Walker, H. M. (1987). Teacher perceptions of the behavioral adjustment of primary grade level handicapped pupils within regular and special education settings. *Remedial and Special Education, 8*(5), 34–39.

Fagen, S. A. (1979). Psychoeducational management and self-control. In D. Cullinan & M. H. Epstein (Eds.), *Special education for adolescents: Issues and perspectives* (pp. 235–271). Columbus, OH: Merrill.

Fagen, S. A., & Long, N. J. (1979). A psychoeducational curriculum approach to teaching self-control. *Behavioral Disorders, 4,* 68–82.

Fagen, S. A., Long, N. J., & Stevens, D. J. (1975). *Teaching children self-control.* Columbus, OH: Merrill.

Farmer, T. W., & Hollowell, J. H. (1994). Social networks in mainstream classrooms: Social affiliations and behavioral characteristics of students with EBD. *Journal of Emotional and Behavioral Disorders, 2,* 143–155.

Farmer, T. W., Stuart, C. B., Lorch, N. H., & Fields, E. (1993). The social behavior and peer relations of emotionally and behaviorally disturbed students in residential treatment: A pilot study. *Journal of Emotional and Behavioral Disorders, 1,* 223–234.

Farrington, D. P. (1986). The sociocultural context of childhood disorders. In H. C. Quay & J. S. Werry (Eds.), *Psychopathological disorders of childhood* (3rd ed.) (pp. 391–422). New York: Wiley.

Farrington, D. P. (1995). The development of offending and antisocial behaviour from childhood: Key findings from the Cambridge Study in Delinquent Development. *Journal of Child Psychology and Psychiatry, 36,* 929–964.

Farson, M. R. (1940). Education of the handicapped child for social competency. *Exceptional Children, 6,* 138–144, 150.

Feeney, T. J., & Urbanczyk, B. (1994). Behavior as communication. In R. C. Savage & G. F. Wolcott (Eds.), *Educational dimensions of acquired brain injury* (pp. 277–302). Austin, TX: Pro-Ed.

Feingold, B. F. (1975). *Why your child is hyperactive.* New York: Random House.

Feingold, B. F. (1976). Hyperkinesis and learning disabilities linked to the ingestion of artificial food colors and flavors. *Journal of Learning Disabilities, 9,* 551–559.

Feldman, D., Kinnison, L., Jay, R., & Harth, R. (1983). The effects of differential labeling on professional concepts and attitudes toward the emotionally disturbed/behaviorally disordered. *Behavioral Disorders, 8,* 191–198.

Feldman, R. S., Salzinger, S., Rosario, M., Alvardo, L., Caraballo, L., & Hammer, M. (1995). Parent, teacher, and peer ratings of physically abused and nonmaltreated children's behavior. *Journal of Abnormal Child Psychology, 23,* 317–334.

Felner, R. D., Brand, S., DuBois, D., Adan, A. M., Mulhall, P. F., & Evans, E. G. (1995). Socioeconomic disadvantage, proximal environmental experiences, and socioemotional and academic adjustment in early adolescence: Investigation of a mediated effects model. *Child Development, 66,* 774–792.

Fenichel, C. (1966). Psychoeducational approaches for seriously disturbed children in the classroom. In P. Knoblock (Ed.), *Intervention approaches in educating emotionally disturbed children* (pp. 5–18). Syracuse, NY: Syracuse University Press.

Fenichel, C. (1974). Carl Fenichel. In J. M. Kauffman & C. D. Lewis (Eds.), *Teaching children with behavior disorders: Personal perspectives* (pp. 50–75). Columbus, OH: Merrill.

Fenichel, C., Freedman, A. M., & Klapper, Z. (1960). A day school for schizophrenic children. *American Journal of Orthopsychiatry, 30,* 130–143.

Fergusson, D. M., & Horwood, L. J. (1995). Early disruptive behavior, IQ, and later achievement and delinquent behavior. *Journal of Abnormal Child Psychology, 23,* 183–199.

Fernald, W. E. (1893). The history of the treatment of the feebleminded. In I. C. Barrows (Ed.), *Proceedings of the National Conference of Charities and Correction.* Boston: G. Ellis.

Fine, A. H. (1991). Behavior disorders in childhood: The psychodynamic interpretation. *Journal of Developmental and Physical Disabilities, 3,* 245–266.

Fishbein, D., & Meduski, J. (1987). Nutritional biochemistry and behavioral disabilities. *Journal of Learning Disabilities, 20,* 505–512.

Fizzell, R. L. (1987). Inside a school of choice. *Phi Delta Kappan, 68,* 758–760.

Fletcher, J. M., Morris, R. D., & Francis, D. J. (1991). Methodological issues in the classification of attention-related disorders. *Journal of Learning Disabilities, 24,* 72–77.

Ford, B. A. (1995). African American community involvement processes and special education: Essential networks for effective education. In B. A. Ford, F. E. Obiakor, & J. M. Patton (Eds.), *Effective education of African American exceptional learners* (pp. 235–272). Austin, TX: Pro-Ed.

Forehand, R., & McKinney, B. (1993). Historical overview of child discipline in the United States: Implications for mental health clinicians and researchers. *Journal of Child and Family Studies, 2,* 221–228.

Forehand, R., Wierson, M., Frame, C. L., Kemptom, T., & Armistead, L. (1991). Juvenile firesetting: A unique syndrome or an advanced level of antisocial behavior? *Behaviour Research and Therapy, 29,* 125–128.

Foreyt, J. P., & Kondo, A. T. (1985). Eating disorders. In P. H. Bornstein & A. E. Kazdin (Eds.), *Handbook of clinical behavior therapy with children* (pp. 309–344). Homewood, IL: Dorsey Press.

Forness, S. R. (1988a). School characteristics of children and adolescents with depression. In R. B. Rutherford, C. M. Nelson, & S. R. Forness (Eds.), *Bases of severe behavioral disorders of children and youth* (pp. 177–203). Boston: Little, Brown.

Forness, S. R. (1988b). Planning for the needs of children with serious emotional disturbance: The national special education and mental health coalition. *Behavioral Disorders, 13,* 127–133.

Forness, S. R., & Kavale, K. A. (1988). Psychopharmacologic treatment: A note on classroom effects. *Journal of Learning Disabilities, 21,* 144–147.

Forness, S. R., Kavale, K. A., & Lopez, M. (1993). Conduct disorders in school: Special education eligibility and comorbidity. *Journal of Emotional and Behavioral Disorders, 1,* 101–108.

Forness, S. R., Kavale, K. A., MacMillan, D. L., Asarnow, J. R., & Duncan, B. B. (1996). Early detection and prevention of emotional or behavioral disorders: Developmental aspects of systems of care. *Behavioral Disorders*.

Forness, S. R., & Knitzer, J. (1992). A new proposed definition and terminology to replace "serious emotional disturbance" in Individuals with Disabilities Education Act, *School Psychology Review, 21,* 12–20.

Forness, S. R., & MacMillan, D. L. (1970). The origins of behavior modification with exceptional children. *Exceptional Children, 37,* 93–99.

Forness, S. R., Sinclair, E., & Russell, A. T. (1984). Serving children with emotional or behavioral disorders: Implications for educational policy. *American Journal of Orthopsychiatry, 54,* 22–32.

Foster, G. G., Ysseldyke, J. E., & Reese, J. H. (1975). "I wouldn't have seen it if I hadn't believed it." *Exceptional Children, 41,* 469–473.

Foster, H. L. (1986). *Ribbin', jivin', & playin' the dozens: The persistent dilemma in our schools* (2nd ed.). Cambridge, MA: Ballinger.

Fowler, M. (1992). *Ch.A.D.D. educators manual: An in-depth look at attention deficit disorders from an educational perspective*. Plantation, FL: Children with Attention Deficit Disorder.

Fox, J. J. (Ed.). (1987). Social interactions of behaviorally disordered children and youth [Special issue]. *Behavioral Disorders, 12*(4).

Franco, D. P., Christoff, K. A., Crimmins, D. B., & Kelly, J. A. (1983). Social skills training for an extremely shy young adolescent: An empirical case study. *Behavior Therapy, 14,* 568–575.

Fredericks, B., & Evans, V. (1987). Functional curriculum. In C. M. Nelson, R. B. Rutherford, & B. I. Wolford (Eds.), *Special education in the criminal justice system* (pp. 189–214). Columbus, OH: Merrill/Macmillan.

Freedman, J. (1993). *From cradle to grave: The human face of poverty in America*. New York: Atheneum.

Freud, A. (1946). *The ego and the mechanisms of defense*. New York: International Universities Press.

Freud, A. (1965). The relation between psychoanalysis and pedagogy. In N. J. Long, W. C. Morse, & R. G. Newman (Eds.), *Conflict in the classroom* (pp. 159–163). Belmont, CA: Wadsworth.

Fridrich, A. H., & Flannery, D. J. (1995). The effects of ethnicity and acculturation on early adolescent delinquency. *Journal of Child and Family Studies, 4,* 69–87.

Frostig, M. (1976). Marianne Frostig. In J. M. Kauffman & D. P. Hallahan (Eds.), *Teaching children with learning disabilities: Personal perspectives* (pp. 164–190). Columbus, OH: Merrill.

Fuchs, D., & Fuchs, L. S. (1994). Inclusive schools movement and the radicalization of special education reform. *Exceptional Children, 60,* 294–309.

Fuchs, D., & Fuchs, L. S. (1995). Special education can work. In J. M. Kauffman, J. W. Lloyd, D. P. Hallahan, & T. A. Astuto (Eds.), *Issues in educational placement: Students with emotional and behavioral disorders* (pp. 363–377). Hillsdale, NJ: Erlbaum.

Fuchs, D., Fuchs, L. S., Fernstrom, P., & Hohn, M. (1991). Toward a responsible reintegration of behaviorally disordered students. *Behavioral Disorders, 16,* 133–147.

Furlong, M. J., & Morrison, G. M. (1994). Introduction to the mini-series: School violence and safety in perspective. *School Psychology Review, 23,* 139–150.

Gadow, K. D. (1986). *Children on medication: Vol. II. Epilepsy, emotional disturbance, and adolescent disorders.* San Diego, CA: College Hill Press.

Gadow, K. D., & Pomeroy, J. C. (1991). An overview of psychopharmacotherapy for children and adolescents. In T. R. Kratochwill & R. J. Morris (Eds.), *The practice of child therapy* (2nd ed., pp. 367–409). New York: Pergamon.

Gadow, K. D., & Sprafkin, J. (1993). Television "violence" and children with emotional and behavioral disorders. *Journal of Emotional and Behavioral Disorders, 1,* 54–63.

Gardner, H., & Hatch, T. (1989). Multiple intelligences go to school: Educational implications of the theory of multiple intelligences. *Educational Researcher, 18*(8), 4–9.

Garmezy, N. (1974). Children at risk: The search for the antecedents of schizophrenia. Part I. Conceptual models and research methods. *Schizophrenia Bulletin, 8,* 14–89.

Garmezy, N. (1987). Stress, competence, and development. Continuities in the study of schizophrenic adults, children vulnerable to psychopathology, and the search for stress-resistant children. *American Journal of Orthopsychiatry, 57,* 159–174.

Garner, D. M., & Parker, P. (1993). Eating disorders. In T. H. Ollendick & M. Hersen (Eds.), *Handbook of child and adolescent assessment* (pp. 384–399). New York: Pergamon.

Garrison, C. Z., Addy, C. L., McKeown, R. E., Cuffe, S. P., Jackson, K. L., & Waller, J. L. (1993). Nonsuicidal physically self-damaging acts in adolescents. *Journal of Child and Family Studies, 2,* 339–352.

Garrison, W. T., & Earls, F. J. (1987). *Temperament and child psychopathology.* Newbury Park, CA: Sage.

Garrison, W. T., & McQuiston, S. (1989). *Chronic illness during childhood and adolescence: Psychological aspects.* Thousand Oaks, CA: Sage.

Gartner, A. F. (1985). Countertransference issues in the psychotherapy of adolescents. *Child and Adolescent Psychotherapy, 2,* 187–196.

Gelfand, D. M., Ficula, T., & Zarbatany, L. (1986). Prevention of childhood behavior disorders. In B. A. Edelstein & L. Michelson (Eds.), *Handbook of prevention* (pp. 133–152). New York: Plenum.

Genaux, M., Morgan, D. P., & Friedman, S. G. (1995). Substance use and its prevention: A summary of classroom practices. *Behavioral Disorders, 20,* 279–289.

Genius, S., & Genius, S. K. (1995). The challenge of sexually-transmitted diseases in adolescents. *Adolescent and Pediatric Gynecology, 8,* 82–88.

Gerber, M. M. (1988). Tolerance and technology of instruction: Implications for special education reform. *Exceptional Children, 54,* 309–314.

Gerber, M. M., & Kauffman, J. M. (1981). Peer tutoring in academic settings. In P. S. Strain (Ed.), *The utilization of classroom peers as behavior change agents* (pp. 155–187). New York: Plenum.

Gerber, M. M., & Semmel, M. I. (1984). Teacher as imperfect test: Reconceptualizing the referral process. *Educational Psychologist, 19,* 137–148.

Gerhardt, P. F., Holmes, D. L., Alessandri, M., & Goodman, M. (1991). Social policy on the use of aversive interventions: Empirical, ethical, and legal considerations. *Journal of Autism and Developmental Disorders, 21,* 265–280.

Germann, G., & Tindal, G. (1985). An application of curriculum-based assessment: The use of direct and repeated measurement. *Exceptional Children, 52,* 244–265.

Gersten, R., Walker, H. M., & Darch, C. (1988). Relationships between teachers' effectiveness and their tolerance for handicapped students. An exploratory study. *Exceptional Children, 54,* 433–438.

Gesten, E. L., Scher, K., & Cowen, E. L. (1978). Judged school problems and competencies of referred children from varying family background characteristics. *Journal of Abnormal Child Psychology, 6,* 247–255.

Gibbs, J. C., Arnold, K. D. Ahlborn, H. H., & Chessman, F. L. (1984). Facilitation of sociomoral reasoning in delinquents. *Journal of Consulting and Clinical Psychology, 52,* 37–45.

Gibbs, J. T. (1987). Identity and marginality: Issues in the treatment of biracial adolescents. *American Journal of Orthopsychiatry, 57,* 265–278.

Giddan, J. J., Bade, K. M., Rickenberg, D., & Ryley, A. T. (1995). Teaching the language of feelings to students with severe emotional and behavioral handicaps. *Language, Speech, and Hearing Services in the Schools, 26,* 3–13.

Gilbert, S. E., & Gay, G. (1985). Improving the success in school of poor black children. *Phi Delta Kappan, 67,* 133–137.

Gilliam, J. E., & Scott, B. K. (1987). The behaviorally disordered offender. In C. M. Nelson, R. B. Rutherford, & B. I. Wolford (Eds.), *Special education in the criminal justice system* (pp. 141–158). Columbus, OH: Merrill/Macmillan.

Gladstone, T. R. G., & Kaslow, N. J. (1995). Depression and attributions in children and adolescents: A meta-analytic review. *Journal of Abnormal Child Psychology, 23,* 597–606.

Glidewell, J. C. (1969). The child at school. In J. G. Howells (Ed.), *Modern perspectives in international child psychiatry.* New York: Brunner/Mazel.

Glidewell, J. C., Kantor, M. B., Smith, L. M. & Stringer, L. A. (1966). Socialization and social structure in the classroom. In L. W. Hoffman & M. L. Hoffman (Eds.), *Review of child development research* (Vol. 2, pp. 221–256). New York: Russell Sage Foundation.

Glidewell, J. C., & Swallow, C. S. (1968, July). *The prevalence of maladjustment in elementary schools.* Report prepared for the Joint Commission on the Mental Health of Children, University of Chicago.

Goldstein, A. P. (1983a). Behavior modification approaches to aggression prevention and control. In A. P. Goldstein (Ed.), *Prevention and control of aggression* (pp. 156–209). New York: Pergamon.

Goldstein, A. P. (1983b). United States: Causes, controls, and alternatives to aggression. In A. P. Goldstein & M. H. Segall (Eds.), *Aggression in global perspective* (pp. 435–474). New York: Pergamon.

Goldstein, A. P. (1987). Teaching prosocial skills to antisocial adolescents. In C. M. Nelson, R. B. Rutherford, & B. I. Wolford (Eds.), *Special education in the criminal justice system* (pp. 215–246). Columbus, OH: Merrill/Macmillan.

Goldstein, A. P. (1990). *Delinquents on delinquency.* Champaign, IL: Research Press.

Goldstein, A. P. (1991). *Delinquent gangs: A psychological perspective.* Champaign, IL: Research Press.

Goldstein, A. P., Carr, E. G., Davidson, W. S., & Wehr, P. (Eds.). (1981). *In response to aggression.* New York: Pergamon.

Goldstein, A. P., & Glick, B. (1994). *The prosocial gang: Implementing aggression replacement training.* Thousand Oaks, CA: Sage.

Goldstein, A. P., & Keller, H. R. (1983). Aggression prevention and control: multi-targeted, multi-channel, multi-process, multi-disciplinary. In A. P. Goldstein (Ed.), *Prevention and control of aggression* (pp. 338–350). New York: Pergamon.

Goldstein, A. P., & Segall, M. H. (Eds.). (1983). *Aggression in global perspective.* New York: Pergamon.

Goldstein, A. P., Sprafkin, R. P., Gershaw, N. J., & Klein, P. (1980). *Skillstreaming the adolescent: A structured learning approach to teaching prosocial skills.* Champaign, IL: Research Press.

Goldstein, A. P., Sprafkin, R. P., Gershaw, N. J., & Klein, P. (1986). The adolescent: Social skills training through structured learning. In G. Cartledge & J. F. Milburn (Eds.), *Teaching social skills to children* (2nd ed.) (pp. 303–336). New York: Pergamon.

Goleman, D. (1995). *Emotional intelligence.* New York: Bantam.

Goodall, K. (1972). Shapers at work. *Psychology Today, 6*(6), 53–63, 132–138.

Goodman, S. H., Gravitt, G. W., & Kaslow, N. J. (1995). Social problem solving: A moderator of the relation between negative life stress and depression symptoms in children. *Journal of Abnormal Child Psychology, 23,* 473–485.

Gordon, B. N., & Schroeder, C. S. (1995). *Sexuality: A developmental approach to problems.* New York: Plenum.

Gottesman, I. (1987). Schizophrenia: Irving Gottesman reveals the genetic factors. *University of Virginia Alumni News, 75*(5), 12–14.

Gottesman, I. I. (1991). *Schizophrenia genesis: The origins of madness.* New York: W. H. Freeman.

Graham, P. J. (1979). Epidemiological studies. In H. C. Quay & J. S. Werry (Eds.), *Psychopathological disorders of childhood* (2nd ed.) (pp. 185–209). New York: Wiley.

Grandin, T. (1995). How people with autism think. In E. Schopler & G. B. Mesibov (Eds.),

Learning and cognition in autism (pp. 137–156). New York: Plenum.

Graubard, P. S. (1964). The extent of academic retardation in a residential treatment center. *Journal of Educational Research, 58,* 78–80.

Graubard, P. S. (1971). The relationship between academic achievement and behavior dimensions. *Exceptional Children, 37,* 755–757.

Graubard, P. S. (1976). The use of indigenous grouping as the reinforcing agent in teaching disturbed delinquents to learn. In N. J. Long, W. C. Morse, & R. G. Newman (Eds.), *Conflict in the classroom* (3rd ed.) (pp. 342–346). Belmont, CA: Wadsworth.

Graubard, P. S., Rosenberg, H., & Miller, M. (1971). Ecological approaches to social deviancy. In E. Ramp & B. L. Hopkins (Eds.), *A new direction for education: Behavior analysis 1971* (pp. 80–101). Lawrence: Kansas University Department of Human Development.

Graziano, A. M., & Dorta, N. J. (1995). Behavioral treatment. In M. Hersen & R. T. Ammerman (Eds.), *Advanced abnormal child psychology* (pp. 171–187). Hillsdale, NJ: Erlbaum.

Green, L., Fein, D., Joy, S., & Waterhouse, L. (1995). Cognitive functioning in autism. In E. Schopler & G. B. Mesibov (Eds.), *Learning and cognition in autism* (pp. 13–31). New York: Plenum.

Greer, R. D., & Polirstok, S. R. (1982). Collateral gains and short-term maintenance in reading and on-task responses by inner-city adolescents as a function of their use of social reinforcement while tutoring. *Journal of Applied Behavior Analysis, 15,* 123–139.

Grenell, M. M., Glass, C. R., & Katz, K. S. (1987). Hyperactive children and peer interaction: Knowledge and performance of social skills. *Journal of Abnormal Child Psychology, 15,* 1–13.

Gresham, F. M., & Little, S. G. (1993). Peer-referenced assessment strategies. In T. H. Ollendick & M. Hersen (Eds.), *Handbook of child and adolescent assessment* (pp. 165–179). New York: Pergamon.

Griffin-Shelley, E. (1994). *Adolescent sex and love addicts.* Westport, CT: Praeger.

Griffiths, W. (1952). *Behavior difficulties of children as perceived and judged by parents, teachers, and children themselves.* Minneapolis: University of Minnesota Press.

Grinder, R. E. (1985). The gifted in our midst: By their divine deeds, neuroses, and mental test scores we have known them. In F. D. Horowitz & M. O'Brien (Eds.), *The gifted and talented: Developmental perspectives* (pp. 5–35). Washington, DC: American Psychological Association.

Grob, G. N. (1973). *Mental institutions in America: Social policy to 1875.* New York: Free Press.

Groden, J., Cautela, J., Prince, S., & Berrryman, J. (1994). The impact of stress and anxiety on individuals with autism and developmental disabilities. In E. Schopler & G. B. Mesibov (Eds.), *Behavioral issues in autism* (pp. 177–194). New York: Plenum.

Grosenick, J. K., George, M. P., & George, N. L. (1987). A profile of school programs for the behaviorally disordered: Twenty years after Morse, Cutler, and Fink. *Behavioral Disorders, 12,* 159–168.

Grosenick, J. K., George, N. L., & George, M. P. (1988). The availability of program descriptions among programs for seriously emotionally disturbed students. *Behavioral Disorders, 13,* 108–115.

Grosenick, J. K., George, N. L., George, M. P., & Lewis, T. J. (1991). Public school services for behaviorally disordered students: Program practices in the 1980s. *Behavioral Disorders, 16,* 87–96.

Grosenick, J. K., & Huntze, S. L. (1979). *National needs analysis in behavior disorders: A model for a comprehensive needs analysis in behavior disorders.* Columbia: University of Missouri, Department of Special Education.

Grosenick, J. K., & Huntze, S. L. (1983). *More questions than answers: Review and analysis of programs for behaviorally disordered children and youth.* Columbia: University of Missouri, Department of Special Education.

Grossen, B. (1993). Child-directed teaching methods: A discriminatory practice of Western education. *Effective School Practices, 12*(2), 9–20.

Grossman, H. (1972). *Nine rotten lousy kids.* New York: Holt, Rinehart, & Winston.

Guerra, N. G., Huesmann, L. R., Tolan, P. H., Van Acker, R., & Eron, L. D. (1995). Stressful events and individual beliefs as correlates of economic disadvantage and aggression among urban children. *Journal of Consulting and Clinical Psychology, 63,* 518–528.

Guerra, N. B., Tolan, P. H., & Hammond, W. R. (1994). Prevention and treatment of adolescent violence. In L. D. Eron, J. H. Gentry, & P. Schlegel (Eds.), *Reason to hope: A psychosocial perspective on violence and youth* (pp. 383–403). Washington, DC: American Psychological Association.

Guetzloe, E. C. (1989). *Youth suicide: What the educator should know*. Reston, VA: Council for Exceptional Children.

Guetzloe, E. C. (1991). *Depression and suicide: Special education students at risk*. Reston, VA: Council for Exceptional Children.

Guevremont, D. C. (1991). Truancy and school absenteeism. In G. Stoner, M. R. Shinn, & H. M. Walker (Eds.), *Interventions for achievement and behavior problems* (pp. 581–591). Silver Spring, MD: National Association of School Psychologists.

Guevremont, D. C., & Dumas, M. C. (1994). Peer relationship problems and disruptive behavior disorders. *Journal of Emotional and Behavioral Disorders, 2,* 164–172.

Gulp, A. M., Clyman, M. M., & Culp, R. E. (1995). Adolescent depressed mood, reports of suicide attempts, and asking for help. *Adolescence, 30,* 827–837.

Gump, P. V. (1975). Ecological psychology and children. In E. M. Hetherington (Ed.), *Review of child development research* (Vol. 5, pp. 75–126). Chicago: University of Chicago Press.

Gunter, P. L., Denny, R. K., Jack, S. L., Shores, R. E., & Nelson, C. M. (1993). Aversive stimuli in academic interactions between students with serious emotional disturbance and their teachers. *Behavioral Disorders, 18,* 265–274.

Guthrie, R. (1984). Explorations in prevention. In B. Blatt & R. J. Morris (Eds.), *Perspectives in special education: Personal orientations* (pp. 157–172). Glenview, IL: Scott, Foresman.

Hagerman, R. J., & Sobesky, W. E. (1989). Psychopathology in fragile X syndrome. *American Journal of Orthopsychiatry, 59,* 142–152.

Haines, T. H. (1925). State laws relating to special classes and schools for mentally handicapped children in the public schools. *Mental Hygiene, 9,* 545–551.

Hallahan, D. P., & Cruickshank, W. M. (1973). *Psychoeducational foundations of learning disabilities*. Englewood Cliffs, NJ: Prentice-Hall.

Hallahan, D. P., Hall, R. J., Ianna, S. O., Kneedler, R. D., Lloyd, J. W., Loper, A. B., & Reeve, R. E. (1983). Summary of research findings at the University of Virginia Learning Disabilities Research Institute. *Exceptional Education Quarterly, 4*(1), 95–114.

Hallahan, D. P., & Kauffman, J. M. (1975). Research on the education of distractible and hyperactive children. In W. M. Cruickshank & D. P. Hallahan (Eds.), *Perceptual and learning disabilities in children: Vol. 2, Research and theory* (pp. 221–256). Syracuse, NY: Syracuse University Press.

Hallahan, D. P., & Kauffman, J. M. (1977). Categories, labels, behavioral characteristics: ED, LD, and EMR reconsidered. *Journal of Special Education, 11,* 139–149.

Hallahan, D. P., & Kauffman, J. M. (1994). Toward a culture of disability in the aftermath of Deno and Dunn. *Journal of Special Education, 27,* 496–508.

Hallahan, D. P., & Kauffman, J. M. (1997). *Exceptional children: Introduction to special education* (7th ed.). Boston: Allyn & Bacon.

Hallahan, D. P., Kauffman, J. M., & Lloyd, J. W. (1996). *Introduction to learning disabilities* (3rd ed.). Boston: Allyn & Bacon.

Hallahan, D. P., Kauffman, J. M., Lloyd, J. W., & McKinney, J. D. (Eds.). (1988). The regular education initiative [Special issue]. *Journal of Learning Disabilities, 21*(1).

Hallahan, D. P., Keller, C. E., & Ball, D. W. (1986). A comparison of prevalence rate variability from state to state for each of the categories of special education. *Remedial and Special Education, 7*(2), 8–14.

Hallahan, D. P., Lloyd, J. W., Kauffman, J. M. & Loper, A. B. (1983). Academic problems. In R. J. Morris & T. R. Krotchwill (Eds.), *The practice of child therapy* (pp. 113–141). New York: Pergamon.

Hallenbeck, B. A., & Kauffman, J. M. (1995). How does observational learning affect the behavior of students with emotional or behavioral disorders? A review of research. *Journal of Special Education, 29,* 45–71.

Hallenbeck, B. A., Kauffman, J. M., & Lloyd, J. W. (1993). When, how, and why educational placement decisions are made: Two case studies. *Journal of Emotional and Behavioral Disorders, 1,* 109–117.

Hallinan, M. T., & Teixeira, R. A. (1987). Opportunities and constraints: Black-white differences in the formation of interracial friendships. *Child Development, 58,* 1358–1371.

Hammill, D. D. (Ed.). (1987). *Assessing the abilities and instructional needs of students.* Austin, TX: Pro-Ed.

Hammond, W. A. (1891). *A treatise on insanity and its medical relations.* New York: Appleton.

Hammond, W. R., & Yung, B. R. (1994). African Americans. In L. D. Eron, J. H. Gentry, & P. Schlegel (Eds.), *Reason to hope: A psychosocial perspective on violence and youth* (pp. 105–118). Washington, DC: American Psychological Association.

Hanson, M., MacKay, S., Atkinson, L., Staley, S., & Pignatiello, A. (1995). Firesetting during the preschool period: Assessment and intervention issues. *Canadian Journal of Psychiatry, 40,* 299–303.

Hanson, M. J., & Carta, J. J. (1996). Addressing the challenges of families with multiple risks. *Exceptional Children, 62,* 201–212.

Hanson, M. J., & Lynch, E. W. (1992). Family diversity: Implications for policy and practice. *Topics in Early Childhood Special Education, 12,* 283–306.

Happe, F. G. E. (1994). An advanced test of theory of mind: Understanding of story characters' thoughts and feelings by able autistic, mentally handicapped, and normal children and adults. *Journal of Autism and Developmental Disorders, 24,* 129–154.

Happe, F. G. E., & Frith, U. (1995). Theory of mind in autism. In E. Schopler & G. B. Mesibov (Eds.), *Learning and cognition in autism* (pp. 177–197). New York: Plenum.

Harden, P. W., Pihl, R. O., Vitaro, F., Gendreau, P. L., & Tremblay, R. E. (1995). Stress response in anxious and nonanxious disruptive boys. *Journal of Emotional and Behavioral Disorders, 3,* 183–190.

Hare, E. H. (1962). Masturbatory insanity: The history of an idea. *Journal of Mental Science, 108,* 1–25.

Haring, N. G. (1968). *Attending and responding.* San Rafael, CA: Dimensions.

Haring, N. G. (1974a). Norris G. Haring. In J. M. Kauffman & C. D. Lewis (Eds.), *Teaching children with behavior disorders: Personal perspectives* (pp. 76–112). Columbus, OH: Merrill.

Haring, N. G. (1974b). Social and emotional behavior disorders. In N. G. Haring (Ed.), *Behavior of exceptional children* (pp. 253–293). Columbus, OH: Merrill.

Haring, N. G., Lovitt, T. C., Eaton, M. D., & Hansen, C. L. (1978). *The fourth R: Research in the classroom.* Columbus, OH: Merrill.

Haring, N. G., & Phillips, E. L. (1962). *Educating emotionally disturbed children.* New York: McGraw-Hill.

Haring, N. G., & Phillips, E. L. (1972). *Analysis and modification of classroom behavior.* Englewood Cliffs, NJ: Prentice-Hall.

Haring, N. G., & Schiefelbusch, R. L. (Eds.). (1976). *Teaching special children.* New York: McGraw-Hill.

Haring, N. G., & Whelan, R. J. (1965). Experimental methods in education and management. In N. J. Long, W. C. Morse, & R. G. Newman (Eds.), *Conflict in the classroom* (pp. 389–405). Belmont, CA: Wadsworth.

Haring, T. G., & Kennedy, C. H. (1990). Contextual control of problem behavior in students with severe disabilities. *Journal of Applied Behavior Analysis, 23,* 235–243.

Harms, E. (1967). *Origins of modern psychiatry.* Springfield, IL: Charles C. Thomas.

Harrington, R. (1993). *Depressive disorder in childhood and adolescence.* New York: Wiley.

Harris, F. C., & Ammerman, R. T. (1986). Depression and suicide in children and adolescents. *Education and Treatment of Children, 9,* 334–343.

Harris, H. F. (1996). Elective mutism: A tutorial. *Language, Speech, and Hearing Services in Schools, 27,* 10-15.

Harris, K. R., Wong, B. Y. L., & Keogh, B. K. (Eds.). (1985). Cognitive-behavior modification with children: A critical review of the state-of-the-art [Special issue]. *Journal of Abnormal Child Psychology, 13*(3).

Harris, S. L. (1994). Treatment of family problems in autism. In E. Schopler & G. B. Mesibov (Eds.), *Behavioral issues in autism* (pp. 161–175). New York: Plenum.

Harris, S. L. (1995a). Autism. In M. Hersen & R. T. Ammerman (Eds.), *Advanced abnormal child psychology* (pp. 305–317). Hillsdale, NJ: Erlbaum.

Harris, S. L. (1995b). Educational strategies in autism. In E. Schopler & G. B. Mesibov (Eds.),

Learning and cognition in autism (pp. 293–309). New York: Plenum.

Harry, B. (1995). African American families. In B. A. Ford, F. E. Obiakor, & J. M. Patton (Eds.), *Effective education of African American exceptional learners: New perspectives* (pp. 211–233). Austin, TX: Pro-Ed.

Hart, B., & Risley, T. R. (1995). *Meaningful differences in the everyday experience of young American children*. Baltimore: Paul H. Brookes.

Hashimoto, T., Tayama, M., Murakawa, K., Yoshimoto, T., Miyazaki, M., Harada, M., & Kuroda, Y. (1995). Development of the brainstem and cerebellum in autistic patients. *Journal of Autism and Developmental Disorders, 25,* 1–18.

Haugaard, J. J. (1992). Epidemiology and family violence involving children. In R. T. Ammerman & M. Hersen (Eds.), *Assessment of family violence: A clinical and legal sourcebook* (pp. 89–107). New York: Wiley.

Hawton, K. (1986). *Suicide and attempted suicide among children and adolescents*. Beverly Hills, CA: Sage.

Hay, L. (1953). A new school channel for helping the troubled child. *American Journal of Orthopsychiatry, 23,* 678–683.

Hayman, M. (1939). The interrelations between mental defect and mental disorder. *Journal of Mental Science, 85,* 1183–1193.

Healy, W. (1915a). *The individual delinquent*. Boston: Little, Brown.

Healy, W. (1915b). *Mental conflicts and misconduct*. Boston: Little, Brown.

Healy, W. (1931). *Reconstructing behavior in youth: A study of problem children in foster homes*. New York: Alfred A. Knopf.

Healy, W., & Bronner, A. F. (1969). *Delinquents and criminals: Their making and unmaking*. New York: Batterson-Smith. (Original work published 1926.)

Helge, D. (1992). Solving special education reform problems in rural areas. *Preventing School Failure, 36*(4), 11–15.

Henry, N. B. (Ed.). (1950). The education of exceptional children. *Forty-ninth yearbook of the National Society for the Study of Education, Part II*. Chicago: University of Chicago Press.

Herbert, M. (1994). Etiological considerations. In T. H. Ollendick, N. J. King, & W. Yule (Eds.), *International handbook of phobic and anxiety disorders in children and adolescents* (pp. 3-20). New York: Plenum.

Hersen, M., & Ammerman, R. T. (Eds.). (1995). *Advanced abnormal child psychology*. Hillsdale, NJ: Erlbaum.

Hersh, R. H., & Walker, H. M. (1983). Great expectations: Making schools effective for all students. *Policy Studies Review, 2*(1), 147–188.

Herson, P. F. (1974). Biasing effects of diagnostic labels and sex of pupil on teachers' views of pupils' mental health. *Journal of Educational Psychology, 66,* 117–122.

Hertzig, M. E., & Shapiro, T. (1990). Autism and pervasive developmental disorders. In M. Lewis & S. M. Miller (Eds.), *Handbook of developmental psychopathology* (pp. 385–395). New York: Plenum.

Herzog, J. R., & Pittman, R. B. (1995). Home, family, and community: Ingredients in the rural education equation. *Phi Delta Kappan, 77,* 113–118.

Hess, R. D., & Holloway, S. D. (1984). Family and school as educational institutions. In R. D. Parke (Ed.), *Review of child development research* (Vol. 7, pp. 179–222). Chicago: University of Chicago Press.

Hetherington, E. M., & Camara, K. A. (1984). Families in transition: The process of dissolution and reconstruction. In R. D. Parke (Ed.), *Review of child development research* (Vol. 7, pp. 398–439). Chicago: University of Chicago Press.

Hetherington, E. M., & Martin, B. (1986). Family factors and psychopathology in children. In H. C. Quay & J. S. Werry (Eds.), *Psychopathological disorders of childhood* (3rd ed.) (pp. 332–390). New York: Wiley.

Heuchert, C. M., & Long, N. J. (1980). A brief history of life-space interviewing. *The Pointer, 25*(2), 5–8.

Hewett, F. M. (1964a). A hierarchy of educational tasks for children with learning disorders. *Exceptional Children, 31,* 207–214.

Hewett, F. M. (1964b). Teaching reading to an autistic boy through operant conditioning. *The Reading Teacher, 18,* 613–618.

Hewett, F. M. (1965). Teaching speech to an autistic boy through operant conditioning. *American Journal of Orthopsychiatry, 35,* 927–936.

Hewett, F. M. (1966). A hierarchy of competencies for teachers of emotionally handicapped children. *Exceptional Children, 33,* 7–11.

Hewett, F. M. (1967). Educational engineering with emotionally disturbed children. *Exceptional Children, 33,* 459–471.

Hewett, F. M. (1968). *The emotionally disturbed child in the classroom.* Boston: Allyn & Bacon.

Hewett, F. M. (1970, November). The Madison Plan really swings. *Today's Education, 59,* 15–17.

Hewett, F. M. (1971). Introduction to the behavior modification approach to special education: A shaping procedure. In N. J. Long, W. C. Morse, & R. G. Newman (Eds.), *Conflict in the classroom* (2nd ed., pp. 360–365). Belmont, CA: Wadsworth.

Hewett, F. M. (1974). Frank M. Hewett. In J. M. Kauffman & C. D. Lewis (Eds.), *Teaching children with behavior disorders: Personal perspectives* (pp. 114–140). Columbus, OH: Merrill.

Hewett, F. M., & Forness, S. R. (1974). *Education of exceptional learners.* Boston: Allyn & Bacon.

Hewitt, L. E., & Jenkins, R. L. (1946). *Fundamental patterns of maladjustment: The dynamics of their origin.* Springfield, IL: State of Illinois.

Hill, H. M., Soriano, F. I., Chen, S. A., & LaFromboise, T. D. (1994). Sociocultural factors in the etiology and prevention of violence among ethnic minority youth. In L. D. Eron, J. H. Gentry, & P. Schlegel (Eds.), *Reason to hope: A psychosocial perspective on violence and youth* (pp. 59–97). Washington, DC: American Psychological Association.

Hinde, R. A. (1986). Some implications of evolutionary theory and comparative data for the study of human prosocial and aggressive behaviour. In D. Olweus, J. Block, & M. Radke-Yarrow (Eds.), *Development of antisocial and prosocial behavior: Research, theories, and issues* (pp. 13–32). New York: Academic Press.

Hinshaw, S. P., Simmel, C., & Heller, T. L. (1995). Multimethod assessment of covert antisocial behavior in children: Laboratory observations, adult ratings, and child self-reports. *Psychological Assessment, 7,* 209–219.

Hirschberg, J. C. (1953). The role of education in the treatment of emotionally disturbed children through planned ego development. *American Journal of Orthopsychiatry, 23,* 684–690.

Hobbs, N. (1965). How the Re-ED plan developed. In N. J. Long, W. C. Morse, & R. G. Newman (Eds.), *Conflict in the classroom.* Belmont, CA: Wadsworth.

Hobbs, N. (1966). Helping the disturbed child: Psychological and ecological strategies. *American Psychologist, 21,* 1105–1115.

Hobbs, N. (1974). Nicholas Hobbs. In J. M. Kauffman & C. D. Lewis (Eds.), *Teaching children with behavior disorders: Personal perspectives* (pp. 142–167). Columbus, OH: Merrill.

Hobbs, N. (1975a). *The futures of children.* San Francisco: Jossey-Bass.

Hobbs, N. (1975b). *Issues in the classification of children* (Vols. I and II). San Francisco: Jossey-Bass.

Hodges, K., & Zeman, J. (1993). Interviewing. In T. H. Ollendick & M. Hersen (Eds.), *Handbook of child and adolescent assessment* (pp. 65–81). New York: Pergamon.

Hodgkinson, H. L. (1995). What should we call people? Race, class, and the census for 2000. *Phi Delta Kappan, 77,* 173–179.

Hoffman, E. (1974). The treatment of deviance by the educational system: History. In W. C. Rhodes & S. Head (Eds.), *A study of child variance: Vol. 3. Service delivery systems* (pp. 81–144). Ann Arbor: University of Michigan.

Hoffman, E. (1975). The American public school and the deviant child: The origins of their involvement. *Journal of Special Education, 9,* 415–423.

Hollinger, J. D. (1987). Social skills for behaviorally disordered children as preparation for mainstreaming: Theory, practice, and new directions. *Remedial and Special Education, 8*(4), 17–27.

Hollister, W. G., & Goldston, S. E. (1962). *Considerations for planning classes for the emotionally disturbed.* Washington, DC: Council for Exceptional Children.

Hops, H., Finch, M., & McConnell, S. (1985). Social skills deficits. In P. H. Bornstein & A. E. Kazdin (Eds.), *Handbook of clinical behavior therapy with children* (pp. 543–598). Homewood, IL: Dorsey Press.

Hops, H., Guild, J. J., Fleischman, D. H., Paine, S. C., Street, A., Walker, H. M., & Greenwood, C. R. (1978). *PEERS (Procedures for Establishing Effective Relationship Skills).* Eugene: University of Oregon, Center at Oregon for Behavioral Education of the Handicapped.

Horowitz, K., Weine, S., & Jekel J. (1995). PTSD symptoms in urban adolescent girls: Compounded community trauma. *Journal of the Academy of Child and Adolescent Psychiatry, 34*, 1353-1361.

Howe, K. R., & Miramontes, O. B. (1992). *The ethics of special education*. New York: Teachers College Press.

Howe, S. G. (1851). On training and educating idiots. The second annual report to the legislature of Massachusetts. *American Journal of Insanity, 8*, 97–118.

Howe, S. G. (1852). Third and final report of the Experimental School for Teaching and Training Idiotic Children; also, the first report of the trustees of the Massachusetts School for Idiotic and Feebleminded Youth. *American Journal of Insanity, 9*, 20–36.

Howell, K. W. (1985). A task-analytical approach to social behavior. *Remedial and Special Education, 6*(2), 24–30.

Howell, K. W. (1987). Functional assessment in correctional settings. In C. M. Nelson, R. B. Rutherford, & B. I. Wolford (Eds.), *Special education in the criminal justice system* (pp. 165–186). Columbus, OH: Merrill/Macmillan.

Howell, K. W., Fox, S. L., & Morehead, M. K. (1993). *Curriculum-based evaluation for teaching and decision making* (2nd ed.). Pacific Grove, CA: Brookes/Cole.

Howells, J. G. (Ed.). (1971). *Modern perspectives in international child psychiatry*. New York: Brunner/Mazel.

Howells, J. G., & Guirguis, W. R. (1984). Childhood schizophrenia 20 years later. *Archives of General Psychiatry, 41*, 123–128.

Howley, C. B., & Howley, A. (1995). The power of babble: Technology and rural education. *Phi Delta Kappan, 77*, 126–131.

Hudley, C., & Graham, S. (1995). School-based interventions for aggressive African-American boys. *Applied and Preventive Psychology, 4*, 185–195.

Huefner, D. S. (1994). The mainstreaming cases: Tensions and trends for school administrators. *Educational Administration Quarterly, 30*, 27–55.

Hultquist, A. M. (1995). Selective mutism: Causes and interventions. *Journal of Emotional and Behavioral Disorders, 3*, 100–107.

Hundert, J. (1995). *Enhancing social competence in young students: School-based approaches*. Austin, TX: Pro-Ed.

Hunter, R., & Macalpine, I. (Eds.). (1963). *Three hundred years of psychiatry, 1535–1860: A history in selected English tests*. London: Oxford University Press.

Hunter, R., & Macalpine, I. (1974). *Psychiatry for the poor. 1851 Colney Hatch Asylum-Friern Hospital. 1973: A medical and social history*. Kent, England: Dawsons of Pall Mall.

Huntze, S. (1985). A position paper of the Council for Children with Behavioral Disorders. *Behavioral Disorders, 10*, 167–174.

Hyman, I. A. (1995). Corporal punishment, psychological maltreatment, violence, and punitiveness in America: Research, advocacy, and public policy. *Applied and Preventive Psychology, 4*, 113–130.

Hymes, J. L. (1949). *Teacher listen: The children speak*. New York: State Charities Aid Association.

Hynd, G. W., Semrud-Clikeman, M., Lorys, A. R., Novey, E. S., Eliopulos, D., & Lyytin, H. (1991). Corpus callosum morphology in attention deficit-hyperactivity disorder: Morphometric analysis of MRI. *Journal of Learning Disabilities, 24*, 141–146.

Idstein, P. (1993). Swimming against the mainstream. *Phi Delta Kappan, 75*, 336–340.

Institute of Medicine. (1989). *Research on children and adolescents with mental, behavioral and developmental disorders: Mobilizing a national initiative*. Washington, DC: National Academy Press.

Isaac, G. (1995). Is bipolar disorder the most common diagnostic entity in hospitalized adolescents and children? *Adolescence, 30*, 273–276.

Itard, J. M. G. (1962). *The wild boy of Aveyron*. New York: Appleton-Century-Crofts (Prentice-Hall).

Iwata, B. A., Pace, G. M., Kalsher, M. J., Cowdrey, G. E., & Cataldo, M. F. (1990). Experimental analysis and extinction of self-injurious escape behavior. *Journal of Applied Behavior Analysis, 23*, 11–27.

Iwata, B. A., Zarcone, J. B., Vollmer, T. R., & Smith, R. G. (1994). Assessment and treatment of self-injurious behavior. In E. Schopler & G. B. Mesibov (Eds.), *Behavioral issues in autism* (pp. 131–159). New York: Plenum.

Jackson, J. F. (1995). Hit by friendly fire: Iatrogenic effects of misguided social policy interventions on African American families. In D. Baumrind, *Child maltreatment and optimal caregiving in social contexts* (pp. 89–99). New York: Garland.

Jacobsen, T. (1995). Case study: Is selective mutism a manifestation of identity disorder? *Journal of the Academy of Child and Adolescent Psychiatry, 34,* 863-866.

James, M., & Long, N. (1992). Looking beyond behavior and seeing my needs: A red flag interview. *Journal of Emotional and Behavioral Problems, 1*(2), 35–38.

Janko, S. (1994). *Vulnerable children, vulnerable families: The social construction of child abuse.* New York: Teachers College Press.

Jarvelin, M. R., Daara, E., Rantakallio, P., Moilanen, I., & Ishohanni, M. (1995). Juvenile delinquency, education, and mental disability. *Exceptional Children, 61,* 230–239.

Jarvis, E. (1852). On the supposed increase of insanity. *American Journal of Insanity, 8,* 333–364.

Jennings, K. D., Mendelsohn, S. R., May, K., & Brown, G. M. (1988). Elementary students in classes for the emotionally disturbed: Characteristics and classroom behavior. *American Journal of Orthopsychiatry, 58,* 65–76.

Jersild, A. T., & Holmes, F. B. (1935). Methods of overcoming children's fears. *Journal of Psychology, 1,* 75–104.

Johnson, J. H. (1986). *Life events as stressors in childhood and adolescence.* Beverly Hills, CA: Sage.

Johnson, J. L. (1969). Special education and the inner city: A challenge for the future or another means of cooling the mark out? *Journal of Special Education, 3,* 241–251.

Johnson, J. L. (1971). Croton-on-campus: Experiment in the use of the behavioral sciences to educate black ghetto children. In N. J. Long, W. C. Morse, & R. G. Newman (Eds.), *Conflict in the classroom* (2nd ed.) (pp. 372–382). Belmont, CA: Wadsworth.

Johnson, L. J., & Blankenship, C. S. (1984). A comparison of label-induced expectancy bias in two preservice teacher education programs. *Behavioral Disorders, 9,* 167–174.

Johnson, W. G., & Hinkle, L. K. (1993). Obesity. In T. H. Ollendick & M. Hersen (Eds.), *Handbook of child and adolescent assessment* (pp. 364–383). New York: Pergamon.

Johnston, H. F., & March, J. S. (1992). Obsessive-compulsive disorders in children and adolescents. In W. R. Reynolds (Ed.), *Internalizing disorders in children and adolescents* (pp. 107–148). New York: Wiley.

Jones, V. R., & Jones, L. S. (1995). *Comprehensive classroom management: Creating positive learning environments for all students.* Boston: Allyn & Bacon.

Jordan, D. (1995). *Honorable intentions: A parent's guide to educational planning for children with emotional or behavioral disorders.* Minneapolis: PACER Center.

Jordan, D., Goldberg, P., & Goldberg, M. (1991). *A guidebook for parents of children with emotional or behavioral disorders.* Minneapolis: Pacer Center, Inc.

Juul, K. D. (1986). Epidemiological studies of behavior disorders in children: An international survey. *International Journal of Special Education, 1,* 1–20.

Kafantaris, V. (1995). Treatment of bipolar disorder in children and adolescence. *Journal of the American Academy of Child and Adolescent Psychiatry, 34,* 732–741.

Kagan, J., Gibbons, J. L., Johnson, M. O., Reznick, J. S., & Snidman, N. (1990). A temperamental disposition to the state of uncertainty. In J. Rolf, A. S. Masten, D. Cicchetti, K. H. Nuechterlein, & S. Weintraub (Eds.), *Risk and protective factors in the development of psychopathology* (pp. 164–178). New York: Cambridge University Press.

Kaminer, Y. (1994). *Adolescent substance abuse: A comprehensive guide to theory and practice.* New York: Plenum.

Kamps, D. M., Leonard, B. R., Dugan, E. P., Boland, B., & Greenwood, C. R. (1991). The use of ecobehavioral assessment to identify naturally occurring effective procedures in classrooms serving students with autism and other developmental disabilities. *Journal of Behavioral Education, 1,* 367–397.

Kane, M. J. (1994). Premonitory urges as "attentional tics" in Tourette's syndrome. *Journal of the American Academy of Child and Adolescent Psychiatry, 33,* 805–808.

Kanner, L. (1943). Autistic disturbances of affective contact. *Nervous Child, 2,* 217–250.

Kanner, L. (1957). *Child psychiatry.* Springfield, IL: Charles C. Thomas.

Kanner, L. (1960). Child psychiatry: Retrospect and prospect. *American Journal of Psychiatry, 117,* 15–22.

Kanner, L. (1962). Emotionally disturbed children. A historical review. *Child Development, 33,* 97–102.

Kanner, L. (1964). *History of the care and treatment of the mentally retarded.* Springfield, IL: Charles C. Thomas.

Kanner, L. (1973a). The birth of early infantile autism. *Journal of Autism and Childhood Schizophrenia, 3,* 93–95.

Kanner, L. (1973b). *Childhood psychosis: Initial studies and new insights.* Washington, DC: V. H. Winston.

Kanner, L. (1973c). Historical perspective on developmental deviations. *Journal of Autism and Childhood Schizophrenia, 3,* 187–198.

Kanner, L., Rodriguez, A., & Ashenden, B. (1972). How far can autistic children go in matters of social adaptation? *Journal of Autism and Childhood Schizophrenia, 2,* 9–33.

Kaplan, B. (Ed.). (1964). *The inner world of mental illness.* New York: Harper & Row.

Kasen, S., Johnson, J., & Cohen, P. (1990). The impact of school emotional climate on student psychopathology. *Journal of Abnormal Child Psychology, 18,* 165–177.

Kashani, J. H., Dahlmeier, J. M., Borduin, C. M., Soltys, S., & Reid, J. C. (1995). Characteristics of anger expression in depressed children. *Journal of the American Academy of Child and Adolescent Psychiatry, 34,* 322–326.

Kaslow, N. J. & Rehm, L. P. (1985). Conceptualization, assessment, and treatment of depression in children. In P. H. Bornstein & A. E. Kazdin (Eds.), *Handbook of clinical behavior therapy with children* (pp. 599–657). Homewood, IL: Dorsey Press.

Kaslow, N. J., & Rehm, L. P. (1991). Childhood depression. In T. R. Kratochwill & R. J. Morris (Eds.), *The practice of child therapy* (2nd ed.) (pp. 43–75). New York: Pergamon.

Katsiyannis, A. (1994). Pre-referral practices: Under Office of Civil Rights scrutiny. *Journal of Developmental and Physical Disabilities, 6,* 73–76.

Kauffman, J. M. (1974a). Conclusion: Issues. In J. M. Kauffman & C. D. Lewis (Eds.), *Teaching children with behavior disorders: Personal perspectives* (pp. 272–286). Columbus, OH: Merrill.

Kauffman, J. M. (1974b). Severely emotionally disturbed. In N. G. Haring (Ed.), *Behavior of exceptional children* (pp. 377–410). Columbus, OH: Merrill.

Kauffman, J. M. (1976). Nineteenth-century views of children's behavior disorders: Historical contributions and continuing issues. *Journal of Special Education, 10,* 335–349.

Kauffman, J. M. (1979). An historical perspective on disordered behavior and an alternative conceptualization of exceptionality. In F. H. Wood & K. C. Lakin (Eds.), *Disturbing, disordered, or disturbed? Perspectives on the definition of problem behavior in educational settings* (pp. 49–70). Minneapolis: Advanced Training Institute, Department of Psychoeducational Studies, University of Minnesota.

Kauffman, J. M. (1980). Where special education for emotionally disturbed children is going: A personal view. *Exceptional Children, 48,* 522–527.

Kauffman, J. M. (1981). Historical trends and contemporary issues in special education in the United States. In J. M. Kauffman & D. P. Hallahan (Eds.), *Handbook of special education* (pp. 3–23). Englewood Cliffs, NJ: Prentice-Hall.

Kauffman, J. M. (1984). Saving children in the age of Big Brother: Moral and ethical issues in the identification of deviance. *Behavioral Disorders, 10,* 60–70.

Kauffman, J. M. (1986a). Educating children with behavior disorders. In R. J. Morris & B. Blatt (Eds.), *Special education: Research and trends* (pp. 249–271). New York: Pergamon.

Kauffman, J. M. (1986b). Growing out of adolescence: Reflections on change in special education for the behaviorally disordered. *Behavioral Disorders, 11,* 290–296.

Kauffman, J. M. (1987). Research in special education: A commentary. *Remedial and Special Education, 8*(6), 57–62.

Kauffman, J. M. (1988). Lessons in the nonrecognition of deviance. In R. B. Rutherford, C. M. Nelson, & S. R. Forness (Eds.), *Bases of severe behavioral disorders of children and youth* (pp. 3–19). Boston: Little, Brown.

Kauffman, J. M. (1989). The regular education initiative as Reagan-Bush education policy: A trickle-down theory of education of the hard-to-teach. *The Journal of Special Education, 23,* 256–278.

Kauffman, J. M. (1992). Foreword. In K. R. Howe & O. B. Miramontes, *The ethics of special education* (pp. xi–xvii). New York: Teachers College Press.

Kauffman, J. M. (1993). How we might achieve the radical reform of special education. *Exceptional Children, 60,* 6–16.

Kauffman, J. M. (1994a). Places of change: Special education's power and identity in an era of educational reform. *Journal of Learning Disabilities, 27,* 610–618.

Kauffman, J. M. (1994b, March 16). Taming aggression in the young: A call to action. *Education Week, 13*(25), 43.

Kauffman, J. M. (1995). Why we must celebrate a diversity of restrictive environments. *Learning Disabilities Research and Practice, 10,* 225–232.

Kauffman, J. M., Boland, J., Hopkins, N., & Birnbrauer, J. S. (1980). *Managing and teaching the severely disturbed and retarded: A guide for teachers.* Columbus, OH: Special Press.

Kauffman, J. M., & Burbach, H. J. (in press). On creating a climate of classroom civility. *Phi Delta Kappan.*

Kauffman, J. M., Cullinan, D., & Epstein, M. H. (1987). Characteristics of students placed in special programs for the seriously emotionally disturbed. *Behavioral Disorders, 12,* 175–184.

Kauffman, J. M., Gerber, M. M., & Semmel, M. I. (1988). Questionable assumptions underlying the regular education initiative. *Journal of Learning Disabilities, 21*(1), 6-11.

Kauffman, J. M., & Hallahan, D. P. (1979). Learning disability and hyperactivity (with comments on minimal brain dysfunction). In B. B. Lahey & A. E. Kazdin (Eds.), *Advances in clinical child psychology* (Vol. 2, pp. 71–105). New York: Plenum.

Kauffman, J. M., & Hallahan, D. P. (1993). Toward a comprehensive service delivery system. In J. I. Goodlad & T. C. Lovitt (Eds.), *Integrating general and special education* (pp. 73–102). Columbus, OH: Merrill/Macmillan.

Kauffman, J. M., & Hallahan, D. P. (Eds.). (1995). *The illusion of full inclusion: A comprehensive critique of a current special educational bandwagon.* Austin, TX: Pro-Ed.

Kauffman, J. M., & Hallahan, D. P. (1997). A diversity of restrictive environments: Placement as a problem of social ecology. In J. W. Lloyd, E. J. Kameenui, & D. Chard (Eds.), *Issues in educating students with disabilities.* Hillsdale, NJ: Lawrence Erlbaum Associates.

Kauffman, J. M., & Kneedler, R. D. (1981). Behavior disorders. In J. M. Kauffman & D. P. Hallahan (Eds.), *Handbook of special education* (pp. 165–194). Englewood Cliffs, NJ: Prentice-Hall.

Kauffman, J. M., & Lewis, C. D. (Eds.). (1974). *Teaching children with behavior disorders: Personal perspectives.* Columbus, OH: Merrill.

Kauffman, J. M., & Lloyd, J. W. (1995). A sense of place: The importance of placement issues in contemporary special education. In J. M. Kauffman, J. W. Lloyd, D. P. Hallahan, & T. A. Astuto (Eds.), *Issues in educational placement: Students with emotional and behavioral disorders* (pp. 3–19). Hillsdale, NJ: Erlbaum.

Kauffman, J. M., Lloyd, J. W., Baker, J., & Riedel, T. M. (1995). Inclusion of all students with emotional or behavioral disorders? Let's think again. *Phi Delta Kappan, 76,* 542–546.

Kauffman, J. M., Lloyd, J. W., Hallahan, D. P., & Astuto, T. A. (Eds.). (1995a). *Issues in educational placement: Students with emotional and behavioral disorders.* Hillsdale, NJ: Erlbaum.

Kauffman, J. M., Lloyd, J. W., Hallahan, D. P., & Astuto, T. A. (Eds.). (1995b). Toward a sense of place for special education in the 21st century. In J. M. Kauffman, J. W. Lloyd, D. P. Hallahan, & T. A. Astuto (Eds.), *Issues in educational placement: Students with emotional and behavioral disorders* (pp. 379–385). Hillsdale, NJ: Erlbaum.

Kauffman, J. M., Lloyd, J. W., & McGee, K. A. (1989). Adaptive and maladaptive behavior: Teachers' attitudes and their technical assistance needs. *Journal of Special Education, 23,* 185–200.

Kauffman, J. M., Mostert, M. P., Nuttycombe, D. G., Trent, S. C., & Hallahan, D. P. (1993). *Managing classroom behavior: A reflective case-based approach.* Boston: Allyn & Bacon.

Kauffman, J. M., & Pullen, P. L. (1996). Eight myths about special education. *Focus on Exceptional Children, 28*(5), 1–12.

Kauffman, J. M., & Smucker, K. (1995). The legacies of placement: A brief history of placement options and issues with commentary on their evolution. In J. M. Kauffman, J. W. Lloyd, D. P. Hallahan, & T. A. Astuto (Eds.), *Issues in educational placement: Students with emotional and behavioral disorders* (pp. 21–44). Hillsdale, NJ: Erlbaum.

Kauffman, J. M., & Wong, K. L. H. (1991). Effective teachers of students with behavioral disorders: Are generic teaching skills enough? *Behavioral Disorders, 16,* 225–237.

Kauffman, J. M., Wong, K. L. H., Lloyd, J. W., Hung, L., & Pullen, P. L. (1991). What puts pupils at risk? An analysis of teachers' judgments of pupils' behavior. *Remedial and Special Education, 12*(5), 7–16.

Kaufman, A. S., & Ishikuma, T. (1993). Intellectual and achievement testing. In T. H. Ollendick & M. Hersen (Eds.), *Handbook of child and adolescent assessment* (pp. 192–207). New York: Pergamon.

Kavale, K. A., & Forness, S. R. (1995). Social skill deficits and training: A meta-analysis of the research in learning disabilities. In T. E. Scruggs & M. A. Mastropieri (Eds.), *Advances in learning and behavioral disabilities* (pp. 119–160). Greenwich, CT: JAI Press.

Kazdin, A. E. (1977). Assessing the clinical or applied importance of behavior change through social validation. *Behavior Modification, 1,* 427–452.

Kazdin, A. E. (1978). *History of behavior modification: Experimental foundations of contemporary research.* Baltimore, MD: University Park Press.

Kazdin, A. E. (1981). Assessment techniques for childhood depression. A critical appraisal. *Journal of the American Academy of Child Psychiatry, 20,* 358–375.

Kazdin, A. E. (1984). *Behavior modification in applied settings* (3rd ed.). Homewood, IL: Dorsey Press.

Kazdin, A. E. (1985). *Treatment of antisocial behavior in children and adolescents.* Homewood, IL: Dorsey Press.

Kazdin, A. E. (1991). Aggressive behavior and conduct disorder. In T. R. Kratochwill & R. J. Morris (Eds.), *The practice of child therapy* (2nd ed., pp. 174–221). New York: Pergamon.

Kazdin, A. E. (1993). Conduct disorder. In T. H. Ollendick & M. Hersen (Eds.), *Handbook of child and adolescent assessment* (pp. 292–310). New York: Pergamon.

Kazdin, A. E. (1994). Interventions for aggressive and antisocial children. In L. D. Eron, J. H. Gentry, & P. Schlegel (Eds.), *Reason to hope: A psychosocial perspective on violence and youth* (pp. 341–382). Washington, DC: American Psychological Association.

Kazdin, A. E. (1995). *Conduct disorders in childhood and adolescence* (2nd ed.). Thousand Oaks, CA: Sage.

Kazdin, A. E., Colbus, D., & Rodgers, A. (1986). Assessment of depression and diagnosis of depressive disorder among psychiatrically disturbed children. *Journal of Abnormal Child Psychology, 14,* 499–515.

Kazdin, A. E., French, N. H., Unis, A. S., Esveldt-Dawson, K., & Sherick, R. B. (1983). Hopelessness, depression, and suicidal intent among psychiatrically disturbed inpatient children. *Journal of Consulting and Clinical Psychology, 51,* 504–511.

Keller, B. B., & Bell, R. Q. (1979). Child effects on adults' method of eliciting altruistic behavior. *Child Development, 50,* 1004–1009.

Kendall, P. C., & Gosch, E. A. (1994). Cognitive-behavioral interventions. In T. H. Ollendick, N. J. King, & W. Yule (Eds.), *International handbook of phobic and anxiety disorders in children and adolescents* (pp. 415-438). New York: Plenum.

Kerbeshian, J., & Burd, L. (1994). Tourette's syndrome: A developmental psychobiologic view. *Journal of Developmental and Physical Disabilities, 6,* 203–218.

Kerfoot, M., Harrington, R., & Dyer, E. (1995). Brief home-based intervention with young suicide attempters and their families. *Journal of Adolescence, 18,* 557–568.

Kerr, M. M., & Nelson, C. M. (1989). *Strategies for managing behavior problems in the classroom* (2nd ed.). Columbus, OH: Merrill/Macmillan.

Kerr, M. M., Nelson, C. M., & Lambert, D. L., (1987). *Helping adolescents with learning and behavior problems.* Columbus, OH: Merrill/Macmillan.

Kerr, M. M., & Zigmond, N. (1986). What do high school teachers want? A study of expectations and standards. *Education and Treatment of Children, 9,* 239–249.

Key, E. (1909). *The century of the child.* New York: Putnam.

King, N. J., Hamilton, D. I., & Murphy, G. C. (1983). The prevention of children's maladaptive fears. *Child and Family Behavior Therapy, 5*(2), 43–57.

King, N. J., Ollendick, T. H., & Tonge, B. J. (1995). *School refusal: Assessment and treatment*. Boston: Allyn & Bacon.

Kingston, L., & Prior, M. (1995). The development of patterns of stable, transient, and school-age onset aggressive behavior in young children. *Journal of the American Academy of Child and Adolescent Psychiatry, 34,* 348–358.

Kinnear, K. L. (1995). *Violent children: A reference handbook*. Santa Barbara, CA: ABC-CLIO.

Kirigin, K. A., Braukman, C. J., Atwater, J. D., & Wolf, M. M. (1982). An evaluation of Teaching-Family (Achievement Place) group homes for juvenile offenders. *Journal of Applied Behavior Analysis, 15,* 1–16.

Kirk, S. A. (1972). *Educating exceptional children* (2nd. ed.). Boston: Houghton Mifflin.

Kirk, W. J. (1976). Juvenile justice and delinquency. *Phi Delta Kappan, 57,* 395–398.

Kittrie, N. N. (1971). *The right to be different: Deviance and enforced therapy*. Baltimore: Johns Hopkins Press.

Klein, M. W. (1995). *The American street gang: Its nature, prevalence, and control*. New York: Oxford University Press.

Klein, R. G., & Last, C. G. (1989). *Anxiety disorders in children*. Newbury Park, CA: Sage.

Klorman, R. (1991). Cognitive event-related potentials in attention deficit disorder. *Journal of Learning Disabilities, 24,* 130–140.

Klorman, R. (1995). Psychophysiological determinants. In M. Hersen & R. T. Ammerman (Eds.), *Advanced abnormal child psychology* (pp. 59–85). Hillsdale, NJ: Erlbaum.

Knapczyk, D. R. (1979). Diet control in the management of behavior disorders. *Behavioral Disorders, 5,* 2–9.

Knapp, M. S. (1995). How shall we study comprehensive, collaborative services for children and families? *Educational Researcher, 24*(4), 5–16.

Knitzer, J. (1982). *Unclaimed children: The failure of public responsibility to children and adolescents in need of mental health services*. Washington, DC: Children's Defense Fund.

Knitzer, J., & Aber, J. L. (1995). Young children in poverty: Facing the facts. *American Journal of Orthopsychiatry, 65,* 174–176.

Knitzer, J., Steinberg, Z., & Fleisch, F. (1990). *At the schoolhouse door: An examination of programs and policies for children with behavioral and emotional problems*. New York: Bank Street College of Education.

Knoblock, P. (Ed.). (1965). *Educational programming for emotionally disturbed children: The decade ahead*. Syracuse, NY: Syracuse University Press.

Knoblock, P. (Ed.). (1966). *Intervention approaches in educating emotionally disturbed children*. Syracuse, NY: Syracuse University Press.

Knoblock, P. (1970). A new humanism for special education. The concept of the open classroom for emotionally disturbed children. In P. A. Gallagher & L. L. Edwards (Eds.), *Educating the emotionally disturbed: Theory to practice* (pp. 68–85). Lawrence: University of Kansas.

Knoblock, P. (1973). Open education for emotionally disturbed children. *Exceptional Children, 39,* 358–365.

Knoblock, P. (1979). Educational alternatives for adolescents labeled emotionally disturbed. In D. Cullinan & M. H. Epstein (Eds.), *Special education for adolescents: Issues and perspectives* (pp. 273–304). Columbus, OH: Merrill.

Knoblock, P. (1983). *Teaching emotionally disturbed children*. Boston: Houghton Mifflin.

Knoblock, P., & Goldstein, A. (1971). *The lonely teacher*. Boston: Allyn & Bacon.

Knoblock, P., & Johnson, J. L. (Eds.). (1967). *The teaching-learning process in educating emotionally disturbed children*. Syracuse, NY: Syracuse University Press.

Kochanska, G. (1995). Children's temperament, mothers' discipline, and security of attachment: Multiple pathways to emerging internalization. *Child Development, 66,* 597–615.

Koegel, L. K., & Koegel, R. L. (1995). Motivating communication in children with autism. In E. Schopler & G. B. Mesibov (Eds.), *Learning and cognition in autism* (pp. 73–87). New York: Plenum.

Koegel, R. L., Frea, W. D., & Surratt, A. V. (1994). Self-management of problematic social behavior. In E. Schopler & G. B. Mesibov (Eds.), *Behavioral issues in autism* (pp. 81–97). New York: Plenum.

Koegel, R. L., & Koegel, L. K. (1990). Extended reductions in stereotypic behavior of students with autism through a self-management treatment package. *Journal of Applied Behavior Analysis, 23,* 119–127.

Koegel, R. L., O'Dell, M. C., & Koegel, L. K. (1987). A natural language teaching paradigm for nonverbal autistic children. *Journal of Autism and Developmental Disorders, 17,* 187–200.

Koegel, R. L., Rincover, A., & Egel, A. L. (1982). *Educating and understanding autistic children.* San Diego, CA: College-Hill.

Kohl, H. (1970). *The open classroom.* New York: Vintage.

Kohn, A. (1993). *Punished by rewards.* New York: Houghton Mifflin.

Koles, M. R., & Jenson, W. R. (1985). Comprehensive treatment of chronic fire setting in a severely disordered boy. *Journal of Behavior Therapy and Experimental Psychiatry, 16,* 81–85.

Kolko, D. J. (1994). Conduct disorder and attention deficit disorder with hyperactivity in child inpatients: Comparisons on home and hospital measures. *Journal of Emotional and Behavioral Disorders, 1,* 75–86.

Kolko, D. J., & Kazdin, A. E. (1986). A conceptualization of fire setting in children and adolescents. *Journal of Abnormal Child Psychology, 14,* 49–61.

Kolko, D. J., & Kazdin, A. E. (1989). The Children's Firesetting Interview with psychiatrically referred and nonreferred children. *Journal of Abnormal Child Psychology, 17,* 609–624.

Kornberg, L. (1955). *A class for disturbed children: A case study and its meaning for education.* New York: Teachers College Press.

Kovacs, M., & Pollock, M. (1995). Bipolar disorder and comorbid conduct disorder in childhood and adolescence. *Journal of the American Academy of Child and Adolescent Psychiatry, 34,* 715–723.

Kozol, J. (1967). *Death at an early age.* New York: Bantam.

Kozol, J. (1972). *Free schools.* Boston: Houghton Mifflin.

Krouse, J. P. (1982). *Peer conformity among delinquent subtypes.* Unpublished doctoral dissertation, University of Virginia.

Krugman, M. (Chairman). (1953). Symposium: The education of emotionally disturbed children. *American Journal of Orthopsychiatry, 23,* 667–731.

Kupersmidt, J. B., & Coie, J. D. (1987). *Preadolescent peer status and aggression as predictors of exter-*
nalizing problems in adolescence. Manuscript submitted for publication, University of Virginia, Charlottesville, VA.

Kupersmidt, J. B., Griesler, P. C., DeRosier, M. E., Patterson, C. J., & Davis, P. W. (1995). Childhood aggression and peer relations in the context of family and neighborhood factors. *Child Development, 66,* 360–375.

Kupersmidt, J. B., & Patterson, C. J. (1987). *Interim report to the Charlottesville Public Schools on children at risk.* Unpublished manuscript, University of Virginia, Charlottesville, VA.

Lahey, B. B., & Carlson, C. O. (1991). Validity of the diagnostic category of attention deficit disorder without hyperactivity: A review of the literature. *Journal of Learning Disabilities, 24,* 110–120.

Landrum, T. J., & Kauffman, J. M. (1992). Characteristics of general education teachers perceived as effective by their peers: Implications for inclusion of children with learning and behavioral disorders. *Exceptionality, 3,* 147–163.

Lane, H. (1976). *The wild boy of Aveyron.* Cambridge, MA: Harvard University Press.

Lantieri, L. (1995). Waging peace in our schools: Beginning with the children. *Phi Delta Kappan, 76,* 386–388.

Lask, B., & Bryant-Waugh, R. (Eds.). (1993). *Childhood onset anorexia nervosa and related eating disorders.* Hillsdale, NJ: Lawrence Erlbaum Associates.

Last, C. G. (1992). Anxiety disorders in childhood and adolescence. In W. R. Reynolds (Ed.), *Internalizing disorders in children and adolescents* (pp. 61–106). New York: Wiley.

Lattimore, P. K., Visher, C. A., & Linster, R. L. (1995). Predicting rearrest for violence among serious youthful offenders. *Journal of Research in Crime and Delinquency, 32,* 54–83.

LaVigna, G. W., & Donnellan, A. M. (1986). *Alternatives to punishment: Solving behavior problems with nonaversive strategies.* New York: Irvington.

Lavigueur, S., Tremblay, R. E., & Saucier, J. (1995). Interactional processes in families with disruptive boys: Patterns of direct and indirect influence. *Journal of Abnormal Child Psychology, 23,* 359–378.

Lawrence, C., Litynsky, M., & D'Lugoff, B. (1982). A day school intervention for truant and delinquent youth. In D. J. Safer (Ed.), *School pro-*

grams for disruptive adolescents (pp. 175–192). Baltimore, MD: University Park Press.

Lee, B. (1971). Curriculum design: The re-education approach. In N. J. Long, W. C. Morse, & R. G. Newman (Eds.), *Conflict in the classroom* (2nd ed.) (pp. 383–394). Belmont, CA: Wadsworth.

Leibowitz, G. (1991). Organic and biophysical theories of behavior. *Journal of Developmental and Physical Disabilities, 3,* 201–243.

Leon, G. R., & Dinklage, D. (1983). Childhood obesity and anorexia nervosa. In T. H. Ollendick & M. Hersen (Eds.), *Handbook of child psychopathology* (pp. 253–275). New York: Plenum.

Leonard, G. (1968). *Education and ecstasy.* New York: Delacorte.

Leone, P. E. (1985). Data-based instruction in correctional education. *Journal of Correctional Education, 36,* 77–85.

Leone, P. E. (1987). Teaching handicapped learners in correctional education programs. In C. M. Nelson, R. B. Rutherford, & B. I. Wolford (Eds.), *Special education in the criminal justice system* (pp. 275–291). Columbus, OH: Merrill/Macmillan.

Leone, P. E., & McLaughlin, M. J. (1995). Appropriate placement of students with emotional or behavioral disorders: Emerging policy options. In J. M. Kauffman, J. W. Lloyd, D. P. Hallahan, & T. A. Astuto (Eds.), *Issues in educational placement: Students with emotional and behavioral disorders* (pp. 335–359). Hillsdale, NJ: Erlbaum.

Leone, P. E., Price, T., & Vitolo, R. K. (1986). Appropriate education for all incarcerated youth: Meeting the spirit of P.L. 94–142 in youth detention facilities. *Remedial and Special Education, 7*(4), 9–14.

Leone, P. E., Rutherford, R. B., & Nelson, C. M. (1991). *Special education in juvenile corrections.* Reston, VA: Council for Exceptional Children.

Leone, P. E., Walter, M. B., & Wolford, B. I. (1990). Toward integrated responses to troubling behavior. In P. E. Leone (Ed.), *Understanding troubled and troubling youth* (pp. 290–298). Newbury Park, CA: Sage.

Lerman, D. C., Iwata, B. A., Zarcone, J. R., & Ringdahl, J. (1994). Assessment of stereotypic and self-injurious behavior as adjunctive responses. *Journal of Applied Behavior Analysis, 27,* 715–728.

Leutwyler, K. (1996). Schizophrenia revisited: New studies focus on malfunctions in the brain. *Scientific American, 274*(2), 22–23.

Levendosky, A. A., Okun, A., & Parker, J. G. (1995). Depression and maltreatment as predictors of social competence and social problem-solving skills in school-aged children. *Child Abuse and Neglect, 19,* 1183–1195.

Levey, J. C., & Lagos, V. K. (1994). Children with disabilities. In L. D. Eron, J. H. Gentry, & P. Schlegel (Eds.), *Reason to hope: A psychosocial perspective on violence and youth* (pp. 197–213). Washington, DC: American Psychological Association.

Levin, H. M., Guthrie, J. W., Kleindorfer, G. B., & Stout, R. T. (1971). School achievement and post-school success: A review. *Review of Educational Research, 41,* 1–16.

Levine, L. W. (1977). *Black culture and black consciousness: Afro-American folk thought from slavery to freedom.* New York: Oxford University Press.

Levy, S. R., Jurkovic, G. L., & Spirito, A. (1995). A multisystems analysis of adolescent suicide. *Journal of Abnormal Child Psychology, 23,* 221–234.

Lewin, P., Nelson, R. E., & Tollefson, N. (1983). Teacher attitudes toward disruptive children. *Elementary School Guidance and Counseling, 17,* 188–193.

Lewinsohn, P. M., Gotlib, I. H., & Seeley, J. R. (1995). Adolescent psychopathology: IV. Specificity of psychosocial risk factors for depression and substance abuse in older adolescents. *Journal of the American Academy of Child and Adolescent Psychiatry, 34,* 1221–1229.

Lewis, C. D. (1974). Introduction: Landmarks. In J. M. Kauffman & C. D. Lewis (Eds.), *Teaching children with behavior disorders: Personal perspectives* (pp. 2–23). Columbus, OH: Merrill.

Lewis, S. Y. (1990). Black teens parenting in the inner city: Problems and recommendations. In A. R. Stiffman & L. E. Davis (Eds.), *Ethnic issues in adolescent mental health* (pp. 208–219). Newbury Park, CA: Sage.

Lewis, W. W. (1982). Ecological factors in successful residential treatment. *Behavioral Disorders, 7,* 149–156.

Lilly, M. S. (1992). Labeling: A tired, overworked, yet unresolved issue in special education. In W. Stainback & S. Stainback (Eds.), *Controversial issues confronting special education: Divergent perspectives* (pp. 85–95). Boston: Allyn & Bacon.

Lincoln, A. J., Kaufman, J., & Kaufman, A. S. (1995). Intellectual and cognitive assessment. In M. Hersen & R. T. Ammerman (Eds.), *Advanced abnormal child psychology* (pp. 137–155). Hillsdale, NJ: Erlbaum.

Linet, L. S. (Ed.). (1995). *Medical letter: 1995 summary of the recent literature*. Bayside, NY: Tourette Syndrome Association.

Linton, T. E. (1969). The European educateur program for disturbed children. *American Journal of Orthopsychiatry, 39,* 125-133.

Linton, T. E. (1970). The European educateur model: An alternative and effective approach to the mental health of children. *Journal of Special Education, 3,* 319–327.

Lipsky, D. K., & Gartner, A. (1991). Restructuring for quality. In J. W. Lloyd, N. N. Singh, & A. C. Repp (Eds.), *The regular education initiative: Alternative perspectives on concepts, issues, and models* (pp. 43–56). Sycamore, IL: Sycamore.

Little, S. A., & Garber, J. (1995). Hyperaggression, depression, and stressful life events predicting peer rejection in children. *Development and Psychopathology, 7,* 845–856.

Lloyd, J. W., Crowley, E. P., Kohler, F. W., & Strain, P. S. (1988). Redefining the applied research agenda: Cooperative learning, prereferral, teacher consultation, and peer-mediated interventions. *Journal of Learning Disabilities, 21,* 43–52.

Lloyd, J. W., Hallahan, D. P., Kauffman, J. M., & Keller, C. E. (1991). Academic problems. In T. R. Kratochwill & R. J. Morris (Eds.), *The practice of child therapy* (2nd ed., pp. 145–173). New York: Pergamon.

Lloyd, J. W., & Kauffman, J. M. (1995). What less restrictive placements require of teachers. In J. M. Kauffman, J. W. Lloyd, D. P. Hallahan, & T. A. Astuto (Eds.), *Issues in educational placement: Students with emotional and behavioral disorders* (pp. 317–334). Hillsdale, NJ: Erlbaum.

Lloyd, J. W., Kauffman, J. M., & Gansneder, B. (1987). Differential teacher response to descriptions of aberrant behavior. In R. B. Rutherford, C. M. Nelson, & S. R. Forness (Eds.), *Severe behavior disorders of children and youth* (pp. 41–52). Boston: College Hill.

Lloyd, J. W., Kauffman, J. M., Landrum, T. J., & Roe, D. L. (1991). Why do teachers refer pupils for special education? An analysis of referral records. *Exceptionality, 2,* 115–126.

Lloyd, J. W., Kauffman, J. M., & Kupersmidt, J. B. (1987, November). *The Virginia Behavior Disorders Project.* Paper presented at Eleventh Annual Conference on Severe Behavior Disorders of Children and Youth, Tempe, AZ.

Lloyd, J. W., Landrum, T. J., & Hallahan, D. P. (1991). Self-monitoring applications for classroom intervention. In G. Stoner, M. R. Shinn, & H. M. Walker (Eds.), *Interventions for achievement and behavior problems* (pp. 201–213). Silver Spring, MD: National Association of School Psychologists.

Lloyd, J. W., Martin, K. R., & Kauffman, J. M. (1995). Teachers' participation in decisions about placement of students with emotional or behavioral disorders. In J. M. Kauffman, J. W. Lloyd, D. P. Hallahan, & T. A. Astuto (Eds.), *Issues in educational placement: Students with emotional and behavioral disorders* (pp. 169–181). Hillsdale, NJ: Erlbaum.

Lloyd, J. W., Singh, N. N., & Repp, A. C. (Eds.). (1991). *The regular education initiative: Alternative perspectives on concepts, issues, and models.* Sycamore, IL: Sycamore Press.

Loeber, R. (1982). The stability of antisocial and delinquent child behavior: A review. *Child Development, 53,* 1431–1446.

Loeber, R., Green, S. M., Keenan, K., & Lahey, B. B. (1995). Which boys will fare worse? Early predictors of the onset of conduct disorder in a six-year longitudinal study. *Journal of the American Academy of Child and Adolescent Psychiatry, 34,* 499–509.

Loeber, R., Green, S. M., Lahey, B. B., Christ, M. A. G., & Frick, P. J. (1992). Developmental sequences in the age of onset of disruptive child behaviors. *Journal of Child and Family Studies, 1,* 21–41.

Loeber, R., & Schmaling, K. B. (1985a). Empirical evidence for overt and covert patterns of antisocial conduct problems: A metaanalysis. *Journal of Abnormal Child Psychology, 13,* 337–352.

Loeber, R., & Schmaling, K. B. (1985b). The utility of differentiating between mixed and pure forms of antisocial child behavior. *Journal of Abnormal Child Psychology, 13,* 315–336.

Loeber, R., Weissman, W., & Reid, J. B. (1983). Family interactions of assaultive adolescents, stealers, and nondelinquents. *Journal of Abnormal Child Psychology, 11,* 1–14.

Loeber, R., Wung, P., Keenan, K., Giroux, B., Stouthamer-Loeber, M., Van Kammen, W., & Maughan, B. (1993). Developmental pathways in disruptive child behavior. *Development and Psychopathology, 5,* 103–134.

Long, N. J. (1974). Nicholas J. Long. In J. M. Kauffman & C. D. Lewis (Eds.), *Teaching children with behavior disorders: Personal perspectives* (pp. 168–196). Columbus, OH: Merrill.

Long, N. J., Morse, W. C., & Newman, R. G. (Eds.). (1965). *Conflict in the classroom.* Belmont, CA: Wadsworth.

Long, N. J., & Newman, R. G. (1965). Managing surface behavior of children in school. In N. J. Long, W. C. Morse, & R. G. Newman (Eds.), *Conflict in the classroom* (pp. 352–362). Belmont, CA: Wadsworth.

Lorion, R. P., Brodsky, A., Flaherty, M. J., & Holland, C. C. (1995). Community and prevention. In M. Hersen & R. T. Ammerman (Eds.), *Advanced abnormal child psychology* (pp. 213–230). Hillsdale, NJ: Erlbaum.

Lovaas, O. I. (1966a). A program for the establishment of speech in psychotic children. In J. K. Wing (Ed.), *Early childhood autism: Clinical, educational and social aspects.* New York: Pergamon.

Lovaas, O. I. (1966b). A behavior therapy approach to the treatment of childhood schizophrenia. In J. P. Hill (Ed.), *Minnesota symposia on child psychology* (Vol. 1, pp. 108–157). Minneapolis: University of Minnesota Press.

Lovaas, O. I. (1969). *Behavior modification: Teaching language to psychotic children* (16mm film). New York: Appleton-Century-Crofts.

Lovaas, O. I. (1977). *The autistic child: Language development through behavior modification.* New York: Irvington.

Lovass, O. I. (1979). Contrasting illness and behavioral models for the treatment of autistic children: A historical perspective. *Journal of Autism and Developmental Disorders, 9,* 315–323.

Lovaas, O. I. (1982). Comments on self-destructive behaviors. *Analysis and Intervention in Developmental Disabilities, 2,* 115–124.

Lovaas, O. I. (1987). Behavioral treatment and normal educational and intellectual functioning in young autistic children. *Journal of Consulting and Clinical Psychology, 55,* 3–9.

Lovaas, O. I., & Koegel, R. L. (1973). Behavior therapy with autistic children. In C. Thoresen (Ed.), *Behavior modification in education.* Chicago: University of Chicago Press.

Lovaas, O. I., Koegel, R. L., & Simmons, J. Q., & Long, J. S. (1973). Some generalization and follow-up measures on autistic children in behavior therapy. *Journal of Applied Behavior Analysis, 6,* 131–166.

Lovaas, O. I., Young, D. B., & Newsom, C. D. (1978). Childhood psychosis: Behavioral treatment. In B. B. Wolman (Ed.), *Handbook of treatment of mental disorders in childhood and adolescence* (pp. 385–420). Englewood Cliffs, NJ: Prentice-Hall.

Lovitt, T. C. (1977). *In spite of my resistance—I've learned from children.* Columbus, OH: Merrill.

Lundman, R. J. (1993). *Prevention and control of juvenile delinquency* (2nd ed.). New York: Oxford University Press.

Lyman, R. D. (1984). The effect of private and public goal setting on classroom on-task behavior of emotionally disturbed children. *Behavior Therapy, 15,* 395–402.

Lynskey, M. T., & Fergusson, D. M. (1995). Childhood conduct problems, attention deficit behaviors, and adolescent alcohol, tobacco, and illicit drug use. *Journal of Abnormal Child Psychology, 23,* 281–302.

Lyons, D. F., & Powers, V. (1963). Follow-up study of elementary school children exempted from Los Angeles City Schools during 1960–1961. *Exceptional Children, 30,* 155–162.

Maag, J. W., & Forness, S. R. (1991). Depression in children and adolescents—identification, assessment, and treatment. *Focus on Exceptional Children, 24*(1), 1–19.

McAdoo, J. L. (1990). Understanding African-American teen fathers. In P. E. Leone (Ed.), *Understanding troubled and troubling youth* (pp. 229–245). Newbury Park, CA: Sage.

McAfee, J. K. (1987). Classroom density and the aggressive behavior of handicapped children. *Education and Treatment of Children, 10,* 134–145.

McCarthy, J. M., & Paraskevopoulos, J. (1969). Behavior patterns of learning disabled, emotionally disturbed, and average children. *Exceptional Children, 36,* 69–74.

McCarthy, M. (1990). The thin ideal, depression and eating disorders in women. *Behavior Research and Therapy, 28,* 205–215.

McCloskey, L. A., Figueredo, A. J., & Koss, M. P. (1995). The effects of systemic family violence on children's mental health. *Child Development, 66,* 1239–1261.

Maccoby, E. E. (1986). Social groupings in childhood: Their relationship to prosocial and antisocial behavior in boys and girls. In D. Olweus, J. Block, & M. Radke-Yarrow (Eds.), *Development of antisocial and prosocial behavior: Research, theories, and issues* (pp. 263–284). New York: Academic Press.

McConaughy, S. H. (1993). Evaluating behavioral and emotional disorders with the CBCL, TRF, and YSR cross-informant scales. *Journal of Emotional and Behavioral Disorders, 1,* 40–52.

McConnell, S. R. (1987). Entrapment effects and the generalization and maintenance of social skills training for elementary school students with behavioral disorders. *Behavioral Disorders, 12,* 252–263.

MacDonald, W. S., Gallimore, R., & MacDonald, G. (1970). Contingency counseling by school personnel: An economical model of intervention. *Journal of Applied Behavior Analysis, 3,* 175–182.

McDowell, R. L., Adamson, G. W., & Wood, F. H. (Eds.). (1982). *Teaching emotionally disturbed children.* Boston: Little, Brown.

McEvoy, M. A., & Odom, S. L. (1987). Social interaction training for preschool children with behavioral disorders. *Behavior Disorders, 12,* 242–251.

Macfarlane, J., Allen, L., & Honzik, M. (1955). *A developmental study of the behavior problems of normal children between 21 months and 14 years.* Berkeley: University of California Press.

McGowan, B. G., & Kohn, A. (1990). Social support and teen pregnancy in the inner city. In A. R. Stiffman & L. E. Davis (Eds.), *Ethnic issues in adolescent mental health* (pp. 189–207). Newbury Park, CA: Sage.

McHugh, J. (1987, April 5). Portrait of trouble: Teen's crimes began early. *The Daily Progress,* pp. A1, A6.

McIntyre, T. (1992). The "invisible culture" in our schools: Gay and lesbian youth. *Beyond Behavior, 3*(3), 6–12.

McIntyre, T. (1993). Behaviorally disordered youth in correctional settings: Prevalence, programming, and teacher training. *Behavioral Disorders, 18,* 167–176.

McIntyre, T. (1994). *McIntyre Assessment of Culture: An instrument for evaluating the influence of culture on behavior and learning.* New York: Hunter College, City University of New York.

McIntyre, T., & Silva, P. (1992). Culturally diverse childrearing practices: Abusive or just different? *Beyond Behavior, 4*(1), 8–12.

Mackie, R. P., Kvaraceus, W. C., & Williams, H. M. (1957). *Teachers of children who are socially and emotionally maladjusted.* Washington, DC: Office of Education, U.S. Department of Health, Education and Welfare.

McKinney, J. D., Mason, J., Perkerson, K., & Clifford, M. (1975). Relationship between classroom behavior and academic achievement. *Journal of Educational Psychology, 67,* 198–203.

McLoughlin, J. A., & Nall, M. (1994). Allergies and learning/behavioral disorders. *Intervention in School and Clinic, 29,* 198–207.

McMahon, R. J. (1984). Behavioral checklists and rating scales. In T. H. Ollendick & M. Hersen (Eds.), *Child behavioral assessment: Principles and procedures* (pp. 80–105). New York: Pergamon.

McManus, M. (1985). *Modification of adolescent students' off-task behaviors using self-monitoring procedures.* Unpublished manuscript, University of Virginia, Charlottesville, VA.

McManus, M. E., & Kauffman, J. M. (1991). Working conditions of teachers of students with behavioral disorders: A national survey. *Behavioral Disorders, 16,* 247–259.

MacMillan, M. B. (1960). Extra-scientific influences in the history of childhood psychopathology. *American Journal of Psychiatry, 116,* 1091–1096.

Maher, C. A. (1987). Involving behaviorally disordered adolescents in instructional planning: Effectiveness of the GOAL procedure. *Journal of Child and Adolescent Psychotherapy, 4,* 204–210.

Mahler, M. S. (1952). On child psychosis and schizophrenia. *Psychoanalytic Study of the Child, 7,* 286–305.

Mahoney, M. J. (1974). *Cognition and behavior modification*. Cambridge, MA: Ballinger.

Mahoney, M. J. (1995). Cognition and causation in human experience. *Journal of Behavior Therapy and Experimental Psychiatry, 26*, 275–278.

Mann, L. (1979). *On the trail of process: A historical perspective on cognitive processes and their training*. New York: Grune & Stratton.

March, J. S. (1995). Cognitive-behavioral psychotherapy for children and adolescents with OCD: A review and recommendations for treatment. *Journal of the American Academy of Child and Adolescent Psychiatry, 34*, 7–18.

Marcus, L. M., & Schopler, E. (1993). Pervasive developmental disorders. In T. H. Ollendick & M. Hersen (Eds.), *Handbook of child and adolescent assessment* (pp. 346–363). New York: Pergamon.

Martin, B. (1975). Parent-child relations. In F. D. Horowitz (Ed.), *Review of Child Development Research* (Vol. 4, pp. 463–540). Chicago: University of Chicago Press.

Martin, E. W. (1972). Individualism and behaviorism as future trends in educating handicapped children. *Exceptional Children, 38,* 517–525.

Martin, J. A. (1981). A longitudinal study of the consequences of early mother-infant interaction: A microanalytic approach. *Monographs of the Society for Research in Child Development, 43* (3, Serial No. 190).

Martin, K. F., Hallenbeck, B. A., Kauffman, J. M., & Lloyd, J. W. (1995). A synopsis of research and professional literature on educational placement. In J. M. Kauffman, J. W. Lloyd, D. P. Hallahan, & T. A. Astuto (Eds.), *Issues in educational placement: Students with emotional and behavioral disorders* (pp. 75–117). Hillsdale, NJ: Erlbaum.

Martin, K. F., Lloyd, J. W., Kauffman, J. M., & Coyne, M. (1995). Teachers' perceptions of educational placement decisions for pupils with emotional or behavioral disorders. *Behavioral Disorders, 20,* 1–6–117.

Martin, R. P. (1992). Child temperament effects on special education process and outcomes. *Exceptionality, 3,* 99–115.

Martin, R. P., Wisenbaker, J., Matthews-Morgan, J., Holbrook, J., Hooper, S., & Spalding, J. (1986). Stability of teacher temperament ratings over 6 and 12 months. *Journal of Abnormal Child Psychology, 14,* 167–179.

Marttunen, M. J., Henriksson, M. M., Heikkinen, M. E., Isometsa, E. T., & Lonnqvist, J. K. (1995). Suicide among female adolescents: Characteristics and comparison with males in the age group 13–22 years. *Journal of the American Academy of Child and Adolescent Psychiatry, 34*, 1297–1307.

Maruskin-Mott, J. (1986). Portrait of Mark Matthews. *Gifted/Creative/Talented, 9*(6), 53.

Marvin, C. A., Beukelman, D. R., Brockhaus, J., & Kast, L. (1994). "What are you talking about?": Semantic analysis of preschool children's conversational topics in home and preschool settings. *Augmentative and Alternative Communication, 10*, 75–86.

Mattison, R. E., & Forness, S. R. (1995). Mental health system involvement and SED placement decisions. In J. M. Kauffman, J. W. Lloyd, D. P. Hallahan, & T. A. Astuto (Eds.), *Issues in educational placement: Students with emotional and behavioral disorders* (pp. 197–211). Hillsdale, NJ: Erlbaum.

Mattison, R. E., Morales, J., & Bauer, M. A. (1992). Distinguishing characteristics of elementary school boys recommended for SED placement. *Behavioral Disorders, 17,* 107–114.

Maudsley, H. (1880). *The pathology of the mind*. New York: Appleton.

Mayer, G. R. (1995). Preventing antisocial behavior in the schools. *Journal of Applied Behavior Analysis, 28,* 467–478.

Mayer, G. R., & Butterworth, T. (1981). Evaluating a preventive approach to reducing school vandalism. *Phi Delta Kappan, 62,* 498–499.

Mayer, G. R., Butterworth, T., Nafpaktitis, M., & Sulzer-Azaroff, B. (1983). Preventing school vandalism and improving discipline: A three-year study. *Journal of Applied Behavior Analysis, 16,* 355–369.

Mayer, G. R., Nafpaktitis, M., Butterworth, T., & Hollingsworth, P. (1987). A search for the elusive settings events of school vandalism: A correlational study. *Education and Treatment of Children, 10,* 259–270.

Mayer, G. R., & Sulzer-Azaroff, B. (1991). Interventions for vandalism. In G. Stoner, M. R. Shinn, & H. M. Walker (Eds.), *Interventions for achievement and behavior problems* (pp. 559–580). Silver Spring, MD: National Association of School Psychologists.

Mayo, T. (1839). *Elements of pathology of the human mind*. Philadelphia: Waldie.

Maypole, D. E., & Anderson, R. B. (1987). Culture-specific substance abuse prevention for blacks. *Community Mental Health Journal, 23,* 135–139.

Mednick, S. A., Moffitt, T., Gabrielli, W., & Hutchings, B. (1986). Genetic factors in criminal behavior: A review. In D. Olweus, J. Block, & M. Radke-Yarrow (Eds.), *Development of antisocial and prosocial behavior: Research, theories, and issues* (pp. 33–50). New York: Academic Press.

Meichenbaum, D. (1977). *Cognitive-behavior modification: An integrative approach*. New York: Plenum.

Meichenbaum, D. (1979). Teaching children self-control. In B. B. Lahey & A. E. Kazdin (Eds.), *Advances in clinical child psychology* (Vol. 2, pp. 1–33). New York: Plenum.

Meichenbaum, D. (1980). Cognitive-behavior modification: A promise yet unfulfilled. *Exceptional Education Quarterly, 1*(1), 83–88.

Meichenbaum, D. (1983). Teaching thinking: A cognitive-behavioral approach. In *Interdisciplinary voices in learning disabilities and remedial education*. Austin, TX: Pro-Ed.

Meichenbaum, D., Bowers, K. S., & Ross, R. R. (1969). A behavioral analysis of teacher expectancy effect. *Journal of Personality and Social Psychology, 13,* 306–316.

Meichenbaum, D., & Goodman, J. (1971). Training impulsive children to talk to themselves. *Journal of Abnormal Psychology, 77,* 115–126.

Menninger, K. (1963). *The vital balance*. New York: Viking Press.

Menolascino, F. J. (1972). Primitive, atypical, and abnormal-psychotic behavior in institutionalized mentally retarded children. *Journal of Autism and Childhood Schizophrenia, 3,* 49–64.

Menolascino, F. J. (1990). The nature and types of mental illness in the mentally retarded. In M. Lewis & S. M. Miller (Eds.), *Handbook of developmental psychopathology* (pp. 397–408). New York: Plenum.

Merrell, K. W. (1994). *Assessment of behavioral, social, and emotional problems: Direct & objective methods for use with children and adolescents*. New York: Longman.

Mesibov, G. B. (1995). Facilitated communication: A warning for pediatric psychologists. *Journal of Pediatric Psychology, 20,* 127–130.

Meyers, A. W., & Cohen, R. (1990). Cognitive-behavioral approaches to child psychopathology. In M. Lewis & S. M. Miller (Eds.), *Handbook of developmental psychopathology* (pp. 475–485). New York: Plenum.

Middleton, M. B., & Cartledge, G. (1995). The effects of social skills instruction and parental involvement on the aggressive behavior of African American males. *Behavior Modification, 19,* 192–210.

Miksic, S. (1987). Drug abuse management in adolescent special education. In M. M. Kerr, C. M. Nelson, & D. L. Lambert, *Helping adolescents with learning and behavior problems* (pp. 226–253). Columbus, OH: Merrill/Macmillan.

Milby, J. B., & Weber, A. (1991). Obsessive compulsive disorders. In T. R. Kratochwill & R. J. Morris (Eds.), *The practice of child therapy* (2nd ed., pp. 9–42). New York: Pergamon.

Miller, D. (1994). Suicidal behavior of adolescents with behavior disorders and their peers without disabilities. *Behavioral Disorders, 20,* 61–68.

Miller, G. E., & Prinz, R. J. (1991). Designing interventions for stealing. In G. Stoner, M. R. Shinn, & H. M. Walker (Eds.), *Interventions for achievement and behavior problems* (pp. 593–616). Silver Spring, MD: National Association of School Psychologists.

Miller, M. S. (1982). *Childstress! Understanding and answering stress signals of infants, children, and teenagers*. New York: Doubleday.

Mira, M. P., & Tyler, J. S. (1991). Students with traumatic brain injury: Making the transition from hospital to school. *Focus on Exceptional Children, 23*(5), 1–12.

Mizes, J. S. (1995). Eating disorders. In M. Hersen & R. T. Ammerman (Eds.), *Advanced abnormal child psychology* (pp. 375–391). Hillsdale, NJ: Erlbaum.

Moffitt, T. E. (1990). Juvenile delinquency and attention deficit disorder: Boys' developmental trajectories from age 3 to 15. *Child Development, 61,* 893–910.

Montague, M., McKinney, J. D., & Hocutt, A. (1994). Assessing students for attention deficit disorder. *Intervention in School and Clinic, 29,* 212–218.

Montee, B. B., Miltenberger, R. G., & Wittrock, D. (1995). An experimental analysis of facilitated communication. *Journal of Applied Behavior Analysis, 28*, 189–200.

Moore, D. R., Chamberlain, P., & Mukai, L. H. (1979). Children at risk for delinquency: A follow-up comparison of aggressive children and children who steal. *Journal of Abnormal Child Psychology, 7*, 345–355.

Moore, K. J., & Chamberlain, P. (1994). Treatment foster care: Toward development of community-based models for adolescents with severe emotional and behavioral disorders. *Journal of Emotional and Behavioral Disorders, 2*, 22–30.

Morenz, B., & Becker, J. (1995). The treatment of youthful sexual offenders. *Applied and Preventive Psychology, 4*, 247–256.

Morgan, D. P. (1993). Substance use prevention and students with behavioral disorders: Guidelines for school professionals. *Journal of Emotional and Behavioral Disorders, 1*, 170–178.

Morgan, D. P., & Jenson, W. R. (1988). *Teaching behaviorally disordered students*. Columbus, OH: Merrill/Macmillan.

Morgan, D. P., Young, K. R., & Goldstein, S. (1983). Teaching behaviorally disordered students to increase teacher attention and praise in mainstreamed classrooms. *Behavioral Disorders, 8*, 265–273.

Morganthau, T., Annin, P., Wingert, P., Foote, D., Manly, H., & King, P. (1992, March 9). It's not just New York. . . . *Newsweek, 119*(10), 25–29.

Morris, R. J. (1985). *Behavior modification with exceptional children*. Glenview, IL: Scott, Foresman.

Morris, R. J., & Kratochwill, T. R. (1983). *Treating children's fears and phobias*. New York: Pergamon.

Morris, R. J., & Kratochwill, T. R. (1991). Childhood fears and phobias. In T. R. Kratochwill & R. J. Morris (Eds.), *The practice of child therapy* (2nd ed., pp. 76–114). New York: Pergamon.

Morrison, G. M., Furlong, M. J., & Morrison, R. L. (1994). School violence to school safety: Reframing the issue for school psychologists. *School Psychology Review, 23*, 236–256.

Morse, W. C. (1953). The development of a mental hygiene milieu in a camp program for disturbed boys. *American Journal of Orthopsychiatry, 23*, 826–833.

Morse, W. C. (1965a). The crisis teacher. In N. J. Long, W. C. Morse, & R. G. Newman (Eds.), *Conflict in the classroom*. Belmont, CA: Wadsworth.

Morse, W. C. (1965b). Intervention techniques for the classroom teacher. In P. Knoblock (Ed.), *Educational programming for emotionally disturbed children: The decade ahead* (pp. 29–41). Syracuse, NY: Syracuse University Press.

Morse, W. C. (1971a). Crisis intervention in school mental health and special classes for the disturbed. In N. J. Long, W. C. Morse, & R. G. Newman (Eds.), *Conflict in the classroom* (2nd ed., pp. 459–464). Belmont, CA: Wadsworth.

Morse, W. C. (1971b). The crisis or helping teacher. In N. J. Long, W. C. Morse, & R. G. Newman (Eds.), *Conflict in the classroom* (2nd ed., pp. 294–296). Belmont, CA: Wadsworth.

Morse, W. C. (1974). William C. Morse. In J. M. Kauffman & C. D. Lewis (Eds.), *Teaching children with behavior disorders: Personal perspectives* (pp. 198–216). Columbus, OH: Merrill.

Morse, W. C. (1985). *The education and treatment of socioemotionally impaired children and youth*. Syracuse, NY: Syracuse University Press.

Morse, W. C. (1994). Comments from a biased point of view. *The Journal of Special Education, 27*, 531–542.

Morse, W. C., Ardizzone, J., MacDonald, C., & Pasick, P. (1980). *Affective education for special children and youth*. Reston, VA: Council for Exceptional Children.

Morse, W. C., Cutler, R. L., & Fink, A. H. (1964). *Public school classes for the emotionally handicapped: A research analysis*. Washington, DC: Council for Exceptional Children.

Morse, W. C., & Wineman, D. (1965). Group interviewing in a camp for disturbed boys. In N. J. Long, W. C. Morse, & R. G. Newman (Eds.), *Conflict in the classroom* (pp. 374–380). Belmont, CA: Wadsworth.

Motto, J. J., & Wilkins, G. S. (1968). Educational achievement of institutionalized emotionally disturbed children. *Journal of Educational Research, 61*, 218–221.

Mountjoy, P. T., Ruben, D. H., & Bradford, T. S. (1984). Recent technological advancements in the treatment of enuresis. *Behavior Modification, 8*, 291–315.

Moustakas, C. E. (1953). *Children in play therapy*. New York: McGraw-Hill.

Moyers, B. (1995, January 8). There is so much we can do. *Parade Magazine*, 4–6.

Moynihan, D. P. (1993). Defining deviancy down. *American Scholar, 62*(1), 17–30.

Mueller, C., Field, T., Yando, R., Harding, J., Gonzalez, K. P., Lasko, D., & Bendell, D. (1995). Under-eating and over-eating concerns among adolescents. *Journal of Child Psychology and Psychiatry, 36*, 1019–1025.

Munk, D. D., & Repp, A. C. (1994). The relationship between instructional variables and problem behavior: A review. *Exceptional Children, 60*, 390–401.

Murphy, D. M. (Ed.). (1986a). Handicapped juvenile offenders [Special issue]. *Remedial and Special Education, 7*(3).

Murphy, D. M. (1986b). The prevalence of handicapping conditions among juvenile delinquents. *Remedial and Special Education, 7*(3), 7–17.

Muskal, F. (1991). Sociological/ecological theories of emotional disturbance. *Journal of Developmental and Physical Disabilities, 3*, 267–288.

National Mental Health Association. (1986). *Severely emotionally disturbed children: Improving services under Education of the Handicapped Act (P.L. 94–142)*. Washington, DC: Author.

National Mental Health Association. (1989). *Invisible Children Project: Final report and recommendations of the Invisible Children Project*. Alexandria, VA: Author.

Neill, A. S. (1960). *Summerhill*. New York: Hart.

Nelson, C. M. (1981). Classroom management. In J. M. Kauffman & D. P. Hallahan (Eds.), *Handbook of special education* (pp. 663–687). Englewood Cliffs, NJ: Prentice-Hall.

Nelson, C. M. (1985). Who's crazy? II. In S. Braaten, R. B. Rutherford, & C. A. Kardash (Eds.), *Programming for adolescents with behavioral disorders* (Vol. 1, pp. 9–15). Reston, VA: Council for Children with Behavioral Disorders.

Nelson, C. M. (1987). Handicapped offenders in the criminal justice system. In C. M. Nelson, R. B. Rutherford, & B. I. Wolford (Eds.), *Special education in the criminal justice system* (pp. 2–17). Columbus, OH: Merrill/Macmillan.

Nelson, C. M., & Pearson, C. A. (1991). *Integrating services for children and youth with emotional and behavioral disorders*. Reston, VA: Council for Exceptional Children.

Nelson, C. M., & Rutherford, R. B. (1983). Timeout revisited: Guidelines for its use in special education. *Exceptional Education Quarterly, 3*(4), 56–67.

Nelson, C. M., & Rutherford, R. B. (1990). Troubled youth in the public schools: Emotionally disturbed or socially maladjusted? In P. E. Leone (Ed.), *Understanding troubled and troubling youth* (pp. 38–60). Newbury Park, CA: Sage.

Nelson, C. M., Rutherford, R. B., Center, D. B., & Walker, H. M. (1991). Do public schools have an obligation to serve troubled children and youth? *Exceptional Children, 57*, 406–415.

Nelson, C. M., Rutherford, R. B., & Wolford, B. I. (Eds.). (1987). *Special education in the criminal justice system*. Columbus, OH: Merrill/Macmillan.

Neuwirth, S. (1994). *Attention-deficit hyperactivity disorder: Decade of the brain*. National Institutes of Health Publication No. 94-3572. Washington, DC: National Institutes of Health.

Newcomb, M. D., & Richardson, M. A. (1995). Substance use disorders. In M. Hersen & R. T. Ammerman (Eds.), *Advanced abnormal child psychology* (pp. 411–431). Hillsdale, NJ: Erlbaum.

Newcomer, P. L., Barenbaum, E., & Pearson, N. (1995). Depression and anxiety in children and adolescents with learning disabilities, conduct disorders, and no disabilities. *Journal of Emotional and Behavioral Disorders, 3*, 27–39.

Newman, B., Buffington, D. M., O'Grady, M., McDonald, M. E., Poulson, C. L., & Hemmes, N. S. (1995). Self-management of schedule following in three teenagers with autism. *Behavioral Disorders, 20*, 190–196.

Nicol, S. E., & Erlenmeyer-Kimling, L. (1986). Genetic factors and psychopathology: Implications for prevention. In B. A. Edelstein & L. Michelson (Eds.), *Handbook of prevention* (pp. 21–41). New York: Plenum.

Nietzel, M. T., & Himelein, M. J. (1986). Prevention of crime and delinquency. In B. A. Edelstein & L. Michelson (Eds.), *Handbook of prevention*. New York: Plenum.

Noll, M. B., Kamps, D., & Seaborn, C. F. (1993). Prereferral intervention for students with emotional or behavioral risks: Use of a behavioral consultation model. *Journal of Emotional and Behavioral Disorders, 1*, 203–214.

O'Brien, F. (1981). Treating self-stimulatory behavior. In J. L. Matson & J. R. McCartney (Eds.),

Handbook of behavior modification with the mentally retarded (pp. 117–150). New York: Plenum.

Odden, A., Monk, D., Nakib, Y., & Picus, L. (1995). The story of the education dollar: No academy awards and no fiscal smoking guns. *Phi Delta Kappan, 77*, 161–168.

O'Donnell, C. R. (1995). Firearm deaths among children and youth. *American Psychologist, 50*, 771–776.

Ogbu, J. U. (1990). Understanding diversity: Summary comments. *Education and Urban Society, 22*, 425–429.

O'Leary, K. D., & Wilson, G. T. (1975). *Behavior therapy: Applications and outcomes*. Englewood Cliffs, NJ: Prentice-Hall.

O'Leary, S. G. (1980). A response to cognitive training. *Exceptional Education Quarterly, 1*(1), 89–94.

O'Leary, S. G. (1995). Parental discipline mistakes. *Current Directions in Psychological Science, 4*, 11–13.

Oliver, C. (1995). Annotation: Self-injurious behaviour in children with learning disabilities: Recent advances in assessment and intervention. *Journal of Child Psychology and Psychiatry, 30*, 909–927.

Ollendick, T. H., & Hersen, M. (1983). A historical overview of child psychopathology. In T. H. Ollendick & M. Hersen (Eds.), *Handbook of child psychopathology* (pp. 3–11). New York: Plenum.

Ollendick, T. H., & Hersen, M. (Eds.) (1993). *Handbook of child and adolescent assessment*. Boston: Allyn & Bacon.

Olweus, D. (1979). Stability of aggressive reaction patterns in males: A review. *Psychological Bulletin, 86*, 852–875.

Olweus, D. (1991). Bully/victim problems among school children: Basic facts and effects of a school-based intervention program. In D. J. Pepler & K. H. Rubin (Eds.), *The development of childhood aggression* (pp. 411–446). Hillsdale, NJ: Erlbaum.

O'Neil, J. (1995). Can inclusion work? A conversation with Jim Kauffman and Mara Sapon-Shevin. *Educational Leadership, 52*(4), 7–11.

O'Neill, R. E., Horner, R. H., Albin, R. W., Storey, K., & Sprague, J. R. (1990). *Functional analysis of problem behavior: A practical assessment guide* (2nd ed.). Pacific Grove, CA: Brooks/Cole.

Ornitz, E. M. (1986). Prevention of developmental disorders. In B. A. Edelstein & L. Michelson (Eds.), *Handbook of prevention* (pp. 75–116). New York: Plenum.

Orr, D. P., Beiter, M., & Ingersoll, G. (1991). Premature sexual activity as an indicator of psychosocial risk. *Pediatrics, 87,* 141–147.

Ortiz, A. A., & Yates, J. R. (1984). Staffing and the development of individualized educational programs for bilingual exceptional students. In L. M. Baca & H. T. Cervantes (Eds.), *The bilingual special education interface* (pp. 187–212). St. Louis: Times Mirror/Mosby.

Orvaschel, H., Ambrosini, P., & Rabinovich, H. (1993). Diagnostic issues in child assessment. In T. H. Ollendick & M. Hersen (Eds.), *Handbook of child and adolescent assessment* (pp. 26–40). New York: Pergamon.

Paget, K. D., Nagle, R. J., & Martin, R. P. (1984). Interrelations between temperament characteristics and first-grade teacher-student interactions. *Journal of Abnormal Child Psychology, 12,* 547–560.

Parke, R. D., & Collmer, C. W. (1975). Child abuse: An interdisciplinary analysis. In E. M. Hetherington (Ed.), *Review of child development research* (Vol. 5, pp. 509–590). Chicago: University of Chicago Press.

Parker, H., & Parker, S. (1986). Father-daughter sexual abuse: An emerging perspective. *American Journal of Orthopsychiatry, 56,* 531–549.

Parkinson, J. (1963). Observations on the excessive indulgence of children, particularly intended to show its injurious effects on their health, and the difficulties it occasions in their treatment during sickness. In R. Hunter & I. Macalpine (Eds.), *Three hundred years of psychiatry, 1535–1860.* London: Oxford University Press. (Original work published in 1807, London: Symonds et al.)

Pataki, C. S., & Carlson, G. A. (1995). Childhood and adolescent depression: A review. *Harvard Review of Psychiatry, 3,* 140–151.

Patterson, C. J., Kupersmidt, J. B., & Griesler, P. C. (1988). *Self-concepts of children in regular education and in special education classes.* Unpublished manuscript, University of Virginia.

Patterson, G. R. (1965a). An application of conditioning techniques to the control of a hyperactive child. In L. P. Ullmann & L. Krasner (Eds.), *Case studies in behavior modification* (pp. 370–375). New York: Holt, Rinehart & Winston.

Patterson, G. R. (1965b). A learning theory approach to the treatment of the school phobic child. In L. P. Ullmann & L. Krasner (Eds.), *Case studies in behavior modification* (pp. 279–285). New York: Holt, Rinehart & Winston.

Patterson, G. R. (1971). *Families*. Champaign, IL: Research Press.

Patterson, G. R. (1973). Reprogramming the families of aggressive boys. In C. Thoresen (Ed.), *Behavior modification in education*. Chicago: University of Chicago Press.

Patterson, G. R. (1975). The aggressive child: Victim or architect of a coercive system? In L. A. Hammerlynck, L. C. Handy, & E. J. Mash (Eds.), *Behavior modification and families* (pp. 267–316). New York: Brunner/Mazel.

Patterson, G. R. (1980). Mothers: The unacknowledged victims. *Monographs of the Society for Research in Child Development, 45* (5, Serial No. 186).

Patterson, G. R. (1982). *Coercive family process*. Eugene, OR: Castalia.

Patterson, G. R. (1986a). The contribution of siblings to training for fighting: A microsocial analysis. In D. Olweus, J. Block, & M. Radke-Yarrow (Eds.), *Development of antisocial and prosocial behavior: Research, theories, and issues* (pp. 235–262). New York: Academic Press.

Patterson, G. R. (1986b). Performance models for antisocial boys. *American Psychologist, 41,* 432–444.

Patterson, G. R., & Capaldi, D. M. (1990). A mediational model for boys' depressed mood. In J. Rolf, A. S. Masten, D. Cicchetti, K. H. Nuechterlein, & S. Weintraub (Eds.), *Risk and protective factors in the development of psychopathology* (pp. 141–163). New York: Cambridge University Press.

Patterson, G. R., DeBaryshe, B. D., & Ramsey, E. (1989). A developmental perspective on antisocial behavior. *American Psychologist, 44,* 329–335.

Patterson, G. R., & Forgatch, M. (1987). *Parents and adolescents living together*. Eugene, OR: Castalia.

Patterson, G. R., Reid, J. B., & Dishion, T. J. (1992). *Antisocial boys*. Eugene, OR: Castalia.

Patterson, G. R., Reid, J. B., Jones, R. R., & Conger, R. E. (1975). *A social learning approach to family intervention: Vol. 1. Families with aggressive children*. Eugene, OR: Castalia.

Patton, J. R., Blackbourn, J. M., Kauffman, J. M., & Brown, G. B. (1991). *Exceptional children in focus* (5th ed.). Columbus, OH: Merrill/Macmillan.

Peacock Hill Working Group. (1991). Problems and promises in special education and related services for children and youth with emotional or behavioral disorders. *Behavioral Disorders, 16,* 299–313.

Pearson, G. H. J. (1954). *Psychoanalysis and the education of the child*. New York: Norton.

Pepler, D. J., & Slaby, R. G. (1994). Theoretical and developmental perspectives on youth and violence. In L. D. Eron, J. H. Gentry, & P. Schlegel (Eds.), *Reason to hope: A psychosocial perspective on violence and youth* (pp. 27–58). Washington, DC: American Psychological Association.

Pescara-Kovach, L. A., & Alexander, K. (1994). The link between food ingested and problem behavior: Fact or fallacy? *Behavioral Disorders, 19,* 142–148.

Peterson, C. C., Peterson, J. L., & Seeto, D. (1983). Developmental changes in ideas about lying. *Child Development, 54,* 1529–1535.

Peterson, R., & Ishii-Jordan, S. (Eds.). (1994). *Multicultural issues in the education of students with behavioral disorders*. Cambridge, MA: Brookline.

Pfeffer, C. R. (1984). Clinical aspects of childhood suicidal behavior. *Pediatric Annals, 13,* 56–61.

Pfiffner, L. J. & O'Leary, S. G. (1987). The efficacy of all-positive management as a function of the prior use of negative consequences. *Journal of Applied Behavior Analysis, 20,* 265–271.

Pfiffner, L. J., Rosen, L. A., & O'Leary, S. G. (1985). The efficacy of an all-positive approach to classroom management. *Journal of Applied Behavior Analysis, 18,* 257–261.

Phillips, E. L. (1967). Problems in educating emotionally disturbed children. In N. G. Haring & E. L. Phillips (Eds.), *Methods in special education* (pp. 137–158). New York: McGraw-Hill.

Phillips, E. L., & Haring, N. G. (1959). Results from special techniques for teaching emotionally disturbed children. *Exceptional Children, 26,* 64–67.

Phillips, L., Draguns, J. G., & Bartlett, D. P. (1975). Classification of behavior disorders. In N. Hobbs (Ed.), *Issues in the classification of children* (Vol. 1, pp. 26–55). San Francisco: Jossey-Bass.

Piacentini, J. (1993). Checklists and rating scales. In T. H. Ollendick & M. Hersen (Eds.), *Handbook of child and adolescent assessment* (pp. 82–97). New York: Pergamon.

Pierce, K., & Schreibman, L. (1995). Increasing the complex social behaviors in children with autism: Effects of peer-implemented pivotal response training. *Journal of Applied Behavior Analysis, 28,* 285–295.

Pilowsky, D. (1995). Psychopathology among children placed in family foster care. *Psychiatric Services, 46,* 906–910.

Plomin, R. (1989). Environment and genes: Determinants of behavior. *American Psychologist, 44,* 105–111.

Plomin, R. (1995). Genetics and children's experiences in the family. *Journal of Child Psychology and Psychiatry, 36,* 33–68.

Poland, S. (1989). *Suicide intervention in the schools.* New York: Guilford Press.

Polirstok, S. R. (1986). Training problematic adolescents as peer tutors: Benefits for the tutor and the school at large. *Techniques: A Journal for Remedial Education and Counseling, 2,* 204–210.

Polirstok, S. R. (1987). A specialized peer tutoring program for academically and behaviorally handicapped adolescents. In J. Gottlieb (Ed.), *Advances in special education* (Vol. 6, pp. 63–74). Greenwich, CT: JAI Press.

Polirstok, S. R., & Greer, R. D. (1977). Remediation of mutually aversive interactions between a problem student and four teachers by training the student in reinforcement techniques. *Journal of Applied Behavior Analysis, 10,* 707–716.

Polirstok, S. R., & Greer, R. D. (1986). A replication of collateral effects and a component analysis of a successful tutoring package for inner-city adolescents. *Education and Treatment of Children, 9,* 101–121.

Polsgrove, L. (Ed.). (1983). Aversive control in the classroom [Special issue]. *Exceptional Education Quarterly, 3*(4).

Polusny, M. A., & Follette, V. M. (1995). Long-term correlates of child sexual abuse: Theory and review of the empirical literature. *Applied and Preventive Psychology, 4,* 143–166.

Postel, H. H. (1937). The special school versus the special class. *Exceptional Children, 4,* 12–13, 18–19.

Potter, H. W. (1933). Schizophrenia in children. *American Journal of Psychiatry, 89,* 1253–1270.

Power, C. (1994). The special role of longitudinal studies. In I. B. Pless (Ed.), *The epidemiology of childhood disorders* (pp. 31–46). New York: Oxford University Press.

Prescott, D. A. (1954). *Emotions and the education process.* Washington, DC: American Council on Education.

Prins, P. J. M. (1994). Anxiety in medical settings. In T. H. Ollendick, N. J. King, & W. Yule (Eds.), *International handbook of phobic and anxiety disorders in children and adolescents* (pp. 267–290). New York: Plenum.

Prior, M., & Werry, J. S. (1986). Autism, schizophrenia, and allied disorders. In H. C. Quay, & J. S. Werry (Eds.), *Psychopathological disorders of childhood* (3rd ed.) (pp. 156–210). New York: Wiley.

Pugliese, M. T., Lifshitz, F., Grad, G., Fort, P., & Marks-Katz, M. (1983). Fear of obesity: A cause of short stature and delayed puberty. *New England Journal of Medicine, 309,* 513–518.

Pullis, M. (1989). Goodness of fit in classroom relationships. In W. B. Carey & S. C. McDevitt (Eds.), *Clinical and educational applications of temperament research* (pp. 117–120). Amsterdam: Swets & Zeitlinger.

Pullis, M. (1991). Practical considerations of excluding conduct disordered students: An empirical analysis. *Behavioral Disorders, 17,* 9–22.

Pullis, M., & Cadwell, J. (1982). The influence of children's temperament characteristics on teachers' decision strategies. *American Educational Research Journal, 19,* 165–181.

Pullis, M., & Cadwell, J. (1985). Temperament as a factor in the assessment of children educationally at risk. *Journal of Special Education, 19,* 91–102.

Putallaz, M., & Heflin, A. H. (1990). Parent-child interaction. In S. R. Asher & J. D. Coie (Eds.), *Peer rejection in childhood* (pp. 189–216). New York: Cambridge University Press.

Quay, H. C. (1975). Classification in the treatment of delinquency and antisocial behavior. In N. Hobbs (Ed.), *Issues in the classification of children* (Vol. 1, pp. 377–392). San Francisco: Jossey-Bass.

Quay, H. C. (1977). Measuring dimensions of deviant behavior: The Behavior Problem Checklist. *Journal of Abnormal Child Psychology, 5,* 277–289.

Quay, H. C. (1986a). Classification. In H. C. Quay & J. S. Werry (Eds.), *Psychopathological disorders of childhood* (3rd ed.) (pp. 1–34). New York: Wiley.

Quay, H. C. (1986b). Conduct disorders. In H. C. Quay & J. S. Werry (Eds.), *Psychopathological disorders of childhood* (3rd ed.) (pp. 35–72). New York: Wiley.

Quay, H. C., & La Greca, A. M. (1986). Disorders of anxiety, withdrawal, and dysphoria. In H. C. Quay & J. S. Werry (Eds.), *Psychopathological disorders of childhood* (3rd ed.) (pp. 73–110). New York: Wiley.

Quay, H. C., Morse, W. C., & Cutler, R. L. (1966). Personality patterns of pupils in special classes for the emotionally disturbed. *Exceptional Children, 32,* 297–301.

Quay, H. C., & Peterson, D. R. (1975). *Manual for the Behavior Problem Checklist*. Coral Gables, FL: Author.

Quay, H. C., & Peterson, D. R. (1987). *Manual for the Revised Behavior Problem Checklist*. Coral Gables, FL: Author.

Quinn, K. P., Epstein, M. H., & Cumblad, C. L. (1995). Developing comprehensive, individualized, community-based services for children and youth with emotional and behavior disorders: Direct service providers' perspectives. *Journal of Child and Family Studies, 4,* 19–42.

Quinsey, V. L., Chaplin, T. D., & Upfold, D. (1989). Arsonists and sexual arousal to fire setting: Correlation unsupported. *Journal of Behavior Therapy and Experimental Psychiatry, 20,* 203–209.

Quintanna, H., & Birmaher, B. (1995). Pharmacological treatment. In M. Hersen & R. T. Ammerman (Eds.), *Advanced abnormal child psychology* (pp. 189–212). Hillsdale, NJ: Erlbaum.

Rabian, B., & Silverman, W. K. (1995). Anxiety disorders. In M. Hersen & R. T. Ammerman (Eds.), *Advanced abnormal child psychology* (pp. 235–252). Hillsdale, NJ: Erlbaum.

Radke-Yarrow, M. (1990). Family environments of depressed and well parents and their children: Issues of research methods. In G. R. Patterson (Ed.), *Depression and aggression in family interaction* (pp. 169–184). Hillsdale, NJ: Erlbaum.

Ramirez, M., & Castaneda, A. (1974). *Cultural democracy: Bicognitive development and education*. New York: Academic Press.

Rank, B. (1949). Adaptation of the psychoanalytic techniques for the treatment of young children with atypical development. *American Journal of Orthopsychiatry, 19,* 130–139.

Rappaport, M. M., & Rappaport, H. (1975). The other half of the expectancy equation: Pygmalion. *Journal of Educational Psychology, 67,* 531–536.

Rappaport, S. R. (1976). Sheldon R. Rappaport. In J. M. Kauffman & D. P. Hallahan (Eds.), *Teaching children with learning disabilities: Personal perspectives* (pp. 344–371). Columbus, OH: Merrill.

Rasanen, P., Hirvenoja, R., Hakko, H., & Vaisanen, E. (1995). A portrait of the juvenile arsonist. *Forensic Science International, 73,* 41–47.

Ray, I. (1846). Observations of the principal hospitals for the insane, in Great Britain, France, and Germany. *American Journal of Insanity, 2,* 289–390.

Raymer, R. (1992, April). Annals of science: A silent childhood. *The New Yorker,* pp. 41–81 (April 13), 43–77 (April 20).

Redl, F. (1959a). The concept of a therapeutic milieu. *American Journal of Orthopsychiatry, 29,* 721–734.

Redl, F. (1959b). The concept of the life space interview. *American Journal of Orthopsychiatry, 29,* 1–18.

Redl, F. (1966). Designing a therapeutic classroom environment for disturbed children: The milieu approach. In P. Knoblock (Ed.), *Intervention approaches in educating emotionally disturbed children* (pp. 79–98). Syracuse, NY: Syracuse University Press.

Redl, F., & Wattenberg, W. W. (1951). *Mental hygiene in teaching*. New York: Harcourt, Brace, & World.

Redl F., & Wineman, D. (1952). *Children who hate*. New York: Free Press.

Redl, F., & Wineman, D. (1952). *Controls from within*. New York: Free Press.

Reed, E. W. (1975). Genetic anomalies in development. In F. D. Horowitz (Ed.), *Review of child development research* (Vol. 4, pp. 59–99). Chicago: University of Chicago Press.

Rees, T. P. (1957). Back to moral treatment and community care. *Journal of Mental Science, 103,* 303–313.

Reid, J. (1993). Prevention of conduct disorder before and after school entry: Relating intervention to developmental findings. *Development and Psychopathology, 5,* 243–262.

Reid, J. B., & Hendricks, A. (1973). Preliminary analysis of the effectiveness of direct home intervention for the treatment of predelinquent boys who steal. In L. A. Hammerlynck, L. C. Handy, & E. J. Mash (Eds.), *Behavior change: Methodology, concepts and practice* (pp. 209–219). Champaign, IL: Research Press.

Reid, J. B., & Patterson, G. R. (1976). The modification of aggression and stealing behavior of boys in the home setting. In A. Bandura & E. Ribes (Eds.), *Behavior modification: Experimental analyses of aggression and delinquency* (pp. 123–145). Hillsdale, NJ: Erlbaum.

Reitman, D., & Gross, A. M. (1995). Familial determinants. In M. Hersen & R. T. Ammerman (Eds.), *Advanced abnormal child psychology* (pp. 87–104). Hillsdale, NJ: Erlbaum.

Rekers, G. A. (1985). Gender identity problems. In P. H. Bornstein & A. E. Kazdin (Eds.), *Handbook of clinical behavior therapy with children* (pp. 658–699). Homewood, IL: Dorsey Press.

Remschmidt, H. E., Schulz, E., Martin, M., Warnke, A., & Trott, G. (1994). Childhood-onset schizophrenia: History of the concept and recent studies. *Schizophrenia Bulletin, 20,* 727–745.

Repp, A. C., & Deitz, D. E. D. (1990). Using an ecobehavioral analysis to determine a taxonomy for stereotyped responding. In S. R. Schroeder (Ed.), *Ecobehavioral analysis and developmental disabilities: The twenty-first century* (pp. 122–140). New York: Springer.

Reynolds, M. C., Wang, M. C., & Walberg, H. J. (1987). The necessary restructuring of special and regular education. *Exceptional Children, 53,* 391–398.

Reynolds, W. M. (1992). Depression in children and adolescents. In W. R. Reynolds (Ed.), *Internalizing disorders in children and adolescents* (pp. 149–253). New York: Wiley.

Reynolds, W. M. (1993). Self-report methodology. In T. H. Ollendick & M. Hersen (Eds.), *Handbook of child and adolescent assessment* (pp. 98–123). New York: Pergamon.

Rezmierski, V. E., Knoblock, P., & Bloom, R. B. (1982). The psychoeducational model: Theory and historical perspective. In R. L. McDowell, G. W. Adamson, & F. H. Wood (Eds.), *Teaching emotionally disturbed children* (pp. 47–69). Boston: Little, Brown.

Rhode, G., Jenson, W. R., & Reavis, H. K. (1992). *The tough kid book: Practical classroom management strategies.* Longmont, CA: Sopris West.

Rhodes, W. C. (1963). Curriculum and disordered behavior. *Exceptional Children, 30,* 61–66.

Rhodes, W. C. (1964). Institutionalized displacement and the disturbing child. In P. Knoblock (Ed.), *Educational programming for emotionally distrubed children: The decade ahead* (pp. 42–57). Syracuse, NY: Syracuse University Press.

Rhodes, W. C. (1967). The disturbing child: A problem of ecological management. *Exceptional Children, 33,* 449–455.

Rhodes, W. C. (1970). A community participation analysis of emotional disturbance. *Exceptional Children, 37,* 309–314.

Rhodes, W. C. (1992). Navigating the paradigm change. *Journal of Emotional and Behavioral Problems, 1*(2), 28–34.

Rhodes, W. C., & Doone, E. M. (1992). One boy's transformation. *Journal of Emotional and Behavioral Problems, 1*(2), 10–15.

Rhodes, W. C., & Head, S. (Eds.). (1974). *A study of child variance: Vol. 3. Service delivery systems.* Ann Arbor: University of Michigan.

Rhodes, W. C., & Paul, J. L. (1978). *Emotionally disturbed and deviant children: New views and approaches.* Englewood Cliffs, NJ: Prentice-Hall.

Rhodes, W. C., & Tracy, M. L. (Eds.). (1972a). *A study of child variance: Vol. 1. Theories.* Ann Arbor: University of Michigan.

Rhodes, W. C., & Tracy, M. L. (Eds.). (1972b). *A study of child variance: Vol. 2. Interventions.* Ann Arbor: University of Michigan.

Rich, H. L., Beck, M. A., & Coleman, T. W. (1982). Behavior management: The psychoeducational model. In R. L. McDowell, G. W. Adamson, & F. H. Wood (Eds.), *Teaching emotionally disturbed children* (pp. 131–166). Boston: Little, Brown.

Richardson, G. A., McGauhey, P., & Day, N. L. (1995). Epidemiologic considerations. In M. Hersen & R. T. Ammerman (Eds.), *Advanced abnormal child psychology* (pp. 37–48). Hillsdale, NJ: Erlbaum.

Richters, J. E., & Cicchetti, D. (1993). Mark Twain meets DSM-III-R: Conduct disorder, development, and the concept of harmful dysfunction. *Development and Psychopathology, 5*, 5–29.

Riddle, M. A., Hardin, M. T., Ort, S. I., Leckman, J. F., & Cohen, D. J. (1988). Behavioral symptoms in Tourette's syndrome. In D. J. Cohen, R. D. Brunn, & J. F. Leckman (Eds.), *Tourette's syndrome and disorders* (pp. 151–162). New York: Wiley.

Rie, H. E. (1971). Historical perspective of concepts of child psychopathology. In H. E. Rie (Ed.), *Perspectives in child psychopathology*. Chicago: Aldine Atherton.

Riggs, P. D., Baker, S., Mikulich, S. K., Young, S. E., & Crowley, T. J. (1995). Depression in substance–dependent delinquents. *Journal of the American Academy of Child and Adolescent Psychiatry, 34*, 764–771.

Rimland, B. (1964). *Infantile autism*. New York: Appleton-Century-Crofts (Prentice-Hall).

Robins, L. N. (1966). *Deviant children grown up*. Baltimore: Williams & Wilkins.

Robins, L. N. (1974). Antisocial behavior disturbances of childhood: Prevalence, prognosis, and prospects. In E. J. Anthony, & C. Koupernik (Eds.), *The child in his family: Children at psychiatric risk* (pp. 447–460). New York: Wiley.

Robins, L. N. (1979). Follow-up studies. In H. C. Quay & J. S. Werry (Eds.), *Psychopathological disorders of childhood* (2nd ed.) (pp. 483–513). New York: Wiley.

Robins, L. N. (1986). The consequences of conduct disorder in girls. In D. Olweus, J. Block, & M. Radke-Yarrow (Eds.), *Development of antisocial and prosocial behavior: Research, theories, and issues* (pp. 385–414). New York: Academic Press.

Robinson, F. J., & Vitale, L. J. (1954). Children with circumscribed interest patterns. *American Journal of Orthopsychiatry, 24*, 755–766.

Rodin, J., Striegel-Moore, R. H., & Silberstein, L. R. (1990). In J. Rolf, A. S. Masten, D. Cicchetti, K. H. Nuechterlein, & S. Weintraub (Eds.), *Risk and protective factors in the development of psychopathology* (pp. 361–383). New York: Cambridge University Press.

Rogers, C. (1983). *Freedom to learn for the 80s*. Columbus, OH: Merrill/Macmillan.

Rogoff, B., & Morelli, G. (1989). Culture and American children. *American Psychologist, 44*, 341–342.

Rolf, J., & Johnson, J. (1990). Protected or vulnerable: The challenges of AIDS to developmental psychopathology. In J. Rolf, A. S. Masten, D. Cicchetti, K. H. Nuechterlein, & S. Weintraub (Eds.), *Risk and protective factors in the development of psychopathology* (pp. 384–404). New York: Cambridge University Press.

Rooney, K. J., & Hallahan, D. P. (1985). Future directions for cognitive behavior modification research: The quest for cognitive change. *Remedial and Special Education, 6*(2), 46–51.

Rosen, L. A. O'Leary, S. G., Joyce, S. A., Conway, G., & Pfiffner, L. J. (1984). The importance of prudent negative consequences for maintaining the appropriate behavior of hyperactive students. *Journal of Abnormal Child Psychology, 12*, 581–604.

Rosenberg, H. E., & Graubard, P. S. (1975). Peer use of behavior modification. *Focus on Exceptional Children, 7*(6), 1–10.

Rosenberg, J. (1994). Direct instruction reaches special-needs students. *Effective School Practices, 12*(4), 5–7.

Rosenblatt, A., & Attkisson, C. C. (1992). Integrating systems of care in California for youth with severe emotional disturbance. I. A descriptive overview of the California AB377 Evaluation Project. *Journal of Child and Family Studies, 1,*, 93–113.

Rosenthal, P. A. & Rosenthal, S. (1984). Suicidal behavior by preschool children. *American Journal of Psychiatry, 141*, 520–525.

Rosenthal, R., & Jacobson, L. (1968). *Pygmalion in the classroom*. New York: Holt, Rinehart & Winston.

Ross, D. M., & Ross, S. A. (1982). *Hyperactivity: Research, theory, action* (2nd ed.). New York: Wiley.

Ross, G. R. (1994). *Treating adolescent substance abuse: Understanding the fundamental elements*. Boston: Allyn & Bacon.

Ross, S., & Jennings, K. D. (1995). Development and psychopathology. In M. Hersen & R. T. Ammerman (Eds.), *Advanced abnormal child psychology* (pp. 49–57). Hillsdale, NJ: Erlbaum.

Rotenberg, K. J. (1991). *Children's interpersonal trust: Sensitivity to lying, deception, and promise violations*. New York: Springer-Verlag.

Rotheram, M. J. (1987). Evaluation of imminent danger for suicide among youth. *American Journal of Orthopsychiatry, 57*, 102–110.

Rothman, D. (1971). *The discovery of the asylum: Social order and disorder in the new republic*. Boston: Little, Brown.

Rothman, E. P. (1967). The Livingston School: A day school for disturbed girls. In P. H. Berkowitz & E. P. Rothman (Eds.), *Public education for disturbed children in New York City* (pp. 30–56). Springfield, IL: Charles C. Thomas.

Rothman, E. P. (1970). *The angel inside went sour*. New York: David McKay.

Rothman, E. P. (1974). Esther P. Rothman. In J. M. Kauffman & C. D. Lewis (Eds.), *Teaching children with behavior disorders: Personal perspectives* (pp. 218–239). Columbus, OH: Merrill.

Rothman, E. P., & Berkowitz, P. H. (1967a). The clinical school—a paradigm. In P. H. Berkowitz & E. P. Rothman (Eds.), *Public education for disturbed children in New York City* (pp. 355–369). Springfield, IL: Charles C. Thomas.

Rothman, E. P., & Berkowitz, P. H. (1967b). The concept of clinical teaching. In P. H. Berkowitz & E. P. Rothman (Eds.), *Public education for disturbed children in New York City* (pp. 327–343). Springfield, IL: Charles C. Thomas.

Rothman, E. P., & Berkowitz, P. H. (1967c). Some aspects of reading disability. In P. H. Berkowitz & E. P. Rothman (Eds.), *Public education for disturbed children in New York City* (pp. 344–354). Springfield, IL: Charles C. Thomas.

Rubenstein, E. A. (1948). Childhood mental disease in America. *American Journal of Orthopsychiatry, 18,* 314–321.

Rubin, R. A., & Balow, B. (1971). Learning and behavior disorders: A longitudinal study. *Exceptional Children, 38,* 292–299.

Rubin, R. A., & Balow, B. (1978). Prevalence of teacher identified behavior problems: A longitudinal study. *Exceptional Children, 45,* 102–111.

Rubin, T. I. (1962). *Jordi, Lisa, and David*. New York: Macmillan.

Rusch, F. R., & Phelps, L. A. (1987). Secondary special education and transition from school to work: A national priority. *Exceptional Children, 53,* 487–492.

Russell, A. T. (1994). The clinical presentation of childhood-onset schizophrenia. *Schizophrenia Bulletin, 20,* 631–646.

Rutherford, R. B., Nelson, C. M., & Wolford, B. I. (1985). Special education in the most restrictive environment: Correctional/special education. *Journal of Special Education, 19,* 59–71.

Rutherford, R. B., Nelson, C. M., & Wolford, B. I. (1986). Special education programming in juvenile corrections. *Remedial and Special Education, 7*(3), 27–33.

Rutter, M. (1991). Age changes in depressive disorders: Some developmental considerations. In J. Garber & K. A. Dodge (Eds.), *The development of emotion regulation and dysregulation* (pp. 273–300). New York: Cambridge University Press.

Rutter, M. (1995). Clinical implications of attachment concepts: Retrospect and prospect. *Journal of Child Psychology and Psychiatry, 36,* 549–571.

Rutter, M., & Bartak, L. (1973). Special educational treatment of autistic children: A comparative study—II. Follow-up findings and implications for services. *Journal of Child Psychology and Psychiatry, 14,* 241–270.

Rutter, M., Maughan, B., Mortimer, P., Ouston, J., & Smith, A. (1979). *Fifteen thousand hours: Secondary schools and their effects on children*. Cambridge, MA: Harvard University Press.

Rutter, M., & Schopler, E. (1987). Autism and pervasive developmental disorders: Concepts and diagnostic issues. *Journal of Autism and Developmental Disorders 17,* 159–186.

Rutter, M., Tizard, J., Yule, W., Graham, P., & Whitmore, K. (1976). Isle of Wight studies, 1964–1974. *Psychological Medicine, 6,* 313–332.

Sabornie, E. J. (1985). Social mainstreaming of handicapped students: Facing an unpleasant reality. *Remedial and Special Education, 6*(2), 12–16.

Sabornie, E. J., Cullinan, D., & Epstein, M. H. (1993). Patterns and correlates of learning, behavior, and emotional problems of adolescents with and without serious emotional disturbance. *Journal of Child and Family Studies, 2,* 159–175.

Sabornie, E. J., & Kauffman, J. M. (1985). Regular classroom sociometric status of emotionally disturbed adolescents. *Behavioral Disorders, 10,* 268–274.

Sack, W. H., Mason, R., & Collins, R. (1987). A long-term follow-up study of a children's psychiatric day treatment center. *Child Psychiatry and Human Development, 18,* 58–68.

Sacks, O. (1995). *An anthropologist on Mars*. New York: Knopf.

Safran, J. S., & Safran, S. P. (1987). Teacher's judgments of problem behaviors. *Exceptional Children, 54,* 240–244.

Safran, S. P. (1995). Peers' perceptions of emotional and behavioral disorders: What are students thinking? *Journal of Emotional and Behavioral Disorders, 3,* 66–75.

Sainato, D. M., Maheady, L., & Shook, G. L. (1986). The effects of a classroom manager role on the social interaction patterns and social status of withdrawn kindergarten students. *Journal of Applied Behavior Analysis, 19,* 187–195.

Sakheim, G. A., & Osborn, E. (1994). *Firesetting children: Risk assessment and treatment.* Washington, DC: Child Welfare League of America.

Sale, P., & Carey, D. M. (1995). The sociometric status of students with disabilities in a full-inclusion school. *Exceptional Children 62,* 6–19.

Salvia, J., & Ysseldyke, J. E. (1991). *Assessment in special and remedial education* (5th ed.). Boston: Houghton-Mifflin.

Sameroff, A. J., & Chandler, M. J. (1975). Reproductive risk and the continuum of caretaking casualty. In F. D. Horowitz (Ed), *Review of child development research* (Vol. 4, pp. 187–244). Chicago: University of Chicago Press.

Sameroff, A. J., Seifer, R. & Zax, M. (1982) Early development of children at risk for emotional disorder. *Monographs of the Society for Research in Child Development, 47* (7, Serial No. 199).

Sampson, R. J., & Laub, J. H. (1993). *Crime in the making: Pathways and turning points through life.* Cambridge, MA: Harvard University Press.

Sanger, D., Maag, J. W., & Shapera, N. R. (1994). Language problems among students with emotional and behavioral disorders. *Intervention in School and Clinic, 30,* 103–108.

Santos, K. E. (1992). Fragile X syndrome: An educator's role in identification, prevention, and intervention. *Remedial and Special Education, 13*(2), 32–39.

Sautter, R. C. (1995). Standing up to violence: Kappan special report. *Phi Delta Kappan, 76,* K1–K12.

Savage, G. H. (1891). *Insanity and allied neuroses: Practical and clinical.* London: Cassell.

Savage, R. C., & Mishkin, L. (1994). A neuroeducational model for teaching students with acquired brain injuries. In R. C. Savage & G. F. Wolcott (Eds.), *Educational dimensions of acquired brain injury* (pp. 393–411). Austin, TX: Pro-Ed.

Savage, R. C., & Wolcott, G. F. (1994). (Eds.). *Educational dimensions of acquired brain injury.* Austin, TX: Pro-Ed.

Schachar, R., & Tannock, R. (1995). Test of four hypotheses for the comorbidity of attention-deficit hyperactivity disorder and conduct disorder. *Journal of the American Academy of Child and Adolescent Psychiatry, 34,* 639–648.

Scharfman, M. A. (1978). Psychoanalytic treatment. In B. B. Wolman (Ed.), *Handbook of treatment of mental disorders in childhood and adolescence* (pp. 47–69). Englewood Cliffs, NJ: Prentice-Hall.

Schill, M. T., & Kratochwill, T. R. (1996). An assessment protocol for selective mutism: Analog assessment using parents as facilitators. *Journal of School Psychology, 34,* 1-21.

Schloss, P. J., Kane, M. S., & Miller, S. (1981). Truancy intervention with behaviorally disordered adolescents. *Behavioral Disorders, 6,* 175–179.

Schopler, E., & Mesibov, G. B. (Eds.). (1987). *Neurobiological issues in autism.* New York: Plenum.

Schopler, E., & Mesibov, G. B. (Eds.). (1994). *Behavioral issues in autism.* New York: Plenum.

Schopler, E., & Mesibov, G. B. (Eds.). (1995). *Learning and cognition in autism.* New York: Plenum.

Schopler, E., Mesibov, G. B., & Hearsey, K. (1995). Structured teaching in the TEACCH system. In E. Schopler & G. B. Mesibov (Eds.), *Learning and cognition in autism* (pp. 243–268). New York: Plenum.

Schreibman, L. (1994). General principles of behavior management. In E. Schopler & G. B. Mesibov (Eds.), *Behavioral issues in autism* (pp. 11–38). New York: Plenum.

Schroeder, S. R. (Ed.). (1990). *Ecobehavioral analysis and developmental disabilities: The twenty-first century.* New York: Springer-Verlag.

Schroeder, S. R., Schroeder, C. S., Rojahn, J., & Mulick, J. A. (1981). Self-injurious behavior: An analysis of behavior management techniques. In J. L. Matson & J. R. McCartney (Eds.), *Handbook of behavior modification with the mentally retarded* (pp. 61–116). New York: Plenum.

Schultz, E. W., & Heuchert, C. M. (1983). *Child stress and the school experience*. New York: Human Sciences Press.

Schultz, E. W., Heuchert, C. M., & Stampf, S. W. (1973). *Pain and joy in school*. Champaign, IL: Research Press.

Schultz, E. W., Hirshoren, A., Manton, A. B., & Henderson, R. A. (1971). Special education for the emotionally disturbed. *Exceptional Children, 38,* 313–319.

Schumaker, J. B., & Deshler, D. D. (1988). Implementing the regular education initiative in secondary schools—a different ball game. *Journal of Learning Disabilities, 21,* 36–42.

Schwartz, I. S., & Baer, D. M. (1991). Social validity assessments: Is current practice state of the art? *Journal of Applied Behavior Analysis, 24,* 189–204.

Schweitzer, R. D., Hier, S. J., & Terry, D. (1994). Parental bonding, family systems, and environmental predictors of adolescent homelessness. *Journal of Emotional and Behavioral Disorders, 2,* 39–45.

Scott-Jones, D. (1993). Adolescent childbearing: Whose Problem? What can we do? *Phi Delta Kappan, 75,* K1–K12.

Seguin, E. (1866). *Idiocy and its treatment by the physiological method*. New York: William Wood.

Shaffer, D., Fisher, P., Hicks, R. H., Parides, M., & Gould, M. (1995). Sexual orientation in adolescents who commit suicide. *Suicide and Life-Threatening Behavior, 25,* 64–71.

Shaffer, D., Gould, M., & Hicks, R. C. (1994). Worsening suicide rates in black teenagers. *American Journal of Psychiatry, 151,* 1810–1812.

Shaffer, D., & Hicks, R. (1994). Suicide. In I. B. Pless (Ed.), *The epidemiology of childhood disorders* (pp. 339–365). New York: Oxford University Press.

Shames, G. H., Wiig, E. H., & Secord, W. A. (Eds.). (1994). *Human communication disorders: An introduction* (4th ed.). New York: Merrill/Macmillan.

Shane, H. C. (Ed.). (1994). *Facilitated communication: The clinical and social phenomenon*. San Diego: Singular Publishing Group.

Shapiro, E. S., & Cole, C. L. (1993). Self-monitoring. In T. H. Ollendick & M. Hersen (Eds.), *Handbook of child and adolescent assessment* (pp. 124–139). New York: Pergamon.

Shaw, J. A., Applegate, B., & Schorr, C. (1996). 21-month follow-up study of school-age children exposed to Hurricane Andrew. *Journal of the American Academy of Child and Adolescent Psychiatry, 35,* 359-364.

Sheehan, S. (1993a, January 11). A lost childhood. *The New Yorker*, pp. 54–85.

Sheehan, S. (1993b, January 18). A lost motherhood. *The New Yorker*, pp. 52–79.

Sheras, P. L. (1983). Suicide in adolescence. In C. E. Walker & M. C. Roberts (Eds.), *Handbook of clinical child psychology* (pp. 587–606). New York: Wiley.

Sherman, J. A., & Bushell, D. (1975). Behavior modification as an educational technique. In F. D. Horowitz (Ed.), *Review of child development research* (Vol. 4, pp. 409–462). Chicago: University of Chicago Press.

Shinn, M. R., & Marston, D. B. (1985). Differentiating mildly handicapped, low-achieving, and regular education students using curriculum-based assessment procedures. *Remedial and Special Education, 6*(2), 31–38.

Shinn, M. R., Ramsey, E., Walker, H. M., Stieber, S., & O'Neill, R. E. (1987). Antisocial behavior in school settings: Initial differences in an at risk and normal population. *Journal of Special Education, 21,* 69–84.

Shores, R. E. (1987). Overview of research on social interaction: A historical and personal perspective. *Behavioral Disorders, 12,* 233–241.

Shores, R. E., Jack, S. L., Gunter, P. L., Ellis, D. N., DeBriere, T. J., & Wehby, J. H. (1993). Classroom interactions of children with behavior disorders. *Journal of Emotional and Behavioral Disorders, 1,* 27–39.

Siegel, A. W., Cousins, J. H., Rubovits, D. S., Parsons, J. T., Lavery, B., & Crowley, C. L. (1994). Adolescents' perceptions of the benefits of their own risk taking. *Journal of Emotional and Behavioral Disorders, 2,* 89–98.

Siegel, B. (1995). Assessing allegations of sexual molestation made through facilitated communication. *Journal of Autism and Developmental Disorders, 25,* 319–326.

Siegel, L. J. (1992). Somatic disorders of childhood and adolescence. In W. R. Reynolds (Ed.), *Inter-*

nalizing disorders in children and adolescents (pp. 283–310). New York: Wiley.

Siegel, L. J., & Ridley-Johnson, R. (1985). Anxiety disorders of childhood and adolescence. In P. H. Bornstein & A. E. Kazdin (Eds.), *Handbook of clinical behavior therapy with children* (pp. 266–308). Homewood, IL: Dorsey Press.

Siegel, L. J., & Senna, J. J. (1994). *Juvenile delinquency: Theory, practice, and law* (5th ed.). St. Paul, MN: West.

Siegel, L. J., & Smith, K. E. (1991). Somatic disorders. In T. R. Kratochwill & R. J. Morris (Eds.), *The practice of child therapy* (2nd ed., pp. 222–256). New York: Pergamon.

Sigafoos, J., Kerr, M., Roberts, D., & Couzens, D. (1994). Increasing opportunities for requesting in classrooms serving children with developmental disabilities. *Journal of Autism and Developmental Disorders, 24,* 631–645.

Sigman, M. (1994). What are the core deficits in autism? In S. H. Broman & J. Grafman (Eds.), *Atypical cognitive deficits in developmental disorders: Implication for brain function* (pp. 139–157). Hillsdale, NJ: Erlbaum.

Sigman, M., Ungerer, J. A., & Russell, A. (1983). Moral judgment in relation to behavioral and cognitive disorders in adolescents. *Journal of Abnormal Child Psychology, 11,* 503–512.

Silberberg, N. E., & Silberberg, M. C. (1971). School achievement and delinquency. *Review of Educational Research, 41,* 17–32.

Silberman, C. E. (1978). *Criminal violence, criminal justice.* New York: Random House.

Silva, R. R., Munoz, D. M., Barickman, J., & Friedhoff, A. J. (1995). Environmental factors and related fluctuation of symptoms in children and adolescents with Tourette's disorder. *Journal of Child Psychology and Psychiatry, 36,* 305–312.

Silver, L. B. (1987). The "magic cure": A review of the current controversial approaches for treating learning disabilities. *Journal of Learning Disabilities, 20,* 498–504, 512.

Simonds, J. R., & Glenn, T. (1976). Folie à deu in a child. *Journal of Autism and Developmental Disorders, 6,* 61–73.

Simpson, R. L. (1987). Social interactions of behaviorally disordered children and youth: Where are we and where do we need to go? *Behavioral Disorders, 12,* 292–298.

Simpson, R. L., & Myles, B. S. (1995). Effectiveness of facilitated communication with children and youth with autism. *Journal of Special Education, 28,* 424–439.

Simpson, R. L., & Zionts, P. (1992). *Autism: Information and resources for parents, families, and professionals.* Austin, TX: Pro-Ed.

Sinclair, E., Forness, S. R., & Alexson, J. (1985). Psychiatric diagnosis: A study of its relationship to school needs. *Journal of Special Education, 19,* 333–344.

Singer, J. D. (1988). Should special education merge with regular education? *Educational Policy, 2,* 409–424.

Singh, A. N., Zemitzsch, A. A., Ellis, C. R., Best A. M., & Singh, N. N. (1994). Seriously emotionally disturbed students' knowledge and attitudes about AIDS. *Journal of Emotional and Behavioral Disorders, 2,* 156–163.

Skinner, B. F. (1953). *Science and human behavior.* New York: Free Press.

Slaughter-Defoe, D. T., Nakagawa, K., Takanishi, R., & Johnson, D. J. (1990). Toward cultural/ecological perspectives on schooling and achievement in African- and Asian-American children. *Child Development, 61,* 363–383.

Slavson, S. R. (1954). *Re-educating the delinquent through group and community participation.* New York: Harper.

Smith, C. R., Wood, F. H., & Grimes, J. (1988). Issues in the identification and placement of behaviorally disordered students. In M. C. Wang, M. C. Reynolds, & H. J. Walberg (Eds.), *Handbook of special education: Research and practice* (Vol. 2, pp. 95–124). New York: Pergamon.

Smith, J., & Prior, M. (1995). Temperament and stress resilience in school-age children: A within-families study. *Journal of the American Academy of Child and Adolescent Psychiatry, 34,* 168–179.

Smith, J. O. (1962). Criminality and mental retardation. *Training School Bulletin, 59,* 74–80.

Smith, K. (1992). Suicidal behavior in children and adolescents. In W. R. Reynolds (Ed.), *Internalizing disorders in children and adolescents* (pp. 255–282). New York: Wiley.

Smith, S., & Couthino, M. (Eds.). (in press). National agenda for achieving better results for children and youth with serious emotional distrubance. *Journal of Emotional and Behavioral Disorders* [special issue].

Smucker, K. S., Kauffman, J. M., & Ball, D. W. (1996). School-related problems of special education foster care students with emotional or behavioral: Comparison to other groups. *Journal of Emotional and Behavioral Disorders, 4,* 30–39.

Snarr, R. W. (1987). The criminal justice system. In C. M. Nelson, R. B. Rutherford, & B. I. Wolford (Eds.), *Special education in the criminal justice system* (pp. 24–48). Columbus, OH: Merrill/Macmillan.

Snow, J. H., & Hooper, S. R. (1994). *Pediatric traumatic brain injury*. Thousand Oaks, CA: Sage.

Snyder, J., & Huntley, D. (1990). Troubled families and troubled youth: The development of antisocial behavior and depression in children. In P. E. Leone (Ed.), *Understanding troubled and troubling youth* (pp. 194–225). Newbury Park, CA: Sage.

Sorenson, S. B., & Bowie, P. (1994). Girls and young women. In L. D. Eron, J. H. Gentry, & P. Schlegel (Eds.), *Reason to hope: A psychosocial perspective on violence and youth* (pp. 167–176). Washington, DC: American Psychological Association.

Soriano, F. I. (1994). U.S. Latinos. In L. D. Eron, J. H. Gentry, & P. Schlegel (Eds.), *Reason to hope: A psychosocial perspective on violence and youth* (pp. 119–132). Washington, DC: American Psychological Association.

Soutter, A. (1996). A longitudinal study of 3 cases of gender identity disorder of childhood successfully resolved in the school setting. *School Psychology International, 17,* 49-57.

Spence, S. H. (1986). Behavioural treatments of childhood obesity. *Journal of Child Psychology and Psychiatry, 27,* 447–453.

Spencer, E. K., & Campbell, M. (1994). Children with schizophrenia: Diagnosis, phenomenology, and pharmacotherapy. *Schizophrenia Bulletin, 20,* 713–725.

Spencer, T., Biederman, J., Harding, M., Wilens, T., & Faraone, S. (1995). The relationship between tic disorders and Tourette's syndrome revisited. *Journal of the American Academy of Child and Adolescent Psychiatry, 34,* 1133–1139.

Spergel, I. A. (1995). *The youth gang problem: A community approach*. New York: Oxford University Press.

Spitz, R. (1946). Anaclitic depression. *The Psychoanalytic Study of the Child, 2,* 313–342.

Spivack, G., & Swift, M. S.(1966). The Devereux Elementary School Behavior Rating Scales: A study of the nature and organization of achievement related disturbed classroom behavior. *Journal of Special Education, 1,* 71–90.

Spivack, G., & Swift, M. S. (1977). The Hahnemann High School Behavior (HHSB) Rating Scale. *Journal of Abnormal Child Psychology, 5,* 299–307.

Sprafkin, J., Gadow, K. D., & Adelman, R. (1992). *Television and the exceptional child: A forgotten audience*. Hillsdale, NJ: Lawrence Erlbaum.

Sprick, R. S., & Howard, L. M. (1995). *The teacher's encyclopedia of behavior management*. Longmont, CO: Sopris West.

Sroufe, L. A., Steucher, H. U., & Stutzer, W. (1973). The functional significance of autistic behaviors for the psychotic child. *Journal of Abnormal Child Psychology, 1,* 225–240.

Stainback, W., & Stainback, S. (1991). A rationale for integration and restructuring: A synopsis. In J. W. Lloyd, N. N. Singh, & A. C. Repp (Eds.), *The regular education initiative: Alternative perspectives on concepts, issues, and models* (pp. 226–239). Sycamore, IL: Sycamore.

Stark, K. (1990). *Childhood depression: School-based intervention*. New York: Guilford Press.

Stark, K. D., Ostrander, R., Kurowski, C. A., Swearer, S., & Bowen, B. (1995). Affective and mood disorders. In M. Hersen & R. T. Ammerman (Eds.), *Advanced abnormal child psychology* (pp. 253–282). Hillsdale, NJ: Erlbaum.

Steele, R. G., Forehand, R., Armistead, L, & Brody, G. (1995). Predicting alcohol and drug use in early adulthood: The role of internalizing and externalizing behavior problems in early adolescence. *American Journal of Orthopsychiatry, 65,* 380–388.

Stein, E., Raegrant, N., Ackland, S., & Avison, W. (1994). Psychiatric disorders of children in care: Methodology and demographic correlates. *Canadian Journal of Psychiatry, 39,* 341–347.

Steinberg, L. (1987). Single parents, stepparents, and the susceptibility of adolescents to antisocial peer pressure. *Child Development, 58,* 269–275.

Stephens, S. A., & Lakin, K. C. (1995). Where students with emotional or behavioral disorders go to school. In J. M. Kauffman, J. W. Lloyd, D. P. Hallahan, & T. A. Astuto (Eds.), *Issues in educational placement: Students with emotional and behavioral disorders* (pp. 47–74). Hillsdale, NJ: Erlbaum.

Stephens, S. A., Lakin, K. C., Brauen, M., & O'Reilly, F. (1990). *The study of programs of instruction for handicapped children and youth in day and residential facilities*. Washington, DC: U.S. Department of Education and Mathematics Policy Research.

Sternberg, R. J. (1991). Giftedness according to the triarchic theory of human intelligence. In N. Colangelo & G. A. Davis (Eds.), *Handbook of gifted education* (pp. 45–54). Boston: Allyn & Bacon.

Stetter, G. M. T. (1995). *The effects of pre-correction on cafeteria behavior*. Unpublished manuscript, University of Virginia.

Stevens, G. E. (1980). Invasion of student privacy. *Journal of Law and Education, 9,* 343–351.

Stevenson, D. L., & Baker, D. P. (1987). The family-school relation and child's school performance. *Child Development, 58,* 1348–1357.

Stevenson-Hinde, J., Hinde, R. A., & Simpson, A. E. (1986). Behavior at home and friendly or hostile behavior in preschool. In D. Olweus, J. Block, & M. Radke-Yarrow (Eds.), *Development of antisocial and prosocial behavior: Research, theories, and issues* (pp. 127–148). New York: Academic Press.

Stevenson-Hinde, J., & Shouldice, A. (1995). 4.5 to 7 years: Fearful behaviour, fears and worries. *Journal of Child Psychology and Psychiatry, 36,* 1027–1038.

Stiffman, A. R., & Davis, L. E. (Eds.). (1990). *Ethnic issues in adolescent mental health*. Newbury Park, CA: Sage.

Stokes, T. F., & Osnes, P. G. (1991). Honesty, lying, and cheating: Their elaboration and management. In G. Stoner, M. R. Shinn, & H. M. Walker (Eds.), *Interventions for achievement and behavior problems* (pp. 617–631). Silver Spring, MD: National Association of School Psychologists.

Stone, F., & Rowley, V. N. (1964). Educational disability in emotionally disturbed children. *Exceptional Children, 30,* 423–426.

Stormont-Spurgin, M., & Zentall, S. S. (1995). Contributing factors in the manifestation of aggression in preschoolers with hyperactivity. *Journal of Child Psychology and Psychiatry, 36,* 491–509.

Stouthamer-Loeber, M., & Loeber, R. (1986). Boys who lie. *Journal of Abnormal Child Psychology, 14,* 551–564.

Strain, P. S. (Ed.). (1981). *The utilization of classroom peers as behavior change agents*. New York: Plenum.

Strain, P. S., & Danko, C. D. (1995). Caregivers' encouragement of positive interaction between preschoolers with autism and their siblings. *Journal of Emotional and Behavioral Disorders, 3,* 2–12.

Strain, P. S., Danko, C. D., & Kohler, F. (1995). Activity engagement and social interaction development in young children with autism: An examination of "free" intervention effects. *Journal of Emotional and Behavioral Disorders, 3,* 108–123.

Strain, P. S., Lambert, D. L., Kerr, M. M., Stagg, V., & Lenkner, D. A. (1983). Naturalistic assessment of children's compliance to teachers' requests and consequences for compliance. *Journal of Applied Behavior Analysis, 16,* 243–249.

Strain, P. S., Odom, S. L., & McConnell, S. (1984). Promoting social reciprocity of exceptional children. Identification target behavior selection, and intervention. *Remedial and Special Education, 5*(1), 21–28.

Strandburg, R. J., Marsh, J. T., Brown, W. S., Asarnow, R. F., & Guthrie, D. (1994). *Schizophrenia Bulletin, 20,* 685–695.

Strauss, A. A., & Kephart, N. C. (1955). *Psychopathology and education of the brain injured child: Vol. 2. Progress in theory and clinic*. New York: Grune & Stratton.

Strauss, A. A., & Lehtinen, L. E. (1947). *Psychopathology and education of the brain injured child*. New York: Grune & Stratton.

Strauss, C. C. (1993). Anxiety disorders. In T. H. Ollendick & M. Hersen (Eds.), *Handbook of child and adolescent assessment* (pp. 239–250). New York: Pergamon.

Strauss, C. C., Forehand, R., Smith, K., & Frame, C. L. (1986). The association between social withdrawal and internalizing problems of children. *Journal of Abnormal Child Psychology, 14,* 525–535.

Strauss, V., & Brown, D. L. (1995, December 13). D.C. teacher reassigned after slapping incident. *The Washington Post*, pp. A1, A23.

Strayhorn, J., Strain, P. S., & Walker, H. M. (1993). The case for interaction skills training in the context of tutoring as a preventative mental health intervention in the schools. *Behavioral Disorders, 19,* 11–26.

Stribling, F. T. (1842). Physician and superintendent's report. In *Annual Reports to the Court of Directors of the Western Lunatic Asylum to the Legislature of Virginia.* Richmond: Shepherd & Conlin.

Stullken, E. H. (1950). Special schools and classes for the socially maladjusted. In N. B. Henry (Ed.), *The education of exceptional children.* Forty-ninth Yearbook of the National Society for the Study of Education, Part II, pp. 281–301. Chicago: University of Chicago Press.

Swaffer, T., & Hollin, C. R., (1995). Adolescent firesetting: Why they say they do it. *Journal of Adolescence, 18,* 619–623.

Swanson, J. M., Cantwell, D., Lerner, M., McBurnett, K., & Hanna, G. (1991). Effects of stimulant medication on learning in children with ADHD. *Journal of Learning Disabilities, 24,* 219–230, 255.

Swap, S. (1974). Disturbing classroom behaviors: A developmental and ecological view. *Exceptional Children, 41,* 163–172.

Swap, S. (1978). The ecological model of emotional disturbance in children: A status report and proposed synthesis. *Behavioral Disorders, 3,* 186–196.

Swap, S., Prieto, A. G., & Harth, R. (1982). Ecological perspectives on the emotionally disturbed child. In R. L. McDowell, G. W. Adamson, & F. H. Wood (Eds.), *Teaching emotionally disturbed children* (pp. 70–98). Boston: Little, Brown.

Swift, M. S., & Swift, G. (1968). The assessment of achievement related classroom behavior: Normative, reliability, and validity data. *Journal of Special Education, 2,* 137–153.

Swift, M. S., & Swift, G. (1969a). Achievement related classroom behavior of secondary school normal and disturbed students. *Exceptional Children, 35,* 677–684.

Swift, M. S., & Swift, G. (1969b). Clarifying the relationship between academic success and overt classroom behavior. *Exceptional Children, 36,* 99–104.

Swift, M. S., & Swift, G. (1973). Academic success and classroom behavior in secondary schools. *Exceptional Children, 39,* 392–399.

Tamkin, A. S. (1960). A survey of educational disability in emotionally disturbed children. *Journal of Educational Research, 53,* 313–315.

Tankersley, M. (1992). *Classification and identification of internalizing behavioral subtypes.* Doctoral dissertation, University of Virginia.

Tannock, R., Ickowicz, A., & Schachar, R. (1995). Differential effects of methylphenidate on working memory in ADHD children with and without comorbid anxiety. *Journal of the American Academy of Child and Adolescent Psychiatry, 34,* 886–896.

Tarnowski, K. J., & Brown, R. T. (1995). Psychological aspects of pediatric disorders. In M. Hersen & R. T. Ammerman (Eds.), *Advanced abnormal child psychology* (pp. 393–410). Hillsdale, NJ: Lawrence Erlbaum.

Tasker, F., & Golombok, S. (1995). Adults raised as children in lesbian families. *American Journal of Orthopsychiatry, 65,* 203–215.

Tate, A. (1993). Schooling. In B. Lask & R. Bryant-Waugh (Eds.), *Childhood onset anorexia nervosa and related eating disorders* (pp. 233–248). Hillsdale, NJ: Lawrence Erlbaum Associates.

Tate, D. C., Reppucci, N. D., & Mulvey, E. P. (1995). Violent juvenile delinquents: Treatment effectiveness and implications for future action. *American Psychologist, 50,* 777–781.

Tattum, D., & Herbert, G. (1990). *Bullying: A positive response.* Cardiff, UK: SGIHE Learning Resources Centre.

Tattum, D. P., & Lane, D. A. (Eds.). (1989). *Bullying in schools.* Stoke-on-Trent, England: Trentham Books.

Taylor, P. D., & Turner, R. K. (1975). A clinical trial of continuous, intermittent, and overlearning "bell and pad" treatments for nocturnal enuresis. *Behaviour Research and Therapy, 13,* 281–293.

Teare, J. F., Smith, G. L., Osgood, D. W., Peterson, R. W., Authier, K., & Daly, D. L. (1995). Ecological influences in youth crisis shelters: Effects of social density and length of stay on youth problem behaviors. *Journal of Child and Family Studies, 4,* 89–101.

Terr, L. C. (1995). Childhood traumas: An outline and overview. In G. S. Everly & J. M. Lating (Eds.), *Psychotraumatology: Key papers and core concepts in post-traumatic stress* (pp. 301-320). New York: Plenum.

Tharp, R. G., & Wetzel, R. J. (1969). *Behavior modification in the natural environment*. New York: Academic Press.

Thomas, A., & Chess, S. (1975). A longitudinal study of three brain damaged children. *Archives of General Psychiatry, 32,* 457–462.

Thomas, A., & Chess, S. (1984). Genesis and evolution of behavioral disorders: From infancy to early adult life. *American Journal of Psychiatry, 141,* 1–9.

Thomas, A., Chess, S., & Birch, H. G. (1968). *Temperament and behavior disorders in children*. New York: New York University Press.

Thomas, A., Chess, S., & Korn, S. J. (1982). The reality of difficult temperament. *Merrill-Palmer Quarterly, 28,* 1–20.

Thomas, E. A., & Rickel, A. U. (1995). Teen pregnancy and maladjustment: A study of base rates. *Journal of Community Psychology, 23,* 200–215.

Thompson, R. A., & Wilcox, B. L. (1995). Child maltreatment research: Federal support and policy issues. *American Psychologist, 50,* 789–793.

Tobin, D. D. (1971). Overcoming crude behavior in a "600" school. In N. J. Long, W. C. Morse, & R. G. Newman (Eds.), *Conflict in the classroom* (2nd ed.) (pp. 465–467). Belmont, CA: Wadsworth.

Tolan, P. H. (1987). Implications of age of onset for delinquency risk. *Journal of Abnormal Child Psychology, 15,* 47–65.

Tolan, P. H., & Thomas, P. (1995). The implications of age of onset for delinquency risk II: Longitudinal data. *Journal of Abnormal Child Psychology, 23,* 157–181.

Tremblay, R. E., Paganikurtz, L., Vitaro, F., Massie, L. C., & Pihl, R. O. (1995). A bimodal preventive intervention for disruptive kindergarten boys: Its impact through mid-adolescence. *Journal of Consulting and Clinical Psychology, 63,* 560–568.

Trent, S. C., & Artiles, A. J. (1995). Serving culturally diverse students with emotional or behavioral disorders: Broadening current perspectives. In J. M. Kauffman, J. W. Lloyd, D. P. Hallahan, & T. A. Astuto (Eds.), *Issues in educational placement: Students with emotional and behavioral disorders* (pp. 215–249). Hillsdale, NJ: Erlbaum.

Trieschman, A. E., Whittaker, J. K., & Brendtro, L. K. (1969). *The other 23 hours*. Chicago: Aldine.

Trippe, M. J. (1970, April). *Love of life, love of truth, love of others*. Presidential address, Annual meeting of the Council for Children with Behavioral Disorders, Gary, IN.

Trosch, L. A., Williams, R. G., & Devore, F. W. (1982). Public school searches and the fourth amendment. *Journal of Law and Education, 11,* 41–63.

Tuma, J. M., & Sobotka, K. R. (1983). Traditional therapies with children. In T. H. Ollendick & M. Hersen (Eds.), *Handbook of child psychopathology* (pp. 391–426). New York: Plenum.

Turnbull, A. P., & Turnbull, H. R. (1990). *Families, professionals, and exceptionality: A special partnership* (2nd ed.). Columbus, OH: Merrill/Macmillan.

Twardosz, S., Nordquist, V. M., Simon, R., & Botkin, D. (1983). The effect of group affection activities on the interaction of socially isolate children. *Analysis and Intervention in Developmental Disabilities, 3,* 311–338.

Tyler, J. S., & Colson, S. (1994). Common pediatric disabilities: Medical aspects and educational implications. *Focus on Exceptional Children, 27*(4), 1–16.

Tyler, J. S., & Mira, M. P. (1993). Educational modifications for students with head injuries. *Teaching Exceptional Children, 25*(3), 24–27.

Ullmann, L., & Krasner, L. (1969). *A psychological approach to abnormal behavior*. Englewood Cliffs, NJ: Prentice-Hall.

Umbreit, J. (1995). Functional assessment and intervention in a regular classroom setting for the disruptive behavior of a student with attention deficit hyperactivity disorder. *Behavioral Disorders, 20,* 267–278.

Underwood, M. (1987). A matter of life or death. *New Jersey School Boards Association: School Leader, 16,* 32–36.

U.S. Department of Education (1991). *Thirteenth annual report to Congress on the implementation of the Individuals with Disabilities Education Act*. Washington, DC: Author.

U.S. Department of Education. (1994). *Sixteenth annual report to Congress on implementation of the Individuals with Disabilities Education Act*. Washington, DC: Author.

U.S. Department of Education. (1995). *Seventeenth annual report to Congress on implementation of the Individuals with Disabilities Education Act*. Washington, DC: Author.

Vaden-Kiernan, N., Ialongo, S., Pearson, J., & Kellam, S. (1995). Household family structure and children's aggressive behavior: A longitudinal study of urban elementary school children. *Journal of Abnormal Child Psychology, 23*, 553–568.

VanDyke, R., Stallings, M. A., & Colley, K. (1995). How to build an inclusive school community: A success story. *Phi Delta Kappan, 76*, 475–479.

Van Hasselt, V. B., & Hersen, M. (Eds.). (1991a). *Journal of Developmental and Physical Disabilities,* [Special issue] *3*(3).

Van Hasselt, V. B., & Hersen, M. (Eds.). (1991b). *Journal of Developmental and Physical Disabilities,* [Special issue] *3*(4).

Veltkamp, L. J., & Miller, T. W. (1994). *Clinical handbook of child abuse and neglect.* Madison, CT: International Universities Press.

Vivian, D., Fischel, J. E., & Liebert, R. M. (1986). Effect of "wet nights" on daytime behavior during concurrent treatment of enuresis and conduct problems. *Journal of Behavior Therapy and Experimental Psychiatry, 17,* 301–303.

Volkmar, F. R., & Cohen, D. J. (1985). The experience of infantile autism: A first-person account by Tony W. *Journal of Autism and Developmental Disorders, 15,* 47–54.

Vollmer, T. R., Marcus, B. A., & Ringdahl, J. E. (1995). Noncontingent escape as treatment for self-injurious behavior maintained by negative reinforcement. *Journal of Applied Behavior Analysis, 28,* 15–26.

Von Isser, A., Quay, H. C., & Love, C. T. (1980). Interrelationships among three measures of deviant behavior. *Exceptional Children, 46,* 272–276.

Votel, S. M. (1985). Special education in France for the emotionally/behaviorally disordered as it relates to that of the United States. In S. Braaten, R. B. Rutherford, & W. Evans (Eds.), *Programming for adolescents with behavioral disorders* (Vol. 2, pp. 127–135). Reston, VA: Council for Children with Behavioral Disorders.

Wagner, B. M., Cole, R. E., & Schwartzman, P. (1995). Psychosocial correlates of suicide attempts among junior and senior high school youth. *Suicide and Life-Threatening Behavior, 25,* 358–372.

Wagner, M. (1991). *Dropouts with disabilities: What do we know? What can we do?.* Menlo Park, CA: SRI International.

Waldman, I. D., & Lillenfeld, S. O. (1995). Diagnosis and classification. In M. Hersen & R. T. Ammerman (Eds.), *Advanced abnormal child psychology* (pp. 21–36). Hillsdale, NJ: Erlbaum.

Walk, A. (1964). The pre-history of child psychiatry. *British Journal of Psychiatry, 110,* 754–767.

Walker, H. M. (1982). Assessment of behavior disorders in school settings: Outcomes, issues, and recommendations. In M. M. Noel & N. G. Haring. (Eds.), *Progress or change: Issues in educating the emotionally disturbed: Vol. 1. Identification and program planning* (pp. 11–42). Seattle: University of Washington.

Walker, H. M. (1983). Application of response cost in school settings: Outcomes, issues, and recommendations. *Exceptional Education Quarterly, 3*(4), 47–55.

Walker, H. M. (1986). The Assessment for Integration into Mainstream Settings (AIMS) assessment system: Rationale, instruments, procedures, and outcomes. *Journal of Clinical Child Psychology, 15,* 55–63.

Walker, H. M. (1995). *The acting-out child: Coping with classroom disruption* (2nd ed.). Longmont, CO: Sopris West.

Walker, H. M., Block-Pedego, A., Todis, B., & Severson, H. (1991). *School Archival Records Search (SARS).* Longmont, CO: Sopris West.

Walker, H. M., & Buckley, N. K. (1973, May). Teacher attention to appropriate and inappropriate classroom behavior. *Focus on Exceptional Children,* 5–12.

Walker, H. M., & Bullis, M. (1991). Behavior disorders and the social context of regular class integration: A conceptual dilemma? In J. W. Lloyd, N. N. Singh, & A. C. Repp (Eds.), *The regular education initiative: Alternative perspectives on concepts, issues, and models* (pp. 75–93). Sycamore, IL: Sycamore Press.

Walker, H. M., Colvin, G., & Ramsey, E. (1995). *Antisocial behavior in school: Strategies and best practices.* Pacific Grove, CA: Brooks/Cole.

Walker, H. M., Greenwood, C. R., Hops, H., & Todd, N. M. (1979). Differential effects of reinforcing topographic components of social interaction: Analysis and direct replication. *Behavior Modification, 3,* 291–321.

Walker, H. M., Hops, H., & Fiegenbaum, E. (1976). Deviant classroom behavior as a function of combinations of social and token reinforcement and cost contingency. *Behavior Therapy, 7,* 76–88.

Walker, H. M., Hops, H., & Greenwood, C. R. (1981). RECESS: Research and development of a behavior management package for remediating social aggression in the school. In P. S. Strain (Ed.), *The utilization of classroom peers as behavior change agents* (pp. 261–303). New York: Plenum.

Walker, H. M., & McConnell, S. (1988). *The Walker-McConnell Scale of Social Competence and School Adjustment: A Social Skills Rating Scale for Teachers.* Austin, TX: Pro-Ed.

Walker, H. M., McConnell, S., Holmes, D., Todis, B., Walker, J., & Golden, N. (1983). *The Walker social skills curriculum: The ACCEPTS program.* Austin, TX: Pro-Ed.

Walker, H. M., & Rankin, R. (1983). Assessing the behavioral expectations and demands of less restrictive settings. *School Psychology Review, 12,* 274–284.

Walker, H. M., Reavis, H. K., Rhode, G., & Jenson, W. R. (1985). A conceptual model for delivery of behavioral services to behavior disordered children in educational settings. In P. H. Bornstein & A. E. Kazdin (Eds.), *Handbook of clinical behavior therapy with children* (pp. 700–741). Homewood, IL: Dorsey Press.

Walker, H. M., Schwarz, I. E., Nippold, M. A., Irvin, L. K., & Noell, J. W. (1994). Social skills in school-age children and youth: Issues and best practices in assessment and intervention. *Topics in Language Disorders, 14*(3), 70–82.

Walker, H. M., & Severson, H. H. (1990). *Systematic Screening for Behavior Disorders (SSBD): A Multiple Gating Procedure.* Longmont, CO: Sopris West.

Walker, H. M., Severson, H. H., & Feil, E. G. (1994). *The Early Screening Project: A proven child-find process.* Longmont, CO: Sopris West.

Walker, H. M., Severson, H. H., Nicholson, F., Kehle, T., Jenson, W. R., & Clark, E. (1994). Replication of the Systematic Screening for Behavior Disorders (SSBD) procedure for the identification of at-risk children. *Journal of Emotional and Behavioral Disorders, 2,* 66–77.

Walker, H. M., Severson, H., Stiller, B., Williams, G., Haring, N., Shinn, M., & Todis, B. (1988).

Systematic screening of pupils in the elementary age range at risk for behavior disorders: Development and trial testing of a multiple gating model. *Remedial and Special Education, 9*(3), 8–14.

Walker, H. M., Shinn, M. R., O'Neill, R. E., & Ramsey, E.(1987). A longitudinal assessment of the development of antisocial behavior in boys: Rationale, methodology, and first year results. *Remedial and Special Education, 8*(4), 7–16.

Walker, L. J., de Vries, B., & Trevethan, S. D. (1987). Moral stages and moral orientations in real-life and hypothetical dilemmas. *Child Development, 58,* 842–858.

Wallace, G., Larsen, S. C., & Elksnin, L. K. (1992). *Educational assessment of learning problems: Testing for teaching* (2nd ed.). Boston: Allyn & Bacon.

Wallerstein, J. S. (1987). Children of divorce: Report of a ten-year follow-up of early latency-age children. *American Journal of Orthopsychiatry, 57,* 199–211.

Walton, F. R., Ackiss, V. D., & Smith, S. N. (1991). Education versus schooling—Project LEAD: High expectations! *Journal of Negro Education, 60,* 441–453.

Warboys, L. M., & Shauffer, C. B. (1990). Protecting the rights of troubled and troubling youth: Understanding attorneys' perspectives. In P. E. Leone (Ed.), *Understanding troubled and troubling youth* (pp. 25–37). Newbury Park, CA: Sage.

Warr-Leeper, G., Wright, N. A., & Mack, A. (1994). Language disabilities of antisocial boys in residential treatment. *Behavioral Disorders, 19,* 159–169.

Waters, E., Hay, D. F., & Richters, J. E. (1986). Infant-parent attachment and the origins of prosocial and antisocial behavior. In D. Olweus, J. Block, & M. Radke-Yarrow (Eds.), *Development of antisocial and prosocial behavior: Research, theories, and issues* (pp. 97–126). New York: Academic Press.

Watkins, C. E., & Schatman, M. E.(1986). Using early recollections in child psychotherapy. *Journal of Child and Adolescent Psychotherapy, 3,* 207–213.

Watt, N. F., Moorehead-Slaughter, O., Japzon, D. M., & Keller, G. G. (1990). Children's adjustment to parental divorce: Self-image, social relations, and school performance. In J. Rolf, A. S. Masten, D. Cicchetti, K. H. Nuechterlein, & S. Weintraub (Eds.), *Risk and protective factors in the development of psychopathology* (pp. 281–303). New York: Cambridge University Press.

Watt, N. F., Stolorow, R. D., Lubensky, A. W., & McClelland, D. C. (1970). School adjustment and behavior of children hospitalized for schizophrenia as adults. *American Journal of Orthopsychiatry, 40,* 637–657.

Webber, J., & Scheuermann, B. (1991). Accentuate the positive . . . Eliminate the negative. *Teaching Exceptional Children, 24,* 13–19.

Webster-Stratton, C. (1985). Comparison of abusive and nonabusive families with conduct-disordered children. *American Journal of Orthopsychiatry, 55,* 59–69.

Webster-Stratton, C. (1990). Stress: A potential disruptor of parent perceptions and family interactions. *Journal of Clinical Child Psychology, 4,* 302–312.

Webster-Stratton, C., & Dahl, R. W. (1995). Conduct disorder. In M. Hersen & R. T. Ammerman (Eds.), *Advanced abnormal child psychology* (pp. 333–352). Hillsdale, NJ: Erlbaum.

Wehby, J. H., Dodge, K. A., Valente, E., and the Conduct Disorders Prevention Research Group (1993). School behavior of first grade children identified as at-risk for development of conduct problems. *Behavioral Disorders, 19,* 67–78.

Weinstein, L. (1969). Project Re-ED schools for emotionally disturbed children: Effectiveness as viewed by referring agencies, parents, and teachers. *Exceptional Children, 35,* 703–711.

Weinstein, R. S., Marshall, H. H., Sharp, L. & Botkin, M. (1987). Pygmalion and the student: Age and classroom differences in children's awareness of teacher expectations. *Child Development, 58,* 1079–1093.

Weiss, G., & Hechtman, L. T. (1993). *Hyperactive children grown up: ADHD in children, adolescents, and adults* (2nd ed.). New York: Guilford Press.

Weiss, R. (1995, June 13). Gene studies fuel the nature-nurture debate. *The Washington Post Health,* pp. 11, 13.

Weiss, R. (1996, January 9). The perfect fat pill is still a long weigh off: As discoveries mount, so does evidence of the body's complexity. *The Washington Post Health,* p. 11.

Weissberg, R. P., & Allen, J. P. (1986). Promoting children's social skills and adaptive interpersonal behavior. In B. A. Edelstein & L. Michelson (Eds.), *Handbook of prevention* (pp. 153–175). New York: Plenum.

Wells, K. C., & Forehand, R. (1985). Conduct and oppositional disorders. In P. H. Bornstein & A. E. Kazdin (Eds.), *Handbook of clinical behavior therapy with children* (pp. 218–265). Homewood, IL: Dorsey Press.

Wenar, C., Ruttenberg, B. A., Kalish-Weiss, B., & Wolf, E. G. (1986). The development of normal and autistic children: A comparative study. *Journal of Autism and Developmental Disorders, 16,* 317–333.

Wentzel, K. R., & Asher, S. R. (1995). The academic lives of neglected, rejected, and controversial children. *Child Development, 66,* 754–763.

Werry, J. S. (1986a). Biological factors. In H. C. Quay & J. S. Werry (Eds.), *Psychopathological disorders of childhood* (3rd ed.) (pp. 294–331). New York: Wiley.

Werry, J. S. (1986b). Organic and substance use disorders. In H. C. Quay & J. S. Werry (Eds.), *Psychopathological disorders of childhood* (3rd ed.) (pp. 211–230). New York: Wiley.

Werry, J. S. (1986c). Physical illness, symptoms and allied disorders. In H. C. Quay & J. S. Werry (Eds.), *Psychopathological disorders of childhood* (3rd ed.) (pp. 232–293). New York: Wiley.

Werry, J. S. (1994). Diagnostic and classification issues. In T. H. Ollendick, N. J. King, & W. Yule (Eds.), *International handbook of phobic and anxiety disorders in children and adolescents* (pp. 21-42). New York: Plenum.

Werry, J. S., McClellan, J. M., Andrews, L. K., & Ham, M. (1994). Clinical features and outcome of child and adolescent schizophrenia. *Schizophrenia Bulletin, 20,* 619–630.

West, R. P., Young, K. R., Callahan, K., Fister, S., Kemp, K., Freston, J., & Lovitt, T. C. (1995). The musical clocklight: Encouraging positive classroom behavior. *Teaching Exceptional Children, 27*(2), 46–51.

Wetzel, R. (1966). Use of behavioral techniques in a case of compulsive stealing. *Journal of Consulting Psychology, 30,* 367–374.

Whalen, C. K. (1983). Hyperactivity, learning problems, and the attention deficit disorders. In T. H. Ollendick & M. Hersen (Eds.), *Handbook of child psychopathology* (pp. 151–199). New York: Plenum.

Whalen, C. K., & Henker, B. (1991). Social impact of stimulant treatment for hyperactive children. *Journal of Learning Disabilities, 24,* 231–241.

Whelan, R. J. (1963). Educating emotionally disturbed children: Reflections upon educational methods and therapeutic processes. *Forum for Residential Therapy, 1,* 9–14.

Whelan, R. J. (1966). The relevance of behavior modification procedures for teachers and emotionally disturbed children. In P. Knoblock (Ed.), *Intervention approaches in educating emotionally disturbed children* (pp. 35–78). Syracuse, NY: Syracuse University Press.

Whelan, R. J. (1974). Richard J. Whelan. In J. M. Kauffman & C. D. Lewis (Eds.), *Teaching children with behavior disorders: Personal perspectives* (pp. 240–270). Columbus, OH: Merrill.

Whelan, R. J., & Gallagher, P. A. (1972). Effective teaching of children with behavior disorders. In N. G. Haring & A. H. Hayden (Eds.), *The improvement of instruction* (pp. 183–218). Seattle: Special Child Publications.

Whelan, R. J., & Haring, N. G. (1966). Modification and maintenance of behavior through systematic application of consequences. *Exceptional Children, 32,* 281–289.

Wickman, E. K. (1929). *Children's behavior and teachers' attitudes*. New York: The Commonwealth Fund, Division of Publications.

Wiener, J. M. (Ed.). (1996). *Diagnosis and psychopharmacology of childhood and adolescent disorders*. New York: Wiley.

Williams, G. J. (1987). Methods of instruction. In N. G. Haring (Ed.), *Assessing and managing behavior disabilities* (pp. 279–302). Seattle: University of Washington Press.

Williams, R. L. M. (1985). Children's stealing: A review of theft-control procedures for parents and teachers. *Remedial and Special Education, 6*(2) 17–23.

Willis, D. J., Swanson, B. M., & Walker, C. E. (1983). Etiological factors. In T. H. Ollendick & M. Hersen (Eds.), *Handbook of child psychopathology* (pp. 41–63). New York: Plenum.

Winzer, M. A. (1993). *The history of special education: From isolation to integration*. Washington, DC: Gallaudet University Press.

Wodarski, J. S., & Feit, M. D. (1995). *Adolescent substance abuse: An empirical-based group preventive health paradigm*. New York: Haworth.

Wolf, M. M. (1978). Social validity: The case for subjective measurement or how applied behavior analysis is finding its heart. *Journal of Applied Behavior Analysis, 11,* 203–214.

Wolf, M. M., Braukmann, C. J., & Ramp, K. A. (1987). Serious delinquent behavior as part of a significantly handicapping condition: Cures and supportive environments. *Journal of Applied Behavior Analysis, 20,* 347–359.

Wolford, B. I. (1983). Correctional education and special education—an emerging partnership, or "Born to lose." In R. B. Rutherford (Ed.), *Monograph in behavioral disorders* (pp. 13–19). Reston, VA: Council for Exceptional Children.

Wolford, B. I. (1987). Correctional education: Training and education opportunities for delinquent and criminal offenders. In C. M. Nelson, R. B. Rutherford, & B. I. Wolford (Eds.), *Special education in the criminal justice system* (pp. 53–82). Columbus, OH: Merrill/Macmillan.

Wolpe, J. (1975). Laboratory-derived clinical methods of deconditioning anxiety. In T. Thompson & W. S. Dockens (Eds.), *Applications of behavior modification* (pp. 33–41). New York: Academic Press.

Wolraich, M. L., Wilson, D. B., & White, J. W. (1995). The effect of sugar on behavior or cognition in children. *Journal of the American Medical Association, 274,* 1617–1621.

Wood, F. H. (1987). Special education law and correctional education. In C. M. Nelson, R. B. Rutherford, & B. I. Wolford (Eds.), *Special education in the criminal justice system* (pp. 85–99). Columbus, OH: Merrill/Macmillan.

Wood, F. H. (Ed.) (1990). When we talk with children: The life space interview. *Behavioral Disorders* [Special section], *15,* 110–126.

Wood, F. H., Smith, C. R., & Grimes, J. (Eds.). (1985). *The Iowa assessment model in behavioral disorders: A training manual*. Des Moines: Iowa Department of Public Instruction.

Wood, M. M., & Long, N. J. (1991). *Life space intervention: Talking with children and youth in crisis*. Austin, TX: Pro-Ed.

Wooden, W. S., & Berkey, M. L. (1984). *Children and arson: America's middle class nightmare*. New York: Plenum.

Worobey, J. (1986). Convergence among assessments of temperament in the first month. *Child Development, 57,* 47–55.

Wright, R. (1995a, March 13). The biology of violence. *The New Yorker, 71*(3), pp. 68–77.

Wright, R. (1995b, August 28). The evolution of despair. *Time 146,*(9), pp. 50–57.

Wright, W. G. (1967). The Bellevue Psychiatric Hospital School. In P. H. Berkowitz, & E. P. Rothman (Eds.) *Public education for disturbed children in New York City* (pp. 78–123). Springfield, IL: Charles C. Thomas.

Wyche, K. F., & Rotheram-Borus, M. J. (1990). Suicidal behavior among minority youth in the United States. In A. R. Stiffman & L. E. Davis (Eds.), *Ethnic issues in adolescent mental health* (pp. 323–338). Newbury Park, CA: Sage.

Yates, A. (1970). *Behavior Therapy*. New York: Wiley.

Younger, A. J., & Boyko, K. A. (1987). Aggression and withdrawal as social schemas underlying children's peer perceptions. *Child Development, 58,* 1094–1100.

Ysseldyke, J. E., & Foster, G. G. (1978). Bias in teachers' observations of emotionally disturbed and learning disabled children. *Exceptional Children, 44,* 613–615.

Yule, W. (1994). Posttraumatic stress disorder. In T. H. Ollendick, N. J. King, & W. Yule (Eds.), *International handbook of phobic and anxiety disorders in children and adolescents* (pp. 223–240). New York: Plenum.

Yung, B. R., & Hammond, W. R. (1994). Native Americans. In L. D. Eron, J. H. Gentry, & P.

Schlegel (Eds.), *Reason to hope: A psychosocial perspective on violence and youth* (pp. 133–144). Washington, DC: American Psychological Association.

Zack, I. (1995, October 11). UVA forums to focus on roles of black males. *The Charlottesville Daily Progress*, pp. B1, B2.

Zayas, L. H. (1995). Family functioning and child rearing in an urban environment. *Developmental and Behavioral Pediatrics, 16*(3, supplement), s21–s24.

Zimmerman, D. (1983). Moral education. In A. P. Goldstein (Ed.), *Prevention and control of aggression* (pp. 210–240). New York: Pergamon.

Zimmerman, J., & Zimmerman, E. (1962). The alteration of behavior in a special class situation. *Journal of the Experimental Analysis of Behavior, 5,* 59–60.

Zionts, P. (1985). *Teaching disturbed and disturbing students*. Austin, TX: Pro-Ed.

Zirpoli, T. J. (1986). Child abuse and children with handicaps. *Remedial and Special Education, 7*(2), 39–48.

Zirpoli, T. J., & Lloyd, J. W. (1987). Understanding and managing self-injurious behavior. *Remedial and Special Education, 8*(5), 46–57.

Zucker, K. J., & Bradley, S. J. (1995). *Gender identity disorder and psychosexual problems in children and adolescents*. New York: Guilford.

Name Index

Subject Index